ORGANIZATIONAL PSYCHOLOGY

ORGANIZATIONAL PSYCHOLOGY

A SCIENTIST-PRACTITIONER APPROACH

Second Edition

Steve M. Jex and Thomas W. Britt

WILEY

JOHN WILEY & SONS, INC.

Library of Congress Cataloging-in-Publication Data

Jex, Steve M.
    Organizational psychology: a scientist-practitioner approach.—2nd ed. / by Steve M. Jex,
Thomas W. Britt.
        p. cm.
    Includes bibliographical references and index.
    ISBN 978-0-470-10976-2 (cloth)
    1. Psychology, Industrial.   I. Britt, Thomas W., 1966-   II. Title.   III. Title: Psychology : a scientist
practitioner approach.
    HF5548.8.J49 2008
    158.7—dc22
                                                                                            2007021315

Printed in the United States of America.

10 9 8 7 6 5 4 3 2 1

Contents

Preface xi

CHAPTER 1
Introduction to Organizational Psychology   1

What Is Organizational Psychology?   2

Organizational Psychology in Context   3

The Scientist-Practitioner Approach   5

Historical Influences in Organizational Psychology   9

The Chapter Sequence   17

Chapter Summary   18

Suggested Additional Readings   20

CHAPTER 2
Research Methods and Statistics   21

Methods of Data Collection   22

Special Issues in Data Collection   34

Statistical Methods in Organizational Psychology   41

Special Issues in Statistical Analysis   48

Chapter Summary   55

Suggested Additional Readings   57

CHAPTER 3
Attraction and Socialization   59

The Recruitment Process: An Organizational Perspective   60

The Recruitment Process: The Applicant's Perspective   63

Organizational Socialization   67

The Impact of Diversity on Organizational Socialization   90

Chapter Summary   92

Suggested Additional Readings   94

CHAPTER 4
Productive Behavior in Organizations   95

Defining Productive Behavior   96

Job Performance   96

Measurement of Job Performance   103

Determinants of Job Performance   109

Organizational Citizenship Behavior   116

Innovation in Organizations   122

Chapter Summary   128

Suggested Additional Readings   130

CHAPTER 5
Job Satisfaction and Organizational Commitment   131

Job Satisfaction   131

Organizational Commitment   152

Chapter Summary   163

Suggested Additional Readings   165

CHAPTER 6
Counterproductive Behavior in Organizations   167

Defining Counterproductive Behavior   167

Ineffective Job Performance   169

Employee Absenteeism   175

Employee Turnover   179

Less Common Forms of Counterproductive Behavior   186

Chapter Summary   195

Suggested Additional Readings   197

CHAPTER 7
Occupational Stress and Employee Health   199

A Brief History   200

Approaches and Terminology   201

Occupational Stress Terminology   202

Occupational Stress Models   205

Workplace Stressors   210

Reducing the Impact of Workplace Stressors   221

Cross-Cultural Occupational Stress Research   226

Generalizability   226

Stressors Experienced   227

Coping with Stress   228

Chapter Summary   229

Suggested Additional Readings   229

CHAPTER 8
Theories of Motivation   233

Defining Motivation and Theoretical Approaches   234

Need-Based Theories of Motivation   235

Cognitive Process Theories of Motivation   239

The Behavioral Approach to Motivation   250

Self-Determination Theory   254

Job-Based Theories of Motivation   256

The Practical Value of Motivation Theories   264

Chapter Summary   265

Suggested Additional Readings   267

CHAPTER 9
Organizational Applications of Motivation Theory   269

Some Basic Assumptions   269

Behaviors Organizations Attempt to Influence   270

Organizational Reward Systems   272

Motivation through the Design of Work   287

Organizational Disciplinary Procedures   298

Chapter Summary   300

Suggested Additional Readings   302

CHAPTER 10
Leadership and Influence Processes   303

Defining Leadership   303

General Approaches to Leadership   306

Modern Theories of Leadership   311

Power and Influence in Organizations   326

Chapter Summary   335

Suggested Additional Readings   338

CHAPTER 11
Group Dynamics and Behavior   339

Why Do People Join Groups?   340

Defining Characteristics of Groups   341

Group Structure   343

Stages of Group Development   349

Intergroup Dynamics and Behavior   355

Types of Intergroup Interactions   355

Predictors of Intergroup Interaction Patterns   358

Intergroup Conflict   362

Improving the Quality of Intergroup Relations   366

Chapter Summary   371

Suggested Additional Readings   373

CHAPTER 12
Team Effectiveness   375

Defining Team Effectiveness   376

Models of Team Effectiveness   378

Determinants of Team Effectiveness   389

Behavioral Processes   396

Enhancing the Effectiveness of Teams   402

The Future of Teams in Organizations   406

Chapter Summary   407

Suggested Additional Readings   409

CHAPTER 13
Organizational Theory and Design   411

What Is an Organizational Theory?   412

Major Organizational Theories   414

Determinants of Organizational Design   421

Recent Innovations in Organizational Design   432

Research on Organizational Design   436

The Future of Organizational Design   437

Chapter Summary   438

Suggested Additional Readings   440

CHAPTER 14
Organizational Culture   441

Defining Organizational Culture   442

Models of Organizational Culture   446

Manifestations of Organizational Culture   447

The Development of Organizational Culture   454

Measuring Organizational Culture   456

Changing Organizational Culture   458

The Impact of Organizational Culture   464

Chapter Summary   468

Suggested Additional Readings   470

CHAPTER 15
Organizational Change and Development   473

What Is Organizational Development and Why Is It Used?   473

A Brief History of Organizational Development   475

Contents

The Theory Base of Organizational Development   477

Organizational-Change Interventions   486

Conditions Necessary for Successful Organizational Change   497

Evaluation of Organizational-Development Programs   502

Special Issues in Client–Consultant Relationships   508

Chapter Summary   511

Suggested Additional Readings   513

References   515

Author Index   587

Subject Index   611

Preface

Organizations are complex social systems that sometimes perform well and sometimes fail miserably. Organizational psychology is a subfield within the larger domain of industrial/organizational psychology that seeks to facilitate a greater understanding of social processes in organizations. Organizational psychologists also seek to use these insights to enhance the effectiveness of organizations—a goal that is potentially beneficial to all.

This book is designed to provide students with a thorough overview of both the science and practice of organizational psychology. It was originally written to serve as the primary text for a course in organizational psychology (graduate, or upper-level undergraduate), but could also meet the needs of an organizational behavior course as well. Because this book will be used at the graduate level, we've invested considerable effort to provide a solid research base in all of the chapters. At the same time, we have also tried to write the book in a style that students will find enjoyable, accessible, and perhaps, at times, even entertaining.

NEW TO THE SECOND EDITION

The most visible change to the second edition of this book is the addition of Dr. Thomas Britt from Clemson University as a coauthor. I met Tom several years ago during a summer while working at Walter Reed Army Institute in Washington, DC. Because Tom's academic training is in social psychology with research interests in organizational psychology, he was really able to improve many of the chapters, particularly those dealing with job attitudes, teams, and leadership. We also found that we had very similar writing styles, and perhaps the best part is that we've worked very well together.

In terms of content, we did not make drastic changes because the feedback I've received during the past 5 years about the first edition has been very positive. As with the first edition, Chapters 1 through 4 provide an introduction to the field of organizational psychology, an examination of the most common research methods used to study behavior in organizations, and the processes by which employees are socialized into organizations and finally become productive members.

Chapters 5 through 8 offer an examination of the processes by which employees develop feelings of satisfaction and commitment toward the organization, an exploration of counterproductive behaviors that they may engage in, how they might come to view the workplace as stressful, and some theories of motivation.

Chapters 9 through 12 include an examination of the various methods organizations use to influence the behavior of employees, leadership and influence processes, and group behavior. Readers will note that two chapters are devoted to groups. One is designed to provide an overview of basic social psychological processes in groups, and the second is focused more specifically on the factors that influence team effectiveness. Some readers may recall that in the first edition there was also a chapter dealing with processes governing interactions *between* teams in organizations. In the second edition the material from this chapter is integrated into the two chapters dealing with groups and team effectiveness.

Chapters 13 through 15 are focused on "macro" or organization-level processes. These include the design of organizations, organizational culture, and organizational change and development.

In terms of content, the major changes involved updating the substantive material in the chapters. Since the first edition many new developments have occurred in the field of organizational psychology, and a great deal of new research has been conducted. We have worked hard to convey these new developments and summarize important new research findings. Another change in the second edition is a section in each chapter where we've asked a prominent researcher to describe how he/she became interested in a particular topic. We felt that these would be interesting to students, and more importantly, put a "human face" on some of the names that are cited in the text.

UNIQUE FEATURES OF THE BOOK

In this second edition we've been careful to retain the features of the first edition of the book that we felt made it unique. For example, we still have a full chapter on research methodology and statistics. Furthermore, since the first edition came out, there have been even more methodological developments in the field—this further validates the decision to include such a chapter in the first edition.

The second edition also covers many topics that are not traditionally part of organizational psychology such as recruitment, job performance, and compensation. As with the first edition, this was done largely because of the belief that there is considerable interrelationship between the "I" and the "O" sides of the broader field of industrial/organizational psychology.

A third and final unique feature that has not changed is the use of "Comment" boxes throughout the book. While the content of many of these boxes has changed, the motivation behind them has stayed the same—*to encourage students to think about and discuss the chapter material*. We both strongly believe that students learn much more when they are highly engaged in the material, and do not feel that reading is a chore. Some of the comments relate current events, some provide extended commentary on chapter material, and others are simply designed to help the reader get to know the authors a little better.

ACKNOWLEDGMENTS

The authors would first like to thank the many colleagues and students who have provided feedback on the first edition since it came out in 2002. Many of you have stopped by to chat about the book at conferences, and this feedback has been extremely valuable. While we cannot guarantee that we've addressed every criticism of the first edition, we've certainly listened and made an effort to do so.

We would also like to thank Tisha Rossi, our editor at Wiley, for her help during the revision process. Tisha provided us with some very valuable editorial feedback, yet also allowed us a considerable amount of discretion on the content of the book. We also greatly appreciate Tisha's flexibility on deadlines.

The authors would also especially like the thank Jason Kain from Bowling Green State University, and Adam Beeco, Lauren Haack, Genevieve Mendes, Brittany Moree, and Kristen Purvis from Clemson University for all of their help during the revision process. Jason read through every chapter and made some very valuable suggestions. He also did a tremendous job organizing the many new citations that were added to this edition. The Clemson students helped conduct literature searches necessary for updating some of the chapters and made suggestions for applied examples.

A NOTE FROM TOM BRITT

I would first like to thank Steve for giving me the opportunity to work with him in the revision of his textbook. I have learned a lot from the process, and find myself becoming even more committed to the field of organizational psychology. I also

have been fortunate to supervise a number of graduate students within Clemson's Industrial/Organizational psychology doctoral program, including Heather Odle-Dusseau, Tiffany Greene-Shortridge, Hailey Herleman, and Eric McKibben. These students continue to provide me with constant sources of energy and support. Most importantly, I would like to thank my twin sons, Noah and Jordan, who continue to remind me of what life is all about.

A NOTE FROM STEVE JEX

I would first like to thank my former colleague Gary Adams for his unwavering friendship and support through the years. I would like to provide a heartfelt acknowledgment to my family. My wife Robin has been a constant source of love and support for over 20 years, and there is certainly no way this book could have been completed without her. I would also like to thank my two sons, Garrett and Travis, for their love and support. They're still my two best friends, and I greatly appreciate the sacrifices they made while I was working on the book.

ORGANIZATIONAL PSYCHOLOGY

Chapter One

Introduction to Organizational Psychology

T he behavior of individuals acting as members of formal organizations has a tremendous impact on many aspects of our lives. Everything—the food we eat, the cars we drive, the houses we live in—depends on the coordinated effort of individuals in organizational settings. This impact, in fact, is so great that we typically take it for granted. In most cases, we only take notice when the results are either very good or very bad. For example, we marvel at the coordinated effort of a professional sports franchise that is highly successful and express disdain when corruption occurs in a government agency. Most of the time, however, the impact of behavior in formal organizations goes relatively unnoticed.

Organizational psychology is a field that utilizes scientific methodology to better understand the behavior of individuals working in organizational settings. This knowledge is also used, in a variety of ways, to help make organizations more effective. Effective organizations are typically more productive, often provide higher-quality services to customers, and are usually more financially successful than less effective organizations. For private organizations, financial success often results in greater job security for employees, and increased shareholder wealth for investors. For public organizations, such as police departments, municipal governments, and public universities, success means higher-quality services and cost savings to taxpayers.

Enhanced organizational effectiveness, and the success that often comes with it, often provides more indirect benefits as well.

Successful organizations provide employment opportunities, which helps to foster the economic well-being of society as a whole. Also, in many instances, employees in successful organizations are more satisfied and fulfilled in their work than employees in less successful organizations. These positive attitudes may carry over to non-work-related roles such as parent and community member. Consumers also benefit from enhanced organizational effectiveness because well-managed, efficient organizations are often able to produce products and provide services at a much lower cost than their less successful competitors. Such cost savings are often passed on to consumers in the form of lower prices. In sum, everyone is a potential winner when organizations function effectively. Organizational psychology seeks to enhance the effectiveness of organizations through scientific research and the application of research findings.

WHAT IS ORGANIZATIONAL PSYCHOLOGY?

This book is designed to provide students with a comprehensive treatment of the science and practice of organizational psychology. In the most general sense, organizational psychology is the scientific study of individual and group behavior in formal organizational settings. Katz and Kahn, in their classic work, The Social Psychology of Organizations (1978), stated that the essence of an organization is patterned human behavior. When behavior is patterned, this implies that some structure is imposed on the behavior of individuals. In organizations this structure typically comes from things such as job descriptions and organizational policies. Many organizations also have a more general set of values that they want employees to abide by. Thus, an organization cannot exist when people just "do their own thing" without any awareness of the behavior of others.

Given Katz and Kahn's defining characteristic of organizations (e.g., patterned behavior), it is easy to see that there are many organizations in this world. A group of five people who regularly play poker on Friday nights would fit this definition, as would a major multinational corporation. Therefore, to further define the field of organizational psychology, it is important to distinguish between formal and informal organizations.

A formal organization is one that exists to fulfill some explicitly stated purpose, and that purpose is often stated in writing. Formal organizations also typically exhibit some degree of continuity over time; that is, they often survive far longer than the founding members do. Business organizations obviously exhibit these defining characteristics of a formal organization, as do many other nonprofit organizations and government agencies.

In contrast, an informal organization is one in which the purpose is typically less explicit than for a formal organization. Going back to the previous example of five poker players, these individuals are obviously spending time together because they enjoy playing poker and, in all likelihood, each other's company. It is doubtful, though, that these reasons for playing poker are formally stated in writing, or even explicitly stated. It is also doubtful (though obviously not impossible) whether this small group would continue to exist if three of the five members moved to another city or simply lost interest in poker.

The field of organizational psychology is concerned with the study of formal organizations. That is not to say that the formal organizations of interest to organizational psychologists are always businesses or profit-making organizations (a common misconception that we have noticed among many of our colleagues trained in other areas of psychology). Throughout the chapters in this book, many studies will be described that have been conducted not only in businesses but also in government agencies, universities, and nonprofit social service agencies.

Another point worth noting is that the focus on formal organizations does not preclude the study of informal organizational processes, or even occasionally informal groups and organizations. It has been shown, for example, that informal friendship ties exist in formal organizations, and they have important implications for employees (Riordan & Griffeth 1995). In this same vein, processes that occur in informal groups and organizations may provide researchers with valuable insights into processes that occur in formal organizations. For example, the manner in which a status hierarchy develops in an informal group such as a sports team may help researchers better understand the emergence of leadership in formal organizations.

Another point of clarification in the previous definition provided has to do with the term psychology itself, since organizational psychology is part of this larger field. Psychology is the scientific study of individual human behavior and mental processes. Two things are important to note about this definition. First, organizational psychologists use methods of scientific inquiry to both study and intervene in organizations. This simply means that organizational psychologists use a systematic, data-based approach to studying organizational processes and solving organizational problems. The "data" used by organizational psychologists may come in a variety of forms, including survey responses, interviews, observations, and, in some cases, organizational records.

The other important part of this definition is that psychology focuses on individual behavior. This may seem a bit odd to some readers, given that a substantial portion of this text is devoted to both group and organizational-level processes. What it means is that regardless of the level at which some phenomenon occurs, psychologists view individual behavior as the most important mediating factor (cf. Porras & Robertson, 1992). Thus, to understand the impact of group and organizational-level variables, we must focus on how they influence, and are influenced by, individual behavior. Groups and organizations don't behave; people do. This strong focus on individual behavior also serves to distinguish organizational psychology from other social science disciplines (e.g., sociology, economics, political science) that attempt to explain organizational processes but are less focused on individual behavior. It is also one way in which organizational psychology differs from the closely related field of organizational behavior (see Comment 1.1).

ORGANIZATIONAL PSYCHOLOGY IN CONTEXT

While organizational psychology represents a legitimate field of study in its own right, it is also part of the broader field of industrial/organizational (I/O) psychology. I/O psychology is defined as the application of the methods and principles of psychology to the workplace (Spector, 2006). Figure 1.1 provides a comparison of the topics that are typically of interest to those in the industrial and organizational portions of the field. Notice that the topics listed on the industrial side are those that are typically associated with the management of human resources in organizations. Contrast these with the topics on the organizational side, which are associated with the aim of understanding and predicting behavior within organizational settings.

Given this distinction between the industrial and organizational sides of the field, it is very tempting to polarize into different "camps" based on one's professional interests. Unfortunately, this "I" and "O" distinction underestimates the considerable interdependence among the topics that constitute each of these subfields.

COMMENT 1.1

ORGANIZATIONAL PSYCHOLOGY VERSUS ORGANIZATIONAL BEHAVIOR:
WHAT'S THE DIFFERENCE?

MANY READERS, PARTICULARLY those who have received at least a portion of their training in a university business school, have heard of the field of *organizational behavior*. What is the difference between organizational psychology and organizational behavior? In all honesty, these two fields are quite similar—so much so, in fact, that many faculty who teach organizational behavior in business schools received their training in departments of psychology. Though less common, there have been some instances where faculty who teach organizational psychology received their training in business schools.

Despite the outward similarities, there are actually subtle differences between organizational psychology and organizational behavior. Moorhead and Griffin (1995) define *organizational behavior* as "the study of human behavior in organizational settings, the interface between human behavior and the organization, and the organization itself" (p. 4). If we focus only on the first part of this definition, there is no difference between organizational psychology and organizational behavior. However, the differences lie in the portion of the definition stating that organizational behavior is concerned with "the organization itself." Specifically, the field of organizational behavior is concerned not only with individual behavior in organizations, but macro-level processes and variables such as organizational structure and strategy are viewed as interesting and worthy of study in their own right.

Organizational psychology is also concerned with the impact of macro-level variables and processes, but only to the extent that such variables and processes have an impact on *individual behavior*. Much of the reason for this difference is that organizational behavior draws from a greater variety of disciplines than does organizational psychology. While organizational psychology draws primarily from various subfields within psychology, organizational behavior draws from a variety of discplines including psychology, sociology, anthropology, economics, and labor relations, to name a few. This greater variety provides organizational behavior with a somewhat more eclectic theoritical base than organizational psychology, although both fields largely study the same phenomena.

Perhaps the most tangible difference between organizational psychology behavior and organizational psychology is in salary levels. Faculty in business schools who teach organizational behavior are typically paid significantly more than faculty who teach organizational psychology within psychology departments. This explains why many who are trained in psychology want to teach organizational behavior in business schools; in fact, a perusal of the background of faculty at business schools will show that many have been trained in psychology. In recent years, however, the hiring of psychologists has waned a bit. This is due to the job market in general, and the fact that business schools now produce more Ph.D.s than they did 25 to 30 years ago.

Source: G. Moorhead and R. W. Griffin. (1995). *Organizational behavior: Managing people and organizations* (4th ed.). Boston: Houghton Mifflin Company.

To illustrate this point, let's say a life insurance company decides to develop a test to select people to sell insurance policies. To do so, this organization would likely conduct some form of job analysis to find out what exactly is involved in selling life insurance policies, develop performance criterion measures based on this job analysis,

FIGURE 1.1

A Breakdown of Topics Associated with the Industrial and Organizational Sides of the Field of I/O Psychology

will see, socialization and occupational stress are important topics within organizational psychology.

This point can also be illustrated by taking an "O" topic and describing the relevance of the "I" side of the field. Let's say the U.S. Army is interested in improving decision-making and communication processes among the small groups that comprise special-forces units. Fortunately, in organizational psychology, there is considerable literature on group effectiveness and processes, and the Army could draw on these sources to help guide its efforts (e.g., Guzzo & Shea, 1992). Can issues that are relevant to the "I" side of the field be ignored? Absolutely not. To be effective, a group must have a certain mix of skills, abilities, and personality traits. Thus, regardless of the team processes that are taught to these units, care must be taken to select the right mix of individuals in the first place. It is also unlikely that decision-making processes would improve unless these teams receive accurate and timely performance feedback. Selection and performance appraisal, of course, are two of the major topics on the "I" side of the field.

develop a selection test to measure things that are thought to be predictive of performance, and ultimately conduct a study to investigate whether performance on the selection test is correlated with the performance criterion measure (Cascio, 1998). Because all of these are "I" activities, what relevance does the "O" side of the field have for the life insurance company in this example? On first glance, it would appear to be very little. However, if you think about it, organizational topics are highly relevant. For example, after these life insurance agents are selected, they must be socialized into the culture of the specific agency in which they will be working, as well as the broader company culture (Bowen, Ledford, & Nathan, 1991; Kristof, 1996). Also, demands of life insurance sales may necessitate the hiring of individuals who will cope well with these demands (Jex, 1998). Thus, the organization needs to understand the unique stressors that are associated with this job, as well as the attributes that facilitate coping. As we

THE SCIENTIST-PRACTITIONER APPROACH

Organizational psychology should be viewed as a science. In fact, much of the content of this book is based on scientific studies of behavior in both organizational and laboratory settings. Organizational psychology, however, is also concerned with the application of scientific knowledge to enhance the effectiveness of organizations. The scientist-practitioner model captures this dynamic interaction between generating scientific knowledge and the application of that knowledge for some practical purpose. At a very general level, the scientist-practitioner model states that science and practice are not independent and, in fact, often feed off each other.

To illustrate how the scientist-practitioner model works, let's say the branch manager of a bank is frustrated by high turnover among tellers. Fortunately, this individual may draw on the findings of many scientific investigations of turnover to guide his or her efforts to reduce it (e.g., Griffeth, Hom, & Gaertner, 2000). Conversely, scientific investigations of organizational phenomena are often motivated by the practical concerns of organizations. For example, the past decade has indicated a considerable rise in research on how organizations can assist employees in balancing the demands of both work and family domains (e.g., Adams, King, & King, 1996; Kossek & Ozeki, 1998). Although certainly useful from a purely scientific standpoint, another important factor motivating this research is that organizations want to avoid losing valuable employees because of difficulties in balancing work and family demands.

Within the general field of I/O psychology, the scientist-practitioner model has become so important that it serves as the underlying philosophy for many if not most graduate training programs in the field. Graduate training guided by the scientist-practitioner model suggests that, first and foremost, students need the skills necessary to conduct scientific research. This explains why virtually all graduate programs in I/O psychology require training in statistics, research methodology, and psychological measurement. The other important implication of the scientist-practitioner model in graduate training is that students are typically provided with some opportunity, through internships or other field experience, to apply what they have learned in real world settings (see Comment 1.2).

The scientist-practitioner model is also quite relevant to the field of organizational psychology, and thus was chosen as the guiding theme for this book. As will become evident as readers proceed through the chapters, research by organizational psychologists has greatly enhanced our understanding of behavior in organizations. For example, research by organizational psychologists has provided valuable insights into things such as group effectiveness, socialization of new employees, and goal-setting processes. At the same time, findings generated from scientific research in these areas have been used to guide interventions designed to help organizations become more effective.

The impact of the scientist-practitioner model also can be seen in the work settings and activities of those trained in organizational psychology. Many hold academic positions—typically, in departments of psychology or management. The primary job duties of most academicians are teaching, scientific research, and service to one's academic department and university. However, many in academia also use their research skills to help organizations solve a variety of practical problems. The careers of both authors of this text have certainly contained this blend of science and practice (see Comment 1.3).

The training of organizational psychologists who pursue academic careers is not drastically different from the training of organizational psychologists who pursue nonacademic careers. Consistent with the scientist-practitioner model, students in graduate programs in I/O psychology and related fields typically receive coursework in research methodology, statistics, and measurement, as well as in specific content areas (e.g., motivation, leadership). It is also common for all students, regardless of their

COMMENT 1.2

TRAINING SCIENTIST-PRACTITIONERS: THE ROLE OF PRACTICAL EXPERIENCE

MOST GRADUATE PROGRAMS in I/O psychology, as well as other fields, incorporate some form of practical experience into their curriculum. This can be accomplished in a variety of ways. Most programs, for example, encourage students to participate in formal internship programs in corporations and consulting firms. Typically, internships span between 6 months and 1 year, and require that students work under the supervision of an experienced I/O psychologist. Other less formal ways that students obtain practical experience include class projects, working with faculty on research and consulting projects, and field-based practicum courses.

The major benefit of students participating in field experiences is that they gain a chance to put what they've learned in their courses into practice in a real organization. Students also benefit in a more subtle way: They develop a greater understanding of how the *real world* actually works. For example, students working on field projects are often surprised at how quickly organizations want things done, as well as the importance of building positive interpersonal relationships with "clients" in organizations. Many students are also surprised that their methodological and statistical training comes in quite handy as they work on these field projects.

Despite the many advantages of practical experience, there can be some disadvantages of incorporating it into graduate programs. The primary single experience by many doctoral programs is that, in some cases, students who take internships never finish their degree. Other problems that can occur are lack of competent supervision and, in some cases, the projects organizations assign to students are not meaningful. Despite these potential disadvantages, carefully monitored practical experience is usually a valuable component of graduate training. It is also an excellent way to teach the scientist-practitioner model to students.

career plans, to conduct research and obtain practical experience.

There are, however, some important components that future academicians typically need to incorporate into their graduate training. For example, it is important for those planning an academic career to become involved in research early in their graduate training. This increases the chances of gaining authorship on journal articles and conference presentations—something that definitely helps in a competitive job market. Research involvement also facilitates the development of close working relationships with faculty. These relationships are crucial in learning how to do research. Another essential component of the training of future academicians is teaching experience. Regardless of the type of institution in which one is employed, teaching is a major component of any academic position and all universities are looking for good teachers. Thus, graduate students who obtain significant teaching experience are much better prepared for academic positions than those with little or no experience.

Typical nonacademic employment settings for organizational psychologists include business organizations, consulting firms, nonprofit research institutes, government agencies and research institutes, and

COMMENT 1.3

SCIENCE AND PRACTICE IN OUR OWN CAREERS

STEVE JEX-WHEN I reflect on my own career, the science-practice theme is very evident. Since receiving my Ph.D. in industrial/organizational psychology in 1988, I have carried on an active program of research in the area of occupational stress. Thus, a good deal of what I do centers around the science. However, in addition to scientific activity, I have conducted a number of projects in organizations that have been designed to solve practical problems. For example, not long after starting my first job out of graduate school, I was the assistant investigator on a project conducted for the U.S. Army Research Institute. This project involved conducting an organizational assessment of the recruiting operations branch of the U.S Army. The Army was interested in ways that the recruiting branch could facilitate the training of field recruiters. Since that first project, I have worked with a number of organizations conducting applied research projects and developing training programs.

What have I learned from working with organizations? Probably most important, I have developed a great deal of respect for those who do applied work on a full-time basis. Applying research findings in organizational settings is tough work that requires considerable skill. Another thing I have learned is that good science has practical value; that is, when projects in organizations are conducted in a scientifically rigorous manner, organizations typically obtain much more useful information than when they are not. Finally, working in organizations has really convinced me of the viability of the scientist-practitioner model. The opportunity to do scientifically meaningful work that has practical value makes the field of I/O psychology very unique and exciting.

Thomas Britt- THE FURTHER INTO my career I get, the more I realize the importance of the scientist-practitioner model. I received my Ph.D. in social psychology in 1994, and then immediately started active duty in the U.S. Army as a research psychologist. I quickly realized that the Army was not necessarily interested in the identity regulation of romantic partners (the topic of my doctoral dissertation), but was interested in how soldiers could be motivated to perform well during stressful military operations. Therefore, I tried to conduct applied research "in the field" that met my own (and journal reviewer's) standards for scientific rigor. I ended up having a lot of fun in the Army conducting research on how the identity images of soldiers as "warriors" and "peacekeepers" influenced motivation and health in different types of operations, how being personally engaged in work could serve as a buffer against many deployment stressors, and how soldiers could possibly derive benefits such as increased self-confidence and appreciation for life as a result of successfully handling the rigors of military operations.

Somewhat to my surprise, I also enjoyed communicating the importance of research findings to military leaders, and thinking about the applied relevance of the research I conducted. I found that leaders were much more likely to take recommendations to heart when they were backed by data collected using a sound research design. I also found that leaders in applied settings appreciated the utility of a well-supported theory in making sense of the findings. Like Steve, I was impressed with how leaders were really willing to devote the time and attention necessary to understand the implications of scientific research for the well-being and performance of their personnel. I find myself being guided by the scientist-practioner even more as I have begun new programs of research on understanding stressors faced by foreign language analysts who work for the U.S. government and how positive motivational states at work can be used to identify employees who thrive under stress.

even market research firms. While actual job duties vary widely by setting, many organizational psychologists employed in nonacademic settings are involved in organizational change and development activities. This might involve assisting an organization in the development and implementation of an employee opinion survey program, designing and facilitating the implementation of team development activities, or perhaps assisting top management with the strategic planning process. The other major activity of those employed in nonacademic settings is research. This is particularly true of those employed in nonprofit research institutes, government research institutes, and market research firms. Given the diversity of these settings, it is difficult to pin down the exact nature of the research that is conducted. However, in the most general sense, these individuals conduct scientific research that is designed to have some practical benefit to the organization or even to society in general.

To prepare for a nonacademic career, graduate students need training in many of the same areas as those pursuing academic careers. These include courses in research methodology, statistics, measurement, and several substantive topical areas. There is one important difference, however: Compared to those seeking academic employment, it is more essential for students planning nonacademic careers to obtain practical experience during their graduate training. This experience can often be gained by assisting faculty with consulting projects, or, in some cases, through formal internship programs (see Comment 1.4). Obtaining practical experience is crucial not only because it enhances a student's credentials, but because it provides valuable opportunities to apply what has been learned in graduate courses.

HISTORICAL INFLUENCES IN ORGANIZATIONAL PSYCHOLOGY

The year 1992 marked the hundredth anniversary of the field of psychology. To mark this centennial, much was written about the history of industrial/organizational psychology. This section, therefore, will not provide a detailed, comprehensive history of the field of organizational psychology. Rather, the intent is to provide a relatively concise summary of some of the people and historical events that have shaped the field.

Historical Beginnings

As Katzell and Austin (1992) point out, interest in the behavior of individuals in organizational settings undoubtedly dates back to ancient times: "In the organizational field, perhaps the earliest recorded consultant was the Midianite priest, Jethro, who advised his son-in-law, Moses, on how to staff and organize the ancient Israelites (Exod. 18)" (p. 803). Formalized attempts to study and influence such behavior, however, have a much more recent history.

In order to understand the more recent historical roots of organizational psychology, we must first examine the beginnings of the broader field of industrial/organizational psychology. Based on most historical accounts of the development of the field of I/O psychology, the industrial side of the field was much quicker to develop than the organizational side. Chronologically, the beginnings of the field of I/O psychology can be traced to work, during the early part of the twentieth century, by pioneers such as Hugo Munsterberg, Walter Dill Scott, and Walter Bingham (Katzell & Austin, 1992). Most of the work at that time dealt with topics such as skill acquisition and personnel

THE INSTITUTE FOR PSYCHOLOGICAL RESEARCH AND APPLICATION (IPRA)

ONE OF THE most important features of the graduate program in I/O psychology at the Bowling Green State University is the experience students receive working on projects through the Institute for Psychological Research and Application (IPRA). IPRA was created by the I/O faculty at Bowling Green in the late 1980s in order to provide graduate students with the opportunity to apply, in actual organizational settings and under the supervision of faculty, what they learn in the I/O program. A secondary pupose of IPRA is to provide graduate students with funding to attend professional conferences.

Typically, local organizations approach the IPRA director (or some other I/O faculty member) with some proposed organizational need that might match the expertise of the I/O faculty at Bowling Green. Examples of projects that have been done through IPRA include employee opinion surveys, training needs assessment, customer service satisfaction surveys, and performance appraisal system development. After an organization has expressed a need, a faculty member is sought to serve as a supervisor on the project. Once a faculty member agrees to supervise a project, a meeting is typically set up with a representative from that organization to obtain more concrete information about the projects. This is typically followed by the submission, to that organization, of a formal proposal that includes the nature of the work to be done, the time frame under which the work will be done, the *deliverables* that the organization will receive at the conclusion of the project, and an itemized budget.

The vast majority of students who graduate from the I/O program at Bowling Green State University feel that their work on IPRA projects was one of the most valuable components of their education; this is particularly true for students who end up working for corporations and consulting firms. Students feel that work on these projects helps them to sharpen their technical skills, provides valuable opportunities to apply what they learn in their classes, and provides a realistic preview of the world of consulting.

---

selection. Very little work dealing with the organizational side of the field was conducted. Table 1.1 provides a chronological summary of some of the major events that shaped the development of the field of organizational psychology in the twentieth century.

Ironically, the beginnings of the organizational side of the field were heavily influenced by the work of several nonpsychologists. Perhaps the best known of these was Frederick Winslow Taylor, who developed the principles of scientific management (Taylor, 1911). Although for many the term scientific management typically conjures up images of time-and-motion study, as well as piece-rate compensation, it was actually much more than that. Scientific management was, to a large extent, a philosophy of management, and efficiency and piece-rate compensation were the most visible manifestations of that philosophy. When one looks past these more visible aspects of scientific management, three underlying principles emerge: (1) those who perform work tasks should be separate from those who design work tasks; (2) workers are rational beings, and they will work harder if provided with favorable economic incentives; and (3) problems in the workplace can and should be subjected to empirical study.

TABLE 1.1

A Chronological Summary of the Major Historical Influences on the Field of Organizational Psychology during the Twentieth Century

Early 1900s	Development and growth of Scientific Management (Taylor); beginning of the scientific study of organizational structure (Weber)
1920s–1930s	Hawthorne Studies; growth of unionization; immigration of Kurt Lewin to the United States
1940s–1950s	WWII; publication of Vitele's book Motivation and Morale in Industry; development of the "Human Relations" perspective; Lewin conducts "action research" projects for the Comission on Community Relations and establishes the Research Center for Group Dynamics at M.I.T.
1960s–1970s	U.S. involvement in Vietnam; Division 14 of the APA is changed to "Industrial/Organizational Psychology"; "multi-level" perspective in organizational psychology; increasing attention to nontraditional topics such as stress, work-family conflict, and retirement.
1980s—1990s	Increasing globalization of the economy; changing workforce demographics; increasing reliance on temporary or contingent employees; redefining the concept of a "job."
2000-Present	Advances in communication technology, continued increases in globalization, greater flexibility in work arrangements, boundaries between "work" and "non work" less clear

In considering the underlying principles of scientific management described previously, the first principle is certainly contrary to much of the thinking in the field of organizational psychology today. Many organizational psychologists, in fact, have recommended that employees be involved in decisions impacting the design of their work (e.g., Hackman & Oldham, 1980). The second principle, namely that employees will respond to financial incentives, has actually received considerable support over the years (Jenkins, Mitra, Gupta, & Shaw, 1998; Locke, 1982). Most organizational psychologists, however, do not believe that financial incentives will completely compensate for extremely dull and repetitive work—something that seems to be an assumption of scientific management. The third principle, empirical study, has been fully embraced by the field of organizational psychology and is clearly the one that establishes the link between the two fields. It is also worth noting that by employing scientific methodology to study production-related processes, Taylor was ahead of his time and is considered a pioneer by some. (Most of his studies dealt with cutting sheet

metal.) Unfortunately, despite the impact of scientific management, many of Taylor's ideas met with a great deal of controversy (see Comment 1.5).

Another early nonpsychologist who contributed greatly to the development of organizational psychology was Max Weber. Weber's academic training was in law and history, but his legacy is largely in the field of organizational design. Weber is best known for his development of the notion of bureaucracy as an organizing principle. The basic idea of a bureaucratic organization is that employees know exactly what they are supposed to be doing, and the lines of authority are clearly stated. Another major principle of bureaucracy is that advancement and rewards should be based on merit and not on things such as nepotism or social class. Many principles of bureaucracy are taken for granted today and are even looked at with a bit of disdain, but these ideas were quite innovative at the time they were proposed by Weber.

Weber was also a pioneer because he went beyond merely giving advice about organization and management issues, and subjected many of his ideas to empirical

COMMENT 1.5

ARTHUR KORNHAUSER: ADVOCATE FOR ORGANIZED LABOR

WHILE THE STUDY of labor unions is generally not considered one of the core areas of industrial/organizational psychology, it has certainly increased dramatically in the past 25 years. Much of the credit for this interest in labor unions can be traced back to the pioneering work of Arthur Kornhauser. Kornhauser received his Ph.D. in psychology from the University of Chicago in 1926, and remained there as a faculty member until 1943. After a brief period in a research position at Columbia University, Kornhauser accepted a full professorship at Wayne State University in 1947 and remained there until his retirement in 1962. Kornhauser died in 1990 at the age of 94.

In a 2003 article published in the *Journal of Applied Psychology*, Mike Zickar provides a fascinating and quite detailed account of the life and work of Kornhauser, which was based on a number of interviews with Kornhauser's colleagues, family, and former students. According to Zickar, Kornhauser was unique in that he was one of the few early industrial/organizational psychologists who conducted research on behalf of labor unions and was an advocate for their interests. Most industrial/organizational psychologists, both early in the development of the field and in the present day, have been interested primarily in issues that are important to the management of organizations—turnover, productivity, and selection, to name few issues.

Unfortunately, Kornhauser's work has not been given the attention of other early figures in the field of industrial/organizational psychology; this is one of the reasons Zickar wrote the article. It is probably a reasonable assumption that Kornhauser's connection to unions, not a mainstream topic in the field, was one reason for this neglect. Other reasons for this neglect, according to Zickar, were that Kornhauser's work was interdisciplinary (he held a joint appointment in the Institute for Labor and Industrial Relations at Wayne State) and that he had only three doctoral students throughout his career.

Note: From Zickar, M. J. (2003) Remembering Arthur Kornhauser: Industrial psychology's advocate for worker well-being. *Journal of Applied Psychology*, 88, 363–369.

investigation. In addition to studying organizational design, Weber wrote extensively on organizational topics such as leadership, power, and norms at a time when these topics were largely ignored by psychologists. This willingness to study organizational issues empirically is one of the major defining characteristics of the field of organizational psychology, and thus represents an important aspect of Weber's legacy.

The Field Takes Shape

Despite the early work of Taylor and Weber, and others, the vast majority of effort in industrial psychology in the early twentieth century was focused on what were described earlier as industrial topics. The event that changed that—an event many see as the beginning of organizational psychology—was the Hawthorne studies. The Hawthorne studies, a collaborative effort between the Western Electric Company and a group of researchers from Harvard University, took place between 1927 and 1932 (Mayo, 1933; Whitehead, 1935, 1938). The original purpose of the Hawthorne studies was to investigate the impact of environmental factors—such as illumination, wage incentives, and rest pauses—on employee productivity.

When one considers the time period in which the Hawthorne studies were initiated (early 1920s), it is not surprising that these topics were investigated because scientific management was the dominant school of managerial thought at the time.

What made the Hawthorne studies so important to the field of organizational psychology were the unexpected findings that came out of this series of investigations. Perhaps the best known were the findings that came from the illumination experiments. Specifically, the Hawthorne researchers found that productivity increased regardless of the changes in level of illumination. This became the basis for what is termed the Hawthorne effect, or the idea that people will respond positively to any novel change in the work environment. In modern organizations, a Hawthorne effect might occur when a relatively trivial change is made in a person's job, and that person initially responds to this change very positively, but the effect does not last long.

The significance of the Hawthorne studies, however, goes well beyond simply demonstrating a methodological artifact. For example, in subsequent studies, Hawthorne researchers discovered that work groups established and strongly enforced production norms. The Hawthorne researchers also found that employees responded differently to different styles of leadership. The overall implication of the Hawthorne studies, which later formed the impetus for organizational psychology, was that social factors impact behavior in organizational settings. This may seem a rather obvious conclusion today, but when considered in the historical context, it was a very novel and important finding. Focusing only on the specific conclusions published by the Hawthorne researchers, as well as the methodological shortcomings of this research (e.g., Bramel & Friend, 1981;

Carey, 1967), misses the much larger implications of this research effort.

During roughly the same time period in which the Hawthorne studies took place, another important historical influence on organizational psychology occurred: unionization. This is somewhat ironic, considering that I/O psychology is often viewed warily by unions (Zickar, 2001), despite the fact that there has been cooperation between the two. However, the union movement in the United States during the 1930s was important because it forced organizations to consider, for the first time, a number of issues that are largely taken for granted today. For example, organizational topics such as participative decision making, workplace democracy, quality of work life, and the psychological contract between employees and organizations are rooted, at least to some degree, in the union movement. Many of these issues were addressed in collective bargaining agreements in unionized organizations. Many nonunionized organizations were forced to address these issues due to the threat of unionization (see Comment 1.5).

During the period of union growth in the 1930s, another event occurred that would prove to be very significant for the development of the field of organizational psychology: Kurt Lewin fled Nazi Germany and ultimately took a post at the University of Iowa Child Welfare Research Station. By the time he immigrated to the United States, Lewin was already a prominent social psychologist who had a variety of research interests, many of which were relevant to the emerging field of organizational psychology. Lewin's ideas, for example, have had a major impact in the areas of group dynamics, motivation, and leadership. Perhaps Lewin's greatest contribution was his willingness to use research to solve practical problems in both organizational and community settings.

The term action research, which is typically associated with Lewin, refers to the idea that researchers and organizations can collaborate on research and use those findings to solve problems. The scientist-practitioner model can be traced to the action research model and thus stands as one of Lewin's most important contributions to the field (see Comment 1.6).

A Period of Growth

World War II had a tremendous impact on the growth of organizational psychology. For example, one of the results of World War II was that women were needed to fill many of the positions in factories that were vacated by the men called into military service. Also, shortly after World War II in 1948,

---

COMMENT 1.6

KURT LEWIN: THE PRACTICAL THEORIST

KURT LEWIN WAS born in 1890 in the village of Mogilno, which was then part of the Prussian province of Posen (now part of Poland). Lewin's father owned a general store, as well as a small farm, so the family was prosperous although not wealthy. In 1905, Lewin's family moved to Berlin, largely to gain better educational opportunities than were available in Mogilno. Lewin entered the University of Frieberg in 1909, initially with the goal of studying medicine. His distaste for anatomy courses contributed to Lewin's abandoning the goal of becoming a physician. He switched his interest to biology. This led to a transfer first to the University of Munich and ultimately to the University of Berlin, where he eventually earned his doctorate in 1916. After returning from military service during World War I, he began his academic career.

The years at Berlin were very productive, and Lewin's work became quite influential. At this time, Lewin began to develop an interest in the application of psychology to applied problems such as agricultural labor, production efficiency, and the design of jobs. Lewin became quite interested in scientific management, particularly the impact of this system on workers. Lewin and his family left Germany in 1933 due to the rise of the Nazi party. He initially received a temporary appointment at Cornell University, and ultimately moved to the University of Iowa Child Welfare Research Station. While at Iowa, Lewin conducted influential studies on a variety of topics, including child development, the impact of social climates, and leadership. Following his years at Iowa, Lewin became deeply involved in the Commission on Community Relations, which was established by the American Jewish Congress. During his involvement, Lewin initiated a number of "action research" projects aimed at enhancing understanding of community problems such as racial prejudice, gang violence, and integrated housing. Remarkably, during this same time, Lewin also founded the Research Center for Group Dynamics at MIT. Lewin's work at the Center continued until his death in 1947, at the age of 56.

In retrospect, it is hard to imagine anyone having a greater impact on the field of organizational psychology than Kurt Lewin. His ideas continue to influence the study of a number of areas such as employee motivation, leadership, group dynamics, and organizational development. However, perhaps Lewin's most enduring legacy was his innovative blending of science and practice.

Source: A. J. Marrow. (1969). *The practical theorist: The life and work of Kurt Lewin.* New York: Basic Books.

President Harry S. Truman made the decision to pursue racial integration of the military. Both events were extremely important because they represented initial attempts to understand the impact of diversity on the workplace, a topic that has become quite pertinent in recent years.

World War II also served as the impetus for major studies of morale and leadership styles. Although Hollywood has managed to portray a somewhat idealized version of WWII, the U.S. military experienced problems with low morale and even desertion. Thus, troop morale and the influence of leadership were issues of great practical importance during this time.

Another very important event in the development of organizational psychology was the publication of Morris Viteles' book *Motivation and Morale in Industry* (1953). This was significant because Viteles' 1932 book, *Industrial Psychology*, had contained very little on the organizational side of the field, largely because there simply wasn't much subject matter at that time. Thus, the 1953 book signified that the organizational side of the field had finally arrived and had a significant role to play in the broader field of industrial psychology. It was also during the post-WWII period that the human relations perspective emerged within the field. Those who advocated this perspective (e.g., McGregor, 1960) argued that the way organizations had traditionally been managed kept employees from being creative and fulfilled on the job. During this time, for example, Herzberg conducted his studies of job design and job enrichment, and major research programs investigating both leadership and job satisfaction were conducted. By the early 1960s, organizational psychology was clearly an equal partner with the industrial side of the field (Jeanneret, 1991).

Another broader social factor impacted the development of organizational psychology during the 1960s and early 1970s: the United States' involvement in the Vietnam War, which led to many cultural changes in America and in other countries. During this period, for example, many young people began to question conventional societal norms and the wisdom of traditional societal institutions such as education, government, and the legal system. Many, in fact, suspected that the federal government was not truthful about many important details of the war. Furthermore, subsequent accounts of the war by historians have proven that many of these suspicions were justified (e.g., Small, 1999). People at that time also began to feel as though they should have much more freedom to express themselves in a variety of ways (e.g., hairstyles, dress, speech).

For organizations, the cultural changes that arose out of the 1960s had major implications. In essence, it was becoming less and less common for people to blindly follow authority. Therefore, organizations had to find methods of motivating employees, other than simply offering financial incentives or threatening punishment. It was also becoming more and more common for employees to seek fulfillment in areas of their lives other than work. Thus, it was becoming increasingly difficult to find employees who were willing to focus exclusively on work.

Maturity and Expansion

From the early 1970s into the 1980s, organizational psychology began to mature as a field of study. For example, during the early 1970s, the name of Division 14 of the American Psychological Association (APA) was formally changed from Industrial Psychology to Industrial/Organizational Psychology. Also during this period, organizational psychologists began to break significant new ground in both theory and research. As just a few examples, Salancik and Pfeffer (1978) proposed Social Information Processing Theory (SIP) as an alternative to more traditional need-based theories of job satisfaction and job design. Also, roughly during this period, organizational psychology began to rediscover the impact of personality and dispositions on things such as job attitudes (Staw & Ross, 1985) and perceptions of job-related stress (Watson & Clark, 1984).

Another noteworthy development that took hold during this period, and continues today, was the recognition that behavior in organizations is impacted by forces at both the group and organizational levels (e.g., James & Jones, 1974; Rousseau, 1985). This multilevel perspective has had major implications for the field in guiding theory development as well as statistical methodology (e.g., Dansereau, Alutto, & Yammarino, 1984; James, Demaree, & Wolf, 1984). During this same period, organizational psychologists began to devote increasing attention to what could be called nontraditional topics. For example, more literature began to appear on work/family issues (e.g., Greenhaus & Buetell, 1985), job-related stress and health (Beehr & Newman, 1978), and retirement (Beehr, 1986). This willingness to explore nontraditional topics was significant because it served as evidence that the interests of organizational psychologists had broadened beyond purely management concerns.

From roughly the late 1980s to the year 2000, a number of trends have impacted the field of organizational psychology. If one takes a global perspective, perhaps the most significant event of this period was the breakup of the Soviet Union and the eventual fall of many Communist regimes. These extraordinary events have implications for organizational psychology because a number of the nations that embraced democracy during this period have also attempted to establish free-market economies. As many of these new democracies found out, managing and motivating employees in state-owned businesses is quite different from doing so in a free-market economy (Frese, Kring, Soose, & Zempel, 1996; Puffer, 1999; Stroh & Dennis, 1994). The science and the practice of organizational psychology can potentially help these nations make this difficult economic transition.

Another important trend that is taking place, both in the United States and worldwide, is the change in the demographic composition of the workforce. The world population is aging rapidly and becoming more ethnically diverse. One of the implications of these demographic shifts is that organizational psychologists will likely devote much more time and attention to understanding the process of retirement (e.g., Adams & Beehr, 1998). Organizational psychologists will likely help organizations as they assist employees in making the retirement transition. The increasing level of cultural diversity will also have wide-ranging implications. Organizational psychologists will increasingly be called upon to investigate the impact of cultural differences on organizational processes such as socialization, communication, and motivation.

A third trend that has become evident during this period is the move away from highly specific jobs, and toward more temporary, project-based work. Some have labeled this dejobbing (Bridges, 1994). This trend has a number of implications for organizational psychology. At the most fundamental level, this trend has impacted and will continue to impact the psychological contract between organizations and employees. What does an organization owe its employees? What do employees owe the organization they work for? In the past, the answers to these questions were rather straightforward; now, they have become increasingly complex.

Another implication of this trend is that many individuals are not employees in the way this word has typically been used in the past. Rather, it has become increasingly common for individuals to hire themselves out on a project or per diem basis. This trend suggests a number of interesting and challenging issues for organizational psychologists. How does an organization maintain a consistent culture and philosophy with a relatively transient workforce? Is it possible to motivate temporary employees to perform beyond an average level of performance? Although some research has been done on temporary, project-based work (Gallagher, 2005), more research clearly needs to be done before these questions can be answered with any degree of certainty.

Recent Past and Beyond

On the morning of September 11, 2001, hijacked commercial aircraft crashed into the World Trade Center in New York City and The Pentagon outside of Washington, DC. In terms of casualties, 9/11 represents one of the worst terrorist attacks in history, and certainly the worst on U.S. soil. Furthermore, for many readers of this text, 9/11 represents the defining moment of their generation, much the same way that the Kennedy assassination was for previous generations.

What are the implications of 9/11 for organizational psychology? This is a difficult question to answer with a high degree of certainty because of the magnitude of these events. Probably the most direct way that many organizations were impacted was in the area of emergency preparedness. That

is, 9/11 made many organizations aware of the need for having plans in place in case of emergencies. Had it not been for the emergency plans of many of the organizations with offices in the World Trade Center, the death toll of 9/11 would likely have been much higher.

Other than 9/11, other recent trends that have had the greatest impact on organizations have been technological change, increasing use of telecommuting and other flexible work arrangements, and increased globalization, to name a few. Advances in communication technology, for example, allow things to be done much quicker in organizations than was possible even 20 years ago. This technology has also allowed employees much greater flexibility in working arrangements, yet at the same time, made it more difficult for them to separate their work and nonwork lives. Considering all of these trends, it is clear that the work world of the recent past and not-too-distant future will be highly complex and fast paced. This may seem rather intimidating, but it is also a very exciting prospect for the field of organizational psychology because it will allow for truly groundbreaking research and practical applications. In fact, this is one of the most exciting times in history to be involved in the science and practice of organizational psychology.

THE CHAPTER SEQUENCE

A textbook should function as a tour guide for the student. In our experience, both as students and course instructors, the best way to guide is in a logical sequential fashion. The sequence of chapters in this book was developed with this consideration in mind. The chapters in Part I provide introductory material on the field of organizational psychology as well as its methodological foundations.

Some students (and maybe even some instructors) may find it unusual to have a chapter on research methodology. I've included it for three primary reasons. First, having at least a rudimentary understanding of research methodology is fundamental to understanding many of the concepts and research findings discussed throughout the text. Second, research methodology is a legitimate area of inquiry within organizational psychology. In fact, a great deal of important research within organizational psychology in recent years has been methodologically oriented. Finally, as a course instructor and supervisor of student research, I have found that students often forget (or perhaps repress) what they learn in research methods courses. Covering research methods in content courses often compensates for this forgetting.

The first seven chapters focus on the behavior of individuals in organizational settings. A close examination of these chapters reveals a sequential ordering. It is assumed that individuals are initially socialized into an organization (Chapter 3), become productive members of that organization (Chapter 4), and derive some level of satisfaction and commitment (Chapter 5). It is also recognized that individuals may engage in behaviors that are counterproductive to their employers (Chapter 6), and that work may have a negative effect on the health and well-being of employees (Chapter 7).

The next three chapters focus on the mechanisms that organizations use to influence employees' behaviors. To this end, Chapter 8 covers the major motivation theories in organizational psychology. In Chapter 9, we examine the various ways in which organizations utilize theories of motivation to actually influence employees' behaviors. Chapter 10 examines the other primary mechanism that organizations use to influence

behavior, namely leadership. Chapter 10 also examines power and influence processes that are at the core of leadership and yet influence many other behaviors in organizations.

In the next two chapters, the focus of the book shifts from the individual to the group level. This is very important, given the increased reliance on teams in many organizations. Chapter 11 introduces the basic concepts underlying group behavior. Chapter 12 describes the factors that have the greatest impact on group effectiveness, as well as the dynamics underlying intergroup behavior.

In the final three chapters, the focus shifts from the group to the organization—the macro level. Chapter 13 reviews several theoretical approaches used to define an organization and examines approaches to organizational design. Chapter 14 probes the concepts of organizational culture and climate. Chapter 15 describes the variety of ways in which organizations engage in planned change with the assistance of behavioral science knowledge.

One topic that readers will notice is not the focus of any one chapter is international or cross-cultural issues. This book examines cross-cultural issues in the context of the various topics covered in the chapters. This was done intentionally because we believe cross-cultural findings are best understood and assimilated in the context of specific topics.

CHAPTER SUMMARY

Organizational psychology is the scientific study of individual and group behavior in formal organizational settings. While it is a legitimate field of study in its own right, organizational psychology is actually part of the broader field of Industrial/Organizational (I/O) psychology. Organizational

PEOPLE BEHIND THE RESEARCH

MIKE J. ZICKAR AND THE HISTORY OF I-O PSYCHOLOGY

I am a firm believer in attacking life with a balance between goal-directed behavior as well as an openness to the moment. I received my Ph.D. from University of Illinois in 1997 and have been at Bowling Green State University since then. My training and primary research has been in psychometric work related to employment testing, a very quantitative area that is about as left-brain dominated as any research area in I-O psychology.

I got into historical research about 10 years ago when I started asking questions about the current state of I-O psychology; these questions were stimulated by a frustration with the way that I-O psychologists ignored certain topics that I viewed important. What function do labor unions have in the day-to-day lives of employees? Why do I-O psychologists, for the most part, focus on improving efficiency more so than improving worker well-being? These questions prompted me to look back in the history of our field.

Historical research relies much more on the right side of the brain compared to quantitative research. I find that balance very stimulating and useful in maintaining my intellectual curiosity. One of my favorite historical pieces is an article about my hero Arthur Kornhauser who was an early progressive I-O psychologist that worked actively with labor unions in the auto industry. When I contacted one of Kornhauser's former students, he seemed unfriendly and impatient until I told him that I wanted to discuss his former advisor. Instantly on hearing his former advisor's name, he warmed up and said in a mournful but pleasant tone, "I always told my wife that if we had had a son, I would have wanted to name him Arthur!"

I did not start off my career interested in historical research, though I now find it an important part of my intellectual identity. Regardless of what path your career takes you, I hope that you will remain open to change and that you stumble occasionally onto new directions and ideas.

Mike J. Zickar
Department of Psychology
Bowling Green State University

psychologists use scientific methods to study behavior in organizations. They also use this knowledge to solve practical problems in organizations; this is the essence of the scientist-practitioner model, the model on which most graduate training in I/O psychology is based. Thus, those with training in organizational psychology are employed in both academic and nonacademic settings. Historically, organizational psychology was slower to develop than the industrial side of the field. The event that is usually considered the historical beginning of organizational psychology was the Hawthorne studies, although many other events and individuals have helped to shape the field over the years and will continue to do so. A constant thread through the history of the field is the dynamic interaction between science and practice—in most cases for the betterment of organizations and their employees.

SUGGESTED ADDITIONAL READINGS

Dunnett, M. D. (1998). Emerging trends and vexing issues in industrial and organizational psychology. *Applied Psychology: An International Review, 47,* 129–153.

Koppes, L. L. (1997). American female pioneers of industrial and organizational psychology during the early years. *Journal of Applied Psychology, 82,* 500–515.

Landy, F. J. (1997). Early influences on the field of industrial and organizational psychology. *Journal of Applied Psychology, 82,* 467–477.

Hyatt, D., Cropanzano, R., Finfer, L. A., Levy, P., Ruddy, T.M., Vandaveer, V., & Walker, S. (1997). Bridging the gap between academics and practice: Suggestions from the field. *Industrial-Organizational Psychologist, 35,* 29–32.

Kanigel, R. (1997). *The one best way: Frederick Winslow Taylor and the enigma of efficiency.* New York: Viking.

Zickar, M. J. (2003). Remembering Arthur Kornhauser: Industrial psychology's advocate for worker well-being. *Journal of Applied Psychology, 88,* 363–369.

Chapter Two

Research Methods and Statistics

Organizational psychologists often design scientific investigations to answer a variety of research questions about behavior in organizational settings; in some cases research is designed to test theories. In order to conduct research, one must make use of research designs, as well as a variety of statistical analyses. As will be shown in this chapter, research methods may range from simple observation of behavior to more elaborate designs. Likewise, statistical methods may range from very simple descriptive measures, to very elaborate model testing.

Research methodology and statistical analysis are also crucial to the practice of organizational psychology. For example, organizational psychologists often use systematic research methods to provide organizational decision makers with information regarding employees' attitudes. In other cases, research methodology and statistical analysis may be used to evaluate some intervention designed to enhance organizational effectiveness. An organization may want to know, for example, whether a team development intervention will enhance the functioning of work groups. This question, and others like it, can also be answered with the aid of typical research methods and statistical analyses used in organizational psychology.

In addition to facilitating the science and practice of organizational psychology, research methodology and statistical analysis have both emerged as legitimate fields of study within organizational psychology. Some organizational psychologists study topics such as job satisfaction, motivation, and organizational change; others have

devoted their attention to methodological and statistical issues. For example, there are organizational psychologists who investigate the validity of self-report measures (e.g., Spector, 1994), as well as the analysis of data from multiple organizational levels (Bliese & Jex, 2002). Both topics will be discussed later in the chapter.

This chapter is designed to provide an introduction to the methods organizational psychologists use to collect data, as well as the statistical techniques used to analyze that data. From the student's perspective, research methodology and statistics are often viewed with some degree of apprehension. Even at the graduate level, courses in research methodology and statistics are often the most feared. Despite these negative perceptions, research methodology and statistics courses are probably the most valuable part of graduate training. Students who are well grounded in research methodology and statistics are in the best position to read and critically evaluate the research literature. They also possess a set of skills that are quite valuable, regardless of the setting in which they choose to work.

METHODS OF DATA COLLECTION

There are literally thousands of research questions that have been, and continue to be, explored by organizational psychologists. Are employees who perceive a high level of autonomy in their work likely to be highly satisfied with their jobs? Does a high level of conflict between work and family responsibilities lead to poor health? Does job performance remain consistent over time? Regardless of the research question being asked, there is a need for relevant data to be collected if the question is ever to be answered. In this section, four data-collection methods will be discussed. These include observational methods, survey research, experimentation, and quasi-experimentation.

Observational Methods

Observational methods actually encompass a variety of strategies that may be used to study behavior in organizations (Bouchard, 1976). *Simple observation*, the most basic of these strategies, involves observing and systematically recording behavior. If one wishes, for example, to investigate decision-making processes used by corporate boards of directors, one might observe these individuals during quarterly meetings and record rele-

vant observations. These observations may reveal that the chairperson has more input into decisions than other board members, or perhaps that younger board members have less input into decisions than their more experienced counterparts.

The primary advantage of simple observation is that it allows behavior to be captured in its natural context. This allows the researcher to avoid the problem of *reactivity*, or changing the phenomenon of interest in the process of measuring it. This is only a potential advantage, however, because the presence of an observer could cause research participants to act differently than they normally would. One way to address this issue is to establish rapport with research participants to the point where they are comfortable enough with the researcher to act naturally. Another option would be to observe the behavior of interest without being detected. For example, if one were interested in the emotions displayed by service employees toward customers, one might sit in a coffee shop and observe as customers' orders are taken. This technique is also used by many retail stores; they send *mystery shoppers* to stores in order to measure the quality of customer service. Observing behavior in this way raises ethical concerns, however, because when it is used, research participants typically are not able to make an informed choice as to whether they wish to participate in the research.

Despite potential advantages, a primary disadvantage of simple observation is that it is a very labor-intensive activity. Observing and recording behavior takes a great deal of time and effort. Also, once observations are recorded, making sense out this information can be very time consuming as well. Another potential disadvantage is that observations are often subjective and may be impacted by the observer's biases. Nevertheless, simple observation can often be quite useful, particularly in the very early stages of a research program. Also, from a practical perspective, managers may find the information generated from observational studies easier to understand, and therefore more useful, than numerical data.

A form of simple observation that may be useful in some cases is *participant observation*. Participant observation is essentially the same as simple observation, except that the observer is also a participant in the event he or she is studying. In the previous example of a researcher studying corporate boards of directors, this could be participant observation if the researcher were also a member of the board. Participant observation can be highly useful, particularly when being a participant in an event provides the researcher with information that may not be obtained otherwise. This point is illustrated well by Van Maanen's (1975) investigation of police recruits as they made the transition from the training academy to regular police work. In conducting this study, Van Maanen participated in the police academy training as a recruit, and thus became a participant in the event he was studying. By doing this, he undoubtedly was able to gather information that would have been unavailable through the use of other methods (see Comment 2.1).

Despite the potential advantages of participant observation, this method also carries some risks. The biggest of these is that by taking on the role of participant, a researcher may change the phenomenon under investigation. This is somewhat ironic, considering that the general advantage of observational methods is that they reduce the risk of reactivity. Being a participant may also lead the researcher to lose his or her objectivity. As previously stated, all observations are subject to distortion, but assuming the role of a participant may compound this problem. In Van Maanen's (1975) study, this problem was dealt with by supplementing his observations with survey data from other police recruits.

Archival Data

A second method for studying behavior in organizations is through the use of *archival data* sources. Archival data represent any form of data or other records that are compiled for purposes that are independent of the research being conducted (Webb, Campbell, Schwartz, Sechrest, & Grove, 1981). Compared to other observational methods, the use of archival data is more prevalent in organizational psychology, largely because of the sheer abundance of archival data sources. Within organizations, records are typically kept on many employee behaviors such as job performance, absenteeism, turnover, and safety, to name a few. In addition, the governments of many countries maintain databases that may be relevant to the study of behavior in organizations. In the United States, for example, the Department of Labor produces the Dictionary of Occupational Titles (DOT), which contains information on the working conditions of a vast number of occupations. This database has been used in several investigations of behavior in organizations (e.g., Schaubroeck, Ganster, & Kemmerer, 1994; Spector & Jex, 1991). Recently, the DOT has been supplemented by a more extensive database in the form of the Occupational Information Network (O*NET). This represents an improvement over the DOT because the occupations that comprise the O*NET are more up to date, and the dimensions on which these occupations are described are more extensive. To date, only a few studies have used O*NET as an archival data source in the same manner

THE PROS AND CONS OF QUALITATIVE RESEARCH METHODS

WITHIN THE GENERAL field of psychology, and organizational psychology in particular, qualitative data collection methods such as observation are not widely used. In other fields such as sociology and anthropology, qualitative methods are used quite frequently. In psychology, we make much greater use of surveys and, to a lesser extent, experimentation and quasi-experimentation (Sackett & Larsen, 1990). In talks with colleagues over the years, the typical disadvantages associated with qualitative methods have been that they are too labor-intensive and too many biases are associated with the observational process.

Unfortunately, because of these disadvantages, many in the field psychology fail to see many of the positive features of qualitative data-collection methods. Chief among these is that observation typically provides a much richer description of whatever one is trying to study than questionnaire data do. For example, observing a group working together for a week is probably more meaningful than knowing that group members rate the group's cohesiveness as 4.3 on a scale of 1 to 6. Another advantage of most qualitative data-collection methods is that they do not require research participants to provide assessments of either

themselves or the work environment. For example, we may be able to determine, through observations, that an employee has a great deal of autonomy built into his or her job. If we were to ask the employee several questions about job autonomy via a questionnaire, the employee's responses might be biased because of a temporary mood state or overall job satisfaction.

In reality, researchers do not have to make either/or decisions in choosing between qualitative and quantitative research methods. For example, in conducting employee opinion surveys, I typically use closed-ended questionnaire items, but I also include space at the end of the survey for employees to write comments that are then analyzed for content. This allows for quantitative analysis of the closed-ended survey items, but employees can express their opinions in their own words. Written comments may also reveal very useful suggestions to organizational decision makers.

Source: P. R. Sackett and J. R. Larsen, Jr. (1990). Research strategies and tactics in industrial and organizational psychology. In M. D. Dunnette & L. M. Hough (Eds.), *Handbook of industrial and organizational psychology* (2nd ed., Vol. 1, pp. 419–490). Palo Alto, CA: Consulting Psychologists Press.

as the DOT (e.g., Liu, Spector, & Jex, 2004), but it is likely that more will follow.

In addition to these common archival data sources, organizational psychologists have also made use of other less common sources to study organizational processes. Sports statistics, in particular, are widely available and can be used to examine (albeit indirectly) organizational processes. Organizational psychologists, for example, have used the performance of professional base-

ball players to study equity theory (Lord & Hohenfeld, 1979), and professional hockey players to study leadership processes (Day, Sin, & Chen, 2004).

The use of archival data offers several advantages to researchers. First, many archival databases are readily available to the public and can be accessed quite easily—in many cases, via the Internet. Second, archival data are nonreactive. Archival data typically are not collected for the researcher's purpose, so there is no chance that participants will distort responses in a way that would impact the validity of the research. Finally, when archival data are used to measure employee behaviors, such records are usually less subject to distortion than self-reports of the same behavior.

Despite these advantages, the use of archival data may present several problems. One is that archival databases contain only indirect measures of the phenomenon of interest to the researcher. Use of databases such as the DOT or O*NET to measure characteristics of employees' jobs illustrates this problem quite well. Information contained in both of these databases is collected at the occupation level, so using it may mask important differences between individuals who may have the same occupation but perform substantially different work, or who perform under very different conditions. For example, a nurse employed in a rural health clinic may have very different job duties than one employed in a large urban hospital, even though they are part of the same occupation.

This issue becomes even more problematic when researchers use sports statistics to study organizational processes. Lord and Hohenfeld (1979), for example, examined the performance of baseball free agents in what is termed the *arbitration* year, or the year prior to going on the free-agent market. Based on the players' performance in this year, and the first year of their new contract, these researchers made inferences about how these players resolved their feelings of underpayment. What these researchers *didn't* do, however, was ask these players *directly* about whether they felt underpaid or how they planned to resolve feelings of underpayment.

Another potential problem with archival data is accuracy. Organizations differ widely in the precision of their record-keeping prac-

tices. Furthermore, there may be instances when an organization has some incentive to distort records. For example, organizations may underreport accidents or other negative incidents in order to avoid negative publicity or increases in insurance costs. Accuracy is probably less of an issue when archival data are obtained from government agencies and well-known academic research institutes. Nevertheless, when using any form of archival data it is always a good idea to ask for some evidence supporting the accuracy of the information.

Survey Research

By far the most widely used form of data collection in organizational psychology is survey research (Scandura & Williams, 2000). Survey research simply involves asking research participants to report about their attitudes and/or behaviors, either in writing or verbally. This form of research is extremely common in our society and is used to gather information for a wide variety of purposes. Most readers have probably participated in some form of survey research.

Before describing the general steps involved in conducting a survey research project, it is useful to consider the purposes of survey research. In some cases, survey research is designed to provide purely descriptive information. For example, the top management team in an organization may wish to know the current level of employee job satisfaction, a government agency may want to assess the income level of working adults, or a research institute may want to know the level of drug use among teenagers. Studies designed for this purpose are often referred to as *prevalence studies*.

Survey research is also conducted to test hypotheses regarding the relationships between variables. For example, a researcher may want to assess whether employees who perceive a great deal of autonomy in their jobs also report a high level of job satisfaction. The researcher in this case is not really concerned with the actual levels of autonomy or job satisfaction, but rather is interested in whether these two variables are related.

As shown in Figure 2.1, the first step in conducting a survey research project is to identify the variables that one will be measuring. For theoretically based research projects, the variables will be directly linked to the research question one is examining. A researcher studying the relationship between interpersonal conflict on the job and employees' satisfaction with their jobs would obviously measure both of these variables. The choice of variables to be measured in

more applied research is often based on the concerns of upper-management personnel or, in some cases, input from employees from all levels of the organization. Determining what to measure in surveys is often achieved through the use of *focus groups* consisting of either top managers or groups of other employees. A focus group is a qualitative data-gathering technique that is often used to generate ideas during the preliminary stages of a research project. For example, to determine what to measure on a survey, a researcher might conduct a focus group with the top management of an organization. The researcher might begin the focus group session by posing a question: "What are the biggest concerns of employees in this organization?" This would be followed by an open-ended discussion, during which the researcher would take note of major issues that come up.

Once the researcher has decided which variables to measure, the next step is to conduct an extensive search of relevant literature on these variables. This is done to determine whether acceptable measures of the variables exist. For many variables of interest to organizational psychologists, several acceptable measures are available. Using previously developed measures saves a researcher considerable time because there is no need to develop new measures. While this can usually be done in theoretically based research projects, using established measures in applied projects such as employee opinion surveys is often more difficult to do. This is because many of the variables measured in employee opinion surveys may be unique to a particular organization. In the present authors' experience, organizations often want survey items *customized* in order to enhance the relevance of the information.

Once a researcher has decided on the variables to be measured and identified

FIGURE 2.1

Steps Involved in Conducting a Survey Research Project

acceptable measures, the next step is to design the questionnaire or survey instrument. This step is extremely important because the quality of the questionnaire will strongly impact the integrity of the data generated. Designing a high-quality survey instrument is a time-consuming, painstaking process. Fortunately, there are excellent sources of information one can refer to for assistance in the questionnaire design process (e.g., Dillman, 2000). One general rule should guide the development of any questionnaire: *It should be easy for the respondent to complete.* That is, instructions should be easy to understand, response categories should be well defined, and the items should be clearly written. It is probably for this reason that more and more researchers have been making use of Internet-based collection of survey data. Respondents need only click the appropriate response categories when completing an Internet-based survey, and simply click a send button when they're done. A potential disadvantage of Internet-based data collection, of course, is that the researcher has little control over who actually completes the survey instrument. It is also possible that samples generated via the Internet may systematically differ (e.g., they may be more educated) from samples generated through other methods.

Another important step in the questionnaire design process is to conduct some form of pilot testing, even if this involves simply asking a colleague to read through the questionnaire. Careful pilot testing may reveal unclear instructions, poorly worded items, or even misspellings.

After the questionnaire is designed and pilot tested, the next step is to determine specifically who the respondents will be. When research is conducted within organizations, this may simply involve asking all employees to complete the survey. In other

cases, it may be necessary to narrow the pool of responding employees. For example, if a researcher were studying customer service behavior among employees, he or she would have to restrict the pool of respondents to those employees who have at least some contact with customers.

In some cases the number of potential respondents may be so large that it is impractical for the researcher to include everyone (e.g., a multi-national corporation with 50,000 employees). If this is the case, some form of *probability sampling* may be utilized. The idea behind probability sampling is that the researcher selects a sample from a larger group (or population) in order to generalize the results to that larger group, within some margin of error (Fowler, 1984). The most basic form of probability sampling is *simple random sampling*. This involves selecting members of a population such that all have an equal and nonzero probability of being included in the sample. As an example, a researcher could randomly select 200 employees from a current employee directory to participate in an organizational survey.

Another form of probability sampling sometimes used is *stratified random sampling*. This essentially represents the application of simple random sampling within identifiable groups or *strata*. Stratified random sampling is often used to increase the precision of estimates (Fowler, 1984); the logic is that if estimates are made within strata and pooled, these will be more precise than applying simple random sampling within an entire population. Stratified random sampling can also be used to increase the representativeness of samples. If, for example, an organization consists of five different employee groups that are represented in equal proportions, proportional stratified random sampling can be used to increase the chances that the sample will reflect this.

A third form of probability sampling that may be useful in some cases is *cluster sampling*. What distinguishes this from the other two forms of sampling previously described is that the unit of sampling is no longer the individual but, instead, some larger unit or *cluster*. An illustration of how cluster sampling can be used comes from a research project one of the authors conducted several years ago for the U.S. Army Recruiting Command (USAREC). This organization is very geographically dispersed and consists of multiple levels (brigades, battalions, companies, and stations). In the initial stages of the project, it was decided that approximately 50 face-to-face interviews needed to be conducted with personnel at brigade, battalion, and company levels. Rather than randomly selecting *individuals* from these three levels, it was decided to first randomly select two battalions within each brigade. Two individuals were interviewed in each battalion, as well as in the company located closest to each battalion.

A major advantage of cluster sampling is that it allows a researcher to cut down on travel time and expense. In the previously described project, imagine if simple random sampling had been used instead of cluster sampling. The 50 individuals selected to be interviewed may have been so geographically spread out that a separate trip would have been required to conduct each interview. Of course, the risk one runs in using cluster sampling is that the sample may not be as representative as it would be if simple random sampling were used. In most cases, though, researchers will accept the risk of decreased representativeness in order to cut down on costs (see Comment 2.2).

Once the researcher determines who the participants will be, the next step is to actually collect data. In collecting survey data, several options are available, and each option has advantages and disadvantages. With written organizational surveys, the ideal way to collect data is to have groups of employees complete the questionnaire in a centralized location and return the completed questionnaire to the researcher upon completion. This is ideal because it provides the best chance for a favorable response rate. A very low response rate is undesirable because it raises concerns about whether the survey results truly represent the target group. For example, in an organization where one of the authors once worked, an employee opinion survey was conducted and the response rate was approximately 10%! This low response rate was revealing in and of itself, but it also raised questions about the validity of the information.

In some cases, centralized data collection is not possible because of employees' schedules or concerns about confidentiality. Other options that are used in some cases are mailing questionnaires to employees' homes, administering a questionnaire verbally by telephone, or e-mailing questionnaires via the Internet or Intranet (i.e., internal system). Although these methods are somewhat less desirable than centralized on-site data collection, there are actually many ways that researchers can use them and achieve very favorable response rates (e.g., Dillman et al., 2000).

The final step in conducting a survey research project is the analysis and presentation of the data. The analysis of survey data is dictated by the purpose of the survey. If the purpose is description (which is usually the case when organizations initiate survey research projects), analyses are relatively simple and straightforward. Descriptive statistics (e.g., means, ranges, percentages) will usually suffice in such situations. In cases where survey data are used for theoretically

COMMENT 2.2

THE COST OF SURVEY RESEARCH

SURVEY RESEARCH IS by far the most commonly used data-collection method in organizational psychology. While survey research has many advantages, it is also true that surveys can be quite costly. Even if a researcher conducts a relatively simple, paper-and-pencil, self-administered survey of 200 employees in an organization, there are monetary costs associated with photocopying, incentives for respondents, and in many cases postage for return envelopes. This type of research project may also require that a researcher spend time personally contacting respondents and reminding them to complete the survey. Internet-based surveys reduce photocopying costs, but the time required to properly design

a web-based data-collection tool is often considerable.

As the size and scope of a survey research project grows, researchers often must hire survey research firms to handle the data collection. This increases efficiency for the researchers, but unfortunately is very costly. For example, it is not unusual for survey research firms to charge several thousand dollars to collect survey data even when sample sizes are relatively modest. Typically when researchers wish to sample very large numbers of respondents, they must seek financial support from government agencies or private foundations in order to cover the costs of these projects.

based hypothesis testing, analyses are conducted to test hypothesized relations between variables. More detailed information on statistical analyses used in hypothesis testing will be discussed later in the chapter. However, it is worth noting here that survey data are typically best for assessing covariation among variables; that is, a change in one variable is associated with a change in another. Assessing whether one variable *causes* a change in another variable is difficult to do with survey data because such data are usually collected at one point in time.

One way to make survey data more amenable to the assessment of causality is to use a *longitudinal* design. An example of this might be measuring employees' job perceptions at one point in time, and then measuring job attitudes 6 months later. Compared to cross-sectional designs, longitudinal research is better because it at least gives the researcher a temporal basis on which to make causal

statements. In the previous example, since job perceptions were measured *prior to* job attitudes it is certainly plausible that job perceptions might have a causal impact on job attitudes. As another example, Britt, Castro, and Adler (2005) examined whether being personally engaged in one's job could buffer soldiers from the adverse effects of working long hours and being away a large number of days for training. These authors found support for this hypothesis by showing that work hours and days training assessed at one point in time predicted health symptoms 3 months later only for soldiers who reported low levels of job engagement. However, an obvious downside to longitudinal research is that it is often impractical because researchers have to keep track of respondents. In recent years, many researchers have begun using very short-term intensive longitudinal designs in which participants provide a large number of observations over a short time period (e.g., Fuller et al., 2003).

Experimentation

Another common form of data collection in organizational psychology is *experimentation*. An experiment is a highly controlled situation that provides a researcher the best opportunity to assess cause-and-effect relationships. This is important because the hallmark of any science is to detect and explain causal relationships.

Because the term *experiment* is very commonly used, students are often unclear about what constitutes a *true* experiment. According to Cook and Campbell (1979), three characteristics distinguish a true experiment from other methods. These are (1) manipulation of an independent variable and measurement of a dependent variable; (2) random assignment to experimental treatment conditions; and (3) maximum control by the experimenter. Let's examine each of these characteristics.

The term *independent variable* is used to designate the variable that is proposed to have some effect on other variables, and hence is typically of primary interest to the researcher. When the independent variable is *manipulated*, this means that research participants experience different levels of this variable. If a researcher were interested in the impact of feedback on performance, for example, the independent variable would be feedback. This variable could be manipulated by providing one group of research participants with feedback after performing a task, while providing no feedback to a second group.

The measurement of the *dependent variable* simply involves some systematic record of the research participants' behaviors or attitudes that may be impacted by the independent variable. Choice of dependent measures is often based on prior research, or accepted practice. In organizational psychology, for example, it is common practice to measure attitudinal-dependent variables with surveys. It is always important, however, to keep in mind that the dependent measure being used is really just an operational definition of a concept. For example, job satisfaction represents whether a person has a positive or negative feeling about his or her job or a job situation. If a five-item scale is used to *assess* job satisfaction, this measure is really being used to represent this conceptual definition.

The second defining characteristic of experimentation, *random assignment*, means that research participants are assigned to groups receiving different levels of the independent variable (also called *treatment conditions*) in a random or nonsystematic fashion. Randomly assigning research participants can be done quite easily—for example, by flipping a coin. The logic behind random assignment is very simple—if research participants are assigned in a truly random fashion, it is likely that the different treatment groups will be similar in all ways except for the independent variable. This allows the researcher to isolate the independent variable as the cause of any differences between treatment conditions on the dependent variable.

The third defining characteristic of an experiment, *maximum control*, means that manipulation of the independent variable and the measurement of the dependent variable are done under controlled conditions. The researcher tries to make sure that all variables other than the independent variable are held constant. Like random assignment, this is done to isolate the independent variable as the cause of any differences among the treatment groups. When experiments are conducted in laboratory settings, researchers can usually achieve a desirable level of control. This is a much greater challenge when experiments are conducted in field settings, though not impossible. Eden (1985), for example, conducted a field experiment in the Israeli Defenses Forces to evaluate the impact of a team development intervention.

Quasi-Experimentation

According to Cook, Campbell, and Perrachio (1990), a quasi-experiment is similar to a true experiment except that it lacks one or more of the essential features previously described. In organizational settings, the independent variable of interest often cannot be manipulated because it is under the control of the organization, or may even be a naturally occurring event. Examples of independent variables that are usually under organizational control would include training programs or the redesign of jobs. Naturally occurring events that could be used as independent variables may include computer shutdowns, changes in government regulations, or mergers. In all of these cases, the researcher has no control over which research participants receive which *treatments*.

Quasi-experimental designs are also used in organizational settings because research participants usually cannot be randomly assigned to treatment conditions. Assignment to training programs provides a good example of nonrandom assignment. Employees typically participate in training programs, either voluntarily or on the basis of an identified training need (Goldstein, 1993). Thus, in most cases, if a researcher were to compare training-program participants to nonparticipants, these two groups could possibly differ in important ways.

Given the constraints that accompany quasi-experimentation, how do researchers set about proving that an independent variable has a causal impact on a dependent

measure? One way is to measure and statistically control variables that may obscure the relationship between the independent and dependent variables. For example, if the average age of a group of employees receiving one level of the independent variable is higher than the age of groups receiving other levels, age can be measured and statistically controlled when comparing the groups. This would be using age as a *covariate*.

Other than statistical control, quasi-experimentation typically requires that researchers systematically identify and rule out alternatives to the independent variable when differences between treatment groups are found. According to Cook and Campbell (1979), there are a variety of explanations, other than the independent variable, that may lead to a difference between a treatment group(s) and a control group in quasi-experimental designs. For example, participants in different groups may be exposed to different historical events, participants may change at different rates, or participants may have differing views about participating in the research.

A researcher conducting a quasi-experiment can never know for sure whether any number of alternative explanations are impacting his or her findings. However, it is often possible to assess the *plausibility* of different alternative explanations. For example, let's say a researcher conducted a quasi-experiment in which the job of bank teller was redesigned at one branch of a bank, but remained the same at another. After 3 months it is found that customer satisfaction is much higher at the branch where the job redesign took place compared to the branch where the job was not changed. The job redesign may have caused the increase in customer satisfaction, but since this was not a true experiment, there may be explanations other than the job redesign. To rule out these alternative explanations, the researcher could begin by comparing these two branches to see whether any preexisting differences between employees in the two branches could have caused the difference in customer satisfaction. If the employees at these two branches were similar in terms of tenure and overall job performance, these could be ruled out as alternative explanations for the findings. The researcher could also gather information on the nature of the customers who frequent each of the two branches. If customers at the two branches tend to be demographically similar, and have similar income levels, this could also be ruled out as an alternative explanation of the difference in customer satisfaction. The researcher, in effect, plays detective in order to identify and rule out alternative explanations for his or her findings. Note that it is never possible to identify *every* possible alternative explanation, so researchers typically attempt to rule out only the most plausible.

Choosing Among Data-Collection Methods

Given the information presented about each method of data collection, readers may wonder how to choose which method to use. Unfortunately, there is no concrete formula for making this choice. Perhaps the best approach is to weigh the advantages and disadvantages of each method. As is illustrated in Figure 2.2, the primary advantage of observational methods is that they provide the researcher with an opportunity to study behavior in its natural context. Unfortunately, observational techniques tend to be highly labor intensive.

Archival data may allow researchers to avoid potential problems associated with self-report measures. An additional advantage of archival data is that they are often

FIGURE 2.2

Summary of the Primary Advantages and Disadvantages Associated with Each of the Four Data Collection Methods

Observational Methods

Advantages	Disadvantages
• Behavior is captured in its natural context.	• May be highly labor intensive.
• Avoids the problem of "reactivity."	• Observations may be subject to bias.
• Some forms of observational data are readily available.	• Some forms of observational data only measure behavior indirectly.

Archival Data

Advantages	Disadvantages
• Easy to obtain	• Measures behavior indirectly.
• Non-reactive	• Not always accurate

Survey Research

Advantages	Disadvantages
• Allows the collection of data from large numbers of participants at low cost.	• Difficult to draw causal interferences from survey data
• Survey data can typically be analyzed with very powerful statistical methods.	• Response rates for some forms of survey data are low.
	• Survey design is a difficult, time-consuming process.

Experimentation

Advantages	Disadvantages
• Best way to assess causal relationships.	• Generalizability of findings may be questionable.
• Best way to isolate the impact of a specific variable.	• Examining a variable in isolation may be unrealistic.
• Gaining compliance of participants is easier compared to survey research.	• Participants may not take the experimental situation serious.

Quasi-Experimentation

Advantages	Disadvantages
• Allows the researcher a way to access causality in naturalistic settings.	• Organizations may be reluctant to allow these to be conducted.
• An excellent way to evaluate the impact of organizational interventions.	• Researchers have very little control.

widely available. The primary disadvantage of archival data is that the researcher usually has little control over how such data were collected. That is, one must take on faith that such data have been properly collected and are accurate.

Survey methodology allows the researcher to obtain data from a large number of participants at a relatively low cost. However, it is typically difficult to draw causal inferences from survey data, especially when the data are cross sectional. Experimentation provides the researcher with the best way to assess causal relationships. In some cases, however, the generalizability of experimental findings may be questionable. Finally, quasi-experimentation, in many cases, offers the researcher a way to assess causal relationships in naturalistic settings. However, quasi-experiments may be difficult to conduct because researchers typically have little control in most field settings.

Given the advantages and disadvantages summarized in Figure 2.2, the choice of a data-collection method depends largely on a researcher's objectives. If establishing causality is of primary importance, then experimentation is likely to be the method of choice. On the other hand, if capturing behavior in its natural context is the primary concern, then observation or quasi-experimentation may be preferred. Ideally, the best course of action is to use multiple methods of data collection (see Comment 2.3).

COMMENT 2.3

THE CASE FOR MULTIPLE DATA-COLLECTION METHODS

UNFORTUNATELY, A SIGNIFICANT portion of research in organizational psychology suffers from what has been termed *mono-operation* bias. This means that, in many studies, all of the variables are measured using only one form of data collection. Often, this one form of data collection is a self-report questionnaire, although it does not have to be. For example, a study would suffer just as much from this form of bias if all variables were measured using simple observation.

Why is it a problem to measure all variables in a study with only one form of data collection? One obvious reason is that the relationships among variables may be inflated because they share a common method (e.g., common-method bias). Another way to view this issue is to think about the positive impact of using multiple forms of data collection in a single study. Let's say a researcher is interested in whether job autonomy is positively related to job satisfaction. Further assume that, in this study, job autonomy is measured through a self-report measure completed by employees, and through archival information collected during a job analysis. Job satisfaction could be measured through a self-report measure and thorough observation of employees through their workday.

After these data are collected, we would likely find that the self-report autonomy measure would be positively related to the self-report job-satisfaction measure. However, what if the archival measure of job autonomy is also related to the self-report job-satisfaction measure? What if the self-report job autonomy is positively related to the observational measure of job satisfaction? If both of these results occur, this would most certainly strengthen the conclusion that job autonomy really does positively relate to job satisfaction. Thus, the real benefit of using multiple data-collection methods is that it allows us to show relationships between variables in multiple ways.

SPECIAL ISSUES IN DATA COLLECTION

Now that the most common methods of data collection have been described, we will explore, in this section, some important contemporary issues related to these methods. Contemporary issues include validity of self-report measures, generalizing laboratory findings to field settings, gaining access to organizations for data collection, and conducting research in different cultures.

Validity of Self-Reports

Self-report measures are used very frequently in organizational psychology. For example, employees are asked to report how much they like their jobs, how much variety they perceive in their work, how committed they are to their employing organization, and how anxious they feel about their jobs—just to cite a few examples. Because self-reports are used so frequently, we often don't give much thought to the assumptions we are making when we use such measures, or whether or not they are valid. Both issues are examined in this section.

Self-report measurement is really based on two implicit assumptions. First, we assume that respondents *know* the information we are asking for in self-report measures. Many of the questions asked in organizational surveys are subjective (i.e., there is no right or wrong answer), so it is pretty reasonable to assume that respondents know this information. Most people know whether they like their job, for example. In other cases, lack of knowledge may compromise the validity of self-report measures. For example, one of the authors once worked in a university system that conducts an annual survey of the job-related activities of faculty. Faculty were asked on this survey to indicate the number of hours in a typical week they devote to course preparation, teaching, research, and university service. While some university faculty may keep detailed logs of what they do each day, most probably have only a very vague idea of the number of hours spent on each of the activities on the survey.

A second assumption underlying self-report measurement is that respondents will be truthful in their responses. Compared to researchers interested in some forms of behavior (e.g., drug use, criminal activity), organizational psychologists are relatively fortunate in this regard. Because most of the items on organizational surveys are not highly sensitive or invasive, employees probably respond truthfully to such items, provided they believe their responses will be held in confidence. In reality, however, employees' comfort levels with surveys vary greatly. For example, when organizational researchers use self-reports to measure things such as absenteeism, turnover intentions, or various forms of counterproductive behavior (e.g., theft, sabotage), employees may not answer truthfully. In such cases, all a researcher can really do is take great care to reassure employees and conduct the survey in such a way that supports the promise of confidentiality. This might include providing employees with stamped envelopes to mail completed surveys to the researcher offsite, or perhaps making sure there is no identifying information contained on the survey instrument itself.

The situation that has generated the most controversy surrounding the use of self-reports is when such measures are used to rate job and organizational conditions. A researcher, for example, may ask respondents about the level of time pressure in their jobs. According to Spector (1994), self-reports often do not correlate well with more *objective* measures of the work environment, such as ratings by job analysts or by others familiar with the same job (Liu, Spector, & Jex, 2004; Spector, Dwyer, & Jex, 1988; Spector & Jex, 1991). Use of self-report measures is also controversial when such measures are correlated with other self-report variables. When this is the case, the correlations between such variables may possibly be inflated due to *common method variance*—a term that is used quite frequently but is rarely explicitly defined. Common method variance represents shared sources of measurement bias between two variables that can be directly tied to the method of measurement being used (Spector, 1987b). As an example, let's say that a researcher is measuring two variables via self-report. Further assume that both of these measures, for some reason, are impacted by social desirability responding (Crowne & Marlowe, 1964)—that is, responses to items in both measures differ in their levels of social desirability. This shared source of measurement bias may lead these two variables to be correlated, even if there is little or no underlying conceptual relationship between the two variables. In cases in which these measures are conceptually related, the presence of common method variance may inflate the magnitude of the relationship between the two variables.

Should researchers be concerned about common method variance? The consensus in the literature seems to be "Yes" (e.g., Podsakoff, MacKenzie, Lee, & Podsakoff, 2003). However, empirical efforts to actually demonstrate the effects of common method bias on relationships between variables have provided only mixed results. Spector (1987b), for example, empirically investigated the prevalence of common method variance in the measurement of job characteristics and job satisfaction. Based on an analysis of sev-eral data sets, he concluded that there was no strong evidence that correlations were inflated due to common method variance.

Spector's (1987) investigation prompted several attempts to replicate his findings; most of these attempts utilized more complex statistical techniques (e.g., Bagozzi & Yi, 1990; Williams & Anderson, 1994; Williams, Cote, & Buckley, 1989). A complete discussion of the findings of these studies is beyond the scope of this chapter, but the general conclusion of these studies was that the impact of common method variance is greater than Spector had estimated. However, as Brannick and Spector (1990) pointed out, there are problems in the use of complex statistical methodology to test for the effects of common method variance.

Perhaps the best way to empirically assess the impact of common method variance is to compare correlations that contain a shared method with those that do not share a method. Crampton and Wagner (1994) conducted a meta-analysis in which they summarized 42,934 correlations from studies using single and multiple methods. Overall, they found that correlations between variables that were both measured via self-report were not appreciably larger than other correlations. In the measurement of some variables, however, correlations based on a single source were larger than others. This suggests that the impact of common method variance is real; however, the magnitude of this effect varies widely, depending on the nature of the variables being measured.

The best conclusion one can draw about the validity of self-report measures is that it depends primarily on the variable being measured, and the research question being asked. For example, if one were interested in measuring employees' feelings about their jobs, then a self-report measure would be quite appropriate. On the other hand, if one were interested in measuring employees' levels of job autonomy, levels of discretion in decision making, or (perhaps) workload, then measuring these variables only with self-report measures is not really appropriate. This is because in all of these examples the researcher is interested in characteristics of the *environment*, not those of the individual employee. When researchers wish to measure characteristics of the work environment, the best course of action is to use multiple measurement methods (e.g., Glick, Jenkins, & Gupta, 1986). Given the reliance

of much organizational research on self-report measurement, it is likely that the pros and cons of self-report measurement are likely to be debated for quite some time (see Comment 2.4).

Generalizing Laboratory Findings

A common criticism of psychology is that it is a science based largely on laboratory studies that investigate the behavior of white rats and college students. Research in organizational psychology tends not to be conducted

---

COMMENT 2.4

THE SELF-REPORT CONTROVERSY

SELF-REPORT MEASUREMENT is undoubtedly the most common form of data collection in organizational psychology. It is also a form of data collection that has evoked a great deal of controversy, particularly when self-reports are used to measure all of the variables in a study. Dr. Steve Jex has followed this issue for over a decade, primarily because it has a great deal of relevance to his own research program in occupational stress, since self-report measures tend to predominate.

On the positive side, self-reports allow us to measure something that is important in determining human behavior—namely, individuals' perceptions of their environments, their emotional states, and, in some cases, their views of other people. Self-report measurement is also very economical. In the time it might take to collect meaningful observations of 20 people, a self-report measure could be distributed to 100 times that many people.

The primary drawback to self-report measurement is that humans are not analytical instruments; thus, self-reports may not always produce accurate information. For example, when we ask employees to provide self-reports

of characteristics of their jobs, these ratings may be biased by internal mood states, social influences of coworkers, or stable internal dispositions (Spector, 1994). These same biases may also influence self-reports of emotional and affective states.

What is the most reasonable conclusion one can draw about self-report measures? In my opinion, it is that self-report measurement, like any other data collection method, has both advantages and disadvantages. Whether one uses self-report measurement should be dictated primarily by the variables one is trying to measure, which are ultimately dictated by the research question one is trying to answer. As a general rule, if one is primarily interested in perceptions, then self-report measurement is a logical choice. However, if one is interested in actual environmental conditions, then self-reports should be supplemented with other forms of data collection.

Source: P. E. Spector. (1994). Using self-report questionnaires in OB research: A comment on the use of a controversial method. *Journal of Organizational Behavior, 15,* 385–392.

as much in laboratory settings in comparison to other areas of psychology (e.g., physiological, cognitive). Laboratory studies do, however, still account for a substantial portion of the research in both organizational psychology and I/O psychology in general (Locke, 1986; Sackett & Larsen, 1990; Scandura & Williams, 2000). The purpose of this section is to examine the issue of whether findings from laboratory investigations can be generalized to *real* organizational settings.

The strongest argument made against laboratory findings' generalizing to field settings is that laboratory situations lack realism. University laboratories are not real organizations; thus, laboratory settings lack what is referred to as *mundane realism*. Realism, however, must also be considered from the perspective of the research participant. It is certainly possible to place a research participant in a situation that lacks mundane realism, yet manipulate variables in such as way that participants react genuinely to the situation. For example, one can be in a completely contrived situation yet still feel pressure to perform well or conform to group norms. When this is the case, it can be said that there is a high degree of *experimental realism* for research participants. Many classic laboratory studies conducted over the years, particularly in social psychology (e.g., Asch, 1957; Milgram, 1974), have lacked mundane realism yet have retained a very high degree of experimental realism.

Another reason laboratory investigations may generalize has to do with the research participants. At the beginning of this section, it was remarked, somewhat facetiously, that laboratory investigations often utilize college students as participants. This often leads to the criticism that, because college students are different from the general population, research findings cannot be generalized. This criticism certainly does have some merit—college students are more intelligent and typically come from higher income levels than the general population (Sears, 1986). However, for the study of many organizational issues, use of college students as research participants probably does not compromise generalizability a great deal. College students, for the most part, represent the cadre of individuals who will hold many of the white-collar jobs in the future. Thus, they may be quite similar to such employees, both in terms of attitudes and abilities, even though they are obviously lacking in relevant organizational experience. By contrast, college students are probably a poor research sample if the aim is to generalize to employees holding blue-collar and manual labor jobs.

Despite these arguments for the generalizability of laboratory experiments, there are clearly important differences between laboratory and field settings. In particular, the high level of experimental control in laboratory settings allows the researcher to isolate the impact of a variable in a way that is impossible in field settings because so many things are occurring that the impact of any single variable may be greatly diluted. Also, when variables are investigated in laboratory settings, they are taken out of their natural context. By taking a variable out of context, the researcher runs the risk of changing the substantive nature of that variable. A good illustration of this point is laboratory research on the effects of ambient temperature on aggression (e.g., Baron & Bell, 1976). In a laboratory setting, it is possible to completely isolate the impact of temperature. In natural settings, however, temperature increases often occur in conjunction with other variables such as loud noise and crowding.

Another important difference to consider is that laboratory settings are typically short term (Runkel & McGrath, 1972). As a result, participants in laboratory investigations have very little time invested and have no reason to form any social ties with others. In contrast, employees in organizations invest a considerable amount of time in their jobs, and often develop important social ties with fellow employees. These differences between laboratory research participants and actual employees may lead to very different reactions to the same situations.

A final important difference between laboratory and field settings is the nature of the tasks performed by research participants. Since laboratory investigations are short term, it is very difficult to match the complexity of the tasks performed by employees in real organizations. Thus, many laboratory studies ask participants to perform relatively simple tasks such as assembling tinker toys, solving anagrams, and putting together puzzles. In contrast, employees in organizational settings perform much more complex tasks.

After examining the pros and cons of laboratory investigations, we are still left with the question of whether laboratory findings generalize to field settings such as organizations. Unfortunately, there is no definitive answer to this question, although it has been examined extensively (e.g., Berkowitz & Donnerstein, 1982; Dipboye & Flanagan, 1979). The most comprehensive analysis of this issue, relevant to organizational psychology, is contained in *Generalizing from Laboratory to Field Settings*, a book edited by Edwin Locke in 1986. The general conclusion one can draw from this book is that well-designed laboratory investigations often do generalize to field settings. A well-designed laboratory investigation is one in which participants are highly engaged in the task being performed and variable(s) of

interest are well simulated. The reader should be cautioned, however, against concluding that all findings do or do not generalize. In the end, generalizability is an empirical question, and the best course of action is to replicate laboratory findings in field settings whenever possible.

Gaining Access to Organizations

One of the biggest challenges from field research is simply gaining access to an organization for data collection. The authors have known, over the years, many colleagues and students who have come up with interesting research questions, but could find no organization in which to collect data. Unfortunately, there is very little in the organizational literature to help guide researchers in their efforts to gain access to organizations. Thus, most of this section is based on both the authors' experience as researchers, and the experiences of fellow organizational researchers.

Before exploring ways to gain access to organizations, consider reasons why organizations would *not* let a researcher gather data. Based on past experience, there are two primary reasons: (1) data collection usually requires employees' time, and (2) organizations are concerned that employees may divulge sensitive or proprietary information about the organization. Organizations that operate in very competitive industries (e.g., consumer products, high technology) are often very concerned with divulging any information that might put them at a competitive disadvantage. In such organizations, the secrecy surrounding activities such as product development often carries over to other activities, regardless of whether the concerns are warranted.

Given these potential objections to the collection of research data, how can organizational researchers still gain access? Perhaps the most fundamental suggestion that can be made in this regard is: Ask. Many researchers who complain about lack of access have actually asked relatively few organizations for their cooperation. They simply assume that they will be unable to collect data. One way to enlist an organization is to contact several organizations by telephone and try to make contact with someone in the human resources department. Another approach is to *mass mail* to organizations, asking for cooperation. T. E. Becker (1992), for example, mailed letters to the presidents of 30 organizations asking for permission to collect data and eventually collected data in one of these.

General appeals or *cold calling* may result in a data-collection opportunity, but it is often much more efficient to use established connections in organizations. Most people have family and/or friends who work in organizations, and such people may be in a position to either authorize the collection of data or put the researcher into contact with someone who has the authority to do so. This suggests that researchers should not be afraid to use established connections in organizations. Researchers should also invest time and energy to develop connections with people who can help with data collection in their organizations in the future. This often takes time and energy but, in the long run, the contact may result in excellent data-collection opportunities (see Comment 2.5).

Let's now assume that a researcher has persuaded an organization to at least consider the possibility of data collection. How can a researcher convince an organization to actually go ahead with data collection? The most useful suggestion that can be made in this regard is: The researcher should offer the organization something in return for its cooperation. For example, researchers often provide a summary of the research findings to the organization, in return for its cooperation. Other researchers may offer to perform some consulting service at no cost to an organization. Organizations typically do not provide a researcher with access to their employees unless the access will provide some tangible benefit in return.

After an organization gives permission to collect data, there is often some negotiation between the researcher and the organization, regarding issues such as research design and measures. At this stage, researchers and organizations often clash, because of their differing goals and objectives. Researchers typically desire a high level of methodological rigor in their investigations because their ultimate goal is to publish their findings in peer-reviewed journals. Unfortunately, methodological rigor may be perceived by the organization as costly in a number of ways. For example, supplementing self-report measures with organizational records may be time consuming and require that employees reveal identifying information. It may also be impossible for an organization to allow a researcher the control needed for experimental or even quasi-experimental investigations. This is a tricky issue for researchers to navigate because just gaining access to organizations is such a challenge. The key is this: The researcher must be willing to accommodate the organization, but not to such an extent that it completely compromises the scientific integrity of the investigation. Unfortunately, researchers often severely compromise the methodological rigor of studies without attempting to persuade organizations of their value. In most cases, a well-designed, methodological, rigorous study will not only help the researcher but will also be more informative to the organization (Campion, 1996).

COMMENT 2.5

GAINING ACCESS TO ORGANIZATIONS: SOME EXAMPLES

STEVE JEX: AS I wrote the section on gaining access to organizations, I thought of the various ways I have gained access to organizations in order to collect data. Like many researchers, I have used family connections. For example, I was able to gain access to an insurance company in Tampa, Florida, to conduct my Master's thesis research while in graduate school. My wife was employed there at the time. To this day, I can't figure out whether my wife was trying to advance science, or just wanted me to get out of graduate school! Another study I conducted, which was ultimately published in the *Journal of Applied Psychology* (Jex, Beehr, & Roberts, 1992), was actually made possible through the efforts of my mother. This study was conducted at a hospital in Saginaw, Michigan (my hometown), where my mother was employed as a nurse. She introduced me to a person in the human resources department who was ultimately able to grant me access to all hospital employees. In this case, I think my mother's help was driven primarily by a desire to see her son get tenure. In addition to using family connections, I have gained access in many other ways. In some cases, current and former students have helped facilitate data-collection efforts. I have also, on occasion, relied on former graduate school classmates, or other colleagues, to provide either data-collection sites or useful contacts.

Is there any underlying theme when I think about the various ways in which I have gained access to organizations? The most obvious theme is that developing and maintaining relationships with people is important. This includes family, students, and professional colleagues. I'm not suggesting that relationships should be initiated only on the basis of what people can do for you. However, the fact is, it is much easier to ask someone for assistance if you've taken the time to maintain an ongoing relationship with him or her. The other important lesson I've learned over the years is simply to ask. We often assume incorrectly that family, friends, and colleagues do not want to be bothered helping with data collection. However, my experience has been that people often are very willing (and even flattered) to help if they're asked.

Thomas Britt: Getting access to samples is a critical issue when trying to do quality organizational research. When I was conducting primarily social-psychological research I took for granted how easy it was to obtain samples by using the subject pool of students taking "Introduction to Psychology." The more I got into organizational psychology, the more I realized the difficulty and tenacity required to gain access to samples. When I was in the U.S. Army as an organizational psychologist, I had a somewhat *captive audience* of soldiers to participate in research projects (although it should be noted that all soldiers provided informed consent to participate). However, even when conducting research with soldiers, it was necessary to convince unit commanders of the importance of the research and why it was worth the time of their soldiers when they could be spending more time training. You also had to provide the commanders with summaries of the results that told them something important, and provide recommendations for what they should do given the results.

Since arriving at Clemson I have continued my ties with the military but have also started collecting data from different applied samples. For example, I have recently begun an assessment of staff at Clemson University examining the influence of positive motivational states at work on well-being and performance. I have worked closely with the administration at all levels to convey the importance of the research (and why we need supervisor ratings of performance in addition to employee reports), and my graduate students and I have spent a great deal of time coordinating with individual units in the university to ensure a high response rate of participation. I have also been struck by the diversity of jobs people have in a university setting (e.g., firefighters, library personnel, campus recreation, facilities). When orienting new graduate students into our Industrial/ Organizational Psychology program, I emphasize that getting access to a quality sample of employees who will be willing to work with you on a research question is often more difficult than coming up with the hypothesis you want to test!

Source: S. M. Jex, T. A. Beehr, and C. K. Roberts. (1992). The meaning of occupational "stress" items to survey respondents. *Journal of Applied Psychology, 77*, 623–628.

Conducting Research in Different Cultures

Given increasing globalization, it is more and more common for organizational psychologists to examine cross-cultural issues. Despite the value of cross-cultural research, data collection in such studies is often challenging for a number of reasons. For example, when self-report measures are used, these often must be translated from one language to another. This may seem rather simple; often, it is not. The typical procedure used to translate self-report measures into different languages is called *back translation*. This involves translating the items on a measure from one language to another (e.g., from English to Chinese), and then back to the original language. The researcher must assess whether the items have retained their meaning to respondents after being translated from a different language.

Another issue researchers must consider in conducting cross-cultural research is sampling. Researchers conducting cross-cultural research often want to compare employees in one culture to employees in another, so it is important to utilize samples that are similar in all aspects except culture (Arvey, Bhagat, & Salas, 1991). The ideal way to accomplish this would be to utilize employees from different cultures who work for the same organization (e.g., De La Rosa, 2006). If this could not be done, a researcher would typically want to select samples from different cultures that work in the same industry and perhaps have similar levels of work experience.

Researchers conducting cross-cultural research must be on the lookout for things that are specific to a given culture and may adversely affect data collection. For example, a researcher utilizing self-ratings of performance must be aware of the fact that, in Asian cultures, it is considered improper to rate oneself high in performance (Fahr, Dobbins, & Cheng, 1991). There may also be vast cultural differences in research participants' degree of comfort when they are asked to provide ratings of persons in positions of authority (Hofstede, 1980).

STATISTICAL METHODS IN ORGANIZATIONAL PSYCHOLOGY

Regardless of the data-collection method used, once data are collected, researchers must analyze those data to assess whether or not their hypotheses are supported. Fortunately for organizational researchers, many statistical methods are available to help make sense out of data. Because a comprehensive review of statistical methodology is beyond the scope of this chapter, we will review, in this section, the statistical methods that are used most frequently in analyzing research data.

Descriptive Statistics

The first thing a researcher needs to do after obtaining a set of data is to get a feel for general trends. For example, if we were to collect data on job satisfaction within an organization, two relevant questions might be (1) what is the *overall level* of job satisfaction in the organization, and (2) are employees very similar in their levels of job satisfaction, or do they vary widely? To answer the first question, some descriptive measure of *central tendency* would be used. The most commonly used measure of central tendency is the mean (also called the *average*), which is calculated by simply adding up all of the scores on a variable and dividing by the total number of scores. Other common measures of central tendency include the median and mode. The *median* is the score on a variable that splits the distribution into two equal halves. Unlike the mean, the median is unaffected by the presence of extremely high or extremely low values. Because of this, the median is useful as a supplement to the mean, in cases in which a distribution contains extreme scores. The *mode* is simply the most frequently occurring score and is typically not very informative unless there is a very dramatic preference for one response over others.

Measures of central tendency are useful because they provide information about the manner in which variables are distributed. This is important because most statistical methods are based on assumptions about the manner in which variables are distributed. Measures of central tendency are also valuable when organizational policy makers

FIGURE 2.3

Graphical Representation of Mean Levels of Four Dimensions Measured in an Employee Opinion Survey.

Notes: Communication = Satisfaction with amount of communication in the organization;
Fairness = Satisfaction with level of fairness in the organization; Benefits = Satisfaction with current fringe benefit package; Commitment = Organizational commitment. Mean values may range from 1 to 4.

are assessing survey results. Figure 2.3, for example, contains a graphical representation of employee opinion survey data collected by one of the authors. This figure graphically represents the mean values of four dimensions contained on the survey. A quick perusal of this figure indicates relatively low satisfaction with the levels of communication and fairness in this organization. On the other hand, employees in this organization appear to be committed to the organization and are reasonably satisfied with their fringe benefits package. While this is certainly not complicated information, it could be important to an organization. In this case, the organization used the information as the basis for interventions to enhance communication and fairness.

In addition to measures of central tendency, researchers often want to know whether responses are uniform or whether there is a great deal of dispersion. The most basic measure of dispersion is the *range*, which is the difference between the highest and lowest value for a particular variable. It is often useful to compare the observed range for a given variable to the possible range. For example, if a variable is scaled such that it may range from 10 to 50 and the observed range is 30 to 50, this indicates potential problems with range restriction.

While the range may be useful in identifying problems with range restriction, it is still a very crude measure of dispersion. More precise and more commonly used measures of dispersion include the *variance* and *standard deviation*. The variance represents the variability of scores around the mean. To calculate the variance, you simply subtract the mean from each score in a distribution, square each value, add up these squared values, and divide by the total number of scores. The standard deviation is simply the square root of the variance.

Given the way in which the variance and standard deviation are calculated, higher values indicate greater dispersion about the mean. The standard deviation is also useful because it can be used in converting raw scores to *standard scores*. A standard score is simply the score on a given variable, expressed (in terms of its distance from the mean) in standard deviation units. The simplest form of standard score is a *z-score*, which is calculated by subtracting the mean from a raw score and dividing the result by the standard deviation. Standard scores can be useful in cases in which the researcher wishes to compare a respondent's scores on different variables that may utilize different scales of measurement (see Comment 2.6).

A final type of descriptive measure that is used in the analysis of research data is *reliability*. Reliability is defined as the extent to which a variable is being measured without error (Nunnally & Bernstein, 1994). What is

COMMENT 2.6

CONFESSIONS OF A STATISTICAL MINIMALIST

IN HIS INITIAL statement as editor of *Journal of Applied Psychology* in 1995, Philip Bobko referred to himself as a "statistical minimalist" (Bobko, 1995, p. 4) in describing his views on statistical analysis. What is a statistical minimalist? Perhaps the best way to understand this is to consider more of Bobko's editorial statement. Specifically, he advised potential authors: "Please look at 'simple' statistics, such as means, standard deviations, correlations, effect sizes, and so forth. And do not just look at them; consider them when attempting to understand and explain what's going on. I believe that one can often (usually?) learn more by looking at these simple statistics with a critical and understanding eye than one can

learn by computing the newest fashion in statistics with an amazed eye" (p. 4).

The important point that Bobko was trying to make in this editorial is that even relatively simple descriptive statistics are important if one's goal is to understand their data. A more subtle message here is that the choice of statistical methods to use should be driven by the question being asked, not by the latest fad. Although not always the case, it is often possible to answer important research questions without resorting to overly complex statistical analyses.

Source: P. Bobko. (1995). Editorial. *Journal of Applied Psychology, 80,* 3–5.

considered error, however, depends on the particular context in which a measure is being used. When multi-item measures are used, which is typically the case in organizational research, it is necessary to assess the *internal consistency reliability*. A measure of internal consistency reliability provides an estimation of the extent to which all items on a scale are measuring the same attribute. Suppose, for example, we constructed a five-item measure of job satisfaction. If internal consistency reliability were estimated to be very high, this would suggest that all five items were measuring the same thing.

In other cases, researchers must provide other reliability estimates. For example, if a variable is going to be assessed at multiple points in time, it is important for the researcher to show that the measure of the variable is not strongly impacted by random fluctuations over time. In this case, an appropriate form of reliability assessment would be *test-retest reliability*, which simply involves administering a measure at two different points in time and calculating the correlation between these scores. If this correlation is high, it suggests that the measure is not strongly impacted by random temporal fluctuations.

Another form of reliability assessment, *interrater reliability*, may be necessary in cases in which multiple raters are utilized to assess some attribute of a person (e.g., performance) or the environment (e.g., job characteristics). There are many ways to assess interrater reliability, but they all basically allow the researcher to assess whether the ratings provided by different raters are similarly ordered. The researcher can also assess whether raters agree on the absolute value of the ratings. This issue will be discussed in greater detail in the final section of the chapter, which deals with aggregation and levels of analysis issues.

Why do researchers need to be concerned about reliability? The answer to that question has to do with the nature of measurement error. Measurement error, by definition, represents sources of influence on the measure other than the hypothesized construct. A *constant* or systematic error would be the tendency of a respondent to answer all items in a way that he or she feels is socially desirable. A *random* error would be a momentary distraction causing as respondent to respond to an item "Strongly Agree" when he or she really meant to respond "Strongly Disagree." When a measure is reliable it is relatively free of random error, though it may still contain considerable constant error. When a measure is unreliable, however, it contains a great deal of measurement error. This is problematic because random error, by definition, is unrelated to other variables; thus, reliability sets an upper bound on the magnitude of relationships between a measure and other variables.

Tests of Mean Differences

After assessing descriptive measures, researchers should hopefully be able to conclude that there are no major distributional problems, and that all variables are measured with a minimal amount of error. If this is indeed the case, the next step is to perform some analysis to test whatever hypotheses are being proposed. There are many different types of hypotheses; a common type of hypothesis involves testing differences in the mean level of a given variable. For example, a researcher may hypothesize that employees in white-collar jobs have higher organizational commitment than blue-collar employees, or that the performance of groups that participate in team-building activities is higher than that of groups not participating. In this section, we cover the two most common statistical tests of mean differences.

Before describing these statistical tests, it is useful to provide a brief overview of the logic behind tests of statistical significance. Regardless of the statistical test being used, a test of statistical significance essentially involves establishing a rule for distinguishing chance from nonchance outcomes. All statistical significance tests begin with the assumption of what is termed the *null hypothesis*, which is another way of saying there is no effect or no relationship between variables. Assuming that the null hypothesis is true, it is possible for a variety of research outcomes to occur simply on the basis of chance. Thus, the researcher needs some decisive rule for determining whether a given result represents a chance occurrence or a legitimate scientific finding. The standard used most often for distinguishing chance from nonchance—the one that has come to be adopted in the behavioral sciences over the years—is 5%. Assuming that the null hypothesis is true, if the probability of a research outcome occurring by chance is 5% or less, scientists typically conclude that it is a legitimate scientific finding (e.g., they reject the null hypothesis). Thus, when the statement is made that a finding is "significant beyond the .05 level," the researcher is saying that it is very unlikely that the finding observed is a chance occurrence.

When testing mean differences, the simplest scenario is testing the difference between two groups. For example, a researcher may wish to test whether the average age of those who participate in training and development activities differs from those who choose not to participate. The statistic most commonly used in this situation would be a *t-test*. The magnitude of the t statistic depends on the absolute difference between means relative to the level of variation within the groups being compared. Thus, even if the absolute difference between the means is substantial, a high degree of variation within the different groups will keep the t value at a relatively low level, and lead the researcher to conclude that there is no meaningful difference between the groups.

There are other instances in organizational research in which the means of more than two groups must be compared. For example, a researcher might want to compare the mean level of job satisfaction in several different work groups that have and have not participated in team development activities. In this case, the statistical procedure used would be *analysis of variance*. The general purpose of analysis of variance is to assess the variation between different groups, relative to the variation within groups. To perform an analysis of variance, it is necessary to calculate several different variance estimates or *mean-squares*. These are used to estimate the variance between groups and the variance within groups. The actual test of statistical significance employed in analysis of variance is the *F-test*, which is simply a ratio of the variance between groups to the variance within groups. When an F is statistically significant, this indicates that the ratio of variance between groups to the variation within groups is very unlikely to have occurred by chance, given the null hypothesis. Recall that the same basic logic is employed with the t-test. If a statistically significant F is found in analysis of variance, this indicates that there is some difference among the means in the groups of interest, although it does not tell the researcher which means are different. To figure this out, follow-up tests would be used to assess the difference within each possible pair of group means.

Given the basic logic behind analysis of variance, this statistical procedure can be used a variety of ways. For example, different forms of analysis of variance can be used to assess (1) the impact of multiple independent variables, (2) repeated measures of dependent variables, and (3) the impact of multiple dependent variables. Readers interested in more detailed information on analysis of variance procedures should consult Keppel and Zedeck (1989).

Correlation and Regression Analysis

Given the prevalence of cross-sectional field surveys in organizational research, hypotheses are often tested by assessing the covariation among the variables of interest. The most commonly used statistical index of covariation is the *Pearson product-moment correlation coefficient*. The correlation coefficient can range from +1.00 to −1.00, but typically falls in between these values. The larger the absolute value of a correlation coefficient, the greater the degree of covariation. This degree is often expressed by squaring the correlation coefficient to obtain the amount of shared variation between two variables. For example, if the correlation between two variables is .30, they share 9% of their variance in common (e.g., $[.30]^2$). When the sign of a correlation is positive, this simply means that two variables covary in the same direction. A negative sign, by contrast, indicates that two variables covary in opposite directions.

The correlation coefficient is useful in testing many hypotheses in organizational research, but it provides very limited information about causal relationships. For example, if job satisfaction were found to be correlated with job autonomy, this could mean that high job autonomy causes employees to be more satisfied with their jobs. On the other hand, it could also mean that a high level of job satisfaction causes employees to see greater levels of autonomy in their jobs. It is also possible that two variables may be correlated primarily because of the influence of a third variable; for example, employees who have higher salaries may be more satisfied and tend to hold jobs with high autonomy. If this is the case, it is said that the relationship is *spurious*.

Correlational analysis is also limited by the fact that only two variables may be examined at a time. In many instances, a researcher may be interested in the extent to which several variables are related to some other variable of interest. For example, a researcher may be interested in the degree to which pay, length of service, level of performance, age, and job type all contribute to employees' overall satisfaction with their employing organization. One way to address this question would be to examine the correlation between job satisfaction and each of these variables individually. Unfortunately, such an analysis does not provide the researcher with information about the extent to which this entire set of variables is related.

The statistical procedure that is used to assess the relation of a set of variables (called predictors) to another variable (called the criterion) is *multiple linear regression* or, simply, multiple regression. Multiple regression is useful because it provides a quantitative estimate of the amount of covariation between a set of predictors and a criterion variable. This is assessed by the multiple R statistic, which is analogous to the correlation coefficient. In most instances, however, researchers report the squared value of multiple R, which serves as a measure of the amount of variance in the criterion variable that is explained by a set of predictors.

Multiple regression is also useful because it allows the researcher to assess the relative impact of each predictor in explaining the criterion variable. When a set of predictors is used to estimate a criterion variable, the criterion is estimated to be a linear function of the predictor set. The general form of this equation is:

$$Y = A + B_1X_1 + B_2X_2 + \ldots B_kX_k$$

where Y is the criterion variable that is being predicted, the Xs represent the predictor variables, A is a constant, and each B-value represents the weighting of a given predictor or the extent to which it contributes to the prediction of the criterion. The advantage of using these statistical weights, as opposed to correlations, is that they are calculated in a way that takes into account the intercorrelations among the other predictor variables in the set. Thus, B-values in multiple regression represent the *unique* contribution of a given variable to the prediction of some criterion measure.

Beyond correlation and regression analysis, many other related methods can be employed for data analysis. Most of these fall under the general category of *multivariate methods* (e.g., Tabachnick & Fidell, 1996) and, due to their complexity, are not covered in this chapter. These methods are quite useful to the researcher, particularly in field investigations. Like all statistical methods, they should be used only if necessary to test a given hypothesis.

Meta-Analysis

A final form of statistical analysis that is being used increasingly in organizational research is *meta-analysis*. Meta-analysis involves the quantitative summary of research findings and is typically used in research domains where a considerable number of studies have been conducted (Rosenthal, 1991). For example, meta-analyses have been con-

ducted on the relation between job satisfaction and job performance (Podsakoff & Williams, 1986), the impact of unemployment on well-being (McKee-Ryan, Song, Wanberg, & Kinicki, 2005), and the impact of different leadership styles (Judge, Piccolo, & Illies, 2004). In all three cases, so many studies have been conducted that it would be difficult to provide an accurate qualitative summary of the findings.

Statistically, meta-analysis essentially involves averaging effect sizes (e.g., from correlation coefficients or differences between two means). Before these effects sizes are averaged, however, researchers typically control for a number of *statistical artifacts*— factors that may lead to differences in the findings between studies. The most basic statistical artifact is sample size. Studies with larger sample sizes need to be weighted more heavily when averaging correlations compared to those with smaller sample sizes. Another common statistical artifact controlled in meta-analyses is measurement unreliability. Earlier in the chapter, *reliability* was defined as the degree to which a variable is measured without error. When measurement procedures are unreliable, this means that they contain considerable error. As was stated earlier, this is important because it sets a lower boundary on the degree to which a variable can be correlated with other variables. Controlling for unreliability puts all variables on a level playing field in terms of measurement error.

The other common statistical artifact controlled in meta-analyses is *range restriction*. In some studies, correlations between variables may be reduced because the values do not cover the entire possible range. This may occur because of a variety of factors (e.g., Johns, 1991), but it always serves to limit the magnitude of correlations. When researchers control for range restriction, they are estimating what the correlations would be if the variables of interest were measured without any range-restriction problems.

Once all relevant statistical artifacts are controlled, two important statistics are typically calculated in meta-analysis. Most researchers calculate some overall estimate of effect size between two variables. This estimate represents the effect size after controlling for the impact of important statistical artifacts, and it provides a good estimate of the *true* relationship between variables. The other statistic typically calculated in meta-analysis is the amount of variation in effect sizes that remains after important statistical artifacts are controlled. Usually, after important statistical artifacts are controlled, there is a relatively small amount of variation between studies' findings. However, if there is still a substantial amount of variation, factors other than statistical artifacts may be contributing to the differences in findings between the studies. Such factors are called *moderator variables*. Some of the more typical moderator variables examined in meta-analyses include aspects of the study design (laboratory experiment versus field study), characteristics of the research samples (employees versus college students), and specific measures used to assess key variables (well-established measures versus measures developed for one study).

SPECIAL ISSUES IN STATISTICAL ANALYSIS

At this point, readers should have a basic understanding of the more typical statistical methods used in organizational psychology. The purpose of statistical methodology is to help researchers answer questions (i.e., it is a means to an end), but it has also become a vibrant field of inquiry in and of itself. In fact, within organizational psychology, many researchers focus on statistical and methodology issues. Because of this focus, several issues in statistical methodology have surfaced over the years and have been the subject of inquiry and debate. In this section, we briefly review four important contemporary issues in the use of statistical methodology in organizational research.

Statistical Power in Organizational Research

Statistical power refers to the sensitivity of statistical tests to detect meaningful treatment effects. To use an analogy, one might think of the statistical power of different tests in the same way as differences between types of microscopes. An inexpensive microscope purchased from a toy store provides some magnification, but extremely small objects (e.g., viruses) cannot be detected. In contrast, an expensive electron microscope provides a much higher level of magnification that allows for the detection of even extremely small particles.

Several factors contribute to statistical power (Cohen, 1992). One is *sample size*. All things being equal, larger sample sizes provide higher levels of statistical power. This is one reason why survey researchers are concerned about nonresponse, and laboratory researchers are concerned about participants not showing up. A second factor impacting power is *effect size*, or the relative strength of the effect a researcher is trying to detect. There are actually several ways to express effect size, but the easiest way to explain it is based on the size of correlations. Generally speaking, if the true correlation between two variables is very small, this effect is much harder to detect than a much larger effect. Smaller-effect sizes require a more powerful "microscope" for detection.

A third factor that impacts statistical power is the *alpha level* chosen in statistical significance testing. The alpha level represents the cutoff for distinguishing chance from nonchance findings. Recall, from the previous discussion of statistical significance testing, that 5% has become the conventional rule in the behavioral sciences. The reason that the alpha level is set so low is to reduce the probability of committing a *Type I error*, or falsely concluding that one has uncovered a legitimate scientific finding. In an organizational setting, an example of committing a Type I error would be falsely concluding that a training program had a positive effect on employee performance. In contrast, a *Type II error* is committed when a researcher fails to detect a legitimate effect when it is present. In the previous example, this would involve

conducting a statistical test and falsely concluding that a useful training program had no impact on employee performance (see Comment 2.7).

As the alpha level becomes more stringent (e.g., smaller than 5%), this reduces the chance of committing a Type I error, but also tends to reduce power and hence increases the chances of committing a Type II error. In contrast, a more liberal alpha level (e.g., 10%) tends to increase power, although this comes at the cost of an increase in the probability of committing a Type I error.

A final factor impacting power is measurement error. Specifically, higher levels of measurement error are associated with low levels of power. This is simply due to the unsystematic nature of measurement error, which was discussed earlier.

COMMENT 2.7

TYPE I VERSUS TYPE II ERROR: WHICH IS THE GREATEST SIN?

GIVEN THE FACT that the alpha level is typically set at .05 or, in some cases, even .01, one would assume that committing a Type I error is a bad thing. Recall that when a Type I error is made, a researcher concludes that a finding is scientifically meaningful when it really is not. Why is this bad? From a scientific point of view, Type I errors are bad because they lead us down *blind alleys*, and ultimately may lead to faulty theories. From a practical point of view, a Type I error may lead an organization to spend a considerable amount of money on a training program that ultimately is not effective. Given these negative effects of a Type I error, we want to minimize the chance that one will occur, so we set alpha at a very low level.

Unfortunately, in minimizing the chances of Type I error, we increase the chances of Type II error. As you recall, Type II error is committed when a researcher fails to uncover a legit-

imate scientific effect. Is it better to make a Type II than a Type I error? It really depends on the situation. Let's say, for example, that a researcher is testing a drug that could potentially neutralize the HIV virus. It would obviously be bad if this researcher were to falsely conclude that this drug was effective (e.g., commit a Type I error). However, consider the implications of committing a Type II error in this case. If this drug is effective, and research does not show it, a great chance to reduce human suffering has been missed.

Ultimately, research should be designed to balance the risks of both Type I and Type II errors. To minimize the risk of Type I error, alpha levels should be set sufficiently low, and proper statistical procedures should be used. On the other hand, Type II error can be minimized primarily by employing adequate sample sizes and reliable measures.

Given the previously described determinants of statistical power, let us now consider the level of statistical power in organizational research. Mone, Mueller, and Mauland (1996) examined this issue in a meta-analysis of the level of power in 26,471 statistical tests from 210 research studies conducted between 1992 and 1994. These authors also explored common practices with respect to the assessment of power prior to conducting research.

The results of the meta-analysis were revealing—and, in fact, somewhat troubling. Given that an acceptable level of statistical power is considered to be 80% (e.g., there is an 80% chance of detecting a true effect; Cohen, 1992), the authors found that across all effect sizes, an acceptable level of power was achieved only 50% of the time. What this means is that across all studies in this meta-analysis, researchers assume a 50% chance of failing to detect a true effect when it is present. This suggests that many studies conducted in organizational research are underpowered.

Low statistical power is especially problematic when researchers are attempting to detect small effect sizes. When Mone et al. (1996) calculated the level of statistical power for small effect sizes, it was found that the percentage of studies achieving an acceptable level of power was only 10%! That is, the vast majority of studies attempting to detect small effects are grossly underpowered. This is unfortunate because small effects are very common in organizational research, due to the vast number of variables impacting employees in organizations.

The results of the survey of authors were also revealing. Perhaps the most important finding was that 64% of the authors surveyed reported that they do not perform any type of power analysis prior to conducting a study. One reason frequently cited for this was that, in many cases, researchers have little or no control over sample sizes in field research. Thus, even if a power analysis indicated that a larger sample size would be desirable, it would not be possible to increase. Many authors in this survey also noted that scholarly journals do not insist on power analysis during the review process, although there are some exceptions (e.g., Campion, 1993). This is unfortunate because scholarly journals serve an important *gate-keeping* function, and insistence on power analysis would serve to heighten awareness of this issue. As it stands right now, there are probably many meaningful effects in organizational psychology that go undetected due to low statistical power.

Detection of Moderator Variables

Recall from the section on meta-analysis that a moderator variable changes the relationship between two other variables (James & Brett, 1984). More specifically, the relationship between two variables differs at different levels of the moderator variable. In organizational psychology, many theoretical models contain moderator variables; thus, it is important to understand the statistical procedures used for assessing whether or not moderated relationships exist.

There are actually several ways to test moderator effects (e.g., see James & Brett, 1984), but the most commonly used procedure is through the use of multiple regression analysis (Cohen & Cohen, 1983). In this procedure, which is known as *cross-product regression*, the independent variable is first entered into the regression equation. In the next step, the moderator variable is entered. In the final step, the cross-product of the independent variable and moderator is entered. The cross-product term is created by multiplying the independent variable by the moderator for each respondent. If the variation explained by the cross-product term is statistically significant, a moderated relationship is present. This means that the relationship between the independent variable and the dependent variable differs as a function of the moderator. This is usually shown visually by plotting the relationship at high (one standard deviation above the mean) and low (one standard deviation below the mean) levels of the moderator. Figure 2.4 illustrates how this is done. In this case, self-efficacy moderates the relationship between work hours and psychological strain. Notice that, when self-efficacy is low, there is a positive relationship between work hours and psychological strain. In contrast, when self-efficacy is high, there is essentially no relationship between these two variables.

The procedure for detecting moderator variables is rather straightforward, but, in practice, the actual detection of moderators is difficult, primarily because of low statistical

FIGURE 2.4

Graphical Representation of a Moderated Relationship

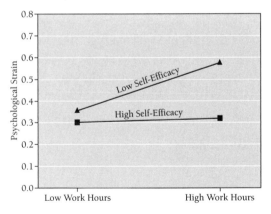

Source: S. M. Jex and P. D. Bliese. (1999). Efficacy beliefs as a moderator of the impact of work-related stressors: A multilevel study. *Journal of Applied Psychology, 84,* 349–361. Copyright © 1999 by the American Psychological Association. Reprinted with permission.

power. This is because moderator effects are typically small, since the variance explained by a moderator effect is that which is left over after the effects of the independent variable and moderator are taken into account. Power is also reduced when the independent variable and the moderator are strongly correlated and, in the case of dichotomous variables (e.g., race, gender), when the proportion differs greatly from 50/50 (Aguinis & Stone-Romero, 1997).

What can be done to increase the power of moderator tests? Given the previous general discussion of statistical power, researchers testing moderator effects should try to employ large samples and highly reliable measures. A somewhat more controversial way to increase power is to increase the alpha level beyond the conventional .05. Recall that the alpha level represents the researcher's decision rule for distinguishing chance from nonchance findings. If a less stringent alpha level of .10 is adopted, for example, this means that results with a 10% or lower probability of occurring by chance are considered legitimate treatment effects.

Given the low power associated with moderator tests, the decision to adopt a less stringent alpha level would appear to be logical. It is not extremely unusual to find researchers using alpha levels of .10 in moderator tests (e.g., Jex & Elacqua, 1999), but the practice is not widespread. This is likely due to the fact that the .05 level is highly ingrained in our thinking. Most students are taught that an alpha level beyond .05 is "cheating," and they are extremely reluctant to raise it.

Beyond statistical considerations in the detection of moderator effects, it is always good practice to have a solid theoretical rationale before searching for moderators. Often, moderator variables that are very intuitively appealing may not be theoretically

COMMENT 2.8

THE ELUSIVE MODERATOR EFFECT

As will become evident as readers make their way through this book, many theories in organizational psychology propose moderator hypotheses; that is, certain relationships may hold under certain conditions, but not under others. Moderator variables are important in theory development because they allow us to specify the precise conditions under which some phenomenon may occur. They also may have a great deal of practical value, for example, by providing an organization with guidance about whether there are certain conditions under which interventions such as job redesign may or may not work.

Despite the theoretical and practical value of moderator variables, they are very difficult to demonstrate empirically. The is primarily due to the fact that moderator variables almost always explain a small portion of the variance-dependent measures and, as a result, statistical power to detect these effects is often very low. Thus, in many cases, researchers propose theoretically sound moderator hypotheses yet come up empty when they test for these effects. What can researchers do to avoid this fate? The most logical steps one can take to increase statistical power of moderator tests are: employ large sample sizes, utilize reliable measures, adopt a reasonable alpha level, and try to cut down on extraneous sources of variation.

justified. Statistical methodology will never compensate for poor theory development (see Comment 2.8).

Use of Causal Modeling

Over the past 20 years, a statistical technique that has become increasingly popular in organizational psychology—and many other fields—is *causal modeling* (James, Mulaik, & Brett, 1982). The logic behind causal modeling is that the researcher derives a set of predictions about how a set of variables relate to one another, and tests all of these relations simultaneously. In practice, this is typically done through the use of either *path analysis* or *structural equation modeling*. With path analysis, the variables that constitute a causal model are the actual variables that are measured. This is illustrated in the simple path model depicted in Figure 2.5. This model proposes that high levels of cognitive ability and work experience lead to high levels of job knowledge, which in turn leads

to high levels of job performance. Structural equation modeling is similar to path analysis except that the variables comprising the causal model are *latent* rather than measured variables. A latent variable is a hypothetical variable that is purported to cause the interrelationships among measured variables. As an example, cognitive ability is a latent variable that might lead to a high intercorrelation among scores on cognitive ability tests and a structured interview. An example of a structural equation model is contained in

FIGURE 2.5
Simple Path Model

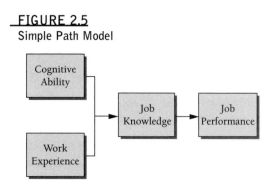

FIGURE 2.6
Simple Structural Equation Model

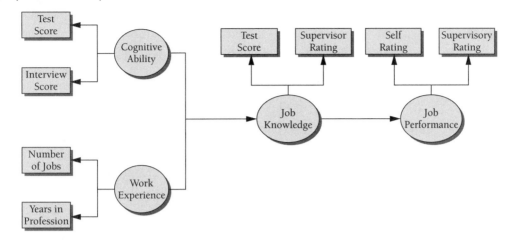

Figure 2.6. The circles are meant to denote latent variables, and the boxes represent measured variables. Continuing with the example from Figure 2.5, scores on a cognitive ability test and a structured interview are used as indicators of the latent variable cognitive ability, and so on. Notice that this is essentially the same model depicted in Figure 2.5. The only difference is that the proposed relationships are among latent rather than measured variables.

Once a model is proposed, the researcher seeks to assess whether the model *fits* the actual data. There are actually several indexes of model fit (Bentler, 1990), but the logic underlying all of them is very similar. When a model is proposed, the researcher is placing certain restrictions on the covariation among the variables of interest. Based on these restrictions, an expected covariance matrix of relations among variables in the causal model can be calculated. This expected covariance matrix is then compared to the actual covariation among the variables in the proposed model. When a model is said to "fit the data well," this means that the actual covariation among the varia-

bles closely matches that which would be expected, based on the proposed relations among the variables.

Causal modeling is a powerful technique because it allows the researcher to simultaneously test all the relations comprising an entire theoretical model. With correlation and regression analysis, it is usually possible to test only *parts* or individual segments of a theoretical model. The use of causal modeling, however, has been somewhat controversial. Some of these controversies are technically beyond the scope of this chapter and are related to things such as parameter estimation methods and the assessing model fit. Some, however, have questioned whether this technique has been overused, and whether model tests have been too data driven and not grounded enough in theory.

Like any statistical technique, causal modeling is neither good nor bad. If applied properly, it can be a very useful part of an organizational psychologist's statistical tool kit. Generally speaking, causal modeling is most powerful when the model being tested has a strong theoretical base, and there is a fairly large sample available. It is only at this point that a researcher has enough insight to propose the complex set of interrelations among variables that comprises most causal models. Thus, it is usually not appropriate to use causal modeling early in a theoretically based research program.

Aggregation and Levels of Analysis

A recent trend in organizational psychology is the exploration of variables at multiple levels of analysis; that is, researchers have increasingly become interested in the impact of variables that are conceptualized not only at the individual level but also at group and even organizational levels. Researchers have also become interested in how variables at different levels of analysis impact each other. This latter type of investigation is known as *cross-level analysis*.

Exploring multiple levels of analysis obviously presents researchers with some important theoretical issues (e.g., Bliese & Jex, 2002; Chan, 1998; Klein, Dansereau, & Hall, 1994). However, with these theoretical considerations come methodological and statistical considerations as well. Let us first consider the issue of *aggregation*. When data are aggregated, this simply means that one value is used to represent the unit of aggregation. An example of this would be using the mean level of job satisfaction within a work group to represent "group-level satisfaction." Note that when a variable is aggregated, all individual differences within the unit of aggregation are suppressed.

When is it appropriate to aggregate individual responses? Generally speaking, researchers must be prepared to justify aggregation on three different levels. First, there must be theoretical justification. The issue here is whether the variable created through aggregation is theoretically meaningful. In the example provided in the previous paragraph, the researcher would need to make the case that the average level of job satisfaction within a work group is a theoretically meaningful variable.

If aggregation is theoretically justified, the researcher must also provide some methodological justification for the decision to aggregate. The most basic methodological question a researcher faces has to do with choosing the unit of aggregation. Most researchers would probably find it acceptable to aggregate the responses of a five-person work group whose members interact frequently. There would likely be less agreement on this issue if one were to aggregate the responses of one division of an organization consisting of 100 members. Unfortunately, there is no hard and fast rule regarding what is and what is not an appropriate unit of aggregation; ultimately it comes down to the variable one is measuring (Bliese & Jex, 2002).

A second methodological issue has to do with the measurement of variables. In many cases, individual responses are aggregated because items make reference to respondent perceptions of the unit of aggregation. For instance, if a researcher were to measure organizational climate (James & Jones, 1974), the items should make reference to the organization and not the individuals responding. This suggests that researchers should make the decision to aggregate before data are collected so items can be reworded appropriately.

Assuming that aggregating is justified theoretically and methodologically, researchers must also be prepared to justify aggregation statistically. In most instances in which individual responses are aggregated, the researcher is doing so in order to measure some attribute of the unit of aggregation. For example, a researcher may want to measure the level of cohesiveness in a group, or the level of trust within an organization. In such cases, it is incumbent upon the researcher to justify aggregation by showing some statistical evidence of agreement in responses within the unit of aggregation. If respondents within a group do not agree on the level of cohesiveness within the group, it usually makes little sense to average their responses. There are several ways to measure interrater agreement, but the most frequently used method has become the r_{wg} statistic (James et al., 1984).

Besides aggregation, the other major issue confronting researchers exploring multiple-level issues is statistical analysis. In any research investigation, the choice of statistical analysis is driven by the research question being asked. Thus, in some cases, the analysis of multilevel data is relatively straightforward. For example, if a researcher were interested in the relation between group cohesiveness and group performance, it would make sense to examine the correlation between aggregate-level measures of both of these variables. The only drawback to this approach, of course, is that it greatly reduces sample size and, hence, statistical power.

In other instances, the analysis of multilevel data is more complex because researchers wish to examine the effects of multiple levels within the same analysis. For example, a researcher may be interested in estimating the relative contribution of individual-level versus group-level effects. In other cases, researchers may be interested in exploring the impact of group- or organizational-level variables on the relation between individual-level variables. In still other cases, researchers may wish to examine the behavior of a small number of research participants over many occasions (e.g., diary studies); such data are *multi-level* because individuals are

nested within time periods or measurement occasions. Fortunately, statistical procedures are available to researchers in order to allow the analysis of data at multiple levels.

To examine cross-level relations, a statistical technique that has become increasingly popular is *random coefficient modeling* (Bliese & Jex, 2002; Byrk & Raudenbush, 1992). Random coefficient modeling can be used, for example, to test whether the magnitude of relations between individual-level variables (represented by regression coefficients) differs as a function of some aggregate-level variable. While both of these techniques are very useful, they are also very complex, and they require the use of special computer software. However, if used appropriately, both can help researchers untangle the complexity of multilevel data.

CHAPTER SUMMARY

This chapter explored the methodological and statistical foundations of organizational psychology. As was shown, organizational psychologists have several options when collecting data about behavior in organizations. These range from simple observation methods to highly complex quasi-experimental investigations. The most frequently used technique, however, is survey research.

In the collection of data in organizations, several important issues must be considered. For instance, researchers need to be cognizant of the limitations of self-report measures and aware of limits on the generalizability of research findings across research settings. When cross-cultural research is attempted, researchers must be attuned to issues of language and sampling. A more practical issue is simply gaining access to organizations to collect research data.

A variety of statistical methods were discussed that can be used to analyze data once they are collected. These range from simple descriptive statistics to more complex correlation and regression analysis. The choice of any statistical technique is dictated by the nature of the question the researcher is attempting to answer.

In the statistical analysis of data, a number of important issues must be considered. Researchers should be aware of the importance of statistical power and attempt to maximize it whenever possible. This is particularly true when researchers are interested

PEOPLE BEHIND THE RESEARCH

PAUL D. BLIESE AND THE IMPORTANCE OF STATISTICS

I've always been attracted to the basic tenets of statistics—the idea that probability can be used to detect patterns in complex data. What fascinated me about the area of multilevel statistics was the idea that researchers and practitioners could make accurate predictions about central tendencies of groups even in cases where the seemingly same data failed to make accurate predictions for individuals. In the Army, this meant that we might be able to predict the average health and well-being of groups of soldiers (platoons, companies) even if we could not necessarily predict the well-being of individual soldiers in the groups.

I became interested in this topic area early in my career when I observed a strong correlation between the average number of hours a group worked and the average well-being of the group members. When I analyzed the same data at the level of individual work hours and

individual well-being, I observed a much weaker relationship. Over the years, I noted that patterns such as those involving work hours and well-being were common in organizational psychology, and I began to explore the conditions that caused correlations to differ across levels (as had many others).

Eventually, this work led me to become interested in the idea that a variable like work hours might actually change meaning when it was averaged within groups. Up to this time, the dominant idea had been that variables maintained the same meaning in both their individual-level form and their aggregated form. For an example of a change in meaning, consider that individual reports of work hours vary for numerous reasons to include work requirements, desire to get ahead and work ethic. When the variable is aggregated by averaging across groups, however, individual differences wash out, and one is left with a group mean that reflects work requirements imposed on the group. In this way, the two variables (average group work hours and individual work hours) have a subtle but important change in meaning across levels.

What have I learned from all this? I guess the answer is that taking the time to track down answers to questions such as "why do two correlations differ?" can lead to an entire career's worth of work.

LTC Paul D. Bliese
Commander, U.S. Army Medical Research Unit-Europe.

in demonstrating the effect of moderator variables. Complex statistical techniques, such as causal modeling, can be useful tools to organizational researchers, provided they are used judiciously and are based on sound theory. The exploration of multilevel data has become increasingly popular in organizational psychology in recent years. Researchers conducting multilevel analysis must be prepared to justify aggregation, and must choose the analytical technique that best represents the substantive issue of interest.

SUGGESTED ADDITIONAL READINGS

Bliese, P. D. (2000). Within-group agreement, non-independence, and reliability: Implications for data aggregatrion and analysis. In K. J. Klein & S. W. Kozlowski (Eds.), *Multilevel theory, research, and methods in organizations* (pp. 349–381). San Francisco: Jossey-Bass.

Dane, F. C. (1990). *Research methods*. Pacific Grove, CA: Brooks-Cole.

De LaRosa, G. M. (2006). *Towards an understanding of individual ratings of cohesion within work units: A multilevel study*. Unpublished master's thesis. Bowling Green State University, Bowling Green: OH.

Hays, W. L. (1988). *Statistics* (4th ed.) Fort Worth, TX: Harcourt Brace Jovanovich.

McCall, M. W., Jr., & Bobko, P. (1990). Research methods in the service of discovery. In M. D. Dunnette & L. M. Hough (Eds.), *Handbook of industrial and organizational psychology* (2nd ed., Vol. 1 pp. 381–418). Palo Alto, CA: Consulting Psychologists Press.

Schaffer, B. S., & Riordan, C. M. (2003). A review of cross-cultural methodologies for organizational research: A best practices approach. *Organizational Research Methods, 6,* 169–215.

Schaubroeck, J., & Kuehn, K. (1992). Research design in industrial and organizational psychology. In C. L. Cooper & I. T. Robertson (Eds.), *International review of industrial and organizational psychology, 1992* (pp. 99–121). Chichester, England: Wiley.

Tabachnick, B. G., & Fidell, L. S. (1996). *Using multivariate statistics* (3rd ed.) New York: HarperCollins.

Chapter Three

Attraction and Socialization

The lifeblood of any social organization is people. For example, a university must have faculty, an auto manufacturer must have design engineers, and a professional baseball team must have players. Thus, to remain viable, all organizations must periodically go through the process of bringing in new employees and training them to become full-fledged organizational members. To begin this process, organizations must first attract potential employees and determine whether their qualifications match organizational needs. This process, however, is not unidirectional—that is, applicants are seeking out and evaluating organizations as potential employers. Once employees enter an organization, they must be trained not only to perform job-specific tasks, but also to learn the culture of the organization. This process is also bidirectional; that is, organizations do things to socialize new employees, and new employees seek out information to help them adjust to their new work environment. Taken together, this entire process can be viewed as attraction and socialization.

This chapter begins with an examination of the first stage of the attraction process, namely recruiting, from the perspective of both the organization and the applicant. As will be shown, organizations use a variety of methods to recruit potential employees, and a number of factors can impact the success of recruiting efforts. At the same time, applicants, or potential employees, evaluate the suitability of potential employers. In general, potential employees attempt to make some determination of the extent to which they fit with an organization.

The focus of the chapter then shifts to employee socialization. Once a recruit accepts employment he or she becomes an official member of an organization. In order to become a full-fledged organizational member, however, a process of socialization is needed. Organizational psychologists have examined the socialization process in an effort to understand the various tactics organizations use to socialize new employees, determine what employees learn as they are socialized, and describe the tactics new employees use to obtain information during the socialization process.

The chapter concludes with a discussion of the impact of diversity on employee socialization. In contemporary organizations, it is quite common for new employees to enter organizations with demographic characteristics, experiences, and values that are far different from those of the majority of employees. Because of this, it may be especially difficult for such individuals to be fully socialized into an organization. Fortunately, there are steps an organization can take to deal with the impact of diversity on the socialization process.

THE RECRUITMENT PROCESS: AN ORGANIZATIONAL PERSPECTIVE

The aim of recruiting is to generate a large pool of highly qualified applicants so that the organization can select those who stand the best chance of becoming successful and remaining with the organization for a long period of time. In college athletics, for example, coaches typically spend most of the off-season recruiting highly prized high school athletes. Although recruiting is usually not considered an *organizational* topic, it is covered briefly in this chapter because it is strongly related to socialization. Successful recruiting increases the chances that the new employees an organization selects will fit well into the culture of the organization and will be socialized more successfully.

Recruitment Planning

Organizations typically do not recruit new employees randomly. Rather, an organization's recruiting efforts are typically based on careful planning as to (1) the number of employees that will be needed in various jobs, (2) when these new employees will be needed, and (3) the present and future supply of potential employees in the labor market. An organization that understands these

three elements of planning will be able to focus its recruiting efforts much more effectively. According to Cascio (1998), this crucial first step in the recruitment process is known as *recruitment planning*.

What type of information does an organization need to develop a sound recruitment plan? First and foremost, recruitment planning should coincide with an organization's *strategic planning*. A strategic plan can be thought of as an organization's plan for "where we're going" and "how we're going to get there." Strategic planning must be linked to recruitment planning because strategic plans often have clear implications for staffing needs. As an example, let's say the coach of a professional football team decides to replace an offensive system that relies heavily on running plays with one that relies primarily on passing. This change in strategy will require players with different skills and thus will have implications for recruiting. The coach would want to focus on obtaining a highly talented quarterback and corps of receivers, either through the college draft or by other means (e.g., trades, free-agent signings).

Another factor that should be considered in developing a recruitment plan is *succession planning*. Succession planning involves making projections as to the likelihood of turnover within various job categories. This is often done on the basis of projected retirements, but may be based on other factors as well (i.e., employees in limited-term jobs, employees returning to school). Based on these projections, an organization can often gear its recruiting efforts toward attracting individuals who have the skills necessary to perform the work of those who may be leaving the organization. As with any prediction, there is some degree of uncertainty in succession planning. For example, since there is no mandatory retirement age for most occupations, organizations are often uncertain as to the retirement plans of senior employees.

A third consideration in recruitment planning is the skills and abilities of current employees. Many organizations ask current employees to periodically complete what is known as a *skills inventory*. A skills inventory may ask employees to document their job experiences, continuing education (if any), and special skills and competencies. If current employees possess the skills and abilities needed by an organization, there is obviously less need to recruit from outside sources. This is important because filling positions internally has certain advantages (i.e., less adjustment for the employee and less cost for the organization) and may create positive incentives for employees.

A final piece of information that is useful for developing a recruitment plan is some assessment of the supply of labor for various job categories. This type of information can often be obtained relatively easily from government agencies, trade associations, and, in some cases, professional organizations. In the field of I/O psychology, for example, the Society for Industrial and Organizational Psychology (SIOP) collects information about the supply of labor in the profession. The basic question an organization is seeking to answer is whether the supply of employees in different job categories is very plentiful or very scarce. For example, the supply of attorneys in the United States has grown to the point where they are quite plentiful in the labor market. In contrast, software developers and computer programmers are in relatively short supply.

Labor market information is useful because it will influence the approach an organization will take in its recruiting efforts, as well as the choice of specific recruiting sources. To fill jobs for which labor is in short supply, organizations may need to be highly aggressive in their recruiting efforts and perhaps offer other incentives (e.g., sign-on bonuses) to attract new employees. Such recruiting efforts may require the assistance of executive search firms and may be international in scope. This is often the case when organizations need to recruit high-level executives or highly skilled technical specialists. In contrast, when the supply of labor is plentiful, organizations may be able to devote fewer resources to recruiting efforts, and may adopt a much less aggressive and costly approach. For example, if many unskilled manual labor positions are open, organizations may rely on referrals from current employees or simply select from walk-in applicants.

Recruiting Methods

Assuming that an organization has developed a sound recruitment plan, the next step is to choose some methods of recruiting. A key decision for any organization that plans to recruit new employees is whether to invite applications from internal and external sources. The primary form of internal recruiting is advertising to current employees (i.e., through job postings). As stated earlier, recruiting internally has many advantages. Internal transfers and promotions are less expensive than bringing in new employees, may provide positive incentives for current employees, and may require less training for those employees who apply and are accepted. It has also been shown that employees recruited internally may be more likely to stay with an organization (Spector, 2006).

On the other hand, new employees recruited from the outside may bring a fresh perspective to the organization. Also, some organizations may be forced to hire outsiders because their current employees have not acquired the skills necessary to perform a given job.

Compared to a current workforce, external recruiting sources are much more plentiful, as indicated in Table 3.1. Although a specific recruiting source may be required because of the nature of the job, some general comments can be made about recruiting sources. For example, the most frequently used recruiting source is some form of advertising—typically, in print or electronic media. Use of the Internet, in particular, has become the preferred method of recruiting for many organizations in the past 10 years (Chapman & Webster, 2003).

The recruiting sources listed in Table 3.1 indicate considerable variation in cost. The least costly recruiting sources are typically walk-ins and employee referrals. In addition to their low cost, employee referrals may be attractive because these applicants typically possess greater knowledge of the organization than other applicants do. This may explain why employees who are referred by organizational members tend to have lower levels of turnover, compared to others (Gannon, 1971; Reid, 1972). An obvious danger in reliance on employee referrals is that it may perpetuate nepotism, and the result may be an overly homogeneous workforce.

Internet advertising is also a relatively inexpensive way for organizations to advertise employment opportunities. According to a survey of human resource professionals conducted by Chapman and Webster (2003), a primary advantage of the Internet is that it allows an organization to develop a very large applicant pool due to its wide availability. It also allows an organization to screen applicants more efficiently through online application procedures, and provides a very visually appealing medium for describing the culture of an organization (Braddy, Meade, & Kroustalis, 2006).

TABLE 3.1
Typical External Recruiting Sources Used by Organizations

1. Advertising: newspapers (classified and display), technical and professional journals, direct mail, television, the Internet, and (in some cases) outdoor advertising.
2. Employment agencies: federal and state agencies, private agencies, executive search firms, management consulting firms, and agencies specializing in temporary help.
3. Educational institutions: technical and trade schools, colleges and universities, coop work/study programs, and alumni placement offices.
4. Professional organizations: technical societies' meetings, conventions (regional and national), and placement services.
5. Military: out-processing centers and placement services administered by regional and national retired officers' associations.
6. Labor unions.
7. Career fairs.
8. Outplacement firms.
9. Walk-ins.
10. Write-ins.
11. Company retirees.
12. Employee referrals.

Source: W. F. Cascio. (1998). *Applied psychology in personnel management* (5th ed.). Upper Saddle River, NJ: Prentice Hall. Reprinted by permission of Pearson Education, Inc., Upper Saddle River, NJ.

Chapman and Webster (2003) also note some potential disadvantages associated with the use of Internet advertising. The biggest of these is that Internet advertising may generate *such* a large applicant pool that screening potential applicants becomes extremely labor intensive. Respondents in this study also noted that using the Internet resulted in somewhat of a "loss of personal" touch in the recruitment process.

The most costly recruiting methods used by organizations are the use of employment agencies and, to a lesser extent, on-campus recruiting. It should be emphasized, however, that the cost of a recruiting source should be weighed against other factors. For example, most organizations are willing to incur the cost of employment agencies or executive search firms when they must select high-level senior executives. Poor hiring decisions at this level may cost an organization millions of dollars. Campus recruiting is typically justified in cases in which organizations are seeking entry-level employees in fields where the supply of labor is relatively low (e.g., engineering, computer science, accounting). This method of recruitment also allows an organization to convey much more detailed information about its culture (Cable & Yu, 2006), which may help applicants make more informed decisions about whether or not they would fit in the organization. This could lead to greater retention in the future.

Other than cost, how else can organizations evaluate the potential usefulness of different recruiting sources? Two commonly used indexes are *yield ratios* and *time lapse data*. A yield ratio is simply the total number of candidates generated by a given recruiting source (Internet advertising, for example), relative to the number of qualified candidates. From an organization's perspective, an ideal recruiting source is one that delivers a large number of candidates who are well qualified for the position the company is attempting to fill. This allows the organization to be highly selective in making its hiring decisions.

Time lapse data represent estimates of the time it takes to go from one step to the next in the recruiting and hiring process. For example, organizations may estimate the time needed for each step that takes place between the initial contact with an applicant and the first day of employment with the organization. Time lapse data help an organization identify *bottlenecks* in the recruitment process that may cause applicants to lose interest (see Comment 3.1). When those bottlenecks are identified, an organization can sometimes take steps to speed up the process; however, this is not always possible. For example, recruitment for government jobs that require security clearance has to be quite lengthy to allow for background investigations.

THE RECRUITMENT PROCESS: THE APPLICANT'S PERSPECTIVE

From the organization's perspective, the recruitment process involves trying to "put our best foot forward" in order to attract potential employees. At the same time, we know that applicants are trying to determine which organizations are most attractive to them. In this section, we examine how, and on what basis, applicants make such judgments about organizations.

In a very general sense, when applicants evaluate potential employers, they are making some judgment as to whether they fit with these organizations. An applicant is really asking himself or herself: "Can I see myself doing this job in this organization?" This question can obviously be answered on

COMMENT 3.1

RESEARCH ON RECRUITING

BECAUSE OF THE importance of recruiting, there has been considerable research on it over the years (see Rynes, 1991). One theme is very evident in recruiting research: The recruiter is not a key factor in whether an applicant decides to accept employment with an organization. Rather, the nature of the job and other conditions of employment (e.g., salary, benefits, promotion potential) appear to be much more important. The one thing about recruiters that does appear to be important, however, is their knowledge of the job that an applicant is seeking. This may be the reason that organizations often select technical specialists to recruit in their technical specialty.

Another very clear theme in the recruiting literature—the way organizations treat applicants during the recruiting process—is important. For example, if an organization treats applicants rudely, or is very lax about keeping them informed, this approach will turn off applicants and make them less likely to accept an offer of employment. Why is this the case? Most recruiting researchers contend that, during the recruiting process, applicants form an impression of a potential employer. Thus, when an applicant is not treated well during the recruiting process, negative *signals* tell the applicant what the organization would be like as an employer.

Most recently, research on recruiting has shown that the image organizations project to potential applicants is very important. In much the same way that consumers form perceptions of different brands of the same product (e.g., different brands of beer), job seekers form perceptions of different employers. Research has also shown that these perceptions are an important determinant of whether or not job seekers pursue employment with a given organization. The practical implication of these recent findings is that organizations need to pay close attention to the image they portray in recruiting materials, company websites, and even advertising.

In summary, research has shown that, in comparison to many other factors, recruiting does not have a large impact on applicants' decision making. Nevertheless, the recruiting process is important, largely because, if not done well, it has the potential to turn off applicants. Organizations should strive to employ knowledgeable recruiters who treat applicants with respect. It is also imperative that organizations attempt to avoid lengthy time delays, and to maintain contact with applicants during the recruitment process. Organizations must also be aware of the image they project to potential applicants, as well as the general public.

Sources: S. L. Rynes. (1991). Recruitment, job choice, and post-hire consequences: A call for new research directions. In M. D. Dunnette and L. M. Hough (Eds.), *Handbook of industrial and organizational psychology* (2nd ed., Vol. 2, pp. 399–444). Palo Alto, CA: Consulting Psychologists' Press; S. L. Rynes, R. D. Bretz, Jr., and B. Gerhart. (1991). The importance of recruitment in job choice: A different way of looking. *Personnel Psychology, 44,* 487–522; Lievens, F., & Highhouse, S. (2003). A relation of instrumental and symbolic attributes to a company's attractiveness as an employer. *Personnel Psychology, 56,* 75–102.

many levels; thus, some explanation is needed as to the bases on which applicants' assessments of fit are made. Perhaps the easiest dimension on which applicants can make an assessment of fit is whether their skills and abilities must match the skills and abilities required to perform a given job (Kristof, 1996). For most faculty positions in universities, for example, a Ph.D. in one's specialty is required, and in many cases, some teaching experience is desired. If a person does not have a Ph.D., he or she obviously would not fit in such a position.

Assuming that an applicant does possess the necessary job-relevant skills and abilities, what other bases does that applicant use to assess his or her fit with a particular organization? According to Schneider's (1987) *Attraction–Selection–Attrition* framework, applicants are attracted to and stay in organizations with cultures that are compatible with their personalities. Compared to judgments about skills, abilities, and credentials, making judgments about an organization's culture is far more difficult. Since applicants are not organizational members, they typically must rely on *secondhand* information sources such as company websites (Cober, Brown, Levy, Cober, & Keeping, 2003), company recruiting brochures (Cable & Yu, 2006), and experiences they have had with an organization as a consumer (Lievens & Highhouse, 2003). Despite the difficulty of making this type of assessment, research has generally supported the ASA framework; that is, members of organizations, and even work groups, tend to be rather homogeneous in terms of personality (George, 1990; Jordan, Herriot, & Chalmers, 1991; Schaubroeck, Ganster, & Jones, 1998; Schneider, Smith, Taylor, & Fleenor, 1998).

To simply say that applicants are attracted to organizations with cultures they perceive to be compatible with their personalities is a rather imprecise statement. Such a statement begs the question: What aspects of personality, and what aspects of organizational culture? To address this question, Judge and Cable (1997) investigated the relationship between the Big Five personality traits (neuroticism, extraversion, openness to experience, agreeableness, and conscientiousness) and job applicants' attraction to organizations with different cultural profiles. Organizational culture can be thought of as the underlying values and basic assumptions that guide much of the behavior of organizational members. (See Chapter 14 for a more extensive examination of organizational culture.)

The results of this study showed that applicants were attracted to organizations with cultural profiles that were congruent with their personalities. As an example of how this works, consider the personality trait of *conscientiousness*. A person who is highly conscientious is dependable and achievement oriented, and plans well. Judge and Cable's (1997) study showed that those who are highly conscientious prefer organizations with cultures that can be described as highly detail oriented, and that place an emphasis on tangible outcomes. This may very well be due to the fact that highly conscientious individuals are meticulous about their work and are likely to produce tangible outcomes.

More recent research has supported Judge and Cable's (1997) findings, with one qualification. Specifically, there is evidence that applicants tend to make judgments about organizations in much the same way that consumers make judgments about different products (e.g., Cable & Turban, 2001). Furthermore, this information may be more salient than judgments about organizational culture when decisions are made whether to pursue employment with a particular organization. According to Lievens and Highhouse (2003), this has important practical implications for recruitment because organizations need to be aware of how they portray themselves in advertisements and other media such as organization websites.

Another way that applicants may judge their fit to a particular organization is on the basis of commonality in perceived values. Values simply represent things that are important to people and organizations. Suppose that a person places a strong emphasis on the value of individual achievement. It is unlikely that this person would be attracted to an organization that places a strong emphasis on the value of teamwork and collective achievement. Several studies have in fact demonstrated that applicants are attracted to organizations that they perceive to have values similar to their own (Chatman, 1991; Dawis, 1990). The major implication is that an organization must be careful to convey accurate information to applicants regarding its values. Obviously, though, applicants base their judgments of an organization's values on more than just recruiting materials. For example, applicants may base such judgments on information from others, encounters with the organization (e.g., as a customer), and the way the organization is portrayed in the media. A broader implication is that organizations must clarify their values and attempt to operate in a way that is consistent with those values. These findings suggest that value clarification is also a useful exercise for applicants (see Comment 3.2).

COMMENT 3.2

VALUE CLARIFICATION: WHAT WOULD YOU WALK THE I-BEAM FOR?

VALUES REPRESENT THINGS, ideas, or goals that are important to people. For one person, acquiring material wealth may be extremely important; for another, the most important thing might be to help other people. There is evidence that when people search for jobs, careers, and organizations, values play a very important role. That is, people want their work lives to be compatible with their values.

Despite the importance of values, many people never take the time to seriously clarify what their values are. However, value clarification occurs very quickly when people have to make choices. Many readers may recall when they were involved in the process of selecting a college to attend. For some, being able to maintain regular contact with family and friends is highly valued, and therefore their choice may be heavily influence by geographical location. For others, the prestige of the institution is most highly valued, and thus they may attend a highly prestigious college located far from home. Of course the most difficult situation is one in which all of one's choices possess highly valued attributes.

An example of a more dramatic way to look at value clarification was encountered by one of the authors while attending a training seminar several years ago. The person leading the seminar described a situation in which an I-beam approximately six inches wide was placed between the roofs of two skyscrapers that were about 50 feet apart. Needless to say, walking across this I-beam would be extremely dangerous. She then asked one of the seminar participants whether he would walk across this I-beam if $100,000 were waiting at the other end. When he quickly responded "No," she then asked whether he had any children. When he replied that he had two sons, ages 5 and 3, she asked whether he would walk this I-beam if his 5-year-old son were stranded on it. As you might guess, his response was now an unequivocal "Yes." (This man obviously didn't have teenagers yet!) Few situations in life require such dramatic value clarification. However, it is a good way to begin thinking about what one really values in life. So the next time you're unsure about your values, asking yourself "What would I walk the I-beam for?" might provide some useful answers.

In addition to personality and values, applicants may make other assessments of fit, based on a variety of other factors. For example, an applicant may have strong feelings about work-family issues, and thus be attracted to organizations that are very progressive regarding work-family initiatives (Cunningham, 2005). Some people seek membership in organizations for more ideological reasons. As an example, enlistment in the armed services is due at least partially to feelings of patriotism.

ORGANIZATIONAL SOCIALIZATION

Assuming that an organization is able to attract a pool of highly qualified applicants, it will obviously utilize some selection procedures, make offers to applicants, and ultimately end up with new employees. When someone is hired, a process of socialization is required to transform the new *outsider* employee into a full-fledged organizational member. In this section, organizational socialization is defined, models of the organizational socialization process are reviewed, and tactics used by both organizations and newcomers during the socialization process are described. The concluding section examines the impact of diversity on organizational socialization efforts.

Defining Organizational Socialization

Organizational socialization represents the process by which an individual makes the transition from *outsider* to *organizational member*. What does a person have to learn in order to make this transition successfully? According to Van Maanen and Schein (1979), in the broadest sense, socialization involves learning the culture of an organization. Thus, socialization is synonymous with the process of *acculturation* of new organizational members. Another important part of the socialization of new members is learning the task-related and social knowledge necessary to be successful members of an organization (Louis, 1990). Stated differently, socialization is about learning to do your job effectively and getting along with others in the organization.

One of the most comprehensive definitions of organizational socialization was provided by Chao, O'Leary-Kelly, Wolf, Klein, and Gardner (1994). Their definition, which contains six dimensions, encompasses elements of task-related learning, knowledge of the social climate, and culture transmission. These six dimensions are presented in Table 3.2.

The first dimension proposed is *history*. As new employees become socialized into an organization, they gradually become familiar with an organization's history, which may include long-held customs and traditions. Many organizations provide newcomers with this information during their initial orientation. New employees at Walt Disney World, for example, learn a great deal about the life of Walt Disney and the traditions of the Disney Corporation in their initial training, which is called "Traditions 101" (Peters & Waterman, 1982).

TABLE 3.2
Six Dimensions of Organizational Socialization (Chao et al., 1994)

1. History.
2. Language.
3. Politics.
4. People.
5. Organizational goals and values.
6. Performance proficiency.

The second dimension of socialization is *language*. All organizations utilize some terminology and jargon that is more familiar to organizational members than to outsiders. Some of this language may reflect the dominant profession within an organization (e.g., a law firm), but in many cases it is also organization specific. Perhaps the best example of organization-specific terminology is in the military. Newcomers to military organizations quickly learn about the reliance on military-specific terminology and acronyms. For example, *presentations* are referred to as *briefings*, and *assignments* are referred to as *missions*. With respect to acronyms, some readers may recall a hilarious scene in the movie *Good Morning, Vietnam,* in which the actor Robin Williams manages to squeeze every possible military acronym into one sentence. Having worked as contractors for the U.S. Army in the past, both authors can personally attest to the reliance on acronyms in the military (see Comment 3.3).

A third aspect of socialization is *politics*. As newcomers become socialized into an organization, they gradually begin to understand the politics or *unwritten rules* that govern behavior within the organization. For example, this may involve learning how to get things done, how to obtain desirable work assignments, and who the most influential people in the organization are. Such things may appear to be obvious at first, but they may actually be more complex. In many organizations, newcomers often find that power and influence are only moderately related to hierarchical level. For example, clerical employees can sometimes become

COMMENT 3.3

ACRONYMS AND MILITARY CULTURE

ONE OF THE biggest shocks for civilians working for or with the military is the heavy reliance on acronyms in the military. For example, the person you are working most closely with is your POC (Point of Contact), and when someone goes to another location temporarily, he or she is TDY (Temporary Duty). Both authors have worked extensively with the U.S. Army, so we're both very familiar with military acronyms. Dr. Britt was an officer in the U.S. Army, so he no doubt was familiarized during basic training. Dr. Jex first encountered military acronyms during work on a year-long research contract for the United States Recruiting Command (USAREC, of course) in the early 1990s. Evidently, the people we were working with on this project were concerned about the contractors' lack of understanding of military acronyms; they provided a booklet explaining the meaning of all military acronyms—the booklet was about an inch thick! However, once everyone working on the project learned some of the more important acronyms, they actually became quite comfortable with this form of communication.

Why does the military make such extensive use of acronyms? Although there is no *official* explanation for this, most likely acronyms were adopted because they facilitate speed of communication, something that might be critical during an actual military operation. Acronyms also serve to distinguish the military from other types of organizations.

very influential because they control the flow of information and access to those at higher levels of the organizations.

The fourth dimension of socialization is *people*. Most organizational newcomers typically belong to some group or unit, so they must establish and maintain good working relationships with others. This may involve establishing relationships both within the work group and in the organization as a whole. Such relationships provide friendship to newcomers, but they also provide valuable information about the organization (Morrison, 2002). For example, they may help a newcomer to understand the history and politics of the organization, help them to master their job tasks, and help clarify their roles within their work groups (Morrison, 2002). In many universities, for example, this process is facilitated by pairing new faculty with senior faculty mentors. These mentoring relationships are important in helping newcomers to adjust to their new surroundings, make contacts within the university, and understand the history of the institution.

The fifth dimension is *organizational goals and values*. Although members of organizations do not become robots who blindly follow orders, they must learn the goals and values of the organization and, to some extent, assimilate them as their own. An employee working for McDonald's, for example, must learn to get at least somewhat *fired up* about the prospect of satisfying customers. As stated earlier, some of this learning is accomplished in the attraction stage because employees tend to be attracted to organizations that they identify with ideologically. However, applicants typically do not have a complete grasp of the goals and values of an organization until they become regular employees.

The final dimension of socialization, according to Chao et al. (1994), is *performance proficiency*. All organizational newcomers must learn to perform their jobs proficiently or they will not be able to maintain their membership for long. Building performance proficiency is a complex process that involves developing an understanding of one's job duties, as well as acquiring the specific skills necessary to perform them. As will be shown later in this chapter, a consistent theme in the organizational socialization literature is that this dimension is the top priority of new employees when they initially enter an organization. This is understandable; rewards and other future opportunities within the organization are often contingent on performance.

The Socialization Process: An Organizational Perspective

The process of organizational socialization can be viewed from two distinct perspectives: (1) the organization and (2) the newcomer. When viewed from an organizational perspective, the focus is on the stages newcomers pass through during the socialization process, and the socialization tactics used by organizations to get them through these stages. When viewed from the perspective of the newcomer, the focus is on the ways in which newcomers learn about and make sense of their new organizational environment. In this section, we examine socialization from an organizational perspective.

Stages of Socialization

Organizational psychologists have tended to view socialization largely in terms of stages that new employees pass through during the socialization process. Feldman (1976, 1981)

FIGURE 3.1
Feldman's (1981) Model of the Stages of
Organizational Socialization

Source: D. C. Feldman. (1981). The multiple socialization of organization members. *Academy of Management Review, 6*, 309–318. Reprinted by permission of
the Copyright Clearance Center.

proposed what has become the most influential stage model of organizational socialization. This model is presented in Figure 3.1.

The first stage in this model is *anticipatory
socialization*, which refers to processes that
occur before an individual joins an organization. This form of socialization typically
occurs during the recruitment phase, when
applicants gather information about the
organization and make some assessment of
whether they would fit within it. As stated
earlier, applicants rely on a number of information sources to make this assessment (e.g.,
recruitment brochures, company representatives, company websites, past experiences as
a consumer). Although all these information
sources are helpful to applicants, they are
obviously not *firsthand* so the accuracy of
this assessment may vary.

In some cases, however, anticipatory socialization may actually occur much earlier
than the recruitment phase. For example,
people often have an opportunity to *try out*
certain occupations through internships,
summer jobs, or other related experiences.
According to Feldman (1981), anticipatory
socialization is most valuable when an applicant has a realistic picture of the organization
and the job he or she will be performing. In
fact, much research has been done on the
value of realistic job previews (RJPs), which
prepare new employees for the realities of
the jobs they will be performing and the
organizations they will be working in (e.g.,
Wanous, 1989). Related to this, it is also
desirable if the applicant actually has the skills
and abilities that are congruent with the job
being sought, and has needs and values that
are congruent with the organization.

As the newcomer moves into the organization and becomes an official member, the
encounter stage begins. According to Feldman (1981), this stage represents the point
at which the newcomer begins to see the job
and organization as they really are. For a
number of reasons, this period may require
considerable adjustment. The newcomer may
have to balance the demands placed on him
or her by the organization with family
demands. A new attorney in a large law firm,
for example, may find that new associates
are expected to work in excess of 80 hours
per week if they want to eventually become
partners. This is also the time when the
new employee is learning the demands of
his or her role within the organization. Often,
this simply requires clarification of role
responsibilities with one's supervisor, but it
may also involve mediating conflicting role
demands.

After new employees become acclimated
to their new roles, they eventually reach the
stage labeled by Feldman as *change and*

acquisition. At this point, the employee has become fairly comfortable with his or her new role both in terms of performing required job tasks and, perhaps more importantly, adjusting to the culture of the organization. At this point, an employee is *firing on all cylinders,* so to speak. For an attorney, this would be the point at which he or she is handling a number of cases and is comfortable doing so. During the change and acquisition phase, the new employee has also come to some resolution regarding role demands; that is, the employee has gained, from his or her supervisor and coworkers, a good understanding of what is and is not expected. At this point employees are also able to achieve some reasonable balance between their work and their personal lives.

To a large extent, when the change and acquisition stage is reached, the new employee has become *socialized,* at least according to the model. To assess the *extent* of socialization, Feldman included behavioral and affective outcomes within the model. At a behavioral level, the extent of socialization can be assessed by whether an employee is capable of carrying out his or her role-related assignments. For example, we would hardly consider the socialization process successful if an employee were unable to perform his or her job.

A second behavioral index of socialization is the extent to which an employee is spontaneously innovative in carrying out role responsibilities, and is cooperative with other employees. According to Van Maanen and Schein (1979), when an employee is socialized into a new role, this may take the form of *custodianship, content innovation,* or *role innovation.* A custodial approach requires simply performing a role exactly *as written,* with little or no deviation. Most readers have undoubtedly heard the phrase "It's not in my job description." Content innovation and role

innovation, on the other hand, imply that the new role occupant may introduce changes into the content or even into the nature of the role. An example of content innovation might be a physician informing patients directly about the results of lab tests rather than having nurses do this. An example of role innovation might be expanding the role of production workers to include not only product assembly, but also quality control and perhaps even communication with product end users. Feldman's model proposes that putting one's stamp on the new role being occupied is an aspect of socialization.

A third behavioral index of the extent of socialization is turnover. If an employee leaves an organization, one could certainly make the case that this represents a breakdown in the socialization process (Feldman, 1981). This is only partially true, however; turnover may occur because of plentiful job opportunities (Carsten & Spector, 1987), or because an employee has exceptional skills and thus may have opportunities in other organizations (Schwab, 1991). It is also possible for an employee to remain in an organization but resist being fully socialized (see Comment 3.4).

Affective outcomes associated with socialization refer to things such as attitudes toward work, level of motivation, and involvement in one's job. According to Feldman's model, when employees are successfully socialized, they tend to exhibit higher levels of job satisfaction, internal work motivation, and job involvement. As with turnover, these outcomes may also be impacted by many factors and are thus imperfect indicators of socialization.

Recently, researchers have proposed that the most immediate outcome of socialization is to increase an employee's sense of *embeddedness* within the organization. Embeddedness reflects the degree to which employees feel

COMMENT 3.4

ORGANIZATIONAL SOCIALIZATION AND CONFORMITY

As NEWCOMERS BECOME socialized into an organization, they begin to understand the organization's culture. Furthermore, once they understand an organization's culture, they begin to assimilate that culture. Thus, it is assumed that one of the signs that an organization is not successful in socializing new employees is turnover. Those who do not conform to an organization's culture end up leaving that organization. This may be true in some cases but, in others, nonconformists end up staying in an organization.

Based on what we know about turnover, there may be situations in which an individual does not embrace the culture of an organization, yet has few other employment options. The nonconforming employee may simply learn ways to cope with working in such an organization. There may also be individuals who do not embrace the culture of an organization, yet may work there for a variety of reasons—compensation, geographical preferences, or simply because it's easier than looking for another job. Such employees may also find ways to cope with working for an organization that they do not fit into.

There may be cases, however, when an employee does not conform and the organization must adapt. If an employee is unusually talented, or possesses a very rare skill, an organization may in some cases be forced to put up with a great deal of nonconformity. A good example of this can be found in Jeffrey Pearlman's 2006 book *Love me, Hate me: Barry Bonds and the Making of an Antihero*. In this book Pearlman describes how the San Francisco Giants have essentially treated Barry Bonds like royalty, despite the fact that the star outfielder is often rude and condescending to fans, members of the media, and at times even his own teammates. If Bonds were unable to hit home runs, it is highly unlikely that the Giants would put up with such behavior. Employees in most organizations have far less freedom to deviate from conventional norms of conduct than Barry Bonds.

Source: Pearlman, J. (2006). *Love me, hate me: Barry Bonds and the making of an antihero.* New York, NY: Harper Collins Publishers, Inc.

connected to others in the organization, feel as though they fit in, and feel as though they would give something up by leaving (Mitchell, Holtom, Lee, Sablynski, & Erez, 2001).

Socialization Tactics

Feldman's (1981) model, which describes the stages employees go through during the socialization process, has received empirical support (e.g., Feldman, 1976), but it does not describe the specific tactics organizations use to socialize newcomers. For example,

what exactly does a police department do to *break in* new recruits after they graduate from the training academy? What methods does a major league baseball team use to help talented minor league players make the difficult transition to playing at the major league level? How does a university help a new professor make the transition from graduate school to faculty status (see Comment 3.5)?

The most comprehensive description of socialization tactics was provided by Van Maanen and Schein (1979) in their review

COMMENT 3.5

SOCIALIZATION INTO ACADEMIA

FOR MOST PROFESSORS, socialization begins during graduate training and continues into the first job out of graduate school. Traditionally, socialization into academia has been a rather informal process; newcomers essentially navigate their own way through. In many graduate programs, advanced students are assigned to teach courses without a great deal of guidance. In some departments, graduate student instructors are assigned a faculty mentor they can go to if they have questions, but they are pretty much on their own in teaching the courses. This same basic approach is often used when graduate students make the transition into faculty positions. Other than some very general guidelines, and occasional advice from a kind senior colleague, most new faculty are left alone to navigate their way through the first years of academia.

In recent years, there has been a trend in many universities to institute formal mentoring programs for new faculty, and for graduate students seeking to pursue academic careers (Perlman, McCann, & McFadden, 1999). In the case of graduate students, formal instruction is provided in teaching and in working with students. New faculty mentoring programs typically involve assigning new faculty to a more senior faculty mentor. A mentor may provide advice on things such as teaching, beginning a research program, the tenure process, and even navigating university politics. Do formal mentoring programs produce better quality faculty? This is a difficult question to answer because few, if any, programs have been systematically evaluated. However, one would assume that most new faculty probably find such programs helpful. The only potential downside to formal mentoring is that if it is too formal, it may decrease the creativity and individuality of new faculty. Although there is a certain amount of comfort in having a senior colleague there to provide advice in difficult situations, navigating those difficult situations alone can result in a great deal of growth and development for new faculty.

Source: B. Perlman, L. I. McCann, and S. H. McFadden. (1999). How to land that first teaching job. In B. Perlman, L. I. McCann, and S. H. McFadden (Eds.), *Lessons learned: Practical advice for the teaching of psychology.* Washington, DC: The American Psychological Society.

---

of the organizational socialization literature. According to these authors, socialization tactics can be described according to the six dimensions that are presented in Table 3.3. Note that these are not specific tactics per se, but dimensions that form a very useful framework for understanding specific tactics. As can be seen, organizations may opt to socialize new organizational members collectively or individually. As an example of collective socialization, an organization might bring in a group of new recruits and put them through an extensive training course together. In state police departments, for example, large groups of individuals are typically hired at the same time, and these

TABLE 3.3
Van Maanen and Schein's (1979) Six Dimensions of Organizational Socialization Tactics

Collective	Individual
Formal	Informal
Sequential	Random
Fixed	Variable
Serial	Disjunctive
Investiture	Divestiture

individuals subsequently attend a training academy as a group or cohort. Among the clear advantages of collective socialization include being more economical from the organization's perspective and providing opportunities for newcomers to develop a sense of cohesion and camaraderie among themselves. Allen (2006), for example, found that collective socialization was associated with stronger feelings of embeddedness among members of a financial services firm. According to Van Maanen and Schein, a potential danger of collective socialization is that it is most likely to produce only a custodial orientation among newcomers; that is, newcomers socialized in this manner may not be particularly innovative in performing their roles.

Examples of individual socialization would include skilled apprenticeship programs and, in a more general sense, mentoring. This form of socialization is typically used when the information a newcomer must learn is very complex, and when socialization takes place over a long period of time. Compared to group socialization, individual socialization allows an organization somewhat more control over the information passed on to the newcomer, and this is more likely to produce outcomes that are desired by the organization. For example, Van Maanen and Schein (1979) point out that those socialized individually are more likely to be innovative in the way they carry out their roles, as compared to those socialized collectively. It has also been shown that individual socialization may lead to greater role clarity (Jaskyte, 2005).

Despite the apparent value of individual socialization, there are some drawbacks. One obvious drawback is cost. For a senior manager to give one-on-one mentoring to a management trainee, or for a master plumber to work with a journeyman, is time consuming

and expensive. Also, in certain occupations, a custodial role orientation encouraged by collective socialization is desirable. For example, if a police officer does not follow proper procedures when making an arrest, the chances of obtaining a conviction may be very slim. Also, if soldiers do not adhere strictly to agreed-on rules of engagement during peacekeeping missions, their actions may result in violations of international law.

The second dimension depicted in Table 3.3 is formal versus informal. Police recruits' attendance at a residential training academy is an example of formal organizational socialization (e.g., Van Maanen, 1975). Note from the previous discussion that this is also collective socialization, although all forms of formal socialization need not be collective. For example, doctoral students are being socialized into their chosen professions in the context of a formal program of study. Within doctoral programs, however, much of the socialization takes place during informal interactions between students and their faculty mentors. The most common form of informal socialization is the very familiar *on-the-job* training. The new employee is not distinguished from more experienced colleagues, but his or her initial performance expectations are obviously lower.

According to Van Maanen and Schein (1979), formal socialization tends to be used in situations in which newcomers are expected to assume new ranks or achieve a certain status in an organization, when there is a large body of knowledge for newcomers to learn, or when errors on the part of a new employee may put others (including the newcomers themselves) at risk. This would certainly apply to law enforcement jobs, as well as many forms of professional training (e.g., law, medicine, dentistry). Informal socialization, on the other hand, is most typical when it is necessary for a newcomer to quickly learn new skills and work methods, or to develop highly specific practical skills. This would apply to a wide variety of workers, such as convenience store clerks, restaurant employees, and production employees in manufacturing.

Formal socialization assures the organization that all newcomers have a relatively standardized set of experiences during the socialization process. In professions such as law, medicine, and dentistry, the commonality in educational programs ensures that those entering these professions have a common base of knowledge. A potential drawback of formal socialization is that it may lead to a custodial approach to one's role. As stated earlier, this is desirable in some cases. In other cases, however, some innovation is desirable even if the role occupant has to acquire a fairly standard set of facts and knowledge. Medical training, for example, involves the formal acquisition of a great deal of information. This is obviously necessary in order to diagnose and treat many illnesses. At times, however, physicians may also need to deviate from doing things *by the book* in order to provide high-quality care for their patients. For example, a patient may have an illness that is a very rare condition and that requires an unconventional form of treatment. Informal socialization allows employees to develop their own unique perspective on their roles, and to introduce changes in those roles when they are able to perform independently.

Socialization tactics can also be viewed in terms of whether they are sequential versus random. For example, to become a physician, one is required to complete a clearly defined sequence of steps: undergraduate training, medical school, internship, and residency. In contrast, for many management positions in organizations, socialization is more random because there is no clear sequence of steps that one must follow. Rather, over time, one gradually acquires the skills and experiences necessary to assume progressively higher levels of managerial responsibility.

According to Van Maanen and Schein (1979), a sequential approach to socialization is typically used when employees are being socialized to move up through a clearly defined organizational hierarchy. In the Army, for example, an officer cannot assume the rank of colonel before passing through lower-level ranks such as captain, major, and lieutenant colonel. Because of these clearly defined steps, sequential socialization tends to produce more of a custodial than an innovative role orientation. In many organizations, for example, employees must *put in their time* at headquarters if they hope to obtain promotions in the future. When socialization is more random, however, new employees may be exposed to a greater variety of views and opinions regarding their roles. As a result, such individuals may be more innovative regarding their specific role responsibilities or perhaps even the way their roles fit into the organization.

Socialization efforts may also be distinguished in terms of being fixed versus variable. When socialization is fixed, a newcomer knows in advance when certain transition points will occur. In many entry-level management training programs, for example, new employees know in advance that they will be rotated through the organization for a specific period of time before being granted a permanent assignment. When socialization is variable, the organization does not tell the new employee when transitions will occur. Instead, the message often given is that a new assignment will be forthcoming "when we feel you're ready to handle it," and no specifics are given as to how and when readiness will be determined.

Fixed socialization patterns are most typically associated with changes in an employee's hierarchical status. In academic institutions, for example, faculty rank is determined in this fashion. Typically, a fixed number of years must be invested before a faculty member can move from assistant to associate, and, finally, to full professor. An advantage of fixed socialization is that it gives an employee greater time to understand his or her role (Jaskyte, 2005), and tends to make an employee feel more a part of the organization (Allen, 2006). It is unlikely, though, that a fixed period of time can be specified before a newcomer in an organization is fully accepted and trusted by his or her coworkers.

According to Van Maanen and Schein (1979), fixed socialization is more likely than variable socialization to facilitate innovative role responses. Variable socialization tends to create anxiety among new employees, and such anxiety acts as a strong motivator toward conformity. Variable socialization also keeps new employees *off balance* and at the mercy of socializing agents within the organization. At first glance, this may appear ideal from the organization's perspective, but it can backfire. If an organization is very arbitrary or vague about the speed of a new employee's career progression, highly talented employees may simply leave for better jobs.

Socialization efforts may also be distinguished as being serial or disjunctive. When socialization occurs in a serial fashion, experienced members groom newcomers to assume similar types of positions in the organization. In most police departments, for example, recruits fresh from academy training are paired with veteran police officers who help them to *learn the ropes*. In addition to fulfilling a training function, serial social-

ization serves to pass on the culture of the organization from one generation to the next. For example, during the socialization process, experienced employees often pass on the history and folklore of the organization to newcomers. Disjunctive socialization, in contrast, occurs when new recruits do not follow in the footsteps of their predecessors, or where no role models are available. This would occur when a new employee occupies a newly created position, or one that has been vacant for some time.

According to Van Maanen and Schein (1979), serial socialization is more likely than disjunctive socialization to facilitate social acceptance into an organization, which is closely related to the previously described term *embeddedness* (Mitchell et al., 2001). In many organizations, it is often necessary to *come up through the ranks* in order to be truly accepted by others. Serial socialization is also useful in situations where moving up in the organizational hierarchy requires some continuity in skills, values, and attitudes. In the military, for example, a person coming from the civilian world might have the necessary managerial and technical skills to assume a high-level rank. However, such a person would likely have difficulty due to a lack of the understanding of military culture and traditions that is needed for such a position. This is also true in academic departments when new graduate students enter each year (Slaughter & Zickar, 2006).

Serial and disjunctive socialization also differ in that serial socialization is more likely than disjunctive socialization to be associated with a custodial role orientation. Disjunctive socialization, on the other hand, is more likely to facilitate innovation. Both approaches to socialization, however, carry certain inherent risks. The custodial role orientation facilitated by serial socialization is desirable if the experienced member of the organization—the person doing the socializing—does his or her job well and projects the correct image of the organization. If this is not the case, a serial approach to socialization may perpetuate a *culture of mediocrity* within the organization. This process can be seen when professional sports teams are unsuccessful year after year. In many cases, veteran players on such teams pass on a culture of losing to newcomers.

An advantage of disjunctive socialization is that it may allow a newcomer to define his or her role in a very innovative and original manner. This, however, requires considerable personal initiative on the part of the employee. An employee who is not highly motivated, or who perhaps lacks confidence, may flounder if socialized in this manner (Gruman, Saks, and Zweig, 2006). Newcomers socialized in this manner may also become influenced by persons in the organization who do not have particularly desirable work habits. If disjunctive socialization is used, organizations may have to do considerable screening during the hiring process, and carefully monitor those who participate in the socialization process.

The final dimension of organizational socialization tactics depicted in Table 3.3 is the distinction between an investiture versus a divestiture approach. When investiture socialization is used, the organization capitalizes on the unique skills, values, and attitudes the newcomer brings to the organization. The organization is telling the newcomer: "Be yourself" because becoming a member of the organization does not require one to change substantially. Many organizations attempt to communicate this message during orientation programs and in a variety of other ways (e.g., giving employees discretion over how they do their jobs). Perhaps the most powerful way to communicate this

message is simply via the way the newcomer is treated in day-to-day interactions. If a newcomer is punished for displaying his or her individuality, this suggests that the organization does not want to capitalize on that employee's unique characteristics.

When divestiture socialization is used, an organization seeks to fundamentally change the new employee. An organization may wish to make the new employee forget old ways of doing things, and perhaps even old attitudes or values. Put differently, the organization is not building on what the new employee brings to the job; instead, it seeks a more global transformation. The first year of many forms of professional training involves a good deal of divestiture socialization. During the first year of doctoral training in many fields (including psychology), for example, students are taught to view problems from a scientific perspective and to base their judgments on empirical data. For many students, this is a form of divestiture socialization (albeit a mild one) because they typically have not thought this way prior to entering graduate training. More dramatic examples of divestiture socialization are used in organizations such as religious cults, radical political groups, and organized crime families. In these cases, new members may be required to abandon all forms of personal identity and give their complete loyalty to the organization.

According to Van Maanen and Schein (1979), divestiture socialization tends to be used when recruits first enter an organization, or when they are striving to gain social acceptance. For example, a new law-school graduate may dramatically change many of his or her attitudes and assumptions during the first transition to practicing law. Changes in lifestyle and spending habits may also be necessary in order to gain social acceptance among other attorneys in a law firm. Failure to make such changes may lead to social isolation and perhaps to disillusionment with one's chosen profession.

Perhaps not surprisingly, research has show that newcomers in organizations tend to react much more favorably to investiture socialization, both in terms of job attitudes and retention (Allen, 2006; Cable & Parsons, 2001). According to Allen, use of investiture socialization tends to make new employees feel embedded within an organization, which makes them more likely to stay. While there may be some extreme cases when divestiture socialization must be used (e.g., intelligence agencies), most organizations are probably much better off using an investiture approach to socialization.

Van Maanen and Schein's (1979) model has proven to be quite useful in facilitating an understanding of the organizational socialization process. Importantly, the authors cite considerable empirical support for many of the propositions in the model. Furthermore, in recent years more empirical reseach has emerged linking specific socialization tactics to a number of socialization outcomes (e.g., Allen, 2006).

Despite its enduring value, a number of things about this model must be kept in mind. First, although the tactics represented by each of the models are described as though they are discreet forms of socialization, in reality they represent opposite ends of a continuum. As an example, most socialization efforts are neither completely formal nor completely informal—they fall somewhere in between. Also, many of the socialization tactics described in this section occur in combination. An organization may socialize new recruits individually, using an informal, serial approach. This highlights the complexity of the organizational socialization process and suggests a possible reason why it is often difficult to predict the outcomes of socialization.

Finally, despite the complexity of organizational socialization tactics, making them explicit is quite useful for organizations. If managers are aware of the tactics that are available for socializing new recruits, the socialization process can be managed more effectively. Organizations can choose those methods of socialization that are likely to provide the most desirable outcomes to both the organization and the new recruit.

The Socialization Process: A Newcomer Perspective

Despite the value of early theory and research on organizational socialization (Feldman, 1976, 1978; Van Maanen, 1975; Van Maanen & Schein, 1979), this literature had a major gap. Specifically, socialization was viewed almost exclusively from an organizational point of view, or as something the organization *does to* the newcomer. Thus, very little research focused on how newcomers make sense of the complex maze of technical and interpersonal information facing them during the socialization process. There was also very little work investigating how newcomers actively seek out information during the socialization process despite the fact that we know that new employees do this. To fill this void, the focus of more recent work on organizational socialization has shifted quite dramatically to the organizational newcomer. More specifically, organizational psychologists have become quite interested in how newcomers gather information about their new organizations and how they make sense out of this information.

Information-Seeking Tactics

According to Miller and Jablin (1991), newcomers actively seek information during organizational socialization, and they do so

FIGURE 3.2
Miller and Jablin's (1991) Model of Newcomer Information-Seeking Behavior

Source: V. D. Miller and F. M. Jablin. (1991). Information seeking during organizational entry: Influences, tactics, and a model of the process. *Academy of Management Review, 16,* 92–120. Reprinted by permission of the Copyright Clearance Center.

in a number of ways. Figure 3.2 presents a model developed by Miller and Jablin to describe the complex process of newcomers' information-seeking processes. As can be seen in the first step in this model, one factor that initially determines information seeking is the newcomer's perceptions of uncertainty. Generally speaking, newcomers put more effort into information seeking when they perceive a great deal of uncertainty in the environment. Newcomers' perceptions of uncertainty depend on a multitude of factors such as the nature of the information one is seeking, individual differences and contextual factors, availability of information sources, and, ultimately, the level of role conflict and ambiguity one experiences. In

actual organizations, the degree of uncertainty varies considerably.

A second factor influencing the choice of newcomers' information-seeking tactics is the social costs associated with these tactics. Social costs really center on the image newcomers want to project to others in the organization, such as supervisors and coworkers. Most readers have probably had the experience of beginning a new job and having coworkers say, "If you have any questions, just ask," or "There's no such thing as a stupid question." Although experienced employees may be completely sincere in making these statements, newcomers may still feel uncomfortable when they must repeatedly ask questions of supervisors or coworkers. In doing so, one incurs an obvious social cost: appearing incompetent in the eyes of one's supervisor and/or coworkers. When the social costs of information seeking are high, newcomers tend to use less overt information-seeking tactics and are more likely to seek out nonthreatening information sources.

Based on perceptions of uncertainty, and on the social costs of information seeking, newcomers choose from a variety of information-seeking tactics. The most straightforward tactic newcomers use to obtain information is *overt questioning*. If a new employee does not know how to use a copy machine, he or she can simply ask someone how to use it. Of all the possible information-seeking tactics, overt questioning is clearly the most efficient. It is also the most likely to yield useful information and may even help the newcomer to develop rapport with others. Despite these advantages, newcomers may incur considerable social costs by using overt questioning because they run the risk of appearing incompetent and may be viewed as an annoyance by some coworkers. Such costs obviously depend on the number of times the same question is repeated and, to some extent, the manner in which the questions are asked. If an employee continues to ask coworkers how to use a copy machine after 6 months on the job, or rudely demands such assistance, he or she would likely be seen as an annoyance.

Another information-seeking tactic newcomers may use is *indirect questioning*: not asking someone to provide the exact information that is needed, but asking a question that gets at it indirectly instead. For example, a new employee hired for a sales position may eventually want to move into a position in the organization's human resources department. As a new employee, this person may feel uncomfortable directly asking his

or her supervisor about the possibility of obtaining a transfer. As an alternative, the new employee may casually ask a question this way: "I have a friend who works for XYZ Corporation and he was initially hired as a purchasing agent but eventually transferred into market research. Does that type of thing happen much here?" By using this approach, the employee reduces the risk of offending his or her supervisor by asking what could be perceived as an inappropriate question. Unfortunately, this type of question may not generate the most accurate information. In the newcomer's organization, transfers from purchasing to market research may be common, but going from sales to human resources is very rare.

A somewhat riskier information-seeking tactic, *testing limits*, may also be used by newcomers. This involves creating situations in which information targets must respond. For example, if a new employee is uncertain about whether attendance at staff meetings is mandatory, he or she may deliberately skip a meeting one week and await the supervisor's reaction. If there is no negative reaction, the employee may presume that attendance is not mandatory. On the other hand, if his or her supervisor reprimands the employee, this signals that attendance is important and should be viewed as mandatory. Assuming that the employee attends subsequent meetings, this one infraction is unlikely to have a negative impact.

Another technique newcomers may use to seek information is through *disguised conversations*. This involves initiating a conversation with someone for a hidden purpose. A new employee may be uncertain about whether employees in the organization are expected to bring work home on the weekends, but is uncomfortable asking about this directly. To obtain the information, the newcomer may strike up a conversation with a fellow employee about what he or she did during the weekend. If the fellow employee states that he or she spent time on a work-related project, this suggests to the newcomer that the organization expects employees to bring work home.

Disguised conversations can be useful because they save the newcomer from having to ask potentially embarrassing questions of others. In the previous example, the newcomer may worry that he or she will be seen as a *slacker* by fellow employees if bringing work home on the weekend is the norm. On the other hand, if this is not the norm, the newcomer may worry that he or she will be perceived as trying to make others look bad (i.e., a *rate buster*) if this question is asked directly. The major disadvantage of disguised conversations is that the newcomer has little control over the response of the information source. That is, the fellow employee in the previous example may be very vague and not divulge whether he or she spent any time working.

One of the major nonverbal information-seeking tactics used by newcomers is *observation*. For example, organizational newcomers typically become keenly aware of the behaviors that are rewarded and punished in the organization. Although newcomers will typically utilize observation to obtain many types of information, they will rely most heavily on this tactic when the social costs of asking the information source directly are high. A new employee may be uncomfortable directly asking his or her supervisor what is considered to be outstanding performance. Observing others may be the safest route to acquiring this information.

Closely related to observation is the use of *surveillance* to gather information. The primary distinction between surveillance and observation is that surveillance is more dependent on retrospective sense mak-

ing, and is more unobtrusive than observation. A newcomer may use surveillance to try to understand organizational norms with regard to the length of the workday. To do this, he or she may pay close attention to the behavior of fellow employees near the end of the day. The use of surveillance allows the newcomer to obtain important information while avoiding the social costs of asking what may be an embarrassing question (e.g., "What hours do we work?"). Unfortunately, this is somewhat risky because the newcomer has no control over the target under surveillance. Thus, newcomers tend to use surveillance in situations of extremely high uncertainty. Newcomers will also tend to use surveillance to a greater degree to obtain information from coworkers rather than supervisors. Newcomers typically have less opportunity to obtain information from supervisors in this manner, and the behavior of coworkers has more information value than supervisory behavior.

A final information-seeking tactic contained in Miller and Jablin's (1991) model is the use of *third parties*, or seeking information from those other than the primary source of information. The use of third parties actually encompasses several of the information-seeking tactics described previously. For example, an employee who is unsure whether a supervisor is pleased with his or her performance may directly or indirectly ask coworkers whether they think the supervisor is pleased. Like other indirect tactics, acquiring information in this way spares an employee potential embarrassment. In the previous example, if the employee's supervisor has not been pleased with his or her performance, asking the supervisor about this directly would obviously be uncomfortable. As with all indirect information-seeking tactics, however, new employees may receive inaccurate information by not going directly to the most relevant information source. In the authors' experience, bitter conflicts in organizations are often started because people do not go to each other directly to obtain information. As anyone who has played the game "Telephone" knows, secondhand information may be highly distorted.

Outcomes of Information-Seeking Tactics and Socialization

Having described the major information-seeking tactics used by newcomers, the next issue addressed in Miller and Jablin's (1991) model is the various outcomes associated with information-seeking tactics. At a general level, different information-seeking tactics provide newcomers with information that varies in both quantity and quality. According to Miller and Jablin, the quality of information is reflected primarily in newcomers' levels of role ambiguity and role conflict. Role ambiguity simply means that an employee is uncertain about his or her role responsibilities. For example, role ambiguity may result if a supervisor is very unclear about performance standards.

Role conflict, on the other hand, occurs when information obtained from different sources is inconsistent. This might occur, for example, if a newcomer receives mixed messages from a supervisor and coworkers regarding performance standards. Levels of role ambiguity and conflict are typically highest when newcomers rely on indirect or covert tactics to acquire information. Because these tactics are far removed from the most relevant information source, they provide newcomers with the least opportunity to verify the accuracy of the information they obtain. Given that both role ambiguity and role conflict are associated with negative outcomes (e.g., Jackson & Schuler, 1985), organizations need to create an environment

in which newcomers feel comfortable using direct information-seeking tactics, such as overt questioning.

Since Miller and Jablin's (1991) review, there has been considerable research on the many aspects of newcomers' information seeking. Ostroff and Kozlowski (1992), for example, examined the relationship between the types of information acquired during socialization, and the use of different information sources. These authors proposed that newcomers use different information sources to acquire different types of information. To acquire task-related information, it was expected that testing (e.g., proposing different approaches to one's supervisor) or experimentation (e.g., performing one's job tasks in different ways and evaluating the effects) would be relied on most heavily. To obtain information about group processes, however, it was expected that coworkers would be the most useful information source. The most important source of information about roles was expected to be observation of the behavior of others.

This study also examined a number of outcomes of the socialization process, as well as changes in the socialization process over time. New employees who considered themselves more knowledgeable about their job-related tasks, role demands, group-level dynamics, and the organization as a whole were expected to be more satisfied with their jobs; be committed to and feel more adjusted to their organization; experience fewer stress-related symptoms; and report lower levels of turnover intent. Over time, knowledge in all areas was expected to increase. The authors proposed that knowledge of the group would initially be greatest but knowledge of the task would equal it over time. Knowledge of the organization as a whole was expected to be the slowest to develop.

Based on data collected at two points in time from 219 individuals who had been business and engineering majors in college, most predictions in this study were supported. For example, observing the behavior of others, which was used most for acquiring knowledge, was followed by interpersonal sources (coworkers and supervisors), experimentation, and objective referents (e.g., consulting written manuals). Also, as predicted, different information sources were used, depending on the type of information respondents were trying to acquire. For information about the role being performed, respondents relied more heavily on supervisors than on coworkers, but tended to rely more on coworkers for information about the internal dynamics of their work group. To obtain information about the task, experimentation was used to a greater extent than interpersonal sources such as supervisors or coworkers.

In terms of knowledge of different domains, at Time 1 respondents reported that knowledge about the group was greater than knowledge of the task, role, and organization. This pattern had changed somewhat at Time 2. At this point, knowledge of the task had surpassed knowledge of the role and group, and knowledge of the organization remained the lowest. There was only one area in which knowledge changed from Time 1 to Time 2: Respondents reported becoming more knowledgeable about the task.

When relationships among information acquisition, knowledge, and outcomes were examined, a number of trends emerged. At both points in time, acquiring knowledge from one's supervisor was associated with higher levels of job satisfaction and commitment, and lower levels of turnover intent. Interestingly, acquiring knowledge from coworkers was associated with high levels of satisfaction and commitment, and low

levels of stress and turnover at Time 1, but these relations were not supported at Time 2. This finding suggests that supervisors are a constant source of information, whereas coworkers may initially be very influential but their influence wanes over time. Acquiring information from observing others and through experimentation was positively related to stress-related symptoms. This may be due to the fact that observing others may provide unclear information and thus may result in role ambiguity. Acquiring information through experimentation may be stressful because it may often result in failure, at least when job tasks are first being learned.

Respondents who believed they possessed more knowledge about all of the domains reported higher levels of satisfaction, commitment, and adjustment. However, the two that stood out as most strongly related to these outcomes were knowledge of task and role domains. It was also found that correlations were stronger between level of knowledge and outcomes than they were between sources of information and outcomes. The implication is that, for newcomers to feel adjusted, it is important that they feel knowledgeable about both their job-related tasks and their work-group role. Where this information is acquired is less important than the fact that it is acquired.

When changes in the relationship among information sources, knowledge, and outcomes were examined, it was found that newcomers who increased the information obtained from supervisors over time also experienced positive changes in satisfaction, commitment, and adjustment. This further reinforces the importance of the supervisor as an information source during the socialization process. It was also found that positive changes in task knowledge were associated with positive changes in both commitment and adjustment and effected a reduction in stress. This finding reinforces the importance of task proficiency to the adjustment of the newcomer.

Ostroff and Kozlowski's (1992) study has a number of important implications. Consistent with Miller and Jablin's (1991) model, the results suggest that newcomers use different methods to acquire different types of information. The results also clearly show that supervisors are important information sources for employees, although newcomers may initially rely just as much on coworkers. Perhaps the most important lesson from this study is that acquiring task knowledge is of paramount importance to the adjustment of new employees. Thus, organizations need to make sure that new employees receive proper training and, in some cases, on-the-job coaching in order to increase their task knowledge over time. A related implication is that organizations should not overload new employees with ancillary duties.

In another longitudinal study of the socialization process, Morrison (1993) collected data, at three points in time, from 135 new staff accountants. In this study, it was proposed that newcomers acquire a number of types of information, most of which were comparable to those in Ostroff and Kozlowski's (1992) study. For example, Morrison proposed that newcomers acquire information on how to perform their job-related tasks. Newcomers also acquire what Morrison described as *referent information*, or information about one's role. Newcomers also must acquire information about how they are performing their jobs (labeled *Performance Feedback*). In many cases, newcomers need to acquire what may be described as *normative information*, or information about the norms within the organization. Finally, newcomers need to acquire *social information*, or information about their level of social integration into their primary work group.

In addition to describing the types of information acquired, this study proposed that there are multiple ways of acquiring each type of information. Consistent with past socialization research, it was proposed that information could be acquired from one's supervisor or from an experienced peer; through monitoring others' behavior; by responses to direct inquiries; or from available written sources. Consistent with Ostroff and Kozlowski (1992), the dimensions of socialization examined were task mastery, role clarification, acculturation, and social integration.

Newcomers seeking greater amounts of technical information and performance feedback were expected to exhibit higher levels of task mastery than newcomers seeking lesser amounts of this information. It was also expected that newcomers seeking greater referent information and performance feedback would report experiencing higher levels of role clarity. With respect to acculturation, it was expected that this would be associated with seeking greater amounts of normative information and social feedback from others. Finally, social integration was also expected to be highest among those seeking greater amounts of normative information and social feedback.

The results of this study partially supported the hypotheses. For example, it was found that technical information (from both supervisors and peers) and written feedback were statistically significant predictors of task mastery. Interestingly, though, the direction of the relation between technical information from peers and task mastery was negative. This may be due to the fact that peers may not always have an adequate mastery of the technical information that is sought by newcomers.

It was also found that to facilitate role clarification, newcomers tended to make use of referent information, performance feedback (through inquiries), and consultants' written feedback. For example, a person new to a work group may pay attention to cues from group members as to whether his or her role performance is satisfactory; informally solicit feedback from the supervisor; and take advantage of written feedback from the initial performance review. Using these information sources makes sense because they are most likely to be relevant to employees' role-related activities.

Social integration was related primarily to the use of normative inquiries and monitoring activities. This finding suggests that new employees may feel uncomfortable asking for direct feedback from either peers or supervisors, in their efforts to determine their level of social integration. Indeed, it is unlikely that most people would feel comfortable asking fellow employees directly about the degree to which they are liked and whether they *fit in* with the work groups. Written sources of feedback would not provide this type of information either.

Finally, for the acculturation dimension, the only significant predictor was monitoring. To some extent, this finding mirrors the findings with regard to social integration. To learn about the culture of the organization, a new employee must primarily observe others in the organization and how things are done. This is likely due to the complexity of culture, but may also be due to the potential social costs associated with more direct forms of information seeking. Because culture is generally taken for granted or internalized (e.g., Schein, 1990), newcomers may run the risk of embarrassment by asking directly about things many experienced organizational members consider to be obvious or mundane. Overall, Morrison's (1993) study,

like that of Ostroff and Kozlowski (1992), suggests that newcomers use a variety of information-seeking tactics, and they use different tactics for acquiring different types of information.

Unfortunately, neither of the studies just described examined whether information seeking during the socialization process has an impact on the success of newcomers. It is clear, for example, that newcomers seek and acquire information, and that they use different information sources to acquire different types of information. What is less clear, however, is whether employees who increase their knowledge over time are ultimately more successful than employees who acquire less information.

Chao et al. (1994) addressed these issues in a longitudinal study of 182 engineers, managers, and professionals, conducted over a 3-year period. Career success in this study was measured by respondents' levels of personal income and career involvement. With respect to personal income, the only socialization dimension that was predictive was knowledge about the politics of the organization. Employees who developed the greatest knowledge of organizational politics tended to have the highest incomes. This may be due to the fact that those who become very knowledgeable about the politics of the organization may be most likely to make the contacts and form the alliances needed to reach levels in the organizational hierarchy that are associated with high levels of income.

In terms of career involvement, the only socialization dimension that was predictive was knowledge of the goals and values of the organization. Specifically, those who indicated having a greater deal of knowledge of the goals and values of the organization reported higher levels of career involvement than those with less knowledge. Looking at this another way, it is difficult for new employees to become highly involved in their careers if they are unsure of what their employers are trying to accomplish. Taken together, these findings suggest that certain aspects of socialization may contribute to affective outcomes (Ostroff & Kozlowski, 1992), and other aspects may be more important in determining success.

Another interesting finding from this study was that changes in the socialization dimensions were related to changes in both measures of career success. Thus, for employees to sustain a high level of success over time, they must continually increase their knowledge in crucial areas of socialization. This finding suggests that, to sustain a high level of success over time, one must never stop learning. Thus, organizations should provide learning opportunities for employees and, when possible, design work in a way that allows employees to learn (Parker & Wall, 1998).

Given the shift in focus of recent socialization research to newcomer information-seeking strategies (e.g., Miller & Jablin, 1991), the influence of other socializing agents and methods has been de-emphasized (e.g., Van Maanen & Schein, 1979). As a result, much less is known about the combined effect of newcomers' information-seeking strategies and the behavior of others (e.g., peers and supervisors) in explaining the socialization of organizational new-comers. Bauer and Green (1998) examined this issue in a very ambitious longitudinal study of 205 newcomers, 364 of their coworkers, and 112 of their managers. Like past socialization research, this study examined newcomer information seeking, several dimensions of socialization (feelings of task proficiency, role clarity, and feelings of being accepted by one's manager), and socialization outcomes such as performance, job satisfaction, and organizational commitment.

What makes the study unique, however, is that the behaviors of managers designed to facilitate socialization were also examined. Thus, this study addresses the need for a dual perspective.

As with the research previously discussed, it was expected that the type of information sought by newcomers and provided by managers would match socialization outcomes. For example, it was predicted that task-oriented information seeking and managers' clarifying behaviors would be related to feelings of task proficiency and role clarity. For feelings of acceptance by one's manager, it was expected that the best predicators would be social information sought by the newcomer, as well as managers' supporting behaviors. For outcomes, it was expected that feelings of task proficiency would predict performance, and feelings of acceptance by one's manager would be predictive of both job satisfaction and organizational commitment. A final prediction examined in this study was that the effects of both information-seeking tactics and managerial behavior on socialization outcomes would be mediated by newcomers' perceived level of socialization.

The results of this study showed that only managerial clarifying behavior at Time 2 predicted role clarity at Time 3. This same result occurred for predicting performance efficacy at Time 3. These findings are interesting because they seem to contradict recent socialization research that has placed such a strong emphasis on the information-seeking tactics of newcomers. Rather, these findings suggest that the behaviors of managers are the most important factor, at least for these outcomes. With respect to feelings of acceptance by one's manager at Time 3, the only variable that was predictive was managers' supportive behaviors at Time 2. Again, employees' information seeking had no impact on this measure. With respect to the mediational hypotheses, no support was found for the mediating role of socialization on the relation between newcomers' information seeking and outcomes. There was, however, evidence that feelings of task proficiency and role clarity fully mediated the relationship between managerial behavior and performance. Role clarity and feelings of acceptance partially mediated the relation between managerial behaviors and organizational commitment. These findings suggest that behaviors of managers, such as providing clarification and support, have a positive impact on things such as newcomers' performance and affective outcomes, but only to the extent that they facilitate the socialization process.

The broader implication of Bauer and Green's (1998) study is that the behavior of individual managers toward new employees is a critical factor in employee socialization. As stated earlier, this study is also noteworthy because the recent organizational socialization literature has focused so heavily on information-seeking tactics and knowledge acquisition of newcomers. Earlier work on organizational socialization focused heavily on the organizational attempts to socialize newcomers. This suggests that a more balanced view of organizational socialization is needed—that is, socialization is the result of a complex interaction between socialization tactics used by organizations and the information-seeking and sense-making processes of newcomers. Ignoring either the organizational or the newcomer perspective provides a limited picture of the organizational socialization process.

A final issue regarding the newcomer perspective is the expectations that newcomers bring to the socialization process. As Feldman's (1981) model showed, there is a period of anticipatory socialization prior to newcomers' formal entry into the organization. One way that prior expectations have been examined is through the study of *realistic job previews (RJPs)* (Wanous, 1989; Wanous, Poland, Premack, & Davis, 1992). As was stated in the earlier section on recruiting, the basic idea behind realistic job previews is that, prior to organizational entry, the newcomer is given a realistic preview of what the job will entail, even if some of this information is negative. Despite the intuitive appeal of RJPs, meta-analyses have shown that they have a very small impact on turnover (McEvoy & Cascio, 1985; Reilly, Brown, Blood, & Malatesta, 1981).

Another approach to dealing with newcomers' expectations is to focus information at a more general level. For example, Buckley, Fedor, Veres, Weise, and Carraher (1998) conducted a field experiment that evaluated the effect of what they described as an *expectation lowering procedure (ELP)* among a sample of 140 employees recently hired by a manufacturing plant. The ELP consisted of lecturing the new employees on the importance of realistic expectations, and how inflated expectations can lead to a number of negative outcomes. This study also included one condition in which employees were provided with a RJP. This allowed the researchers to test the impact of an RJP against the more general ELP.

The results of this study indicated that both the RJP and ELP had positive effects. For example, employees in those two conditions initially had lower expectations than those who received neither intervention, although there was no difference after 6 months. Most importantly, lower levels of turnover and higher levels of job satisfaction were found in the RJP and ELP conditions, compared to those receiving neither intervention. It was also found that expectations mediated this effect; that is, both RJP and

ELP interventions lowered turnover because they first lowered employees' expectations.

An important implication of this study is that organizations may not have to develop job-specific realistic previews for newcomers in order to facilitate realistic expectations. Rather, the expectations of newcomers can be changed to be more realistic by more general interventions of the type conducted by Buckley et al. (1998). From a practical point of view, this is encouraging because developing RJPs is more time-consuming than more general interventions such as ELP. RJPs must be job-specific; thus, many RJPs must be developed, depending on the number of jobs in an organization. The more general point to be gleaned from this study is that newcomers do much better when they come into a new organization with realistic expectations of both their jobs and their future lives within the organization. Thus, it's always a good idea to have as much information as possible before choosing a job or career (see Comment 3.6).

COMMENT 3.6

HOW TO DEVELOP REALISTIC EXPECTATIONS

THERE IS CONSIDERABLE research evidence to support the value of having a realistic picture of the job one will be performing, as well as life in the organization in which one will be working. Despite the value of realistic expectations, many readers might be wondering how to gain this type of information while still in college. Many students do so through internships, participation in cooperative education programs, and summer employment. Many university placement offices post (and keep records of) these types of jobs at local, national, and international levels. Recent research has also shown that college students, and job seekers in general, make considerable use of company websites (Braddy, Meade, & Kroustalis, 2006), as well as their experiences with an organization as a consumer (Lievens & Highhouse, 2003).

A somewhat less conventional way to obtain information is to set up an informational interview with a member of the profession you wish to pursue, or an employee of the organization you would like to work for. This involves simply contacting such an individual and asking for about 30 minutes of his or her time. Before the meeting, it's a good idea to prepare a list of questions about the profession or the organization. Although time may not always permit an informational interview, professional people are often very willing to talk about their profession to an eager college student.

What, then, is the best way to develop realistic expectations? In this author's opinion, direct experience with a member of an organization is most likely to provide the most accurate and timely information. Despite the accessibility of company websites, one must remember that organizations control the information on these sites, and therefore they may provide an overly optimistic picture. It has also been shown that users of company websites form impressions of an organization based not only on the actual content of the website, but also by it's design (e.g., how easy it is to use, how visually appealing it is; Cober, Brown, Levy, Cober, & Keeping, 2003). Relying on one's experiences as a consumer may also lead to inaccurate information about a job and particular organizations. For example, many organizations are highly customer focused so they often may treat consumers much better than they do their employees.

The Socialization Process: An Interactionist Perspective

As previously stated, early research on employee socialization was focused primarily on the tactics organizations use to socialize newcomers. The focus then shifted somewhat; that is, researchers became interested in understanding the manner in which newcomers acquire and use information during the socialization. While both types of research continue, the most recent trend in socialization research has been to understand the interaction between organizational tactics and the methods newcomers use to acquire information. This is an exciting development in socialization research because it represents the most realistic view of what actually happens when employees first enter an organization. In this section we briefly review research that has been guided by this interactionist perspective to socialization.

One issue that researchers have recently examined is whether the impact of organizational socialization tactics differs depending on the degree to which newcomers seek information. Gruman et al. (2006), for example, found in a study of 140 university students that organizational socialization tactics were more strongly related to socialization outcomes among newcomers who exhibited less feedback-seeking and information-seeking behaviors. Kim, Cable, and Kim (2005) found similar results in a study of 279 employee-supervisor pairs from seven organizations located in South Korea. These researchers also found that socialization tactics had little effect on employees who proactively developed strong relationships with their supervisors.

Taken together, both of these studies suggest that organizational socialization tactics may in fact not be needed in many cases. When newcomers are highly proactive about seeking information and feedback, and when they develop strong working relationships with their immediate supervisors, organizations may simply not need to do a great deal to socialize them.

Another issue that has been examined in recent socialization research is the manner in which employees are socialized into work teams. Given the prevalence of teams in organizations (Kozlowski & Bell, 2003), and the fact that an employee's ties to his or her work group are often stronger than they are to the organization as a whole (Meyer & Allen, 1997), this is clearly an important issue. As an example of this research, Chen G. (2005) examined the socialization process in 104 project teams from three high-technology organizations. The most important findings of this study were that employee empowerment and the expectations of team members were both positively related to newcomer performance. More specifically, new employees performed the best when they felt empowered and when their teams expected them to perform well.

It has also been shown that the manner in which team members are socialized into the organization as a whole may have an impact on the overall effectiveness of teams. For example, Oh, Chung, and Labianca (2004) conducted a study of 77 work teams from 11 organizations in Korea and found that teams whose members had more social relationships with members of other teams were more effective than teams whose members had fewer such relationships. While this finding may be somewhat specific to the Korean context, it suggests that employees should not only be socialized into a team but also to the organization as a whole.

In summary, this section provided a small sampling of recent socialization research examining the dynamic interaction between organizational socialization tactics and newcomer information seeking. While more research clearly needs to be done, this research has already contributed to a greater understanding of employee socialization than examining organizational socialization tactics or newcomer information seeking in isolation. Future organizational socialization research will likely follow this interactionist framework.

THE IMPACT OF DIVERSITY ON ORGANIZATIONAL SOCIALIZATION

Given increasing levels of diversity in the workplace, organizations are understandably concerned about how this may impact the socialization process. Research has in fact shown that women and ethnic minorities are more strongly attracted to organizations they perceive as managing diversity more effectively (Ng & Burke, 2005) and providing more opportunities to minorities (Perkins, Thomas, & Taylor, 2000). Thus, such concerns are well founded.

Jackson, Stone, and Alvarez (1992) reviewed the literature on the impact of diversity on socialization into groups and came up with a number of propositions, many of which are relevant to the broader issue of organizational socialization. According to these authors, the primary dilemma posed by diversity is that many individuals who are perceived as *different* must still be socialized and assimilated into organizations. This would be the case, for example, if a female executive were promoted to an all-male top-management group. Not only does such an individual tend to stand out, but it may also be difficult for such individuals to become accepted and seen as "part of the team." According to Jackson et al., this occurs simply because people tend to like, and feel more comfortable around, persons

perceived to be similar to themselves (e.g., Byrne, 1971).

Because people are attracted to, and feel more comfortable with, those who are similar to themselves, those perceived as *different* are often at a disadvantage during the socialization process. According to Jackson et al. (1992), newcomers who are dissimilar are often less likely to form the social ties and receive, from experienced organizational members, the feedback necessary to assimilate well into organizations. Experienced organizational members may not deliberately exclude those who are demographically different, but there is a subtle tendency to shy away from such individuals. This often puts women and racial minorities at a disadvantage because, in many organizations, the most influential members are white males.

How can organizations facilitate the socialization of a demographically diverse workforce? Jackson et al. (1992) suggested a number of strategies that might help to facilitate the socialization process. For example, they recommended that when several minority employees enter an organization at the same time, collective socialization processes should be used, if possible. Recall from Van Maanen and Schein's (1979) description of organizational socialization tactics that collective socialization has the benefit of generating communication and support among those socialized in the same cohort. This type of socialization may help women, racial minorities, and perhaps older employees feel less isolated, and may facilitate the development of social support networks within the organization. In professional baseball, for example, the socialization of players from Latin American countries is greatly enhanced by the formation of these types of social support networks (see Comment 3.7).

Another recommendation of Jackson et al. (1992) is for organizations to develop

COMMENT 3.7

"THE CHAIN"

IMAGINE BEING 17 years old and living on your own in a foreign country where you don't speak the language and have little familiarity with the culture. Worse yet, you are under tremendous pressure on your job—in fact, if you don't perform well you will be sent back to your native country and more than likely live in poverty. Sounds like a pretty far-fetched scenario, right? Actually it's a pretty common experience for many talented young baseball players who come to the United States from Latin American countries such as the Dominican Republic, Panama, Venezuela, and Puerto Rico with the dream of becoming major league stars.

How do Latin players cope with their difficult circumstances? Actually, many do not adjust well and end up returning to their native countries. For those who do survive, an important coping mechanism is support from each other. As Omar Vizquel of the San Francisco Giants explains, "Latin players tend to band together in the States and help each other. Some people call it *La Cadena*—Spanish for *The Chain*. It's nothing formal; just a feeling of obligation the older players have toward the younger ones." Examples of this might be helping a younger player secure housing, or simply explaining to them how to order a meal in English.

Source: Vizquel, O. (with Bob Dyer). (2002). *Omar! My life on and off the field.* Cleveland, OH; Gray & Company Publishers.

---

training programs aimed at both newcomers and established organizational members. For newcomers, such training programs might be aimed at increasing awareness of some of the problems they may face in the socialization process, and further helping them to develop coping strategies. For established organizational members, such training may help to increase awareness of some of the challenges women and racial minorities face when they are being assimilated into the organization. As Jackson et al. point out, however, such *diversity training* programs may have the unintended consequence of highlighting the differences rather than the similarities between people. It is also possible that if such programs are forced on employees, they may create less favorable attitudes toward diversity.

A third recommended strategy is the use of valid procedures in the selection of female and minority employees. Assimilating any newcomer into an organization will be much easier if the individual has the skills and abilities needed to do the job (Ostroff & Kozlowski, 1992). Although socialization of female and minority employees may initially be difficult, organizations are typically pragmatic enough to accept those who are capable of performing their jobs well and making a positive contribution. This also suggests that no one benefits when organizations hire and promote unqualified individuals on the basis of gender or racial preferences. This became very obvious to one of the authors several years ago when teaching a course composed primarily of African Americans, many of whom worked in professional positions in the auto industry. When the issue of racial quotas was discussed during class, the vast majority of these African American students were strongly opposed to this method of addressing past racial discrimination. Most expressed a strong desire to be seen as having *made it* on the basis of their own talents, and not because of a government-mandated program.

Finally, performance appraisal and reward systems can go a long way toward assimilating female and racial minority employees into organizations. For example, managers in organizations should be evaluated, at least to some degree, on the extent to which they develop all of their subordinates. If female and minority employee subordinates continually have a difficult time adjusting, this should reflect poorly on the evaluation of a manager. If an organization rewards on the basis of the performance of work groups, it is in a group's best interest to maximize the talents of all group members, regardless of gender, race, or age. This may explain the relative success of the military, at least in comparison to civilian organizations, in providing opportunities for racial minorities (Powell, 1995). *Mission accomplishment* is the highest priority in military organizations, and those who contribute positively to the mission are likely to be rewarded and accepted, regardless of race.

CHAPTER SUMMARY

In this chapter, we examined the ways that organizations attract new organizational members, and the process by which they are socialized. Organizations utilize a variety of methods to recruit potential newcomers; the choice of method is dependent on a number of factors such as the nature of the job, cost, relative quality of candidates generated, and time considerations. Regardless of the method chosen, recruiting research suggests that organizations are best served by providing recruits with accurate information, and treating them with respect and courtesy.

Recruiting obviously is not a one-sided process. Job seekers, who are the targets of organizational recruiting efforts, evaluate the messages put out by organizations and make some judgment as to the attractiveness of the organization. Research suggests that judgments of organizational attractiveness are made primarily on the basis of job seekers' judgments of *fit* with the organization. That is, job seekers make some judgment as to whether several aspects of the organization fit with their abilities, values, and personality. It has also been shown more recently that job seekers evaluate organizations in much the same way that consumers evaluate different products. The major implication for organizations is that it is in their best interest to provide an accurate portrayal of their culture to potential employees.

Once an individual is hired, the process of organizational socialization begins. Although many definitions of socialization have been provided, most see it as the extent to which a new employee is able to do his or her job, get along with members of the work group, and develop some understanding of the culture of the organization. Organizations may use a variety of tactics to socialize organizational newcomers. The choice of tactics depends, to a large extent, on the nature of the job a newcomer will assume in the organization and the ultimate goals of the socialization process.

Like recruiting, socialization is a two-way process. Organizational newcomers actively seek information about the organization and may use a variety of tactics in order to obtain information. The choice of tactics depends largely on the level of uncertainty, the nature of the information being sought, and the perceived social costs of obtaining it. A consistent finding in recent socialization research is that newcomers initially put their efforts into obtaining information that will help them to

DEREK CHAPMAN AND THE MECHANISMS UNDERLYING RECRUITMENT

I think one of the main things that attracted me to doing research on recruiting was how it seemed to be relevant for just about everyone and yet we knew very little about it. We all look for jobs at some point in our lives and have to make hard choices about what to do and where to work. Furthermore, every company has to worry about finding and competing for good employees so the broad appeal of recruiting was compelling to me. Despite this fact, the area seemed to be nearly wide open for investigation, and I found the opportunity to explore the unexplored to be very interesting. For me, the route to conducting recruiting research was somewhat indirect.

In the mid 90's I was doing my Ph.D. in I/O Psychology under the supervision of Pat Rowe at the University of Waterloo. Pat had been doing interview research since the mid 1950's and quickly interested me in looking at the dynamic interpersonal processes in employment interviews. In the course of doing interview research with Pat I noticed that many applicants did not like the rigorous and highly valid structured interview formats that most academics recommend. I became more and more interested in how applicants reacted to

those interviews as well as how they reacted to various interview media (telephone, videoconference etc.). I was also curious about how those reactions affected their impressions of organizations. This ultimately led me to spend more and more time thinking about recruiting and job choice. This interest led me to sign up for a session with Sara Rynes in the late 1990's at a doctoral consortium with a small group of Ph.D. students interested in recruiting research. Rynes pointed out that the recruiting field was still in its infancy, and I was immediately struck by the large number of unexplored areas that really needed attention. She recommended a recruiting book by Allison Barber that had just been published. The combination of Rynes' encouragement and Barber's book motivated me to focus more on my recruiting research stream.

I think I have learned a lot about recruiting from conducting research, speaking with professional recruiters, and from talking to people who are going through the job choice process. One of the things that has intrigued me the most has been the role that recruiters play in our job choice decisions. For a long time the collective wisdom of researchers had been that recruiters didn't matter much—it was all about pay and location. Some of my work has refuted this premise by taking a look at the mechanisms by which recruiters influence our thinking. Rather than having direct effects on our decisions, recruiters appear to play a role in influencing our perceptions of job and organizational attributes as well as providing us with signals about what it might be like to work for their organization. We also found that recruiters had the most influence on the best candidates—those who had to choose among multiple job offers. Now, with my students at the University of Calgary, I am looking at integrating the persuasion literature with the recruiting literature. I believe there is considerable overlap in these areas that could help us understand what employers can do to improve recruiting.

I now live and work in Calgary, Canada, a beautiful city near the Canadian Rockies that is home to a booming oil and gas industry. Unemployment here is approaching zero and finding skilled tradespeople in this city of 1 million people is extremely difficult. With billions of dollars in oil and gas projects depending on finding qualified people to do the work, I get a great deal of satisfaction seeing how the fundamental research in recruiting can be used to help real companies develop scientifically based strategies to compete in one of the tightest labor markets in North America.

Derek S. Chapman
Department of Psychology
University of Calgary

perform their job tasks competently, and that will enable them to get along with members of their immediate work group. Once they are able to perform their job tasks competently, the focus of information seeking shifts to broader issues such as the culture of the organization. Recent research has begun to examine the interaction between organizational socialization tactics and newcomer information seeking.

A final issue examined was the impact of diversity on the socialization of organizational newcomers. Those perceived as *different* by established organizational members may face a number of unique challenges in the socialization process. In the extreme, such individuals run the risk of being marginalized and never really fitting in. Organizations can, however, take steps to facilitate the socialization of older employees, females, and racial minorities. Through facilitating the development of support networks, providing training programs, using valid selection procedures, and placing an emphasis on performance and employee development, organizations can make sure that these individuals are accepted and their talents are fully utilized.

SUGGESTED ADDITIONAL READINGS

Allen, D.G. (2006). Do socialization tactics influence newcomer embeddedness and turnover? *Journal of Management, 32,* 237–256.

Barber, A. E. (1998). *Recruiting employees: Individual and organizational perspectives.* Thousand Oaks, CA: Sage.

Braddy, P. W., Meade, A. W., & Kroustalis, C. M. (2005). Organizational recruitment website effects on viewers' perceptions of organizational culture. *Journal of Business and Psychology, 20,* 525–543.

Chen, G. (2004). Newcomer adaptation in teams: Multilevel antecedents and outcomes. *Academy of Management Journal, 48,* 101–116.

Kim, T., Cable, D. M., & Kim, S. (2005). Socialization tactics, employee productivity, and person-organization fit. *Journal of Applied Psychology, 90,* 232–241.

Slaughter, J. E., & Zickar, M. J. (2006). A new look at the role of insiders in the newcomer socialization process. *Group & Organization Management, 31,* 264–290.

Chapter Four

Productive Behavior in Organizations

As new employees gradually become acclimated to their work environments, they eventually reach a point where they are capable of engaging in behavior that contributes positively to organizational goals and objectives. As examples, an accountant becomes capable of handling the tax returns of several clients of an accounting firm, a retail store employee becomes capable of operating a cash register with minimal supervision, and a scientist becomes capable of independently carrying out his or her own original research investigations. The behaviors described in the examples may be thought of collectively as *productive behavior*, which is the focus of this chapter.

After thoroughly defining productive behavior, the chapter shifts to a discussion of job performance. This is, by far, the most common form of productive behavior in organizations, and organizational psychologists have devoted considerable attention to its study. Much work, for example, has been devoted to simply understanding what is meant by job performance, and in determining performance dimensions that are common across jobs.

After addressing models describing the different aspects of basic job performance, we then address the critical issue of how job performance has been measured by organizational psychologists. The effective measurement of job performance is critical if we hope to better understand the predictors of employees who excel versus falter at work. Organizational psychologists encounter a number of challenges in trying to effectively

measure job performance, including such issues as all employees being given high ratings (restriction of range) and the performance of employees varying over time as a result of personal and environmental factors.

Having addressed the basic dimensions of job performance and how to assess these dimensions, we then move to the important area of the causes of job performance. Considerable work has been devoted to determining the relative contribution of abilities, skills, motivation, personality, and situational factors in explaining performance differences across employees. As researchers have found, the interaction among all of these predictors is complex. Fortunately, the amount of research done allows us to draw some fairly definitive conclusions about what predicts employees who perform well versus poorly.

The chapter then addresses the second major form of productive behavior at work, which is when employees do things that are not required in their formal job descriptions. For example, organizations may at times need employees to provide assistance to each other, even though this activity is not part of their formal job descriptions. These types of behaviors have been defined as *organizational citizenship behaviors* (OCBs). Research into OCB has focused primarily on understanding the factors that lead employees to perform OCBs.

Finally, we address a third form of productive behavior at work: innovation. For example, to remain competitive, a computer manufacturer may need employees to consistently design new computer models that have innovative designs and features. There is considerable research on creativity in the general psychological literature, but organizational psychologists have also examined organization-specific innovation and creativity. Like other forms of productive behavior, innovation and creativity result from a complex interaction between characteristics of individual employees and the organizational environments in which they work.

DEFINING PRODUCTIVE BEHAVIOR

For the purposes of this chapter, *productive behavior* is defined as employee behavior that contributes positively to the goals and objectives of the organization. When an employee first enters an organization, there is a transition period during which he or she is not

contributing positively to the organization. For example, a newly hired management consultant may not be generating any billable hours for his or her consulting firm. From an organizational perspective, a new employee is actually a liability because he or she is typically being compensated during this unproductive period. The organization is betting, however, that, over time, the new employee will reach a point where his or her behavior contributes positively to the organization. When productive behavior is viewed in financial terms, it represents the point at which the organization begins to achieve some return on the investment it has made in the new employee. In the sections that follow, we take an in-depth look at three of the most common forms of productive behavior in organizations: job performance, organizational citizenship behavior (OCB), and innovation.

JOB PERFORMANCE
Defining Job Performance

Job performance is a deceptively simple term. At the most general level, it can be defined simply as "all of the behaviors employees engage in while at work." Unfortunately, this is a rather imprecise definition because employees often engage in behaviors at work that have little or nothing to do with job-specific tasks. For example, in a study of enlisted military personnel, Bialek, Zapf, and McGuire (1977) found that less than half of the work time of these individuals was spent performing tasks that were part of their job descriptions. Thus, if performance were defined simply in terms of employee behaviors performed while at work, many behaviors that have no relation to organizational goals would be included (e.g., talking with coworkers about last night's game). On the other hand, if job performance were confined only to behaviors associated with the technical aspects of the basic tasks employees perform, much productive behavior in the workplace would be excluded.

According to Campbell (1990), job performance represents behaviors employees engage in while at work that contribute to organizational goals. This definition is obviously more precise than simply defining performance as all behaviors that employees perform at work. It is also not too restrictive; job performance is not confined only to behaviors directly associated with task performance. One other important aspect of this definition is that job performance represents behaviors that are formally evaluated by the organization as part of the employee's responsibilities and duties. This aspect of the definition distinguishes job performance from the other forms of productive behavior we address later in the chapter.

In defining job performance, it is important that we distinguish it from several related terms. According to Campbell (1990), job performance should be distinguished from effectiveness, productivity, and utility. *Effectiveness* is defined as the evaluation of the results of an employee's job performance. This is an important distinction because employee effectiveness is determined by more than just job performance. For example, an employee who is engaging in many forms of productive behavior may still receive a poor performance rating (a measure of effectiveness) because of performance rating errors, or simply because he or she is not well liked by the person assigned to do the rating.

Productivity is closely related to both performance and effectiveness, but it is different because productivity takes into account the cost of achieving a given level of performance

or effectiveness. For example, two salespeople may perform equally well and ultimately generate the same level of commissions in a given year. However, if one of these individuals is able to achieve this level of sales at a lower cost than the other, he or she would be considered the more productive of the two. A term that is closely related to productivity, and is often used interchangeably, is *efficiency*. This refers to the level of performance that can be achieved in a given period of time. If a person is highly efficient, he or she is achieving a lot in a relatively short period of time. Given that "time is money," one can consider efficiency a form of productivity. Some organizations, in fact, are highly concerned with efficiency. United Parcel Service (UPS), for example, places a strong emphasis on the efficiency of the truck drivers who deliver packages to customers.

Finally, *utility* represents the value of a given level of performance, effectiveness, or productivity for the organization. This definition may seem redundant alongside the description of effectiveness. Utility is somewhat different, however. An employee may achieve a high level of effectiveness (i.e., the results of his or her performance are judged to be positive), but utility still could be low. An organization simply may not place a high value on the level of effectiveness achieved by the employee. In large research universities, for example, faculty research productivity and grant writing are typically given higher priority than teaching performance. Consequently, it is possible to be denied tenure at such universities even though one is a superb teacher.

At first glance, distinguishing among performance, effectiveness, productivity, efficiency, and utility may appear to be a rather trivial exercise. On the contrary, these distinctions are extremely important if one is interested in understanding and ultimately predicting performance. Many studies in organizational psychology purport to predict "performance" when they are actually predicting "effectiveness" or "productivity" (Jex, 1998). Employees typically have more control over performance than they do over effectiveness or productivity, so studies often fail to adequately explain performance differences among employees. This gap may ultimately lead to erroneous conclusions about the determinants of performance differences.

Models of Job Performance

Efforts to model job performance are aimed at identifying a set of performance dimensions that are common to all jobs. Given the vast number of jobs that exist in the world of work, trying to determine a relatively small number of dimensions underlying job performance is a challenging task. However, modeling job performance is vitally important because so much research and practice in organizational psychology centers around performance prediction. A major reason for studying many of the variables that we do (e.g., motivation, leadership, stress) is their potential impact on performance. Even though models of job performance contain many different dimensions, two major categories of job performance can be found across models: *in-role (task) performance* and *extra-role (contextual) performance* (Borman & Motowidlo, 1993; Conway, 1999). In-role performance refers to performance on the technical aspects of an employee's job. For example, a nurse would be required to perform specific tasks such as drawing blood, ensuring proper delivery of medication, and so on. Likewise, a truck driver has to know how to effectively load and handle cargo, operate complex machinery, and perform other technical types of tasks. Extra-role per-

formance refers to nontechnical abilities such as being able to communicate effectively, exhibiting motivation and enthusiasm at work, and being a good team member.

The distinction between in-role and extra-role performance can be seen in Campbell's (1990, 1994) comprehensive model of job performance. Campbell developed his model of job performance by analyzing a diverse set of jobs performed by soldiers in the U.S. Army. Based on an analysis of the performance dimensions of multiple jobs, he argued that performance on all jobs can be broken down into the eight dimensions listed in Table 4.1. We would argue that the first two dimensions in Campbell's model reflect the importance of in-role or task performance. The first dimension is *job-specific task proficiency*, and it includes behaviors associated with the core tasks that are unique to a particular job. For example, behaviors such as counting money, recording deposits, and cashing checks would represent some of the job-specific tasks of a bank teller. On the other hand, examples of the core job tasks of a teacher at a day-care center may include scheduling activities, maintaining discipline, and communicating with parents.

The second dimension reflective of in-role performance in this model is *nonjob-specific task proficiency*. This dimension is represented by behaviors that must be performed by some or all members of an organization, but that are not specific to a particular job. For example, the primary job-related activities of a college professor are teaching and research in a given substantive area (e.g., physics). However, regardless of one's specialty, most professors are required to perform common tasks such as advising students, serving on university committees, writing grants, and occasionally representing the university at ceremonial

TABLE 4.1
Campbell's (1990, 1994) Model of Job Performance According to the In-Role Extra-Role Distinction

Performance Dimensions	Description
In-Role	
1. Job-Specific-Task Proficiency	Technical aspects of job performance
2. Non-Job-Specific Task Proficiency	Common tasks performed by different employees
Extra-Role	
3. Written and Oral Communication	Ability to write and communicate effectively
4. Demonstrating Effort	Going the "extra mile" at work
5. Maintaining Personal Discipline	Refraining from negative behaviors, following through on tasks
6. Facilitating peer and team performance	Being a good team member; working well with other members
7. Supervision/Leadership	Effectively supervising and leading others
8. Management/Administration	Effectively organizing and keeping track of critical information

events such as commencement. In the military, soldiers must not only be able to carry out the technical aspects of their job (e.g., fire patriot missiles, ensure adequate quantities of helmets and ammunition), but they must also be proficient on tasks common to all soldiers (e.g., knowing how to react upon a chemical weapons attack, knowing how to read a map and navigate in an unfamiliar environment).

Both the first and second dimensions of Campbell's model reflect tasks that must be performed within a given occupational position and therefore represent in-role performance. The remaining six dimensions address the extra-role or contextual dimensions of performance that tend to cut across different jobs.

The third dimension is labeled *written and oral communication task proficiency.* Inclusion of this dimension acknowledges that incumbents in most jobs must communicate either in writing or verbally. For example, a high school teacher and an attorney obviously perform very different job-specific tasks. Both, however, must periodically communicate, both orally and in writing, in order to do their jobs effec-

tively. A high school teacher may need to communicate with parents regarding students' progress, and an attorney may need to communicate with a client in order to verify the accuracy of information to be contained in a legal document such as a trust or divorce agreement.

The fourth and fifth dimensions are labeled *demonstrating effort* and *maintaining personal discipline,* respectively. Demonstrating effort represents an employee's level of motivation and commitment to his or her job tasks. Regardless of whether one performs the job of dentist, firefighter, or professional athlete, it is necessary to exhibit commitment to one's job tasks. It may also be necessary at times to demonstrate a willingness to persist in order to accomplish difficult or unpleasant tasks. Professional athletes, at times, may have to *play through* nagging injuries in order to help their teams. Maintaining personal discipline is abiding by specified rules and refraining from negative behaviors such as substance abuse or other forms of unproductive behavior. Taken together, these two dimensions essentially represent the degree to which an employee is a *good citizen* in the workplace.

The sixth dimension is labeled *facilitating peer and team performance*. One aspect of this dimension is the degree to which an employee is helpful to his or her coworkers when they need assistance. This could involve assisting a coworker who is having trouble meeting an impending deadline, or perhaps just providing encouragement or boosting the spirits of others. This dimension also represents the degree to which an employee is a *team player*, or is working to further the goals of his or her work group. As Campbell (1990) points out, this dimension would obviously have little relevance if one worked in complete isolation. Today, when so many companies place strong emphasis on teamwork, working alone is more the exception than the rule (see Comment 4.1).

The seventh and eighth dimensions are labeled *supervision/leadership* and *management/administration*, respectively. Both of these dimensions represent aspects of job performance that obviously apply only to jobs that carry some supervisory responsibilities. Whether one is a supervisor in a retail outlet, a hospital, or a factory, certain common behaviors are required. For example, supervisors in most settings help employees set goals, teach employees effective work methods, and more generally attempt to model good work habits. Many supervisory positions also require a multitude of administrative tasks such as monitoring and controlling expenditures, obtaining additional resources, and representing one's unit within an organization.

When we consider each of these dimensions of job performance, it becomes clear that all eight dimensions would not be relevant for all jobs. In fact, Campbell (1990) argued that only three (core task proficiency, demonstrating effort, and maintenance of personal discipline) are major performance components for all jobs. This model is still quite useful because it provides a common metric for examining performance across jobs. For example, using this model, we could compare employees from two completely different jobs on the dimension of demonstrating effort. In addition, the performance of different types of jobs could be compared across the dimensions. Having such a common metric is tremendously helpful in trying to understand the general determinants of job performance.

A second model of job performance was proposed by Murphy (1994). His model was specifically developed to facilitate an understanding of job performance in the U.S. Navy, but the performance dimensions are also relevant to many civilian jobs. As can be seen in Table 4.2, this model breaks performance down into four dimensions instead of eight. The first of these is labeled *task-oriented behaviors*, which closely mirrors the job-specific task proficiency dimension in Campbell's (1990, 1994) model. It is also reasonable to assume that, for supervisory jobs, this label would include the dimensions related to supervision and management/administration. In essence, this represents performing the major tasks associated with one's job. This dimension is also the only component of Murphy's model that refers explicitly to in-role performance. The remaining dimensions refer to extra-role performance. The second dimension, labeled *interpersonally oriented behaviors*, represents all of the interpersonal transactions that occur on the job. These might include a retail store clerk answering a customer's question, a nurse consulting a doctor about a patient's medication, or an auto mechanic talking to a service manager about a repair that must be done on a car. Because many interpersonal transactions in the workplace are task-related, this dimension mirrors facilitating peer and team performance in J. Campbell's

COMMENT 4.1

BEING A GOOD TEAM MEMBER

OF THE EIGHT dimensions of job performance described in Campbell's (1990) model, one of the most interesting, and potentially most important, is "Facilitating peer and team performance." One obvious reason is that more and more organizations are making use of *teams* for both projects and even as a basis for organizational structure. Given this greater use of teams, it is not surprising that much recent organizational research has focused on team effectiveness. However, one aspect of team effectiveness that has not been given great attention is identifying the characteristics of a good team member. According to Susan Wheelan, in her book *Creating Effective Teams: A Guide for Members and Leaders*, there are a number of behavioral characteristics of effective team members. These include:

- not blaming others for group problems
- encouraging the process of goal, role, and task clarification
- encouraging the adoption of an open communication structure
- promoting an appropriate ratio of task and supportive communications
- promoting the use of effective problem-solving and decision-making procedures
- encouraging the establishment of norms that support productivity, innovation, and freedom of expression

- going along with norms that promote group effectiveness and productivity
- promoting group cohesion and cooperation
- encouraging the use of effective conflict-management strategies
- interacting with others outside of the group, in ways that promote group integration and cooperation within the larger organizational context
- supporting the leader's efforts to facilitate group goal achievement

This list is obviously not meant to be exhaustive, but it illustrates the specific behaviors that contribute to effective team performance. As is evident from the list, most of these behaviors transcend technical specialties and even organization types. This is consistent with Campbell's notion that there is a general set of performance dimensions.

Source: J. P. Campbell. (1990). Modeling the performance prediction problem in industrial and organizational psychology. In M. D. Dunnette and L. M. Hough (Eds.), *Handbook of industrial and organizational psychology* (2nd ed., Vol. 1, pp. 687–732). Palo Alto, CA: Consulting Psychologists Press; and S. A. Wheelan. (1999). *Creating effective teams: A guide for members and leaders.* Thousand Oaks, CA: Sage.

TABLE 4.2
Murphy's (1994) Model of Job Performance According to the In-Role Extra-Role Distinction

Performance Dimensions	Description
In-Role	
1. Task-Oriented Behaviors	Performing major tasks associated with job
Extra-Role	
2. Interpersonally oriented Behaviors	All interpersonal transactions that occur on job
3. Down-time Behaviors	Behaviors outside of work that affect job performance (e.g. drug/alcohol use, extra jobs)
4. Destructive/Hazardous Behaviors	Safety violations, sabotage, accidents

model. Not all interpersonal transactions in the workplace are task related. For example, employees may start off Monday mornings with *small talk* about what they did over the weekend. This dimension therefore also represents the extent to which employees generally maintain positive interpersonal relations with coworkers. This aspect of job behavior is not explicitly part of Campbell's model, although it is clearly an important aspect of performance (see Comment 4.2). The distinction between task-oriented performance and performance that occurs in the context of the job has also been highlighted by Van Scotter and Motowidlo (1996).

The third dimension, *down-time behaviors*, represents behaviors that may lead the job incumbent to be absent from the worksite. These include counterproductive behaviors, such as drug and alcohol abuse, and other violations of the law. They are considered aspects of performance because an employee with a substance abuse problem, for example, may be frequently absent from work and is therefore not performing well. A closely related set of behaviors is included in the fourth category, *destructive/hazardous behaviors*. These would include such things as safety violations, accidents, and sabotage. The down-time behaviors and destructive/

COMMENT 4.2

MAINTAINING POSITIVE INTERPERSONAL RELATIONS AT WORK

MAINTAINING POSITIVE INTERPERSONAL relationships with others is a performance dimension that is rarely noticed unless someone is unable to do it. Research over the years has shown, relatively consistently, that interpersonal conflict is perceived negatively by employees and leads to a number of negative outcomes (e.g., Spector & Jex, 1998). Specifically, when there are frequent interpersonal conflicts in the work environment, employees tend to dislike their jobs and feel anxious and tense about coming to work.

Another aspect of interpersonal relations that has been explored less frequently, but may be just as important, is the impact of interpersonal relations on promotions in organizations. Having worked in different organizations and taught many courses over the years, a frequent theme we have heard is that relatively few individuals fail to get promoted due to lack of technical skills. More often than not, a lack of mobility in organizations is due

to an inability to get along with others. In fact, many organizations invest considerable amounts of money in individual coaching programs that are often aimed at individuals who have a great deal of technical prowess but are lacking in interpersonal skills. Why is it so important to get along with others in organizations? The likely reason is that much of what gets done in any organization gets done through people. If someone has a hard time getting along with others, it is quite possible that he or she will have a hard time gaining others' cooperation and assistance—factors that are often necessary to get things done in organizations.

Source: P. E. Spector and S. M. Jex. (1998). Development of four self-report measures of job stressors and strain: Interpersonal Conflict at Work Scale, Organizational Constraints Scale, Quantitative Workload Inventory, and Physical Symptoms Inventory. *Journal of Occupational Health Psychology, 3,* 356–367.

hazardous behaviors dimensions are most closely related to the dimension of maintaining personal discipline in Campbell's (1990, 1994) model. In some cases, though, destructive/hazardous behaviors may result from a lack of effort (e.g., not taking the time to put on safety equipment), so this dimension may overlap with the demonstrating effort dimension in Campbell's model.

Compared to Campbell's (1990, 1994) eight-dimension model, Murphy's (1994) four-dimension model is somewhat less useful, for two reasons. First, this model was developed to explain job performance—specifically, among U.S. Navy personnel. Campbell's objective was to describe performance in a broader spectrum of jobs, although his model could certainly be used to describe job performance among military personnel. Second, the performance dimensions described by Murphy are considerably broader than those described by Campbell. Because they are so broad, it is more difficult to determine the factors that led to differences among employees on these performance dimensions. Despite these disadvantages, this model again provides us with a set of dimensions for comparing performance across jobs. The importance of looking for cross-job dimensions of performance has also been emphasized by Viswesvaran (2002), who has argued that most models of job performance include a more general measure of performance followed by more specific measures depending on the theorist. Although not all researchers agree on the exact subdimensions of job performance, there is a general recognition that job performance is more than just the technical aspects of performing narrowly defined tasks, and that how employees interact with others and in other ways contribute to the organization need to be considered.

MEASUREMENT OF JOB PERFORMANCE

The prior section dealt with models organizational psychologists have developed to capture the important dimensions on which job performance should be assessed. The next critical step in understanding what causes employees to perform well or poorly is developing reliable and valid measures of job performance. Having good measures of job performance allows us to better understand those variables related to performance. In the present section we examine how job performance has been measured, as well as challenges researchers have faced in developing reliable and valid measures of job performance. Specifically, three areas are discussed: (1) measures of job performance, (2) restriction in the variability of job performance, and (3) instability in job performance over time.

Measures of Job Performance

By definition, job performance is behavior, so job performance is rarely measured directly. More typically, what is measured is some external assessment of job performance. According to Murphy (1989a), performance can be assessed in eight different ways: (1) paper/pencil tests, (2) job skills tests, (3) on-site hands-on testing, (4) off-site hands-on testing, (5) high-fidelity simulations, (6) symbolic simulations, (7) task ratings, and (8) global ratings. By far, the two most common methods of performance assessment in organizations are ratings of employees' performance on specific tasks and ratings of overall performance on the job.

An example of the latter performance rating was used by Van Dyne and LePine (1998). These authors assessed in-role and extra-role performance by having employees, their coworkers, and supervisors respond to items assessing different aspects of performance. Sample items from the measure are presented in Table 4.3. In-role performance was assessed by items referring to the extent that employees met their performance expectations and performed well at the tasks that made up the employees' job. Extra-role performance was assessed through nontask behaviors that nevertheless are expected of the employee, such as helping others in his or her group and attending scheduled functions.

The literature on performance rating is vast (e.g., Landy & Farr, 1980; Murphy, 2004; Murphy & Cleveland, 1990), and will not be reviewed in detail here. However, two general points can be made. First, there are many potential sources of error in performance ratings. For example, a rater may not have an adequate opportunity to observe performance, ratings may be biased by the degree to which the rater likes or dislikes the ratee, or different raters may employ different internal performance standards. These are just three of many potential sources of error. Rating errors are problematic because they ultimately mask meaningful differences in actual job performance, and thus may weaken the relationship between job performance and other variables.

A second point is that steps can be taken to reduce error in performance ratings. For example, rater training has been shown to increase accuracy in performance ratings (Pulakos, 1984). Another way to circumvent the problems with performance ratings is to seek more *objective* performance measures, such as output produced or sales commissions. Unfortunately, these more objective performance measures may have serious flaws of their own. The most obvious flaw is that most are really measures of effectiveness or productivity and not actual job performance (Campbell, 1990). Another disadvantage is that employees may lack control over objective performance indicators. For example, even a very skilled real estate salesperson would probably not sell many houses if the mortgage interest rates rose to 20%.

Some researchers have attempted to deal with the biases inherent in performance ratings by constructing *behaviorally anchored rating scales* that clearly reflect those employee behaviors that constitute poor, average, and superior performance (see Campbell, 1990). For example, consider a paralegal's ability to prepare a legal brief for a courtroom session. Instead of rating the paralegal on a scale from "very poor" to "very good," a behaviorally anchored rating scale would include such terms as "fails to

---

TABLE 4.3
Van Dyne and LePine's Measure of In-Role and Extra-Role Performance

Sample of In-Role Performance Items
1. "This particular worker fulfills the responsibilities specified in his/her job description"
2. "This particular worker performs the tasks that are expected as part of the job"

Sample of Extra-Role Performance Items
3. "This particular worker assists others in this group with their work for the benefit of the group"
4. "This particular worker speaks up in the group with ideas for new projects or changes in procedure"
5. "This particular worker attends functions that help the work group"

Source: Van Dyne, L.V., & LePine, J.A. (1998). Helping and voice extra-role behaviors: Evidence of construct and predictive validity. *Academy of Management Journal, 41,* 108–119.

incorporate necessary details into the legal brief" and "produces a report that summarizes the major points of the brief without additional unnecessary material." Anchoring the scale with specific behaviors is presumed to take some of the subjectivity out of the performance assessment.

The major point of considering performance measurement is simply that we must always keep in mind that performance is not the same thing as the measurement of performance. Furthermore, because measuring anything will inevitably involve some degree of error, our understanding of performance and our ability to predict it will always remain imperfect.

Restriction in the Variability of Job Performance

Researchers face a number of challenges in adequately assessing job performance among a population of employees. We first consider the issue of restriction in the variability of performance among employees. For a variety of reasons, the variability in performance levels within organizations is often restricted. To better understand restriction in performance variability, it is useful to distinguish between *artifactual restriction* in performance variability and *true restriction*. Artifactual restriction in performance variability results from factors such as errors in performance ratings or the performance measurement system. Even though there may be real differences among employees' levels of job performance, these may be masked because of an error in the performance rating process. For example, employees within an organization may really differ from each other in how well they are performing, with some doing very well and some doing very poorly. However, supervi-

sors may give all employees high ratings because of a concern they will be laid off if ratings are less than stellar. True restriction in performance variability, on the other hand, occurs when measures of performance are relatively accurate but there is a true lack of meaningful variation in actual job performance. It may simply be the case that all employees are performing at a high or low level within an organization because of such factors as leadership or the inherent difficulty of the tasks being performed. In this section, reasons for true restriction in performance variability are discussed.

According to Peters and O'Connor (1988), there are four reasons why variation in individual performance may be restricted. First, organizations simply may have very low performance standards. If organizations do not expect much, this standard will tend to discourage high levels of performance, and employees will gravitate toward *minimally acceptable* levels of performance. The end result of this process is often a great reduction in the variability of performance. A good example is the commonly held stereotype that performance standards for government employees are low. Many readers have probably heard the expression "Good enough for government work," which implies that work must only be done at a minimally acceptable level.

A second factor, which is related to low performance standards, is that organizations vary in the degree to which they value high levels of individual job performance. Organizations either may fail to recognize the contributions of those who perform well or tolerate individuals who consistently perform poorly. Some organizations may even inadvertently create situations in which low levels of performance are actually rewarded, and high levels of performance are punished. For example, in many organizations, employees who perform well are often *rewarded* with greater responsibility and heavier workloads, but receive no additional compensation or promotions. The current authors have also seen managers rid themselves of incompetent employees by recommending that they be promoted to positions in other departments.

A third factor restricting performance variability is the degree to which organizations excuse employees for low levels of performance. This factor is related to low performance standards but operates somewhat differently. According to Peters and O'Connor (1988), organizations may develop what they describe as a "culture of justification" (p. 117); that is, employees are routinely allowed to "explain away" instances of poor performance. A somewhat more irreverent way of describing this is the familiar acronym *CYA*, otherwise known as "cover your a**!"Such a culture takes away the incentive to perform well and ultimately restricts performance to mediocre levels.

A final cause of restriction in performance variability is variation in organizational resources. Having limited resources often leads to situational constraints that ultimately reduces the variability in performance (Peters & O'Connor, 1980). For example, it is difficult for an auto mechanic to perform well if he or she has no tools. On the other hand, if organizational resources are extremely plentiful, this may also reduce the variability in performance. In this case, everyone in an organization may perform up to his or her full potential and, as a result, the variability in performance will be restricted.

A somewhat different explanation as to why the variation in actual performance levels may be restricted is that selection and retention in organizations are not random processes. According to Johns (1991), most organizations require that employees pass through relatively rigorous screening processes before they are hired. For example, those who wish to become police officers typically must pass through a series of tests before even being selected for academy training. In many other occupations, such as law, medicine, and engineering, much of this screening is done by universities during professional training. As a result of these screening processes, the variation in skill and ability levels among employees may be quite restricted, which may ultimately restrict the variability in job performance. Employees who perform poorly or who simply do not fit well with an organization's culture often select themselves out and leave voluntarily (Ployhart, Weekly, & Baughman, 2006; Schneider, 1987). Like formal socialization processes, this again tends to create uniformity in job performance.

Despite all of the factors that may restrict performance variability, empirical evidence suggests that performance variability in organizations is still meaningful. For example, Schmidt and Hunter (1998) point out that even though performance variability in organizations is somewhat restricted, a substantial portion still remains. If this were not the case, it is unlikely that selection tools such as cognitive ability tests, personality measures, and biodata instruments would be related to performance.

Instability in Job Performance over Time

A second challenge in assessing the job performance of employees includes the extent to which performance is stable versus fluctuating. There has been considerable debate, over the years, concerning the relative stability of performance criterion measures (e.g., Ackerman, 1989; Austin, Humphreys, &

Hulin, 1989; Barrett, Caldwell, & Alexander, 1985; Henry & Hulin, 1987, 1989). Some contributors have claimed that performance is relatively stable over time; many others have argued (quite forcefully at times) that performance is more dynamic. The weight of the evidence seems to support the position that performance criteria are dynamic. For example, Deadrick and Madigan (1990) examined the stability in performance of sewing machine operators over time and found that the correlations between performance levels were quite strong when the time interval was very short. However, the correlation between performance at one point in time and 23 weeks later was considerably weaker. Thus, because of a variety of factors, employee performance tends to fluctuate over time. In fact, this inconsistency may explain why people are so impressed when a high

level of consistency is displayed. In sports, for example, great honors are bestowed on athletes for breaking records that indicate consistency and longevity (see Comment 4.3).

Ployhart and Hakel (1998) pointed out that although evidence supports the dynamic nature of performance, correlations between levels of performance at different points in time provide little insight into how the performance of individuals changes over time. Furthermore, we know very little about variables that predict distinct patterns of change in performance over time. To address this issue, these researchers examined 8 years' worth of performance criterion data from a sample of 303 securities analysts.

Using a statistical procedure known as *latent growth curve modeling*, which allows the modeling of patterns of change over time,

---

COMMENT 4.3

THE INTERACTION BETWEEN DECLARATIVE AND PROCEDURAL KNOWLEDGE

Is DECLARATIVE KNOWLEDGE a necessary precondition to obtaining procedural knowledge? That is, do you have to know about something in order to know how to do something? For some tasks, it is fairly obvious that declarative knowledge is a precursor to procedural knowledge. For example, it would be very difficult to fly a jet airplane if one had absolutely no knowledge of jet propulsion.

For some types of human performance, however, it is unclear whether declarative knowledge must precede procedural knowledge. For example, it is not unusual for athletes to understand how to do things but not necessarily know the principles behind what they are doing (perhaps that's where Nike

came up with the slogan "Just Do It"). There are also instances of great musicians who are unable to read music but are able to play musical compositions based on their auditory memory.

Perhaps those instances when one can achieve procedural knowledge without first obtaining declarative knowledge are relatively rare. However, it would be useful to develop a greater understanding of the interaction between these two forms of knowledge. Many training and educational programs are based on the premise that declarative knowledge must come first, so a greater understanding of this interaction may pave the way for interesting new training and educational methods.

they found that, on average, performance among these securities analysts approximated a basic learning curve. Initially, performance rose steadily; eventually, it reached a leveling-off point. They also found that, within the sample, not all curves were the same. For example, there were differences in how quickly performance initially accelerated. There were also differences in how quickly performance reached a leveling-off point. Most importantly, they found that patterns of change in performance over time were predictable; for example, those who described themselves as persuasive and empathetic exhibited the quickest initial rate of acceleration in sales. They also found that these two variables predicted whether there would be a drop in performance. Those who described themselves as persuasive were more likely to exhibit a drop in performance early in the second year of employment, and those describing themselves as empathetic were less likely to exhibit this drop. At a practical level, this finding suggests that exhibiting empathy toward clients may be a more effective sales technique than trying to persuade them.

Ployhart and Hakel's (1998) study provides important insight into the issue of performance stability. At least for the sample employed, it suggests that although performance is not stable over time, it does not fluctuate randomly. More importantly, this study suggests that it is possible to identify and statistically model patterns of change in performance over time. It also suggests that there may be individual differences that predict patterns of performance variability over time. An important practical implication of this possibility is that an organization may be able to identify a desired temporal pattern of performance and select individuals who are likely to exhibit that pattern. For example, it may be possible to screen out individuals whose performance peaks very quickly and then declines.

Job performance variability over time can also be explained by characteristics of the job itself. Murphy (1989b) proposed that jobs are characterized by what he termed *maintenance* stages and *transition* stages. During maintenance stages, the tasks comprising the job become somewhat routine and automatic for the job incumbent. For example, once a person learns to drive an automobile, the steps necessary to perform this task become so routine that little conscious thought is required. When this level of proficiency is achieved, it is as if people are on *automatic pilot* when they are performing the task. This may explain why, during morning commutes over the years, the author has witnessed drivers applying makeup, eating breakfast, or reading newspapers!

When a job is in the transition stage, the tasks comprising the job become novel and the incumbent cannot rely on automatic routines while performing them. Transition periods in jobs may occur during the introduction of new technology or perhaps when a major change in laws impacts the job being performed. For example, due to new manufacturing technology, the jobs of many production employees have changed dramatically in the past 10 years (Parker & Wall, 1998). Also, many employees in nursing homes and other long-term healthcare facilities have recently experienced profound changes in their jobs because of changes in Medicare billing procedures (Campbell, 1999).

Murphy (1989b) notes that, because transition periods require adjustments on the part of the employee, they lead to some level of disruption and instability in performance. Another consequence of transition points is that general cognitive ability is a more important determinant of performance during these periods (compared to performance during the maintenance period). This makes sense, given the well-established finding that general cognitive ability is a stronger predictor of performance in complex jobs. If this is true, it follows that general cognitive ability should be more strongly related to performance during these periods. Unfortunately, this proposition has not yet received empirical scrutiny.

More recent research by Sturman, Cheramie, and Cashen (2005) has also emphasized the importance of job characteristics in examining the stability of performance over time. These authors also examined whether job performance was assessed with subjective ratings or more objective indicators. The authors found that test-retest correlations for job performance over the course of a year were highest (r = .83) for jobs that were low in complexity and assessed through subjective ratings, and were lowest (r = .50) for jobs that were high in complexity and assessed through objective indicators. The authors pointed out that even in the latter case the correlation between job performance assessed at different time periods was relatively high.

DETERMINANTS OF JOB PERFORMANCE

Having discussed how organizational psychologists define and measure job performance, we now consider those factors predictive of whether employees perform well or poorly. In trying to explain behavior such as job performance, organizational psychologists have at times engaged in heated debates over the relative impact of the person versus the environment (e.g., nature versus nurture). In such cases, these debates are resolved by the rather commonsense notion

that most behaviors are the result of a complex interaction between characteristics of people and characteristics of the environment.

Generally speaking, differences in job performance are caused by the interaction among ability, motivation, and situational factors that may facilitate or inhibit performance. Thus, for an employee to perform well, he or she must possess job-relevant abilities. Ability alone will not lead to high levels of performance, though, unless the employee is motivated to perform well and does not experience severe situational constraints. Of course, in some cases, a high level of one of these three factors will compensate for low levels of the others (e.g., a highly motivated employee will overcome situational constraints), but usually all three conditions are necessary.

This section begins with an examination of a well-known theoretical model of the determinants of job performance, followed by an exploration of empirical evidence on determinants of job performance. Given the vast number of factors that influence job performance, the exploration of the empirical literature will currently be limited to individual differences or characteristics of persons that explain performance differences. Environmental factors that influence job performance (e.g., leadership, motivation, situational constraints) will be covered in more detail in subsequent chapters.

Campbell's Model of Job Performance

Campbell (1990, 1994) proposed that job performance is determined by the interaction among *declarative knowledge, procedural knowledge/skill,* and *motivation* (see Fig. 4.1).

FIGURE 4.1
Campbell's (1990, 1994) Model of the
Determinants of Job Performance

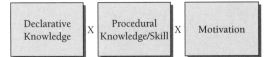

Adapted from J. P. Campbell. (1990). Modeling the performance prediction problem in industrial and organizational psychology. In M. D. Dunnette and L. M. Hough (Eds.), *Handbook of industrial and organizational psychology* (2nd ed., Vol. 1, pp. 687–732). Palo Alto, CA: Consulting Psychologists Press. Modified and reproduced by permission of the publisher.

Declarative knowledge is simply knowledge about facts and things. An employee with a high level of declarative knowledge has a good understanding of the tasks that are required by his or her job. As an example, a medical technician with a high level of declarative knowledge knows the steps necessary to draw blood from a patient. According to Campbell, differences in declarative knowledge may be due to a number of factors, such as ability, personality, interests, education, training, experience, and the interaction between employee aptitudes and training. Many forms of professional and academic training, at least in the early stages, stress the acquisition of declarative knowledge. The first year of medical school, for example, requires considerable memorization of information about human anatomy and physiology.

Once an employee has achieved a high degree of declarative knowledge, he or she is in a position to acquire a high level of procedural knowledge/skill. When this is achieved, the employee understands not only what needs to be done but also how to do it, and is able to carry out these behaviors. A medical technician who has achieved a high level of procedural skill or knowledge not only knows the steps involved in drawing blood, but is also able to perform this task. According to Campbell, differences in the acquisition of procedural knowledge/skill are determined by the same factors that lead to differences in declarative knowledge. In academic and professional training, the acquisition of procedural knowledge/skill tends to be emphasized at later stages or, typically, after a sufficient degree of declarative knowledge has been acquired. Medical training, for example, becomes more hands on during the third and fourth years.

When an employee has reached a high level of procedural knowledge/skill, he or she is capable of high levels of job performance. Stated differently, the employee has performance potential. Whether this potential actually leads to high levels of job performance depends on motivation. According to Campbell (1990, 1994), motivation reflects an employee's choices regarding (1) whether to expend effort directed at job performance, (2) the level of effort to expend, and (3) whether to persist with the level of effort that is chosen. Thus, even if an employee has achieved a very high level of procedural knowledge/skill, low motivation may prevent the skill from being translated into a high level of performance. For example, a highly capable employee may simply decide not to put forth any effort, may not put in enough effort, or may put forth the effort but lack the willingness to sustain it over time.

The primary value of Campbell's (1990, 1994) model is that it states, in precise terms, the factors within the person that determine performance, and the interplay among those factors. Furthermore, it has received empirical support (e.g., McCloy, Campbell, & Cudeck, 1994). The model also reminds us that the interaction among the factors that determine performance is complex. For example, a high level of motivation may compensate for a moderate level of procedural knowledge/skill. On the other hand, a low level of motivation may negate the potential benefits of a high level of procedural knowledge/skill. This model can also be used to generate ideas and hypotheses about performance and its determinants (see Comment 4.4).

Given all the factors that have been proposed to explain differences in job performance, a logical question may be: What is the relative contribution of all of these factors to performance? Indeed, so much research has examined this question over the years that a comprehensive review of this literature is clearly beyond the scope of the chapter. It is possible, however, to draw some conclusions, at least with respect to individual difference predictors of performance. As stated earlier, situational factors that impact performance will be covered in other chapters.

General Mental Ability as a Predictor of Job Performance

By far the one individual difference variable that has received the most attention as a determinant of job performance is *general mental ability*. Numerous definitions have been offered, but the common element in most definitions of general mental ability is that it reflects an individual's capacity to

---

COMMENT 4.4

WHAT IS JOB EXPERIENCE?

JOB EXPERIENCE IS a variable that is used so frequently in organizational psychology that it is easy to take its importance for granted. Typically, most researchers don't pay too much attention to job experience because they are measuring it either for descriptive purposes, or to use as a control variable in statistical analyses. In the vast majority of studies, experience is measured simply as the number of months or years that a person has been employed in a particular job or in a particular organization.

Tesluk and Jacobs (1998) pointed out that organizational or job tenure is not likely to capture the complexity of job experience. They point out, for example, that the same length of tenure may be very different in terms of both the density and the timing of job-related experiences. A good example of the density dimension would be a surgeon performing in a war zone. This individual would typically be doing surgeries around the clock, and would thus acquire more surgical experience in three months than a surgeon at a regular civilian hospital would acquire in twice the time. A good example of timing would be a manager's having to take over a poorly performing department immediately after completing his or her training. Such an experience would undoubtedly have a greater impact on this individual now than it would later in his or her career.

Many organizations recognize complexity of experience and attempt to structure the assignments of high-potential managers in a way that maximizes their developmental value. For the most part, however, researchers have treated experience in a very simplistic fashion. In the future, this is likely to be a very fruitful area of research in organizational psychology.

Source: P. E. Tesluk and R. R. Jacobs. (1998). Toward an integrated model of work experience. Personnel Psychology, 51, 321–355.

process and comprehend information (Murphy, 1989b; Waldman & Spangler, 1989). Research has consistently shown, over many years, that general mental ability predicts performance over a wide range of jobs and occupations. The most comprehensive demonstration of this was a meta-analysis conducted by Schmidt and Hunter (1998), in which nearly 85 years of research findings on various predictors of job performance were summarized. Their analysis indicated that the corrected correlation between general mental ability and performance across jobs was .51—that is, over 25% of the variance in performance across jobs is due to differences in general mental ability. A recent meta-analysis of 283 independent samples conducted in the United Kingdom also revealed validity coefficients between general mental ability and performance in the .5 to .6 range (Bertua, Anderson, & Salgado, 2005). In addition, recent research suggests that meta-analyses of the relationship between general mental ability and job performance have not sufficiently adjusted for the problem of range restriction in mental ability (i.e., individuals very low in mental ability are likely not to be hired), and may actually underestimate the correlation by 25% (Hunter, Schmidt, & Huy, 2006). When one considers the numerous other factors that can influence job performance (e.g., motivation, leadership, situational constraints), the fact that mental ability is such a strong predictor is truly impressive.

Why is general mental ability such a key to explaining differences in job performance? According to Schmidt, Hunter, and Outerbridge (1986), the intermediate link between general mental ability and job performance is *job knowledge*; that is, employees who possess higher levels of general mental ability tend to develop a greater understanding of their job duties than individuals with lower levels. For example, a very intelligent airplane pilot would likely possess greater knowledge of all that goes into flying a plane than a pilot who was less intelligent. In essence, those with high levels of mental ability are able to extract more relevant information from the job environment than those with lower levels of general mental ability.

Another consistent finding in this literature is that general mental ability is a better predictor of performance in jobs that have a high level of complexity compared to jobs lower in complexity (Bertua et al., 2005; Hunter, Schmidt, & Judiesch, 1990). Although there is no standard definition, most researchers agree that job complexity is strongly influenced by the mental demands and information-processing requirements placed on job incumbents (Wood, 1986). For example, the job of a corporate executive requires the use of *higher-order* cognitive skills such as planning and synthesizing large amounts of information. On the other hand, the job of a convenience store clerk typically requires what might be considered *lower-level* cognitive skills such as following established guidelines and procedures. General mental ability predicts good performance in complex jobs, primarily because such jobs place higher-level information-processing demands on incumbents. Thus, compared to those with lower levels, incumbents who possess high levels of general mental ability are better able to meet those demands.

Although mental ability is a strong predictor of job performance, researchers have also found that there are large ethnic group differences on such tests, which may contribute to biased selection and subsequent litigation (Van Rooy, Dilchert, & Viswesvaran, 2006). Therefore, researchers have become interested in assessing other forms of intelligence, such as emotional intelligence. Baron, Handley, and Fund (2006) describe emotional intelligence as being able to understand and express yourself; understand and relate with others; manage and control emotions; change, adapt, and solve problems of a personal and interpersonal nature; and finally the ability to generate positive mood and to be self-motivated. Although emotional intelligence shows fewer ethnic group differences, meta-analyses reveal it only accounts for 2% of the variance in performance after controlling for general intelligence (Van Rooy & Viswesvaran, 2004).

Job Experience as a Predictor of Job Performance

Job experience is an individual difference variable that has been examined frequently as a general predictor of job performance. It would seem logical that a person with a higher level of relevant job experience would perform better than others who possess little or no job experience. Empirical evidence has, in fact, shown that experience, like general mental ability, is positively related to job performance over a wide range of job types (McDaniel, Schmidt, & Hunter, 1988; Schmidt & Hunter, 1998). Like general mental ability, the relation between experience and job performance appears to be mediated by job knowledge (Schmidt et al., 1986). Researchers have also found that the relationship between experience and job performance depends on job complexity. For example, McDaniel et al. (1988) found that experience was a better predictor of performance in low- rather than high-complexity jobs. They attributed this difference to the fact that experience is really the only preparation for low-complexity jobs. For example, there is no way to learn how to perform the job of convenience store clerk

other than by actually working at it. With high-complexity jobs, however, education may compensate for a lack of experience. Note that the form of this interaction effect is exactly the opposite of that found for general mental ability.

There is also evidence that the importance of job experience in explaining performance differences tends to diminish over time. For example, McDaniel et al. (1988) found that the correlation between experience and performance was strongest in samples in which the average level of job experience was less than 3 years, but the correlation was considerably less for samples in which the average level of experience was higher. This suggests that there is a *law of diminishing returns* with respect to the influence of job experience on job performance.

Research on the influence of job experience on job performance should be viewed cautiously, however, because most studies have measured job experience as the number of years in an organization or job. Quinones Ford, and Teachout (1995) pointed out that job experience can be viewed not only in terms of quantity but also quality. Years of experience is a quantitative measure of experience. If job experience is viewed qualitatively, this has to do with the job tasks performed and the relevance of situations one has been exposed to on the job. For example, if an individual has several years of experience as an accountant, but has conducted few field audits, that person will not necessarily perform better in an auditing position than an individual who has less general accounting experience.

Building on the work of Quinones et al. (1995), Tesluk and Jacobs (1998) proposed that job experience can also be viewed in terms of both the density and timing of job-related experiences. When experience has high density, the employee is exposed to many *developmental experiences* in a relative short period of time. These may include increased responsibilities, and perhaps even being required to perform under very difficult conditions. The timing dimension has to do with the fact that certain experiences might have more, or less, developmental value, depending on whether they occur at the beginning, middle, or latter stage of one's career. For most employees, mistakes have a greater developmental impact when they occur at the early (as opposed to later) stages of one's career. The more important point from the work of Quinones et al. (1995) and Tesluk and Jacobs (1998) is that job experience is a complex variable, and much theoretical and empirical work needs to be done before we fully understand and appreciate it (see Comment 4.5).

Personality as a Predictor of Job Performance

Along with general mental ability and job experience, there has been a recent wave of research on personality as a predictor of job performance. The personality trait consistently found to predict job performance over a wide range of jobs is *conscientiousness* (Barrick & Mount, 1991, 2005; Dudley, Orvis, Lebiecki, & Cortina, 2006; Ones, Viswesvaran, & Schmidt, 1993; Thoresen, Bradley, Bliese, & Thoresen, 2004). A person who is conscientious can be described as dependable, goal oriented, planful, and achievement oriented. Barrick and Mount (1991) found that the corrected correlation between conscientiousness and performance, across a wide variety of jobs, was .22. Ones et al.

COMMENT 4.5

CONSISTENCY OF PERFORMANCE IN BASEBALL

SOME OF THE most highly regarded records in the world of sports reflect consistency of performance. In baseball, for example, a record that has stood for over 50 years is New York Yankee Joe DiMaggio's 56-game hitting streak. More recently, Cal Ripken, Jr., of the Baltimore Orioles, made history by playing in 2,632 consecutive games. Why are these two records so highly regarded? DiMaggio's record is remarkable when one considers all of the factors that work against obtaining a base hit in that number of consecutive games. One would think that the skill of pitchers at the major league level, minor injuries, and general fatigue would make such a streak highly unlikely. Thus, this record is a reflection of DiMaggio's skill as a hitter, and his determination.

One reason Ripken's streak is so unusual is simply that few players last that long at the major league level. It is also unusual for players to avoid serious injuries for that period of time. Furthermore, because of the number of games played in a major league season (162), and minor injuries, most players want an occasional day off. Thus, Ripken's streak is a reflection of a number of factors, including consistency in performance, rigorous off-season conditioning, and a high level of motivation.

What do these baseball records tell us about stability and consistency of performance? If anything, they highlight the fact that stability and consistency, over time, are more the exception than the rule. Because of external constraints, fluctuations in motivation, and just plain good/bad luck, performance in most domains is often quite variable. However, when it does remain consistent for a long period of time, it is often highly rewarded.

(1993) found that the mean corrected correlation between integrity tests (which many presume are measures of conscientiousness) and job performance, across jobs, was .34.

There are three explanations for why conscientiousness is a robust predictor of performance. According to Schmidt and Hunter (1998), the variable that links conscientiousness and job performance is job knowledge. Recall that this was the same variable proposed to mediate the relation between both general mental ability and experience and performance. In this case, however, the process has to do primarily with motivation rather than with ability. Individuals who are highly conscientious presumably put time and effort into acquiring high levels of job knowledge, and hence will perform better than those who are less conscientious.

Another explanation for the relation between conscientiousness and performance is goal setting. In a study of sales personnel, Barrick, Mount, and Strauss (1993) found that goal setting mediated the relation between conscientiousness and job performance. Specifically, those who were highly conscientious exhibited a greater tendency for setting performance-related goals than those who were less conscientious. This proclivity for setting goals facilitated, in turn, higher levels of job performance. This adds to the findings of Schmidt and Hunter (1998) regarding why highly conscientious people tend to perform well, regardless of the job.

A final explanation for the relationship between conscientiousness and performance is motivational. Barrick, Stewart, and Piotrowski (2002) found that conscientiousness was related to performance ratings of employees through the employee striving to accomplish more at work and reach a higher status. After these motivational variables were controlled, conscientiousness no longer predicted job performance. This research supports a model in which conscientiousness gives rise to increased motivation, which leads employees to perform better.

It is also worth noting that, in addition to conscientiousness, other personality traits are more likely to predict performance in particular types of jobs. Barrick and Mount (2005) point out that the personality traits of *extraversion* and *agreeableness* (the tendency to avoid conflict and be easy to get along with) are especially predictive of job performance for jobs requiring employees to interact with other people on a frequent basis. *Openness to experience*, the tendency to be open to new ideas and experiences, is an important predictor for jobs that require employees to continuously adapt to change.

A more recent approach to personality and job performance involves combining traits into a larger factor that predicts job performance. Erez and Judge (2001) argued that *self-esteem, locus of control, generalized self-efficacy*, and *neuroticism* all tap a person's *core self-evaluation*, which they define as "basic conclusions or bottom-line evaluations that represent one's appraisal of people, events, or things in relation to oneself" (p. 1,270). Self-esteem is a person's overall attitude toward himself or herself. Locus of control refers to whether individuals believe the causes of their behavior are either due to their own actions (internal locus of control) or the environment (external locus of control). Generalized self-efficacy refers to whether people think they can generally accomplish the tasks they face. Finally, neuroticism refers to a lack of emotional stability and the tendency to experience negative affective states. Neuroticism contributes negatively to an individual's core self-evaluation.

Erez and Judge (2001) found that the four separate personality traits all contributed to the one larger trait of core self-evaluation. More importantly, the authors found that this larger trait was predictive of performance in both student samples (r = .35) and insurance salesmen (r = .34 for sales volume and r = .44 for rated performance). The correlations between core self-evaluations and performance were greater than any of the correlations between the four traits that made up the larger trait. Finally, core self-evaluations are related to performance even when controlling for conscientiousness. In a recent review, Judge, Van Vianen, and De Pater (2004) provided support for the core self-evaluation personality trait, and also provided a shorter scale that can assess the variable.

Summarizing the state of knowledge regarding the predictors of job performance, the most important individual difference variables influencing job performance are general mental ability, job experience, and conscientiousness. Furthermore, the primary mechanisms linking these variables to job performance are job knowledge and, to a lesser extent, goal setting and motivation. Finally, many of these relations appear to be influenced by job complexity. Figure 4.2 summarizes these propositions.

Readers will undoubtedly note that Figure 4.2 does not contain a number of situational factors such as motivation, leadership, and organizational climate. This was done largely for pedagogical reasons, because the link between these situational factors and performance will be covered in later chapters. It is important to note, however, that although few studies have examined the joint effect of individual differences and situational factors, it has been demonstrated empirically that both do contribute to job performance (see Barrick & Mount, 2005;

FIGURE 4.2

Summary of the Most Important Individual Difference Predicators of Job Performance

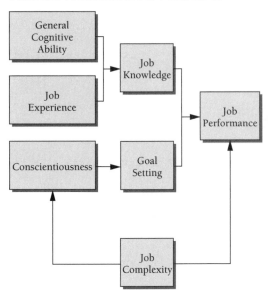

Colarelli, Dean, & Konstans, 1987; Day & Bedeian, 1991). Thus, organizations must do more than simply hire smart, experienced, conscientious people in order to facilitate high levels of employee performance.

ORGANIZATIONAL CITIZENSHIP BEHAVIOR

The second form of productive behavior to be discussed in this chapter is organizational citizenship behavior (OCB) (Organ, 1977, 1994). Generally speaking, OCB refers to behaviors that are not part of employees' formal job descriptions (e.g., helping a co-worker who has been absent; being courteous to others), or behaviors for which employees are not formally rewarded. Even though such behaviors are not formally mandated by organizations, in the aggregate they are believed to enhance the effectiveness of groups and organizations (George & Bettenhausen, 1990; Katz & Kahn, 1978; Podsak-off, Ahearne, &

MacKenzie, 1997). Recall from the previous models of job performance (Campbell, 1990, 1994; Murphy, 1994) the distinction between in-role and extra-role performance, and how extra-role performance represented those aspects of job performance not tied to specific tasks relevant to one's primary area of expertise (e.g., teamwork, dedication, communication ability). The distinction between extra-role performance and OCB is rather blurred. Technically, the key distinction is that OCBs are not evaluated as part of the formal appraisal system used to assess employees. In addition, the antecedents of OCB are different from those of in-role and extra-role performance.

One way of classifying OCB has been adopted by Organ (1977, 1994), where OCB in organizations can be categorized into five different types:

1. *Altruism* represents what we typically think of as "helping behaviors" in the workplace. This form of OCB is sometimes referred to as *prosocial behavior*. An example of altruism would be an employee's voluntarily assisting a co-worker who is having difficulty operating his or her computer.
2. *Courtesy* represents behaviors that reflect basic consideration for others. An example of behavior within this category would be periodically "touching base" with one's coworkers to find out how things are going, or letting others know where one can be reached.
3. *Sportsmanship* is different from other forms of OCB because it is typically exhibited by not engaging in certain forms of behaviors, such as complaining about problems or minor inconveniences.
4. *Conscientiousness* involves being a good citizen in the workplace and doing things such as arriving on time for meetings.

5. *Civic virtue* is somewhat different from the others because the target is the organization—or, in some cases, the work group—rather than another individual. An example of this form of OCB would be attending a charitable function sponsored by the organization.

Although this classification scheme represents a reasonable way of *carving up* OCB, other researchers have organized OCB differently. For example, Organ and Konovsky (1989) distinguished OCB that helped others at work when they had a problem (altruism) from following rules and doing whatever is needed to get the job done (compliance). Finally, McNeely and Meglino (1994) distinguished OCBs that are directed at helping others (OCBI) from those that are directed toward the organization as a whole (OCBS). These latter types of distinctions are typically guided by a researcher's specific interest in comparing the predictors of different types of OCB.

Reasons for OCB

Why do employees engage in OCB? There are actually three different explanations. According to the first, the primary determinant is positive affect, typically in the form of job satisfaction. Theoretically, this view comes from a fairly long history of social–psychological research showing that a positive mood increases the frequency of helping and of other forms of spontaneous prosocial behavior (see George & Brief, 1992). Furthermore, positive mood and helping behavior are actually mutually reinforcing because helping others usually makes people feel good. Bettencourt, Gwinner, and Meuter (2001) found that positive job attitudes were related to different types of OCB in service-oriented employees. Researchers have also found that job involvement, a correlate of job satisfaction, is positively correlated with supervisor ratings of OCB (Diefendorff, Brown, & Kamin, 2002).

A second explanation for OCB has to do with cognitive evaluations of the fairness of employees' treatment by an organization. This view is theoretically rooted in *Equity Theory* (Adams, 1965), which states that employees evaluate their work situations by cognitively comparing their inputs to the organization with the outcomes they receive in return. (Equity Theory will be covered in more detail in Chapter 8.) If employees perceive that the organization is treating them fairly or justly, then they are likely to reciprocate the organization by engaging in OCB. It seems, however, that certain forms of fairness or justice predict OCB better than others. For example, Moorman (1991) found that the best predictor of OCB was *interactional justice*, or the manner in which supervisors treat employees as they carry out organizational policies and procedures. In contrast, other studies have found that *procedural justice* is a better predictor of OCB than is *distributive justice* (e.g., Konovsky & Pugh, 1990). Procedural justice refers to employees' perceptions of the fairness of procedures used to make decisions such as pay raises; distributive justice refers to perceptions of fairness of the outcomes one receives as a result of those procedures. Recent research suggests that perceptions of organizational justice are especially important predictors of OCB for employees who are classified as *entitled* (Blakely, Andrews, & Moorman, 2005). These types of employees like their outcomes to be greater than other employees even when inputs are comparable. These individuals may be especially likely to base their decision to engage in OCB on the extent to which they feel they are being treated fairly by the organization.

A third explanation for OCB is that it is due to dispositions. According to this viewpoint, certain personality traits predispose individuals to engage in OCB. In other words, some people are naturally more helpful than others are. Compared to the first two explanations of OCB, the dispositional viewpoint has received much less attention in the OCB literature because proponents of this view have been vague as to the specific personality traits that should be related to OCB. This has been a criticism of dispositional explanations of other forms of employee attitudes and behavior (Davis-Blake & Pfeffer, 1989).

Other than affect, fairness, and dispositions, a handful of other factors have been proposed to explain the performance of OCB, although none of these has received extensive empirical scrutiny. For example, Chattopadhyay (1998) found evidence that OCB is predicted by the demographic composition of work groups. It has also been found that the performance of OCB may be influenced by factors such as job-related stressors (Jex, 1998; Jex, Adams, Bachrach, & Rosol, 2001) and employees' level of organizational commitment (Williams & Anderson, 1991). Wang, Law, Hackett, Wang, and Chen (2005) have recently shown that leadership is an important predictor of OCB. Using employees from organizations throughout the People's Republic of China, these authors found that positive perceptions of and trust in leaders were related to a greater tendency to perform OCB. Finally, Finkelstein and Penner (2004) found that motives surrounding the desire to help co-workers and possessing a citizenship-role identity (e.g., "helping the company is an important part of who I am") were more strongly related to OCB than motives associated with impression management.

FIGURE 4.3
Summary of the Major Antecedents of
Organizational Citizenship Behavior (OCB)

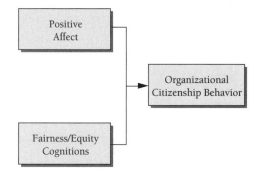

To evaluate the relative impact of various antecedents of OCB, Organ and Ryan (1995) conducted a meta-analysis of 55 studies. Their results suggest that job satisfaction and perceived fairness were correlated with OCB at approximately the same magnitude. The results for dispositional predictors of OCB were rather disappointing, however. For example, personality traits such as conscientiousness, agreeableness, positive affectivity, and negative affectivity were all unrelated to OCB. As Figure 4.3 summarizes, the most logical conclusion to be drawn from Organ and Ryan's meta-analysis is that affective and cognitive influences combine in an additive fashion to determine OCB.

Special Issues in OCB Research

Since Organ (1977) first introduced the concept of OCB, there has been considerable research on the topic. As with most well-researched topics, many issues have generated controversy and debate among researchers in this area. In this section, four of these issues are discussed briefly.

The underlying premise behind OCB research is that this form of productive behavior is necessary in order for organizations to be effective (Katz & Kahn, 1978).

What is typically argued is that if employees performed their jobs exactly as written, and did nothing beyond that, organizations would not be able to function effectively. Surprisingly, this claim had received virtually no empirical scrutiny until very recently. It has now been shown empirically, at least for groups, that OCB is positively related to effectiveness (Karambayya, 1989; Podsakoff et al., 1997). As would be expected, groups in which members engage in more OCBs tend to be more effective than groups in which members engage in fewer of these behaviors. For example, researchers have found that OCB is related to aspects of organizational effectiveness (e.g., profit, customer satisfaction) among bank branches in Taiwan (Yen & Niehoff, 2004).

What is still not clear from research on OCB and its effectiveness is the direction of causality underlying this relationship. Researchers have largely operated under the assumption that OCB has a causal impact on group and organizational effectiveness. However, it is also possible that the direction of causality could be reversed. Members of effective groups may report high levels of OCB, regardless of whether they actually exist. When a group is successful, group members may perceive high levels of OCB as they bask in the glow of this success. In a related study, Staw (1975) found that group members' retrospective reports of group cohesiveness could be manipulated based on false feedback about group performance. In this study group, members who were told that their group had been successful reported higher levels of cohesiveness than did group members who were told that their group had been unsuccessful. Using the same paradigm as Staw (1975), Bachrach, Bendoly, and Podsakoff (2001) recently found evidence that retrospective perceptions of OCB may be influenced by group performance. This issue will undoubtedly be addressed in future OCB research.

A second issue concerns the validity of the OCB concept itself. As originally defined by Organ (1977), OCB represents behavior that is above employees' formal job responsibilities, and for which there are no formal rewards. With regard to the first issue, it is becoming increasingly questionable that, in performing their day-to-day activities, employees make the *job descriptive* versus *nonjob descriptive* distinctions upon which OCB is based. This suggests that many employees view activities, such as helping other employees, being courteous to others, and occasionally attending functions on behalf of their organization, as part of their formal role responsibilities. This reasoning is supported by Morrison (1994), who found, in a sample of clerical employees, that many behaviors that are considered OCB were classified by these employees as part of their normal job responsibilities. She also found that there was very little correlation between employees' and supervisors' classifications of OCBs. Thus, many of the behaviors that supervisors consider OCB may simply represent employees' doing things that they consider to be part of their jobs.

Another interesting finding from Morrison's (1994) study was that employees were most likely to classify OCBs as in-role behaviors when they reported high levels of both job satisfaction and affective organizational commitment. Building on this finding, Bachrach and Jex (2000) conducted a laboratory study in which they used a mood-induction procedure to investigate the impact of mood on the categorization of OCB for a simulated clerical position. In this study, it was found that inducing a positive mood state had no impact on classification of OCB. Interestingly, though, subjects who experienced a negative mood-induction procedure classi-

fied fewer of the OCBs as being part of their regular roles, compared to those in the positive or neutral mood conditions. These findings suggest that negative affect may result in a more narrow definition of one's role. Taken together with Morrison's study, these findings call into question the *in-role* versus *extra-role* distinction that has been implicit in OCB research.

A third issue in OCB research is whether employees really engage in OCB without the expectation that such behaviors will be rewarded. Despite Organ's (1977) initial claim, recent evidence suggests that this assumption may be rather questionable. For example, it has been shown empirically that performing OCB positively influences formal performance appraisals (Eastman, 1994), and it is doubtful that employees are unaware of this. According to Bolino (1999), when OCB is performed with the expectation of future rewards, it then becomes a form of *impression management* (see Chapter 10) rather than truly altruistic behavior. Impression management behaviors are simply tactics people use to influence others' views of them. According to Bolino, OCB is most likely to be used as an impression management tool when it is highly visible to others, particularly those responsible for the dispensation of rewards. As an example, an employee may help other employees only when his or her supervisor is around to observe.

One could certainly argue that as long as OCB is performed, the motivation is irrelevant. However, the reasons behind such behavior are important if organizations want to influence the performance of OCB. If employees perform OCB primarily because they are satisfied with their jobs, or feel that they have been treated fairly, organizations can influence the performance of OCB by treating employees fairly and taking steps to enhance satisfaction. On the other hand, if OCB is performed with the expectation of rewards, or for impression management purposes, organizations should directly or indirectly link rewards to the performance of OCB. In essence, this suggests that OCB should be explicitly recognized as another form of job performance.

A final issue in OCB research is whether OCB will remain a viable concept in the workplace of the future. Bridges (1994), among others, has pointed out a clear trend in recent years: Organizations have been moving away from formal job descriptions. In fact, Bridges has predicted that the concept of a *job* will eventually cease to exist (see

Comment 4.6). This has not occurred as yet, but it is true that the work of employees in many organizations has become increasingly project driven, and their activities revolve more and more around project completion rather than fulfilling their job duties. Given this trend, one may ask whether the *in-role/extra-role* distinction upon which OCB rests will be relevant in the workplace of the future. Behaviors considered to be OCB will still be necessary in a *dejobbed* environment, but employees in the future will tend to consider them "part of the job," at least to the extent that they facilitate project completion. As Morrison's (1994) study shows, this is already occurring but will probably

---

COMMENT 4.6

A WORLD WITHOUT JOBS

WILLIAM BRIDGES, IN his 1994 book *JobShift: How to Prosper in a Workplace without Jobs*, argues that, in the near future, the concept of a "job" will cease to exist. That is, rather than having a formalized job description that lays out one's duties, each person in an organization will be given project-based objectives and expected to accomplish them. One of the implications of having no formalized jobs is that organizations will be able to make much greater use of temporary and contingent employees; that is, an organization will be able to bring in specialists on an "as needed" basis to complete specific projects. This will give organizations considerable flexibility and allow them to operate with much lower labor costs. Another implication of this trend is that more and more people will become "independent contractors" rather than permanent employees of a given organization.

According to Bridges, this trend toward doing away with jobs has thus far been most evident in organizations that operate in high-

technology sectors. This is largely due to the speed at which things are done in these sectors, and the need for constant innovation. Will other types of organizations eventually do away with jobs? Although it's certainly possible, there are reasons to believe that many organizations will not do away with jobs. For example, defending the legal soundness of selection and promotion procedures depends, to a large degree, on the job-relatedness of those procedures. Thus, an organization without job descriptions would be in a very difficult position if its selection and promotion procedures were challenged. One would also assume that unions would be very wary of doing away with job descriptions since they help in establishing wage rates and essentially serve as a "contract" as to the job duties employees are expected to perform.

Source: W. Bridges. (1994). JobShift: How to Prosper in a workplace without Jobs. Reading, MA: Addison-Wesley.

become a more pronounced trend because many employees may not have formal job descriptions to guide their behaviors.

INNOVATION IN ORGANIZATIONS

The third and final form of productive behavior to be examined in this chapter is innovation. Like OCB, innovation is really an aspect of job performance, but it is unique enough that a distinct literature examining its antecedents has developed. Although no standard definition of innovation exists, this form of productive behavior may be thought of as instances in which employees come up with very novel ideas or concepts that further the goals of the organization. Hellstrom and Hellstrom (2002) coined the term *organization ideation* to refer to "the process of creating useful conceptual novelty, and the circulation and taking on of that novelty in an organization" (p. 108). The most visible forms of these types of employee innovation in organizations are new products and services, and there are many examples of these. The Dell Computer Company, for example, has been an innovator in the marketing and distribution of personal computers. Saturn has been an innovator in both the distribution and service of automobiles. Not all innovations, however, take the forms of products and services. For example, an employee or employees may come up with a unique organizational structure, a more efficient production method, or some other cost-saving administrative procedure.

In the organizational innovation literature, there are four distinct streams of research (Damanpour, 1991). For the first stream, some researchers have examined the process by which employees come up with innovative ideas; others are more interested in determining the characteristics that dis-

tinguish highly innovative employees from others. Note that, in both cases, the focus is on the employee or employees responsible for the innovation. This view is also reasonably congruent with the definition of innovation proposed in this chapter. For the second stream, innovation is viewed from a more macro perspective; that is, many innovation researchers focus on what is described as the *diffusion* of innovations throughout an organization (see Greenhalgh, Robert, & McFarlane, 2004). An example of this might be the manner in which computers come to be utilized companywide. For the third stream, innovation researchers tend to focus on what can be described as the *adoption* of innovations (Frambach & Schillewaert, 2002). Viewed from this perspective, the focus is on an organization's initial decision on whether to adopt some innovation. Finally, a fourth stream emphasizes the importance of individuals and organizations in innovation. Hellstrom and Hellstrom (2002) have recently emphasized how individual workers and facilitating organizational conditions come together to breed innovation. The authors argue that "organizational highways, alleys, and by-lanes (p. 107)" can be created within an organization to spread innovation throughout the organization. See Comment 4.7 for an example of organizational innovation in the business of baseball.

Employee Attributes that Contribute to Creativity and Innovation

If innovation is viewed from the individual employees' perspective, a logical question is: Are there predictors of whether employees will be innovative? According to Amabile (1983), several variables are predictive of creative production in individuals. Because creativity and innovation are closely linked,

COMMENT 4.7

MONEYBALL APPLIED TO INNOVATION IN ORGANIZATIONS

MICHAEL LEWIS, IN his 2004 book "Moneyball: The Art of Winning and Unfair Game," describes the art of managament and winning in the world of baseball. Although the book was written about the business of recruiting and managing talented baseball players, a number of organizational scholars recognized the relevance of the principles described in the book to the overall field of human resource management and organizational innovation. A lead article in Human Resource Management (2006) was devoted to the implications of the book for organizations, and several other organizational scholars commented on this lead article.

Perhaps the biggest lesson to be gained from "Moneyball" is the importance of not maintaining practices that are based purely on speculation, intuition, and tradition, but recognizing the need to be innovative to deal with the demands facing the organization. Lewis tells the story of how general manager Billy Beane turned the Oakland Athletics into a highly effective team with a third as much money as the wealthiest baseball teams. One of the underlying themes is how Beane had to

be innovative in order to identify, acquire, and keep talent in ways that other baseball teams with more money did not. Beane used a number of principles from psychology in order to make decisions for which baseball players to recruit, including the best predictor of future performance being past performance and statistical indicators of performance being superior to hunches or intuition in identifying players who would excel. Although this approach seems reasonable, at the time it represented a strong deviation from the status quo of identifying talented players, and was viewed as a highly radical approach. Of course, the method ultimately paid off and the Oakland A's thrived as a baseball team and organization. The story of Moneyball has implications for how organizations in general recruit and retain employees, emphasizing the use of objective data as opposed to subjective perceptions when making decisions.

Source: M. Lewis. (2004). Moneyball: The art of winning an unfair game. New York, NY: W.W. Norton & Company.

these variables are also relevant to predicting innovation in organizational settings. According to Amabile, creativity is due to *task-relevant skills, creativity-relevant skills, and task motivation.*

The area of task-relevant skills is related to the previously discussed variable of general mental ability, but it is more than that. To be creative, an individual must have a high level of general mental ability, but must also have more specific abilities. For example, a scientist developing a new vaccine must not only be intelligent, but must also

know specific information about the behavior of microorganisms and be able to apply this knowledge in his or her work. Specific knowledge and technical skills are dependent on a certain level of general mental ability. Often, however, individuals must acquire these through some type of formal education; for example, most successful scientists have completed graduate training in their respective fields. Creative talent may also be developed apart from formal education. In the creative arts, for example, many successful people learn through informal means such as one-on-one tutoring, or they may even be self-taught.

Despite the importance of task-relevant skills, many people possess them but do not produce creative, innovative work. For example, despite the large number of individuals holding the doctoral degree in industrial/organizational psychology and related fields (e.g., Organizational Behavior, Human Resource Management), a relatively small proportion become highly productive researchers (e.g., Long, Bowers, Barnett, & White, 1998; Ones & Viswesvaran, 2000). Keep in mind that individuals holding Ph.D. degrees in these fields all have reasonably equivalent education and training, and have achieved a certain level of competence in their specialty. Why, then, are some highly productive while others are not? The answer to this question may lie in the area of creativity-relevant skills and task motivation.

Creativity-relevant skills are essentially *meta-skills* that individuals use in the creative process. One crucial skill in the creative process is a cognitive style that is conducive to creativity. According to Amabile (1983), creative people are able to understand the complexities in a problem and are able to *break set* during problem solving. Stated differently, being creative requires being able to see a problem from multiple perspectives and having the willingness needed to *break the mold* in order to solve a problem. A good historical example of this principle not being applied can be seen in retrospective accounts of the Vietnam War (McNamara, Blight, Brigham, Biersteker, & Schandler, 1999). In hindsight, it is clear that American and North Vietnamese decision makers viewed the conflict from completely different perspectives and were unwilling to deviate from these perceptions. On the American side, Vietnam was viewed as the "First Domino" in a Communist plan to dominate Southeast

Asia. The North Vietnamese, on the other hand, equated American intervention with the colonialism of the French. If either side had been willing to deviate from these perspectives, it is possible that the conflict could have been settled before the war escalated to a level that was so destructive for both sides.

Another important creativity-relevant skill is a work style that is conducive to creativity. Creative people are able to concentrate their efforts on a given problem for long periods of time. Stated differently, creativity requires hard work. Creative people, for example, are often able to work long hours at a time without stopping. Another aspect of work style is that creative people are able to engage in what Amabile (1983) described as *productive forgetting*—the ability to abandon unproductive searches, and temporarily put aside stubborn problems. Clear examples of this can be found in the sciences, where *breakthroughs* are typically achieved only after many failures.

The creativity-relevant skills described up to this point may be acquired from training, but there are more dispositional factors that contribute to creativity. Although researchers have been unable to isolate a *creative personality*, some personality traits do seem to be associated with creative activity. These include self-discipline, ability to delay gratification, perseverance in the face of frustration, independence, an absence of conformity in thinking, and lack of dependence on social approval.

The issue of task motivation has not been examined extensively in creativity research, largely because of the strong focus on intrinsic factors associated with creativity. It is likely, however, that at least some of the variation in creativity can be explained by the level and nature of the motivation one has toward the task being performed. According to Amabile (1983), creativity requires that individuals genuinely enjoy what they are doing, and perceive that they are performing the task because they want to, rather than because of external pressures. These perceptions of enjoyment and intrinsic motivation depend on one's initial level of intrinsic motivation toward the task being performed, the presence or absence of external constraints in the social environment, and the individual's ability to block out or minimize external constraints.

Organizational Determinants of Creativity and Innovation

Given our discussion of the determinants of creativity in individuals, what can organizations do to foster creativity and innovation among employees? The short answer to this question is to hire creative people. Although this suggestion makes sense, there are other things organizations can do. For example, to enhance creativity-relevant skills, organizations can provide training in the use of creative problem-solving methods such as brainstorming. A typical activity in such a training program might be for participants to come up with as many different uses for a paper clip as they can think of in 5 minutes (there are actually quite a few, if you think about it!). Such forms of training will obviously not completely compensate for a lack of innate ability; however, they may help talented employees realize their creative potential.

Another way that organizations can foster creativity and innovation is through influencing task motivation. A more comprehensive discussion of motivation is contained in Chapter 8 but in the present context, there appear to be things organizations can do to enhance task enjoyment and intrinsic motivation. One way is to attempt to place employees into jobs that they genuinely enjoy. This is not always possible, but if it can be done, it can lead to higher levels of creativity. Another way organizations can enhance task motivation is through the identification and removal of external constraints (Peters & O'Connor, 1988). Even though some individuals may be able to temporarily circumvent external constraints, employees stand a greater chance of developing the intrinsic motivation necessary to be creative if they are not there in the first place.

Kauffeld, Jonas, and Grote (2004) attempted to develop a structured measurement tool to assess an organization's climate for innovation. The authors found four major factors: activating leadership (having leaders that encouraged and modeled innovation), continuous questioning (encouraging employees to always question current practices), consequential implementation (seeing that the implementation of innovations had real consequences for the employee and organization), and professional documentation (clearly indicating and describing the innovation). The authors found that a climate for innovation was related to variables such as quality of developed solutions for organizational problems and product innovations.

Amabile and Conti (1999) have also extended Amabile's work on individual creativity into organizations, and explicitly recognizes the importance of the organizational context in facilitating the creativity of employees. She argues that five environmental factors in organizations can contribute to creativity in employees: encouraging creativity, autonomy and freedom, resources (the opposite of removing constraints), pressures (increasing positive challenges and reducing such factors as workload), and obstacles to creativity (e.g., conservatism and conflict). Amabile, Conti, Coon, Lazenby, and Herron (1996) found that the presence of facilitating factors is related to the creativity of Research and Development projects in a high-tech company.

As stated earlier, much of the innovation literature has adopted a macro focus; that is, researchers have focused on identifying characteristics of organizations that facilitate or impede the adoption or diffusion of innovation in those organizations. The most comprehensive examination of organizational-level predictors of the adoption of innovation was a meta-analysis by Damanpour (1991), in which he combined data from 23 studies. Before describing the findings from this meta-analysis, it is important to note that Damanpour distinguished between *technical innovations* and *administrative innovations*. Technical innovations pertain to innovations in products, services, and production process technology. An organization adopting a new production process would be adopting a technological innovation. Administrative innovations focus on organizational structure and administrative processes. An example of this would be an organization's decision to switch to a team-based organizational structure.

The results of this study suggest there are several organizational-level predictors of innovation. The strongest predictor, not surprisingly, was technical knowledge resources. Organizations are more likely to adopt innovations when they have employees who possess the technical expertise to understand and facilitate the implementation process. A possible explanation for this finding is that without technical expertise, there would be no innovations for organizations to adopt in the first place. Thus, an organization needs to hire individuals with high levels of technical knowledge.

The second most powerful predictor of innovation was the organization's level of specialization. An organization that is highly specialized, such as the manufacturer of a small number of products, likely has individuals with high levels of technical expertise. Having many technical specialists simply brings more talent to bear on important problems and may facilitate the cross-fertilization of ideas, both of which ultimately lead to innovation.

A third notable predictor of innovation identified in this meta-analysis was the level of external communication in an organization. Examples of this predictor would be technical experts' presenting their research findings at conferences and sharing their ideas with individuals in other organizations. Organizations that encourage frequent communication with the external environment are likely to increase the chances of bringing in innovative ideas from the outside. External communication also provides members of organizations with an opportunity to test the validity of their ideas on those outside of the organization. For those in many technical specialties, external communication may in fact be the only way to obtain unbiased feedback on their ideas. One recent study found that employees in project-based and knowledge-intensive organizations are more innovative at work when they are embedded in social structures relevant to a given project or area of knowledge outside the organization (Staber, 2004).

A fourth predictor of innovation was identified as *functional differentiation*. A high level of functional differentiation simply means that distinct and identifiable functional specialties exist within an organization. As an example, an organization with a high degree of functional differentiation may have a research and development division with a departmental structure based on technical specialties. A high level of functional differentiation leads to innovation because groups of employees who belong to the same functional specialty are better able to elaborate on ideas and hence to develop innovations. In many cases, this is helpful because specialty-based coalitions may help to facilitate administrative changes and innovations.

The four variables described previously were the strongest predictors of innovation identified in this meta-analysis. Other less powerful, though statistically significant, predictors of innovation were professionalism (.17), centralization (−.16), managerial attitudes toward change (.27), administrative intensity (.22), slack resources (.14), and internal communication (.17). These results suggest that innovation is fostered by employees who have a strong identification with their profession, a low level of centralization, positive managerial attitudes toward change, a high concentration of administrative employees, available slack resources, and a high level of communication.

More recent research has supported the validity of these factors as predictors. Thomas, McDonnell, McCulloch, While, Bosanquet, and Ferlie (2005) examined innovation in Primary Care Groups within the healthcare system in England. These authors found that an organization's capacity for innovation was driven by such factors as having multiple opportunities for employees to reflect and learn and communicate with other employees within the organization, having both clinicians and managers in positions of leadership to provide multiple perspectives, and being sure to time a particular innovative initiative correctly given the demands facing a particular work group. Caldwell and O-Reilly (2003) conducted interviews with senior executives and found that factors such as support for risk-taking, being tolerant of mistakes, high levels of teamwork, and being able to implement decisions quickly were seen to lead to increased innovation (see also Mohamed, 2002).

Given these findings, organizations wishing to encourage innovative behavior certainly need to recruit and hire the best technical talent possible. It is also important that organizations allow talented individuals to communicate with others outside of the organization, to develop and test ideas. This can be done through a variety of mechanisms: attending professional conferences, publishing in peer-reviewed journals, and, in some cases, bringing in experts from the outside. Ironically, some organizations are hesitant to do this, for fear that external communication will compromise proprietary information. This is particularly true for organizations operating in highly competitive industries (e.g., consumer products, food). This is a valid concern, but one could argue that the potential benefits of such forms of external communication far outweigh the risks.

Influencing managerial attitudes toward change is a complicated issue, but an organization can approach it in several ways. One way is to select management employees who have positive attitudes toward change. This may be difficult if the assessment must be done during the hiring process. Another approach may be to influence management attitudes through training and development activities. Ultimately, the most powerful influence on attitudes toward change is the way managers are treated. In many organizations, employees are punished for or discouraged from trying new things. Thus, the best way to improve attitudes toward change may be to encourage managers to try new things and to take risks. By doing this, organizations can take the threat out of change. Consequently, managers themselves may be more receptive to change and innovation.

This latter point emphasizes the importance of leadership in positive attitudes and actions toward innovation. Mumford and

Licuanan (2004) discussed the importance of leaders in facilitating the teamwork necessary for creative innovation to occur, and reviewed research showing that leaderless teams are less effective because of this lack of facilitation. These authors point out that leaders who are effective at encouraging innovation and creativity tend to have high levels of technical expertise and creative thinking skills. Finally, the authors note that because employees involved in innovative work tend to be more intrinsically motivated to perform their tasks, the primary role of leaders is to create the conditions that can funnel motivation to a given area of creativity.

CHAPTER SUMMARY

In this chapter, we examined productive behavior, or employee activities that contribute to the goals of the organization. The most common form of productive behavior in organizations is job performance, and this has been studied extensively for a number of years. There have even been attempts to describe dimensions of performance that are common to most jobs. Such efforts to model job performance continue to evolve, and they hold great promise in helping us to understand the substantive nature of job performance. Although there are differences between proposed models, one distinction that cuts across all of them is in-role (technical aspects of a given job) versus extra-role (skills that transcend the specific content of a job such as communication skills and being a team player) performance.

Because of its complexity, a number of factors complicate the attempts to measure job performance. These include the amount of instability in job performance over time and the fact that a number of forces tend to restrict the variability in job performance

within organizations. Despite all of these complicating factors, organizational researchers have still learned a great deal about the determinants of job performance. Research accumulated over the years has led to the conclusion that three variables stand out as predictors of performance, regardless of the job: (1) general cognitive ability, (2) level of job experience, and (3) the personality trait of conscientiousness. Furthermore, these variables appear to influence performance largely through the acquisition and utilization of job knowledge and the motivation to perform well.

Organizational Citizenship Behavior (OCB) represents the second form of productive behavior examined in the chapter. Although it can take several forms, OCB is defined as behavior that is not part of employees' formal job responsibilities. Research has shown that employees engage in OCB primarily because of positive affect and perceptions of the level of fairness with which they are treated by the organization. Only recently have researchers begun to empirically examine the assumption that OCB enhances organizational performance, to question the *in-role/extra-role* distinction that lies at the heart of OCB, and to probe the underlying motivation for the performance of OCB.

The third form of productive behavior discussed was innovation. We examined the characteristics of individuals who are likely to engage in innovative or creative behavior, and we explored macro influences on the innovation process. Drawing on individual-level studies of creativity, it appears that creativity and innovation can be explained on the basis of domain-relevant skills, creativity-relevant skills, and task motivation. Macro-level studies suggest several influences on the innovation process in

JOHN CAMPBELL AND THE MODELING OF JOB PERFORMANCE

For 100 years the focus of I/O Psychology has been on two major dependent variables, individual job performance and individual job satisfaction. While hundreds of studies have been devoted to the modeling and measurement of job satisfaction, no such literature existed for performance itself, until recently (i.e. after 1990). We had no "theory of performance." Performance measures typically were "criteria of convenience," and virtually all available indicators (e.g. college professor grant dollars or realtor sales volume) are susceptible to many sources of variation besides the actions of the individual. An outlandish example was a suggestion by a researcher to use "death rates" as a measure of physician performance. Over a 20-year period my goal was to correct this situation and give our most important dependent variable its due as a scientific construct.

Two projects made this possible. First, my colleagues and I compiled every study ever done on the determinants of, and the measurement of, individual manager performance. It resulted in the 1970 book, *Managerial Behavior, Performance, and Effectiveness*, which made a clear distinction between (a) the things managers actually do, and (b) the outcomes of what they do (i.e. the bottom line), which are virtually always influenced by many things besides the manager's behavior.

The second was the largest project in the history of applied psychology (Project A), which dealt with the U.S. Army's selection and classification system. Three years were devoted to development of multiple measures of performance, using every known measurement technology. Two cohorts of 10,000 new recruits were followed for six years. Performance was assessed at the end of technical training, after 3 years, and after 6 years on the job.

With this much data it was possible to model empirically the substantive nature of performance in this population of occupations. I then proposed a comprehensive model of individual performance for all jobs (e.g. Campbell, McCloy, Oppler, & Sager, 1992).

This was the first model of its kind, and the intent was to provide a meaningful specification of performance that can guide research, inform human resource practices, and provide a framework for integrating the existing literature. It felt good then. It still does.

John P. Campbell
Department of Psychology
University of Minnesota

organizations. The most general predictors of innovation appear to be technical knowledge resources, external communication, and managerial attitudes toward change. As with individual-level attributes, organizations have several levels of influence at the macro level in order to encourage both the development and adoption of innovation.

SUGGESTED ADDITIONAL READINGS

Barrick, M. R., & Mount, M. K. (2005). Yes, personality matters: Moving on to more important matters. *Human Performance, 18,* 359–372.

Hellstrom, C., & Hellstrom, T. (2002). Highways, alleys and by-lanes: Charting the pathways for ideas and innovation in organizations. *Creativity and Innovation Management, 11,* 107–114.

Podsakoff, P. M., & MacKenzie, S. B. (1997). Impact of organizational citizenship behavior on organizational performance: A review and suggestions for future research. *Human Performance, 10,* 133–151.

Ree, M. J., Earles, J. A., & Teachout, M. S. (1994). Predicting job performance: Not much more than g. *Journal of Applied Psychology, 79,* 518–524.

Sackett, P. R., Gruys, M. L., & Ellingson, J. L. (1998). Ability-personality interactions when predicting job performance. *Journal of Applied Psychology, 83,* 545–556.

Viswesvaran, C. (2002). Assessment of individual job performance: A review of the past century and a look ahead. In N. Anderson, D. S. Ones, H. P. Sinangil, & C. Viswesvaran (Eds.), *Handbook of industrial, work, and organizational psychology, Volume 1: Personnel psychology.* Thousand Oaks, CA: Sage Publications.

Chapter Five

Job Satisfaction and Organizational Commitment

Everyday experience suggests that humans are evaluative creatures; they look at much of their experience in terms of liking and disliking. Most of us, for example, have developed very clear preferences regarding the people we socialize with, the activities we engage in, and even the foods we choose to eat. In the workplace, this propensity for evaluation leads employees to develop feelings of liking or disliking toward the jobs they are performing. Most people have some opinion, be it positive or negative, about their job and the organization in which they work.

One could argue that another human tendency is to develop feelings of attachment or commitment. Indeed, many of us develop feelings of commitment toward other people, ideas, and even institutions. In the workplace, this tendency is manifested as employees' level of commitment toward the employing organization. Employees may be committed to their employing organizations for varying reasons, but there is no doubt that such feelings of commitment have important consequences for both the individual employee and the organization as a whole.

In this chapter, we cover two topics that many believe lie at the core of organizational psychology: (1) job satisfaction and (2) organizational commitment. Job satisfaction essentially represents employees' overall evaluation of their jobs, including feelings of positive affect toward their jobs or job situations. Organizational commitment, which is closely related to job satisfaction, represents employees' feelings of attachment and loyalty toward an organization. Both of these variables have

been studied extensively in organizational psychology, largely because they are related to a number of outcomes that are important for both theoretical and practical reasons.

JOB SATISFACTION

Job satisfaction is, without a doubt, one of the most heavily studied topics in organizational psychology, as well as in the broader field of industrial/organizational psychology. To emphasize this point, many authors have referred to Locke's chapter in the *Handbook of Industrial and Organizational Psychology*

(1976), where he reported that studies dealing with job satisfaction numbered in the thousands. That was approximately 25 years ago, so the figure cited by Locke has grown considerably. A recent search of Psychinfo with the keywords "Job Satisfaction" revealed 21,375 references on the topic. Incidentally, this high level of research attention has not escaped the notice of many inside and outside the field of I/O psychology. For example, the first author can remember as a graduate student one of the nonI/O faculty stating that I/O psychology was defined as "One hundred and one ways to ask people how they like their jobs. . . . " Although this individual was being a bit facetious (he was actually being *very* facetious), there is certainly a grain of truth in his statement.

Defining Job Satisfaction

Job satisfaction can be defined as an employee's overall evaluation of his or her job as favorable or unfavorable (e.g., Locke, 1976; Spector, 1997a). In this sense, job satisfaction is basically an employee's attitude toward his or her job (see Eagly & Chaiken, 1993). Like all attitudes, job satisfaction consists of feelings, thoughts, and behaviors individuals have relevant to their jobs. Most authors emphasize the emotional component of job satisfaction. However, cognitive and behavioral components of job satisfaction are important aspects of the construct as well.

The cognitive aspect of job satisfaction represents an employee's beliefs about his or her job or job situation; that is, an employee may believe that his or her job is interesting, stimulating, dull, or demanding—to name a few options. Note that although these represent cognitive beliefs, they are not completely independent of the previously described affective component. For example,

a statement or belief that "My job is interesting" is likely to be strongly related to feelings of positive affect.

The behavioral component represents an employee's behaviors or, more often, *behavioral tendencies* toward his or her job. An employee's level of job satisfaction may be revealed by the fact that he or she tries to attend work regularly, works hard, and intends to remain a member of the organization for a long period of time. Compared to the affective and cognitive components of job satisfaction, the behavioral component is often less informative because one's attitudes are not always consistent with one's behavior (Fishbein, 1979). It is possible, for example, for an employee to dislike his or her job but still remain employed there because of financial considerations.

Measurement of Job Satisfaction

Given the importance of job satisfaction to organizational psychologists, it is crucial to develop measures of the construct that are reliable and valid. As we learned with the study of job performance, it is impossible to study something if you can't measure it. Fortunately for organizational psychologists, several reliable and valid measures of job satisfaction are available for their use. In this section, four of the most widely used measures are described. However, before describing specific measures, we briefly review the process by which measures come to be seen as valid.

Although the measures that are described in this section are viewed by many as *construct valid* measures of job satisfaction, it is really incorrect to say that any measure is or is not construct valid. Construct validity is a matter of degree. Research has strongly supported the construct validity of the measures described in this section—in most cases, this evidence has been accumulated over several decades. Because of this accumulated evidence, researchers can use these measures with a great deal of confidence that they are indeed measuring employees' levels of job satisfaction.

How do we provide evidence for the construct validity of a measure? In general, there are three tests of construct validity (Campbell & Fiske, 1959; Nunnally & Bernstein, 1994). First, for a measure to be construct valid, it must correlate highly with other measures of the same construct. Stated differently, a measure must exhibit *convergence* with other measures of the same construct. For example, if two different organizational researchers develop separate measures of job satisfaction with different items, these two measures should correlate highly with each other. A second test of construct validity is that a measure must be distinct from measures of other variables. Another name for this is *discrimination*. For example, we may want to show that job satisfaction is not simply a function of differences between people in their tendency to evaluate everything in their world either positively or negatively. A third way that researchers typically show evidence of construct validity is through theoretically grounded predictions; that is, researchers typically develop a theoretically based *nomological network* of proposed relationships between the measure being developed and other variables of interest. To the extent that these relations are supported, the construct validity of the measure is supported. For example, much of the research we review in the following paragraphs illustrates the theoretical relationships between job satisfaction and other variables, such as job characteristics and personality. Given the thousands of studies conducted on job satisfaction, the nomological network for the construct is quite elaborate.

Several measures are widely considered to be construct valid measures of job satisfaction. Again, they are not construct valid in an absolute sense. Rather, so much favorable evidence has accumulated over the years that they are widely accepted measures of the job satisfaction construct. Given the large number of construct valid job satisfaction measures currently in use, a comprehensive coverage would be beyond the scope of this chapter. However, a handful of job satisfaction measures have been used widely over the years. Four of these are described in this section.

One of the first measures of job satisfaction that enjoyed widespread use was the *Faces Scale* developed by Kunin in the mid1950s (Kunin, 1955). As can be seen in Figure 5.1, this scale consists of a series of faces with differing emotional expressions. Respondents are asked simply to indicate which of the five faces best represents their feelings of overall satisfaction toward the job. The primary advantages of the Faces Scale are its simplicity and the fact that respondents need not possess a high reading level in order to complete it. This would be an excellent scale to use, for example, if a researcher were surveying a sample of employees who were known to have a very low level of education.

FIGURE 5.1
The Faces Scale of Job Satisfaction

Put a check under the face that expresses how you feel about your job in general, including the work, the pay, the supervision, the opportunities for promotion, and the people you work with.

Source: T. Kunin. (1955). The construction of a new type of attitude measure. *Personnel Psychology, 8,* 65–67. Reprinted by permission.

A potential disadvantage of the Faces Scale is that it does not provide the researcher with any information about an employee's satisfaction with different facets of the job. If an employee endorses one of the lower values on the Faces Scale (a "Frown"), this does not tell the researcher whether the source of this dissatisfaction is pay, supervision, or the content of the work itself. Thus, if a researcher is interested in pinpointing the source of satisfaction or dissatisfaction, the Faces Scale is of more limited value.

Another scale that has enjoyed extremely widespread use is the *Job Descriptive Index (JDI)* developed in the late 1960s by Patricia Cain Smith and her colleagues at Cornell University (Smith, Kendall, & Hulin, 1969). Sample items from the JDI are presented in Table 5.1. One thing to notice immediately is that the JDI is aptly named because the scale does require that respondents describe their jobs. Also, in contrast to the Faces Scale, users of the JDI obtain scores for various facets of the job and the work environment. The JDI provides scores for the individual facets of work, pay, promotion opportunities, supervision, and coworkers. Although some users of the JDI combine the facet scores to form an overall satisfaction index, this practice is not recommended by the developers of the JDI.

The primary advantage of the JDI is that a great deal of data supports its construct validity. Furthermore, research still continues in an effort to improve this scale (see Comment 5.1). Thus, the initial development and continued research on the JDI are exemplary. One consequence of this longstanding research effort is that considerable *normative data* on the JDI have been accumulated over the years. Thus, if a researcher or consultant were to use the JDI to measure job satisfaction among a sample of nurses, he or she would be able to compare their scores to a normative sample from the same occupation. Norm group comparisons can often be extremely useful if top managers want to know how the satisfaction levels of their employees compare to those of employees in similar occupations or employees within the same industry.

Given the vast amount of research associated with the JDI, not many disadvantages are associated with this scale. However, one issue has come up with the JDI: the lack of an overall satisfaction scale. As stated earlier, in

TABLE 5.1
Sample Items from the Job Descriptive Index (JDI)

Think of your present job. In the blank beside each word of phrase, write:
Y for "Yes" if it describes your job
N for "No" if it does not describe your job
? if you cannot decide

Work	*Pay*	*Promotions*
——Fascinating	——Barely live on income	——Opportunities somewhat limited
——Pleasant	——Bad	——Promotion on ability
——Can see results	——Well paid	——Regular promotions

Source: P. C. Smith, *The Job Descriptive Index, Revised.* Copyright, 1975, 1985, 1997, Bowling Green State University. Licensing for the JDI and related scales can be obtained from: Department of Psychology, Bowling Green State University, Bowling Green, Ohio 43403. Reprinted by permission.

COMMENT 5.1

THE LEGACY OF THE JDI

THE JOB DESCRIPTIVE Index (JDI) is undoubtedly one of the most popular and widely used measures of job satisfaction. One of the reasons for such wide use is the considerable research and development that has gone, and continues to go, into this instrument. The JDI was developed by Patricia Cain Smith and colleagues at Cornell University in the early 1960s. When Dr. Smith relocated from Cornell to Bowling Green State University in the mid-1960s, she founded the JDI research group, which consisted of both faculty and graduate students.

Over the years, the JDI research group has conducted research aimed at further refinement of the instrument, as well as development of national norms. This group continues such efforts to the present day, and has developed a number of other measures that are based on the JDI. The JDI research group at Bowling Green has also served as a clearing-house for research data using the JDI. As a result, the group has assembled an impressive data archive consisting of dozens of data sets, collected over a 25-year period and containing over 12,000 cases. Recently, the group has begun to make a portion of these data available to researchers outside of Bowling Green who are interested in job satisfaction and related areas such as occupational stress, retirement, and job design.

Overall, the JDI represents one of the most comprehensive and exemplary scale development efforts ever conducted in the field of industrial/organizational psychology. It also serves as a good example of how scale developers, and the entire field, can benefit by making data available to the research community.

Source: http://www.bgsu.edu/departments/psych/JDI.

some cases, researchers merely wish to measure employees' levels of overall satisfaction, and the JDI does not allow for this. To address this issue, developers of the JDI created what is termed the *Job in General (JIG) Scale* (Ironson, Smith, Brannick, Gibson, & Paul, 1989). The JIG is modeled after the JDI except that it consists of a number of adjectives and phrases about the job in general rather than about specific job facets. The JIG has been used less frequently than the JDI, but some recent research has contributed to the scale's validity (Skibba & Tan, 2004). In addition, Russell and his colleagues (2004) have recently developed a shorter form of the measure that should be appealing to organizational researchers.

A third job satisfaction measure that has enjoyed widespread acceptance and use within organizational psychology is the *Minnesota Satisfaction Questionnaire (MSQ)*. The MSQ was developed by a team of researchers from the University of Minnesota at roughly the same time the JDI was being developed (Weiss, Dawis, England, & Lofquist, 1967). The long form of the MSQ consists of 100 items that are designed to measure the 20 facets of work that are presented in Table 5.2. There is also a *short* form of the MSQ, consisting of 20 items. The short form, however, is not designed to provide facet satisfaction scores.

The items comprising the MSQ consist of statements about various facets of the job,

TABLE 5.2

A Listing of the Facets Measured by the Minnesota Satisfaction Questionnaire (MSQ)

Activity	Ability utilization
Independence	Company policies and practices
Variety	Compensation
Social status	Advancement
Supervision (human relations)	Responsibility
Supervision (technical)	Creativity
Moral values	Working conditions
Security	Coworkers
Social service	Recognition
Authority	Achievement
Supervision (human relations)	Company policies and practices

Source: D. J. Weiss, R. V. Dawis, G. W. England, and L. H. Lofquist. (1967). *Manual for the Minnesota Satisfaction Questionnaire* (Minnesota Studies in Vocational Rehabilitation, No. 22). University of Minnesota, Minneapolis.

and the respondent is asked to indicate his or her level of satisfaction with each. For example, a respondent is presented with an item having to do with activity level, such as "Being able to keep busy all the time," and is asked to indicate his or her level of satisfaction with the statement. Compared to the JDI, the MSQ is more of an affect-based measure; that is, responses indicate liking or disliking rather than description.

Like the JDI, considerable research has gone into the development and construct validation of the MSQ. The MSQ also provides quite extensive information on employees' satisfaction with various facets of the job or work environment. As stated earlier, this type of information may be especially useful when organizations are conducting internal employee opinion surveys. For example, if it is found that satisfaction with a certain facet is much lower compared to the others, this suggests that an organization may need to makes changes in this area. The only major disadvantage of the MSQ is its length. At 100 items, the full version of the MSQ is very difficult to administer, especially if a researcher wishes to measure other variables.

Even the shortened version (20 items) is still considerably longer than many other measures of satisfaction available.

A final job satisfaction measure that has not been used as extensively as the others described, but that has considerable evidence supporting its psychometric properties, is the *Job Satisfaction Survey (JSS)*. This scale was originally developed by Spector (1985) as an instrument to measure job satisfaction levels of Human Service employees. The JSS consists of 36 items designed to measure nine facets of the job and work environment. The facets measured by the JSS are listed in Table 5.3.

Compared to the other measures described in this section, the JSS is fairly typical; that is, the items represent statements about a person's job or job situation. Respondents are then asked to indicate the extent to which they agree with each item. Given this type of scaling, the JSS is more similar to the JDI because it is more descriptive in nature than the MSQ. Unlike the JDI, however, an overall satisfaction score can be computed for the JSS by summing the facet scores.

TABLE 5.3
A Listing of the Facets Measured by the Job Satisfaction Survey (JSS)

Pay	Promotion
Supervision	Benefits
Contingent rewards	Operating procedures
Coworkers	Nature of work
Communication	

Source: P. E. Spector. (1997). *Job satisfaction: Application, assessment, causes, and consequences.* Thousand Oaks, CA: Sage. Reprinted by permission of Sage Publications, Inc.

Compared to the JDI and MSQ, not as much supporting data are available for the JSS, but the evidence supporting the psychometric properties of this scale is still impressive (Spector, 1997a). Furthermore, Spector has assembled a fairly comprehensive normative database for the JSS; it includes a variety of job types, many different organizations, and even different countries.

In conclusion, a number of valid measures exist to measure overall job satisfaction and satisfaction with different aspects of one's job. The normative information on many of these scales is especially useful for organizational psychologists who want to be able to compare their employees to employees from similar occupations and organizations. Now that we have addressed the prediction and measurement of job satisfaction, we address the important question of outcomes predicted by job satisfaction.

Predictors of Job Satisfaction

A substantial portion of the research conducted on job satisfaction over the years has been devoted to explaining what exactly determines employees' levels of job satisfaction. Understanding the development of job satisfaction is certainly of theoretical importance to organizational psychologists. It is also of practical interest to organizations as they attempt to influence employees' levels of job satisfaction and, ultimately, other important outcomes.

There are three general approaches to explaining the development of job satisfaction: (1) *job characteristics*, (2) *social information processing*, and (3) *dispositional* approaches. According to the job characteristics approach, job satisfaction is determined primarily by the nature of employees' jobs or by the characteristics of the organizations in which they work. According to this view, employees cognitively evaluate their jobs and organizations and make some determination of their relative level of satisfaction.

Over the years, several models have been proposed to explain the precise manner in which job satisfaction develops in response to job conditions (see Hulin (1991) for a summary). There are differences among these models, but the common theme running through most of them is that job satisfaction is largely determined by employees' comparison of what the job is currently providing them and what they would like it to provide. For each facet of a job—pay, working conditions, supervision—employees make some assessment of what they are currently receiving. These assessments are meaningful only when they are compared with what an employee feels he or she should be receiving from a particular facet. These perceptions are based on a number of factors: the employees' skills, the amount of time they have put into the job, and the availability of other employment opportunities.

If employees perceive what they are currently receiving to be at or above what they feel they should be receiving, then they are satisfied. If not, then feelings of dissatisfaction are evoked. As a relatively simple example of how this works, suppose an employee's current yearly salary is $42,000. If the employee believes that he or she should be receiving an annual salary of approximately $40,000, then the salary will evoke feelings of satisfaction. On the other hand, if the employee believes, for some reason, that he or she deserves an annual salary of $100,000, then the current salary will evoke feelings of dissatisfaction. The importance of comparisons in pay satisfaction can be seen in a recent meta-analysis by Williams, McDaniel, and Nguyen (2006). These authors examined the antecedents and consequences of pay level satisfaction by combining the results of over 203 studies. The authors found that one of the biggest predictors of pay level satisfaction was how well an employee's current pay compared to other employees in the same organization. Clearly, employees base their satisfaction with their pay on comparisons with others. What makes these findings even more convincing is that the actual pay of employees was controlled in the analyses.

The notion that job satisfaction depends on an employee's comparison of what he or she is currently receiving versus what is desired is reasonable. However, according to Locke (1976), this is an oversimplification because it does not account for the fact that employees differ in the importance they place on various facets of work. For one employee, it may be extremely important to have pay and fringe benefits that meet his or her expectations; for another, it may be essential to have a job that provides an opportunity for challenging assignments.

To explain how such differences influence the development of job satisfaction, Locke (1976) proposed what has become known as *range of affect theory*. The basic premise of range of affect theory is that facets of the work are differentially weighted when employees make their assessments of job satisfaction. For example, if pay is very important to an employee, the fact that his

or her current pay is close to what was expected would have a large positive impact on his or her overall assessment of job satisfaction. In contrast, if pay is relatively unimportant, the fact that expectations were met or unmet would have a relatively small impact on employee job satisfaction.

The job characteristics approach to job satisfaction is strongly ingrained in organizational psychology (e.g., Campion & Thayer, 1985; Griffin, 1991; Hackman & Oldham, 1980). Furthermore, the weight of empirical research from a variety of areas strongly supports the idea that characteristics of the job and the job situation are robust predictors of employees' levels of job satisfaction (e.g., Ellickson, 2002; Fried & Ferris, 1987; Williams et al., 2006). Thus, by the mid1970s, the job characteristics approach had clearly become entrenched as the dominant approach to job satisfaction within organizational psychology.

The first major challenge to the job characteristics approach came in the late 1970s in the form of Social Information Processing (SIP) theory (Salancik & Pfeffer, 1977, 1978). Salancik and Pfeffer criticized the job characteristics approach to job satisfaction on two counts. First, they proposed that the job characteristics approach was inherently flawed because it was based on the assumption that job characteristics were objective components of the work environment. According to these authors, jobs are "social constructions" that exist in the minds of employees and are not objective entities. Second, they pointed out that the job characteristics approach was based on the idea of need satisfaction. The problem with this, according to Salancik and Pfeffer, is that little evidence has supported the utility of needs in the prediction of employee outcomes.

Salancik and Pfeffer (1978) proposed two primary mechanisms by which employees develop a feeling of satisfaction or dissatisfaction. One of these mechanisms states that employees look at their behaviors retrospectively and form attitudes such as job satisfaction in order to make sense of it. This view is based on Bem's (1972) *Self Perception Theory*, which is a more general social psychological theory of attitude formation. According to this view, for example, an employee who has been working in an organization for 30 years may say to himself or herself, "I've worked here for a long time, therefore I must really like my job . . . " This view challenges whether employees actually hold stable attitudes toward their jobs based on objective features of the environment, and instead suggests that employees' job satisfaction may fluctuate and be determined based on features of the situation.

The other explanation—the one most closely linked to social information processing theory—is that employees develop attitudes such as job satisfaction through processing information from the social environment. This view is based largely on Festinger's (1954) *Social Comparison Theory*, which states that people often look to others to interpret and make sense of the environment. According to this view, for example, a new employee who happened to interact with other employees who were dissatisfied with their jobs would also likely become dissatisfied. The practical implication of this, of course, is that organizations must be careful not to allow new employees to be *tainted* by dissatisfied employees during the socialization process.

Within organizational psychology and other related fields, the initial development of Social Information Processing theory had a strong impact. This was undoubtedly due to the fact that the job characteristics approach had been dominant up to that point. As evidence of this impact, a flurry of research activity designed to test this theory was conducted in the late 1970s and throughout the 1980s, (e.g., Adler, Skov, & Salvemini, 1985; O'Reilly & Caldwell, 1979; Weiss & Shaw, 1979; White & Mitchell, 1979). Most of these investigations found that social information, usually in the form of verbal comments about task characteristics, had at least as powerful an impact on job satisfaction and perceptions of task characteristics as the objective characteristics of the task. Field tests of Social Information Processing theory, however, have been much less supportive than laboratory investigations (e.g., Jex & Spector, 1989).

Given the inability to demonstrate Social Information Processing effects outside of laboratory settings, it is tempting to conclude that this is nothing more than an interesting laboratory phenomenon (e.g., Jex & Spector, 1988). However, common sense and everyday experience suggest that social information does play a role in the formation of our attitudes. If the impact of social influence is ubiquitous, why then is the influence of social information on job satisfaction so difficult to demonstrate outside of laboratory settings? According to Hulin (1991), laboratory investigations of social information processing effects are typically more successful than field studies because they grossly simplify the social influence process. For example, in most laboratory studies, participants are given either "positive" or "negative" social information about the task they are being asked to perform. In organizational settings, employees rarely receive such discrete levels of social information about their jobs or organizations. For example, employees may receive social information covering a variety of levels of favorability, and may at times receive conflicting information from the same source. In the future, organizational psychologists must develop more creative ways of studying the

COMMENT 5.2

SOCIAL INFORMATION PROCESSING RESEARCH

WHEN GERALD SALANCIK and Jeffrey Pfeffer introduced the Social Information Processing (SIP) approach to job satisfaction in the late 1970s, they caused a great deal of controversy among job satisfaction researchers. The reason for this controversy is that Salancik and Pfeffer challenged the widely held belief that job satisfaction was due primarily to characteristics of the jobs and organizations in which employees work. One of the results of this controversy was that different *camps* developed—those who favored the job characteristics approach, and those who favored the social information processing approach.

As so often happens when different camps develop, each tried to provide empirical evidence supporting its position. Thus, in the late 1970s and early 1980s, a number of the laboratory studies conducted essentially pitted the job characteristics and social information

processing approaches against each other. More specifically, researchers manipulated characteristics of laboratory tasks and, at the same time, provided social cues (usually by using a confederate) about the desirability of the task. The objective was then to see which of these manipulations explained the most variance in task satisfaction.

What many of these so-called *race horse design* studies showed, not surprisingly, was that the task satisfaction of laboratory subjects was influenced by both task design and the social cues that were provided about the task. Since that time, researchers have generally accepted the fact that both job characteristics and social information have an impact on job satisfaction. In the future, the key is to determine the situations in which each of these (along with dispositions) may exert the greatest impact.

impact of social information on job satisfaction (see Comment 5.2).

One recent attempt to examine the influence of the social context on ratings of job satisfaction examined how the variability in personality within an organization is related to employee reports of job satisfaction (Ployhart, Weekley, & Baughman, 2006). These authors found that employees working in organizations where people differed widely in their personalities reported lower levels of job satisfaction than employees who worked in organizations where people were similar in their personalities, especially on the traits of agreeableness and extraversion. The average level of a personality trait in an organization was also related to job satisfaction. Employees reported higher job satisfac-

tion when they were in organizations where employees reported higher levels of emotional stability, conscientiousness, and extraversion. This study illustrates that the types of people and similarities between people in the employees' environment are predictive of job satisfaction.

The most recent approach to explaining job satisfaction is based on *internal dispositions*. The basic premise of the dispositional approach to job satisfaction is that some employees have a tendency to be satisfied (or dissatisfied) with their jobs, regardless of the nature of the job or organization in which they work. The use of dispositions to explain behavior and attitudes is often portrayed as a very recent phenomenon, but the dispositional approach to job satisfaction can actually be traced back to the work of Weitz (1952). Weitz was interested in whether an individual's general affective tendencies would interact with job satisfaction to impact turnover. Thus, Weitz was not interested in explaining job satisfaction by dispositions per se, but his work was clearly suggestive of that notion.

The study that brought about renewed interest in dispositions was Staw and Ross's (1985) investigation of the stability of job satisfaction among a national sample of working males. This study found that there was a statistically significant correlation between job satisfaction at one point in time, and job satisfaction 7 years later. Because many of those in the sample had changed jobs—and, in some cases, careers—the authors argued that the level of stability that was found suggested that job satisfaction was at least partially determined by dispositions. Subsequent research by Staw, Bell, and Clausen (1986) provided even more impressive evidence of stability by showing that job satisfaction in adolescence was predictive of job satisfaction in adulthood.

Perhaps the most interesting evidence for the dispositional approach to job satisfaction was provided in a study conducted by Arvey, Bouchard, Segal, and Abraham (1989). In this study, the authors examined job satisfaction among pairs of monozygotic twins and estimated the extent to which job satisfaction was similar within pairs. Using a statistic called the *intraclass correlation coefficient*, these authors found that approximately 30% of the variance could be attributed to genetic factors. Although this study was subsequently criticized on methodological grounds (e.g., Cropanzano & James, 1990), it is nevertheless consistent with a dispositional approach to job satisfaction. In addition, other researchers have recently replicated the heritability of job

satisfaction using a stronger methodology. Ilies and Judge (2003) estimated a heritability coefficient of .54 for job satisfaction, again indicating approximately 29% of the variance in job satisfaction was a function of genetic factors.

A major limitation of early work on the dispositional approach to job satisfaction was that it was imprecise as to exactly which dispositions are related to job satisfaction (Davis-Blake & Pfeffer, 1989). Recall that Staw and Ross (1985) demonstrated that job satisfaction was stable over time, but they did not specify which dispositional traits accounted for this consistency. Subsequent dispositional research focused on documenting relations between specific traits and job satisfaction. As an example, Levin and Stokes (1989) found that *negative affectivity* was negatively associated with job satisfaction, and explained variance that was independent of job characteristics (see also Connolly & Viswesvaran, 2000). Negative affectivity is a dispositional trait having to do with the predisposition to experience negative emotionality and distress (Watson & Clark, 1984). It has also been found that positive analogues to negative affectivity, such as *dispositional optimism* and *positive affectivity*, are positively related to job satisfaction (e.g., Connolly & Viswesvaran, 2000; Jex & Spector, 1996). Bono and Judge (2003) also examined the relationship between the personality trait of core self-evaluation (discussed in Chapter 4) and job satisfaction, and found a correlation of .48 between the two variables.

Judge and his colleagues have conducted some of the most comprehensive research on the dispositional contributors to job satisfaction. Judge, Heller, and Mount (2002) conducted a meta-analysis on over 163 samples and found that the *big five* personality traits of extraversion, conscientiousness, openness to experience, agreeableness, and neuroticism collectively correlated .41 with job satisfaction. The highest correlations were between job satisfaction and neuroticism (such that higher neuroticism was related to low job satisfaction), extraversion, and conscientiousness. Furthermore, Ilies and Judge (2003) examined whether the *Big Five* personality traits and Positive and Negative Affectivity would account for the genetic influences on job satisfaction. According to this approach, genetic factors produce differences in personality and affectivity, which then leads individuals to report different levels of job satisfaction. The authors found that Positive and Negative Affectivity accounted for 45% of the genetic influence on ratings of job satisfaction, and that the Big Five personality traits accounted for 24%. These types of analyses do a good job of unifying research on the dispositional approach to job satisfaction, showing how various factors within the individual can influence ratings of job satisfaction in the absence of any additional information about a person's job!

One issue that dispositional researchers as yet have failed to resolve is determining the practical implications of dispositional effects. At first glance, it might be assumed that if job satisfaction is linked to specific traits, organizations would be justified in using that information to select individuals who are likely to be satisfied. This recommendation, however, ignores the fact that situational effects still exert a stronger impact on job satisfaction than dispositions (e.g., Gerhart, 1987; Levin & Stokes, 1989). Also, given the fact that, in many instances, job satisfaction is not strongly related to performance (Podsakoff & Williams, 1986), selecting employees who are most likely to be satisfied may have adverse legal ramifications. More research is needed before dispositional findings are applied in organizational settings. Of course, it may be helpful

for managers to be aware of this research, so they realize that some individuals are prone to report high or low job satisfaction irrespective of job conditions.

In this section, we have covered three general approaches to explaining employees' levels of job satisfaction in organizations: job characteristics, social information processing, and dispositions. After examining each of these approaches, it is tempting to ask: "Which of these approaches is correct?" The weight of empirical evidence favors the job characteristics approach, yet it would be premature to conclude that this approach is "right" and the other two approaches are "wrong." As was pointed out earlier, modeling social influence with a high degree of fidelity in laboratory settings is extremely difficult (Hulin, 1991). Furthermore, in the case of dispositions, research is still in its infancy, and much still needs to be learned. Thus, the most appropriate conclusion, which is summarized in Figure 5.2, is that job satisfaction is a joint function of job characteristics, social information processing, and dispositional effects. This figure also illustrates that by viewing these approaches as predicting different aspects of job satisfaction, we improve our ability to understand this important job attitude. Finally, we would like to

FIGURE 5.2
Summary of the Determinants of Job Satisfaction

point out that organizational researchers have recently recognized the importance of national culture in the prediction of job satisfaction.

Job Satisfaction: A Cross-Cultural Perspective

Like many issues in organizational psychology, the study of job satisfaction has taken place primarily in the United States and Western European countries. This is obviously a *blind spot* in our knowledge because work is a universal activity, and, presumably, so is the development of positive or negative feelings toward work. In this section, we briefly examine recent evidence on the possibility of cross-cultural differences in levels of job satisfaction, and potential reasons for these differences.

Given the dearth of cross-cultural research in general, relatively few studies have examined cross-cultural differences in job satisfaction. For example, Griffeth and Hom (1987) found that Latin American managers were more satisfied than European managers. In a comparison of Dominican and American employees working for the same company, Marion-Landis (1993) found that the Dominicans were more satisfied than their American counterparts. Several studies have also shown that Japanese employees tend to be less satisfied than American employees (e.g., Smith & Misumi, 1989).

Direct cross-national comparisons in job satisfaction are interesting, but they often provide little insight into why the differences exist. To understand the basis of such differences, it is useful to frame the issue in terms of the three approaches to job satisfaction discussed at the beginning of this chapter. When viewed from the job characteristics perspective, there are several plausible explanations for cross-cultural differences in job satisfaction. For example, considerable evidence exists for cross-cultural differences in *values*. Hofstede (1984) investigated differences in values—including *individualism/collectivism, masculinity, power distance,* and *uncertainty avoidance*—in 40 different countries. The individualism/collectivism dimension reflects the extent to which people are concerned with their own interests and needs, rather than those of other people or of members of important collective units (e.g., family, work group). Masculinity reflects the degree to which there is a focus on achievement and performance as opposed to the wellbeing and satisfaction of others. Power distance reflects the degree to which those with high levels of authority and status are distinct from those with lower levels. Finally, uncertainty avoidance reflects the extent to which people are comfortable working in uncertain environments.

Hofstede's (1984) findings have shown rather clearly the existence of cross-national differences on each of these four values. For example, the United States and countries in Western Europe tend to place a very high value on individualism, while Hispanic and Asian countries tend to place a relatively high value on collectivism. With respect to masculinity, Scandinavian countries tend to place a relatively high value on this dimension compared to other countries. Power distance tends to have very high value in Hispanic countries, but the opposite is true in countries such as Australia and Israel. Uncertainty avoidance was found to be highest in countries such as Greece and Portugal, and lowest in Singapore and Denmark.

The primary implication of these cross-national differences in value preferences is that cross-cultural differences in job satisfaction may be due to differences in what employees desire from their jobs. Recall from the beginning of this chapter that job satisfaction has been purported to result from a comparison between what people perceive their jobs provide and what they desire. Thus, when viewed from this perspective, cultural differences can be at least partially attributed to the fact that employees in different cultures seek different things from their jobs, and may place different levels of importance on different job facets.

While there is undoubtedly some merit to this argument, cross-cultural differences in job satisfaction may also be influenced by cross-national differences in actual job conditions. Because of economic and political differences, employees in different countries may differ greatly in the quality of their on-the-job experiences. In the former Soviet Union, for example, it is unlikely that employees in state-run organizations had much decision-making authority over many aspects of their jobs. In contrast, employees in countries that embrace free-market economics typically have greater participation in decision making and are more strongly encouraged to engage in proactive behaviors.

Cross-cultural differences can also be viewed through the lens of the social information processing approach to job satisfaction. For example, it is possible that in addition to value differences, cross-cultural differences may exist in the degree to which social influence processes are salient to employees. One might speculate that in an individualistic society such as the United States, social information may have a relatively minimal impact, and job satisfaction may be only weakly related to prevailing cultural values. In contrast, in a more collectivist society such as Japan, social influence processes may be much more important.

Compared to the job characteristics and social information processing approaches, the dispositional approach to job satisfaction would appear to be less helpful in explaining crosscultural differences in job satisfaction.

However, it is possible that the prevalence of certain dispositional traits that influence job satisfaction may differ across cultures. A recent study highlighting cultural influences on job satisfaction can be found in Comment 5.3.

Outcomes of Job Satisfaction

Although job satisfaction is important for its own sake, researchers and managers are interested in job satisfaction primarily because of its possible relationship to other variables of interest. Given the sheer volume of research on job satisfaction that has been conducted over the years, it would be nearly impossible to discuss all of the correlates of job satisfaction. Thus, this section describes relations between job satisfaction and four types of variables that have both theoretical and practical importance: attitudinal variables, absenteeism, employee turnover, and job performance.

Attitudinal Variables: By far, job satisfaction has been found to correlate most strongly with other attitudinal variables. These variables reflect some degree of liking or disliking; that is, they are affective in nature. Examples of common attitudinal variables used in organizational research include job involvement, organizational commitment (described later in the chapter), frustration, job tension, and feelings of anxiety. Notice that all of these variables, to a large degree, reflect levels of affect. For job involvement and organizational commitment, this affect is positive. The other variables reflect feelings of negative affect.

Considerable empirical research has supported the relationship between job satisfaction and attitudinal variables. For example, in a comprehensive meta-analysis of 124 published studies, Mathieu and Zajac (1990) found that the corrected correlation between

COMMENT 5.3

NATIONAL CULTURE AND JOB SATISFACTION

HUANG AND VAN DE VLIERT (2004) recently conducted a study of the determinants of job satisfaction among individuals from 39 different countries. Their total sample size was 129,087, and the authors were able to determine how characteristics of the country, such as the degree of collectivism versus individualism, influenced the relationship between other factors and job satisfaction. The extent to which a country was collectivistic versus individualistic was determined by three different indexes, based on Diener, Diener, and Diener (1995^{Q7}). The first was an index reflecting individualism versus collectivism provided by Hofstede (1991) in his study of values in different countries. The second was the ranking of a country's individualism by another leading researcher in the field, Harry Triandis. Finally, each country's divorce rate was calculated between 1995 and 1998. The reasoning behind this third indicator was that countries with higher divorce rates are likely more individualistic, as these nations recognize the rights of individuals over collective values of duty and obedience.

Huang and Van de Vliert argued that a country's level of individualism versus collectivism may influence how factors such as job level and characteristics relate to job satisfaction. For example, some researchers have found that white-collar workers report higher

job satisfaction than blue-collar workers, because the former employees have more complex and interesting jobs. In the present study the authors found that the tendency for white-collar workers to report higher job satisfaction only occurred in more individualist countries (e.g., the United States and the United Kingdom), and not in more collectivist countries (e.g., China and Indonesia). Furthermore, job level and individualism/collectivism interacted with job characteristics to predict job satisfaction. The relationship between job level and job satisfaction was found primarily among jobs where individuals reported an opportunity to use their skills and abilities at work, and this effect was especially pronounced in individualistic cultures. Having a white-collar job was actually negatively related to job satisfaction when individuals did not feel they had an opportunity to use their skills and abilities at work, and this relaitonship was especially true in collectivistic cultures.

The results of this study indicate the importance of examining how culture-level factors can influence the prediction of job satisfaction. In general, organizational researchers are beginning to question how well results obtained with employees from a single culture will generalize to employees in different cultures.

organizational commitment and job satisfaction was .53. It has also been found that job satisfaction is positively related to a multitude of other measures that reflect positive affect, such as job involvement, positive mood, and organization-based self-esteem, to name a few (e.g., Spector, 1997a). With respect to negative attitudes, numerous occupational stress studies have shown that job satisfaction is

strongly and negatively related to variables such as frustration, anxiety, and tension (Jackson & Schuler, 1985; Jex & Spector, 1996; Spector & Jex, 1998).

Although there is little debate that job satisfaction is related to other attitudinal variables, the precise mechanisms underlying many of these relations remain unclear because much of the research on job satisfaction has relied on self-report measures and cross-sectional designs. For example, a high level of job satisfaction may cause employees to have other positive feelings toward their jobs, and may lead to lower levels of negative feelings. Conversely, it is also possible that other positive and negative attitudes cause high or low levels of job satisfaction. For example, a high level of job involvement, coupled with a low level of frustration, may lead employees to feel satisfied toward their jobs. It is also possible that such relations are the result of shared common causes such as job conditions (Fried & Ferris, 1987; Jackson & Schuler, 1985; Mathieu & Zajac, 1990). Only the use of longitudinal designs will allow researchers to investigate the causal direction between job satisfaction and other job attitudinal variables (Zapf, Dormann, & Frese, 1996).

Absenteeism: The study of absenteeism is important for both theoretical and practical reasons. From a theoretical perspective, absenteeism represents a common way in which employees may withdraw from their jobs (Hulin, 1991). From a practical perspective, absenteeism is a very costly problem to many organizations. When employees are absent, work may not get done or may be performed by less experienced employees.

It is certainly intuitively plausible that an employee's absence from work would be one reaction to a high level of job dissatisfaction. Despite its intuitive plausibility, empirical research has provided only weak support for the relation between job satisfaction and absenteeism. For example, Hackett and Guion (1985) conducted a meta-analysis of 31 studies and found the corrected correlation between job satisfaction and absenteeism to be only $-.09$. This suggests that job satisfaction may play some role in employee absences, but that role is marginal.

Hackett and Guion (1985) offer a number of explanations for the weak relation between job satisfaction and absenteeism. One reason is the measurement of absenteeism itself. Although at first glance absenteeism would appear to be a rather simple variable, it is actually quite complex. For example, when measuring absences, one can distinguish between excused and unexcused absences. Excused absences would be allowed for events such as illnesses and funerals. In unexcused absences, the employee simply does not show up at work. One could argue that job satisfaction would be more likely to play a role in unexcused than in excused absences.

Another reason for the weak relation between satisfaction and absenteeism is that job satisfaction represents a general attitude, whereas absenteeism is a specific form of behavior. For example, a person's attitude toward organized religion (a general attitude) would probably not be a good predictor of attendance at a worship service on one particular day. According to the *Theory of Planned Behavior* (Ajzen[Q6] 1988, 2001), a complex pathway links general attitudes (such as job satisfaction) to actual behavior. For example, variables such as subjective norms (the employee's perception of whether important others expect him or her to go to work) and attitudes toward the behavior of missing work on different occasions may be stronger predictors of absenteeism than overall job satisfaction. Thus, job satisfaction may be weakly related to absenteeism because of a failure to account for unmeasured variables such as normative standards surrounding attendance, as well as attitudes toward being absent from work.

Finally, an issue that absenteeism researchers typically confront is that absenteeism is a behavior that has a low *base rate* (i.e., it doesn't occur frequently). Predicting a variable with a low base rate is problematic because most of the statistical procedures used by organizational psychologists, particularly correlation and regression analysis, are based on the assumption that variables are normally distributed. In most instances in organizational research, the variables examined are not exactly normally distributed, but they do not deviate so far that conventional statistical procedures are seriously biased. However, in the case of absenteeism, distributions may be so skewed that the true relationship between job satisfaction and absenteeism is seriously underestimated when commonly used statistical procedures are used.

Employee Turnover: Another correlate of job satisfaction that is of considerable interest to both researchers and managers is employee turnover. Some turnover in organizations is inevitable and, in some cases, may even be desirable. However, very high levels of turnover can be costly to organizations since they must begin the process of recruiting, selecting, and socializing a new employee. High levels of turnover may also have an adverse impact on the public image of an organization, and hence increase the difficulty of recruiting.

Given the importance of turnover, organizational psychologists have devoted considerable attention to understanding its antecedents. Although some of the work on turnover has been aimed at simply documenting its relation with job satisfaction, much more has been aimed at modeling the role job satisfaction plays in employees' turnover decisions. One of the earliest, and ultimately most influential, models of the turnover process was developed by Mobley (1977). As can be seen in Figure 5.3, this model proposes that employees' decisions to leave a job are complex and consist of multiple stages. In the first stage, an employee evaluates his or her

FIGURE 5.3
Mobley's Model of the Turnover Process

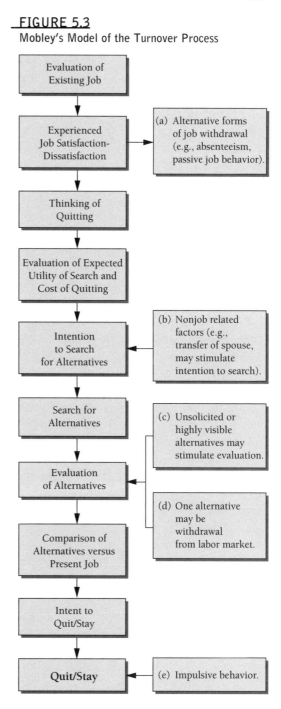

Source: W. H. Mobley. (1977). Intermediate linkages in the relationship between job satisfaction and employee turnover. *Journal of Applied Psychology, 62,* 237–240. Copyright © 1977 by the American Psychological Association. Reprinted with permission.

existing job and, depending on this evaluation, experiences either satisfaction or dissatisfaction. After this evaluation, if the employee is satisfied, the process is unlikely to go further. If the employee is dissatisfied, however, this may lead to thoughts of quitting his or her job. Notice, however, that the model allows for the possibility that employees may express job dissatisfaction through other forms of withdrawal, or by simply putting forth less effort.

Once a dissatisfied employee begins to think about quitting his or her job, the next step in the model is some cognitive evaluation of whether a search will be successful, and the various costs associated with quitting the present job. Even if a person is extremely dissatisfied with a job, leaving entails certain costs—moving to a new location and perhaps giving up benefits accrued in the present job. If an employee decides either that a search would be unsuccessful, or that the cost of leaving the job is too high, the process will end and the employee may simply find ways to adapt to the present situation.

On the other hand, if the employee believes that a search will be successful, and the costs associated with leaving are not prohibitive, he or she will then progress to the next stage in the model: an intention to search for alternatives. This is the point at which a person begins planning the job search, and, in all likelihood, an intention to search will translate into actual search behavior. The employee may post his or her resume on internet job sites such as "Monster.com," seek the services of an employment agency, or attend job fairs, hoping to find alternative employment opportunities. The model allows for the possibility that the intention to search will be motivated by factors other than job dissatisfaction (e.g., desire to live in another location).

After searching for alternatives, a person may find that none is available. This outcome obviously depends on a person's level of qualifications and the availability of jobs in his or her profession. If a person finds no alternatives, he or she may have no choice but to adapt to the present job. If alternatives are available, the next step is to evaluate them. It is also possible that an individual may be presented with employment alternatives suggested in unsolicited offers.

In evaluating different employment alternatives, the model proposes two standards of evaluation. Alternatives are evaluated against the employee's internal standards for judging the acceptability of jobs, as well as his or her present job. Given these two evaluative standards, it is possible that alternatives may exceed a person's internal standards, yet still not measure up to his or her present job. If this is the case, the job search may remind the employee that the "Grass is not necessarily greener on the other side," and the present job may be viewed in a more favorable light. Another possibility, which is acknowledged in the model, is that the individual may withdraw from the labor market completely. For example, a dissatisfied employee may decide to become a stay-at-home parent.

The job search may also result in one or more alternative employment offers that are perceived to be more attractive than the present job. According to the model, if this is the case, the person forms intentions regarding whether to quit the present job. Why don't people automatically quit their present jobs if a better alternative is found? Based on the previously discussed Theory of Planned Behavior, a person may decline a more attractive job offer simply because he or she does not have a positive attitude toward the act of changing jobs. Normative influences may come into play as well. For example, a person may come from a family in which both parents worked for the same organization during their entire careers, and thus may experience subtle (or not so subtle) normative pressure to remain employed with the same organization and not be a *job hopper*.

Another reason that intentions may not translate into actual behavior is that the act of quitting one's job is much different from the idea of quitting. In Figure 5.3, Mobley's (1977) model proposes that, relatively early in the process, an employee should evaluate the costs associated with quitting. It is important to note, however, that early in the process, *quitting* is an abstract concept and not a concrete choice that a person is faced with. Thus, although the model is not very explicit, some reevaluation of the costs of quitting one's job is likely to take place between the intention to quit and the actual quitting. A person may get *cold feet* when faced with a concrete job offer, and may decide that the costs associated with leaving the present job for a better one are not worth it after all. As a final note, the model allows for the possibility that the decision to quit may be made impulsively. Perhaps some readers have had the experience of making an *on-the-spot* decision to quit a job.

Empirical research over the years has supported Mobley's model in two ways. First, studies that have tested the original model, or variants of it, have generally provided support (e.g., Hom, Caranikas Walker, Prussia, & Griffeth, 1992; Michaels & Spector, 1982; Mobley, Griffeth, Hand, & Meglino, 1979). In a recent examination of a similar model, KammeyerMueller, Wanberg, Glomb, and Ahlburg (2005) conducted a study where they examined employees over five distinct points in time over a 2-year period to assess those variables that predicted who left versus remained with the organization. Using Hierarchical Linear Modeling, the authors found that employees who left the organization showed reductions

in work satisfaction and commitment to the organization across the five data-collection periods. In addition, these employees showed increases in work withdrawal behaviors and searching for alternative jobs across the five time periods.

The model has also been supported more indirectly through studies examining the correlation between job satisfaction and turnover. Carsten and Spector (1987) conducted a meta-analysis of 42 studies and found that the corrected correlation between job satisfaction and turnover was −.24. The corrected correlation between behavioral intentions and actual turnover was .32. Tett and Meyer (1993) also conducted a meta-analysis and estimated the correlation to be .27. One would expect intentions to be more strongly correlated with turnover than with job satisfaction because intent is a more proximal cause of job satisfaction (see Figure 5.3).

These authors also examined, albeit indirectly, whether the availability of employment alternatives would influence the relationship between job satisfaction and turnover. Specifically, the authors obtained data on the levels of unemployment that existed in the localities at the time when data for each of the studies were collected. As expected, the corrected satisfaction–turnover and intentions–turnover correlations were both stronger during periods of low (as opposed to high) unemployment. This is presumably due to the fact that alternative employment opportunities are much more plentiful when unemployment is low.

These findings are consistent with the role that job satisfaction is proposed to play in the turnover process. In fact, when one considers that job satisfaction is actually a very distal cause of turnover, and turnover is a low base-rate event, an overall corrected correlation of −.24 to .27 between these two variables is actually quite remarkable. At a more conceptual level, these findings suggest that the desire to find more satisfying work is often a driving force behind job changes. Therefore, organizations wishing to keep turnover to manageable levels cannot ignore job and organizational conditions that impact job satisfaction.

Job Performance: The third correlate of job satisfaction is job performance. Of the numerous variables that researchers have correlated with job satisfaction over the years, job performance has perhaps the longest history. In fact, the attempt to link job satisfaction with job performance can actually be traced back as far as the Hawthorne Studies. Based on their findings, the Hawthorne researchers came to the relatively naïve conclusion that one way to make employees more productive was to make them more satisfied. Stated differently, "A happy worker is a productive worker." This notion that job satisfaction influenced job performance became widely accepted and helped to usher in what was described in Chapter 1 as the *Human Relations* movement within organizational psychology.

Toward the end of the 1950s and in the early 1960s, another trend in organizational psychology—reliance on cognitive processing models—would eventually change the prevailing views on the relationship between job satisfaction and job performance. Vroom's (1964) Expectancy Theory, for example, proposed that employees would put forth more effort if they believed that effort would translate into high levels of performance, and higher performance would lead to valued outcomes. If performance is viewed from this perspective, there is no reason to assume that job satisfaction should play a causal role in determining job performance. On the other hand, if high levels of job performance ultimately lead to

desirable outcomes, employees should be most satisfied with their jobs when they perform well and are rewarded for it. If viewed from this perspective, one would conclude that job performance causes job satisfaction. Thus, rather than trying to make employees happy, organizations would be much better off helping employees develop the skills they need to perform well, and linking rewards to performance.

Unfortunately, much of the early debate surrounding the relation between job satisfaction and job performance was based on opinion instead of empirical data. That basis began to change in the 1970s and 1980s, when there were more empirical investigations of the relation between job satisfaction and job performance. In the mid1980s, many of these empirical studies were summarized in comprehensive meta-analyses by Iaffaldano and Muchinsky (1985) and, later, by Podsakoff and Williams (1986). In the Iaffaldano and Muchinsky investigation, the corrected correlation between job satisfaction and job performance was found to be .17. Podsakoff and Williams obtained very similar results.

Podsakoff and Williams (1986) also found that the satisfaction–performance relation was moderated by the degree to which rewards were linked to performance. In studies where rewards were closely tied to performance, the corrected correlation between job satisfaction and performance was .27. In contrast, in studies where rewards were not closely tied to performance, the corrected correlation was weaker (r = .17). This moderator effect is important because it suggests that when job satisfaction and performance are related, the most plausible causal sequence is from performance to job satisfaction, rather than the reverse. More specifically, if rewards are tied closely to performance, job satisfaction may be a natural byproduct of receiving rewards.

Just when organizational researchers were beginning to doubt whether job satisfaction was a sufficiently strong predictor of job performance, Judge, Thoresen, Bono, and Patton (2001) reviewed past meta-analyses and argued there were limitations with the studies. The authors conducted a new meta-analysis with over 54,000 participants from 312 samples and found the true correlation between job satisfaction and performance was .30. The authors also pointed out that the correlations between job satisfaction and performance varied widely between studies, suggesting there are other variables that determine the strength of the job satisfaction–performance relationship. In their meta-analysis, Judge et al. found that the relationship was especially high when employees had highly complex jobs. Judge et al. proposed an integrative model of the satisfaction–performance relationship that emphasized reciprocal relationships between the two variables as well as mediators and moderators of the satisfaction to performance and performance to satisfaction relationships. The authors argued that future researchers should focus their attention on examining how job satisfaction is related to job performance and factors that enhance versus reduce the strength of the relationship.

Schleicher, Watt, and Greguras (2004) followed these suggestions and uncovered an important moderator of the satisfaction–performance relationship: the affective-cognitive consistency (ACC) of job satisfaction. The authors noted that prior research in the field of attitudes has shown that people who report discrepancies between the affective and cognitive components of an attitude object evidence lower correlations between that attitude and behavior (Kraus, 1995). This point emphasizes that individuals reporting the same level of job satisfaction may hold that attitude with different levels of strength, and that we

should not expect job satisfaction to predict performance if individuals do not exhibit consistency between the different components of job satisfaction.

Remember at the beginning of the chapter we emphasized that job satisfaction entails both positive affect or feelings about one's job as well as cognitive beliefs about one's job. Schleicher et al. (2004) argued that job satisfaction would not predict job performance well when there was inconsistency between these two components (e.g., when employees reported positive affect for their job but exhibited negative thoughts). In fact, the authors found a reasonably strong relationship between job satisfaction and performance when ACC was high, but virtually no relationship when ACC was low. These findings highlight the importance of considering the nature (strength) of job attitudes when examining the ability of job attitudes to predict outcomes like performance, absenteeism, and turnover.

Based on the accumulated empirical research, it is tempting to conclude that the job satisfaction–job performance relationship is unpredictable and variable. However, according to Ostroff (1992), this conclusion may be erroneous because the vast majority of studies examining the relationship between job satisfaction and job performance have been conducted at the individual level of analysis. Ostroff points out that although employees who are highly satisfied with their jobs may not necessarily perform better than employees who are more dissatisfied, this relation may be stronger at the organizational level of analysis. Organizations containing employees who are highly satisfied will tend to perform better than organizations containing employees who are highly dissatisfied. When employees are highly satisfied, they may not be more productive as individuals, but they may nevertheless engage in behaviors that facilitate the effectiveness of the organization as a whole.

Ostroff (1992) tested this hypothesis by examining relations between job satisfaction and several performance indexes in a national sample of 298 junior and senior high schools. As can be seen in Table 5.4, aggregate-level job satisfaction was significantly related to every performance indicator, and the magnitude ranged from −.11 to .44. Many of these correlations are considerably higher than those found in individual-level studies (Iaffaldano & Muchinsky, 1985; Podsakoff & Williams, 1986). Interestingly, Ostroff argued that, at the organizational level, satisfaction likely causes higher levels of performance, which is counter to individual-level studies (Podsakoff & Williams, 1986). Unfortunately, since this study was cross-sectional, the issue could not be addressed.

TABLE 5.4

Correlations between Organization-Level Job Satisfaction and Organization-Level Performance Measures

Performance Measure	Correlation
Reading achievement	.30
Math achievement	.31
Social science achievement	.24
Percentage of students passing courses	.20
Administrative performance	.24
Percentage of students dropping out	−.28
Percentage of students attending	.24
Percentage of students with discipline problems	−.27
Vandalism costs (in dollars)	−.11
Student satisfaction with teachers	.24
Overall student satisfaction	.44

Note: All correlations are statistically significant beyond the .05 level.
Source: C. Ostroff. (1992). The relationship between satisfaction, attitudes, and performance: An organization-level analysis. Journal of Applied Psychology, 77, 963–974. Copyright © 1992 by the American Psychological Association. Adapted with permission.

However, a recent study by Schneider, Hanges, Smith, and Salvaggio (2003) challenges the argument that job satisfaction determines performance at the organizational level. These authors studied 35 companies over 8 years and assessed job satisfaction and objective indexes of company performance (i.e., financial and market share indexes). First of all, the authors found there were significant influences of the company on individual reports of job satisfaction. Secondly, the pattern of relationships between job satisfaction and company performance over time suggested that high levels of company performance were more likely to precede increases in job satisfaction than job satisfaction preceding company performance. These results suggest that highly performing companies end up with employees who are more satisfied than employees who perform poorly. Clearly, organizational psychologists will need to conduct additional research to better understand the causal direction between job satisfaction and job performance at the individual and group levels, as well as variables that influence both relationships. A recent approach to job attitudes as a predictor of important behaviors in organizations combines job satisfaction and organizational commitment into a single measure of job attitude (Harrison, Newman, & Roth, 2006). This approach is considered in the following section on organizational commitment.

ORGANIZATIONAL COMMITMENT

In addition to feelings of satisfaction or dissatisfaction for one's job, employees may develop feelings of attachment or commitment toward the organizations in which they are employed. As with satisfaction or dissatisfaction, a strong case can be made that the tendency to develop attachment or commitment ties extends far beyond the workplace. For example, people commit to each other through marriage and other forms of kinship. Many people also faithfully commit themselves to activities such as exercising, institutions such as churches, and political ideologies such as democracy. Given these vast numbers of commitments, it is not surprising that employees also develop feelings of commitment and attachment toward the organizations in which they work.

Defining Organizational Commitment

At a very general level, *organizational commitment* can be thought of as the extent to which employees are dedicated to their employing organizations and are willing to work on their behalf, and the likelihood that they will maintain membership. Note that in this general definition, one can distinguish between affective commitment and behavioral commitment (Mowday, Porter, & Steers, 1982). Commitment represents both the feelings and the behavioral tendencies that employees have toward the organization.

Meyer and Allen (1991) further refined the definition of organizational commitment by pointing out there can be multiple bases of commitment—that is, employees may be committed for different reasons, and these reasons constitute unique forms of commitment. They proposed a three-component model of commitment consisting of *affective, continuance,* and *normative* commitment. Affective commitment reflects the extent to which employees identify with the organization and feel a genuine sense of loyalty toward it. In contrast, continuance commitment is based on employees' perceptions of the relative investments they have made in the organization, and the relative costs associated with seeking membership in another organization. Normative commitment is based on an employee's feeling of obligation to the organization, wherein remaining a member is the morally right thing to do.

In addition to having multiple bases, employee commitment may be focused at different levels within the organization and may even be directed to outside groups. For example, an employee may feel a sense of commitment toward his or her organization as a whole, the primary work group to which he or she belongs, and perhaps the leader of the group. Many employees in organizations also feel a sense of commitment toward the profession to which they belong. For example, physicians who work for Health Maintenance Organizations (HMOs) are likely to have some level of commitment to their employing organization, but are committed to the medical profession as well.

Meyer and Allen (1997) illustrate the multiple forms of commitment that can occur in a matrix in which the three bases of commitment (affective, continuance, and normative) are crossed with six distinct foci. As can be seen in Figure 5.4, an employee may have feelings of affective, continuance, and/or normative commitment toward any number of foci within the organizational environment. This reflects the fact that, for employees in most organizations, commitment is a multidimensional, complex construct. Thus, if one were to come up to an employee and ask, "How committed are you?" the employee would most likely have a multipart answer.

Measurement of Organizational Commitment

As with most subjective attitudinal variables, organizational commitment is measured with self-report scales. Historically, the first

FIGURE 5.4
The Relationship between Bases and Foci of Commitment

Source: J. P. Meyer and N. J. Allen. (1997). *Commitment in the workplace: Theory, research, and application.* Thousand Oaks, CA: Sage. Reprinted by permission of Sage Publications, Inc.

organizational commitment scale to gain widespread use was the Organizational Commitment Questionnaire (OCQ; Mowday, Steers, & Porter, 1979). The original OCQ primarily reflected what Meyer and Allen (1991) described as affective commitment and, to a lesser extent, normative commitment. The original OCQ also contained one item measuring an employee's turnover intentions. The inclusion of this item prompted criticism, particularly when the OCQ was used to predict turnover. Most researchers who have used the OCQ in recent years have eliminated the turnover intent item. In many cases, researchers have also used shorter versions of the original measure.

In general, there is evidence that the OCQ has desirable psychometric properties. Mathieu and Zajac (1990), in their meta-analysis of 124 organizational commitment studies, reported that the mean internal consistency reliabilities for various forms of the OCQ were all over .80. In this same study, the OCQ was found to correlate appropriately with conceptually related variables, thus providing some support for its construct validity. The major limitation of the OCQ is that it measures primarily the affective component of organizational commitment, and

thus provides very little information on the continuance and normative components. This is an important limitation because these different forms of commitment are associated with different outcomes.

More recently, Allen and Meyer (1990) developed an organizational commitment measure that contains three subscales that correspond to the affective, continuance, and normative components of commitment. An example of an affective commitment item is: "This organization has a great deal of personal meaning to me." An example of a continuance commitment item is: "It would be too costly for me to leave my organization in the near future." Finally, an example of a normative commitment item is: "I would feel guilty if I left my organization now."

Because the Allen and Meyer (1990) scale has been developed more recently than the OCQ, comparatively less evidence has accumulated to support both its reliability and its validity. However, the evidence accumulated to date has been very encouraging. For example, Meyer and Allen (1997) reported that the median internal consistency reliabilities for the affective, continuance, and normative commitment scales are .85, .79, and .73, respectively. They also report that all three scales have exhibited reasonably high levels of temporal stability.

In terms of construct validity, there is also impressive supporting evidence. For example, several studies have supported the three-factor structure of the scale (summarized in Meyer & Allen, 1997). There is also evidence that these forms of commitment are empirically distinguishable from related constructs such as job satisfaction, values, and occupational commitment. The construct validity of Meyer and Allen's measure has also been supported by the pattern of its relationships with other variables. (These will be described in more detail in a later section.) The important point is that the three subscales corresponding to the three different forms of commitment appear to correlate with other variables in an expected manner.

Other than the OCQ and the Allen and Meyer (1990) scales, a handful of other measures of organizational commitment have surfaced, but none has been used extensively. One recent measure worth noting was developed by Becker (1992). In this study, organizational commitment was measured in terms of multiple bases (as per Meyer and Allen) and multiple foci. Few other studies have done this, so there is little empirical evidence on the viability of this approach to measuring commitment. However, in the future, it may be useful to measure commitment in this fashion if, indeed, different outcomes are associated with different combinations of bases and foci of commitment.

Development and Predictors of Organizational Commitment

What determines employees' levels of commitment toward their organizations? Given the complexity of the organizational commitment construct, this is not an easy question to answer. Most researchers have ap-

proached this issue by examining the development of each of the three bases of commitment proposed by Meyer and Allen (1991). If one considers affective commitment, a prediction might be that employees will tend to develop this type of commitment if they perceive that the organization is being supportive and/or treating them in a fair manner (Meyer & Allen, 1991). In fact, research has shown that affective commitment is positively related to variables such as perceived organizational support (POS) and procedural justice. POS simply represents the extent to which the organization is seen as helpful to the employee; in effect, it is "on the employee's side." Recall from the previous chapter that procedural justice reflects the fairness of the procedures organizations use in dealing with employees. Recent research with hospital nurses has revealed that a supportive organizational culture is predictive of affective commitment, especially the culture of the specific ward in which the nurses work (Lok & Crawford, 2001).

Another factor that may influence the development of affective commitment is whether the organization is seen as a source of rewarding outcomes. Research has shown, for example, that a positive relationship exists between affective commitment and variables such as job scope, participative decision making, job autonomy, and perceived competence (Meyer & Allen, 1997). One way to interpret such findings is based on a belief that employees develop feelings of affective commitment if they see the organization as a place where they feel they are important and competent.

Another way some researchers have sought to explain affective commitment is through behavioral commitment and retrospective sense making. Put differently, one might say that employees develop feelings of affective commitment as a retrospective mechanism to justify their tenure in the organization and the level of effort they have expended on its behalf. This explanation of commitment is consistent with Salancik and Pfeffer's (1978) Social Information Processing theory, described earlier in the chapter. In general, retrospective explanations of affective commitment have met with very limited support. However, as Meyer and Allen (1997) point out, this mechanism is quite subtle and thus may be very difficult to test empirically. A study examining this type of explanation would have to be longitudinal, and employees would need to be assessed on multiple occasions (see Zapf et al., 1996).

Compared to affective commitment, explaining the development of continuance commitment is much more straightforward. Most explanations of continuance commitment rely on Becker's (1960) notion of *side bets* as a mechanism committing one to a course of action. If, for example, a person has wagered a bet that he or she would lose 20 pounds over the next 6 months, this would commit the person to that course of action. When this concept is applied to the workplace, we can see very clearly that, over time, employees accumulate a number of *side bets* that commit them to their current employer. For example, the accrual of seniority means that employees may be entitled to special benefits or privileges. If the employee were to leave and work for another employer, such benefits would be forfeited. Also, many employees develop numerous social relationships with their coworkers, and these bonds help to facilitate feelings of belonging and comfort. These feelings would be forfeited in a switch to another employer.

Another proposed determinant of continuance commitment is the extent to which employees *perceive* other viable alternatives to the present employer. The word *perceive* is italicized because it really doesn't matter whether actual alternatives exist; the important thing is an employee's perceptions. Perceptions of alternatives may be influenced by factors in the environment, such as the unemployment rate, but may also be affected by other more subjective factors. For example, an employee's perception of his or her overall competence, level of training, and mobility will all enter into the perception of alternatives. As one might guess, continuance commitment will tend to be higher among employees who perceive few alternatives to the present employer.

Compared to affective and continuance forms of commitment, much less is known about the development of normative commitment. According to Meyer and Allen (1997), personal characteristics and the nature of an employee's transactions with the organization may influence the development of normative commitment. At a personal level, individuals may differ in terms of whether their early socialization emphasized the development of strong loyalty and a sense of moral obligation to their employers. Meyer and Allen also point out that the organization may attempt to instill in employees, during the initial socialization process, a strong sense of moral obligation to the organization.

Perhaps the most powerful determinant of normative commitment is the manner in which an organization treats its employees. When employees enter an organization, an implicit agreement, or a *psychological contract*, exists between them and the organization (e.g., Schein, 1980). A psychological contract essentially represents an employee's perceptions of what he or she feels is reasonable treatment as a member of the organization. One would assume that normative commitment is highest when an employee perceives the organization as honoring its end of the psychological contract. More research, however, is needed before more conclusions can be drawn about the development of this form of commitment.

More recent research has emphasized cross-cultural and ethnic influences on organizational commitment. This type of research has involved examining the level of organizational commitment across countries and assessing whether models of organizational commitment developed with largely United States and western European samples generalize to other populations. Gelade, Dobson, and Gilbert (2006) examined national differences in affective organizational commitment across 49 different countries. The authors also examined country-level predictors of organizational commitment, such as personality attributes, socioeconomic indicators, and values. These authors found that organizational commitment did vary across the 49 countries, with approximately 11% of the variance in scores being a function of nation.

The authors found the highest levels of organizational commitment were shown in countries that were extraverted, low in neuroticism, high in happiness, high in egalitarian values, and low in societal cynicism. The authors found no relationship between affective commitment and gross national income per capita, indicating that making more money does not, by itself, account for organizational commitment across nations.

An example of Meyer and Allen's commitment model being applied to other countries can be found in a study conducted by Lee, Allen, Meyer, and Rhee (2001). These authors examined whether the three-component model discussed previously applied to employees in South Korea. In the first study the authors found that the original Meyer and Allen measure assessing the three forms of commitment

did not generalize well to South Korea, with the Continuance Commitment scale showing especially low reliability. The authors then used items developed by Meyer and his colleagues that avoided North American expressions and were therefore more amenable to translations into other languages. Lee and his colleagues found that with this set of new items the underlying structure (and therefore meaning) of organizational commitment was similar across the two cultures. These results illustrate the importance of ensuring proper translation of organizational constructs when examining cross-cultural similarities and differences.

Consequences of Organizational Commitment

As with job satisfaction, researchers and managers are interested in organizational commitment largely because of its relationship with other variables. In this section, we briefly review evidence on the relationship between organizational commitment and attitudinal variables, absenteeism, turnover, and performance.

Attitudinal Variables: Given Meyer and Allen's (1991) distinction among affective, continuance, and normative commitment, the correlates of each of these forms of commitment are examined separately. Affective commitment has been shown to be strongly related to other work-related attitudes. As mentioned earlier in the chapter, Mathieu and Zajac (1990) found that the mean corrected correlation between affective organizational commitment and job satisfaction was .53. Other consistent attitudinal correlates of affective commitment found in this meta-analysis included job involvement (.36), occupational commitment (.27), union commitment (.24), and stress (.29).

Compared to affective commitment, less empirical work has examined the relation between attitudinal correlates of either continuance or normative commitment (Meyer & Allen, 1997). Based on the little evidence that is available, however, it appears that continuance commitment is correlated with many of the same variables as affective commitment, yet there are some important differences. Mathieu and Zajac (1990), for example, found that affective commitment was more strongly related to job satisfaction and job involvement than was continuance commitment. A more recent meta-analysis by Cooper-Hakim and Viswesvaran (2005) concluded that job satisfaction correlated .47 with affective commitment, .09 with continuance commitment, and .29 with normative commitment.

Absenteeism: Compared to attitudinal correlates, much less evidence exists on the relation between each form of organization commitment and absenteeism. Mathieu and Zajac (1990) found that the corrected correlation between affective commitment and attendance was .12 and the correlation with lateness was .11. These findings suggest that those with high levels of affective commitment tend to exhibit lower levels of absenteeism, but this trend is quite weak. Recall from the previous section that the correlation between absenteeism and job satisfaction is of a similar magnitude (e.g., Hackett & Guion, 1985). As with job satisfaction, this weak relationship may be due to variation in the measurement of absenteeism, as well as more general issues in attitude–behavior consistency. Also, from a conceptual point of view, a high level of affective commitment indicates a desire to contribute to an organization—a desire that may at times be negated by situational contingencies.

Again, compared to affective commitment, little evidence exists on the relations between either continuance or normative commitment and absenteeism. Studies that have been done, however, have shown neither of these forms of commitment to be related to absenteeism (Meyer & Allen, 1997). From a conceptual point of view, these findings are somewhat surprising. For example, if an employee's commitment is of the continuance variety, it is in his or her best interest to attend work on a regular basis; failure to do so could jeopardize his or her membership in the organization. This argument of course is based on the assumption that organizational policy is such that frequent absenteeism would be met with negative consequences. With respect to normative commitment, frequent absenteeism would seem to be inconsistent with commitment based on a strong moral obligation toward one's employing organization. Given the little research that is available, both of these possibilities await examination in future research.

Employee Turnover: Given the nature of organizational commitment, considerably more evidence exists on the relation among all three forms of commitment and turnover. As might be expected, research has generally shown a negative relation among all three forms of commitment and turnover (Allen & Meyer, 1996; CooperHakim & Viswesvaran, 2005; Mathieu & Zajac, 1990). The fact that all forms of commitment are negatively associated with turnover would appear to be a positive thing for organizations. However, this may not be true in some cases. For example, consider an employee who remains in an organization primarily because he or she has a high level of continuance commitment. Is this necessarily good for the organization, or even for the employee? Such an individual may adopt an attitude of doing the bare minimum and may be very unhappy in his or her job. The same may be true for an employee who remains in an organization primarily out of a sense of moral obligation (e.g., normative commitment).

A recent study on organizational commitment and turnover adopted a longitudinal approach, assessing employees at five points over a 2-year period (Kammeyer-Mueller et al., 2005). At each point the authors assessed perceived costs of leaving the company, organizational commitment, critical events experienced by the employee (e.g., mistreatment), and other factors. Using survival analysis, the authors found that organizational commitment (assessed by Mowday & Steer's measure) was a significant predictor of turnover over time.

Job Performance: Much research over the years has investigated the relation between organizational commitment and job performance. In general, affective commitment has been shown to be positively related to job performance, although the magnitude of this relation is not strong (CooperHakim & Viswesvaran, 2005; Mathieu & Zajac, 1990; Meyer & Allen, 1997). Determining the mechanism(s) behind these relations is difficult, however, because these studies have used a wide variety of performance criterion measures. For example, some have used supervisors' ratings of overall performance (e.g., Konovsky & Cropanzano, 1991), others have used objective indexes such as cost control (e.g., Shim & Steers, 1994), and others have utilized self-ratings of performance (e.g., Baugh & Roberts, 1994). One commonality among these studies, however, is that the relation between affective commitment and performance is mediated by employees' effort. Employees who possess

high levels of affective commitment tend to work harder and exert more effort than employees who possess lower levels of affective commitment. In some cases, this higher level of effort will translate into higher levels of performance, although this is not always the case (Campbell, 1990, 1994).

This link between affective commitment and effort suggests that commitment is positively related to performance when employees possess adequate ability, when performance is primarily determined by motivation, and when employees have some level of control over performance. This explains why researchers have generally found that affective commitment predicts organizational citizenship behavior (OCB) better than inrole performance (Meyer & Allen, 1997; Organ & Ryan, 1995). Recall from the previous chapter that because OCB is largely motivationally based, employees have greater control over it than they do over inrole performance.

Compared to affective organizational commitment, considerably less research has examined the performance-related implications of either continuance or normative commitment. Meyer and Allen (1997) point out, however, that most of the available empirical research has shown that neither of these forms of commitment is strongly related to either inrole performance or OCB (see also Cooper-Hakim & Viswesvaran, 2005). Furthermore, it is difficult to come up with a conceptual justification for why they would be related to performance. For example, there is no reason why continuance commitment would prompt an employee to exert high levels of effort or go appreciably beyond his or her required job duties.

It is somewhat more plausible that high levels of normative commitment would engender high levels of effort toward organizational goals. One can also make an equally plausible counter argument that commitment based on employees' feelings of obligation would not necessarily lead to greater levels of effort on behalf of the organization. To the contrary, one can even imagine that an employee who feels compelled to remain in an organization out of a sense of obligation may even grow to resent that organization and perhaps be compelled to engage in counterproductive behaviors (see Chapter 6).

Sinclair, Tucker, Cullen, and Wright (2005) have recently examined the interesting idea that profiles on affective and continuance commitment may be associated with in-role and extra-role performance. These authors pointed out that no prior research has examined how combinations of affective and continuance commitment might predict outcomes. The authors used cluster analysis to identify four different employee profiles relevant to commitment: allied (medium affective and continuance commitment), free agents (medium continuance and low affective commitment), devoted (high affective and continuance commitment), and complacent (medium affective and low continuance). The authors found relatively strong correlations between affective and continuance commitment and in-role and extra-role performance. In addition, the authors found that the *devoted* employees were rated especially high by their supervisors on measures of in-role and extra-role performance compared to the other groups.

Combining Organizational Commitment and Job Satisfaction to Predict Performance

So far in this chapter we have treated organizational commitment and job satisfaction as two separate constructs, in keeping with the vast majority of thinking and research in organizational psychology. However, a recent

meta-analysis by Harrison et al. (2006) examined the effects of combining organizational commitment and job satisfaction into an *overall job attitude*. These authors then assessed the ability of this overall job attitude to predict a combined measure of work-relevant behavior assessing such behaviors as task performance, extra-role performance, and turnover. The logic behind this approach is similar to that described earlier in the chapter by Ajzen (1988), who argued that general measures of attitudes will be most related to general measures of behavior. Harrison et al. found that a measure of overall job attitude correlated with overall work-relevant behavior at .59, providing strong evidence that job attitudes are linked to broad measures of behaviors that employees engage in at work. There is no doubt that this recent finding will reinvigorate research on the importance of job attitudes.

Practical Applications of Commitment Research

One way to view the applications of organizational commitment research is to examine various ways in which organizations may engender high levels of commitment among their employees. Meyer and Allen (1997) describe several different human resources policies that may influence employee commitment. For example, it has long been recommended that during the selection and recruitment processes, organizations provide realistic information to potential employees (Wanous, 1973). Retention has typically been cited as the rationale for using realistic job previews, but Meyer and Allen point out that realistic job previews may also engender employee commitment. Employees who are provided with candid information will presumably feel that the organization has "laid its cards on the table," and the employees are able to make informed choices about whether to join the organization. Such feelings of free choice may enhance employees' feelings of commitment to the organization.

Providing realistic job previews may also facilitate commitment for more symbolic reasons. If an organization is honest, even about the undesirable aspects of a job, recruits have a signal that the organization is going to treat them in a fair and honest manner in the future. When these recruits become employees, they will likely *reciprocate* such honesty and fairness with high levels of commitment. Conversely, if an employee feels that he or she was provided with an overly positive picture of the job prior to being hired, this signals a lack of fairness and honesty in the organization.

After employees enter an organization, their initial socialization and training experiences may have a strong impact on their ultimate level of commitment. Recall from Chapter 3 that organizations use a multitude of strategies to socialize new employees (Van Maanen & Schein, 1979), and that new employees may use a variety of strategies to obtain information (Miller & Jablin, 1991). Meyer and Allen (1997) point out that an investiture approach to socialization is likely to lead to greater feelings of organizational commitment than a divestiture approach. Recall that when an investiture approach is used, the organization does not require the newcomer to completely give up his or her old self. Rather, the organization allows the newcomer to be a full-fledged member while still maintaining some individuality. What message does this convey? The newcomer receives a message of affirmation and a willingness, on the part of the organization, to respect the rights of employees. Employees will often respond to this message with

greater feelings of commitment toward the organization.

A divestiture approach to socialization, in contrast, requires the newcomer to essentially give up many aspects of his or her prior identity and "fall in line" in order to assume full membership in the organization. This form of socialization may suggest to the newcomer that the organization is *elite*, and that achieving membership should be viewed as a great privilege. On the other hand, it may also convey an unhealthy mistrust of outsiders and a condescending view of newcomers. Given these mixed messages, it would seem possible that divestiture socialization could lead to either very high or very low levels of commitment.

In most recent empirical research on the socialization process (e.g., Chao et al., 1994; Ostroff & Kozlowski, 1992), a consistent finding is that the greatest initial concern of newcomers is to acquire task-related information. Before newcomers learn about things such as the political climate of the organization they want to be able to carry out their job-related tasks in a competent manner. Given these initial concerns, organizations must make sure that new employees receive the training they need in order to do their jobs. Such training may require a formal training program or more informal on-the-job coaching activities.

Training may enhance organizational commitment because it conveys to newcomers that the organization is supportive and has a vested interest in their success. Another reason is: If training ultimately facilitates an employee's success, this will likely result in positive outcomes for the employee (e.g., pay increases, promotions). If employees recognize that the training they have received has contributed to their success, they are likely to be grateful to the organization. Such feelings of gratitude may very well enhance the employee's affective or normative commitment.

Training may also contribute to enhanced feelings of continuance commitment. If an employee received training that was highly specific to a particular organization, this would greatly enhance the cost associated with leaving the organization. As an example, much of the training that military personnel receive is so highly specialized that it does not transfer well to civilian jobs. For some individuals, this may enhance feelings of continuance commitment and ultimately contribute to a decision to pursue a longterm military career.

Given this apparent tradeoff between providing general versus highly specific training, which course of action should an organization choose? Training that is highly transferable will likely engender feelings of affective commitment toward the organization. A potential drawback, however, is that such training often does enhance employees' marketability. Highly specific training will enhance employees' job performance, and thus may have the potential to enhance feelings of affective or normative commitment. This form of training may also heighten feelings of continuance commitment, and thus enhance employee retention. However, organizations probably do not want employees to remain in the organization primarily because of feelings of continuance commitment. Ultimately, it is probably best for organizations to have some balance between general and organization-specific training programs.

The development of internal promotion policies is another area in which organizations can make tangible use of organizational commitment research. As Meyer and Allen (1997) point out, promoting from within an organization facilitates higher levels of commitment among employees. If an organization does pursue an internal promotion policy, some important issues must be addressed. Perhaps most important, any internal promotion initiatives should be publicly made available to all employees. If employees see internal promotion practices as being unfair and secretive, the unintended effect may be a reduction of employees' commitment. It also makes little sense to make promotional opportunities available to employees if the organization fails to help them acquire the skills necessary to be competitors for such opportunities. As was discussed previously, skill acquisition can certainly be facilitated by formal training programs. However, to provide employees with meaningful developmental experiences, organizations may utilize other methods, such as lateral transfers or job rotation.

Organizations often utilize organizational commitment research in the area of compensation and benefits. Although there is some degree of variation, most organizations tie their forms of compensation to employee tenure. It is quite common, for example, for organizations to require that employees accrue some minimum years of service before they can be vested in pension programs and receive matching contributions in 401(k) savings plans. Such requirements may enhance commitment, but it is primarily of the continuance variety. Thus, having such requirements may induce employees to remain in the organization but will not necessarily motivate them to work harder on its behalf.

A more creative way that organizations may use compensation to enhance employees' commitment is through the use of profit sharing or employee stock ownership plans (ESOPS; Lawler & Jenkins, 1992). The idea behind such plans is that employees benefit from the increased profitability of the organization as a whole. This presumably helps employees to see *the big picture* and work for the good of the entire organization. It is also possible that such compensation programs may enhance all three forms of organizational commitment. Having *ownership* in the organization may evoke feelings of pride and identification that may ultimately facilitate the employee's affective commitment. Feelings of ownership may also evoke a strong sense of responsibility and moral obligation toward the organization; hence, normative commitment may be heightened. Because employees in such compensation systems stand to lose financially if they leave the organization, continuance commitment may also be enhanced. These plans are discussed in more detail in Chapter 9.

CHAPTER SUMMARY

In this chapter, we examined employee job satisfaction and the related topic of organizational commitment. Both topics are important, for theoretical and practical reasons. Job satisfaction is generally defined as employees' feelings of affect toward their jobs or job situations, but may also contain cognitive and behavioral components. Given the way job satisfaction is defined, the vast majority of measures of job satisfaction have come in the form of self-reports. Measures range from the very general Faces Scale to other measures that allow researchers to assess employees' satisfaction with various facets of the work environment. As with any scales, measures of job satisfaction must be evaluated on the basis of construct validity. Two scales for which considerable evidence of construct validity has accumulated are the Job Descriptive Index (JDI) and the Minnesota Satisfaction Questionnaire (MSQ). More recently, the Job Satisfaction Survey (JSS) has shown considerable potential as a valid measure of job satisfaction.

Traditionally, the characteristics of jobs, and other aspects of the work environment, have explained differences in job satisfaction. In general, job satisfaction tends to be highest when the characteristics of a job match the employees' expectations in areas that are deemed important. In recent years, it has been proposed that job satisfaction is due to cues from the social environment, as well as stable dispositions. In reality, job satisfaction is likely the result of a complex interaction among job characteristics, social cues, and dispositions, in addition to the culture in which employees are raised.

Research has shown that job satisfaction is consistently related to other measures of positive and negative affect. Evidence suggests, however, that job satisfaction is only a very weak predictor of absenteeism. Job satisfaction has been found to be related to turnover, albeit indirectly and only when employees perceive the existence of alternative employment opportunities. In general, research suggests that the relationship between job satisfaction and job performance is not strong. Under certain conditions, such as when rewards are directly tied to performance, there is evidence that the two may be more strongly related. Evidence also suggests that job satisfaction is a much better predictor of organizational citizenship behavior than it is of inrole performance. It has also been shown that the satisfaction–performance relationship may be stronger at the aggregate rather than the individual level.

Organizational commitment reflects employees' feelings of loyalty toward the organization and their willingness to maintain membership. Employees may be committed because they have positive feelings toward the organization (affective), because they realize that the costs of leaving outweigh the benefits (continuance), or because they feel morally obligated to stay (normative).

PEOPLE BEHIND THE RESEARCH

PAUL SPECTOR AND OUTCOMES OF JOB SATISFACTION

Soon after I completed graduate school in 1975, I read *Work and Well-Being* by Peter Warr and Toby Wall that talked about the link between stressful job conditions and employee health and well-being. Inspired by that book, I conducted a study that showed how job satisfaction related to physical health symptoms. Unfortunately, I did not have much luck publishing that study as the field was not very interested in the new area of job stress. I then turned my attention to the link between job satisfaction and turnover with better publication success.

From this work we learned that job dissatisfaction is an important antecedent to turnover; people who dislike their jobs are likely to quit. However, the relationship between job satisfaction and turnover is moderated by the job market. In other words, unhappy people can only quit when they can find other work. Thus job dissatisfaction can produce a desire to quit, but people will only quit when they find alternative employment.

In the middle 1980s I returned to studying the role of job satisfaction in the job stress process. This has resulted in a research program of more than 20 years linking job satisfaction to other variables, including stressful job conditions, counterproductive work behavior (e.g., aggression at work, sabotage, and theft), negative emotions, and physical health symptoms. Much of the early work was done with one of this book's authors, Steve Jex. We looked at interpersonal conflict and organizational constraints, two stressful conditions of work that were not being studied. We showed how they related, not only to job satisfaction, but both behavior and health as well. We also to research showing that the personality variable of neuroticism had a complex role in the process linking stressful job conditions to job satisfaction. For example, we learned that people high in neuroticism tended to be found in jobs that were of lower quality than people who were low in neuroticism. Thus individuals high in this personality trait have good reason to be less satisfied with their jobs.

Although I have studied many variables in the workplace, most of my studies have included a measure of job satisfaction. This is because job satisfaction is a contributor to many important human phenomena in the workplace.

Paul E. Spector
Department of Psychology
University of South Florida

Affective and normative commitment can be explained largely on the basis of equity theory. Feelings of commitment represent employees' desires to reciprocate what they consider fair and equitable treatment at the hands of the organization. Continuance commitment, on the other hand, is due largely to employees' perceptions of *sunk costs* and the extent of alternatives.

Historically, the most popular measure of organizational commitment has been the Organizational Commitment Questionnaire (OCQ). A major limitation of the OCQ, however, is that it measures only affective commitment. More recently, Allen and Meyer (1990) have developed a scale that measures all three forms of commitment. Although this scale is relatively new, evidence to date has shown that it has excellent psychometric properties. This scale will likely be the most widely used measure in future organizational commitment research.

Commitment has also been studied in order to predict other variables. Affective commitment has been found to be consistently related to other attitudinal variables. Research, however, has not supported a strong link with absenteeism. This form of commitment has been found most strongly related to turnover—a finding that is not surprising, given the nature of this construct. Affective commitment appears to be related to performance only to the extent to which it increases employee effort. Although considerably less research has been conducted on continuance and normative commitment, most studies have shown that these are primarily related to turnover. Recent research suggests that profiles of employees on different types of commitment may be an especially strong predictor of performance. In addition, recent research highlights the importance of potentially combining job satisfaction and organizational commitment into an overall measure of job attitude.

Commitment research also has a number of practical applications. Organizations may impact employees' feelings of commitment during the socialization process, as well as through other human resources manage-ment policies. In general, human resources management practices that convey a high level of organizational support tend to be associated with high levels of affective and normative commitment. Practices that increase employees' *sunk costs* tend to engender feelings of continuance commitment. Organizations are typically best served by achieving some balance among affective, continuance, and normative commitment among their employees.

SUGGESTED ADDITIONAL READINGS

CooperHakim, A., & Viswesvaran, C. (2005). The construct of work commitment: Testing an integrative framework. *Psychological Bulletin, 131,* 241–259.

Harrison, D. A., Newman, D. A., & Roth, P. L. (2006). How important are job attitudes? Metaanalytic comparisons of integrative behavioral outcomes and time sequences. *Academy of Management Journal, 49,* 305–325.

Ilies, R., & Judge, T. A. (2003). On the heritability of job satisfaction: The mediating role of personality. *Journal of Applied Psychology, 88,* 750–759.

Judge, T. A., Thoresen, C. J., Bono, J. E., & Patton, G. K. (2001). The job satisfaction-job performance relationship: A qualitative and quantitative review. *Psychological Bulletin, 127,* 376–407.

Meyer, J. P., Allen, N. J., & Smith, C. A. (1993). Commitment to organizations and occupations: Extension and test of a three-component conceptualization. *Journal of Applied Psychology, 78,* 538–551.

Sanchez, J. I., Korbin, W. P., & Viscarra, D. M. (1995). Corporate support in the aftermath of a natural disaster: Effects on employee strains. *Academy of Management Journal, 38,* 504–521.

Chapter Six

Employees typically behave in ways that contribute positively to the goals of their employing organizations. That is, employees perform their jobs to the best of their abilities, occasionally go above and beyond the call of duty, and may even come up with innovative and creative ideas on their own. Employees tend to engage in such productive behaviors because organizations are selective in their hiring and, as will be shown in subsequent chapters, often set up motivational and leadership systems that encourage such forms of behavior.

However, employees may also, at times, engage in behaviors that run counter to organizational goals. Common forms of counterproductive behavior in organizations include ineffective job performance, absenteeism, turnover, and unsafe behavior. Other forms of counterproductive behavior include antisocial behaviors such as theft, violence, substance use, and sexual harassment. Although less common, these forms of behavior may be quite destructive and ultimately costly to organizations.

This chapter examines counterproductive behavior in organizations. In covering these forms of behavior, the emphasis will be on understanding both the causes and the consequences of such behaviors. A related objective is to explore ways in which an organization can eliminate these behaviors or at least keep them at a level that is not too destructive to the goals of the organization.

Counterproductive Behavior in Organizations

DEFINING COUNTERPRODUCTIVE BEHAVIOR

Most readers have probably received poor service at a restaurant, or experienced the inconvenience of a long wait, brought about by poor scheduling or staffing shortages, at a doctor's office. While obviously annoying, these experiences represent relatively mild forms of counterproductive behavior in organizations. More dramatic forms of counterproductive behavior, such as criminal activity or violence, may have very negative consequences and become very newsworthy events. For example, when a government employee commits espionage, national security may be compromised, and media attention surrounding such a crime is typically intense. Likewise, when a disgruntled employee enters an organization and fatally assaults several coworkers, lives are permanently altered, and the event receives considerable media attention.

The specific examples in the preceding paragraph are all different, but each represents a form of *counterproductive behavior* in organizations. For the purposes of this chapter, *counterproductive behavior* will be defined as behavior that explicitly runs counter to the goals of an organization. This definition is based on a number of underlying assumptions. For example, it is assumed that organizations have multiple goals and objectives. A major goal of private organizations is profitability, but such organizations may have many others as well. These may include a high level of customer service, a harmonious work environment, and the reputation of being socially responsible. According to the previous definition, if an employee engages in behaviors that make it more difficult for an organization to achieve any of its goals, the employee is engaging in counterproductive behavior.

The previous definition also makes no assumptions regarding the motives underlying counterproductive behavior, although much of the research on counterproductive behavior is focused on this very issue (Schat & Kelloway, 2005). A retail employee who steals merchandise from his or her employer is obviously doing it intentionally and, most likely, for personal gain. On the other hand, it is entirely possible for an employee to engage in counterproductive behavior without intending to. For example, an employee who is poorly trained or who lacks job-related abilities may want very badly to perform well, but may not accomplish that goal.

Finally, the previous definition makes no assumption as to the causes underlying counterproductive behavior. Recall from Chapter 4 that productive behaviors likely result from a complex interaction between characteristics of individuals and characteristics of the environment. This same perspective is adopted in the examination of counterproductive behavior. In fact, one can make a strong argument for a person-by-environment interaction for literally all forms of counterproductive behavior (Fox & Spector, 1999). When an employee performs his or her job poorly, this may be due to limited ability, but may also be partially caused by poor task design. Likewise, when an employee engages in a violent act at work, this may be due to deep-seated psychiatric problems, but may also be exacerbated by an authoritarian organizational climate.

Based on the definition provided, there are undoubtedly many forms of counterproductive behaviors in organizations. In organizational psychology, however, only a handful of these behaviors have received empirical scrutiny. The most commonly studied counterproductive behaviors have been ineffective job performance, absenteeism, turnover, and accidents. More recently, organizational researchers have begun to examine several other forms of counterproductive behavior that are less common, but are potentially more devastating to organizations. These include theft, violence, substance use, and sexual harassment.

INEFFECTIVE JOB PERFORMANCE

Most people who go to work each day want to do their jobs well, and for good reason. High levels of performance are often associated with positive tangible outcomes such as merit increases, cash bonuses, promotional opportunities, and the like. Performing well may also lead to intangible rewards such as praise and admiration from others, and a heightened sense of personal accomplishment. Despite all the logical reasons for performing well, some employees do not perform up to par. Ineffective job performance is often a difficult issue for organizations, for a number of reasons. For example, in many cases, it may be difficult for an organization to detect ineffective performance in the first place. Once detected, it is often challenging to diagnose the cause of the performance problem. Finally, organizations often struggle with the issue of how to respond to, and prevent, instances of ineffective performance. Each of these issues is discussed in the following paragraphs.

Detection of Ineffective Performance

Recall from Chapter 4 that models of job performance propose that behaviors constituting job performance may be categorized into a number of different types, such as core tasks that are specific to the job, and more general or peripheral tasks. Ideally, all organizations would have in place performance measurement systems that would allow assessment of the many behaviors that constitute the performance domain. If this were the case, a routine performance appraisal would be quite useful in the detection of ineffective performance. Unfortunately, most performance measurement systems typically provide information about the *impact* of employee behavior, but far less information about the behaviors themselves.

Performance-related data that organizations typically collect may be classified into four different types: *personnel data, production data, subjective evaluations,* and more recently *electronic performance monitoring.* Personnel data include items such as absences, sick days, tardiness, disciplinary actions, and safety violations. Some of these, as will be shown later in the chapter, are counterproductive behaviors for which personnel data provide a direct measure. Personnel data may also, at times, provide useful information in the diagnosis of the cause of performance problems. For example, an employee who is absent or late may have a substance abuse problem that ultimately negatively impacts his or her performance.

Production data provide an organization with useful information about tangible outcomes associated with job performance. The most commonly used form of production data is probably sales commissions, although production indexes may be used in many other settings. As a means of detecting ineffective job performance, there are clearly advantages to using production data. Such data provide organizations with an objective performance metric that an employee cannot dispute (i.e., numbers don't lie). Such data are also typically not costly to obtain because they are often collected for multiple purposes.

A potential drawback with production data is that they often provide an overly simplistic view of employee performance. A salesperson may exhibit reduced sales commissions in a particular year, yet these numerical data provide an organization with little information about the source of the performance problem. Also, in the first author's experience, reliance on production

COMMENT 6.1

THE IMPORTANCE OF PERFORMANCE FEEDBACK

WITHOUT A DOUBT, one of the least favorite tasks of managers and supervisors is conducting annual or semiannual performance reviews. This is particularly true when an employee is performing poorly. Ironically, though, performance reviews have the potential to provide the greatest benefit to those employees who are not performing well—provided they are done well.

Research on conducting performance reviews has shown that there are several attributes of an effective performance review. One of the most important of these, particularly for a poorly performing employee, is that the tone of the review should be constructive rather than punitive. An employee who is performing poorly is likely to respond much more favorably to a supervisor who says, "What can I do to help you improve?" than to a supervisor who lists all of the things that the employee is doing poorly.

It is also very important that the feedback provided to an employee is specific and is focused on behavior. Telling a poorly performing employee that he or she has a "bad attitude" doesn't provide that employee with much diagnostic information. On the other hand, telling the same individual that he or she often does not thank customers after completing a transaction is much more specific and, more importantly, is something the individual can change.

Finally, research has also shown that performance reviews should be conducted separately from salary reviews. When the performance and salary reviews are conducted together (which is common), most people tend to focus disproportionately on the size of their salary increase. Unfortunately, what ends up receiving much less attention in comparison is performance feedback and, if necessary, suggestions for improvement. This is particularly unfortunate for employees performing poorly; these individuals stand to benefit the most from focusing on performance.

Source: H. H. Meyer, E. Kay, and J. R. P. French, Jr. (1965). Split roles in performance appraisal. *Harvard Business Review, 43*, 123–129.

data may lead supervisors to adopt a somewhat callous attitude toward subordinates who are experiencing a performance problem. The response to reduced sales commissions may be: "Increase your sales, or else!"

By far the most common form of employee performance data comes from subjective appraisals. Most typically, an employee's immediate supervisor(s) completes some performance appraisal instrument on an annual or semiannual basis. In considering subjective appraisals, it is important to keep in mind that what is actually being measured in most cases is the result of employees' behavior, or, more specifically, employee

effectiveness (Pritchard, 1992). To be sure, some organizations may invest the time and effort required to develop and implement elegant behaviorally based performance appraisal systems. Most organizations, however, still tend to rely on performance appraisal instruments that utilize rather general dimensions of employee performance and engage in rather minimal efforts to train raters (Cascio, 1998).

As a method of detecting ineffective performance, subjective appraisals have certain advantages when compared to either personnel data or production indexes. Compared to production data, a supervisor's thoughtful consideration of an employee's performance may provide considerably greater insight into the root causes of ineffective employee performance. Also, if appraisals are performed well and the information is regularly transmitted to employees (e.g., Meyer, Kay, & French, 1965), they may prevent ineffective performance before it occurs (see Comment 6.1).

Despite these potential advantages, subjective appraisals are often of marginal value in the detection of ineffective performance. Because many organizations still utilize performance appraisal instruments that assess very global performance dimensions, such ratings may often fail to reveal performance problems. Also, despite the considerable technical advances in performance appraisal methodology over the past 25 years (e.g., Borman, 1991; Murphy & Cleveland, 1990), many organizations still administer performance appraisals very poorly or simply ignore them.

A final method of detecting ineffective performance, and in some cases other forms of counterproductive behavior, is *electronic performance monitoring* (Zweig & Webster, 2002). It is common, for example, for employees in customer service call centers to be monitored by supervisors when they interact with customers on the telephone. Research has shown that electronic performance monitoring can be an effective method of detecting ineffective performance, particularly when employees know in advance that it is taking place (Hovorka-Mead, Ross, Whipple, & Renchin, 2002). However, it has also been shown that many employees view it as an invasion of privacy (Aiello & Kolb, 1995).

Causes of Ineffective Performance

Let's assume for the moment that an instance of ineffective performance has been detected. A salesperson has failed to meet his or her quota for 3 consecutive months; a clerical employee repeatedly makes mistakes on his word-processing assignments; a university professor repeatedly receives negative assessments of his or her teaching performance. In each of these cases, all we know is that the employee is not performing up to par. What is often *not* known is why the employee is performing poorly.

In many organizational settings, the underlying causes of ineffective performance are often unclear. As a result, the cause(s) of ineffective performance must be determined by attributional processes; that is, after observing some instance of ineffective performance, a supervisor must make some judgment about the cause(s) of this behavior. *Attribution theory* suggests that people make use of several pieces of information when determining the causes of another person's behavior (Kelley, 1973). For instance, people examine the consistency of behavior over time, between different settings or contexts, and in comparison to others. Thus, if an instance of poor performance were encountered, a supervisor would ask questions such as: Is the poor performance consistent with this employee's past performance? Does he/she perform poorly on all aspects of the job or just certain ones? Is the level of performance poor compared to other employees?

If a supervisor is able to find answers to these three questions, he or she is likely to make some determination as to the cause of the ineffective performance. Generally speaking, if the ineffective performance is consistent over time and settings, and is seen as poor in relation to others, a logical conclusion would be that the ineffective performance was due to a lack of ability or motivation, both of which are internal to the employee. In contrast, if the ineffective performance is not a consistent pattern over time and settings, and is not seen as being poor in relations to others, a supervisor would likely conclude that the ineffective performance was due to factors external to the individual (e.g., poor task design, interruptions from others).

Unfortunately the attribution process is not always accurate. Furthermore, people may in fact hold certain biases in assessing the causes of others' behavior. The best known of these is termed the *fundamental attribution error* (Ross, 1977) and refers to the bias toward attributing the causes of others' behavior to internal, as opposed to external, causes. Although the reasons for this bias are complex, the basic issue is that, in most situations, people are more distinctive than the situations they are in. Thus, when any behavior occurs, there is a tendency to focus on personal (as opposed to situational) factors being the cause.

There is evidence that the fundamental attribution error may impact diagnoses of ineffective performance, although several factors may influence it. For example, in a laboratory study, Mitchell and Kalb (1982) found that supervisors who lacked experience in the tasks their subordinates performed tended to attribute poor performance to internal causes. In contrast, those with more task experience made more external attributions. In another laboratory study, Ilgen, Mitchell, and Frederickson (1981) found that supervisors who were highly interdependent with subordinates tended to make more external attributions for ineffective performance; supervisors who saw little interdependence tended to make more internal attributions.

Understanding the attributional processes involved in determining the causes of ineffective performance is important because such attributions may have a strong impact on supervisory responses to ineffective performance. For example, if a supervisor sees the cause of the ineffective performance as being poor task design, his or her response may be quite different than if it is seen as due to a lack of effort. Ilgen et al. (1981) found that supervisors responded to ineffective performance more favorably when they attributed it to external (versus internal) causes. It has also been shown that supervisors react more favorably to ineffective performance when they perceive it as being caused by a lack of ability, as opposed to a lack of motivation (Podsakoff, 1982). This is presumably because employees have less control of the former than the latter.

For the moment, we'll take as a given that determining the cause(s) of ineffective performance often requires the use of imperfect attributional processes. What then are the most common causes of ineffective performance? To answer this question, it is useful again to think back to Chapter 4 and the discussion of the causes of productive behaviors, such as job performance. Based on this vast literature, it can be concluded that ineffective performance may be due to employees' inability to perform their jobs effectively (e.g., lack of ability, lack of skills, poor training), lack of willingness to perform effectively (e.g., unwilling to put forth or sustain effort, putting efforts in the wrong direction), or aspects of the environment that prevent the employee from performing well (e.g., poor task design, ineffective co-workers).

In examining each of these causes of ineffective performance, there are tangible organizational activities that may contribute to them. Despite the advances that have been made in employee selection (Guion & Highhouse, 2004), selection is still an imperfect process. As a result *selection errors* may result in organizations hiring individuals who lack either the skills or the abilities necessary to perform their jobs. Selection errors may also occur when employees possess the requisite skills and abilities necessary to perform their jobs, but simply do not fit well into the culture of the organization (Kristof, 1996).

How can organizations avoid selection errors? At the risk of sounding overly simplistic, organizations simply need to put a systematic effort into employee hiring. While many organizations clearly do this, many others do not. More to the point, many organizations simply fail to gather and utilize data that would help them make more informed hiring decisions. Although a complete exploration of the employee selection is clearly beyond the scope of this chapter (see Guion & Highhouse, 2004, for complete coverage), selection errors may often be avoided by the systematic use of tests, personal history information, and background/reference checks.

Another way in which organizations may contribute to ineffective performance is through *inadequate socialization and training*. As was pointed out in Chapter 3, when employees first enter an organization, they typically need to be trained on specific job-related skills, as well as more general information about the culture of the organization (Goldstein & Ford, 2002). Employees who receive either inadequate training or no training at all may be set up for failure when they enter an organization. In such an environment, only those who have very high levels of ability and self-confidence may survive.

With respect to socialization, organizations may make a number of errors that could lead to poor performance among employees. Specifically, failing to provide new employees with information about important aspects of the culture of the organization may lead to failure. For example, if the

culture of an organization is such that timely completion of work is highly valued, a new employee may inadvertently perform poorly by not completing work on time. Typically, this type of situation is resolved when the new employee realizes the value of timeliness.

A more problematic situation occurs when new employees receive *mixed signals* about the culture of the organization and how this relates to performance expectations. Both authors have found that this is a typical problem for faculty at medium-size regional universities. Because such institutions do offer a limited number of doctoral programs, some faculty and administrators feel that an organizational culture that places a strong emphasis on research is appropriate. On the other hand, many institutions this size have historically placed a strong emphasis on undergraduate education, so many others feel that the culture should place a strong emphasis on teaching excellence and availability to undergraduate students. Although such differences in philosophy may sometimes lead to insightful dialogue, they often prove to be very confusing to new faculty members who must decide where to focus their efforts.

Finally, in some cases, employees may want to perform well but are prevented from doing so because of constraints in the environment. For example, an employee's job tasks may be designed in a way that makes it difficult to perform well, or in a way that is incompatible with the organization's reward systems (Campion & Berger, 1990; Campion & Thayer, 1985). For example, if it is crucial for an employee to make independent judgments in order to perform effectively, it would not make sense to design the job in a way that denies this employee decision-making authority. Even if tasks are designed properly, other constraining forces in the work environment may hinder performance (Peters & O'Connor, 1980; Spector & Jex, 1998). For example, employees may be unable to perform well because of interruptions from others, poor tools or equipment, and perhaps poor information from others.

Management of Ineffective Performance

Given the multitude of factors that may contribute to ineffective performance, managers need to investigate its causes when it occurs. Thus, as a first step toward investigating ineffective performance, managers should talk to the employee. Perhaps more importantly, such discussions should involve considerable listening on the part of the manager (Meyer et al., 1965). Depending on the outcome of the conversation with the poorly performing employee, a number of corrective actions may be utilized by the manager to improve performance. In some cases, it may be possible to improve an employee's performance through relatively straightforward *training interventions*. For example, if an employee is consistently producing poor-quality written reports, a logical way to improve performance might involve some form of training aimed at improving his or her written communication skills.

In other cases, the underlying cause(s) of ineffective performance may not be as obvious. Let's say, for example, that a real estate salesperson is failing to produce acceptable commissions. For a sales manager to accurately diagnose the cause of this particular performance problem, he or she may need to actually observe the employee trying to close a sale. This type of activity may be thought of as *on-the-job coaching* of the employee. Coaching is a form of training, but it is much more extensive and time consum-

ing. The manager who provides coaching to employees is engaged in a form of active learning that may involve examining all aspects of the employee's performance-related behavior. Another option in dealing with ineffective performance is the use of *counseling* and *employee assistance programs (EAPs)* (Cooper, Dewe, & O'Driscoll, 2003). Employees do not *compartmentalize* their lives; thus, problems outside of work may manifest themselves in the workplace. Marital or financial problems may have a negative impact on the performance of even highly competent employees. If this option is considered, however, managers must be very careful how they approach the employee. Even if such efforts are well intentioned, the suggestion that employees need to seek such services may be met with considerable resistance on the part of an employee. Despite these potential caveats, providing counseling or EAPs may be very useful ways of dealing with some instances of ineffective performance.

As is evident by now, organizations have a variety of ways of dealing with ineffective performance when it occurs. Ideally, though, organizations usually prefer to prevent ineffective performance before it occurs. A first step toward preventing ineffective performance is the utilization of scientifically based selection programs. There is considerable evidence that some variables—most notably, general cognitive ability, conscientiousness, and prior experience—predict performance across a variety of job types (Barrick & Mount, 1991; Schmitt, 2004; Schmidt & Hunter, 1998). Thus, organizations that employ rigorous selection programs increase the probability that employees enter with the skills, abilities, and personality traits necessary to perform their jobs.

Once employees enter an organization, steps must also be taken to nurture employees' skills and abilities so they are translated into performance (Colarelli et al., 1987). As stated earlier, one way of addressing this issue is through proper training and socialization. The manner in which organizations conduct initial training and socialization varies widely (see Chapter 3). Organizations that take the time to properly socialize and train new employees clearly stand a good chance of avoiding performance problems in the future.

A final step toward the prevention of performance problems is having a systematic performance measurement and feedback system. This helps to keep employees on track with respect to performance, and serves to communicate performance expectations. In many cases, ineffective performance may simply be due to the fact that employees do not know what the organization (or their immediate supervisor) expects. Regular performance evaluations also signal to employees that performance matters.

EMPLOYEE ABSENTEEISM

The second form of counterproductive behavior examined in this chapter is employee absenteeism. Recall from the previous chapter that absenteeism was discussed, but only as a potential consequence of job dissatisfaction and low organizational commitment. In this section, we approach absenteeism from a somewhat broader perspective and examine other predictors, as well as various ways in which organizations can reduce the incidence of employee absenteeism.

Defining and Measuring Absenteeism

Absenteeism appears to be a relatively simple variable to define and measure; that is, *absenteeism* can simply be defined as not showing up for work. However, defining absenteeism

in such a general way is problematic when the goal is to predict and control absenteeism. In the absenteeism literature, researchers typically make some distinctions with respect to the types of absences. The most common distinction is between excused and unexcused absences. Excused absences would be those due to reasons that the organization deems as acceptable (e.g., illness, caring for a sick child). In contrast, unexcused absences would be those that are either due to unacceptable reasons (e.g., decided to go shopping) or cases in which an employee has not followed proper procedures (e.g., neglected to call in to one's supervisor). Making distinctions between types of absences is important because different types may be caused by different variables. To underscore this point, Kohler and Mathieu (1993) examined a number of predictors of seven different absence criterion measures among a sample of urban bus drivers and found different predictors for different criteria. For example, they found that absences due to nonwork obligations (e.g., caring for children, transportation problems) were most strongly related to variables such as dissatisfaction with extrinsic features of the job, role conflict, role ambiguity, and feelings of somatic tension. On the other hand, absences due to stress reactions (e.g., illnesses) were most strongly related to dissatisfaction with both internal and external features of the job, feelings of fatigue, and gender (women were absent more frequently).

To measure absenteeism, the most common indexes are *time lost measures* and *frequency measures* (Hammer & Landau, 1981). When a time lost measure is used, absenteeism is represented by the number of days or hours that an employee is absent for a given period of time. As an example, if an employee is absent from work 3 days over a 3-month period, that employee's level of absenteeism would be 3 days or 24 hours (assuming that each workday is 8 hours).

If a frequency metric is used, absenteeism represents the number of absence occurrences for a given period of time. An occurrence can range from 1 day to several weeks. In the previous example, if each of the 3 days that the employee is absent occurs in a different month, the time lost and the frequency metrics would be identical. However, if the employee was absent for 3 consecutive days, the absence would be recorded as only one occurrence if a frequency metric is used.

Although both time lost and frequency measures of absenteeism have been used in studies of absenteeism (e.g., Hackett & Guion, 1985; Steel & Rentsch, 1995), time lost measures are generally more desirable because they exhibit greater variability than frequency measures (Hammer & Landau, 1981). Thus, it is generally more difficult to predict absenteeism when using frequency-based absenteeism measures.

Another important issue in the measurement of absenteeism is the time frame used to aggregate absences. In terms of aggregation periods, studies can be found in which absenteeism data are aggregated over periods ranging from as short as 1 month to as long as 4 years (Hammer & Landau, 1981; Steel & Rentsch, 1995). The primary advantage to using longer aggregation periods is that the distributions of such measures are not as likely to be skewed as those from shorter periods. Given that absenteeism is a low base-rate event (as are many other forms of counterproductive behavior) even for relatively long periods of time, aggregating absenteeism data over a very short period of time may pose researchers with some vexing statistical problems.

Predictors of Absenteeism

For many years organizational psychologists have focused on affective predictors of absenteeism, such as job satisfaction and organizational commitment. As was shown in Chapter 5, however, meta-analytic reviews have generally found the relationship between affect and absenteeism to be rather weak (e.g., Hackett, 1989; Hackett & Guion, 1985; Mathieu & Zajac, 1990). These findings can be attributed at least in part to the issues discussed previously (e.g., choice of absenteeism measures, aggregation periods). They also may be due to the fact that there may be other variables that predict absenteeism better. In this section, we go beyond affective variables and review other predictors that have been explored in the absenteeism literature.

As a first step toward understanding absenteeism, it is useful to consider employee attendance decisions in a general sense. According to Steers and Rhodes (1978), two general factors—the ability to attend and the desire to attend—determine employees' attendance. Ability to attend is determined largely by an employee's health but may also be due to factors such as nonwork responsibilities, reliability of transportation, and weather. The desire to attend work is determined to a large extent by employees' feelings about the organization or job, but may also be due to other factors. For example, an employee may like his or her job but choose not to attend because of some more attractive nonwork alternative. For example, an employee may choose to be absent on a particular day in order to go holiday shopping.

Based on this view of absenteeism, three nonaffective variables have been shown to stand out as consistent predictors of absenteeism. For example, it has been consistently found that women tend to be absent from work more frequently men (Farrell & Stamm, 1988; Steel & Rentsch, 1995; VandenHeuvel & Wooden, 1995). Based on Steers and Rhodes (1978), this is probably because women are more likely than men to be in situations that constrain their ability to attend work. For example, it has been shown that, even in dual-career situations, women tend to assume primary responsibility for childcare and household chores (Hochschild, 1989).

Another important nonaffective predictor of absenteeism is the nature of an organization's *absence-control policies*. Some organizations are quite lenient; they choose not to even record employees' absences. At the other extreme, some organizations require extensive documentation for the reason for absences, and respond with strict disciplinary actions when employees are absent frequently. As one might expect, the frequency of absenteeism tends to be lower in organizations that have more strict absence-control policies (Farrell & Stamm, 1988; Kohler & Mathieu, 1993; Majchrzak, 1987). It is important to note, however, that simply having a strict absence-control policy in place may not always reduce absenteeism. For example, Majchrzak (1987) found that in Marine Corps units where the absence-control policy had been communicated clearly and applied consistently, unauthorized absences were reduced significantly over a 6-month period. In contrast, absences remained constant in units where no policy existed, or where the policy was not communicated clearly.

Another important nonaffective predictor of absenteeism is *absence culture*. The term was originally defined by Chadwick-Jones, Nicholson, and Brown (1982) as "the beliefs and practices influencing the totality of absence frequency and duration—as they currently occur within an employee group or organization" (p. 7). There are two things to note about this definition. First, absence culture is a group- or organization-level construct, and thus must be measured at the appropriate level (e.g., group or organization). Second, because organizations typically consist of multiple groups, several absence cultures may in fact be operating simultaneously in the same organization.

Given that normative standards serve as an important guide for the members of any social unit (Hackman, 1992), one would expect that group members' absenteeism would tend to be consistent with the prevailing absence culture. Unfortunately, to date, there has been relatively little empirical investigation of the absence culture construct or of its effects on absenteeism. One exception is a study in which Mathieu and Kohler (1990) examined the impact of group-level absence rates on individual absences. Using a sample of transit operators employed by a large public transit authority, they found that the level of absences in the various garages in which these employees worked predicted absenteeism using a time-lost measure.

A more direct test of the effect of absence culture comes from a study conducted by Martocchio (1994). Unlike the method in the Mathieu and Kohler (1990) study, Martocchio actually assessed absence culture within groups and investigated the impact of this variable on absenteeism. Based on a sample of clerical employees at a Fortune 500 company, Martocchio found that group-level beliefs regarding absenteeism (e.g., absence culture) were predictive of individual employees' absenteeism, measured in terms of the frequency of paid absences. Individuals' beliefs regarding absenteeism predicted only the frequency of unpaid absences. Figure 6.1 summarizes all of the

FIGURE 6.1
Summary of the Major Determinants of Employee Absenteeism

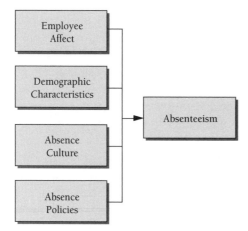

factors that have been shown to influence employee absenteeism.

Overall, the research on absenteeism provides fairly clear guidance for organizations wishing to reduce absenteeism. More specifically, organizations need to have in place absence-control policies that are fair, yet at the same time, discourage employees from unnecessary absences. It is also important for organizations to foster a positive absence culture in the organization as a whole, as well as within work groups. Finally, in some cases organizations can prevent absences by helping employees overcome barriers to attendance. Benefits such as sick child care, flexible schedules, and telecommuting may allow employees to reduce absences that are due to nonwork demands.

Cross-Cultural Differences in Absenteeism

Like most phenomena studied by organizational psychologists, absenteeism has been examined largely in samples of either American or Western European employees. Despite calls for cross-cultural absenteeism research (e.g., Martocchio & Harrison,

1993), few studies have examined cross-cultural differences in absenteeism. One notable exception is a study by Johns and Xie (1998). Employees from the People's Republic of China and from Canada were compared on a number of aspects of absenteeism, such as perceptions of their own absence levels in comparison to those in their work groups; manager–subordinate agreement on absence norms; and legitimacy of reasons for absenteeism.

The most notable cross-cultural difference found in this study was that Chinese employees were more likely than Canadians to generate estimates of their own absenteeism that favored their work group. This suggests that absence norms may be a more powerful predictor of absenteeism among the Chinese. Along these same lines, it was found that Chinese managers were in greater agreement with their work groups on absence norms than were Canadian managers. Finally, with respect to reasons for absence, the Canadians were less likely than the Chinese to see domestic reasons as a legitimate excuse for absences. In contrast, the Chinese were less likely than the Canadians to see illness, stress, and depression as legitimate excuses.

Johns and Xie (1998) attributed their findings to well-documented differences in values between Western and Eastern societies. Most notably, in Eastern societies, the strong collectivist orientation suggests that social norms regarding such behavior may have a more powerful effect than they do in Western societies. This may also explain why those in collectivist societies may see absences due to family reasons as more legitimate than do those in more individualistic societies. In contrast, in Eastern societies, norms surrounding the expression of feelings may prohibit absenteeism based on poor mental or physical health. The results of this study are provocative; they suggest that cross-cultural absenteeism research may be a fruitful area of research in the future.

EMPLOYEE TURNOVER

Like absenteeism, employee turnover was discussed in the previous chapter as a correlate of job satisfaction and organizational commitment. Furthermore, compared to absenteeism, employee affect has been shown to be a stronger predictor of turnover decisions. Therefore, the focus in this section will be to examine employee turnover from a more macro perspective (e.g., the impact of turnover on organizations), explore nonaffective predictors of turnover, and, finally, explore a recent model that has applied behavioral decision theory to the study of turnover.

The Impact of Turnover on Organizations

Like many variables explored in this book, employee turnover has been studied from a very micro perspective; that is, researchers have sought to more fully understand the individual-level decision-making processes that characterize turnover decisions. Organizational researchers have generally paid much less attention to examining the impact of employee turnover on organizational effectiveness. Abelson and Baysinger (1984), distinguished between *optimal ternover* and *dysfunctional turnover*. Optimal turnover occurs when poorly performing employees decide to leave an organization. These authors also suggest that, in some cases, turnover may be optimal even if a high-performing employee leaves because the cost of retaining that individual may be too high. This situation occurs frequently in professional sports when play-

ers from teams in relatively small markets become free agents. These teams want to retain their star players, but they simply do not have the financial resources to do so.

Like optimal turnover, dysfunctional turnover can be viewed in multiple ways. If an organization's rate of turnover is extremely high, this can be very dysfunctional. High rates of turnover translate into increased costs associated with constantly having to recruit and train new employees. A consistently high rate of turnover may also serve to tarnish the image of the organization (see Highhouse and Hoffman, 2001) and thus make it even harder to attract new employees. In most industries, there are organizations that have a reputation of "chewing up and spitting out" employees.

Turnover is also dysfunctional if there is a consistent pattern whereby good employees leave. As stated previously, in some cases the cost of retaining high-performing employees may be prohibitive; thus, some level of turnover among high-performing employees is inevitable. Unfortunately, if this is a consistent pattern then an organization will be losing valuable human capital.

Another way to view the impact of turnover on organizations is to distinguish between what might be termed *avoidable turnover* and *unavoidable turnover*. Turnover is avoidable when there are steps that an organization could have taken to prevent it. As argued previously, this is somewhat subjective and involves weighing the costs of losing employees versus the benefits of retention. Unavoidable turnover, on the other hand, is illustrated by situations in which an organization clearly cannot prevent an employee from leaving. This may occur when an employee's spouse is transferred to another location, or when there is simply no need for the employee's services. In other cases, turnover may be unavoidable simply because an employee decides to withdraw from the labor force.

Nonaffective Predictors of Turnover

One nonaffective predictor that has actually received a fair amount of attention in the turnover literature is performance. Organizations obviously prefer that turnover is highest among lower-performing employees. Furthermore, empirical evidence has supported such a negative relation between performance and turnover (e.g., McEvoy & Cascio, 1987; Williams & Livingstone, 1994), although this relation is not strong. The relative weakness of the performance-turnover relation may be due to a number of factors. As Hulin (1991) has argued quite forcefully, turnover is a low base-rate event, and studies employing typical parametric statistical procedures may underestimate the true relation between turnover and other variables. This becomes even more problematic when performance is examined as a predictor of turnover because, due to a variety of factors, the variability in job performance measures may be severely restricted (e.g., Jex, 1998; Johns, 1991).

A more substantive variable that may impact the performance-turnover relation is organizational reward contingencies. One of the assumptions underlying the prediction that turnover is negatively related to performance is that low performers will receive fewer organizational rewards than high performers. Because of this, low-performing employees are likely to become dissatisfied and seek employment elsewhere. Given that organizations vary widely in the extent to which they reward on the basis of performance, this would certainly account for the weak performance-turnover relation. Furthermore, in one meta-analysis of the performance-turnover relation (Williams & Livingstone, 1994), the average correlation

between performance and turnover was strongest in studies conducted in organizations where rewards were tied to performance.

A third factor that may impact the performance-turnover relation is the form of this relationship. As in most studies in organizational psychology, it has been assumed that the performance-turnover relation is linear. Jackofsky (1984), however, has argued that the performance-turnover relation may in fact be *curvilinear* and best described by a U-shaped function. This means that turnover should be highest among employees performing at very low and at very high levels. Jackofsky (1984) argued that, in most cases, very low performers are not going to be rewarded very well and thus may become dissatisfied. As performance moves toward medium levels, employees are probably being rewarded at a level that keeps them from becoming extremely dissatisfied, and thus seeking alternative employment. As performance increases, however, there is a greater likelihood that employees will have attractive alternative employment opportunities and thus may be more likely to leave an organization. This may even be true in organizations that reward on the basis of performance. Employees who are extremely talented may be receiving top salaries in a particular organization, but organizations simply may not be able to match what another organization is willing to pay in order to lure the employee away.

To date, Jackofsky's (1984) curvilinear hypothesis has not received a great deal of empirical investigation, although it has received some support. Schwab (1991) investigated the relation between performance and turnover among faculty at a large university, and found a negative relation between performance (measured by number of publications) and turnover among nontenured faculty. In contrast, among tenured faculty, there was a positive relation between performance and turnover.

The negative relation between performance and turnover among nontenured faculty is likely due to the fact that low-performing individuals, knowing they probably will not receive tenure, leave before they are denied tenure. Among tenured faculty, those performing at low levels are more likely to remain with the organization because their jobs are secure, and they are likely to have relatively few alternatives. High-performing tenured faculty, in contrast, often have very attractive employment alternatives so they may be lured away by other universities.

In addition to Schwab's (1991) study, more direct tests of the curvilinear hypothesis have supported this relationship (e.g., Trevor, Gerhart, & Boudreau, 1997), as did the previously mentioned meta-analysis conducted by Williams and Livingstone (1994). Trevor et al. also found that this curvilinear relation is more pronounced if salary growth is low and rates of promotion are high. When salary growth is low, both low and high performers have the most to gain by seeking other employment. When rates of promotion are high, low performers are likely to be dissatisfied and look elsewhere. High performers who are promoted rapidly are going to be more marketable in the external labor market than high performers who are promoted more slowly.

A second nonaffective variable that may impact turnover is the external labor market. Most people do not leave their present job until they have secured other employment, so turnover should be highest when job opportunities are plentiful. Steel and Griffeth (1989), for example, performed a meta-analysis and found the corrected correlation between perceived employment opportunities and turnover to be positive but relatively modest (r = .13). Gerhart (1990), however, found that a more objective index of employment opportunities (regional unemployment rates) predicted turnover better than perceptions of employment opportunities. The fact that these findings are at odds suggests that the objective state of the external labor market, and individuals' perceptions of opportunities, may operate independently to influence turnover decisions.

This issue was addressed in a somewhat different way by Steel (1996) in a sample of U.S. Air Force personnel. He examined the impact of objective labor market indexes and perceptions of employment opportunities on reenlistment decisions. The results of this study showed that reenlistment decisions could be predicted with a combination of perceptual and objective labor market variables. Turnover was highest among individuals who reported that they had strong regional living preferences and believed there were a large number of employment alternatives. The one objective labor market measure that predicted reenlistment was the historical retention rate for each Air Force occupational specialty in the study. Those in occupational specialties with high retention rates were more likely to re-enlist.

Although Steel's study is quite useful in combining perceptual and objective data, its generalizability may be limited by its use of a military sample. In civilian organizations, employees are not bound to a certain number of years of service; thus, they may leave the organization at any time. One might surmise that labor market conditions (both objective and perceptive) might be more salient for military personnel because they have a window of opportunity; they can choose between staying and leaving the organization. As with any finding, generalizability is ultimately an empirical issue. Thus, these findings must be replicated in a non-military setting.

A final variable—job tenure—may directly and indirectly impact turnover. As discussed in the previous chapter, longer job tenure is associated with higher levels of continuance commitment and, hence, lower levels of turnover (Meyer & Allen, 1997). Job tenure may also have an indirect effect because turnover may be influenced by different variables at different points in an employee's job tenure. Dickter, Roznowski, and Harrison (1996) examined both job satisfaction and cognitive ability as predictors of quit rates in a longitudinal study conducted over a period of approximately 4 years. Their findings indicated that the impact of job satisfaction on turnover is strongest when employees have been on the job about 1 year, and this effect gradually decreases over time. It was also found that a high level of cognitive ability was associated with decreased risk of turnover. However, as with job satisfaction, this relationship diminished over time.

The results of Dickter et al. (1996) suggest that job satisfaction may drive turnover decisions early in an employee's job tenure. However, as an employee builds up job tenure, the costs associated with leaving one's employer become greater. Also, as job tenure increases, it is likely that a greater number of nonwork factors will come into play when one is deciding whether to leave one's present employer. For example, employees with children in school may not wish to change jobs if doing so involves a geographical move.

The fact that cognitive ability has less impact on turnover over time is also significant. Cognitive ability is associated with job performance (e.g., Schmidt & Hunter, 1998), and this supports the notion that the relation between performance and turnover is nonlinear only among those who have

been employed a relatively short period of time. Performance may not be related to turnover among longer-tenured employees for a number of reasons. For example, the level of performance among those who stay in an organization may be restricted, and this may prevent performance from being related to turnover among this group. This essentially represents a *self-selection effect*.

It is also possible that true performance differences exist among longer-tenured employees, but other factors are at work. For example, when employees have been employed in an organization for several years, managers may be reluctant to highlight their performance differences. It is also possible that, over time, the experience employees gain may compensate for what they may be lacking in cognitive ability.

An Alternative Turnover Model of the Turnover Process

As discussed in the previous chapter, Mobley's (1977) model of the turnover process, and variants of it, have dominated the turnover literature for the past 25 years. Although there are some differences among these models, they all basically have two things in common. First, all propose that employee affect (mainly job satisfaction) plays a key role in the turnover process. That is, a lack of satisfaction or feelings of low commitment set in motion the cognitive processes that may eventually lead an employee to quit his or her job. Second, because of the emphasis on employee affect, an implicit assumption in most turnover models is that employee turnover is usually due to willingness to get away from the present job rather than attraction to other alternatives.

According to Lee and Mitchell (1994), the dominant process models in the turnover literature have been useful, but they have also ignored some basic properties of human decision-making processes. Based largely on behavioral decision theory (Beach, 1993), they developed the *Unfolding Model* of the turnover process. A basic assumption of the Unfolding Model is that people generally do not evaluate their job or job situation unless forced to do so. Lee and Mitchell refer to events that force people to evaluate their jobs as "shocks to the system." Shocks may be negative events (e.g., a major layoff), but they are not necessarily. A shock is simply any event that forces an employee to take stock and review his or her job situation (Holtom, Mitchell, Lee, & Interrieden, 2005). For example, a promotion may also be a shock to the system, according to Lee and Mitchell's definition.

Once an employee experiences a shock to the system, a number of outcomes are possible. One possibility is that the employee may have a preprogrammed response to the shock, based on previous experience. For example, an employee may have previously worked in a company that was acquired by a competitor, and decided it was best to leave the company. If this same event happens in later years, the employee may not even have to think about what to do; he or she may simply implement a preprogrammed response.

Where a preprogrammed response does not exist, an employee would engage in *controlled cognitive processing* and consciously evaluate whether the shock that has occurred can be resolved by staying employed in the current organization. To illustrate this point, Lee and Mitchell (1994) provide the example of a woman who becomes pregnant unexpectedly (a shock to the system). Assuming that this has not happened before, this woman would probably not have a pre-programmed response (quit or stay), and most likely would not have a specific job alternative. Rather, she would be forced to evaluate her attachments to both the organization and her career. Such an evaluation may also involve deciding whether continuing to work in the organization is consistent with her image of motherhood.

A third type of situation involves a shock to the system without a preprogrammed response, but with the presence of specific job alternatives. An example of this situation would be where an employee receives an unsolicited job offer from another organization. This job offer may be considered a shock to the system because it forces the employee to think consciously about his or her job situation and to compare it to the outside job offer. Note that, in this type of situation, the employee may be reasonably happy in his or her job but may ultimately leave because another job is simply better.

A final alternative is where there is no shock to the system but turnover is *affect initiated*—that is, over time, an employee may simply become dissatisfied with his or her job for a variety of reasons. For example, the job may change in ways that are no longer appealing to the employee. Alternatively, the employee may undergo a change in his or her values or preferences, and may no longer see the job as satisfying. According to Lee and Mitchell (1994), once a person is dissatisfied, this may lead to a sequence of events, including reduced organizational commitment, more job search activities, greater ease of movement, stronger intentions to quit, and a higher probability of employee turnover. This proposed sequence of events is very consistent with dominant affect-based models of the turnover process (e.g., Mobley, 1977).

Lee and Mitchell's (1994) Unfolding Model is relatively new, so it has not received nearly the empirical scrutiny of more traditional affect-based process models. However, empirical tests of this model have met with some success (Lee, Mitchell, Holtom, McDaniel, & Hill, 1999; Lee, Mitchell, Wise, & Fireman, 1996). As with any model, it is likely that further refinements will be made as more empirical tests are conducted. Nevertheless, the Unfolding Model does represent an important development in turnover research.

In recent years a major concept that has come out of work on the Unfolding Model of turnover is that of *embeddedness*. Mitchell et al. (2001) define embeddedness as the combination of forces (in one's both personal and professional life) that keep a person from changing his or her employer. A person would be highly embedded in a professional sense, for example, if he or she had a large social role in his or her current organization. A high level of embeddedness in one's personal life may result from one's family situation and perhaps a high level of community involvement. Research has in fact shown that embeddedness is a fairly good predictor of voluntary turnover, as well as behaviors (e.g., Lee, Mitchell, Sablynski, Burton, & Holtom, 2004).

Accidents

Accidents represent a very serious and costly form of counterproductive behavior in organizations. For example, in the United States alone, the most recent estimate is that there were 4.7 million recorded workplace injuries in the United States in 2002, and in this same year 5,524 of these were fatal (U.S. Bureau of Labor Statistics, 2004). Furthermore, it has been estimated that accidents cost organizations $145 billion per year (U.S. Department of Health and Human Services (2002)). Another indication of the importance of safety in the workplace is that many

nations have enacted legislation dealing with safety standards, and many have also created government agencies to oversee compliance with these standards. In the United States, for example, the Occupational Safety and Health Act provides employers with a set of legal standards regarding safety in the workplace. This legislation also led to the creation of the Occupational Safety and Health Administration (OSHA) to enforce employment safety and health standards.

Determinants of Accidents

As one might imagine, accidents are more common in certain types of work settings than in others. Employees who work in agriculture and mining are particularly at risk, while those who work in sales or service industries are least likely to be involved in accidents (U.S. Bureau of Labor Statistics, 2004). Work settings, however, do not completely explain variation in accident rates. Because of this, considerable effort over the years has been devoted to gaining a better understanding of other causes of accidents, and, perhaps more importantly, how organizations can take proactive steps to make the workplace safer.

Research on accidents has a long history, although much of it has not been conducted by organizational psychologists. For example, industrial engineers have focused on the design of machinery and the physical layout of the workplace as possible causes of workplace accidents (Wickens & Hollands, 2000). Within psychology, early accident research focused largely on developing a profile of "the accident-prone employee." This research identified a number of characteristics that were occasionally correlated with accidents, but researchers were never able to consistently document a cluster of characteristics that were consistently associated with accident prevalence (see Hansen, 1988). This is not surprising, given that much of this research was largely devoid of any theoretical underpinnings.

Research examining personal characteristics associated with accidents has become more theoretically grounded over the years, and, in fact, has yielded some useful results. For example, Hansen (1989) studied predictors of accident frequency among employees of a large petrochemical processing company and found that accidents were most frequent among employees who were younger, highly distractible, and who scored high on a measure of general social maladjustment. More recently, Frone (2003) found similar personality traits to predict accidents among high-school-age employees, so there does appear to be some consistency in characteristics that lead to accidents.

In recent years, there has been a noticeable shift in accident research, from investigating characteristics of individual employees, to characteristics of group and organizational climates. According to Griffin and Neal (2000), *safety climate* consists of employees' perceptions of the policies, procedures, and practices relating to safety in an organization. Others (e.g., Zohar, 2003) view safety climate as more of an aspect of an organization's culture with regard to safety. Regardless of the definition, two fundamental questions are at the core of safety climate: Is employee safety considered a high-level organizational priority? And does this get communicated to employees through formal organizational policies and managerial actions?

In the past 10 years a considerable amount of research has been done on the relationship between safety climate and both accident frequency as well as behaviors associated with safety. Clarke (2006) recently summarized much of this literature in a meta-analysis of 32 studies and found that a positive safety climate was associated with lower accident involvement, compliance with safety procedures, and participation in more proactive safety behaviors. The strongest of these relationships was between positive safety climate and participation in proactive safety behaviors.

This recent shift in emphasis toward safety climate is important for a number of reasons. At a general level, it offers a productive departure from a long history of accident research that has clung rather dogmatically to individual characteristics as predictors. This is not to say that individual characteristics have no bearing on accidents; for example, the results of Hansen's (1989) and Frone's work would suggest otherwise. However, given the considerable effort that has gone into the investigation of individual predictors, the actual insight gained about accidents and accident prevention has been rather disappointing.

Safety climate research also represents a recognition that employees work in a social context and that this impacts safety (Neal & Griffin, 2006). Thus, information communicated via the social environment may have a powerful impact on employees' behaviors. Granted, research on safety climate is still in its infancy and a number of issues are still to be resolved (e.g., Does safety climate operate equally at the group and organizational levels? How does safety climate develop in the first place? Do personal characteristics of employees interact with safety climate to impact actual safety behavior?). Despite these unresolved issues, safety climate represents a fruitful new approach that may yield considerable insight into safety and ultimately provide organizations with concrete guidance on reducing the incidence of workplace accidents.

Accident Prevention

Given the research reviewed, an organization can take one of four different approaches to the prevention of accidents. First, based on human factors and industrial engineering research, an organization may choose to focus on physical factors. For example, an effort might be made to design equipment so it is easier to use and make other features of the physical environment safer for employees. This approach can be quite useful, given that some accidents can be prevented by better equipment design. It may also be quite costly, depending on the modifications that may be needed within the physical environment.

A second approach, and one that is used frequently, is *behavior modification* (see Chapter 9) that encourages employees to use safe work practices and discourages employees from being unsafe. This involves the use of reinforcements for safe behaviors and the use of sanctions or punishment for unsafe behaviors. An organization, for example, might offer cash bonuses to employees who have the best safety records in a particular year. This is an approach that has been successfully in a number of organizations (e.g., Komaki, Barwick, & Scott, 1978; Komaki, Heinzmann, & Lawson, 1980). On the negative side, organizations may take disciplinary actions (e.g., written reprimands, suspensions) against employees who engage in unsafe work practices or who consistently have poor safety records.

A third approach is to use selection as a means of screening out employees who are likely to be unsafe. If unsafe behavior is viewed as part of a general pattern of deviant antisocial behavior, then organizations may have a number of useful predictors at their disposal. For example, based on Hansen's (1989) study, described earlier, general social maladjustment and distractibility would

appear to be two predictors that organizations could use to screen out employees who may have poor safety records. On the positive side, organizations may consider the use of personality traits such as conscientiousness in selection as a positive step toward improving safety (Barrick & Mount, 1991; Tett, Jackson, & Rothstein, 1991).

A final method of preventing accidents is by changing or improving the safety climate of the organization. Some possible ways of doing this might be publicizing the importance of safety within the organization and making supervisors and managers accountable for the safety records within their units (Hofmann & Morgeson, 1999; Zohar, 2000). Over time, as more research on the safety climate construct is conducted, organizations will likely be provided more guidance in their efforts to improve safety climate.

LESS COMMON FORMS OF COUNTERPRODUCTIVE BEHAVIOR

Up to this point in the chapter, we have covered the most common forms of counterproductive behavior in organizations. Most organizations must deal frequently with ineffective employee performance, absenteeism, turnover, and employee safety issues. These, however, are clearly not the only forms of counterproductive behavior in organizations. In this concluding section, we explore less common forms of counterproductive behavior in organizations. These include: employee theft, workplace violence and mistreatment, substance use, and sexual harassment.

Employee Theft

Employee theft may be defined simply as employees taking things from the organization that don't belong to them. Based on this definition, theft could range from relatively minor acts, such as employees taking inexpensive office supplies, to more serious forms, such as a government employee's theft of classified documents. Most of the literature on employee theft has focused on what could be described as *moderate* forms of employee theft: retail store employees stealing merchandise, or convenience store employees skimming money from the cash register.

Research on the frequency of employee theft has shown that it does occur with enough frequency to be problematic for many organizations. For example, it has been estimated that approximately 35% of employees steal from their employers, and the financial losses from theft are in the billions (Kuhn, 1988). In a more recent estimate, it was found that 52% of people reported taking property from work without permission, and 25% reported falsifying receipts to get reimbursements for money they didn't spend (Bennett & Robinson, 2000). Unfortunately, because the costs of employee theft are often passed on to consumers, the impact of this behavior reaches far beyond the organizations in which it occurs.

A review of the literature on the causes of employee theft reveals two clear themes. The first, and by far the strongest, is that theft is due largely to characteristics of the individual (e.g., Collins & Schmidt, 1993; Jones & Boye, 1992; Ones et al., 1993). Furthermore, publishers of integrity tests have conducted much of this research. This is potentially problematic because such organizations may lack the motivation to rigorously evaluate the predictive capabilities of their products. Despite these concerns, Ones et al.'s (1993) meta-analysis showed fairly clearly that integrity tests do in fact predict employees' theft. Because most integrity tests

measure the personality trait of conscientiousness, this suggests that the employees most likely to steal have a low level of this trait; in other words, they are unreliable, lack self-discipline, and have a disregard for rules and authority. Other than conscientiousness, it has also been shown that theft tends to be higher among employees who have very tolerant attitudes toward theft and other forms of dishonesty (Jones & Boye, 1992).

A second theme in the literature is that theft is impacted by conditions in the environment such as unfair or frustrating organizational conditions. Greenberg (1990), for example, conducted a study in which a pay-reduction policy was implemented in two separate locations of a large manufacturing organization. In one of these locations, little explanation was provided as to why the policy was being implemented, and this explanation was given with little remorse or sensitivity. In the other location, however, management provided employees with a more extensive explanation as to why the policy had to be adopted, and did so with much greater sensitivity. This study showed that the rate of theft in the plant where the inadequate explanation was provided was significantly higher compared to the plant given the adequate explanation and a third plant where no pay reduction had been implemented.

According to Spector (1997b), employee theft is also caused by organizational conditions that induce frustration among employees. Frustration is essentially the emotion evoked in people when things in the environment are blocking their goals. In organizations, these barriers may include environmental constraints such as poor equipment, unnecessary rules and regulations, and other policies that end up wasting employees' time. Thus, Spector has proposed

FIGURE 6.2
Spector's Model of the Impact of Locus of Control
on the Relationship between Frustration and
Counterproductive Behavior

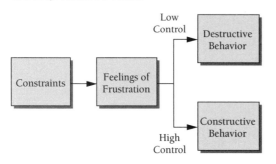

Source: P. E. Spector. (2000). *Industrial and organizational
psychology: Research and practice* (2nd ed.). New York: John
Wiley & Sons, Inc. Reprinted by permission.

that employees may vent their frustrations
toward the organization through acts of theft
and sabotage. As with many relations, the
link between frustration and theft may be
influenced by other factors. For example,
employees who are frustrated may feel like
stealing but do not act on such impulses
either because they have no opportunity or
they are afraid of the consequences of such
behavior. According to Spector, one variable
that may moderate the relation between frustration and theft is employees' *locus of control.*
Locus of control represents beliefs regarding
the control people have over reinforcements
in their lives (Rotter, 1966). A person
described as having an internal locus of control generally believes that he or she has
control over reinforcements. In contrast, an
external locus of control is associated with
the belief that one has little control over
reinforcements.

The potential moderating effect of locus
of control on the relation between frustration
and theft is depicted in Figure 6.2. As can be
seen, this model proposes that frustration is
most likely to lead to destructive behaviors
such as theft among employees who have an
external locus of control. Those with an
external locus of control tend to respond to
frustration through theft and other forms of
destructive behavior because they do not
believe that frustrating organizational conditions can be changed through more constructive means. In contrast, those with an
internal locus of control are more likely to
believe that they are able to change frustrating organizational conditions constructively.
These individuals, for example, may choose
to exert their influence through participative
management practices or labor-management
committees. Spector's (1997b) hypothesis
has received some empirical scrutiny and
in general has been supported (Chen &
Spector, 1992; Spector & O'Connell, 1994;
Storms & Spector, 1987).

Workplace Violence and Mistreatment

Like employee theft, workplace violence is a
relatively infrequent event. However, in
recent years, there has been an alarming
increase in the number of violent incidents
in the workplace. For example, it has
recently been estimated that in the United
States nearly two million people may experience physical attacks in the workplace each
year (Barling, 1996). Even more alarming is
the fact that homicides are the second leading cause of job-related deaths (U.S. Bureau
of Labor Statistics, 1999). In addition to
overt violence, many employees experience
other forms of mistreatment in the workplace such as rudeness, verbal abuse, and
social exclusion. Both workplace violence
and more general mistreatment are covered
in the following.

***Workplace Violence and Generalized
Mistreatment.*** Like other phenomena
that either have been or will be covered in

this book, what is considered workplace violence is quite broad. For the purposes of this chapter, *workplace violence* is defined as physical acts of aggression by members of an organization, carried out in organizational settings. Notice that no attempt is made to specify or restrict the target of the aggression. For example, a violent act could be directed at (or instigated by) a fellow employee, one's supervisor, or even a customer. Since most research on workplace violence and aggression has focused on the violent acts of employees toward other employees (see Schat & Kelloway, 2005 for a review), the focus in this section will be on violent acts committed by employees toward other employees. However, it has been shown that clients and customers also commit many of the violent and antisocial acts against employees in organizations (e.g., Bussing & Hoge, 2004).

To explain violent acts on the part of employees, there have generally been three foci in the literature: (1) the physical environment; (2) characteristics of the individual; and (3) the organizational environment. If the focus is on the physical environment, we are able to draw on the social-psychological literature that has linked aggression to violent cues in the environment, as well as factors that induce frustration (Worchel, Cooper, Goethals, & Olson, 2000). Considerable research has also linked stress-related symptoms to monotonous machine-paced work (e.g., Broadbent, 1985). Unfortunately, neither of these characteristics has been linked to workplace violence.

Given that little empirical research has examined the link between the physical environment and workplace violence, we can only speculate that environment may play a role. However, it is interesting to note that some of the most highly publicized acts of violence on the part of employees have taken place in work environments that many would consider somewhat noxious. In the U.S. Postal Service, for example, much of the work is highly monotonous and paced by the speed of machines. Factories and other manufacturing facilities are often noisy and hot. This link is obviously pure speculation, but over time, as more data are collected about violent incidents, it may be possible to assess more clearly the contribution of the physical environment.

A second focus in the workplace violence literature is identification of the characteristics of those who may be predisposed to violent acts. Given that workplace violence is a low base-rate event, this is obviously not an easy task. Nevertheless, research has show that certain personal characteristics may indicate heightened risk of violence. Day and Catano (2006) summarized this literature and concluded that the primary predictors of violent behavior tend to be past history of violent behavior, alcohol and drug abuse, lack of conscientiousness, low agreeableness, and low emotional stability. There has also been evidence that individuals who are high on hostility may be predisposed to aggressive behavior in the workplace (Judge, Scott, & Ilies, 2006).

A third focus of workplace violence research has viewed the organizational environment as a possible factor precipitating violent acts. Much of what can be said here mirrors the previous section on theft. Organizations that treat employees unfairly and ignore their frustrations may be at greater risk for violence than organizations that emphasize fairness and support (Greenberg, 1990; Spector, 1997b). It has also been shown recently that leaders who are very passive and unwilling to take action may allow antisocial and aggressive behaviors to occur in their work groups (Skogstad, Einarsen, Torsheim, Aasland, & Hetland,

2007). These could potentially escalate the level of physical violence.

In considering the research on the organizational environment, it must be remembered that, even in the worst organizational environments, very few employees engage in acts of violence. Thus, a negative organizational environment will probably not have a strong main effect on the incidence of workplace violence. Rather, the best way to think of the contribution of the organizational environment is in combination with personal factors. For example, a person who is prone to aggression and violence may take out his or her frustrations through violent acts if treated in an unfair or arbitrary manner by the organization.

Generalized Mistreatment. While workplace violence is clearly an important form of counterproductive behavior in organizations, we also know that physical violence does not occur frequently in organizations. On the other hand, it is far more common for employees to experience rudeness, verbal attacks, invasions of their privacy, and in some cases even malicious attempts to sabotage their performance.

In organizational psychology such behaviors have received a variety of labels, including workplace incivility, bullying, mobbing, social undermining, and workplace deviance (see Bowling & Beehr, 2006). While we do not view all of these as being the same, we also believe that these all have a great deal in common and therefore discuss them collectively under the label of *generalized mistreatment*.

What do we know about generalized mistreatment in organizations? Bowling and Beehr (2006) conducted a meta-analysis on consequences of many forms of generalized workplace mistreatment that included 90 samples. One clear finding from this study is that people react to mistreatment in a variety of negative ways, including increased depression and anxiety and decreased job satisfaction. The findings also indicated that individuals who experience high levels of mistreatment report higher levels of physical symptoms and may be absent from work more frequently.

While the effects of mistreatment are pretty clear, less research has addressed its causes. Nevertheless, it has been shown that leaders or supervisors may play a key role in whether this type of behavior occurs (Skogstad et al., 2007). Individuals who are hostile, feel they are treated unfairly by their organization, are dissatisfied, and who feel emotionally exhausted may be more likely to lash out at others (Blau & Andersson, 2005; Judge et al., 2006). These findings, though limited in scope, suggest that the way organizations treat employees is clearly a major contributing factor. Of course it has also been suggested (see Andersson & Pearson, 1999) that mistreatment in the workplace is merely a symptom of a general trend toward lower levels of civility and decorum on society in general (Comment 6.2).

Substance Use

According to Frone (2006), approximately 14% of the U.S. work force (17.7 million workers) reports some use of illicit drugs, and approximately 3% (3.9 million) report using on the job. Use of alcohol, which is obviously legal, is undoubtedly much higher. These numbers represent a serious concern for organizations because employees who use alcohol and illicit drugs may be absent from work more frequently and may be more likely than nonusers to engage in a variety of other counterproductive behaviors (Frone, 2004). We also know that substance use is related, either directly or indirectly, to

INCIVILITY ON TELEVISION

IN THEIR 1999 review, Andersson and Pearson (1999) both defined what is meant by workplace incivility and developed a model to explain why it occurs and how it might escalate into more serious forms of aggression. Essentially, *workplace incivility* was defined as "low intensity deviant behavior with ambiguous intent to harm the target, in violation of workplace norms for mutual respect. Uncivil behaviors are characteristically rude, discourteous, displaying a lack of respect for others." (p. 1)

While there are a multitude of factors within the workplace that may lead to incivility, Andersson and Pearson also suggest that this is a reflection of a more general societal trend. Nowhere is this more apparent than on television. In the highly popular show "American Idol," for example, contestants are not only eliminated from the competition, but they are also frequently humiliated and made fun of by the judges. Other reality TV shows often highlight arguments and even physical confrontations among the contestants.

Why has there been such a rise in the phenomenon of "incivility as entertainment"? The most obvious answer is that people seem to enjoy it. Television programming is driven largely by viewer ratings, so as long as people watch programs that highlight uncivil behavior networks will continue to put them on. Perhaps out of concern for the effect of such programs on children (or simply because these programs will get boring), people will communicate to television networks that they want to see examples of more civil behavior on television. Hopefully this will translate into more civil behavior in society in general, and the workplace more specifically.

Source: Andersson, L., Pearson, C. (1999). Tit for tat? The spiraling effect of incivility in the workplace. *Academy of Management Review, 24,* 452–471.

negative outcomes such as traffic fatalities, domestic abuse, and violent crimes. Research examining the impact of substance use in organizations has produced some fairly consistent findings. For example, it has been shown that employees who are problem drinkers and users of illicit drugs may exhibit a number of negative outcomes, such as performance decrements, increased absenteeism, greater frequency of accidents, greater job withdrawal, and more antagonistic behavior toward others (Frone, 2004; Roman & Blum, 1995). Given these findings, the more pressing issues appear to be (1) identifying those who may have substance use problems, and (2) deciding what to do when employees show signs of substance use problems.

The prediction of substance use has been addressed in two basic ways. As with theft and violence, substance use is seen by many as part of a more general pattern of antisocial behavior (e.g., Hogan & Hogan, 1989). Given this conceptualization, efforts have been made to predict substance use based on personality traits more generally associated with antisocial behavior. McMullen (1991), for example, found that the reliability scale from the Hogan Personality Inventory (HPI; Hogan & Hogan, 1989) was negatively related to self-reports of both off- and on-the-job substance use among college students. Interestingly, in this same study, in an applicant sample, this scale distinguished those who passed and those who failed a urinalysis drug screening.

Other than personality, research has also investigated personal characteristic predictors in the form of personal history. Lehman, Farabee, Holcom, and Simpson (1995) investigated a number of personal background characteristics as predictors of substance use among a sample of municipal workers, and produced a number of meaningful findings. Those at the greatest risk for substance use were young males who reported low self-esteem, had a previous arrest history, came from a family with substance use problems, and tended to associate with substance-using peers.

Another line of inquiry has examined environmental predictors of substance use. In this line of research, the variable that has been examined most is stressful job conditions. For the most part, this research has shown that although holding a stressful job may increase one's risk of substance use, this effect does not appear to be large (e.g., Cooper, Russell, & Frone, 1990). A more recent line of inquiry has examined the social norms surrounding substance use in organizations. Recall that this idea has also been explored, with some success, in the study of both absenteeism and accidents. An example of this type of research can be seen in a study by Bennett and Lehman (1998), in which the impact of a workplace drinking climate was measured. It was found that in groups where a drinking climate was positive, individuals reported higher levels of both their own and coworkers' drinking activity. These findings suggest that social factors within work groups, and perhaps even within professions, may contribute to problem drinking.

More recent findings seem to be consistent with the idea that the social environment plays a key role in substance use. Frone (2006), for example, found that the prevalence of substance use differed considerably by occupation, which suggests that some work environments or occupational cultures differ with regard to norms surrounding substance use; this could also reflect differences in availability. This was also shown in other research on substance use among high-school-aged employees as well (Frone, 2003).

Based on the empirical research, what can organizations do to prevent substance use among employees? As with prevention of theft and violence, research on substance use suggests that organizations should focus on both screening out potential substance users and creating a social environment that does not promote substance use. *When screening out potential employees, employers must take into account the fact that recovering alcoholics are protected under the Americans With Disabilities Act of 1990 and cannot be discriminated against.* Given the multitude of counterproductive behaviors that are associated with low conscientiousness (e.g., Hogan & Hogan, 1989; Ones et al., 1993), assessing this trait would appear to have some merit. A thorough preemployment background check would also seem to be a logical step toward preventing substance use problems (Lehman et al., 1995). As stated earlier, organizations obviously must make sure that such checks do not violate the rights of applicants.

Another method of preventing substance use has become increasingly popular: requiring applicants, and even current employees, to submit to drug screening, most typically through urinalysis. Drug screening is both expensive and controversial (Rosen, 1987), so organizations must think very carefully about its use. Nevertheless, research has shown that people are not strongly opposed to the use of preemployment drug testing for jobs in which the safety of others could be put at risk by a drug-using employee

COMMENT 6.3

JUICING THE GAME: BASEBALL AND STERIODS

WHEN MOST PEOPLE think about substance use in the workplace, they think about alcohol and illicit drugs such as marijuana. In major league baseball, however, the primary substance use issue in recent years has been players' use of anabolic steroids. In his 2005 book *Juicing the Game: Drugs, Power, and the Fight for the Soul of Major League Baseball*, journalist Howard Bryant provides an informative and insightful account of this issue. As Bryant explains, steroid use presented major league baseball with a very difficult dilemma. Despite the well-known dangers of steroid use, it is also true that offensive production (e.g., home-runs) in baseball increased considerably when steroid use was the heaviest. Increases in offensive production, of course, translate into greater attendance and revenues. Given the increased publicity surrounding anabolic steroids in the past 5 years, major league baseball has instituted mandatory testing for anabolic steroids, and increased the penalties for those caught.

Source: Bryant, H. (2005). *Juicing the game: Drugs, power, and the fight for the soul of major league baseball.* New York: Viking.

(Murphy, Thornton, & Reynolds, 1990), but have less favorable attitudes in jobs without these characteristics. Research has also shown that attitudes toward drug-screening programs are more positive when such programs are seen as procedurally fair (Konovsky & Cropanzano, 1991). Important procedural issues in drug testing include the basis on which employees or applicants are required to submit to such tests, as well as whether retesting is allowed.

Perhaps the most critical issue surrounding drug testing is an organization's response to confirmed employee substance use. An organization essentially has two choices in deciding how to respond to such employees: punishment or treatment. Some organizations have what could be described as *zero tolerance* policies with respect to drug use. In the military, for example, evidence of illicit drug use will automatically disqualify a recruit and will result in immediate disciplinary action against active duty personnel. In other cases, when substance use problems among employees are discovered, organiza-

tions seek to provide these individuals with treatment—typically, through Employee Assistance Programs (EAPs) and referrals. This is obviously a difficult issue. A recent example of this is the difficulty major league baseball has had in deciding how to respond when players are caught using anabolic steroids (see Comment 6.3).

Although cogent arguments can be made for either approach, research suggests that drug testing is viewed more favorably if those identified as having substance use problems are provided with at least some form of treatment (Stone & Kotch, 1989). The provision of treatment makes a drug-testing program appear to have a greater level of fairness compared to programs that have only punitive outcomes. A possible downside to treatment is that an organization may run the risk of conveying an overly tolerant attitude toward substance use. In dealing with substance use, an organization is best served by pursuing a policy that combines clearly stated consequences with compassionate options that assist with treatment and recovery.

Sexual Harassment

Sexual harassment has become a highly visible issue in organizations ranging from corporations to universities. *Sexual harassment* is defined as "unwelcome sexual advances, requests for sexual favors, and other verbal or physical contact when (a) submission to the conduct is either explicitly or implicitly a term or condition of an individual's employment, (b) submission to or rejection of such conduct by an individual is used as a basis for employment decisions affecting that individual, and/or (c) such conduct [that] has the purpose or effect of unreasonably interfering with work performance, or creating an intimidating, hostile, or offensive working environment" (Equal Employment Opportunity Commission, 1980). The term *quid pro quo sexual harassment* is often used to denote situations in which an employee's advancement or performance is adversely impacted by refusing the sexual advances of a supervisor or other employee who exerts power over the employee. This form would apply primarily to the first two parts of the definition provided previously.

The second form of sexual harassment, often referred to as *hostile work environment*, refers primarily to the third part of the definition. In this form, there is no overt attempt to manipulate or threaten. Rather, the existence of sexual harassment is based on the general behavior of others in the workplace. Vulgar comments, telling "off-color" jokes, the display of pornographic images, and even nonverbal gestures that elicit discomfort may provide the basis for sexual harassment based on the hostile work environment argument. This category is important because it highlights the fact that even behavior intended to be for fun can be perceived as offensive to others. Destructive intent is not a prerequisite for sexual harassment.

Given the variety of behaviors that may constitute sexual harassment, estimating its prevalence is a challenge. In a recent review of the sexual harassment literature, Bates, Bowes-Sperry, and O'Leary-Kelly (2005) report that, in 2002, the number of formal sexual harassment charges handled by the U.S. Equal Opportunity Commission was 14,396, which was a 37% increase from 1992. Interestingly, these authors also report that some studies have shown that nearly 75% of women surveyed report unwanted sexual attention, and nearly 50% have experienced gender-related harassment. Thus, a logical conclusion one may draw is that very blatant sexual harassment is not a common occurrence in organizations. On the other hand, more subtle forms of sexual harassment occur quite frequently.

Organizational research on sexual harassment has examined a number of issues, including prevalence (Fitzgerald, Drasgow, Hulin, Gelfand, & Magley, 1997), causes (Gruber, 1998; Gutek, Cohen, & Konrad, 1990), ways to respond to sexual harassment allegations, and methods of prevention (Fitzgerald, 1993). Consistent with government estimates, this research suggests that sexual harassment is quite prevalent, it is much more likely to be experienced by women than men, and that victims are often in positions of unequal power and heightened visibility in relation to the perpetrators (e.g., women who work in largely male groups).

More recent research on sexual harassment suggests that sexual harassment is part of a more general pattern of mistreatment and harassment in organizational settings. For example, Lim and Cortina (2005) found that sexual harassment and more general incivility in the workplace tend to be positively associated. It has also been shown that minority women tend to experience higher levels of sexual harassment than do white women (Berdahl & Moore, 2006). These findings suggest that organizations wishing to reduce sexual harassment need to focus not only on sexual harassment, but also on the more general social climate of the organization.

Probably the most effective way for organizations to prevent sexual harassment is to have in place a clearly articulated sexual harassment policy (Bates, Bower-Sperry, & O'Leary-Kelly, 2005). Such a policy serves the dual purposes of letting employees know what is considered sexual harassment, and the steps an organization will take if harassment occurs. Letting employees know what is considered sexual harassment is often easier said than done. Given the wording of sexual harassment statutes, employees may often be confused as to what is and what is not sexual harassment. However, based on the authors' experience, getting people to agree on what is appropriate and inappropriate behavior in mixed-gender company may not be nearly as difficult as it may seem. Given common sense and knowledge of the prevailing societal codes of morality, the vast majority of adults know what is and what is not proper behavior in mixed-gender company. Ignorance is not a viable defense against charges of sexual harassment.

Sexual harassment policies also need to communicate to employees that sexual harassment is a serious matter, and that those who engage in such behavior will encounter severe consequences. Ultimately, however, the most powerful way to communicate an organizational sexual harassment policy is through an organization's response to such behavior. If organizations respond to such behavior in a manner that is consistent with their policy, and do so regardless of the parties involved, this sends the powerful message that the organization will not tolerate such behavior.

CHAPTER SUMMARY

This chapter examined counterproductive behaviors, or those actions on the part of employees that explicitly run counter to the goals of an organization. The most common form of counterproductive behavior is ineffective job performance. Nevertheless, ineffective performance is often difficult to detect due to external constraints on performance and deficiencies in organizational performance measurement systems. Based on models of job performance, ineffective performance may be due to characteristics of the employee as well as environmental factors. Organizations may respond to poor performance in a number of ways, including training, coaching, and, if all else fails, punishment. A key issue in deciding the response to poor performance is the underlying causes of performance difficulties.

Absenteeism and turnover are the other two most common forms of counterproductive behavior in organizations. Absenteeism has long been viewed by organizational psychologists as a behavioral response to negative feelings about one's job or job situation. Over time, however, this somewhat narrow view has given way to a broader view of the causes of absenteeism. The most promising of these appears to be group norms regarding absenteeism. This is due largely to the recognition that absenteeism is a complex phenomenon and thus may be impacted by a variety of factors.

Like absenteeism, turnover has been viewed largely as a response to negative affect. Here too, more contemporary turnover research has expanded and investigated other nonaffective predictors of turnover. The external labor market, as well as employees' job performance, are two nonaffective variables that have been shown to have an important impact on employee turnover.

Another important advance in this area is the use of findings from behavioral decision theory to model the turnover process. The concept of *embeddedness*, which has grown out of this research, appears to be a promising predictor of turnover.

Less common forms of counterproductive behavior examined in the chapter included accidents, theft, violence and mistreatment, substance use, and sexual harassment. Many years of research have failed to uncover a clear profile of the "accident-prone" employee, but more recent research in this area has provided some important insights. The "safety climate" within an organization, in particular, appears to be an important predictor of accident frequency. Attention to this climate, coupled with a focus on the physical environment and characteristics of employees, is likely to be the best strategy for preventing accidents in organizations.

Theft and violence, when considered together, can be considered *antisocial* behaviors in organizations. Although both are relatively low-frequency events, they can nevertheless be quite damaging to organizations. Lower-level forms of mistreatment, such as rudeness or verbal abuse, occur with much greater frequency. Like most forms of behavior, all of these forms of counterproductive behavior can be explained by characteristics of both the employee and the environment. With respect to theft, considerable evidence has accumulated suggesting that employees with a combination of a low level of conscientiousness and tolerant attitudes toward theft are most likely to steal. Research has been much less conclusive about personal characteristics indicative of violence and mistreatment, although it is likely that violence is often indicative of underlying psychopathology.

With respect to environmental characteristics, there is some evidence that treating employees unfairly, and failing to address frustrations, may heighten the risk of all of these antisocial behaviors. This is particularly the case when employees believe they have no control over events that impact them. Thus, organizations wishing to prevent antisocial behavior should combine thorough preemployment screening with efforts to treat employees fairly and remove barriers to performance.

Substance use is a form of counterproductive behavior that may be quite damaging, particularly when employees perform dangerous work or are entrusted with the safety of others. The causes of substance use are complex; however, it is interesting to note that personality traits predictive of other forms of antisocial behavior are also predictive of substance use. Prediction and prevention of substance use often pose a dilemma for organizations because issues of employee privacy and public relations are involved.

The final form of counterproductive behavior examined in this chapter was sexual harassment. Sexual harassment may occur in the form of direct acts, or more indirectly through behaviors that, in the aggregate, create a "hostile work environment." Research has shown that women are typically the victims of sexual harassment, and it is most likely to occur in work situations in which women are in the minority and fill positions of lower power than men. The best way to prevent this form of counterproductive behavior is to have in place a clearly articulated sexual harassment policy, and to heighten employees' awareness of the issue. More recent research also suggests that sexual harassment may be part of a more general pattern of mistreatment; thus, organizations may also decrease sexual harassment by promoting a social climate of respect and civility towards others.

PEOPLE BEHIND THE RESEARCH

MICHELLE DUFFY AND THE DARK SIDE OF WORKPLACE RELATIONS

I first became interested in social undermining after conducting interviews (as part of my job at the time) with a number of employees in various occupations who were experiencing a multitude of physical health symptoms such as chronic colds, flues, headaches, stomach pain, and sleeplessness. One thing that struck me was how frequently the direction of the interview turned to a focus on interpersonal workplace relationships. The power of these workplace relationships and the meaning they had in peoples' lives stayed with me. Although people would talk about positive aspects of their relationships and workplace interactions, often they seemed to strictly focus on the negative aspects of these interpersonal interactions. Across different occupations and ranks, I heard stories that were quite similar regarding the power of *negative* workplace interpersonal interactions in peoples' work lives. People described interactions in which they were ridiculed, insulted, ignored, delayed, hampered, and misled by their own coworkers and supervisors. The power of these undermining behaviors was destructive and seemingly toxic.

At that time, much of the research focus was on positive and supportive workplace interactions. There was much less known about the impact of negative interactions on employee health and well-being. I decided to study these types of interactions for my dissertation. I found that undermining behaviors were indeed associated with a variety of undesirable employee outcomes such as lower physical and emotional well-being, lower performance and poor job attitudes. More interesting to me, however, was the fact that undermining behaviors were *more* predictive of employee outcomes than were supportive behaviors. In terms of how they affect peoples' lives, a negative workplace event carries much more weight than a positive event. Beyond this, I also found people have the most difficult time dealing with coworkers who frequently engaged in **both** positive and negative behaviors (rather than just negative behavior). With these people, you never know where you stand and the inconsistency in their behavior is very damaging to a person's well-being.

Michelle Duffy
Carlson School of Management
University of Minnesota

SUGGESTED ADDITIONAL READINGS

Berdahl, J. L., & Moore, C. (2006). Workplace harassment: Double jeopardy for minority women. *Journal of Applied Psychology, 91,* 426–436.

Bowling, N. A., & Beehr, T. A. (2006). Workplace harassment from the victim's perspective: A theoretical model and meta-analysis. *Journal of Applied Psychology, 91,* 998–1012.

Clarke, S. (2006). The relationship between safety climate and safety performance: A meta-analytic review. *Journal of Occupational Health Psychology, 11,* 315–327.

Frone, M. R. (2006). Prevalence and distribution of illicit drug use in the workforce and in the workplace: Findings and implications from a U.S. national survey. *Journal of Applied Psychology, 91,* 857–869.

Chapter Seven

O
ccupational stress is a topic that has generated a tremendous volume of research (Beehr, 1995; Jex, 1998), and a great deal of that research has focused on the physical and mental health of employees (Hofman & Tetrick, 2003). Stress is also a topic that has been the focus of a great deal of popular media attention, and it comes up frequently in everyday conversation. (Who doesn't have a stressful job!) Despite all this attention, the scientific study of occupational stress does not have a long history. Furthermore, despite the considerable progress that has been made over the years, we still have much to learn about the impact of stress on the health and well-being of employees.

A question that is often asked about occupational stress is: Does it really have an aversive effect on individuals and organizations, or are those who study occupational stress "making mountains out of molehills"? There is evidence that being consistently exposed to stressful work conditions is harmful to employees and may have a negative impact on organizational effectiveness. Consider, for example, that the amount of money extracted from the U.S. economy due to occupational stress has been estimated to be in the billions of dollars (e.g., Aldred, 1994; Ivancevich & Matteson, 1980; Matteson & Ivancevich, 1987; Mulcahy, 1991). Such estimates are based on the assumption that stress plays a role in negative outcomes such as increased healthcare costs, higher rates of absenteeism and turnover, more on-the-job accidents, and reduced productivity.

Occupational Stress and Employee Health

Another indication of the harmful effects of occupational stress is the increasing trend toward stress-related workers' compensation claims (National Council on Compensation Insurance, 1988, 1991; DeFrank & Ivancevich, 1998). In the past, compensation for work-related injuries was limited to physical injuries caused by some physical event or stimulus. Increasingly, however, more and more states are recognizing the legitimacy of physical and even psychological injuries that may be caused by some stressful aspect of the work environment that is not physical in nature (e.g., an overly demanding supervisor).

Occupational stress is also important because of its impact on society as a whole. It is unlikely that a person experiencing constant stress on the job will function effectively in his or her other roles, such as husband/wife, parent, neighbor, and community member. Failure to perform these roles effectively may not have direct economic costs but may, in the long run, have a tremendously negative impact on society. Thus, occupational stress is clearly not the "cause of all societal ills," but it does have an important and real impact on individuals, organizations, and society.

A BRIEF HISTORY

The earliest scientific investigations related to the field of occupational stress were conducted by the well-known physiologist Walter Cannon in the early part of the twentieth century (e.g., Cannon, 1914). Cannon's work focused on the relationship between emotions and physiological responses, and is considered the earliest work in the field of psychosomatic medicine (the relationship between psychological states and physical illness). Cannon, however, is best known for having coined the term *homeostasis*. Homeostasis represents the body's effort to restore normal physiological functioning when some deviation is required. When the body is exposed to extreme cold, for example, the physiological changes that are evoked are designed to maintain a constant internal body temperature. Stressful conditions on the job are typically perceived as aversive events that require some adaptive response designed to return the employee to normal functioning.

The first actual scientific investigations of stress are attributed to Hans Selye (1956), who is considered by many to be the "Father of Stress." Selye, an endocrinologist, was conducting research on reproductive hormones in animals. During the course of this research, he was required to expose these animals to a number of aversive stimuli, such as temperature extremes and radiation. While doing this, Selye observed a great deal of predictability in these animals' efforts to adapt to the aversive stimuli. From this, Selye reasoned that humans do much the same in their efforts to cope with the challenges of everyday life, and he developed the *general adaptation syndrome* to describe this process.

The general adaptation syndrome consists of three distinct stages: alarm, resistance, and exhaustion. In the alarm stage, the physiological resources of the body are mobilized, in wholesale fashion, to deal with an impending threat. In the resistance stage, the body recognizes that not all of its resources may be needed, and thus continues to mobilize only those that are necessary. Finally, in the exhaustion stage, the body realizes that its physiological resources are depleted and, as a result, makes another attempt to mobilize. If this second attempt at mobilizing physiological resources does not neutralize the threat, this may lead to permanent damage to the organism, or what Selye termed *diseases of adaptation*. While the general adaptation syndrome tends to be accepted as a general framework by stress researchers, it has not been submitted to extensive empirical test in humans. Furthermore, it has recently been argued that this response is more appropriate for males than it is for females (Taylor et al., 2000).

Selye's work was undoubtedly pioneering, but it must be remembered that he focused primarily on physiological reactions to aversive physical stimuli. He was not focusing specifically on stress in the workplace. The first large-scale program of research focusing specifically on stress in the workplace was undertaken at the University of Michigan's Institute for Social Research in the early 1960s. What is particularly noteworthy about this research effort is that the focus was on *psychosocial factors* in the workplace that may be stressful to employees. Psychosocial factors represent aspects of the work environment having to do with interactions with other people. In particular, the Michigan researchers focused much of their attention on what they termed *role stressors* (to be discussed in more detail later in the chapter), which are aversive working conditions associated with behaviors expected of each employee in an organization (e.g., Caplan, Cobb, French, Harrison, & Pinneau, 1975; Kahn, Wolfe, Quinn, Snoek, & Rosenthal, 1964).

Despite the contributions of the University of Michigan research program, occupational stress did not attract a lot of interest among organizational psychologists in the late 1960s and early 1970s. This changed in 1978, due in large part to a comprehensive review and analysis of the occupational stress literature. The authors of the review, which appeared in the journal *Personnel Psychology,* were Terry Beehr and John Newman. The Beehr and Newman (1978) compilation is generally regarded as an important scholarly work and has been cited frequently, but its greatest contribution may have been to alert those in the field of organizational psychology that occupational stress was an issue worthy of attention.

Evidence of the impact of Beehr and Newman's review can be seen in the steep increase in the volume of occupational stress research after its publication (Beehr, 1995, 1998). Since then, several books, chapters, and comprehensive reviews have continued to summarize this vast literature (e.g., Cartwright & Cooper, 1997; Cooper & Dewe,

2004; Jex, 1998; Jex & Beehr, 1991; Kahn & Byosiere, 1992; Smith & Sulsky, 2005; Sullivan & Bhagat, 1992).

APPROACHES AND TERMINOLOGY

Organizational psychologists have certainly contributed much to the study of occupational stress, but a perusal of the occupational stress literature will show that important contributions have also been made by physicians, clinical psychologists, engineering psychologists, labor economists, epidemiologists, and nurses, to name a few. To capture the interdisciplinary nature of occupational stress, Beehr and Franz (1987) proposed that occupational stress can be approached from four different perspectives: (1) medical, (2) clinical/counseling, (3) engineering psychology, and (4) organizational psychology. The distinguishing feature of the *medical approach* to occupational stress is a focus on the contribution of stress in the workplace to employee health and illness. When viewed from this perspective, stressful aspects of the work environment may be considered pathogenic agents that contribute to disease conditions. Not surprisingly, many researchers who approach occupational stress from this perspective are physicians or have received their academic training in some other health-related field (e.g., health education, nursing, public health).

The *clinical/counseling approach* to occupational stress emphasizes the impact of stressful working conditions on mental health outcomes (e.g., depression, anxiety). Beehr and Franz (1987) also point out that, compared to the others, this approach tends to focus more on treatment than on research. That is, rather than focusing on why stressful work conditions lead to problems, adherents of this approach tend to focus on developing methods to relieve stress-related symptomatology (e.g., Beehr, Jex, & Ghosh, 2001). As one would expect, the clinical/counseling approach is dominated by those trained in clinical or counseling psychology.

The *engineering psychology approach* to occupational stress focuses on sources of stress that originate from the physical work environment. Examples of these might include work schedules, pace of work, or perhaps the design of employees' workstations. This emphasis on the physical environment as a source of stress is not surprising, given that the discipline of engineering psychology (also termed *human factors*) focuses on the interface between employees and the physical environment. Another distinctive feature of this approach, according to Beehr and Franz (1987), is that it emphasizes the performance-related implications of stress in the workplace. It is also true, though not pointed out by Beehr and Franz, that much of the occupational stress research guided by this approach has examined health-related outcomes such as physiological changes (Frankenhaeuser, 1979) or fatigue (Sparks, Cooper, Fried, & Shirom, 1997).

The *organizational psychology approach* to occupational stress is characterized by a number of distinctive features. For one thing, this approach tends to focus on what were previously defined as psychosocial sources of stress in the workplace. This implies two things. First, this approach tends to focus heavily on *cognitive appraisal*, or the process by which employees perceive the work environment and decide whether it is stressful. Second, as was pointed out earlier, this approach tends to focus on sources of stress that emanate from interactions with others (i.e., they are social in nature). Another distinguishing feature of this approach, as compared to the others, is

that researchers tend to be interested in the impact of occupational stress on employee outcomes that directly impact organizational effectiveness.

In recent years, these four approaches have largely converged under one umbrella known as Occupational Health Psychology (OHP; Barling & Griffiths, 2003). OHP is essentially a new interdisciplinary field that is concerned with using the theories and methods of psychology (and closely related fields) to enhance the health, safety, and well-being of employees. It should be pointed out that, although occupational stress is only one aspect of OHP, it is a very key one because of the impact that stress has on employee health and safety (see Comment 7.1).

OCCUPATIONAL STRESS TERMINOLOGY

For many years occupational stress researchers have adopted (and, at times, struggled with) unique terminology. In this section, the terminology used in occupational stress research is briefly reviewed. No term has evoked more controversy and discussion than the term *stress* itself (see Comment 7.2). It can be defined in a number of ways, but researchers have tended to adopt a stimulus, response, or stimulus–response definition. A *stimulus* definition implies that stress is some type of force acting upon the individual. In everyday conversation, this definition might be reflected in the following sentence: "Bob has had his share of stress at work during the past year." Notice in this statement that the term stress is used to refer to negative aspects of the work environment that may be troublesome to the individual.

A *response* definition implies that stress is synonymous with the way in which

COMMENT 7.1

OCCUPTIONAL HEALTH PSYCHOLOGY: DEVELOPMENT OF A NEW FIELD

ONE OF THE most significant developments in the study of occupational stress and health has been the emergence of the field of Occupational Health Psychology (OHP). According to Tetrick and Quick (2003), the purpose of OHP is to "develop, maintain, and promote the development of employees directly and the health of their families" (p. 4). They go on to state that many areas of psychology (e.g., clinical, industrial/organizational, health, human factors), as well as other health-related disciplines (e.g., occupational medicine, public health), have developed theories and methods that have the potential to positively impact employee health and well-being, particularly when members of these disciplines work together. Thus, the field of OHP can best be described as an interdisciplinary approach to the enhancement of employee health and well-being.

While the field of OHP is still very new, it has grown quickly and is international in scope. Many universities offer concentrations in OHP as part of the doctoral training in psychology, and there are now two major professional organizations associated with OHP (European Association of Occupational Health Psychology; Society for Occupational Health Psychology). There is also a scientific journal devoted exclusively to OHP (*Journal of Occupational Health Psychology*), and several professional conferences have focused on this field.

Source: Tetrick, L.E., & Quick, J.C. (2003). Prevention at work: Public health in occupational settings. In J.C. Quick & L.E. Tetrick (Eds.), *Handbook of occupational health psychology* (3–18). Washington, DC: American Psychological Association.

employees react to stressful job conditions. Consider the following statement: "Barbara is feeling a lot of stress because of her upcoming performance review." Stress is used here to represent the feelings that are evoked by something in the work environment that the employee obviously considers to be aversive.

When a *stimulus–response* definition is used, the term *stress* is used merely to refer to the overall process by which the work environment may negatively impact employees. Rather than using the term *stress* to refer something in the work environment or the response of an employee, the term *stressor* is used to represent aspects of the work environment that may require some adaptive response on the part of employees. For example, one might note that a person

appears to be experiencing many stressors on his or her job. (Later in the chapter, a number of common organizational stressors will be described.)

The other term associated with the stimulus–response definition, *strain*, refers to a multitude of maladaptive ways employees may react to stressors. For example, one might observe that because of working long hours (a stressor), an employee appears to be showing a great deal of strain. Occupational stress researchers typically classify strains in three categories: psychological, physical, and behavioral. Psychological strains include affective or emotional responses to stressors. Common examples of these from the occupational stress literature include anxiety and frustration (Spector, Dwyer, & Jex, 1988), hostility (Motowidlo, Packard, & Manning,

COMMENT 7.2

THE MEANING OF THE WORD *STRESS*

LIKE MANY OTHER researchers in various fields of study, occupational stress researchers have struggled considerably with terminology over the years. Variance in terminology makes it more difficult for researchers to communicate and more generally decreases the rate of progress within any scientific endeavor. This can also be a big problem if those who participate in occupational stress studies have their own definitions of important terms and concepts.

Several years ago, the first author conducted a study, in collaboration with Terry Beehr and Cathy Roberts, in which we were interested in a simple question: "How do survey respondents tend to interpret the word 'stress' when it is used on self-report questionnaires?" Our data seemed to indicate that respondents had a tendency to use what is termed a *response* definition. In other words, if you ask people about their current "stress level," chances are they will answer in terms of the reactions they are having to the stressful conditions they are experiencing in their job.

The practical implication of this study is actually quite simple: Unless there is a compelling reason to do so, it is probably not a good idea to use the word *stress* in questionnaire items. If it is used, researchers should be very clear as to how they are defining it.

Source: S. M. Jex, T. A. Beehr, and C. K. Roberts. (1992). The meaning of occupational "stress" items to survey respondents. *Journal of Applied Psychology, 77,* 623–628.

1986), and depression (Heinisch & Jex, 1997).

Physical strains include responses that are related to employees' physical health and well-being. These have received considerable attention in recent years (e.g., Ganster & Schaubroeck, 1991) because of the escalating costs associated with healthcare. The most common method of measuring physical strain has been self-reported physical symptoms (e.g., Frese, 1985; Spector & Jex, 1998). Other methods that can be found in the occupational stress literature include the assessment of physiological indexes (e.g. blood pressure, heart rate; Fried, Rowland, & Ferris, 1984; Schaubroeck & Merritt, 1997) and diagnosed disease conditions (Sales & House, 1971).

Behavioral strains have been explored the least in occupational stress research. This is likely due to the difficulties associated with obtaining behavioral indexes, as well as a lack of understanding of the many forms of behavior in organizations (e.g., Campbell, 1990). Perhaps the most relevant form of behavioral strain in organizations is impaired job performance. The majority of occupational stress studies that have examined the impact of stressors on job performance have measured it through the use of supervisory ratings (Jex, 1998). Other behavioral strains that have been examined, with varying degrees of success, include absenteeism, turnover, and substance abuse.

Despite the multitude of strains that have been studied over the years, it is important to keep in mind that not all reactions to stressors are negative. A tight deadline may be seen as challenging, or perhaps a vaguely defined role may provide an employee the opportunity to carve out her niche in an organization. In fact, in recent years, psychologists have begun to systematically study the more positive effects of many types of stressors (Britt, Adler, & Bartone, 2001; Nelson & Simmons, 2003).

OCCUPATIONAL STRESS MODELS

As was pointed out in Chapter 21, a theoretical model is simply a description of the relevant variables impacting some phenomenon and the relationships among these variables. Theoretical models are quite useful in guiding behavioral science research and its applications. Over the years, a number of theoretical models of occupational stress have been developed to help guide both research and organizational efforts to reduce stress. Those that have had the greatest impact are described in the following.

Institute for Social Research (ISR) Model

One of the earliest occupational stress models came out of the previously mentioned program of research at the University of Michigan's Institute for Social Research (French & Kahn, 1962; Katz & Kahn, 1978). For this reason, it has come to be known as the ISR model of occupational stress. As can be seen in Figure 7.1, this model begins with the objective environment. This includes anything in an employee's work environment: the number of hours worked, the amount of responsibility, the extent to which interaction with others is required, and so on.

The next step in this model is labeled the psychological environment. At this step, the employee perceives the objective environment. The employee at this point is appraising aspects of the work environment and making some judgment as to whether or not they are threatening (Lazarus, 1966). As was stated in the previous discussion of approaches to occupational stress, the appraisal process is a key component of the organizational psychology approach.

FIGURE 7.1
The ISR Model of Occupational Stress

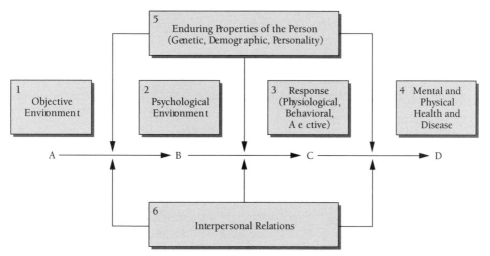

Source: Adapted from: D. Katz and R. L. Kahn. (1978). *The social psychology of organizations* (2nd ed.). New York: Wiley. Reprinted by permission.

Once the environment is appraised, the model proposes that the result may be immediate physiological, behavioral, and emotional responses on the part of the employee. Physiological changes that are commonly evoked by stressful stimuli include increases in heart rate, elevated blood pressure, and increased respiration rate (Fried et al., 1984). Immediate behavioral responses may include decreased effort, or perhaps an inability to concentrate (Jex, 1998). Emotional responses may include increases in both anxiety and depressive symptoms, and a decrease in job satisfaction (Heinisch & Jex, 1997; Spector et al., 1988).

Depending on the severity and duration of the immediate responses, the result may be adverse changes in mental and physical health. For example, an employee whose initial response to a stressor (such as an impending deadline) is increased anxiety may end up feeling anxious all the time. On the physical side, an employee who experiences a short-term elevation in blood pressure in response to this same stressor may eventually develop chronic hypertension or coronary heart disease.

The next two components in the ISR model (5 and 6) are meant to illustrate the impact of individual differences on all of the processes depicted in the model. For example, people obviously differ considerably in terms of genetic makeup, demographic characteristics, personality traits, and the quality of their interpersonal relations with others. Furthermore, any or all of these factors may impact the manner in which people perceive the objective environment, their immediate responses to perceived stressors, and, ultimately, whether stressors lead to adverse mental and physical health.

While the ISR model has not been explicitly tested, it has served as a conceptual guide for a substantial portion of the occupational stress research conducted over the years, and for that reason it has been quite influential. The primary weakness of this model is its generality, which is probably the main reason it hasn't been empirically tested. The model also does not provide specifics about each of the steps in the process. One could also argue that important variables and processes have been left out of the model. For example, the model does not explicitly account for employees' efforts to cope with stressors, or acknowledge that stressors may impinge on the employee from outside of the organization.

Beehr and Newman's Facet Model

In addition to providing a comprehensive review of the occupational stress literature, Beehr and Newman (1978) proposed a model of the occupational stress process. The primary reason for proposing this model, according to these authors, was to serve as a guide to categorizing the occupational stress literature. Thus, like the ISR model, this model was meant to be a guide for researchers rather than a model to be empirically tested. As can be seen in Figure 7.2, this model proposes that the occupational stress process can be broken down into a number of "facets" that represent categories of variables to be studied. Going from left to right in the model, the Personal facet represents the stable characteristics that employees bring with them to the workplace. Examples of variables included here would be demographic characteristics (e.g., age, gender, race) and personality.

The Environmental facet, in contrast, represents those stimuli in the work environment that individual employees must confront. Variables comprising this facet would include characteristics of the work performed (e.g., level of complexity) as well as

FIGURE 7.2
Beehr and Newman's Facet Model of Occupational Stress

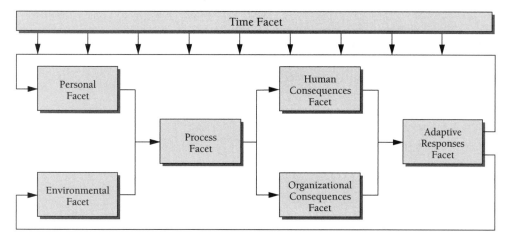

Source: Adapted from: T. A. Beehr and J. E. Newman. (1978). Job stress, employee health, and organizational effectiveness: A facet analysis, model, and literature review. *Personnel Psychology, 31,* 665–699. Reprinted by permission.

the nature of job-related interpersonal relations. It is in the Process facet that characteristics of the person and the situation interact. This is the point at which employees appraise the work environment and ultimately decide whether it is harmful.

If the employee perceives stressors to be present after the environment is appraised, there may be a variety of consequences for both the individual employee and the organization as a whole. The Human Consequences facet represents the multitude of ways in which employees may respond to stressors that primarily have implications for each individual employee (e.g., health problems, substance abuse). In contrast, the Organizational Consequences facet represents employee responses that primarily have implications for organizational functioning (e.g., higher rates of absenteeism and turnover, impaired employee job performance).

Depending on the consequences for the individual and the organization, some response may be required. The Adaptive

Response represents efforts on the part of individuals and organizations to respond adaptively to stressors. An adaptive response for an individual may be to exercise when he or she feels tense or anxious. An organization may respond to increased absenteeism by instituting flexible work hours.

The final facet in this model is Time. As is evident from Figure 7.2, this facet has an impact on all other facets in the model. It exhibits recognition of the fact that the process of employees' appraising the environment, determining what aspect(s) are stressful, and ultimately responding to those perceived stressors, is embedded in a temporal context. In some cases, this process may be very short; at other times, it may occur over a period of several years. As Beehr and Newman (1978) aptly pointed out, this is probably the least understood of all the facets because of the reliance on cross-sectional research designs. (See McGrath and Beehr, 1990, for a more extensive discussion of the role of time in occupational stress research.)

Demands—Control Model

A model of occupational stress that is much more specific than the others presented to this point is known simply as the Demands–Control model. This model, which was proposed by Robert Karasek in the late 1970s, posits that the most stressful situations in the workplace are those in which employees face heavy job demands but, at the same time, are given little control over their work. (Karasek [1979] used the term *Job Decision Latitude* to denote control.) A good example would be the situation of a typical factory worker in the Scientific Management era. Recall from Chapter 1 that one of the major principles of Scientific Management was to provide production employees with challenging goals, usually in the form of production standards. At the same time, proponents of Scientific Management argued that these same employees should have little control over things such as the design of work methods and the scheduling of rest breaks. Factory employees during this period also had little control over the reliability of machinery or the motivation levels of their fellow employees.

Most research using the Demands-Control model as a theoretical framework has examined health and physiological outcomes (e.g., Fox, Dwyer, & Ganster, 1993; Karasek, Baker, Marxer, Ahlbom, & Theorell, 1981; Perrewe & Ganster, 1989). This limits the scope of the model somewhat, although it is certainly possible that the scope of the Demands–Control model could be broadened. In fact, some research that tested the Demands–Control model has investigated psychological outcomes (e.g., Spector, 1987a).

It is also worth mentioning that recent tests of the Demands–Control model have shown that the interaction between job demands and control may be more complex than Karasek

originally proposed. Most notably, Schaubroeck and Merritt (1997) found, in predicting blood pressure, that the interaction between demands and control that is predicted by Demands–Control theory was observed only for employees who reported high self-efficacy. This suggests that having control over one's work tasks is helpful to an employee only if he or she feels able to perform those tasks (i.e., has high self-efficacy). Some research has also shown that the proposed Demands-Control interaction may be less likely to occur among employees who have high levels of social support (Jonsson, Rosengren, Dotevall, Lappas, & och Wilhelmsen, 1999); in fact, some now refer to this model as the *Demands-Control-Support* model.

Person—Environment Fit Model

This model of occupational stress actually has implications for many organizational phenomena (e.g., selection, socialization). The historical roots of the Person–Environment (P–E) Fit approach can be traced back to Kurt Lewin and his notion of *interactional psychology*. Lewin simply believed that human behavior is a function of the interaction between characteristics of the person and characteristics of the situation. One aspect of this interaction that is relevant to occupational stress is the degree to which there is a fit between the person and the situation. According to this approach, an employee perceives the work environment as stressful when there is a lack of fit (Caplan, 1987; French, Caplan, & Harrison, 1982).

The general notion of P–E Fit is rather simple but there are many ways in which fit (and misfit) between an employee and the work environment can occur. According to Kristof (1996), fit (and misfit) may indicate the degree to which an employee's skills and abilities match the requirements of the job he or she is performing. An employee who lacks the skills and abilities necessary to perform a job may feel overwhelmed and inadequate. Conversely, when job requirements are well below an employee's capabilities, the results may be boredom, frustration, and dissatisfaction. In either case, it is very likely that such an employee will perceive the job as stressful.

The concept of P–E Fit (and misfit) may also occur at a more "macro" level of analysis. More specifically, one can speak of the degree of fit between characteristics of the employee and characteristics of the organization. For example, suppose an employee who places a very high value on individual accomplishment goes to work for an organization that places a very high value on teamwork. This would obviously be a poor fit and it is likely that such an individual would ultimately find working in such an environment stressful.

The P–E Fit approach has proven to be quite useful to occupational stress researchers. Over the years, considerable refinements have been made both in conceptualizing fit (e.g., Edwards, 1994; Kristof, 1996) and in the statistical analysis of P–E Fit data (Edwards & Parry, 1993). Perhaps the major limitation of the P–E Fit approach is that, compared to the Environment component, we seem to be much further ahead in the measurement of the Person component of the model. That is, psychologists have devoted considerable time and energy to conceptualizing and measuring individual characteristics such as abilities, skills, and personality. Far less attention has been given to conceptualizing and measuring unique characteristics of organizations.

Effort-Reward Imbalance

This model has been developed fairly recently, and has become quite influential in guiding occupational stress research in Europe. The model was developed by Johannes Siegrist in Germany, who proposed that the most stressful situations are those in which an employee's efforts are out of proportion with the rewards that his or her job is providing him or her (Siegrist, 2002); put differently, an employee is putting more into the job than he or she is getting out of it. One can think of many occupations in our society that would likely fit this "high effort–low reward" profile (e.g., teaching, social work, nursing). Siegrist also proposed that people who are extremely committed to work are most likely to experience this imbalance because it is unlikely that the rewards they receive will ever match their efforts.

Since the Effort-Reward Imbalance model has been developed fairly recently, it has not been empirically tested as much as the Demands-Control or P–E Fit models. However, it has been shown that those experiencing high Effort-Reward Imbalance are most susceptible to symptoms of poor health (Peter, Geibler, & Siegrist, 1998; Siegrist, 1996; Siegrist et al., 2004).

Comparison of Occupational Stress Models

Having described the four occupational stress models, some comparison of the relative merits of each is in order. In terms of usefulness, all of the models presented have some merit. However, over the years, the ISR model and the model proposed by Beehr and Newman (1978) have guided the bulk of occupational stress research. This suggests that both models have served as road maps to guide occupational stress researchers' efforts. It is relatively easy to use each of these models to guide a specific research investigation or to clarify the focus of a stress-related organizational intervention.

Of all the occupational stress models, the Demands-Control model (Karasek, 1979) has clearly received the most empirical scrutiny, and the results have been mixed (e.g., Fox et al., 1993; Perrewe & Ganster, 1989; Spector, 1987a). As was stated earlier, this may be due to the fact that the conditions under which demands and control interact are more complex than those Karasek originally proposed (e.g., Schaubroeck & Merritt, 1997). The P–E Fit approach has also received a fair amount of empirical testing, though not all of this testing has been in the context of occupational stress research. In this case, the results have generally been favorable (e.g., Kristof, 1996). Since the Effort-Reward Imbalance model has been developed only recently, it has not been subject to a great deal of empirical testing so more research is needed. However, tests of this model that have been conducted have supported it (Siegrist, 2002).

WORKPLACE STRESSORS

A *stressor* represents anything in the job or organizational environment that requires some adaptive response on the part of the employee. One of the difficulties in covering stressors is simply deciding which ones to describe when there are so many in the workplace. The stressors covered in this section represent two general types: (1) those that have been commonly studied or have received considerable attention in the occupational stress literature, and (2) those that have received less attention but have more recently become the focus of attention.

Commonly Studied Stressors

Role Stressors: In the history of occupational stress research, role stressors have been given far more attention than any

other type. A *role* is essentially a set of behaviors that are expected of an individual. Most people have multiple roles (e.g., parent, employee, student, spouse), so it stands to reason that people also have multiple sets of role demands. In complex social systems such as organizations, roles serve the important function of bringing order and predictability to the behavior of individuals (Katz & Kahn, 1978). Roles also help individual employees gauge whether they are doing what they are supposed to be doing.

Employees in organizations receive role-related information through both formal and informal sources. In many organizations, the most common formal source of role-related information is a written job description. Other common sources are verbal and written communications with one's immediate supervisor. All of these formal sources may provide important information, but they may also be limited in defining an employee's role. For example, written job descriptions are often very general and become outdated quickly. In addition, supervisors' job knowledge may be lacking, and communication is often imprecise.

To compensate for limitations in formal sources of information, employees may look to informal sources as they define their organizational roles. These may include informal interactions with coworkers at the same level, as well as encounters with subordinates and even with persons outside the boundaries of the organization (e.g., customers, suppliers, regulatory agencies). The term *role set* encompasses the various sources of information, both formal and informal, that employees utilize in defining their roles in organizations.

The communication of role-related information should be a smooth process in which the various members of a role set provide clear and consistent information to employees. However, we know that this does not always happen. When role-related information is unclear, this may lead to a stressor known as *role ambiguity* (Kahn et al., 1964; King & King, 1990). In the most general sense, role ambiguity exists when an employee is unsure of what he or she is supposed to do. This uncertainty can be manifested in a variety of ways: unclear performance standards (Beehr, Walsh, & Taber, 1980), uncertainty regarding scheduling and work methods (Breaugh & Colihan, 1994), and so on. A common example of role ambiguity experienced by students is professors' lack of clarity regarding grading standards.

Another common problem that may occur is a lack of consistency in the role-related information provided by the various members of an employee's role set. When this occurs, the stressor that may result is known as *role conflict* (Kahn et al., 1964; King & King, 1990). Role conflict usually results from inconsistent information or conflicting demands provided by different members of an employee's role set. It is also possible that the same individual within an employee's role set may communicate inconsistent information or requests over time. For many college professors, their teaching responsibilities and research activities form a common source of role conflict. The more time they spend on teaching, the less time they have available for research, and vice versa.

A third role stressor that has been examined, though not nearly as much as role ambiguity and conflict, is *role overload*. This stressor is defined by Jones, Flynn, and Kelloway (1995) as occurring when "an employer may demand more of an employee than he or she can accomplish in a given time, or simply, the employee may perceive the demands of work as excessive" (p. 42).

Given the generality of this definition, it is possible that an employee may feel overloaded for two reasons. First, feelings of role overload may be due to the sheer volume of the demands emanating from an employee's role set (this is referred to as *quantitative role overload*). During tax season, for example, many accountants experience this type of role overload. Second, role overload may be due to the difficulty of the demands, relative to the skills and abilities of the employee (this is referred to as *qualitative role overload*). This form of role overload is becoming very common in all of the armed services because the skill requirements of new technology often exceed those of enlisted personnel.

A great deal of occupational stress research has been grounded in role theory, so it is not surprising that more empirical research has been done on role stressors than on any of the other stressors covered in this chapter. Several meta-analyses have been conducted to summarize this vast literature (Abramis, 1994; Fisher & Gitelson, 1983; Jackson & Schuler, 1985; Tubre, Sifferman, & Collins, 1996). Overall, the results from these meta-analyses have been quite consistent in showing that role ambiguity and role conflict are correlated with a variety of strains. Table 7.1, for example, shows corrected correlations from Jackson and Schuler's study. As can be seen, high levels of role ambiguity and role conflict are associated with low job satisfaction, high anxiety and tension, and a higher probability of turnover. Correlations with behavioral outcomes such as absenteeism and job performance, however, are very small.

Compared to role ambiguity and role conflict, much less research has examined the effects of role overload. The few studies that have been done, however, have shown this stressor to be related to higher levels of

TABLE 7.1
Corrected Correlations Between Role Stressors and Both Affective and Behavioral Outcomes

Outcome	Role Ambiguity	Role Conflict
Job satisfaction	−.46	−.48
Tension/Anxiety	.47	.43
Turnover intent	.29	.34
Absences	.13	−.02
Performance ratings	−.12	−.11

Source: S. E. Jackson and R. S. Schuler. (1985). A meta-analysis and conceptual critique of research on role ambiguity and role conflict in work settings. *Organizational Behavior and Human Decision Processes, 36,* 16–78.

both psychological and physical strain (e.g., Caplan et al., 1975; Caplan & Jones, 1975; Jex, Adams, Elacqua, & Bachrach, 1998). Interestingly, some evidence suggests that quantitative role overload may actually be positively associated with job performance (Beehr, Jex, Stacy, & Murray, 2002). Employees who perform their jobs well may receive a disproportionate share of work assignments. Also, in some jobs (e.g., sales), the volume of work one has to contend with is directly proportional to one's success. Qualitative workload, however, is associated with lower performance ratings, at least in a training context (Britt, Thomas, & Dawson, 2006).

Workload: Workload is typically defined as the amount of work an employee has to do in a given period of time. This definition, however, is deceptively simple. For example, for many jobs it is necessary to distinguish between perceptions of workload and objective workload. In a purely objective sense, two employees may have exactly the same volume of work but perceive their respective workloads quite differently. Another complicating factor in attempting to understand the impact of

workload is that it is cyclical. Employees in retail stores, for example, experience a sharp increase in workload as the end-of-year holiday season approaches, but this peak is followed by a decline in January. Finally, as with role overload, it is necessary to distinguish between the sheer volume of work one is required to perform (quantitative workload) and the difficulty of that work (qualitative workload).

In general, studies of the impact of workload have focused heavily on physical outcomes. In one of the earliest studies of workload, Buell and Breslow (1960) found that working more than the typical 40 hours per week doubled the chances of mortality from coronary heart disease in men. Subsequent research, over several years, has shown that working long hours is associated with a variety of indicators of ill health, although the effects appear to be rather modest (Sparks et al., 1997). The negative physical effects associated with long hours are most likely due to physiological changes that occur during periods of overwork. According to research conducted in Sweden by Frankenhaeuser (1979), the level of adrenaline and other catecholamines increases predictably during periods of long work hours. If these adrenal hormones remain consistently elevated over an extended period of time, the risk of a number of illnesses may increase. To date, however, longitudinal research linking cyclical elevations in adrenal hormone levels to illness is lacking (Jex & Beehr, 1991).

This type of effect has also been shown with indices of workload other than work hours. Rau (2004), for example, had job analysts independently assess the demands of a sample of white-collar employees in Germany. Furthermore, demands measured in this way were associated with elevations in blood pressure during the work day. Interestingly, blood pressure returned to normal levels after the work day only for those who also had a great deal of control over how they did their jobs.

In addition to physical strains, studies have examined both the psychological and the behavioral effects using a variety of workload indexes. Spector and Jex (1998) recently summarized the results of several studies that examined perceived workload, and found it to be related to high anxiety and frustration, reduced job satisfaction, and increased turnover intentions. These authors also found that perceived workload was positively related to job performance ratings. Recall that this was also true for quantitative role overload (Beehr et al., 2000), suggesting that not all stressors lead to negative outcomes. In the long run, however, this relationship might be detrimental. Employees who perform well and thus have to shoulder a disproportionate share of the workload may eventually tire of such conditions and leave the organization.

Interpersonal Conflict: Most jobs require at least a minimal amount of interaction with other people (e.g., coworkers, customers, contractors). Such social interactions are often a source of satisfaction and personal fulfillment (Nielsen, Jex, & Adams, 2000; Riordan & Griffeth, 1995). Interactions with others can also make work more stressful if *interpersonal conflict* (Keenan & Newton, 1985; Spector, 1987), defined as negatively charged interactions with others in the workplace, develops. Negative interactions can range from something as minor as a momentary dispute over a parking space to heated arguments (see Comment 7.3). At extreme levels, interpersonal conflicts may even escalate to physical violence (O'Leary-Kelly, Griffin, & Glew, 1996).

Research suggests that there may be several potential causes of interpersonal conflict. Perhaps the most widely cited precursor to conflict is competition among people (Forsyth, 1999). In many organizations, employees must compete for rewards such as pay raises, promotions, and competitive budget allocation processes (e.g., the more Department A receives, the less Department B receives). This policy of one person's (or department's) gain is another's loss often fosters a high level of competition.

Another factor that may lead to interpersonal conflict is rude or contentious behavior on the part of employees. This may occur, for example, when one person tries to influence another through threats or coercion (Falbe & Yukl, 1992), although such behavior may at times be directed at no one in particular (Andersson & Pearson, 1999). As Falbe and Yukl point out, employees who are the target of contentious influence tactics typically do not respond favorably; in fact, they may retaliate. In either case, the odds that interpersonal conflict will occur are heightened.

Interpersonal conflict may also occur in response to behavior that is not intentionally directed at another individual, but ultimately has a negative effect. An example of this type of behavior is "free riding" in groups (Albanese & Van Fleet, 1985; Roberts, 1995). Free riding occurs when one or more members of a work group do not "pull their weight" and, as a result, other group members must pick up the slack. Those who must pick up the slack may resent the free rider, and this resentment may ultimately come out in the form of strained interpersonal relations. What's important to note about this example is that the person who is perceived to be a free rider may have had no intention of angering his or her fellow group members. This person, in fact, may not even realize that he or she is free riding.

COMMENT 7.3

THE COMPLEXITY OF INTERPERSONAL CONFLICT

INTERPERSONAL CONFLICT IS a stressor that has not been studied for a long period of time but has been shown to negatively impact employees (e.g., Spector & Jex, 1998). In fact, if you talk to people working in organizations, this is often mentioned as a very important source of stress. People strongly dislike coming to work when they don't get along with others, or when fellow employees are embroiled in conflicts.

Given the effects of interpersonal conflict, it is important that occupational stress researchers get a better handle on all of the forms in which interpersonal conflict can manifest itself in organizations. Most studies, to date, have assessed relatively mild forms of interpersonal conflict. However, we know that what constitutes interpersonal conflict ranges widely from minor arguments to physical violence.

Another aspect of interpersonal conflict that has yet to be explored is its active versus passive forms. Active conflict, which has been the focus of most of the research, includes arguments and saying rude things to others. More passive forms of conflict might include not returning a fellow employee's phone calls, or perhaps "forgetting" to invite a coworker to a meeting.

In summary, interpersonal conflict is an important variable that is much more complex than current research would seem to indicate. A great deal more conceptual work needs to be done before we are able to get a clear picture of the impact of interpersonal conflict in organizations.

Source: P. E. Spector and S. M. Jex. (1998). Development of four self-report measures of job stressors and strain: Interpersonal Conflict at Work Scale, Organizational Constraints Scale, Quantitative Workload Inventory, and Physical Symptoms Inventory. *Journal of Occupational Health Psychology, 3,* 356–367.

Compared to role stressors, considerably less research has been conducted on the effects of interpersonal conflict in organizations. Probably the most comprehensive summary of the impact of interpersonal conflict was provided by the previously described meta-analysis by Spector and Jex (1998). This meta-analysis showed that interpersonal conflict is correlated with a number of psychological, physical, and behavioral strains. The most notable finding from the meta-analysis was that interpersonal conflict was most strongly related to feelings of anxiety at work. This would appear to be a logical finding, given that anxiety is an emotion felt in anticipation of future problems and challenges (Spielberger, 1979). Those who experience high levels of interpersonal conflict at work may spend time ruminating over the possible effects of past conflicts, and may worry over future conflicts before they even occur.

Organizational Constraints: Organizations have a vested interest in facilitating the job performance of their employees. To the extent that individual employees are effective, the more effective the organization will ultimately become. However, anyone who has worked in any organization knows that organizational conditions do not always facilitate performance. In fact, organizational conditions may even detract from or constrain employee performance. For example, it is not unusual for employees to have difficulty doing their jobs because of unnecessary rules and procedures, a lack of resources, or interruptions from fellow employees.

Peters and O'Connor (1980) used the term *situational constraints* to describe a variety of organizational conditions that may prohibit employees from performing up to their capabilities. (In this section, the term *organizational constraints* is used in recognition of the fact that constraints are not always tied to specific situations.) To more fully define organizational constraints, Peters and O'Connor (1980) proposed a classification system consisting of 11 different categories of organizational constraints. These include (1) job-related information, (2) budgetary support, (3) required support, (4) time and materials, (5) required services and help from others, (6) task preparation, (7) time availability, (8) the work environment, (9) scheduling of activities, (10) transportation, and (11) job-related authority.

For any of these categories of constraints, the inhibiting effect on performance may be due to unavailability, inadequacy, or poor quality (or some combination of these). Consider the category of *job-related information*. Employees, in some cases, may lack the information needed to accomplish job-related tasks. In other cases, there may be information available, but not enough to accomplish required tasks. In still other cases, there may be plenty of information available, but the information is of such poor quality that it is of limited value; hence, employee performance is constrained.

Since Peters and O'Connor (1982) first introduced the concept, many studies have examined relations between organizational constraints and a variety of stress-related outcomes. In fact, so many studies have been conducted that two recent meta-analyses have summarized their findings (Spector & Jex, 1998; Villanova & Roman, 1993).

The specific outcomes examined in these meta-analyses differ somewhat, but the major conclusion from both is that organizational constraints are most strongly related to negative emotional reactions on the part of employees. These include things such as job dissatisfaction, frustration, and anxiety.

One finding is common to both meta-analyses (which is somewhat puzzling): the lack of a relation between organizational constraints and job performance. Organizational constraints are things in the environment that inhibit performance, so one would expect a much stronger relation. However, Peters and O'Connor (1988) point out that in most organizations several factors work against such a relation. For instance, performance appraisals are often conducted poorly and may ultimately restrict the variability in such measures (Cascio, 1998). Also, in many organizations, performance standards are very low, and employees are offered little incentive to perform above these standards.

The lack of a relationship between organizational constraints and performance may also be due to the fact that measures of *in-role* performance have been used. Jex, Adams, Bachrach, and Sorenson (2003) found that the presence of organizational constraints was negatively related to altruistic or helping behaviors among employees. This suggests that when employees experience organizational constraints they may do what they *have* to do (e.g., fulfill their basic job requirements), but may not go beyond this.

Perceived Control: The human desire to maintain control over the environment, even if this control is illusory, has been well documented in the behavioral sciences literature (e.g., Averill, 1973; Friedland, Keinan, & Regev, 1992). Compared to the other stressors covered in this chapter, perceived control is much more general and thus can be manifested in a variety of ways. According to Spector (1986), the two primary ways that perceived control is manifested in organizations are through *job autonomy* and *participative decision making*. A high level of job autonomy indicates that an employee has discretion over how his or her job tasks are to be performed, and perhaps over things such as starting and ending times (Hackman & Oldham, 1980). As an example, university professors have considerable autonomy (some would say, too much!) over many aspects of their jobs, while manual laborers and convenience store clerks typically have little autonomy.

Participative decision making is defined by Lowin (1968) as an organizational form of decision making in which those responsible for implementing decisions have some input in their formulation. This participation could take a variety of forms but is most typically identified with labor-management committees, quality circles, job enrichment, and other shared governance policies (Cotton, 1995). As an illustration of how participative decision making might be carried out, several years ago one of the authors and a colleague assisted a medium-size producer of dairy products in conducting a company-wide employee opinion survey. All phases of this project were conducted in collaboration with an "Employee Committee," which consisted of approximately 12 individuals, from several divisions of the company, who were responsible for representing the interests and views of their fellow employees.

Like other stressors covered in this section, meta-analyses have summarized the effects of both job autonomy and participative decision making. For example, Spector (1986) summarized the findings of 88 studies conducted between 1980 and 1985. A summary of the results of this meta-analysis is provided in Table 7.2. As can be seen, both

manifestations of perceived control are positively correlated with job satisfaction and negatively related to a number of strains. For example, employees who perceive a lack of control also tend to report being emotionally distressed and experiencing physical symptoms; exhibit lower levels of performance; and are more likely to quit their jobs.

Since Spector's (1986) investigation, other meta-analyses have focused more specifically on participative decision making (e.g., Wagner, 1994; Wagner & Gooding, 1987). Most of the outcomes examined in these meta-analyses, with the exception of job satisfaction and job performance, are not relevant to occupational stress. However, in both studies, participative decision making was strongly and positively related to job satisfaction, suggesting that a lack of participation may lead to negative attitudinal reactions.

Contemporary Organizational Stressors

The stressors discussed in the previous section are those that have received the greatest

TABLE 7.2
Corrected Correlations between Two Measures of Perceived Control and Affective, Health, and Behavioral Outcomes

Outcome	Job Autonomy	Participation
Job satisfaction	.37	.44
Emotional distress	−.37	−.18
Physical symptoms	−.33	−.34
Turnover intent	−.26	−.20
Turnover	−.25	−.38
Performance	.26	.23

Source: P. E. Spector. (1986). Perceived control by employees: A meta-analysis of studies concerning autonomy and participation at work. *Human Relations, 39,* 1005–1016. Copyright © The Tavistock Institute, 1986. Reprinted by permission of Sage, Ltd.

attention in the occupational stress literature. These stressors are also somewhat *timeless* in that they have been present in the workplace for many years and will likely be there for quite some time into the future. The stressors covered in this section, in contrast, have received comparatively less attention because their increased importance is related to more recent trends. These contemporary stressors include work–family conflict, mergers and acquisitions, layoffs and job insecurity, and emotional labor.

Work–Family Conflict: Conflict between work and family is certainly not a new stressor. In recent years, however, there are reasons that work–family conflict has indeed increased in importance as a stressor. For example, it has been reported that 85% of employees have some day-to-day family responsibilities that they must balance with work (Bond, Galinsky, & Swanberg, 1998).

Also, extended families are becoming more geographically dispersed and generally are having less contact with each other, compared to previous generations. Thus, it appears that, for employees today, the demands from work and family domains are competing more than ever. At the same time, sources of support that have traditionally been available to help balance those demands (i.e., extended family) are increasingly unavailable.

In describing work–family conflict, researchers make the distinction between what is termed *work–family conflict*, and what is termed *family–work conflict*. Work–family conflict occurs when the demands of work interfere with one's family responsibilities. For example, an unexpected meeting late in the day may prevent a parent from picking up his or her child from school. In contrast, family–work conflict occurs when the demands of family interfere with one's work

responsibilities. A very common example would be a parent's need to leave his or her work in order to take care of a sick child.

Another distinction often made in the work–family conflict literature is between *time-based conflict, strain-based conflict*, and *behavior-based conflict*. With time-based conflict, the time demands in one domain make it more difficult to attend to one's responsibilities in the other. Since the typical workweek is now well over 40 hours per week (Sparks et al., 1997), this is often the reason why work interferes with family. This would be "time-based, work–family conflict." On the other hand, family demands can be very time-consuming and may interfere with work. Any parent of infant or preschool children would certainly attest to the time demands associated with this role. This would be "time-based, family–work conflict."

Strain-based conflict occurs when the *strain* due to stressors in one domain impairs a person's functioning in the other. Like time-based conflict, this can occur in two directions. For example, if a person is anxious and tense because of an increase in his or her workload, this response may have a negative impact on the quality of interactions with family members. In contrast, an employee who is emotionally distraught over having to care for an elderly parent may have difficulty concentrating on work, and his or her performance may suffer.

Behavior-based conflict occurs when the behaviors required in one domain conflict with those required in the other. For example, the tough and demanding persona that a football coach may need to project to his players may conflict with the tenderness and patience needed as a parent. Like the other forms of conflict, this one could also go in the opposite direction as well. A summary of the various forms of work–family conflict is presented in Table 7.3.

TABLE 7.3
A Taxonomy of Different Forms of Work-Family Conflict

		Direction of Conflict	
Basis of Conflict	Time	Time-Based, Work-Family Conflict	Time-Based, Family-Work Conflict
	Strain	Strain-Based, Work-Family Conflict	Strain-Based, Family-Work Conflict
	Behavior	Behavior-Based, Work-Family Conflict	Behavior-Based, Family-Work Conflict

Although work–family conflict is a relatively new research domain, there has been a fair amount of empirical research on the effects of this stressor. Kossek and Ozeki (1998) summarized much of this research in a meta-analysis and found that work–family and family–work conflict were both negatively associated with job and life satisfaction. Interestingly, though, work–family conflict was more strongly correlated with both job and life satisfaction than was family–work conflict. The major implication of this finding is that employees may find it more stressful to have their work interfere with their family life than the reverse. Another interesting finding from this study was that work–family conflict was more strongly related to job and life satisfaction among women than it was among men. Thus, when the demands of work interfere with family responsibilities, women evidently find it more stressful than do men. This may reflect the fact that despite recent societal changes, women still take on a greater share of family responsibilities than men do (Hochschild, 1989).

Recent research has also been conducted looking more closely at the causes of employee perceptions of work–family conflict. Judge and Colquitt (2004), for example, found that employees who perceived that they were treated fairly by their employing organizations tended to perceive lower levels of work–family conflict. Along this same vein, Lapierre and Allen (2006) found that support from supervisors tended to be associated with lower levels of work–family conflict. Both findings suggest that organizations may be able to do a great deal to reduce conflict between the work and family domains.

Mergers and Acquisitions: The trend for organizations to engage in mergers and acquisitions started in the mid-1980s and has continued since. Mergers occur when two separate organizations combine to form one. An acquisition, on the other hand, occurs when one company (which is typically larger) obtains a controlling financial interest in another company (which is typically smaller). The acquirer then assumes a dominant role over the acquired. Hogan and Overmeyer-Day (1994) point out that, in practice, it is often difficult to clearly distinguish between mergers and acquisitions. Acquiring organizations often want to convey the impression that the two organizations are equal partners. Given this fuzzy boundary, mergers and acquisitions are discussed here as one stressor.

According to Hogan and Overmeyer-Day (1994), much of the research on mergers and acquisitions has focused on the financial and strategic implications of these transactions. A somewhat smaller body of literature has examined the stress-related implications (e.g., Buono & Bowditch, 1989; Rentsch & Schneider, 1991; Schweiger & DeNisi, 1991). Related research efforts have also been aimed at recommending strategies to help employees cope with mergers and acquisitions (e.g., Ivancevich, Schweiger, & Power, 1987).

From the limited empirical literature, the most reliable stress-related correlates of mergers and acquisitions are employees' feelings of anxiety, uncertainty, and job insecurity. Considering that even rumors of mergers and acquisitions evoke considerable speculation among employees as to how the merger or acquisition will be handled, this finding is not surprising. Ivancevich et al. (1987) recommended that organizations engaging in mergers and acquisitions should make an effort to communicate to employees as much information as possible. Given that mergers and acquisitions will continue in the future, more research is needed on the stress-related implications of this important organizational activity.

Layoffs and Job Insecurity: Like mergers and acquisitions, layoffs became a fact of life in the 1980s. A survey by the American Management Association indicated that 66% of U.S. firms with more than 5,000 employees reported reducing their workforce through layoffs in the late 1980s (Henkoff, 1990). This trend continued into the 1990s and is likely to continue for years to come (Kozlowski, Chao, Smith, & Hedlund, 1993).

Layoffs are somewhat different from the other stressors discussed in this chapter. Like the other stressors, layoffs occur in an organizational context, but their most direct impact is felt outside of the organizational context (Leana & Feldman, 1992). It is important to note, though, that layoffs often impact those who do not lose their jobs. Employees who survive layoffs may have feelings of vulnerability, and even guilt (Brockner, Grover, Reed, & DeWitt, 1992; Brockner, Grover, Reed, DeWitt, & O'Malley,

1987), and may experience an increase in workload because the amount of work typically stays the same.

How do layoffs impact those who lose their jobs? The evidence is rather unequivocal: Job loss is bad for one's mental and physical health. For example, research over the years has shown that job loss is strongly related to decreases in both psychological and physical well-being. This was shown rather clearly in a recent comprehensive meta-analysis of over 437 effects sizes (McKee-Ryan et al., 2005).

Research has also shown rather clearly that the negative impact of job loss is mitigated by reemployment (Eden & Aviram, 1993; Vinokur, van Ryn, Gramlich, & Price, 1991), and the manner in which individuals cope with job loss. For example, Wanberg (1997) found that unemployed individuals who employed *active coping* techniques (e.g., they actively searched for employment) fared better than those who avoided looking for work. An obvious reason is: Active coping is likely to speed reemployment.

Compared to job loss, relatively less is known about the impact of job insecurity. A recent meta-analysis, however, showed that job insecurity has a negative impact on employee emotions and well-being (Sverke, Hellgren, & Naswall, 2002). With respect to emotional reactions, it is likely those who survive a layoff may respond with reduced trust and commitment toward their employing organization (Buch & Aldrich, 1991). Seeing fellow employees laid off may signify a potential breach of the implicit *psychological contract* between employees and the organization (Morrison & Robinson, 1997). Layoff survivors may also find that their job duties have been expanded, leading to feelings of being overworked (Byrne, 1988; Tombaugh & White, 1990).

Another issue may confront layoff survivors: To remain employed, they may be forced to accept job transfers that require relocation. This may be very difficult, particularly for dual-career families (Gupta & Jenkins, 1985). Children may also perceive job insecurity in parents, and such perceptions may have a negative impact. For example, Barling, Dupre, and Hepburn (1998) found that college students perceived their parents' job insecurity, and these perceptions were associated with attitudes about the world of work. Students who perceived high levels of job insecurity among their fathers reported lower levels of both the Protestant work ethic (i.e., hard work pleases God) and humanistic work beliefs. Given the prevalence of layoffs in recent years, the long-term implications of these findings are troubling (see Comment 7.4) and suggest that more research on job insecurity is needed.

Emotional Labor: During the past 50 years, the structures of the U.S. economy and the economies of other countries have changed dramatically. Once dependent on heavy manufacturing, the service sector now dominates the economies of the United States and many other nations. This shift undoubtedly has enormous implications for many organizational phenomena, but it has clearly changed the content of people's jobs. As a result, many employees are faced with a very different set of stressors than were their forefathers who worked in factories a half-century ago.

The term _emotional labor_, initially coined by Hochschild (1979, 1983), refers to the emotional demands that employees face on

---

COMMENT 7.4

THE IMPACT OF OCCUPATIONAL STRESS ON CHILDREN

IN A RECENT study, Barling, Dupre, and Hepburn (1998) found that parental job insecurity had a negative impact on children's beliefs about the value of hard work as well as beliefs about humanistic values in the workplace. Stated differently, parents' job insecurity led their children to question the value of hard work and to believe that the workplace was rather cold and unforgiving.

This study is interesting for two reasons. First, the occupational stress literature offers very little data on the impact of stressors beyond the person experiencing them. It seems logical, though, that if an employee is experiencing stressors at work, the effects of these stressors will be felt by his or her spouse and children. People cannot simply block out work when they leave. Second, this study suggests that children whose parents worry about job security may develop a rather cynical attitude toward the workplace and may question whether there is any value in hard work. This finding is troubling, because hard work and commitment are needed for societies to be productive.

Perhaps, as time goes by and people do not expect to be with one employer for a long period of time, job insecurity will become less of an issue, and children may be less impacted by it. However, in the meantime, the study by Barling et al. (1998) reminds us that children are keen observers of their parents' work lives, and they form many long-lasting attitudes based on these observations.

Source: J. Barling, K. E. Dupre, and C. G. Hepburn. (1998). Effects of parents' job insecurity on children's work beliefs and attitudes. Journal of Applied Psychology, 83, 112–118.

the job. Emotional labor can take many forms, but two stand out as being particularly relevant to the study of occupational stress. In the first form, employees are forced to confront negative emotions. Examples of this would occur when a grocery store clerk must interact with a dissatisfied customer, or when a physician must interact with a grieving family. In another relevant form of emotional labor, an employee may be forced to suppress his or her true emotional state in order to further the goals of the organization. The term that has been used to describe such a situation is *surface acting* (Grandey, 2000). Many occupations have "display rules" that tell the employee the appropriate emotion to display to customers or clients (Ekman, 1973). Employees who work directly with the public encounter this type of situation every day. For example, a waiter at a restaurant may be having a bad day yet must be pleasant to customers because his job demands it. In contrast, a bill collector may be feeling happy yet must act very tough in order to get people to pay their bills.

Research on emotional labor is still relatively new, but there is evidence linking it to stress-related outcomes. The most common stress-related outcomes associated with emotional labor have been poor work attitudes and increased emotional exhaustion (Ashforth & Humphrey, 1993; Brotheridge & Grandey, 2002; Grandey, 2003). Higher emotional labor requirements are associated with heightened feelings of emotional exhaustion. Ashforth and Humphrey, however, point out that the relation between emotional labor and emotional exhaustion (and possibly other strains) may be quite complex. For example, if the emotional display rules of a job are congruent with how an employee is actually feeling, this may not be harmful: Being cordial to a customer will not be difficult for a salesperson who is in a good mood.

Recent research has shown other factors that may impact employees' reactions to emotional labor. Grandey, Fisk, and Steiner (2005) found that employees with high levels of job autonomy tended to react less negatively to emotional labor compared to those with less control. These authors also compared the reactions of French and American employees and found that in general Americans reacted more negatively to emotional labor. The authors of this study reasoned that this occurred because the French culture allows more personal control over the expression of emotions as compared to American culture.

Emotional labor appears to be a very fruitful area for further occupational stress research, considering the large number of service sector employees. It also may be useful to broaden the scope of emotional labor research to include jobs outside of the service sector, because even these jobs may have differing emotional display rules that impact employees.

REDUCING THE IMPACT OF WORKPLACE STRESSORS

The focus of the chapter so far has been on understanding the relationship between specific stressors and strains (i.e., understanding what is stressful on the job). At this point, we shift the focus to examining ways to use that knowledge to improve the health and quality of life of employees in the workplace. Organizational efforts to reduce the impact of job-related stressors generally take one of five forms: (1) stress management training, (2) reduction of stressors, (3) alternative work schedules and telecommuting, (4) family-friendly benefits, and (5) health and fitness programs. Each of these approaches is discussed in the following paragraphs.

Stress Management Training

Perhaps the most common method of combating the effects of workplace stressors is referred to as *stress management training* or, more commonly, stress management (Murphy, 1984). Stress management training is designed to help provide employees with the resources necessary to cope more effectively when they are faced with stressors. Note that the purpose of stress management training is not to eliminate or even minimize the stressors themselves; their existence is basically taken for granted.

The content of stress management training programs varies widely from organization to organization (Beehr et al., 2001; Bellarosa & Chen, 1997), but there are some common program components. For example, most programs have some educational component; that is, employees are provided with information regarding the nature of stress and its effects. It is also very common for such programs to include some form of training that is designed to help employees reduce the physical effects of stressors. In many cases, this involves some form of *relaxation training*, in which employees learn to release the muscular tension that often accompanies stressful encounters at work. Among other interventions, in *biofeedback training*, employees learn to control physiological responses (e.g., heart rate and respiration) to stressors with the aid of physiological monitoring equipment (Smith, 1993).

Another common component of stress management training programs involves teaching techniques that are designed to help employees alter their appraisals of the work environment. As noted at the beginning of this chapter, the manner in which the work environment is cognitively appraised is a key factor in determining whether it is considered a stressor. One commonly used method of accomplishing this is Meichenbaum's (1977) *Stress-Inoculation Training*, which consists of three distinct phases (see also Driskell, Salas, & Johnston, 2006).

In the first phase, participants are provided with information about stress, as well as a conceptual framework for understanding the phases of the treatment that will follow. In the second phase, participants learn and rehearse various coping strategies, which are typically taught in the form of "self-statements." The idea underlying this phase is that people often engage in dysfunctional self-statements when they encounter stressors, and these may ultimately exacerbate the effect of the stressor. As an example, before making an important sales presentation, a person may say to himself or herself: "I'm no good at speaking in front of other people . . . " Needless to say, negative self-statements make the situation more uncomfortable. According to Meichenbaum (1977), it is possible to replace such negative self-talk with more functional statements. For example, when making a sales presentation, the person could instead learn to say: "One step at a time; you can handle the situation" (p. 155). This type of self-statement is likely to be more functional and can have a calming effect on the individual.

The final phase of Stress Inoculation is referred to as *Application Training*. In this phase, participants learn to apply and use positive self-statements in everyday situations. This involves developing an awareness of situations that are perceived as stressful and of the negative self-statements that accompany such situations. Once this is done, participants learn to substitute self-statements that facilitate coping. One thing to note about this process: Consistent use of these positive self-statements may require considerable practice and rehearsal.

In recent years stress management programs, particularly in European countries, have become more comprehensive and wider in scope. According to Aust and Ducki (2004), many German companies have begun using an approach to stress management known as *health circles*. In a typical health circle, employees meet periodically (e.g., once a month) to discuss ways to reduce stress and improve overall employee health; these discussions typically lead to recommendations to top management. Some readers will recognize the similarity of this approach to *quality circles*, which are used by some manufacturing firms to improve product quality. Unfortunately, little research has been conducted to evaluate health circles, but this is an innovative approach to stress management that may grow in the future.

Reduction of Stressors

Another approach to dealing with occupational stress is to attempt to reduce the levels of the stressors themselves. This approach is much less popular than stress management training, most likely because it's more difficult. However, if an organization is truly interested in reducing the effects of stressors, this approach has greater potential for improving employees' well-being and quality of life, rather than simply treating the effects of stressors (Hurrell, 1995).

There may be many interventions that would reduce stressors—some may even have a preventative effect. Examples might include (but are not limited to) redesigning a job to increase autonomy (Griffin, 1991; Hackman & Oldham, 1980), providing employees with opportunities for greater participation in organizational decision making (Lowin, 1968; Wagner, 1994), training managers to communicate more effectively with subordinates, and training

employees to use more effective conflict-resolution techniques.

The interventions previously mentioned, when implemented in organizations, are typically not labeled as *stress reduction* efforts. In many cases, these interventions are offered as training programs, or as part of a comprehensive organizational development strategy (see Chapter 15). The result of many organizational development interventions, however, is a decrease in stressors and, consequently, an increase in employees' well-being. This point is illustrated very clearly in a study conducted by Schaubroeck, Ganster, Sime, and Ditman (1993), in which a Responsibility Charting intervention in a university was evaluated. Responsibility Charting is an activity that is typically conducted during team-building interventions. It helps a work group clarify who is responsible for what, within the group (French & Bell, 1995). One of the effects of Responsibility Charting, found in this study, was a reduction in role ambiguity.

This approach to stress management has also been used quite successfully to reduce stressors associated with the physical environment, or what are often termed *ergonomic* stressors. This includes things such as repetitive motions, poorly designed equipment that leads to back pain, and computer screens that lead to eye strain. This approach has been used to improve the physical conditions of employees in the meat packing industry (May & Schwoerer, 1994), as well as office workers (May, Reed, Schwoerer, & Potter, 2004).

Alternative Work Schedules and Telecommuting

In many cases, stressors are the result of time-based conflicts. For example, an employee may be required to be at home when his or her child arrives home from school in the afternoon. Unfortunately, this may conflict with regular work hours. To help employees cope with this form of conflict, an increasing number of organizations are implementing policies allowing *alternative work schedules*. An alternative work schedule is defined as any deviation from the typical 5-day, 8:00–5:00 or 9:00–5:00 work schedule. Given this rather broad definition, there are numerous forms alternative work schedules can take. The two most typical forms are *flextime* and the *compressed workweek*.

In a typical flextime arrangement, all employees are required to be present during some portion of the day. This time period is referred to as the *core hours*. Beyond the core hours, employees are allowed to choose their own hours, as long as they work an 8-hour day and their choice of hours is relatively consistent. To illustrate, an organization could mandate that all employees must be present between 10:00 A.M. and 3:00 P.M. Beyond these core hours, an employee may choose to start work at 7:00 A.M. and leave work at 3:00 P.M. An employee also has the option of starting his or her workday at 10:00 A.M. and leaving work at 6:00 P.M.

Because many organizations have adopted flextime arrangements (Johnson & Packer, 1987), a number of empirical studies have evaluated the impact of this form of alternative scheduling (e.g., Pierce & Newstrom, 1982; Pierce, Newstrom, Dunham, & Barber, 1989). Most of these empirical studies have found that employees respond positively to flextime arrangements in terms of job satisfaction, performance, and absenteeism. Pierce and Dunham (1992), however, suggested that flextime arrangements that have a small number of core hours and allow for changes in the pattern of hours are likely to be most appealing to employees.

In a typical compressed workweek arrangement, employees work four 10-hour days instead of five 8-hour days. In such an arrangement, an employee could work 4 consecutive days (e.g., Monday through Thursday) or arrange to have a day off in the middle of the week. Compressed scheduling has been found to have positive effects because it allows employees greater scheduling flexibility (Latack & Foster, 1985; Pierce & Dunham, 1992). One potential problem with compressed scheduling, however, is that the fatigue associated with working longer days may offset the increased flexibility (Goodale & Aagaard, 1975). According to Pierce and Newstrom (1992), the best way to avoid this problem is to implement the compressed schedule so that employees work 4 days and then have 4 days off. The key to making compressed scheduling work is to allow employees enough time to recover from the longer days.

Because of advances in communication technology, many organizations have allowed employees to engage in *telecommuting* arrangements. In a typical telecommuting arrangement, an employee is allowed to do a portion of his or her work at home. It has recently been estimated that in the United States alone there are over 28 million telecommuters, and this figure is likely to rise (International Telework Association and Council, 2001).

Given the relative recency of telecommuting, there is not a great deal of empirical research on its effects. Interestingly, though, research that has been done suggests that telecommuting may have both positive and negative effects. On the positive side, telecommuters may be better able to prevent work demands from interfering with family demands (LaPierre & Allen, 2006). Unfortunately, however, telecommuters may be more subject to nonwork interruptions, and this is particularly true for employees with large families (Golden, Veiga, & Simsek, 2006). Future research on telecommuting will likely focus on ways to maximize its positive effects, while minimizing the negative.

Family-Friendly Benefits

To help employees cope with the often conflicting demands of work and family, many organizations offer what have been termed *family-friendly* benefits. There is no standard definition of what constitutes a family-friendly benefit. Generally, these benefits are specifically designed to help employees balance the demands of work and family. Typical family-friendly benefits include flexible spending accounts, child care and elder care referrals, part-time work options, and on-site day care facilities. Both flexible work schedules and telecommuting, which were discussed in the previous section, are also considered family-friendly benefits in many cases.

Unfortunately, a widely held misconception about family-friendly benefits is that they are exclusively for women. Such benefits may be more salient to women (Kossek & Ozeki, 1998), but they are designed to benefit both men and women. In fact, in a survey of human resources executives, Milliken, Martins, and Morgan (1998) found that the percentage of females in an organization was not indicative of whether an organization offered family-friendly benefits. This study found that the best predictor was whether the executives felt that work–family issues would impact organizational effectiveness.

There is considerable testimonial evidence on the value of family-friendly benefits, but methodologically rigorous evaluations have been rare. Thomas and Ganster (1995), for example, conducted a study of the stress-related impact of family-friendly benefits among hospital employees. They found that those who worked in organizations offering family-friendly benefits reported higher levels of job satisfaction and lower levels of depression and somatic complaints. They were also found to have lower cholesterol than employees working in organizations that did not offer such benefits. This study also showed that family-friendly benefits, particularly flexible schedules, have a positive impact because they enhance employees' perceptions of control and reduce feelings of work–family conflict.

One final point—one that complicates evaluation of the impact of family-friendly benefits—must be considered: The implementation of such benefits is often at the discretion of individual managers. Furthermore, Casper, Fox, Sitzmann, and Landy (2004) found that supervisors were not equally aware of the existence of family-friendly benefits and, as a result, varied in the number of employees referred to them. As a result, the mere existence of a family-friendly benefit does not guarantee that all employees will have equal access. For example, an organization may institute a policy that makes it possible for employees to switch from full-time to part-time status. If this policy is at the discretion of individual managers, all employees may not have the opportunity to benefit. This raises the general point that perhaps the key to helping employees balance the demands of work and family does not lie in *official* solutions such as family-friendly benefits (Goff, Mount, & Jamison, 1990). Rather, the most important factor may be the flexibility, understanding, and compassion of individual managers (LaPierre & Allen, 2006). At a more general level, the overall culture of an organization with respect to work-family issues may also be more crucial than particular package of family-friendly benefits (Cunningham, 2005).

Health and Fitness Programs

An increasing number of organizations are offering a variety of programs designed to improve employees' physical health and fitness. Such programs can range from something as simple as providing information about health-related topics to extensive on-site fitness facilities (O'Donnell, 1986). For most organizations, the primary motivation for offering health and fitness programs is to reduce employees' healthcare costs (Falkenberg, 1987; Jex, 1991). Indeed, several studies conducted over the years have shown that health and fitness programs do reduce healthcare costs (see Pelletier, 1991, for a summary). Another common reason is that employees who are healthy and physically fit are less likely to be absent due to illness. As with healthcare costs, there is empirical evidence showing that health and fitness programs do indeed lead to reductions in employee absenteeism (Cox, Shephard, & Corey, 1981; Kerr & Vos, 1993; Tucker, Aldana, & Friedman, 1990).

Some studies have also attempted to link participation in health and fitness programs to outcomes such as psychological strain (e.g., anxiety, depression, job satisfaction). Compared to the studies examining healthcare costs and absenteeism, evidence linking fitness programs to psychological strain is much more equivocal. According to Jex and Heinisch (1996), this is largely due to methodological flaws in the design of many studies examining the impact of health and fitness programs. For example, many such studies do not employ control groups. Even in studies that do employ control groups, fitness program participants often drop out prior to program completion, or participate at a very minimal level.

Perhaps the most accurate conclusion to be drawn about health and fitness programs

is that they are useful for improving the physical health of employees and, as a result, may lead to decreased absenteeism. Based on the available empirical evidence, however, it is unclear whether participation in health and fitness programs has a great deal of impact on other stress-related outcomes. In the future, methodologically sound evaluations of health and fitness programs will be needed to provide more definitive evidence on this issue.

CROSS-CULTURAL OCCUPATIONAL STRESS RESEARCH

The majority of what we know about occupational stress comes from studies of employees in the United States and, to a lesser extent, Great Britain, Germany, and Scandinavia. As a result, very little evidence exists regarding basic issues such as whether occupational stress models generalize across cultures, whether cultural factors impact the stressors employees experience, and whether there are cultural differences in coping strategies. In this final section of the chapter, we briefly review research that has investigated these issues. Readers interested in a more comprehensive coverage of cross-cultural issues in occupational stress should consult Liu and Spector (2005).

GENERALIZABILITY

Very little evidence exists regarding the generalizability of occupational stress theories. This is not a trivial issue, given that most occupational stress theories have been developed in the United States or other Western countries. Xie (1996) examined this issue by testing Karasek's (1979) Demands–Control model in the People's Republic of China (PRC). According to Xie, it would be tempting to predict that Karasek's model would not apply in a collectivist nation like the PRC, since this model focuses on personal control. However, as Xie points out, there are clear differences between blue- and white-collar workers within the PRC. Blue-collar workers " . . . are generally less educated and less exposed to Western influences. Therefore, they are more likely to maintain the traditional values which impede the desire of individuals for personal control" (p. 1,600). White-collar workers, on the other hand, have had greater exposure to Western values, one of which is valuing personal control. These individuals, compared to blue-collar workers, have also benefited much more from recent economic changes in the PRC.

Based on a sample of 1,200 respondents, the interaction between demands and control that would be predicted by Karasek's model was found only for white-collar employees for most of the outcomes in the study. This supports Xie's hypothesis and suggests, more importantly, a potential limitation on this very popular occupational stress model. Recall that Schaubroeck and Merritt (1997) also found that this model was supported only for those with high self-efficacy.

One potential reason for this finding is that the meaning of control may differ between Chinese and Western cultures. According to Spector, Sanchez, Siu, Selgado, and Ma (2004), personal control beliefs in collectivist cultures such as China do not center on the person exerting direct control over the environment. Rather, in collectivist cultures such beliefs are focused on (a) adapting one's self to the environment and (b) exercising control through one's relationships with others. If this is true then many of the control measures used by occupational stress researchers, which center on personal control over the environment, may not be appropriate for collectivist cultures.

STRESSORS EXPERIENCED

Another important issue that has lent itself to cross-cultural research is whether there are cultural differences in the perceptions of stressors. This issue was addressed in a cross-cultural study of role stressors among managers from 21 nations, conducted by Peterson et al. (1995). These authors found that perceptions of role stressors (ambiguity, conflict, and overload) varied considerably across nations. They also found that levels of role stressors could be predicted from characteristics of different national cultures. Perceptions of role stressors differed with respect to power distance (degree of segregation by levels of power), level of masculinity, degree of individuality, and degree to which individuals try to decrease uncertainty.

For example, managers from nations low in power distance (e.g., industrialized, Western countries) reported high levels of role ambiguity and low levels of role overload. The pattern of results was exactly the opposite in nations characterized as high on power distance (e.g., Latin American and Far Eastern countries). This finding suggests that Western managers may not have problems with the sheer volume of work but may be uncertain about their responsibilities. Non-Western managers, in contrast, may be clear about their responsibilities but see the sheer volume of work as a stressor.

These findings, according to Peterson et al. (1995), suggest that "Role conflict, ambiguity, and overload contain a core of meaning wrapped up in the nature of formal relationships within formal organizations" (p. 447). The mistake often made in occupational stress research is to assume that the meaning of organizational events is consistent across cultures. In the future, more of this type of cross-cultural comparative research may reveal other important differences in stressors across cultures.

A second example of cross-cultural occupational stress research was provided in a study by Van De Vliert and Van Yperen (1996) in which cross-national comparisons in role overload were examined. These authors contended that the cross-national differences in role overload reported by Peterson et al. (1995) could be explained, at least in part, by cross-national differences in ambient temperature. That is, nations characterized as low in power distance by Peterson et al. were located in geographical areas in which the ambient temperature tended to be comparatively higher. They proposed that differences in ambient temperature, rather than in power distance, could have led to differences in reports of role overload.

These authors reanalyzed the data from Peterson et al. (1995), along with two other cross-cultural data sets. It was found, as predicted, that controlling for ambient temperature eliminated the relationship between power distance and role overload. Thus, these authors concluded that the relationship between power distance and role overload might be due entirely to cross-national differences in ambient temperature. These findings suggest that certain cultural characteristics may be determined, to a certain degree, by climate, and that such characteristics may then impact organizations.

More recently, Liu (2003) examined differences in stressful incidents between employees from China and the United States. She found that employees from both countries reported many common stressors, but there were also differences. For example, compared to the employees from the United States, Chinese reported mistakes at work and evaluations as greater sources of stress. In contrast, employees from the United States reported lack of personal control as a source of stress more frequently than the Chinese employees.

COPING WITH STRESS

Coping represents the manner in which employees attempt to adapt to the stressors they experience. While people may cope with stressors in numerous ways (Latack & Havlovic, 1992), in general people either try to do something about the stressor they are experiencing, or they simply try to adapt to it. Given the apparent differences in the meaning of personal control between individualistic and collectivist cultures (Spector et al., 2004), one might expect that there would be cultural differences in how directly employees confront stressors.

Research does support this, at least indirectly. For example, employees in the United States have been shown to confront conflict more directly than Taiwanese (Trubisky, Ting-Toomey, & Lin, 1991) and Arab Middle Eastern employees (Elsayed-Ekhouly & Buda, 1996). In a similar vein, Liu (2003) found that the American and Chinese employees differed in the types of conflicts they had with others. Americans reported more direct conflicts (e.g., being rude to others), whereas the conflicts reported by the Chinese were more indirect (e.g., doing things behind people's backs).

In summary, this section has provided a very brief sampling of recent cross-cultural occupational stress research. While more research obviously needs to be done, it is clear that cultural factors may play an important role in the stress process. Many of the theories, models, and variables that were once thought to be universal may not be. As organizations continue to expand globally, the importance of further cross-cultural occupational stress research cannot be overstated.

CHAPTER SUMMARY

This chapter examined occupational stress, a topic that is becoming increasingly important both to organizations and to society as a whole. The roots of occupational stress research can be traced to the early twentieth century, although the first large-scale research program did not begin until the 1960s. Furthermore, a great deal of occupational stress research has been conducted only within the past 25 years.

Occupational stress researchers have, at times, struggled with terminology. This is largely due to the fact that the study of occupational stress has always been interdisciplinary in nature. Organizational psychology has certainly contributed, but important contributions have also been made by those in medicine, clinical psychology, and engineering psychology.

Several models of the occupational stress process have been proposed over the years, and four of these were discussed. The ISR model is probably the most influential because it has guided a great deal of occupational stress over the years. Other models discussed included Karasek's Demands–Control Model, Beehr and Newman's Facet Model, the P–E Fit Model, and finally the Effort-Reward Imbalance model.

Stressors represent things in the job or organization that require some type of adaptive response on the part of employees. The most commonly studied stressors are those associated with employee roles, although researchers have also examined workload, interpersonal conflict, organizational constraints, and perceived control. Stressors that have increased in importance in recent years include work–family conflict, mergers and acquisitions, job insecurity, and emotional labor.

Organizations wishing to reduce the impact of stressors have generally tried to do so in five different ways. The most common method is the development of stress management training programs that teach employees how to cope more effectively with stressors. Other less common methods include reducing stressors, offering alternative work schedules, making family-friendly benefits available, and offering employees health and fitness programs.

Occupational stress has clearly lagged behind in cross-cultural research. Recently, however, there appears to be some progress in this area. For example, research conducted in the People's Republic of China has shown that the Demands–Control Model may not apply to all cultures, most likely due to differences in the meaning of personal control. It has also been shown that culture may have an impact on the types of stressors that are perceived, as well as the coping methods used by employees. A great deal more cross-cultural research is needed, however.

SUGGESTED ADDITIONAL READINGS

Aust, B., & Ducki, A. (2004). Comprehensive health promotion interventions at the workplace: Experiences with health circles in Germany. *Journal of Occupational Health Psychology, 9,* 258–270.

Judge, T. A., & Colquitt, J. A. (2004). Organizational justice and stress: The mediating role of work-family conflict. *Journal of Applied Psychology, 89,* 395–404.

Lapierre, L. M., & Allen, T. D. (2006). Work-supportive family, family-supportive supervision, use of organizational benefits, and problem-focused coping: Implications

PEOPLE BEHIND THE RESEARCH

GARY ADAMS AND THE CONSIDERATION OF WORK IN THE CONTEXT OF LIFE

It would be nice to be able to say that since deciding to become and I/O psychologist (way back when I was a sophomore in college) I always wanted to study topics related to occupational stress and health but that just wouldn't be true. I was originally interested in personnel selection. I had learned about the notion of person—environment fit and the idea that when there is a good fit, good things tend to happen for people and the organizations where they work. I thought I would make my career as a consultant helping organizations put that principle into practice. I earned a master's degree and then took a position in human resources. I enjoyed that work and like to think it went well but my mentor inspired me to pursue a Ph.D.

As I went back to school one of the main ideas I took from the work I had been doing, as well as my time in the Army and other positions, is that the impact of work on the individual (and vice versa) extends well beyond the office or factory door. Thus, while keeping in mind that idea of person environment fit, the major direction of my work shifted to a focus on the relationship between work and non-work. This can be seen in some of my research on the relationship between work and retire-ment, which I had originally thought of as trade-off between work and leisure. It can be seen in the research I've done on social support and the relationship between work and family. It can also be seen in my research regarding the after effects of both traumatic events (post-traumatic stress disorder) and chronic stress at work. The other change that took place while I was pursuing the Ph.D. was a shift from wanting to pursue consulting as my full-time employment to a greater interest in becoming a full-time academician. Again, this was something inspired by a mentor along the way.

The "what have I learned" question is a tough one. It may be better to ask, "what I am still learning," and then a few things come to mind. First, work is just one part of a larger puzzle called life and it's important to people and organizations for those pieces of the puzzle to fit together well. I know that sounds cliché but larger contexts do matter. I also learned that people often talk about happy and productive workers but forget that neither of these two is likely to occur when the worker (and/or the work) is unhealthy. Regarding advice to those who may be just beginning a career in I/O, I would suggest learning all you can, especially in the area of methodology. It is important to find good, relevant research questions, use good methods to study them, and then be able to communicate the answer you find to others. On a more personal level, I have found that I am fortunate to work in a field that provides a variety of opportunities and the flexibility to pursue them. I have also found that it's nice to be in field that is populated by so many good people. Again, larger contexts really do matter.

Gary A. Adams
Department of Psychology
University of Wisconsin-Oshkosh

for work-family conflict and employee well-being. *Journal of Occupational Health Psychology, 11,* 169–181.

Bond, J. T., Galinsky, E., & Swanberg, J. (1998). *The 1997 National Study of The Changing Workforce.* New York: Families and Work Institute.

Brotheridge, C., & Grandey, A. (2002). Emotional labor and burnout: Comparing two perspectives of "people work." *Journal of Vocational Behavior, 60,* 17–39.

DeFrank, R. S., & Ivancevich, J. M. (1998). Stress on the job: An executive update. *Academy of Management Update (1998) 12*(3): 55–66.

Hofmann, D. A., & Tetrick, L. E. (2003). The etiology of the concept of health: Implications for "organizing" individual and organizational health. In D. A. Hofmann and L.E. Tetrick (Eds.), *Health and safety in organizations: A multilevel perspective* (pp. 1–28). San Francisco: Jossey-Bass.

International Telework Association and Council. (2001). Telework America report. Retrieved November 20, 2007, from http://www.workingfromanywhere.org/telework/twa2001.htm.

Peter, R., Geissler, H., & Siegrist, J. (1998). Associations of effort-reward imbalance at work and reported symptoms in difference groups of male and female public transport workers. *Stress Medicine, 14,* 175–182.

Liu, C., & Spector, P. E. (2005). International and cross-cultural issues. In J. Barling, E. K. Kelloway, & M. R. Frone (Eds.), *Handbook of work stress* (pp. 487–516). Thousand Oaks, CA: Sage.

Siegrist, J. (1996). Adverse health effects of high-effort/low-reward conditions. *Journal of Occupational Health Psychology, 1,* 27–41.

Siegrist, J. (2002). Effort-reward imbalance at work and health. In P. L. Perrewe & Ganster, D. C. (Eds.), *Historical and current perspectives on stress and health* (pp. 261–291). Amsterdam: JAI Elsevier.

Siegrist, J., Starke, D., Chandola, T., Godin, I., Marmot, M., Niedhammer, I., & Peter, R. (2004). The measurement of Effort-Reward Imbalance at work: European Comparisons. *Social* Science & Medicine, *58, 8,* 1483–1499.

Sulsky, L., & Smith, C. (2005). *Work Stress.* Belmont, CA: Thomson Wadsworth.

Thomas, L. T., & Ganster, D. C. (1995). Impact of family-supportive work variables on on work-family conflict and strain: A control perspective. *Journal of Applied Psychology, 80,* 6–15.

Chapter Eight

Theories of Motivation

M otivation is concerned with a question: Why do people "do what they do?" Whether we realize it or not, all of us are "naïve scientists" who often attempt to figure out the motives behind the behavior of others. We may read a newspaper and wonder why a person committed a violent crime, or perhaps why an athlete maintained a consistently high level of performance during his or her career. Within organizational psychology, the study of employee motivation represents one of the most important topics in the discipline, and there are several reasons for this. First, motivation is a key to understanding many forms of behavior in organizations. Understanding what motivates employees helps us to understand the dynamics underlying such important behaviors as job performance, absenteeism, turnover, and even counterproductive behaviors.

Second, an understanding of the dynamics underlying various forms of behavior enhances our ability to predict these same behaviors. For example, if an organization's leaders understand the motivation underlying performance, they can predict their employees' future performance. This is important when organizations are initially selecting new employees, but it may also be helpful when current employees are being considered for promotional opportunities.

In addition, understanding an employee's motivation for performing at work can allow leaders to structure the work environment to encourage productive work behavior and discourage counterproductive work behavior. For example, if an organization

knows that employees are highly motivated by financial incentives, this knowledge can be used to influence performance through the strategic use of raises. However, if leaders realize that having control over job performance is especially important for motivating employees, then the work environment can be structured to allow employees sufficient autonomy over what they do. All organizations, in one way or another, attempt to influence employees' behaviors. Organizations that are armed with a clear understanding of motivation are in a better position to influence employee behavior than are organizations that lack this knowledge.

This chapter provides an overview of the theories of motivation that have been most influential in organizational psychology. In Chapter 9, we will examine how motivation theories are applied within organizations to influence employee behavior. Before examining specific motivation theories, however, we will briefly review the important issue of how motivation is defined and the classification of theories that have been applied to work motivation. As will become evident, this is important because different theories conceptualize motivation in somewhat different ways.

DEFINING MOTIVATION AND THEORETICAL APPROACHES

Definitional Issues in Motivation

According to Kanfer (1990), motivation is a *hypothetical construct*—we cannot see it or feel it. However, we can observe the effects or by-products that are indicative of differing levels of motivation. To use an analogy, motivation is a bit like gravity. We cannot see or feel gravity, but its effects would become very clear if one were to jump out of a window of a five-story building.

Pinder (1998) argued that motivation determines the form, direction, intensity, and duration of work-related behavior. The form of behavior refers to the types of activities an employee would choose to engage in at work. For example, some employees may choose to focus on task-based performance, whereas other employees choose to invest their efforts on building interpersonal relationships and facilitating group cohesion. The direction of motivation refers to the specific path employees take in accomplishing the goals they set for themselves. For example, a nurse may have a predetermined

schedule for the various tasks he or she needs to accomplish within a given time frame, and this schedule serves to guide behavior during the course of the day. The intensity component of motivation addresses the vigor and amount of energy put into goal-directed work performance. A market analyst can approach the tasks he or she faces with intense energy or detached resignation. Finally, duration refers to how long an individual pursues a particular course of direction at work, perhaps persisting even when facing obstacles. In a related definition, Steers, Mowday, and Shapiro (2004) recently defined *motivation* as "factors or events that energize, channel, and sustain human behavior over time" (p. 379).

By observing these dimensions of behavior, we can draw some conclusions about the influence of motivation on employees' behaviors. Based on Pinder's proposition, a major question for organizational psychologists studying employee motivation is: What dependent variable should be studied in empirical research? As readers will see, common dependent measures for theories of motivation include employees' effort, choice, or, in some cases, persistence. In addition, researchers have often examined motivation as a predictor of well-being and performance. Although factors other than motivation (e.g., ability, lack of critical resources) can certainly influence well-being and performance, researchers have shown that motivation has important implications for these dependent variables.

A final issue to consider in defining and understanding employee motivation is determining what forms of behavior organizations wish to influence. This will become particularly important when applications of motivation theories are described in Chapter 9, but it is also important in understanding different motivation theories. As will be shown, motivation theories can be distinguished in terms of whether they ultimately predict outcomes most relevant to performance, employee citizenship, or simply the propensity to maintain organizational membership.

Theoretical Approaches to Motivation

Given the importance of motivation in psychology, numerous theories of human motivation have been developed over the years. Many of these, however, either were not developed to explain behavior in the workplace, or are simply difficult to apply in the work domain. The theories that are covered in this chapter have been developed specifically to explain employee motivation or have been applied successfully to the study of work behavior. It is possible to place motivation theories into five general categories:

1. Need-based theories explain work motivation in terms of the extent to which employees satisfy important needs in the workplace.
2. Cognitive process theories emphasize the decisions and choices that employees make when they allocate their efforts.
3. The behavioral approach emphasizes applying principles of learning to the work environment.
4. Self-determination theory emphasizes the importance of the distinction between motivation being driven by extrinsic factors (e.g., need for approval, money) versus intrinsic factors (e.g., interest in the work itself).
5. Job-based theories place the source of motivation primarily in the content of jobs that employees perform.

The first four categories described represent theories of motivation that were developed in the broader field of psychology and were subsequently applied to motivation at work. The final category covers theories that were developed within the specific context of the work environment. When taken together, these separate theories provide a comprehensive explanation of employee motivation at work.

NEED-BASED THEORIES OF MOTIVATION

By definition, a *need* indicates some deficient state within an individual. We know, for example, that humans need things such as oxygen and water in order to survive. Psychologists have also proposed that humans have psychological needs that serve to drive much of human behavior. Murray (1938), for example, was one of the first psychologists to propose a systematic taxonomy of human needs (e.g., achievement, power, affiliation, intimacy). He proposed that these needs are evoked by different stimuli in the environment, and subsequently drive behavior (see Comment 8.1).

Maslow's Need Hierarchy

Building on the work of Murray (1938), Maslow (1943) proposed his well-known *Need Hierarchy* as an explanation of the forces driving human behavior. It is important to note that Maslow's theory was not designed specifically to explain behavior in the workplace. Rather, Maslow attempted to create a *universal* theory that would explain the driving forces behind all purposeful behaviors. It is also important to consider that Maslow developed his Need Hierarchy based largely on clinical observations rather than systematic

COMMENT 8.1

DO HUMANS REALLY HAVE PSYCHOLOGICAL "NEEDS"?

THEORIES OF MOTIVATION that emphasized need satisfaction once strongly dominated the field of organizational psychology. Over time, however, need theories have generally fallen out of favor. At the present time, they are considered more for their historical value than anything else. One obvious reason for this demise is that need theories have not stood up well under empirical scrutiny. Another reason is that the concept of psychological *needs* is rather controversial.

Although it is rather easy to make a case that humans have physiological needs, the idea that psychological needs exist is more debatable. For example, it could be argued that although things such as social belonging are *valued*, people typically do not suffer dire consequences if they have less social contact than they desire. On the other hand, it has been shown that social isolation may lead to certain forms of psychopathology and contribute to developmental disabilities (e.g., Bowlby, 1973). From this point of view, one could

mount a rather convincing argument that psychological needs do exist.

Baumeister and Leary (2005) have recently argued that all humans have a need to belong to social groups, and that an individual's self-esteem is a subjective indicator of the extent to which an individual is securely included in valued groups (Leary, Tamber, Terdel, & Downs, 1995). These authors have argued that when the need to belong is thwarted many negative consequences occur. Haslam and his colleagues (2004) have also argued that the work group can be an important part of an employee's self-concept and therefore motivate behavior at work so that the employee maintains secure inclusion in the work group or organization.

Source: J. Bowlby. (1973). *Separation: Anxiety and anger.* New York: Basic Books. Baumeister, R.F., & Leary, M.R. (1995). The need to belong: Desire for interpersonal attachments as a fundamental human motivation. *Psychological Bulletin, 117,* 497–529.

empirical research. Despite these caveats, Maslow's theory has become quite influential in a variety of areas of psychology, including organizational psychology.

Figure 8.1 presents the five need levels that comprise Maslow's Need Hierarchy. At the bottom of the hierarchy are *physiological needs*. This level represents the needs for food, oxygen, and water—attributes that are physiologically necessary to sustain life. These needs are at the lowest level because they will motivate behavior only if they are unsatisfied. Thus, a person who lacks such basic necessities will be motivated primarily to obtain them. The closest most of us have come to being motivated by physiological

needs is a late-night excursion to a fast-food restaurant. In some parts of the world, however, basic physiological sustenance is one of the major forces driving not only work behavior, but many other behaviors as well.

When physiological needs are satisfied, a person then "moves on" to the next level in the hierarchy: *safety needs*, which include things such as shelter from the elements and protection from predators. As with all needs, Maslow proposed that safety needs would motivate behavior only to the extent that they are unmet. Compared to physiological needs, it is a bit easier to illustrate how safety needs may motivate work behavior. For example, work may allow a person to

FIGURE 8.1
Maslow's Need Hierarchy

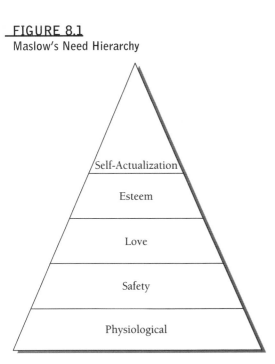

provide his or her family with adequate housing in a safe neighborhood, as well as the security of having a guaranteed retirement income.

If safety needs are satisfied, the next level that becomes salient is *love* and *belonging needs*. This level represents the need to form meaningful social relationships with others and the desire to feel a sense of belonging. Although love needs may be satisfied in a variety of ways, for most people work represents an important context for satisfying this type of need. People often develop close social ties with coworkers and derive considerable satisfaction from these affiliations. These social ties may also help employees to cope with many negative aspects of the work environment (Cohen & Wills, 1985).

After love needs are met, the next level that becomes important in motivating behavior is *esteem needs*. Esteem needs are linked to a desire to feel a sense of competence and mastery. As with social/belongingness needs, esteem needs may potentially be satisfied in

a variety of ways. For example, one may feel a sense of esteem or competence by being a good parent, cultivating a productive garden, or having a neat and clean house. For many people, the workplace represents a primary setting in which esteem and competence needs are satisfied (Baumeister, 1991). For example, an accountant may feel a sense of pride and accomplishment when he or she completes a client's tax return quickly and accurately.

The highest need level that can be reached in Maslow's hierarchy is *self-actualization*. According to Maslow (1943), to self-actualize is to realize one's potential and fulfill one's capacities. Maslow pointed out that few people ever completely "satisfy" the need for self-actualization. Compared to the other levels of needs, self-actualization is a bit more difficult to describe because researchers differ considerably in how they define the variable. Nevertheless, it is certainly possible that work could provide the opportunity for self-actualization. A teacher, for example, may feel actualized by educating future generations.

When viewed as a complete theory, Maslow's Need Hierarchy is certainly intuitively appealing and represents an insightful statement about human nature. The theory, however, initially fared very poorly as a predictor of work behavior (Locke & Henne, 1986). Empirical research did not support the number of levels in the theory or the notion that lower levels in the hierarchy must be satisfied before higher-level needs will motivate behavior (e.g., Hall & Nougaim, 1968). In addition, reviews of motivation theory in the 1990s included Maslow's theory primarily for historical value and because it has served as the basis for more elaborate theories of work motivation (e.g., Ambrose & Kulik, 1999; Austin & Vancouver, 1996; Kanfer, 1990). However, Latham and Pinder 2001 recently argued that Maslow's theory has seen a resurgence in the study of work motivation. Ronen (2001) studied employees from 15 different countries and found support for the discrimination among levels in Maslow's hierarchy. Importantly, Maslow's theory has also inspired other researchers to consider the roles that needs play in employee motivation.

ERG Theory

The most direct descendant of Maslow's Need Hierarchy was Alderfer's (1969) *ERG Theory* of motivation. The acronym ERG stands for *existence, relatedness,* and *growth.* Essentially, Alderfer collapsed Maslow's five need levels into three. Existence encompasses both the physiological and the safety/security needs from Maslow's theory. Relatedness corresponds to the social/belongingness level in Maslow's theory. Growth represents the esteem and self-actualization levels from Maslow's theory.

ERG theory also deviates from the Need Hierarchy in other important ways. Unlike Maslow's theory, ERG Theory allows for the possibility that needs do not have to operate in a strict hierarchical fashion (Alderfer, 1969). For example, an artist may be trying to scratch out a living and, at the same time, to achieve his or her artistic potential. ERG also allows for the possibility that people may regress if their needs at one level are not satisfied. Suppose an artist fails to achieve his or her potential. According to Alderfer, such a person may become more focused on satisfying "lower level" needs. The artist may become focused on making friends and connecting with people socially. Recall that Maslow's theory is focused only on moving up through the hierarchy of needs. It says little about situations in which needs are thwarted.

When it was first proposed, ERG Theory was seen as an improvement to Maslow's theory, but it has fared only slightly better in terms of empirical support. Alderfer's (1969) original work supported the theory, but subsequent tests have offered only mixed support (e.g., Wanous & Zwany, 1977). However, like Maslow's theory, ERG Theory has served as a foundation for future theories in which need satisfaction is proposed to be a central component.

Need for Achievement Theory

A third need-based theory of motivation, *Need for Achievement Theory* (Atkinson, 1964; McClelland, 1965), has proven to be somewhat more useful than the two previously discussed. Need for Achievement draws its historical roots from the early work of Murray (1938). However, rather than focusing on multiple needs, the emphasis has been primarily on the Need for Achievement in explaining differences between people in goal-directed behavior.

The work of McClelland and others has identified some consistent distinguishing characteristics of those who have a high need for achievement. For example, they tend to choose moderate levels of risk, have a strong desire for knowledge of results or feedback, and have a tendency to become very absorbed in their work. In the work environment, this may be reflected in the tendency of such individuals to set moderately difficult performance goals, seek jobs that readily provide performance feedback, and perhaps work long hours.

McClelland also proposed that Need for Achievement has consequences for entire societies as well as for individuals. For example, in his book *The Achieving Society*, McClelland (1961) proposed that societies differed in terms of their absolute levels of Need for Achievement, and that such differences may explain differences in economic growth. Thus, one way to promote economic development in poor countries, according to McClelland, is to promote higher levels of Need for Achievement among native or indigenous populations.

Compared to the other two need-based theories, Need for Achievement Theory is clearly narrower in focus. Rather than trying to account for all needs and all forms of behavior, this theory focuses on only one need and a very specific form of behavior (e.g., achievement). This tighter focus makes Need for Achievement Theory somewhat more useful in organizations. For example, if a manager knows that one of his or her subordinates has a high need for achievement, this knowledge may be useful in determining job assignments and the frequency with which performance-related information should be communicated.

The narrow focus of Need for Achievement Theory is also problematic in some respects. McClelland acknowledged that factors other than Need for Achievement influence behavior, but then does not go on to indicate how Need for Achievement is related to these additional variables. However, it is important to keep in mind McClelland's narrow focus and that he was not attempting to develop a full-blown theory of human motivation.

COGNITIVE PROCESS THEORIES OF MOTIVATION

Another way that we can view employee motivation is in terms of the *cognitive processes* underlying motivation. *Cognition*, of course, means thought. What are some of the thought processes that go along with

employee motivation? As readers will see in the theories described in this section, employees make judgments about how fairly they are being treated, choose where they will direct their efforts, and are able to anticipate future rewards associated with different levels of goal accomplishment. An understanding of these cognitive processes provides a great deal of insight into employee motivation.

When one looks at the history of psychology, the closest the field has ever come to having what might be described as a *dominant paradigm* was during the 1960s and 1970s, when behaviorism was at the height of its popularity. Thought processes such as decision making and choice were not considered under the realm of psychology, because these could not be directly observed.

This view began to change in the late 1970s, and the changes ushered in what many have referred to as the *Cognitive Revolution* in psychology. During this period, psychologists began to focus on the thought processes underlying phenomena such as problem solving, choice, and even psychopathology. Another factor that facilitated the development of cognitive process theories was the growth in computer use. This is important because with this revolution came an increasing trend, particularly in memory research, to equate human information processing with computer information processing. As readers will notice, the "mind as computer" metaphor is evident, particularly in the more recent cognitive process theories of motivation.

Equity Theory

According to Homans (1958), humans tend to view social interactions as being much like economic transactions. That is, we tend to view relationships with others, as well as transactions with institutions (e.g., work, government), in terms of what we give and what we receive. Based on this notion, *social exchange theory* was developed to explain how we weigh and balance what we give and receive from our interactions with others (Kelley & Thibaut, 1978).

Equity Theory is a type of social exchange theory that focuses on how people determine the fairness of social exchanges (Adams, 1965). Although Equity Theory can really be applied to any form of social exchange, in describing this theory we focus on the work context. A basic assumption of Equity Theory is that employees bring to the workplace what they perceive to be a number of inputs. Given that Equity Theory focuses on cognition, an input is essentially anything an employee decides it is. Job-relevant inputs would include factors such as a person's academic credentials, years of prior experience, and job-related skills, as well as the level of effort given to his or her employer.

The other important component of Equity Theory is outcomes. Outcomes represent those things that an employee feels he or she is receiving from the employment relationship. The most tangible of these is monetary compensation, but outcomes may also include intangibles such as praise from one's supervisor, feelings of accomplishment, or even feelings of camaraderie among one's coworkers. Like inputs, outcomes are cognitive representations, and thus may differ from employee to employee.

According to Adams (1965), employees cognitively compare their ratio of inputs-to-outcomes to the perceived ratio of some comparative standard. A comparative standard could be another employee employed in the same job in the same organization, someone performing a similar job in a different organization, or perhaps even the focal employee at a different point in time. If an employee perceives that the ratio of his or her inputs to outcomes is equal to the ratio of the comparative other, a *state of equity* is said to exist. This means that the employee is reasonably satisfied with the current exchange relationship with his or her employer. When these ratios are different, however, a *state of inequity* is said to exist. In this case, the employee is not satisfied with the current state of the exchange relationship, and therefore is motivated to bring it back into balance.

According to Equity Theory, the most common form of inequity is referred to as *underpayment*. This occurs when the ratio of inputs to outcomes is perceived as less favorable than the comparative standard. For example, if an employee perceives that he or she is working much harder than a fellow employee who is paid the same salary, this may engender feelings of underpayment. According to Adams (1965), an employee can use a number of strategies in an attempt to restore equity when feelings of underpayment exist. These strategies are summarized in Table 8.1.

One way for an employee to restore equity would be to attempt to increase his or her outcomes. In the previous example given, the employee could go to his or her supervisor and ask for a raise in order to compensate for his or her higher level of work effort. This may have the effect of restoring equity if the employee is successful, but it may also be risky. If the employee's request for a raise is denied, he or she may feel worse than before. This is especially true if the employee regards the effort required to request the raise as an additional input.

In a second strategy to restore equity, the employee may reduce inputs so that the ratio becomes equal to that of other workers, and the underpayment is rectified. For example, an employee may reduce effort to a level that

TABLE 8.1
A Summary of the Mechanisms That Can Be Used to Restore Equity

Mechanism	Example
Increasing outcomes	Asking one's supervisor for an increase in salary
Reducing inputs	Decreasing the level of effort devoted to work tasks
Cognitive adjustments	Changing the perception of the value of one's inputs or outcomes, to restore equity
Changing the "comparative standard"	Choosing a different person to compare the ratio of inputs to outcomes
Leaving the field	Obtaining a job that provides a more favorable ratio of inputs to outcomes

is perceived as commensurate with outcomes. This strategy also carries some degree of risk. Reduced effort on the part of an employee may be perceived negatively by a supervisor or coworkers. This may, in turn, result in even fewer outcomes for the employee.

A third strategy is to cognitively adjust one's perceptions of inputs and outcomes in a way that restores equity. For example, employees may cognitively reevaluate their outcomes and decide that they are more favorable than was first thought. For example, an employee who perceives he or she is being paid poorly may consider that his or her cost of living is lower than employees in other cities. The employee could also reevaluate his or her inputs and decide that they do not have as much value as first thought, or perhaps decide that there are additional outcomes that were not considered initially. The inputs and outcomes of the comparison standard may also be cognitively adjusted in order to bring the two ratios into balance.

Of all the strategies listed in Table 8.1, cognitive adjustment of the perceptions of inputs and outcomes clearly requires the least amount of effort on the part of an employee, and it is the least risky. For example, the employee does not have to make an effort to increase his or her outcomes, and

does not incur the risk that goes along with reducing his or her inputs. A potential drawback with this strategy is that it may result in an employee being taken advantage of. There are situations in organizations where people are treated unfairly, and cognitively adjusting one's perceptions does not change unfair treatment.

The fourth possibility listed in Table 8.1 is that an employee who perceives underpayment may change his or her *comparative standard* so that the ratio is perceived more favorably. For example, if the authors were to use a professional baseball player as a comparative standard in making equity judgments, this would undoubtedly lead to strong feelings of inequity, at least with regard to salary. On the other hand, changing the comparative standard to "associate professors in psychology departments" would provide a greater chance of restoring equity. Keep in mind, though, that even within the same occupation or profession, multiple comparisons may be possible. For example, among academic I/O psychologists, distinctions can be made between those in psychology departments and those in business schools. Even within psychology departments, a distinction can be made between those teaching in doctoral programs and those employed at the master's level (see Comment 8.2).

COMMENT 8.2

SALARY EQUITY IN PROFESSIONAL SPORTS

ONE AREA IN which the effects of Equity Theory can be observed quite readily is professional sports. It's almost comical, for example, to see a professional athlete who is being paid $5 million per year complain bitterly that he is being treated unfairly because he is not being paid $10 million. Most of us would be ecstatic to be paid even a fraction of either of those amounts. However, if one keeps in mind the *comparative standard* used by a professional athlete, such feelings of inequity become much easier to understand. More specifically, highly paid professional athletes compare their earnings to other highly paid professional athletes of the same stature. When these types of comparisons are made, the fact that one is a multimillionaire is really irrelevant.

What's important is how one's salary compares to these other players.

A related issue that Equity Theory can help to explain is how highly paid professional athletes reconcile the fact that they are paid a great deal more than physicians, teachers, scientists, and others who perform work that is extremely important to society. Here's one somewhat speculative answer: A major league baseball player making $10 million may reason that he is deserving of this because of all the years he spent developing his skills, the years he spent playing in the minor leagues, and the fact that his career could be ended at any time by an injury. In Equity Theory terms, what this player is doing is cognitively adjusting his inputs relative to his outcomes.

A final way that an employee may respond to underpayment inequity was described by Adams (1965) as exiting the field of play, or withdrawing from the inequitable exchange. In an employment setting, this would typically take the form of employee turnover, although it could take more subtle forms. For example, an employee who is feeling inequitably treated may psychologically withdraw from the organization. This may simply involve very minimal participation or reduced feelings of organizational commitment (see Chapter 5). As Adams pointed out, leaving the field is a step that is typically taken after other methods of resolving inequity are exhausted. In certain cases, however, this may be an employee's best option. For example, if there is little chance that equity can be restored, it may be best for an employee to seek other employment.

Recall that Equity Theory also proposes that feelings of inequity will arise when the ratio of a person's inputs to outcomes is more favorable when held to the comparative standard. This is referred to as *overpayment*. Given that feelings of underpayment largely represent feelings of unfairness or injustice, how then can we describe the quality of feelings of overpayment? According to Adams (1965), feelings of overpayment are uncomfortable, as are feelings of underpayment. Qualitatively, feelings of overpayment are probably best described as guilt rather than unfairness.

According to Adams (1965), an employee experiencing overpayment may use the same basic strategies that can be used to restore equity when feelings of underpayment exist. For example, one could increase one's inputs to make them proportional to one's outcomes, attempt in some way to decrease one's outcomes, cognitively adjust one's inputs or outputs, change the comparative standard, or even leave the exchange. Of all these strategies, the most common is cognitive adjustment, most likely because it is easier and more feasible than most of the others.

In general, research has supported Equity Theory very well, particularly with respect to the underpayment condition. It has been shown, for example, that perceptions of underpayment inequity are unpleasant and will motivate employees to do something about the inequity (e.g., Greenberg, 1990; Lord & Hohenfeld, 1979). In recent years, equity theorists have distinguished between equity with respect to the outcomes employees receive, and the procedures used to determine those outcomes. Perception of the equity of one's outcomes is referred to as *distributive justice*. The term *procedural justice* is used to denote perceptions of equity with respect to the procedures used to determine outcomes (Folger & Cropanzano, 1998). Some researchers have also argued for a separate category of *interactional justice*, which refers to the perception that an employee has been treated with dignity and respect in regard to a particular transaction (Colquitt, Conlon, Wesson, Porter, & Ng, 2001). Research has supported the distinctions between these three forms of justice (Cohen-Charash & Spector, 2000).

Collectively, these three forms of justice are often referred to as *fairness perceptions*, and a great deal of recent research has been conducted on the outcomes of these perceptions (e.g., Sweeney & McFarlin, 1997). Fairness perceptions have been especially related to engaging in counterproductive work behaviors, including theft (Greenberg, 2002), workplace revenge (Trip, Biese, & Aquino, 2002), and sabotage (Ambrose, Seabright, & Schminke, 2002). Clearly,

organizations should not want employees to be motivated by a lack of perceived fairness at work.

The weakest support for Equity Theory has typically come from studies that have examined the overpayment condition (Pritchard, 1969). While it has been shown in a laboratory setting that feelings of overpayment can be induced (e.g., Lawler, Koplin, Young, & Fadem, 1968), there is very little evidence of this effect in organizational settings. This may be due to the fact that the whole notion of overpayment is rather questionable. At least with respect to salary, it simply may be unlikely that many people see themselves as overpaid. It is also possible that people may be able to cognitively adjust their perceptions very quickly to alleviate feelings of overpayment. For example, a person who is being paid what he or she considers too much may rationalize this by adjusting his or her perceptions of inputs (e.g., "My experience is a little better than I thought") or outputs ("With today's prices, that salary is not as great as it seems").

Expectancy Theory

One of the things that is unique about humans, at least with respect to cognition, is their ability to anticipate the future and adjust their behavior accordingly. *Expectancy Theory* is based on this uniquely human characteristic, and is focused on the cognitive processes that drive employees' decisions regarding where they will direct their efforts (Vroom, 1964, 1995). The basic premise of Expectancy Theory is that employees will generally direct their efforts toward behaviors or courses of action when:

1. There is a high probability that they will be able to perform the behavior if they try.

2. There is a high probability that the be-havior or course of action will lead to some outcome.
3. The outcome that will result from the behavior or course of action has value to the person.

If any of these three conditions is lacking, a person is unlikely to direct his or her efforts toward that particular course of action.

According to Vroom (1964, 1995), the belief that one's efforts will allow one to perform a given behavior is referred to as *expectancy* and is typically denoted as effort-to-performance (E $\emptyset$ P). Because expectancy is a belief about the future, Vroom proposed that this is a probability function and, as such, may range from 0 to 1. An expectancy of zero essentially means there is no way that a person's efforts will result in a given level of performance. In contrast, an expectancy of close to 1 indicates that an employee has considerable confidence that, if he or she puts forth effort, a given level of performance can be achieved. Expectancy beliefs may be based on a number of factors: a person's innate ability, his or her level of training, or the existence or lack of significant performance constraints.

The belief that a given behavior or level of performance will be associated with a given outcome is referred to as *instrumentality* and is typically denoted as performance-to-outcome (P $\emptyset$ O). Like expectancy, instrumentality is a probability function. For example, an employee may perceive the instrumentality for the relationship between a given level of performance and a pay increase to be zero if salary raises are across the board or are determined by collective bargaining. On the other hand, a high instrumentality would indicate a strong possibility that a given level of performance would be rewarded with a given pay increase. Instru-

mentality beliefs are based, to a large extent, on stated organizational reward policies (i.e., the existence of merit pay), but are also based on the manner in which such policies are carried out.

The value of the outcomes that an employee may obtain is referred to as *valence*. According to Vroom, because of a number of factors, people differ on the value they attach to outcomes that can be obtained for different levels of performance. One person, for example, may place a high value on monetary compensation; thus, a high raise may have considerable valence. Another person, in contrast, may place greater value on feelings of mastery and praise from others. One interesting thing about valence is that it can take on negative values, and this has implications for predicting the direction of effort. Consider, for example, all of the things that may occur if an employee performs his or her job very well. Pay raises, praise from one's supervisor, recognition from others, and feelings of accomplishment are outcomes that most people would find at least moderately desirable. In contrast, those who perform their jobs well often end up having to perform a greater proportion of the work, and their higher salaries may encounter resentment from fellow employees. These outcomes would be considered by most people to be at least moderately undesirable.

Vroom proposed that Expectancy, Instrumentality, and Valence can be combined, in equation form, to explain employee motivation. This equation is presented in Table 8.2. The variable that this equation predicts is labeled *force*, which represents the level of effort that an employee will direct toward a given level of performance. Readers should be clear that force is not the same as performance. A person may direct his or her efforts in a way that is consistent with Expectancy Theory, yet not perform

TABLE 8.2
The Equation Representing How the Components of Expectancy Theory Interact to Determine Motivational Force

$$F = E (\Sigma\ I \times V)$$

F = Motivational force
E = Expectancy (E → P)
Σ = Summing over all possible outcomes
I = Instrumentality (P → O)
V = Valence

well because of a lack of innate ability or performance-related constraints.

As is shown in Table 8.2, for each possible outcome that can result from a given level of performance, instrumentality is multiplied by the valence. These values are then summed, and this sum is then multiplied by expectancy. Given this equation, force will be highest when employees believe that effort will lead to a given level of performance, and that the level of performance will lead to valued outcomes. Conversely, if any of these values are near zero, the motivational force will be considerably lower. For example, let's say an employee believes there is a high probability that effort will lead to a given level of performance, and that the outcomes that are possible are highly valued. If this employee does not believe that these outcomes are contingent on performance (e.g., instrumentality is low), then force will be low.

As another example, consider an employee who believes that effort will lead to a given level of performance, and that performance will lead to a number of outcomes. In this case, force may still be low if the outcomes have little value to the employee. The possibility of a promotion, or perhaps of praise, does not mean much to the employee.

Finally, an employee could believe that performance leads to highly valued outcomes, but he or she does not believe that the effort

will lead to performance (e.g., expectancy is low). For example, many marathon runners believe that setting a world record would lead to a number of highly valued outcomes (e.g., money, fame, feelings of accomplishment), yet do not believe they can achieve this level of performance, even with considerable effort.

Since its development in 1964 by Vroom, Expectancy Theory has become one of the dominant motivational theories in organizational psychology. As a result, considerable research has examined expectancy theory predictions. Van Eerde and Thierry (1996) performed a meta-analysis of 77 studies that have tested Expectancy Theory predictions, and examined the correlations between expectancy theory components and outcomes such as performance, effort, intention, preference, and choice.

The results of this study showed mixed support for Expectancy Theory. For example, although individual components such as expectancy and instrumentality were correlated with a number of outcomes, multiplying terms together, as suggested by Expectancy Theory, did not result in greater prediction. Another important finding from this meta-analysis was that correlations based on studies employing *within-subjects designs* were stronger than correlations from studies employing *between-subjects designs*. In a within-subjects design, Expectancy Theory would be used to predict a particular individual's choice among different levels of performance or different courses of action. In a between-subjects design, Expectancy Theory would be used to predict performance or effort from a large number of individuals. This finding supports the contention that the theory is useful in predicting how people will direct their efforts when faced with a number of different choices (e.g., Mitchell, 1974; Muchinsky, 1977).

In addition to direct empirical tests, Expectancy Theory has received indirect support from studies that have examined the impact of financial incentives (Jenkins et al., 1998; Lawler, 1990; Lawler & Jenkins, 1992). Although financial compensation will be discussed in greater depth in Chapter 9, suffice it to say that considerable evidence has shown that financial incentives can be a powerful motivator. Although this in itself does not constitute direct support for Expectancy Theory, it is certainly consistent with many of its propositions.

Goal-Setting Theory

The idea that human behavior is motivated and regulated by goals and aspirations has long been recognized by psychologists (Austin & Vancouver, 1996). Thus, like Expectancy Theory, the conceptual under-pinnings of *Goal-Setting Theory* can be traced back many years. Organizational psychologists, most notably Edwin Locke, have elaborated on the basic notion of goal-setting and have described how this drives behavior in organizations.

Before describing the specifics of Goal-Setting Theory, it is important to consider why goals motivate employees' behaviors. According to Locke (1968), goals have motivational value for three reasons:

1. Goals serve to direct our attention and focus our efforts in a particular direction. A student who has a goal of obtaining an A in a course is likely to direct much of his or her attention toward that course.
2. Goals help us to maintain task persistence. This is important because, in many cases, people will fail or get sidetracked when they are trying to accomplish something.

3. The existence of goals tends to facilitate the development of task strategies. For example, the student in item 1 may devise very innovative methods of studying his or her course material in order to enhance retention.

Having described the functions served by goals, we now examine the attributes of goals that make them motivating. One attribute that has been supported very strongly over the years is *goal difficulty* (e.g., Locke & Latham, 1990a). Generally speaking, goals that are difficult are more motivating than easier goals. For example, a salesperson is going to be more motivated if he or she has a goal of making $100,000 in commission, rather than a goal of $50,000.

The second attribute that must be present for a goal to have motivational value is *goal acceptance*. To a large extent, goal acceptance hinges on a person's belief that a goal is attainable. If a person does not believe he or she can attain a particular goal, this goal will probably not be accepted. Over the years, it has been suggested that employee participation in goal setting is a necessary condition for goal acceptance. Latham and Locke (1991), however, point out that evidence has shown that assigned goals can be just as motivating as jointly set goals, as long as they are accepted.

The third condition necessary for goals to be motivating is *goal specificity*. Goals are much more motivating when they specify a particular level of performance (e.g., "Sell 20 cars in the next month"), as opposed to being vague (e.g., "Be a good salesperson"). Because of the importance of goal specificity, many goal setting studies have what is referred to as a "do your best" condition in which participants are given no concrete performance goals.

Fourth, it has generally been recognized that employees must receive feedback in order for goals to motivate performance. Attaining a goal is often an incremental process; thus, it is important that employees receive feedback regarding their progress. Furthermore, according to Latham and Locke (1991), the relation between goals and feedback is actually reciprocal; that is, feedback helps employees to keep on track with respect to goal attainment. Conversely, the existence of goals helps to put feedback into a meaningful context.

In terms of research support, goal setting is one of the most well-validated theories in all of organizational psychology. Over 30 years of research has supported the motivational value of goals in both laboratory and field settings (e.g., Locke & Latham, 1990a, 1990b). Because of this wide support, the focus in the past 15 years has largely been on explaining the mechanisms underlying goal setting, as well as identifying boundary conditions of the theory and moderators of some of the key relationships predicted by the theory.

With respect to mechanisms underlying goal setting, considerable research has been conducted on goal commitment, goal acceptance, feedback, and self-efficacy (Ambrose & Kulik, 1999). It has been found, for example, that monetary incentives can be used to enhance goal commitment and acceptance (Wright, 1992), and that both feedback and self-efficacy are necessary conditions for goal setting to be effective (Latham & Locke, 1991; Locke & Latham, 2006). It makes sense that employees will not be able to translate their goals into high levels of performance if they are not given adequate feedback regarding the extent to which their behaviors are contributing to performance. A great deal of recent research has revealed the importance of both employees seeking feedback regarding their performance (Ashford & Black, 1996; Bernichon, Cook, & Brown, 2003) and managers providing feedback to employees (Ilgen & Davis, 2000).

In terms of boundary conditions, several studies have indicated that goal setting may not work in all situations. Because goals tend to narrow one's focus, they may actually be counterproductive in situations in which an employee may need to alter a poorly designed task (Staw & Boettger, 1990). Also, those who are assigned specific goals may be less likely to spontaneously help coworkers (Wright, George, Farnsworth, & McMahan, 1993). This tendency for goals to lead to *tunnel vision* may be counterproductive in organizations of the future, since it has been predicted that role boundaries will be much less well defined (Bridges, 1994).

Another boundary condition of goal setting is that there may be a *law of diminishing returns* with respect to the number of goals that an employee can use to guide his or her behavior: As the number of goals begins to increase, the probability of conflict between goals increases (Gilliland & Landis, 1992). Furthermore, when an employee has a large number of goals, the probability increases that he or she may not even be able to keep track of them all. Given that goal specificity is a key element of the theory, it is unlikely that an employee will be able to retain the specifics of an excessive number of performance-related goals.

A final boundary condition that has been examined in recent years is task complexity. Research has shown that goal setting may be more effective for simple (as opposed to complex) tasks (Mone & Shalley, 1995). The most frequently cited reason for this is that if they are going to motivate performance, goals require a portion of a person's cognitive resources (e.g., Kanfer, Ackerman, Murtha, Dugdale, & Nelson, 1994). Devoting cognitive resources to goals will have a detrimental effect when one is performing a complex task (e.g., preparing an annual budget). Also, when goal setting is used for complex tasks, goals are often set at inappropriate levels. Setting very distal goals will probably not be very helpful when one is performing a complex task. For example, if a research scientist were to set a very distal goal (e.g., "I want to obtain three scientific breakthroughs in the next 10 years"), this may have very little impact on performance. On the other hand, if a person performing this job were to set more proximal goals (e.g., "Read three important research articles this week"), this could potentially facilitate task performance. Given the increasing complexity of future jobs, this is an issue that clearly warrants more attention in goal-setting research.

Self-Regulation

In many areas of psychology, a trend in recent years has been to explain behavior in terms of self-regulation mechanisms. Some of these theories will be discussed in the following paragraphs.

Control Theory

Control theory represents a very general theory that attempts to explain self-regulation processes underlying motivation (Carver & Scheier, 1981; Powers, 1973a, 1973b, 1978b). Control theory is typically discussed within the organizational psychological literature in the context of goal setting, where individuals attempt to reduce the discrepancy between a desired end state (i.e., goal) and their current level of progress

toward that end state (e.g., Klein, 1989; Latham & Pinder, 2004).

According to Powers (1973a), any control system consists of four distinct parts:

1. A *sensor* is a component that gathers important information about the control system. For humans, the sensor represents one's observations and perceptions.
2. A *standard* represents some state that a system attempts to maintain or achieve. In terms of motivation, this would most likely be some type of goal, such as a level of performance or perhaps a more general aspiration (e.g., wanting to become a doctor).
3. A *comparator* or *discriminator* represents the mechanism by which information that is obtained by the sensor is compared to the standard. For example, a person may cognitively compare his or her rate of progression toward a desired goal.
4. An *effector* represents the mechanism by which the system can interact with its environment. With humans, the effector mechanism makes it possible, for example, to adjust one's effort if it is determined that progression toward a given goal is too slow.

Control theory conceptualizes motivation as an ongoing process by which people cognitively monitor their progress toward some goal or standard, and may make adjustments based on whether they are making progress toward that goal or standard (Scheier & Carver, 1988; see also Nelson, 1993). This is a negative discrepancy model, where individuals are motivated to minimize the discrepancy between a current and desired end state. Furthermore, individuals obviously have many goals they are pursuing at any point in time, and these goals are hierarchically organized. According to

Carver and Scheier, the highest level of feedback loop is the idealized self-image, which represents the ideal images individuals have set for themselves. For example, an individual may have an idealized self-image of being a good and decent person. The next highest level of feedback involves principles, which when achieved contribute to the idealized self-image. Principles can be seen as similar to values, in that they provide guidelines for behavior. Examples of principles may be kindness, altruism, courage, or achievement. The lowest level of feedback involves programs, which are the specific behaviors that are carried out in order to achieve the principles an individual has adopted. For example, an individual who endorses the principle of achievement would constantly enact programs where achievement was possible (e.g., excelling on particular tasks at work).

Given its generality, control theory could be used to explain essentially any form of purposeful behavior (e.g., weight loss, progress in psychotherapy, accumulation of wealth). As stated earlier, organizational psychologists have used control theory primarily as a means of explaining the mechanisms underlying goal setting (e.g., Klein, 1989; Lord & Hanges, 1987), although it has also been used in other areas, such as occupational stress (e.g., Edwards, 1992).

According to Klein (1989), control theory augments goal setting in many ways. For example, control theory provides a more elegant description of the process by which feedback influences goal-setting processes. In control theory terms, feedback represents a sensor that facilitates the process by which an individual compares his or her performance to a given goal, and makes adjustments as necessary. Control theory also provides a plausible explanation for why a person may revise his or her goals in the face of repeated failure.

Beyond the implications for goal setting, control theory also serves as a useful framework for examining many other types of behavior in organizations. For example, an employee who suddenly begins to put forth more effort may be doing so because he or she feels that the current level of effort matches what is considered to be the effort of a "good employee." An employee who decides to change jobs may feel that the current job does not match his or her perception of what a job should be providing. Finally, an employee may decide to decrease his or her hours at work and spend more time at home because this is more congruent with his or her perception of being a "good parent."

Carver and Scheier have accumulated evidence for control theory within the context of their theory of self-regulation. However, less research has been conducted using control theory separate from goal setting within an organizational setting. The overwhelming support for goal-setting theory over the years certainly bodes well for the viability of control theory. In the future, there is likely to be more research on goal setting performed from a control theory perspective. It is also quite possible that organizational researchers will examine other employee behaviors from a control theory perspective.

Social Cognitive Theory (SCT)

Albert Bandura was one of the main pioneers of the cognitive revolution in psychology, and his SCT emphasized that cognitive variables mediate the relationships between environmental events and behavioral consequences (Bandura, 2001). A central component of Bandura's model is the construct of self-efficacy, which he initially defined as "beliefs in one's capabilities to organize and execute the courses of action required to produce given attainments" (1997, p. 3). This definition emphasizes the confidence the individual has to complete his or her task. Stajkovic and Luthans (1998) expanded on Bandura's original definition and defined self-efficacy as, "an individual's confidence about his or her abilities to mobilize the motivation, cognitive resources, and courses of action needed to successfully execute a specific task within a given context" (p. 63). These authors argue that self-efficacy affects several aspects of motivation, including behavior initiation, effort, persistence, and success. In measuring self-efficacy, it is important to remember that the construct is domain-specific, and therefore should be assessed with reference to performance on a specific task (Latham & Pinder, 2005).

In addition to the concept of self-efficacy, Bandura (2001) has also contributed to theoretical work on self-regulation through his emphasis on dual control systems that determine goal-directed behavior. Bandura argues that goal-directed behavior involves two control systems. The first system involves the creation of a positive discrepancy between an individual's current state and a desired future goal. The second is the negative discrepancy model discussed earlier, where individuals attempt to reduce the discrepancy between the desired goal and the steps required to reach the goal. Bandura's model can be integrated with goal-setting theory by noting that setting difficult goals involves creating a negative discrepancy control system where a high goal is to be mastered.

THE BEHAVIORAL APPROACH TO MOTIVATION

The underlying assumption of the behavioral approach to motivation is that behavior is largely a function of its consequences. For example, when working with laboratory animals, the frequency with which a rat presses a bar is largely a function of the consequences of performing that behavior. If the consequence is positive for the rat (e.g., a food pellet), this will increase the probability of the behavior occurring in the future. On the other hand, if the consequence is either negative (e.g., an electric shock) or neutral (e.g., nothing happens), this will decrease the probability of the behavior occurring in the future.

The behavior of people in work settings is much more complicated than the behavior of laboratory rats. However, at a very basic level, the general principle described also governs behavior in organizations; that is, people in organizations generally try to behave in ways that produce positive outcomes, and avoid behaving in ways that produce negative or neutral outcomes. In the remainder of this section, we will examine some of the mechanisms underlying behavioral explanations of motivation in organizations.

One of the major principles that can be used to influence behavior in organizations is *reinforcement*. Reinforcement can be defined as any stimulus that increases the probability of a given behavior. If an employee writes a good report and receives verbal praise from his or her supervisor, the verbal praise could be considered reinforcement. Readers will notice that this definition is not conceptual; rather, we define reinforcement primarily in terms of its function or consequences.

One of the key issues in the use of reinforcement to influence behavior is how it is administered. According to Luthans and Kreitner (1985), *schedules of reinforcement* describe various strategies that can be used to administer reinforcement. A general distinction that can be made about reinforcements is between those that are continuous and those that are intermittent. If reinforcement is provided continuously, this simply means that a person is constantly receiving reinforcement for his or her actions. This type of reinforcement schedule is rarely used in organizations, but may have some use when new employees are initially learning their jobs. For example, a supervisor may initially reinforce a new employee every time he or she successfully completes a work assignment.

An obvious problem with continuous reinforcement is that it is inefficient for the organization. Also, if reinforcement is provided continuously, it may eventually lose value to the employee. Thus, in most cases, reinforcement in organizations is provided according to intermittent schedules. One common form of intermittent reinforcement is a fixed-interval schedule—the administration of reinforcement according to predictable time periods. Paying employees once a month is an example of such a schedule in an organization. A key decision to be made when using a fixed-interval schedule is the length of time between administrations of reinforcement. For example, when employees are first learning a task, it is common for intervals between reinforcement to be very small. Gradually, however, the intervals between administrations of reinforcement become larger. That is, an employee may receive a compliment or other reward perhaps once every few days. One problem with a fixed-interval schedule is the well-established tendency for organisms to slack off performing immediately following the reinforcement.

A variable-interval reinforcement schedule is also the administration of reinforcement over time. However, unlike the fixed-interval schedule, when a variable-interval schedule is used, the time interval between administrations of reinforcement varies. For example, an employee may receive compliments from his or her supervisor twice in the same week, but may not receive another compliment during the next 3 weeks. The power of variable reinforcement lies in the fact that the employee does not know exactly when it is coming. Some rewards cannot be administered this way (e.g., salary), but variable schedules can be a powerful way to motivate behavior using other more intangible reinforcers.

Intermittent reinforcement can also be administered after a given number of times a desired behavior is performed; such schedules are referred to as *ratio schedules*. For example, in a laboratory setting, a rat may receive a food pellet for pressing a bar a certain number of times. In an organizational setting, an employee may receive a reward based on the performance of a given behavior (e.g., selling a car, or a certain number of cars). If a fixed-ratio schedule is used, reinforcement is administered after a behavior has been performed a given number of times. For example, employees working at a manufacturing plant may be given a bonus for every 50 products delivered.

As with the fixed-interval schedule, a key decision is the number of behaviors that must be performed before the employee may receive the reward. In many cases, the number of behaviors required to obtain reinforcement has to do with the skill level of employees. For example, when employees are first learning a task, the number of behaviors required to obtain reinforcement will generally not be very high. Over time, as the employee becomes more skilled, more behaviors are typically required in order to obtain reinforcement.

When a variable-ratio reinforcement schedule is used, reinforcement is also administered based on the behavior performed. However, unlike the fixed-ratio schedule described previously, the number of behaviors required to obtain reinforcement varies. An employee may be reinforced after performing a given behavior twice, and then not reinforced again until the behavior is performed five more times. Some readers will recognize this as the reinforcement schedule on which gambling is based. Given the number of people who become addicted to gambling, it is fair to say that this is a very powerful schedule of reinforcement. Like the variable-interval schedule described previously, some rewards cannot be administered according to this schedule for ethical reasons. However, rewards such as praise and recognition certainly can be, and often are, administered in this manner.

A second major principle of the behavioral approach to motivation is that of *punishment,* or any consequence that has the effect of reducing the probability of a behavior occurring. In organizational settings, punishment may be used to influence behavior, but typically it is used much less often than reinforcement. The most common use of punishment in organizations is to decrease the frequency of counterproductive behaviors. Thus, punishment primarily motivates behavior by discouraging negative behavior. The most common forms of punishment in organizations are docking employees' pay, suspension, demotion, being given undesirable work assignments, and, in extreme cases, termination.

Although punishment may have a powerful effect, there are important issues to consider before organizations use it to influence employee behavior. For example, although punishment may produce the desired outcome in the short run, it may also produce considerable resentment and distrust among employees. In addition, it is well known that punishment tends to suppress undesirable behavior rather than eliminate it completely. Another danger in using punishment to influence behavior is that an organization may adopt it as the primary mode of influence. Typically, in this mode, employees are not praised when they do something well but are punished when they do something wrong. The overuse of punishment may also lead to negative perceptions of fairness, which, as discussed previously, result in a host of dysfunctional consequences.

In many cases, the behavior of employees in organizations may meet with neither positive nor negative consequences—that is, nothing happens. This should lead to a phenomenon is known as *extinction*, where the occurrence of the given behavior declines until it is not performed at all. The influence of extinction on organizational behavior may be positive or negative, depending on the nature of the behavior under consideration. For example, if an employee is rude and obnoxious during meetings, extinguishing such behavior is positive. On the other hand, if an employee is very helpful to others and never receives any acknowledgment, there is a chance that the positive behavior will be extinguished. Of course, in such cases, some employees may feel a sense of internal satisfaction and thus may keep performing helpful behaviors for that reason. However, when such behavior is no longer internally rewarding, it may cease.

Probably the most important implication of extinction is that organizations must think about the behaviors they want to encourage and the behaviors they want to see minimized. Too often, rewards in organizations are administered in a way that encourages behaviors that are only minimally important, and extinguishes those that are the most crucial to organizational success. Consider, for example, an organization that administers rewards primarily on the basis of seniority. In behavioral terms, such an organization is saying that the most valuable commodity is the length of service of employees. Under this type of system, an employee who performs very well but has not been employed a long period of time has little incentive to maintain a high level of performance. In Chapter 9 we focus more on the strategic use of reinforcement to motivate employees.

In many companies, behavioral principles are used in training employees to learn new skills and to adopt new behaviors. Particularly when an employee is learning a novel behavior, the behavioral principle of *shaping* comes into play. Essentially, shaping has to do with the reinforcement of successive approximations of a particular behavior, rather than the entire behavioral sequence. Probably the best example of the use of shaping is in the training of animals. Readers who have been to Sea World have undoubtedly enjoyed the tricks performed by sea lions and killer whales. To teach those tricks, trainers must work many hours and reinforce the slightest movements that are seen as leading to the ultimate behavior.

In organizational settings, shaping may be used in ways that have implications for employee motivation. For example, when employees are first learning job tasks, reinforcing "successive approximations" of ultimate task performance will keep an employee from getting discouraged. In many academic departments, faculty are often reinforced for taking preliminary steps that may lead to desired outcomes, such as publication and external grants. By reinforcing behaviors such as building relationships with those at funding agencies, and establishing collaborative relationships with other researchers, it is hoped that such activities will ultimately lead to grants and publications.

A final behavioral principle that has important implications for motivation is *feedback*. When employees engage in any form of behavior (or in performance-related behavior in particular), it is helpful to have some feedback about that behavior (Kluger & DeNisi, 1996). Feedback has motivational value, particularly when it is positive. Most employees enjoy hearing positive feedback when they perform well, and such feedback often serves as an incentive to maintain a high level of performance. Feedback can also have considerable diagnostic value when employee performance is lacking. When an employee is performing poorly, feedback serves the important function of letting the person know that he or she is seen as not performing well. Sometimes, it is quite obvious when performance is lacking (e.g., a comedian tells a bad joke), but in many cases, it is not (e.g., a manager who is making poor strategic decisions). Thus, in many instances, feedback about performance must be given by some external agent or the employee simply will not know that he or she is performing poorly.

Perhaps the most important diagnostic function of feedback is that it communicates to employees where specific performance deficiencies exist. Simply having the knowledge that one is not performing well is certainly useful. However, it is more useful to receive feedback on what specific aspects of performance are lacking. Once these aspects are established, it is possible to go even further and diagnose the root cause of the performance problem.

In organizations, the application of behaviorism is known as *Organizational Behavior Modification (OBM)*, and this approach has been used to influence a number of behaviors, such as safety, suggestive selling, and production efficiency. In general, evidence supporting the effectiveness of OBM is impressive (Weiss, 1990). That is, using behavioral principles has been shown to influence the behaviors listed above in ways that are favorable for organizations. One limitation of OBM, and thus of the behavioral approach, is that it appears to work best when it is applied to relatively simple forms of behavior. That is, when jobs are relatively simple, it is much easier to keep track of desirable and undesirable behaviors, and apply reinforcement accordingly. With more complex tasks, however, this becomes much more difficult to do.

As an example, suppose we tried to use reinforcement principles to motivate a scientist who is working on mapping the entire human genetic structure. Because of the complexity of this type of scientific activity, it would likely be quite difficult to get a good handle on all of the steps necessary to ultimately accomplish this goal. Also, because progress in this type of scientific activity is very slow and incremental, reinforcement may be so infrequent that it would have little impact on motivation.

Another issue has been raised about behaviorism: the ethics underlying this approach. Some critics, for example, have charged that by systematically analyzing the contingencies underlying behavior and manipulating the environment to impact behavior, people are robbed of their choice and free will. B. F. Skinner, in his 1971 book, *Beyond Freedom and Dignity*, countered such charges by stating that environmental contingencies will govern behavior whether or not we choose to intervene. Behaviorism, in his view, represented nothing more than a systematic attempt to use those environmental contingencies in a way that was beneficial to society.

SELF-DETERMINATION THEORY

Thus far the motivation theories we have considered have viewed the employee as a calculating individual who is motivated by the desire to pursue positive consequences and avoid negative consequences. These types of theories are collectively referred to as *hedonic theories* of motivation, with an emphasis on needs, cognitive processes, and behavioral consequences being used in the service of allowing an individual to maximize pleasure and avoid pain (Ryan & Deci, 2001). In contrast, *organismic theories* of motivation "assume that humans are inherently motivated to develop their interests and skills, to connect and contribute to other people, and to move toward their fullest potential" (Sheldon, Turban, Brown, Barrick, & Judge, 2003, p. 358). Organismic theories are growth-oriented, emphasizing human beings' innate need to develop.

Self-determination theory (SDT) is an organismic theory that has been very influential in areas outside of organizational psychology, but it has only recently been applied to employee motivation at work (Sheldon et al., 2003). Sheldon and his colleagues note that SDT is actually a collection of a number of smaller theories that all emphasize the importance of individuals performing tasks out of intrinsic interest or a sense that task performance is relevant to important aspects of an individual's identity. Deci (1975) initially emphasized the importance of *intrinsic motivation* for task enjoyment and persistence, where an individual performs a task because of an inherent enjoyment in the task itself, rather than for extrinsic reasons such as pleasing others or making money. Deci argued that intrinsically motivating tasks feel autonomous, coming from the individual, whereas extrinsically motivating tasks feel controlled, with performance having more to do with external demands than one's inherent interests. Employees who truly enjoy the work they do will feel more autonomy at their job, which should lead them to persist in their work even when external factors, such as being monitored by a boss, are absent.

Later research emphasized the importance of how an individual interprets the motivation behind the various tasks he or she performs. *Cognitive Evaluation Theory* made the important point that how individuals interpret or evaluate the reasons for their behavior determines whether that behavior ends up feeling autonomous versus controlled (Deci & Ryan, 1985). For example, two different employees may get a bonus for performing at a certain level. One employee may interpret the bonus as an attempt by management to control his or her behavior, whereas another employee may interpret the bonus as recognition for a job well done. The latter employee is likely to feel greater autonomy at work, and therefore exhibit greater task persistence and enjoyment.

SDT appears to work well with inherently interesting jobs where individuals can gain enjoyment from the job itself, but what about really boring jobs that provide little inherent interest? For example, it is hard to imagine employees showing intrinsic motivation for tasks that are highly monotonous and uninteresting (e.g. checking for errors in database after database). Recent modifications to SDT accommodate these types of tasks. Ryan and Deci (2000) present an elaborated version of SDT where extrinsic motivation is separated into four separate types: *external motivation* (where the individual is performing for external rewards), *introjected motivation* (where the individual is performing in order to avoid feeling guilty about not living up to obligations), *identified motivation* (where the individual is performing a task because it expresses his or her values or is otherwise personally important), and *integrated motivation* (where various sources of identified motivation are integrated into a

coherent self-conception). Ryan and Deci argue that external and introjected motivation are both perceived by the individual as controlling, but that identified and integrated motivation is perceived as autonomous, because the individual "owns" the behavior.

Sheldon et al. (2003) discuss how these forms of motivation can be applied to an employee who builds computers. Although it is unlikely that many employees have an intrinsic interest in putting computers together, an employee may build a computer to get a paycheck (external), to avoid being seen as a bad worker (introjected), or because he or she takes pride in producing a quality computer (identified). The authors argue that employees motivated through identification will be more satisfied at work and will maintain superior performance in the absence of supervision by others.

SDT is just beginning to be applied to employee motivation within organizational psychology. In the context of work motivation, Sheldon et al. (2003) detailed how the theory could be used to provide insights into the areas of goal commitment and training motivation. The authors point out that most conceptualizations of goal commitment emphasize commitment to goals as a function of expectancy of achieving the goal and the attractiveness of the goal. A SDT approach emphasizes the importance of the internalization of the goal as personally important in predicting goal commitment. Sheldon and his colleagues have found that individuals are more likely to attain goals when they have internalized the goals and are pursuing them for autonomous reasons (Sheldon & Elliot, 1998; Sheldon & Houser-Marko, 2001).

Judge and his colleagues have recently used a model based on SDT to understand the relationship between core self-evaluation and job satisfaction (Judge, Bono, Erez, & Locke, 2005). Recall from Chapter 4 that employees with high levels of core self-evaluation have high self-esteem, high self-efficacy, an internal locus of control, and low levels of neuroticism. These authors conducted a longitudinal study where core self-evaluations and the motivation underlying the pursuit of work goals were assessed at Time 1 and job satisfaction and the attainment of work goals were assessed at Time 2 (60 days later). The authors found that core self-evaluation was related to a higher level of autonomous motivation for work goals (pursing work goals for intrinsic and identified reasons). In addition, higher levels of autonomous motivation at Time 1 were related to higher goal attainment and higher levels of job satisfaction at Time 2. Future research is needed to examine the ability of SDT to predict performance related outcomes at work.

JOB-BASED THEORIES OF MOTIVATION

Job-based theories propose that the key to understanding motivation lies in the content of employees' jobs. Job-based theories are closely related to need-based theories, due to the fact that need satisfaction is often offered as an explanatory mechanism linking job content and motivation. Job-based theories, however, are more likely than need-based theories to have been developed specifically for the workplace. Also, focusing on job content as the lever for influencing behavior is inherently more practical than focusing on need satisfaction.

Motivation-Hygiene Theory

From a historical perspective, the first job-based theory to appear on the scene

was Herzberg's *Motivation-Hygiene Theory* (Herzberg, 1968). The basic premise behind Herzberg's theory, as with all job-based theories, was that the primary source of motivation in the workplace was the content of people's jobs. At the time that Motivation-Hygiene Theory was developed, most organizations were highly influenced by Scientific Management. Recall that the primary method of motivation in Scientific Management was through compensation and financial incentives. Herzberg, and others, were of the opinion that financial incentives had the power to "motivate" people in the sense that they kept them on the job and perhaps prevented them from complaining. Using terminology from SDT, motivation was completely external. However, Herzberg believed that, in order to truly motivate employees, the content of the jobs that people perform was key.

Herzberg proposed that the work environment could be divided into two general categories. The first of these, *hygiene factors*, included aspects of the work environment, such as pay, fringe benefits, relations with coworkers, and essentially everything else that is distinct from the content of an employee's work. Herzberg used the term *hygiene factors* because these factors are necessary to keep employees from being dissatisfied but do not have the power to truly motivate them. To use a health-related analogy, maintaining proper dental hygiene does not make a person's teeth any better, but it prevents problems such as tooth decay and gum disease.

Herzberg labeled the second category of the work environment *motivators*. In contrast to hygiene factors, motivators reside primarily in the content of a person's job. Motivators include things such as the amount of challenge inherent in one's work, the amount of discretion one has in carrying out one's job

FIGURE 8.2
Summary of Hygiene Factors and Motivators

Hygiene Factors	Motivators
Pay	Level of Challenge
Fringe Benefits	Level of Autonomy or Discretion
Relations with Coworkers	Intrinsic Interest
Physical Working Conditions	Opportunities for Creativity

tasks, and perhaps how intrinsically interesting the work is. According to SDT discussed earlier, these factors all promote a more intrinsic orientation to performing at work. According to Herzberg, in order to motivate an employee, an organization must design work in a way that builds in motivators and thus makes work content intrinsically rewarding to employees. A summary of hygiene factors and motivators is contained in Figure 8.2.

In terms of empirical support, Motivation-Hygiene Theory has not fared particularly well. Herzberg, Mausner, and Snyderman (1959) provided what has probably been the strongest support for Motivation-Hygiene Theory. In their study, engineers and accountants employed by the City of Pittsburgh were asked to describe critical incidents that were illustrative of being "very satisfied" or "very dissatisfied." Consistent with Motivation-Hygiene Theory, hygiene factors were mentioned more often than motivators when describing dissatisfaction. The reverse was true when describing satisfaction.

After the Herzberg et al. (1959) study, other attempts were made to test the theory (summarized by Locke, 1976), but most were unsuccessful. Since the mid-1970s, very little research has used Motivation-Hygiene Theory as a framework. (For an exception, see Maidani, 1991.) The reason most analysts have given for the inability to replicate the theory is the critical incident method used in Herzberg's original study. Specifically, in describing critical incidents, respondents tended to attribute highly satisfying incidents to aspects of the job that were most closely associated with themselves (e.g., the degree of challenge in the job) and to attribute dissatisfying incidents to aspects of the work environment that were most closely associated with others (e.g., social relations with coworkers). Thus, many have argued that Herzberg's findings represented a methodological artifact rather than support for Motivation-Hygiene Theory. (See Locke, [1976] for an example of one of the most vigorous criticisms of the theory.)

Despite the lack of empirical support for his theory, one can certainly argue that Herzberg was a pioneer because he was one of the first organizational psychologists to focus on job content as a source of employee motivation. This point has often been lost over the years. In focusing on the methodological shortcomings of Motivation-Hygiene Theory, many in the field have failed to give Herzberg credit for being ahead of his time and providing the foundation for many practices that are commonplace in organizations today. In addition, the critical distinction emphasized by Herzberg between external and intrinsic motivation has gained a great deal of support through SDT described previously.

Job Characteristics Theory

Although Herzberg was one of the first to emphasize the importance of job content in motivating employees, his theory had some important limitations. For example, Motivation-Hygiene Theory was rather imprecise as to how to build "motivators" into employees' jobs. Herzberg also provided no tangible measures of these job dimensions. Another problem with Motivation-Hygiene Theory is that it was based, at least implicitly, on the assumption that all employees want the same things from their work.

Job Characteristics Theory (Hackman & Oldham, 1976, 1980), to a large extent, addressed the deficiencies in Motivation-Hygiene Theory and has become the most influential job-based theory of motivation in organizational psychology. Before describing its major components, we should note that Job Characteristics Theory has evolved over several years. For example, Turner and Lawrence (1965) proposed the concept of *Requisite Task Attributes*—essentially, a set of job

dimensions that they believed to be motivating to employees. Building on this work, Hackman and Lawler (1971) proposed what is generally considered the most immediate precursor to what eventually became Job Characteristics Theory. Job Characteristics Theory extended this earlier work by proposing the mediating linkages between job characteristics and outcomes, and by specifying moderators of individual differences.

As can be seen in Figure 8.3, the starting point in the theory is labeled *core job dimensions*. These represent characteristics of a person's job and include the following dimensions: *skill variety, task identity, task significance, autonomy*, and *feedback*. Skill

FIGURE 8.3
Job Characteristics Theory of Motivation

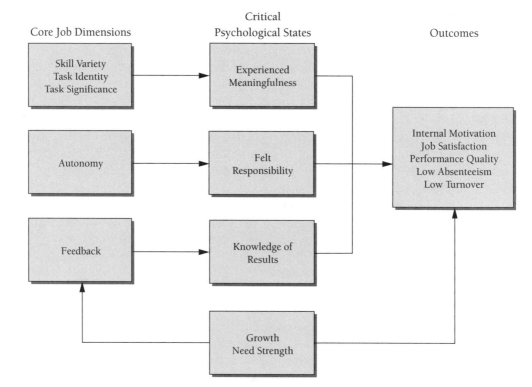

Source: J. R. Hackman and G. R. Oldham. (1980). Work redesign. Reading, MA: Addison-Wesley. Reprinted by permission of Pearson Education, Inc. Upper Saddle River, NJ.

variety represents the extent to which a job requires that a person must use many different skills. A good example of a job with high skill variety would be that of a corporate executive. A person performing this job may have to utilize quantitative skills to prepare a budget, interpersonal skills to manage conflicts among others, and high-level analytical skills to develop a long-term strategic plan. On the other end of the spectrum, a manual labor job may require primarily heavy lifting and a very minimal amount of independent judgment.

Task identity represents the extent to which a job requires that a person must complete a whole identifiable piece of work, as opposed to a small fragment of it. Conducting research is an example of a job with high task identity because it requires a person to be involved in all steps in the process: reviewing the literature, developing measures, collecting and analyzing data, and writing a report. Low task identity might be found in a traditional assembly-line job. An employee may be responsible for adding one part to a product, and thus will have only a vague idea of how he or she contributes to the finished product.

Task significance represents the degree to which performing the job is important or "counts for something." In a sense, all jobs in the workforce are important, but it is possible to argue that some are more significant than others. For example, most readers would probably agree that the task significance for a research scientist studying the molecular structure of the HIV virus is higher than that of a clerk in a retail store. Nevertheless, this core job dimension is still a bit more subjective than the other two.

Autonomy represents the degree to which employees have control and discretion over things such as how they perform their job tasks and schedule their work.

Comparatively speaking, college professors represent a professional group with an extremely high level of autonomy. As most readers know, professors have considerable control over their hours of work, choice of work activities, and method of approaching their work activities. At the other extreme might be a person performing telemarketing. Most telemarketing companies provide very explicit instructions (e.g., scripts) to telemarketing representatives and instruct them not to deviate from these instructions.

The final core job dimension, feedback, represents the extent to which performing a job provides information about the performance of the job incumbent. As a rule, comedians know very quickly whether their audience considered a particular joke funny. Dead silence and a sea of blank stares are pretty good indicators that a joke has "bombed." At the other extreme, years may pass before a corporate executive receives feedback about certain aspects of his or her performance. For example, the "correctness" of a decision to enter a new market may not be known until the company has been in that market for several years.

Notice in Figure 8.3 that the core job dimensions are immediately linked to the next step, which is labeled *critical psychological states*. These states represent what employees experience, on a psychological level, by performing a job with a given set of core job dimensions. According to the model, when jobs have high levels of skill variety, task identity, and task significance, the corresponding psychological state is *experienced meaningfulness*. Having these three dimensions present leads employees to psychologically experience their jobs as meaningful.

The critical psychological state associated with autonomy is labeled *felt responsibility*. If an employee has autonomy over how he or she performs a job, this will evoke feelings of responsibility for the outcomes that result from that work. An executive who has complete autonomy to determine the strategic direction of an organization will also likely feel a strong sense of responsibility for the success or failure of that organization. Conversely, an employee who simply "follows orders" is unlikely to feel a great deal of responsibility for the outcomes of his or her work.

The core job dimension of feedback is linked to the critical psychological state of *knowledge of results*. Thus, an employee whose job provided considerable feedback will psychologically possess knowledge of the results of his or her performance. Conversely, employees who receive little feedback have a correspondingly vague knowledge of the results of their performance.

According to the next step in the model, critical psychological states are linked to *personal and work outcomes*. This means that experiencing the three previously described critical psychological states will lead to a number of outcomes, one of which is high internal work motivation. Note also in Figure 8.3 that the critical psychological states are also associated with high levels of job satisfaction and performance quality, and low levels of absenteeism and turnover.

The final aspect of Job Characteristics Theory is the role of *growth-need strength*. Growth-need strength represents the extent to which employees see their job as a mechanism for satisfying "growth" needs such as personal achievement and self-actualization (Alderfer, 1969; Maslow, 1943). The specific role played by growth-need strength is that of moderating the relations between the core job dimensions and the critical psychological states, and between the critical psychological states and the personal and work outcomes. More specifically, Hackman and Oldham proposed that the core job dimensions will

evoke the critical psychological states only for those with a high level of growth-need strength. Similarly, the theory proposed that the critical psychological states will lead to the proposed personal and work outcomes only among those who have a high level of growth-need strength. For those with a low level of growth-need strength, core job dimensions will have little impact on critical psychological states, and these states will have little impact on outcomes.

Over the years, Job Characteristics Theory has been subjected to considerable empirical testing. Fried and Ferris (1987) conducted a comprehensive meta-analysis of job characteristics studies and reported a number of findings that were supportive of Job Characteristics Theory. For example, all of the core job dimensions were found to be related to outcomes such as job satisfaction, motivation, absenteeism, and turnover. Fried and Ferris's data, however, are a bit more equivocal with respect to the role of the critical psychological states proposed by Hackman and Oldham. Specifically, the core job dimensions do not correlate predictably with their proposed critical psychological states. In addition, the magnitude of the correlations between the core job dimensions and the critical psychological states is not stronger than with outcomes. This is important because if the critical psychological states are key mediators, as proposed by Hackman and Oldham, the core job dimensions should be more strongly correlated with them than with more distal outcomes (Baron & Kenny, 1986).

Although the Fried and Ferris (1987) meta-analysis is informative, very few studies have tested the Job Characteristics Model as a whole. This was done in Hackman and Oldham's (1975, 1976) early work, but most researchers after that have tested only parts of the theory. One exception is a study in which Champoux (1991) tested the entire theoretical model utilizing canonical correlation analysis. The results of this study supported both the causal flow of the model and the proposed moderating effects of growth-need strength. Subsequent studies, however, have been less supportive of the moderating effects of growth-need strength (Evans & Ondrack, 1991; Johns, Xie, & Fang, 1992; Tiegs, Tetrick, & Fried, 1992), as well as the mediating influence of the critical psychological states (e.g., Renn & Vandenberg, 1995). It is worth noting that cross-cultural research on job characteristics and job satisfaction has taken advantage of some of the key distinctions presented in Hackman and Oldham's work (see Comment 8.3).

Campion's Multidisciplinary Approach. One of the assumptions underlying the two previously described job-based theories was that job content appeals to employees at a psychological level and this, in turn, results in positive employee outcomes. This would appear to be a valid assumption, but it is also true that employees view their jobs from more than just a psychological/motivational perspective. Consistent with this point, the design of jobs is an issue that is of interest to other disciplines, such as industrial engineering, human factors/ergonomics, and biomechanics.

Based on this notion, Campion developed the *Multidisciplinary Approach to Job Design* (Campion & McClelland, 1991; Campion & Thayer, 1985). Strictly speaking, this is not a theory of motivation, but an approach to guide the design and redesign of jobs. It is covered as a theory here because

COMMENT 8.3

CULTURAL DIFFERENCES IN THE IMPORTANCE OF INTRINSIC JOB CHARACTERISTICS

JOB CHARACTERISTICS THEORY emphasizes the importance of intrinsic job characteristics such as autonomy and meaningfulness. Are intrinsic job characteristics more important determinants of job satisfaction for some cultures than others? That question was addressed in a large mutli-national study conducted by Huang and Van de Vliert (2003). These authors examined questionnaire responses from over 107,000 employees in 49 different countries. Employees in each country responded to the extent to which their job contained intrinsic characteristics such as being interesting and promoting autonomy. The country of the employees was coded along such dimensions as Gross National Product (GNP), individualistic versus collectivistic, and degree of power distance. The authors found that intrinsic job characteristics were stronger predictors of job satisfaction for employees in richer counties, more individualist countries, and countries with smaller power distance (less hierarchically organized). The authors reasoned that intrinsic work characersitics may not be as important predictors of job satisfaction in countries where such characteristics are not necessarily valued. This research highlights the importance of considering country-level influences on motivational processes.

Source: Huang, X., & Van de Fliert, E. (2003). Where intrinsic job satisfaction fails to work: National moderators of intrinsic motivation. Journal of Organizational Behavior, 24, 159–179.

the different approaches that are described by Campion ultimately represent a desire for different end states. Thus, even though this is typically presented only as a method of job design, at its core it is really a theory of motivation.

According to Campion, organizations can use four different approaches to design jobs, and each approach is associated with certain outcomes for both individual employees and the organization as a whole. As can be seen in Table 8.1, the *motivational* approach has been emphasized by those in psychology and closely related fields (e.g., human resources, organizational behavior). Recall from the previously described job-based theories that the emphasis is on making job content intrinsically interesting and meaningful to employees. Positive outcomes associated with this approach include increased job satisfaction, internal motivation, higher-quality performance, and fewer withdrawal behaviors. Designing jobs in this fashion also comes at a cost. For example, these types of jobs are more complex and thus may require higher skill levels, longer training periods, and higher levels of compensation. Such jobs may also be stressful because of the high levels of responsibility and the complexity of the interpersonal interactions that are required.

The next job design approach presented in Table 8.1 is *mechanistic*. This approach derives its roots from scientific management and, in more modern times, has been the province of industrial engineering. Consistent with scientific management, the emphasis in the mechanistic approach is to design jobs with maximum efficiency in mind. Job tasks are simplified and work cycles are generally made to be short. The primary benefit of the mechanistic approach is that employees performing jobs designed in this way will

be efficient, particularly if one defines *efficiency* in terms of speed of production. Jobs designed in this fashion will also, generally, be easier to staff, and training time will be short due to low-level skill requirements. The primary disadvantage of the mechanistic approach is that jobs designed in this way may foster boredom and alienation among employees, which ultimately could lead to a number of counterproductive behaviors such as absenteeism, lack of effort, and even sabotage.

The third approach to job design presented in Table 8.1 is *biological*. This approach is focused on designing jobs to maximize the physical comfort of employees. Those trained in ergonomics and biomechanics tend to emphasize this form of job design. By emphasizing employees' physical comfort in the design of jobs, organizations may reap important benefits such as reduced health care costs and lower numbers of workers' compensation claims. These outcomes may ultimately translate into higher levels of job satisfaction, but designing jobs in this fashion may require a considerable investment on the part of the organization. There may also be instances where employees' physical comfort detracts from their performance, particularly in tasks that require sustained attention to detail and vigilance.

The fourth and final approach to job design in Table 8.1 is *perceptual motor*. In this case, jobs are designed primarily with task-related information-processing demands in mind. As such, this approach tends to be emphasized primarily by those trained in human factors engineering. The primary advantage of this approach is that it may cut down on errors and fatigue, particularly for jobs that have heavy information-processing requirements. Airline pilots, air traffic controllers, and anesthesiologists are three groups whose jobs would be relevant. Despite these advantages, a potential drawback to this approach might be high levels of boredom, if information is highly simplified. Also, like the biological approach, this approach to job design may require considerable research and development costs.

Beyond specifying the four different approaches to job design, the underlying message in Campion's model is that decisions regarding job design require that organizations weigh certain costs and benefits, and ultimately make some trade-offs. For example, if efficiency is a very high priority within an organization, the mechanistic approach would probably be preferred, despite its inherent costs. Campion's theory also reminds us that organizational psychology is not the only discipline that has something to contribute in the realm of job design.

Since it has been developed more recently, much less empirical work has been done on the Multidisciplinary Approach than on Job Characteristics Theory. It appears, however, that many of the premises of this theory have been supported. For example, Campion and McClelland (1991) found that job changes according to the different disciplinary orientations led to many of the predicted outcomes. Also, Campion and Berger (1990) demonstrated that redesigning jobs according to different approaches had a number of predicted implications for compensation. Over time, it is likely that more research will examine many of the propositions in this useful approach to job design.

Summary of Job-Based Theories

When viewed in a historical context, job-based theories represent a major theoretical breakthrough in organizational psychology. Prior to Herzberg, much of motivational theory within organizational psychology was focused on need satisfaction. Furthermore, outside of the field, because of the influence of Scientific Management, much of the theory and practice in motivation was focused only on the use of financial incentives. This is not to say that financial incentives are irrelevant. Rather, the advent of job-based theories led to the realization that job content can have a potent impact (positive or negative) on people.

A problem that is common to all three job-based theories is that all assume, to a large extent, that job content is an objective attribute (Salancik & Pfeffer, 1977). It has been shown, however, that "objective" indexes of the work environment often do not correlate well with self-report measures of the same attributes (e.g., Spector & Jex, 1991). Another weakness in the job-based theories described in this section is that they are somewhat deficient with regard to process issues. For example, in Job Characteristics Theory, the core job dimensions lead employees to experience critical psychological states, and these states lead to a number of outcomes. The theory is not very explicit, however, as to the reasons underlying these propositions. Given the time period in which Job Characteristics Theory was developed (mid-1970s), and the proposed moderating role of growth-need strength, one might deduce that the mechanism is need satisfaction (Hackman & Oldham, 1976). However, it is also possible that jobs high on the core job dimensions also have higher levels of compensation and prestige. Both of these factors, rather than need satisfaction, may be necessary for the steps in the model. The more general point is that by focusing so heavily on job content, these theories have come up a bit short on the processes by which job content is translated into outcomes.

THE PRACTICAL VALUE OF MOTIVATION THEORIES

Having reviewed what are generally considered to be the major theories of employee motivation, we now ask: How valuable are these theories to managers in organizations? We do not believe it would be possible or worthwhile to rank-order the theories in this chapter in terms of practical value. However, it is possible to draw some general conclusions about the practical usefulness of the five general types of theories described. Generally, Need Theories probably fare the worst. Needs may be highly specific to individual employees, so it may be extremely difficult for a manager to either determine a given employee's level of need satisfaction or take steps to respond to it. Also, because a given need may be satisfied in multiple ways, motivating on this basis would be quite time-consuming and cumbersome for managers.

Job-based theories, in contrast, fare considerably better in terms of practical value. Job content is something that most managers can relate to, and in fact have some control over. Thus, if a manager sees that an employee lacks autonomy in his or her job, steps may be taken to increase autonomy. In a similar manner, the insights provided by SDT stress the importance of crafting jobs so that employees experience ownership and believe in the personal importance of their work. On the other hand, in some cases, changing a person's job is simply not practical. For example, job content may be governed by a union contract, or perhaps changing one employee's job would have such wide-ranging effects throughout an organization that the cost would be prohibitive.

Cognitive process theories may also have considerable practical value, although the exact value varies considerably for each theory. Expectancy Theory, for example, has much to offer managers in designing reward systems and in the diagnosis of performance problems; that is, performance-based rewards will be effective only if employees are able to see a connection between their performance and the level of rewards they attain (e.g., Instrumentality). Similarly, a performance problem may be linked to a belief that effort will make no difference (e.g., low expectancy), a belief that performance will make no difference (e.g., low instrumentality), or the fact that an employee simply does not value the rewards that an organization is providing. Goal-setting theory has also proven to be very useful and, in fact, is employed extensively in organizations.

Equity Theory, at least in its original form, probably has less practical value than Expectancy Theory and Goal Setting. Because perceptions of inputs and outcomes represent cognitions, they may be highly individualized and thus may be of little help to managers in motivating people. Also, readers will recall that many Equity Theory predictions are negative; that is, Equity Theory predicts that in some situations employees will reduce effort, or perhaps even leave a situation, in order to resolve feelings of under-reward. However, for most managers, motivation is a positive enterprise and trying to prevent negative behaviors is not nearly as useful. Nevertheless, recent developments and research in Equity Theory focusing on fairness perceptions of treatment and policies emphasizes the negative organizational consequences that can occur when employees believe they are not being treated fairly.

The behavioral approach to employee motivation may also be very useful to managers. Principles of behaviorism are relatively easy for most managers to grasp, even if they do not have behavioral science training. Particularly when jobs are not highly complex, it is not difficult to determine the contingencies governing different behaviors. Finally, from a practical point of view, the best thing about the application of behavioral principles is that it works.

Locke and Latham (2004) have recently illustrated how current theories of motivation could be improved. One important recommendation involves integrating the different motivation theories into a comprehensive model of work motivation. Given the diversity of theories discussed in the present chapter, this task is easier said than done. However, it is worth emphasizing that all of the theories proposed likely address a part of what we mean by work motivation, and therefore each theory yields novel recommendations for managers in order to motivate employees to perform well and feel good about their work. Well-articulated and well-supported theories provide managers with considerable informed guidance as they attempt to motivate employees. If no theories of motivation were available, managers' attempts to motivate people would essentially be random, or perhaps would be based on each manager's idiosyncratic view of the world. In the next chapter, we examine how these motivation theories are applied in organizations in order to influence a multitude of employee behaviors.

CHAPTER SUMMARY

In this chapter, we reviewed what are considered the major theories of motivation in organizational psychology. These theories were organized into five general categories: Need-Based Theories, Cognitive Process Theories, The Behavioral Approach, Self-Determination Theory, and Job-Based Theories. According to Need-Based Theories, mo-

tivation is largely rooted in the human desire to satisfy needs. Theories falling under this category included Maslow's Need Hierachy, Alderfer's ERG Theory, and Achievement Motivation Theory. In general, support for Need-Based Theories has been rather weak, due largely to the difficulty of conceptualizing and measuring needs.

Cognitive Process Theories are aimed at describing the cognitive processes involved in employee motivation. These theories, for example, focus on things such as decision making, levels of aspiration, and self-regulation. Theories discussed under this category included Equity Theory, Expectancy Theory, Goal Setting, and Control Theory. Although all of these theories have been supported, Goal Setting has clearly received the greatest support and has had the most impact within organizations. In the future, as Cognitive Process Theories become more complex, a challenge will be to translate these into a form that can be readily used by managers.

The Behavioral Approach to employee motivation involves using principles adapted from behaviorism in order to influence behavior in organizations. The principle used most frequently is reinforcement, although others, such as punishment, shaping, and extinction, may be used in certain situations. Applications of the behavioral approach in organizations, in the form of Organizational Behavior Modification (OBM), have produced impressive results. This approach, however, appears to work best in situations where the jobs being performed are not highly complex.

Self-determination theory emphasizes the importance of not only the quantity, or amount, of motivation, but the quality of that motivation. Proponents of this theory of employees driven by autonomous motivation at work will be more satisfied and perform better than employees who experience their behavior as controlled by others. This theory has received a great deal of support outside of the organizational context, and will likely be applied to organizational psychology in coming years.

According to Job-Based Theories, the content of employees' jobs is the key factor influencing motivation. Theories covered under this category included Herzberg's Motivation-Hygiene Theory, Job Characteristics Theory, and Campion's Interdisciplinary Approach to Job Design. Job-Based Theories have proven quite useful and have generally been supported much better than Need-Based Theories. One problem that plagues Job-Based Theories is the distinction between objective and subjective attributes of jobs.

In the concluding portion of the chapter, we examined the value of motivation theories to managers in organizations. This may

PEOPLE BEHIND THE RESEARCH

EDWIN LOCKE AND AN EVIDENCED-BASED THEORY OF GOAL SETTING

I first became interested in goal setting when I read about a study done in 1935 in England by C. A. Mace. Some of his results were reported in Art Ryan's and Pat Smith's 1954 text, *Principles of Industrial Psychology*. Both were professors at Cornell where I was working towards my Ph.D. in the early 1960's. At the same time Ryan was writing a book *Intentional Behavior,* eventually published in 1970, and I got to read drafts of some of the chapters.

It was an unpleasant time in the field of psychology, because it was then dominated by the doctrine of behaviorism (with B. F. Skinner as its leader). This very irrational doctrine had dominated psychology for most of the century.

It held that consciousness was an epiphenomenon, that human action could be understood without reference to consciousness, and that people were determined by their environment. Neither Ryan, nor Smith, nor I accepted this doctrine (which started to collapse in the 1970's) but we were in the minority then.

I decided, in agreement with Ryan, that looking at conscious goals or intentions was a good way to begin the study of human motivation—that is, by looking at proximal causes. So I did my dissertation on goal setting and started a program of research. Gary Latham discovered goal setting independently based on some field research, and then we began to work together—which we have done off and on for over 40 years.

The most important thing we learned? Build theories inductively based on the accumulation of a great many studies over a long period of years. Don't base them on deduction or on just a few empirical studies. Another important point: Always use your independent judgment. Don't accept doctrines or theories just because they are popular. Look at the evidence and draw your own conclusions.

Edwin A. Locke
R.H. Smith School of Business
University of Maryland

vary from theory to theory, but it was concluded that, in general, motivation theories can be quite useful to managers. Specifically, theories provide managers with a "road map" for motivating employees. Without motivation theories, managers would be forced to rely entirely on intuition and their own implicit theories of human behavior. We continue to explore the importance of motivation in the next chapter as we examine the specific tactics used by organizations to influence employee motivation.

SUGGESTED ADDITIONAL READINGS

George, J. M. (1995). Asymmetrical effects of rewards and punishments: The case of social loafing. *Journal of Occupational and Organizational Psychology, 68*, 327–338.

Griffin, R. W., & McMahan, G. C. (1994). Motivation through work design. In J.Greenberg (Ed.), *Organizational behavior: The state of the science* (pp. 23–43). Hillsdale, NJ: *Erlbaum*.

Latham, G. P., & Pinder, C. (2005). Work motivation at the dawn of the twenty-first century. *Annual Review of Psychology, 56*, 485–516.

Locke, E. A., & Latham, G. P. (2002). Building a practically useful theory of goal setting and task motivation: A 35 year odyssey. *American Psychologist, 57*, 705–717.

Locke, E. A., & Latham, G. P. (2004). What should we do about motivation theory? Six recommendations for the twenty-first theory. *Academy of Management Review, 29*, 388–403.

Chapter Nine

Organizational Applications of Motivation Theory

F or any organization to be successful, employee behavior must be channeled in directions that contribute positively to that success. As examples, a car dealership wants its salespeople to work hard to sell cars, and an elementary school wants its teachers to strive to educate students. Organizations also want to prevent employees from engaging in behaviors that stand in the way of organizational success. For example, a construction company wants to discourage its employees from being late to work, and an auto manufacturer wants employees to refrain from drug use on the job.

The purpose of this chapter is to build on Chapter 8 by describing the various ways in which organizations apply motivation theories in order to influence employee behavior. It should be noted at the outset that the methods described in this chapter are not the only ways that organizations can influence behavior. Indeed, an organization could manipulate, coerce, and even physically threaten its employees in order to influence their behavior. However, in the long run, these methods tend to have undesirable effects. Thus, organizations typically use more positive methods.

This chapter describes methods that are either directly or indirectly based on the theories of motivation described in Chapter 8. An obvious advantage of doing this is that it serves to maintain continuity from chapter to chapter. A more important reason, which will hopefully be brought out in this chapter, is that methods of influence that are firmly grounded in well-supported motivation theories are generally more effective than

those based purely on intuition or speculation.

SOME BASIC ASSUMPTIONS

Before getting into specific methods that organizations use to influence employees' behaviors, it is useful to examine some basic assumptions surrounding this process. One underlying assumption, which is so basic that we rarely question it, is that an organization has the right to influence the behavior of its employees. In essence, the relationship between organization and employee is viewed as a *psychological contract* whereby each is entitled to certain things (e.g., Morrison & Robinson, 1997). From an employee's perspective, the employment relationship typically carries with it certain entitlements such as pay, fringe benefits, and, possibly, other perquisites. In return, an organization expects employees to behave in ways that benefit the organization. When their behavior is not benefiting the organization, employees are expected to modify their behaviors.

Another assumption is that employees have at least some freedom of choice regarding the behaviors they are capable of engaging in that positively or negatively influence an organization's performance. If employees had no freedom of choice, organizations would have very little to do in the way of *motivating* their employees. In fact, if employees had no freedom of choice, all an organization would have to do is order employees to behave in ways that supported organizational goals. This would obviously make life much simpler in organizations. (It would also make for a very short Chapter 9.) In reality, though, employees in most organizations do have some level of control. Certain forms of behavior (i.e., attending work) may be required to maintain organizational membership. The choice to go beyond these basic behaviors typically rests with the employee.

A third assumption underlying applications of motivation theory is there are no major internal or external constraints on employees' behaviors. Internal constraints would be things such as a lack of job-relevant skills or abilities among employees. As was shown in Chapter 4, motivation is only one determinant of productive behavior in organizations. When an organization attempts to influence employees' behaviors through compensation, for example, it is assumed (not always correctly) that employees have

the skills and abilities necessary to perform their jobs well.

External constraints, on the other hand, represent factors in the external organizational environment that make it difficult for employees to translate their skills and abilities into performance (Peters & O'Connor, 1988). Although situational constraints is a topic that has typically been explored in the occupational stress literature (see Chapter 7), it is relevant here as well. When organizations attempt to motivate employees by providing higher levels of job autonomy, for example, an implicit assumption is that there are no organizational conditions blocking the increase in autonomy.

A final underlying assumption of organizational attempts to motivate employees is that behavior is at least somewhat malleable. Put differently, it is assumed that people are capable of changing their behaviors. This seems like a fairly commonsense notion, but the evidence in the psychological literature regarding behavior change is not clear-cut. For example, Hellervik, Hazucha, and Schneider (1992) conducted an extensive review of the behavior change literature and concluded that, in general, empirical evidence supports the notion that behavior is amenable to change. They were quick to point out, however, that behavior cannot be changed quickly or easily (see Comment 9.1).

BEHAVIORS ORGANIZATIONS ATTEMPT TO INFLUENCE

Figure 9.1 contains four forms of behavior that are most typically targeted by organizational influence attempts. If we take a sequential view of motivation, organizational attempts to influence behavior begin before employees actually become organizational members. Specifically, organizations first try to influence behavior during the attraction

CAN PEOPLE CHANGE?

BEHAVIOR CHANGE IS an important issue that has been studied and debated by psychologists for many years. The importance of behavior change, however, goes far beyond psychology and other behavior sciences. For example, people's views about behavior change have implications for the relationships that we develop with others and, in many cases, public policy decisions. Many people also spend a considerable amount of money in order to change what they consider to be undesirable behaviors (e.g., smoking, overeating, being sedentary).

What does psychological research have to say about behavior change? Hellervik, Hazucha, and Schneider (1992) conducted a comprehensive review of the behavior change literature and came up with a number of interesting conclusions. The good news is that research evidence generally supports the notion that it is possible for people to change behavior. Their review contained studies showing evidence that people are able to change behaviors such as level of knowledge, job performance, safety behavior, and mental health. However, their review also showed that behavior change is complex and depends on a number of factors—perhaps most importantly, the behavior one is trying to change. For example, it is unlikely that underlying traits such as cognitive ability and personality traits can be changed. On the other hand, much simpler things, such as interpersonal skills, probably can be modified.

Another important conclusion from this review is that behavior change is not easy. People have to be motivated to change, and interventions designed to change behavior need to be well designed and, in many cases, need to take place over a fairly long period of time. So, yes, it is possible for people to change some forms of behavior, but such change does not occur overnight. Failing to recognize this could lead to problems if organizations either attempt to change behaviors that cannot be modified, or fail to use proper interventions to change other behaviors that must be modified.

Source: L. W. Hellervik, J. F. Hazucha, and R. J. Schneider. (1992). Behavior change: Models, methods, and a review of the evidence. In M. D. Dunnette and L. M. Hough (Eds.), *Handbook of industrial and organizational psychology* (2nd ed., Vol. 3, pp. 823–895). Palo Alto, CA: Consulting Psychologists Press.

stage. Through tangible means such as salary and benefits, and more intangible means such as promotion potential and organizational image, organizations strive to influence skilled individuals to seek membership in the organization, and ultimately to become members of the organization.

Once an individual becomes an employee, there are a number of behaviors that organizations attempt to influence. The most visible of these, and the one that has been explored the most in the motivation literature, is productive behavior. Organizations want employees to perform their basic job tasks well and, in some cases, go beyond and perform extra-role behaviors (e.g., helping other employees, striving extra hard). They would also like employees to come up with innovative and creative ideas for the organization's benefit, and, given the increasing competition and rates of change, organizations often want employees to learn new things and periodically update their skills.

FIGURE 9.1
Types of Behaviors That Are Typically the Focus of Applications of Motivation Theories in Organizations

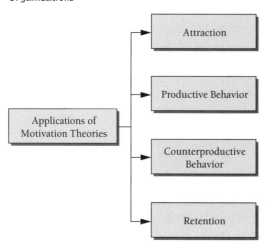

This strong focus on performance in the motivation literature has unfortunately shifted the focus away from other behaviors the organizations wish to influence. For example, organizations obviously want to discourage employees from being absent frequently, and from engaging in a multitude of counterproductive behaviors such as theft, substance use, and sabotage—to name a few. Although we typically don't think of these behaviors as the focus of organizational motivation programs, they really are in the sense that organizations are trying to persuade employees not to engage in them.

Another behavior that is frequently the focus of organizational applications of motivation theory is retention. In comparison to other behaviors, motivating employees to retain their membership in an organization is a bit different because it requires the organization to balance a number of factors. As is often the case with compensation, an organization may be in the position of having to make difficult choices when deciding which employees are worth retaining, and how much the organization is willing to pay to keep them. If an organization retains one employee by providing a large pay increase, this may very well prompt other employees to look elsewhere. Thus, an organization is often in the unenviable position of having to weigh the cost of internal harmony against the cost of a skilled employee's leaving.

Regardless of the behavior organizations wish to influence, applying motivation theories involves some choice on the part of an organization, and such choices are often value driven. For example, the founder of an organization may make a very conscious choice to reward his or her employees on the basis of performance. In other cases, the values communicated by motivational practices are far more implicit and, in some cases, are in conflict with the espoused values of the organization (Kerr, 1975; Lawler, 1990). Many organizations say they value performance and even institute reward systems that are meant to reflect this philosophy. However, despite the espoused value of performance, rewards in many organizations are only very weakly related to performance. Thus, in exploring the application of motivation theories, we must keep in mind that such applications always involve important value-laden choices on the part of organizations.

ORGANIZATIONAL REWARD SYSTEMS

By far, the most common method of motivating and influencing employee behavior is through *organizational reward systems*. There could potentially be an infinite number of ways an organization could reward its employees, so it is useful to distinguish between two types of rewards: tangible and intangible. Tangible rewards are those that are most familiar to readers: salary, fringe benefits, and bonuses. Intangible rewards include things such as recognition, praise, and increased freedom for employees. Tangible rewards will be discussed first. Organizational reward systems draw primarily from the behavioral approach to motivation described in Chapter 8, with the logic being that rewarding desired behaviors will lead to an increased likelihood of their occurrence.

Tangible Rewards

One misconception within organizational psychology, perhaps due to the rise of job-based theories over the years, is that money does not motivate people in the workplace (Flannery, Hofrichter, & Platten, 1996; Lawler, 1990). Quite to the contrary, few people would work for an organization for no salary. Furthermore, people engage in a variety of illegal behaviors, ranging from selling illegal drugs to selling government secrets, primarily to make money. Why is money important? In a general sense, money is obviously important because it provides the means for people to purchase life's necessities and luxuries. In the workplace, employees' salaries are important because they communicate something about the employees' value to the organization. Within a given organization, if one employee has an annual base salary of $20,000 and another employee is paid $100,000, it is fairly evident that the second employee is more highly valued than the first. Salary is also important because many people use it as at least an indirect barometer of their career success. For example, a person may define *success* as having a six-figure salary before the age of 40. Given the informational and practical value of money, it is not surprising that money is linked to employee performance and retention (Stajkovic & Luthans, 1997, 2003).

Despite the importance of pay, it is also true that pay is one of many motivating factors in the workplace. In fact, when people are asked about the most important things they are looking for in a job, pay tends to be ranked lower than things such as a chance to do interesting work, and an opportunity to use their skills (Hugick & Leonard, 1991).

As an attraction mechanism, pay can be highly effective. According to Gerhart and Milkovich (1992), research evidence shows that organizations who adopt a strategy of paying top dollar for talent have greater success in attracting skilled employees than organizations choosing not to do so. The reasons for this would appear to be rather obvious. When all other things are equal, many applicants will choose to work for an organization that pays them well. In addition, organizations that pay premium salaries tend to develop a positive reputation; thus, more applicants will be attracted to them (see Comment 9.2).

Despite the apparent utility of paying top salaries to attract top talent, this strategy can be quite risky for organizations. Given the high payroll costs involved, those hired must perform extremely well in order to justify this cost (Lawler, 1990). In addition, if several organizations within the same industry adopt this strategy, salaries may be driven to a much higher level than would be warranted by normal market forces (e.g., scarcity of labor). This has clearly been the case in professional sports, where salaries have reached astronomical levels. It has become increasingly difficult for *small market* teams to compete for talent and ultimately to be successful. It should be noted, also, that many teams with huge payrolls have been unsuccessful (see Comment 9.3).

Pay is also frequently used as a mechanism for motivating behaviors such as performance and retention in organizations.

COMMENT 9.2

BEING KNOWN AS A HIGH-PAYING COMPANY

IT'S CLEAR FROM the compensation literature that organizations known to pay very high wages tend to be more successful in recruiting employees, compared to organizations that are less generous. Therefore, it may be especially important for organizations to convey this in their various recruiting tools. In Chapter 3 we discussed how applicants to organizations make judgments about organizations in much the same way that consumers make judgments about different products. Leivens and Highhouse (2003) have emphasized that how organizations portray themselves in advertisements and other media may strongly affect the ability of the organization to recruit employees. Being known as a high-paying company may be an important aspect of company image.

On the surface, the reason for this seems rather obvious: Who doesn't want a high salary? Paying high wages also helps with recruiting, for other reasons. For example, the fact that an organization pays well may be seen by potential employees as a sign that the organization "takes care of its employees," and may even give the organization a somewhat elite image among potential applicants. Attracting a great number of applicants may allow an orga-

nization to be highly selective, and, ultimately, to hire the best talent available.

So why don't all organizations attempt to be known as high-paying companies? One reason is that many organizations simply can't afford the expense. Paying premium wages is costly, and that cost tends to compound over time. Typically, only large organizations and those that have been extremely successful can afford to have such high payroll costs. Another reason some organizations do not choose this strategy is that wages can get out of control if many organizations in the same industry choose to adopt this strategy. In fact, this strategy may drive wages to a level that is out of line with the skills and talents of those who are being hired. (See the section on executive compensation.) Furthermore, when organizations are paying everyone well, employees must be able to contribute almost immediately, and there may be little time for newcomers to ease into their roles.

Source: B. Gerhart and G. T. Milkovich. (1992). Employee compensation: Research and practice. In M. D. Dunnette and L. M. Hough (Eds.), *Handbook of industrial and organizational psychology* (2nd ed., Vol. 3, pp. 481–569). Palo Alto, CA: Consulting Psychologists Press.

The most common way of doing this is through *merit pay*; that is, employees receive an annual percentage increase in their pay, based on the outcome of a formal performance review (Lawler & Jenkins, 1992). Ideally, in a merit pay system, employees who receive the most favorable performance reviews receive the greatest percentage increases. From an organizational viewpoint, the hope is that employees will see the connection between performance and the size of their annual increase.

According to Lawler and Jenkins (1992), there is ample evidence that a well-designed and properly administered merit pay program can be highly effective in motivating employees. Merit pay systems, however, are often not effective because they are either poorly designed or administered improperly. A clear theme in the compensation literature is that pay systems should be designed to support the strategic objectives of an organization (Flannery et al., 1996; Lawler, 1990; Wilson, 1995). Thus, if an

CAN MONEY BUY ORGANIZATIONAL SUCCESS?

BESIDES THE HIGH costs that go along with paying high wages, this strategy is risky for another reason: An organization paying high wages must be very successful in order to justify those costs.

In professional sports, this is a particularly relevant issue, given that salaries have become so high and success is so cut and dry. Do teams that pay enormous salaries to players tend to be more successful than teams paying lower salaries, due either to a lack of resources or simply a refusal to pay high salaries? There are certainly a number of examples to support this hypothesis. In major league baseball, the New York Yankees have traditionally had one of the higher payrolls, and they have been quite successful of late. In professional basketball, the Chicago Bulls were quite successful during the period when they had one of the highest paid players (Michael Jordan) on their team.

There are, however, notable examples of professional sports teams that have been unsuccessful in trying to spend their way to success. In professional football, for example, the San Francisco 49ers in 1999 had the distinction of having one of the highest payrolls and one of the worst records in the conference. In their case, injuries, combined with age-related declines, contributed to this dubious distinction. In professional baseball, the Baltimore Orioles spent a considerable amount of money on free-agent players in 1999, and ended up losing nearly as many games as they won. In addition, as discussed in Chapter 4, Michael Lewis (2003) describes how Billy Beane, general manager of the Oakland Athletics, was able to put together a top-notch team without keeping their highest paid players.

In professional sports, as with any other type of organization, buying a deep supply of talent is necessary but not always sufficient for success. Thus, organizations need to be concerned not only with acquiring talent, but with things such as how that talent will mesh together, and how to design a system in which that talent will be best used.

organization's strategy is focused on customer service, the merit pay system should encourage positive customer service behavior. A common mistake in many organizations is that very little thought is put into exactly what behaviors are being encouraged by the merit pay system.

For the proper administration of a performance-based merit pay system, three factors are particularly crucial. First, for such a system to work, an organization must be able to accurately measure and document performance differences among employees. This can be done in some companies, but, more often, it is nearly impossible to do with any level of accuracy, particularly when jobs require a great deal of collaboration or interdependence. If performance cannot be accurately measured and documented, a performance-based merit pay system will be doomed to failure. In fact, where performance cannot be measured well, a performance-based merit system may do more harm than good because employees may see merit pay decisions as being very arbitrary.

Second, the system must be administered fairly; that is, employees must believe there is some validity to the performance-based pay decisions that result from the system (Eskew & Hennenman, 1996; Scarpello & Jones, 1996). This is related to, but goes beyond, the first point. Fairness involves not only the accuracy of performance measurement, but also whether employees perceive that merit increases reflect actual performance differences. This obviously mirrors the actual administration of the merit pay system, but it also depends heavily on communication. In many cases, merit pay procedures are ineffective simply because organizations fail to adequately explain the basis for merit increases.

Third, for a merit pay system to motivate performance, the amount of money available to fund merit increases has to be enough to allow the amount of the increases to be perceived as meaningful (Lawler, 1990). What is seen as a meaningful pay increase is somewhat subjective; it depends on many factors, such as the current rate of inflation and what other comparable organizations are paying. However, a clear trend during the past 20 years has been for organizations to reduce the size of merit pay increases (Lawler & Jenkins, 1992). Thus, many merit pay systems that are well designed in some respects have only a negligible impact on employee performance simply because the amount of the merit increases is not meaningful to employees.

In addition to these factors, Shaw and his colleagues have recently examined the importance of positive affectivity (PA) in how employees respond to merit pay increases (Shaw, Duffy, Mitra, Lockhard, & Bowler, 2003). These authors argued that employees high in PA are especially sensitive to rewards, and will therefore react positively to even modest pay increases. On the other hand, individuals low in PA are not especially sensitive to rewards, and therefore require larger increases in merit pay to *register* a positive reaction. This reasoning lead to the hypothesis that the relationship between merit pay raise size and reactions to the pay raise would be less strong among individuals high

in PA. The authors tested this hypothesis in a longitudinal study of employees at a large hospital representing diverse job types (e.g., physician, administrative). The authors were able to objectively determine the amount of merit pay increase between the Time 1 and Time 2 assessments (which were separated by 4 months). The authors found strong support for their hypotheses. There were no relationships between size of merit pay and affective (how happy they were) and behavioral (intentions to work harder) reactions for individuals high in PA. These individuals tended to report positive affective and behavioral reactions irrespective of the merit pay size. On the other hand, strong relationships were obtained between size of the merit pay increase and affective and behavioral reactions among employees low in PA. These results emphasize the importance of examining the role of personality in reactions to motivational incentives.

As an alternative or supplement to merit pay, some organizations have shifted toward pay for performance, through the use of *incentive pay*. In a typical incentive pay system, an employee's pay is directly linked to a quantifiable level of performance. The most common form of incentive pay, which dates back to Scientific Management, is piece-rate compensation. Under a typical piece-rate system, employees are paid a certain amount based on the number of products or parts produced. It is also common, in piece-rate systems, for employees to have a chance to earn *bonuses* by producing at a very high level. For sales jobs, a familiar form of incentive pay is described as sales commissions.

Bonuses are another way that organizations often attempt to tie pay to performance. In principle, bonuses are very similar to incentive pay; however, bonuses are often given out based on different criteria. For example, a manager may receive an annual bonus that is contingent on his or her department's meeting a given performance goal. Another difference is that bonuses are often distributed as lump-sum payments, whereas incentive pay is typically distributed from paycheck to paycheck.

Compared to merit pay, an advantage of incentive pay and bonus compensation is that both are more concretely tied to performance. For example, a real estate agent knows that variations in his or her paycheck are linked to the number of homes sold. A manager who receives an annual bonus typically knows why it is being paid. Because of the timing of merit pay, it is often difficult for employees to draw any connections between their increase and their performance. Another advantage, at least with lump-sum bonuses, is that they are more psychologically meaningful to employees. When an employee receives a 5% merit increase (which is fairly typical), this makes only a negligible difference in take-home pay and is often taken for granted. In contrast, a lump-sum payment of 5% of one's annual salary is more likely to attract the attention of the employee.

Incentive pay and bonuses are also advantageous to organizations for financial reasons because these systems make it much easier for the organizations to link their labor costs with their ability to pay (Lawler, 1990). For example, under incentive and bonus systems, employees are paid well when the organization is financially successful. During lean years, however, incentive and bonus payments are much lower.

At least in the case of incentive pay, research clearly supports a positive impact on performance. Jenkins et al. (1998) conducted a meta-analysis of 39 studies conducted in both laboratory and field settings and found the corrected correlation between financial incentives and performance quantity to be .34. Financial incentives had no impact on performance quality. This meta-analysis also revealed that the impact of financial incentives was greatest in experimental simulations and when studies were conceptually grounded in either expectancy or reinforcement theory. It has also been shown that financial incentives work well in comparison to other methods of increasing employee productivity (Guzzo, Jette, & Katzell, 1985).

More recently, Peterson and Luthans (2006) conducted a quasi-experimental study to investigate the impact of financial incentives (in the form of bonus pay) and non-financial incentives on multiple dimensions of business-unit performance. The non-financial incentives are addressed in the next section of the chapter. In the study the experimental condition of financial incentives involved individual restaurants receiving a bonus of increasing amounts based on the performance of a specified number of objective behaviors. Employees were educated about the bonus program, learning that the restaurant receiving the bonus would mean that they could expect between $25 and $75 being added to their paycheck based on engaging in the desired behaviors. A control group of restaurants did not receive any intervention. The authors measured multiple dimensions of performance at four time periods: before the intervention, and 3, 6, and 9 months following the intervention. Performance was assessed in terms of gross profit of the restaurant, average amount of time taken by a drive-through order (a key predictor of customer satisfaction), and turnover of employees. The authors found that restaurants receiving the financial intervention did not differ from the control group before the intervention. However, compared to the control group, those restaurants receiving the financial incentive evidenced a higher gross profit, faster drive-through time, and lower turnover at all time periods after the intervention. These results reveal the strong effects of a relatively modest financial incentive.

Despite the positive aspects of incentives and bonuses, some clear negatives are associated with these methods of motivating employees' performance. Though not a problem in all incentive and bonus systems, some of these systems can lead to adversarial relations between employees and management. Historically, this has been most typical in the implementation of piece-rate compensation systems. In a typical piece-rate system, employees are expected to produce a certain amount, considered the *standard*, and are paid more if they produce more than the standard. In many companies, there is considerable disagreement over what is an appropriate standard, and employees may intentionally slow down production while the standard is being determined. Management sometimes exacerbates this problem by arbitrarily raising the standard if they feel that the employees are making too much money. Ultimately, the focus can be more on "beating the system" than on increasing productivity.

Problems may also occur when some jobs in an organization are covered by incentive and bonus systems and others are not. The employees who do not work under such plans may resent the employees who do. Employees who work under such a system may be reluctant to accept a transfer to other job responsibilities for which they may be better suited, because they would have to take a pay cut to do so.

One thing that merit pay, incentives, and bonuses all have in common is that most are typically based on an individual employee's performance. Many of today's organizations, however, want employees to take a broader perspective and focus their efforts on enhan-

cing the success of the work group or organization. One of the most common ways that organizations tie rewards to organizational performance is through *employee stock ownership plans*, commonly referred to as ESOPs (Rosen, Klein, & Young, 1986). Although the ownership of stock is often associated only with executive compensation, many organizations make wider use of this form of compensation. Perhaps the most notable example of this policy is Wal-Mart discount stores, where hourly employees have always been allowed to purchase stock in the company. In addition, UPS has used ESOPs to encourage motivation among all its employees (Soupata, 2005).

From an organization's point of view, there are many advantages to having employees share an ownership stake through stock purchases. For example, if an organization is performing well financially, this can be an excellent way to attract talented employees. Also, because the value of stock often appreciates over time, employees may lose out financially if they leave the organization after a short period of time. Therefore, stock ownership can also be a way of enhancing retention. It is also possible that stock ownership will encourage positive attitudes and a sense of responsibility among employees (Klein, 1987)—things that many organizations try to promote by designating employees as *owner-representatives*. Finally, from a purely financial point of view, having employees own stock is beneficial because it is a good way for an organization to raise capital and thus avoid hostile takeovers from larger organizations or investors (Lawler & Jenkins, 1992).

Hallock, Salazar, and Venneman (2004) reviewed research suggesting that ESOPs were related to reduced absenteeism and turnover, and increased employee productivity, firm profitability, and firm stock performance. These authors argued that in order for ESOPs to serve as effective motivators of performance, employees need to see some connection between their individual performance and the stock market performance of their organization. Therefore, Hallock et al. (2004) examined the determinants of employee satisfaction with ESOPs among employees in a trucking firm located in the United States. The authors found that the primary predictors of satisfaction with the ESOP were employee's perceived influence over stock performance, perceived influence over decision making, and age. Employees were most satisfied with the program when they felt their efforts influenced the company's stock performance, when they had influence over various decisions related to such issues as working conditions and supervisors, and when they were older.

Although ESOPs have been shown to predict employee performance, they are probably less likely to motivate employees when compared to other financial incentives that establish a clearer connection between the employee's performance and an outcome (see Kraizberg, Tziner, & Weisberg, 2002). With the exception of high-level executives, most employees are unable to see a strong connection between their own performance and the organization's stock price. This has been particularly true in recent years' increased volatility in financial markets. Furthermore, in most ESOPs, participation is not based on performance. The only criterion employees must meet before they are able to purchase shares of company stock is that they must be employed for a certain period of time (6 months, for example).

Organizations also attempt to motivate employees' organizational performance through *profit-sharing* and *gain-sharing* programs. According to Florkowski (1987), in a typical profit-sharing program, an organiza-

tion designates a target profit margin that it wishes to achieve. When profits exceed this target margin, a percentage of these *excess* profits is shared with employees. For example, if an organization decides that a 5% profit margin is acceptable and the actual profit margin is 7%, a portion of the additional 2% is shared with employees. Profit sharing has the potential to decrease competition and enhance cooperation among employees. Employees under such a system stand to gain much more by working together for the good of the organization as a whole, rather than trying to outdo each other. Also, like ESOPs, profit sharing may help in attracting and retaining high-quality employees. Although there has not been a great deal of research evaluating profit sharing, there is some evidence that it is associated with such positive effects as enhanced organizational productivity and positive employee attitudes (Florkowski, 1987; Florkowski & Schuster, 1992).

Profit sharing, however, is also unlikely to be a powerful motivator of individuals' performance. As with ESOPs, most employees fail to see a strong connection between their own behavior and the profitability of their organization. Some organizations can address this issue by basing profit-sharing payments on divisional or even unit profitability, although this can't always be done. The other problem with profit sharing as a motivational tool is that profit-sharing programs often pay out only once or twice a year. Thus, even if an employee is able to see the connection between his or her performance and profits, the temporal lag between performance and the profit-sharing payment makes it very difficult for such payments to have much motivational impact.

Gain sharing is similar to profit sharing in that some portion of pay is based on the performance of the organization as a whole.

According to Lawler (1990), however, it is different in two respects. First, the payments made to employees from gain-sharing programs are based on cost savings rather than on profits. For example, an organization might determine, based on past data, that losing 10% of cost, due to production defects, is acceptable. Given this 10% target, if a lower percentage can be achieved, some portion of the additional savings will go to employees.

Second, gain sharing is a comprehensive organizational change intervention; profit sharing is strictly a compensation program. Given the objectives of gain sharing, this makes sense. Cost reduction typically requires the efforts of individuals at many levels of an organization's hierarchy; thus, input from all employees is vital.

Evidence on the effects of gain-sharing programs has been positive (e.g., Hatcher & Ross, 1991; Petty, Singleton, & Connell, 1992). Specifically, such programs have been shown to result in significant cost reductions, and may in fact have positive effects on employees' attitudes. It is much easier for employees to see the connection between their behaviors and cost reduction, as opposed to their impact on stock prices or profit margins. Also, compared to profit sharing, gain sharing represents a more fundamental change in management values, so employees working under gain-sharing programs may find that many other aspects of their work situation improve.

One potential drawback to gain sharing is that, in some cases, it is difficult for an organization to establish cost-reduction benchmarks. If an organization is relatively new, for example, or has not collected a great deal of historical data, the cost-reduction benchmarks that are set may be regarded by employees as being arbitrary. If this is the case, such a plan may do a great deal more harm than good. Gain sharing can only work if the cost-reduction benchmarks are seen as being objective. If they are seen as being arbitrary, employees may feel a great deal of resentment.

Up to this point, all the forms of tangible compensation that have been described involve either direct cash payments to employees or the prospect of some future payment. However, not all forms of tangible compensation involve direct cash payments to employees. *Fringe benefits* represent a significant portion of most employers' total compensation costs. The most typical fringe benefits offered by employers include health and dental insurance, some form of life insurance coverage, and pension benefits. Some organizations also offer their employees benefits such as 401(k) plans, vision coverage, and tuition reimbursement.

Unfortunately, very little research has examined the motivational impact of fringe benefits. However, the research that has been done suggests that their impact may be fairly minimal. Often, employees simply lack knowledge about their organization's fringe benefits program (Milkovich & Newman, 1990), and they typically underestimate its financial value (Wilson, Northcraft, & Neale, 1985). Given that barrier, it is hard to imagine that fringe benefits would have much motivational value.

Fringe benefits, however, can have a positive impact on the attraction and retention of employees (Gerhart & Milkovich, 1992). For example, given the high cost of health care, even small differences in health coverage plans can have significant financial implications for employees. Thus, a very good health coverage plan may potentially provide an organization with a competitive advantage when it tries to attract employees and is reasonably competitive with respect to salary. The same can also be said for retirement and pension plans.

With regard to retention, pension plans probably have the greatest impact because the value and portability of one's benefits often depend on organizational tenure. Organizations must deal with one question, however: Is it desirable to attempt to retain employees primarily on the basis of their *sunk costs* in a pension program? Such plans may help to retain employees, but employees who remain in an organization primarily for that reason may not be highly productive or particularly motivated (Meyer & Allen, 1997).

Another common form of noncash compensation comes in the form of *perquisites*, more commonly know as *perks*. The specific perks offered by organizations vary widely and depend, to a large extent, on the level of each employee. For example, for servers in fast-food restaurants, typical perks include meal discounts and free uniforms. Most retail stores offer employees discounts on merchandise. At the other end of the spectrum, perks for high-level executives can reach almost outrageous proportions. For example, it is not unusual for executives to receive perks such as country club memberships, free use of a company-owned resort, transportation to and from work, and travel via a corporate aircraft. Organizations have cut back on executive perks in recent years, due to changes in tax laws, but most executives are still treated very well by their organizations (see Comment 9.4).

As with fringe benefits, very little research has examined the impact of perks in organizations. It is doubtful, however, that perks have a great impact on employees' day-to-day behaviors because, for most people, perks represent a relatively small portion of their compensation. In addition, within most industries, the nature of the perks provided to employees is fairly standard. For high-level employees, however, perks may make

a difference, particularly when a company needs their skills. For example, to lure away an executive from a competing firm, an organization may attempt to "sweeten the deal" with perquisites. This is also a very common practice in professional sports. For example, when the Los Angeles Dodgers signed free-agent pitcher Kevin Brown in 1998, a clause in his contract called for unlimited use of a corporate jet to fly to his home in Georgia.

Intangible Rewards

Although organizations often reward employees with tangible resources such as money and fringe benefits, these represent only a subset of the rewards organizations may use to influence employees' behaviors. Many organizations recognize employees' performances with what can be described as intangible rewards. An *intangible reward* is defined as one from which the employee does not realize financial or material gain. Although clearly not as powerful as financial rewards, intangible rewards are used frequently and, in many cases, are highly valued by employees. Intangible rewards are relevant to many of the theories of motivation described in Chapter 8. They serve as a source of reinforcement in the context of the behavioral approach, they satisfy the needs of employees for belonging and competence, and they promote a more autonomous orientation to work.

One of the most common intangible rewards in organizations is a combination of *recognition and awards*. In some companies, recognition and citations come with tangible rewards attached, but the tangible reward is often less meaningful to the employees than the recognition and appreciation that are conveyed. For example, many organizations formally recognize employees after a certain

---

COMMENT 9.4

EXECUTIVE PERKS: LIFE IS GOOD AT THE TOP

PERQUISITES (*PERKS* FOR short) are special privileges that employees receive over and above their salary and fringe benefits. For most employees, perks represent a relatively small and insignificant portion of their total compensation. For high-level executives, however, perks can represent a significant portion of total compensation and may be quite lavish. Common perks for executives include a car and driver, country club membership, use of company-owned vacation properties, first-class travel privileges, and separate dining facilities, to name a few. In many organizations, top executives are almost treated like royalty.

In recent years, however, organizations in the United States have become somewhat less extravagant in granting perks to executives.

One of the reasons for this is that, in the mid-1990s, the Internal Revenue Service ruled that some perks represented a form of income to executives and thus were subject to income tax. Another reason is that more and more organizations are trying to create an egalitarian atmosphere in which all employees are treated equally. Granting lavish perks only to executives serves to highlight status differences within organizations, and thus runs counter to an egalitarian philosophy. Finally, public outrage over executive compensation in general has probably led organizations to be a bit more judicious about the perks they grant to executives.

Despite these cutbacks, perks still offer a very comfortable existence to executives in most organizations.

---

number of years of service, or when they have achieved some change in status, such as a promotion. Awards may also be given out for specific work-related accomplishments such as coming up with a novel work process or a cost-saving measure.

One large organization that uses recognition and awards to a great extent is the U.S. Military. The Armed Services have a hierarchically structured series of awards ranging from awards reflecting good discipline to the Medal of Honor, awarded for the highest acts of courage and self sacrifice. When used consistently to reward superior performance, these awards can be effective motivators of service member behavior under extremely stressful conditions. Castro and his colleagues (Castro, 2006; Thomas & Castro, 2003) have discussed the fair distribution of awards and recognition in supporting service member motivation, retention,

and performance. Recently Britt and his colleagues examined job recognition as a predictor of morale among soldiers deployed on a peacekeeping mission to Kosovo (Britt, Dickinson, Moore, Castro, & Adler, 2007). The authors found that when soldiers felt they were recognized for their contributions, they were more likely to report higher levels of morale during the operation. Morale during the operation then predicted deriving benefits from participating in the operation months after it was over. Although the judicious use of awards and recognition in the military can sustain motivation, it is also worth emphasizing that the administration of awards that do not appear contingent on performance can negatively affect motivation (see Thomas & Castro, 2003).

Another frequently used intangible reward is *praise*. For example, a supervisor may verbally praise a subordinate when a work assignment is well done. The use of praise should have some impact on an employee's behavior because it is likely that praise from one's immediate supervisor has some reinforcement value (Latham & Huber, 1992) and may enhance employees' feelings of competence (Bandura, 1986). Key issues, however, are the timing and sincerity of supervisory praise. Praise is likely to have the greatest impact when it follows closely after the desired behavior. If a supervisor praises a subordinate for a report that was written 6 months earlier, this is likely to have little effect on the employee. The effect will undoubtedly be much greater if the praise is delivered on the day after the report is completed.

Praise from a supervisor is also much more effective if employees believe that it is sincere. Undoubtedly, a number of factors can determine sincerity, but two are particularly important. The first has to do with the frequency with which praise is given out. If a supervisor is constantly praising his or her subordinates, the motivational value of this praise will likely diminish over time. On the other hand, if praise is very rarely given out, subordinates may become highly suspicious on those few occasions when they do receive it. Thus, for praise to be effective, supervisors must strike a balance between giving too much or too little.

A related issue, though no less important, is the level of performance that must be achieved in order to receive praise. If supervisors heap lavish amounts of praise on subordinates for mediocre performance, this will decrease the value of praise when high levels of performance are actually achieved. Praise is also typically more effective if employees feel that they have some control over the behavior for which they are being praised (Koestner, Zuckerman, & Olsson, 1990). It is unlikely, for example, that an employee would be influenced if

praise were given for something he or she had little control over.

In the section on tangible awards we introduced a study by Peterson and Luthans (2006) investigating the impact of financial incentives on the performance of restaurants. These authors also examined the effects of non-financial incentives on performance through the use of performance feedback and social recognition. Specifically, the authors had managers develop a chart for employees reflecting key performance measures (average time at the drive-through, cash register errors) for performance feedback. For social recognition, the managers were instructed to praise groups of employees based on meeting and exceeding performance standards. Managers were also instructed to give positively toned weekly memos to each employee reflecting how pleased they were with the employees meeting group goals.

Compared to a control group of restaurants that received no intervention, restaurants that received the intervention focused on recognition and praise had higher gross profits, faster drive-through times, and reduced employee turnover 6 and 9 months after the intervention. In terms of comparing the impact of financial versus nonfinancial incentives, at 6 and 9 months following the intervention, there were no differences between the two intervention groups in terms of gross profits or drive-through times. Both had resulted in equivalent improvements in performance. However, financial incentives did have a stronger positive impact on employee retention compared to non-financial incentives.

Another intangible reward that organizations sometimes use to motivate employees is *status symbols*. Status symbols are simply ways that organizations communicate an employee's worth or value to the organization. Typical status symbols include the size and location of one's office, an impressive-sounding title, and, in some areas, the location of one's parking space. Unfortunately, there is very little research on the impact of status symbols on employees' behaviors. One would assume, however, that these probably do not have a great deal of impact on employees. Most people tend to take status symbols for granted, although they may be happy with them initially. Also, status symbols often go hand in hand with other more tangible forms of compensation.

A final intangible reward that organizations sometimes use to influence employees' behaviors is *increased autonomy and freedom*. Over time, as employees become more proficient and demonstrate that they can be trusted, supervisors may grant them increased autonomy and freedom (Spector, Dwyer, & Jex, 1988). This may be done in a number of ways. For example, supervisors may give employees broad latitude on how they perform their work, and perhaps allow employees the freedom to choose their own hours or even to work at home on occasion. Although supervisors granting this type of autonomy and freedom do not see it as being a reward, it is quite possible that subordinates do see it that way.

One of the clear benefits of granting increased autonomy and freedom is that it will likely enhance job satisfaction and perhaps decrease employees' stress (e.g., Fried & Ferris, 1987; Spector, 1986). It is also possible that this will enhance performance and retention, although little empirical evidence exists to support either outcome. Granting increased autonomy and freedom may have a positive effect on performance, especially when employees are highly talented and motivated. Increased autonomy and freedom may help these employees to reach their full potential.

Autonomy and freedom may contribute to retention as well. Often, autonomy and freedom are perks that employees have acquired over time by demonstrating their talent and loyalty within an organization. Thus, if an employee were to leave his or her present organization, it is unlikely that the same degree of autonomy and freedom would be present at the new company, at least initially. The autonomy and freedom that employees have in a given career keep them from taking other career paths. This is undoubtedly one of the reasons why many university professors choose to stay in academia rather than pursue more lucrative careers in business or government. When people have experienced a great deal of freedom in their jobs, it is very difficult to give it up, even if they will be paid significantly more elsewhere.

Executive Compensation

Up to this point, we have covered the major types of rewards that organizations use to influence employees' behaviors. These same rewards are typically used to influence the behavior of executives, but the compensation of executives is quite unique, for a number of reasons. One reason is the amount of compensation of executives, compared to other employees. Although executive salaries vary by type of organization, it is not at all unusual for the total compensation of executives in private organizations to exceed several million dollars per year (Crystal, 1995).

Other than the sheer amount of compensation, another difference is that executives' compensation is typically based more on the performance of the organization than is the compensation of other employees. In fact, executives may receive 50% or more of their total compensation in the form of bonuses, or through stock options. Bonuses are often determined by the profitability of the company; typically, the company must perform well for an executive to benefit handsomely from exercising his or her stock option. Thus, compared to other organizational employees, a greater portion of executives' compensation is at risk if the organization does not perform well (Gomez-Mejia, 1994).

Given the high level of compensation that is received by executives, many have raised the issue of whether this reward is deserved (e.g., Crystal, 1991). Arguments in favor of high executive salaries typically center around two facts: (1) high-level executive skills are in relatively short supply, and (2) decisions made by these individuals can have a tremendous financial impact on an organization and its shareholders.

On the other hand, it has also been argued that executive compensation packages have become excessive and are out of line with the actual impact that executives have on organizational effectiveness (Barkema & Gomez-Mejia, 1998; Crystal, 1991). According to this argument, executive skills are scarce but not scarce enough to warrant the levels of compensation currently given to executives. For example, even though the salaries of professional athletes are often viewed as excessive, it could be argued that the skills possessed by these individuals are much rarer than the skills possessed by executives. For example, it is likely that far fewer people possess the basketball skills of Michael Jordan or the baseball skills of Alex Rodriguez, in comparison to the administrative skills of Michael Eisner.

Another reason for treating executive compensation separately is that, even within the same organization, the processes typically used to set executive compensation levels are often quite different from those used to determine compensation for other employees. According to Crystal (1991), high-level executive compensation packages typically result from negotiations between the executive and the compensation subcommittee of the organization's board of directors. This negotiation process is often aided by an outside compensation consultant who determines whether the board is compensating the executive at a level that is commensurate with executives employed at comparable organizations.

Given these procedures for determining executive compensation levels, there may be reasons why executives are at a distinct advantage in this process. Members of corporate boards of directors are often executives who inhabit the same social circles as the organization's executives. Such similarity may positively bias board members in favor of the executives. Also, many board members have their compensations determined in the same fashion, so it is certainly in their interest to have members of their peer group well compensated. Thus, members of corporate boards may not be the most objective judges of what is a fair level of compensation. Interestingly, research has not shown a relationship between the composition of compensation committees and executive compensation (Daily, Johnson, Ellstrand, & Dalton, 1998), a finding these authors attribute to pressure from shareholders to curb executives' salaries.

Another aspect of this process that often favors executives is the use of external compensation consultants. As stated earlier, the role of a compensation consultant is typically to assess an executive's compensation in relation to the compensation of executives in comparable organizations. On the surface, then, it would appear that compensation consultants would be the most objective players in the whole process. Keep in mind, however, that compensation consultants must give their recommendations to executives and board members who typically want to see the level of executives' compensations rise. If a compensation consultant does not recommend a highly lucrative compensation package, he or she may not be hired the next time compensation is determined (Crystal, 1991).

Within organizational psychology, research on executive compensation is relatively new, although some consistent findings have begun to emerge. For example, the amount of executives' compensation is only weakly related to the performance of organizations (Finkelstein & Hambrick, 1988; Gerhart & Milkovich, 1990). This finding would appear to be a bit disconcerting, given the vast amounts of money paid to executives. However, it could simply be a statistical artifact, due to the restriction of range in executive salaries. It may also be due to the fact that even though executives are important, their actions represent one of a multitude of factors that contribute to organizational success. For example, even if top executives make sound strategic decisions, these will not lead to success if an organization lacks the necessary talent, at lower levels, to translate these decisions into higher levels of profitability. Organizations are also impacted by a number of external forces that are outside of executives' control: economic cycles, changes in government regulations, shifts in consumer preferences, and so on.

Another stream of research has begun to examine the various determinants of executive compensation. One fairly consistent finding is that executive compensation is positively related to organizational size (Finkelstein & Hambrick, 1988; Gomez-Mejia, 1994; Gomez-Mejia & Welbourne, 1989). Larger organizations have greater financial resources, and thus are simply able to pay higher salaries than small organizations. It has also been found that executives

appear to be paid, to a large extent, based on the amount of discretion they have over decision making in their organizations (Finkelstein & Boyd, 1998). This makes a good deal of sense, considering that when executives have a great deal of discretion in decision making, they have a much greater chance of impacting (positively or negatively) organizational performance.

More recently, Wasserman (2006) examined differences in financial compensation for executives who were founders versus non-founders of new venture companies. Wasserman noted that most prior work on executive compensation has been focused on *agency theory*, where executives are paid handsomely to work on behalf of the organization because there may be times when the interests of the executives and principal members of the organization diverge. Agency theory is argued to be more relevant to non-founders of an organization who do not have an intrinsic interest in the viability and profitability of the company.

In contrast, *stewardship theory* refers to the tendency for executives to be motivated less by self-interest, and more by an intrinsic desire for the organization to succeed. According to Wasserman (2006), founders of an organization are much more likely to be ego invested in an organization, and therefore may require less financial compensation to motivate behavior to maximizing the effectiveness of the organization. The author argues that founders will accrue more *psychic* rewards by seeing their organization succeed. The motivational forces underlying agency versus stewardship theory are similar to the distinction made in Chapter 8 between controlled and autonomous motivation in the context of Self-Determination Theory.

Wasserman (2006) conducted a study in which he examined the predictors of executive salary (plus bonuses) among 1,238 executives from 528 private companies. His primary hypotheses were that founders would receive less financial compensation than non-founders, that a greater number of employees would be related to higher levels of compensation, and that the relationship between number of employees and compensation would be stronger for non-founders than founders. The logic for the last hypothesis was that because of a founder's stewardship motivation, he or she would be less likely to require additional compensation because of factors such as increasing employees. Wasserman found support for his hypotheses. On average, founders were paid $25,000 less than non-founders. The number of employees in a company was also positively related to compensation of the executive. Finally, the relationship between number of employees and compensation was much stronger for non-founders than for founders. These results indicate that even in the high-stakes realm of executive pay, psychological motivators of commitment and responsibility can decrease (somewhat) the need for financial motivation.

We return now to a question that was asked about other types of compensation: What impact does executive pay have on employees' behaviors? It appears fairly obvious that executive compensation has a great deal of impact on attraction. In fact, without such compensation packages, most organizations would find it difficult to attract high-level executive talent. The impact of executive compensation on attraction is closely tied to its impact on retention; that is, organizations must compensate executives very well in order to retain their services. There are, however, certain ways that executive compensation packages can be structured to have a greater impact on retention. For example, when granting an executive stock options, a board of directors has

some discretion over the length of time the stock shares must be held before the executive may sell them (Crystal, 1991). Thus, to retain an executive, a board may specify a relatively long period of time before the stock options may be exercised.

Another common way for corporate boards to enhance executive retention is by granting executives so-called *golden parachutes*—lucrative pension benefits that are contingent on remaining with the organization for a given period of time. Although job tenure is a feature built into most pension programs, with executives the stakes are so high that remaining with an organization may make a difference of millions of dollars in pension benefits. However, some executives may be so wealthy that the loss of pension benefits may mean very little if another organization is more competitive with its offer of compensation.

Finally, does executive compensation have any impact on performance? As stated earlier, there is a very weak connection between the amount of an executive's compensation and organizational performance. However, because so many factors contribute to organizational performance, it is still possible that compensation does motivate executives. Executive compensation packages are typically heavily loaded with stock options, and such packages are likely to motivate executives to make decisions that will increase stock prices. This can obviously be done through increasing profits, but it may also be done by more negative means such as layoffs or ill-advised acquisitions.

MOTIVATION THROUGH THE DESIGN OF WORK

Although reward systems represent the major mechanism for influencing employees' behaviors, organizations also attempt to motivate employees through the design of work; that is, they try to design employees' jobs, departmental structures, and even the whole organization itself in ways that engender high employee involvement and motivation. In this section, we focus primarily on the design of employees' jobs as a motivational tool used in organizations. More macro-level approaches to the design of work will be covered in Chapter 14. In discussing increasing motivation through job designs, a number of theories discussed in Chapter 8 will be relevant. Obviously, job-based theories are the primary approach emphasized in considering how to best design jobs to maximize motivation. However, we will also see that Self-Determination Theory also underlies attempts to maximize autonomy and personal importance at work, and that many attempts to redesign work recognize the needs that employees have in a work context.

Job Design: A Brief History

According to Moorhead and Griffin (1998), prior to the nineteenth century, most nations were agrarian societies. Families farmed and were largely self-sufficient. Gradually, this model of self-sufficiency gave way to what might be described as *general craft* work. Specifically, people gradually reduced their production of food and instead concentrated their efforts on the production of goods (e.g., clothing, furniture) that were then traded for food. Over time, this *general craft* model gave way to greater specialization. For example, in the production of clothing, people began specializing in weaving, sewing, and tailoring.

The single event that had the greatest impact on the design of work was the Industrial Revolution, which occurred in the United States in the late 1800s, and had spread throughout Europe in the late 1700s and early 1800s. With the Industrial Revolution came systematic study of job specialization by men such as Adam Smith and Charles Babbage. Their work ultimately led to the development of the assembly line and, eventually, to the introduction of Taylor's Scientific Management system. As readers may recall, the primary motivational mechanism used in Scientific Management was compensation; employees were paid on the basis of the amount they produced. Job design was also a key part of motivating employees under the Scientific Management system. To the extent that jobs were designed so employees could maximize their efficiency, this would lead to higher wages because employees were being paid on the basis of how much they produced.

Due largely to worker dissatisfaction over Scientific Management, there eventually emerged an approach to work design that is typically identified with the Human Relations school of thought. According to advocates of this approach, work should be designed in ways that provide employees with an opportunity to have input and to fully maximize their skills and abilities. A major assumption behind this approach was that people work not only to make money but also for more intrinsic reasons such as intellectual stimulation and creative expression. Although a number of work design interventions came out of the Human Relations movement, a common thread running through most was that jobs were designed to be more interesting and to give employees greater discretion over work-related decisions.

Since the Human Relations era, the focus has been on refining this basic approach. For example, Hackman and Oldham's (1980) Job Characteristics Model brought greater specificity to the design of jobs and produced a tool for the diagnosis of the motivational properties of jobs (the Job Diagnostic Survey). Campion's interdisciplinary approach to job design has represented the melding of approaches to job design that come from disciplines other than organizational psychology. We now consider specific approaches to the design of work.

Humanistic Job Design

One of the simplest forms of humanistic job design is *job rotation*. With job rotation, the actual content of jobs is not changed; however, employees are allowed to periodically rotate among different jobs. The reasoning behind job rotation is that performing different jobs will provide an employee with greater variety and, perhaps, an opportunity to learn new skills. Although job rotation has been shown to produce some positive outcomes and is still used (Campion, Cheraskin, & Stevens, 1994), the content of employees' jobs does not actually change. This type of job design is probably most effective for relatively simple jobs that can become boring over time. For example, amusement parks will frequently rotate employees from one ride to another in order to prevent boredom and maintain vigilance.

A second approach to job design, stemming directly from humanistic principles, is *job enrichment*. The term *job enrichment* was first coined by Frederick Herzberg and was used to describe those aspects of people's jobs that were labeled as *motivators*. (Recall the description of Motivation-Hygiene Theory in the previous chapter.) Motivators were linked to the content of people's work, such as the amount of control workers had over decisions, the level of intellectual challenge in the work, and the level of creativity workers were able to use in performing the work. Job enrichment represented an attempt to build greater levels of motiva-

tors into jobs and, hence, to make them more motivating.

The primary mechanism used for the enrichment of jobs was termed *vertical loading*, which simply means providing employees with more tasks to perform, as well as greater freedom and discretion as to how they perform those tasks. As an example of how vertical loading might work, the job of a janitor might be vertically loaded by allowing this individual to schedule his or her cleaning tasks and to assume responsibility for ordering new cleaning supplies. In this way, the job has been changed by adding tasks and allowing the employee to assume the responsibility for tasks that may have been previously performed by a supervisor.

Although few empirical studies have evaluated the design of jobs according to Herzberg's principles of job enrichment, there is some indication that this approach was successfully implemented in some organizations. For example, Ford (1973) reported positive outcomes, such as increased productivity and reduced turnover, resulting from the enrichment of clerical jobs at AT&T. Texas Instruments also had a great deal of success with the enrichment of janitorial jobs (Weed, 1971). Finally, Campion and McClelland (1991) reported positive motivational consequences (e.g., increased job satisfaction) of enlarging employees' jobs to provide them with more responsibility.

Not all of the early job-enrichment programs were successful, however (Griffin & McMahan, 1994). One of the reasons is that early job-enrichment programs were conducted under the assumption that everyone would be motivated by having their jobs enriched. Given the vast number of ways in which humans differ, this would appear to be a rather naïve assumption at best. Early job enrichment represented a rather narrow and imprecise way of designing jobs to enhance motivation. Although vertical loading may make sense in some cases, there may also be other ways that jobs could be changed in order to enhance motivation. It is largely in response to these two criticisms of job enrichment that the next approach to job design evolved.

The Job Characteristics Approach to Job Design

As you'll recall from Chapter 8, Hackman and Oldham's (1980) Job Characteristics Theory posits that most jobs can be described according to these *core* dimensions: autonomy, variety, significance, feedback, and identity. Furthermore, to the extent that these core dimensions are present, people will tend to experience their jobs as psychologically meaningful, feel a sense of responsibility about their work, and have an understanding of how they are performing their jobs. If people experience these positive psychological states, a number of positive outcomes will occur, one of which is high internal motivation. Hackman and Oldham proposed that this model would only be applicable for those with high growth-need strength, and, more recently, it has been proposed that satisfaction with the work context (e.g., pay, working conditions) is also a key moderator. For over 25 years, Job Characteristics Theory has served as the theoretical foundation for a great deal of applied work on job design in organizations. It is to that aspect of Job Characteristics Theory that we now direct our focus.

According to Hackman and Oldham (1980), an important first step in any potential job redesign effort is some form of diagnosis of the job (or jobs) within an organization that might be the target of such an effort. Fortunately, in the course of developing Job Characteristics Theory, Hackman

and Oldham also developed the *Job Diagnostic Survey (JDS)*, which can be used to measure each of the components in the theory. The JDS has undergone a number of refinements over the years and, at present, is a reasonably good psychometric instrument.

When used for a preliminary diagnosis, the pattern in the measures of the five core job dimensions is most important. Let's say, for example, that a group of employees holding similar clerical positions completed the JDS, and the pattern of results resembled those in Figure 9.2. In this case, the scores that we see reflect a reasonably high level of significance, variety, and feedback. However, it is clear that the employees performing this job feel that they lack both autonomy and task identity. In clerical jobs, it is not unusual for incumbents to have little autonomy over how their work is done, and the low task identity may reflect a feeling that they are only contributing to the goals of the organization in a very narrow way.

Now that a diagnosis has been done and we have some indication of how a job might be changed, Hackman and Oldham (1980) recommend that the next step is to assess the feasibility of job redesign. Although a

FIGURE 9.2
Sample Profile of Core Job Dimension Scores from the Job Diagnostic Survey (JDS)

number of factors influence feasibility, the general categories to examine are the employees and the organizational system. With respect to employees, a major issue is whether employees want their jobs redesigned. Also, because job redesign often increases the skill requirements of jobs, the skill levels of employees must be taken into account (e.g., Campion & McClelland, 1991). If employees either do not want job redesign, or possess very limited skills, job redesign is unlikely to be successful.

Some of the organizational factors that would likely influence the decision of whether to pursue job redesign would be the presence of union representation of employees, the prevailing management philosophy of the organization, and the likely cost of redesigning jobs. Although the presence of a union does not automatically mean that jobs cannot be redesigned, it does make it much more difficult because collective bargaining agreements often cover the content of jobs that employees perform. Thus, if an organization decides to redesign jobs, a union may see this as the organization's attempt to get more work out of its members without raising their pay.

The prevailing management and control mechanisms in an organization are important because job redesign interventions often involve granting employees greater discretion over how they perform their jobs. Thus, at some level, job redesign often requires that managers and supervisors delegate some of their authority to subordinates. If the prevailing management philosophy in an organization is very authoritarian, there is a good chance that most forms of job redesign will not work—they simply will not fit the organization. Thus, the prevailing management culture within an organization must not view delegation of authority negatively if job redesign is to work.

Redesigning jobs in an organization can be a costly undertaking. Job redesign often necessitates the use of outside consultants, requires training employees in new skills and work methods, and may introduce changes in jobs that interface with those being redesigned. Generally speaking, if an organization must completely redesign its production processes or technology in order to redesign a job or set of jobs, this may make the cost of job redesign prohibitive.

When the conditions in an organization appear to favor job redesign, a major choice organizations face is how to implement this change. Although it is possible to simply mandate the redesign of jobs, it is generally advisable to involve those organizational members who are major *stakeholders* in the job redesign process. A stakeholder is anyone who may be influenced by the redesign of a job. The obvious set of stakeholders in any job design effort are job incumbents—workers whose lives will be changed by the redesign of the job. Other common stakeholders are supervisors, union representatives, and anyone else in the organization who must regularly interact with job incumbents. There is no standard way to involve stakeholders, but a common mechanism is to create a temporary committee or task force composed of major stakeholders to provide oversight of the job redesign process.

Assuming that there is cooperation from major stakeholders, the next step in this process is to decide on specific changes to be made in jobs. These changes should obviously be driven by the initial diagnosis. It is also useful to have additional information about the job (from a job analysis, if available). According to Hackman and Oldham (1980), jobs can be redesigned in a number of different ways, depending on the core job dimension that one is trying to enhance. A common method of changing jobs, and one that is really based on the principle of job enrichment, is *vertical loading*. In the Job Characteristics Theory approach to job redesign, vertical loading is essentially the same as it was in Herzberg's approach; that is, employees are given more tasks and greater levels of control and discretion over how they perform their job duties.

If one thinks back to Job Characteristics Theory, vertically loading a job could influence nearly all of the core job dimensions, although the greatest impact is typically increased autonomy, because employees are provided with higher levels of discretion. However, this intervention may potentially have a positive impact on the other core dimensions of skill variety, task identity, and task significance, as well. Skill variety is often enhanced because, when one has greater control, this often necessitates the use of skills that were previously not used. Task identity may be enhanced because vertical loading often makes it possible for employees to complete a whole cycle of work rather than a small fragment. Task significance is enhanced because, when a job is vertically loaded, it is often easier for an employee to see the importance of the work he or she is performing.

Another common job design intervention based on Job Characteristics Theory is *combining tasks*. This simply involves combining small, specialized tasks into larger units of work. For example, a clerical employee whose job has involved primarily word processing may have filing and phone coverage added to his or her job duties. Combining tasks undoubtedly has the greatest influence on the core job dimension of skill variety because the employee is doing different things that may require different skills. It is possible, however, that combining tasks may also influence task identity if the combination of tasks represents a more integrated experience for the employee.

A third intervention based on Job Characteristics Theory is that of *forming natural work units*. This is similar to combining tasks, but, in practice, operates quite differently. Forming natural work units involves giving an employee responsibility for a logical, identifiable body of work. For example, an insurance company could redesign the jobs of claims adjusters so that, instead of handling claims on an ad hoc basis, each adjuster could have primary responsibility for the claims of a certain group of clients. This type of job change often allows higher levels of task identity to be built into jobs because, when natural work units are formed, employees are more likely to complete a job from *start to finish* and to see the job as an integrated whole. This intervention also has the potential to increase task significance because doing an integrated piece of work helps employees to see the *big picture*—that is, to understand how their work contributes to the more general mission of the organization.

A fourth job redesign intervention is *establishing client relationships*. This simply involves making it possible for an individual who is performing a job to interface directly with internal or external customers. A manufacturer may use this type of intervention by providing a phone number on a finished product so that, if there is a problem, the customer can contact the individual or team that produced the product. From the employees' perspective, this may enhance autonomy by giving the job a somewhat entrepreneurial feel. It also has the potential to enhance skill variety, since the skills necessary to interface with customers may be quite different from those required for other aspects of the job. Establishing client relationships is also an excellent way to build greater levels of feedback to any job.

Connecting employees and clients may also provide the setting for employees to see the beneficial effects of their work on others. Grant and his colleagues have recently developed a model emphasizing how illustrating the positive impact that employees have on others can sustain motivation and lead to an increase in performance (Grant, in press; Grant et al., in press). Grant refers to interventions designed to increase employees' awareness of the positive impact of their work on others as *relational job design*, and provides convincing evidence that such interventions can increase employee persistence and performance. Grant et al. conducted a longitudinal study among employees in a fundraising organization. Callers in the primary intervention condition interacted with a beneficiary of their fundraising efforts (an undergraduate student who received a scholarship as a result of fundraising efforts). Employees in a *letter-only* control condition received a letter from a beneficiary containing essentially the same information as the interpersonal contact. Employees in the second control condition had no contact with students. One month later the authors examined pre- to postintervention change in the length of phone time with potential donors and the amount of money raised. In a dramatic illustration of the impact of contact with the beneficiary, those in the primary intervention group increased their phone time by 142%, and ended up raising 171% more money. Those in the control groups did not show an increase on either measure. Future research will undoubtedly continue to examine the benefits of relational job design on motivation and performance.

A final intervention based on Job Characteristics Theory is *opening feedback channels*. This simply involves redesigning a job in a way that provides employees with an opportunity to receive feedback on their performances. In manufacturing, this may simply involve providing employees with access to quality control data on a regular basis. It may also involve the elimination of feedback from supervisors, in favor of direct feedback to employees. This intervention is targeted specifically at the core job dimension of feedback.

Hackman and Oldham (1980) reported the results of several studies that showed the successful implementation of job redesign based on Job Characteristics Theory, and others were published over the years (e.g., Griffin, 1991; Griffin & McMahan, 1994; Parker & Wall, 1998). Generally speaking, redesigning a job based on Job Characteristics Theory has been shown to have a fairly robust effect on job satisfaction (i.e., satisfaction tends to increase when jobs are redesigned), although the impact on actual job performance is somewhat mixed. For example, Griffin (1991) examined the redesign of jobs for bank employees and found that immediately after the job redesign performance actually went down. Over time, however, performance ultimately exceeded initial levels. This suggests that it may take time for employees to learn redesigned jobs, but ultimately redesigning jobs may enhance performance.

Despite the successes, Hackman and Oldham (1980) also note instances in which the redesign of jobs based on Job Characteristics Theory has been unsuccessful (e.g., Frank & Hackman, 1975). Although there may be numerous reasons for job redesign failures, there are likely to be some common themes. For example, organizations often do not anticipate the complexities of job redesign. A common mistake in this regard is failing to anticipate *ripple effects*, or the wider impact when a job is redesigned. For example, when a job is vertically loaded, many of the decisions that were previously in the hands of the supervisor are *passed down* to the employee. If supervisors are not informed of this at the beginning of a job redesign project, they may ultimately not be cooperative.

A second common reason for difficulties in job redesign is failure of the organization to do the necessary preliminary work. For example, if a proper diagnosis is not conducted, a job may be redesigned when it does not need to be or when employees do not want it. An organization may also make the mistake of failing to involve key stakeholders in the job redesign process. If, for example, an organization were to attempt to redesign a job without consulting a union, it is very likely that the redesign would not be successful.

The Interdisciplinary Approach to Job Redesign

Given its relatively recent development, less has been written about the application of the interdisciplinary approach, at least in comparison to Hackman and Oldham's (1980) Job Characteristics Theory. Nevertheless, this approach has been used successfully in organizations. When job design is guided by the interdisciplinary approach, the first step in the process is a thorough diagnosis of the job(s) that is being considered for redesign. In the process of developing the interdisciplinary approach, Campion and colleagues developed the *Multimethod Job Design Questionnaire* to assess jobs on each of the four disciplinary approaches (e.g., Campion & Thayer, 1985), although research suggests that it measures more than four dimensions (Edwards, Skully, & Brtek, 1999). This instrument can be used, for example, to highlight whether a job may be lacking on the motivational, mechanistic, biological, or per-

ceptual motor approaches to job design. Recall that the motivational approach focuses on increasing autonomy and employee participation; the mechanistic approach focuses on specialization and efficiency; the biological approach focuses on preventing physical problems and environmental stressors; and the perceptual approach focuses on facilitating effective information processing. A diagnosis may indicate, for example, that a job is well designed for efficiency and speed of information processing, but lacks characteristics that will facilitate internal motivation and physical comfort.

If a job is lacking in one or more of the four approaches to job design, an organization must decide whether the costs of enhancing the job on that approach would be offset by the benefits of improvement. In some cases, the choice is relatively obvious. For example, if a job is lacking on the biological approach, and several workers' compensation claims have been filed as a result, an organization may have little choice but to improve the physical comfort level of those performing this job.

In other cases, however, the choices are not as clear-cut. For example, if a job is lacking on the motivational approach, enhancing it may lead to desirable outcomes such as high job satisfaction and internal motivation, and decreased absenteeism and turnover. Changing a job in this manner, however, may also increase the skill requirements, which may force the organization to pay higher wages (Campion & Berger, 1990). In some cases, this is a trade-off that is favorable for an organization; in other cases, it is not.

Assuming that a diagnosis was performed and an organization decided to enhance a job on any of the four approaches to job design, how would the organization do it? In the motivational approach, the previous section on the Job Characteristics Theory approach to job design answers the question. Making changes—such as vertical loading, combining tasks, forming natural work units, establishing client contact, and opening feedback channels—will likely maximize outcomes associated with this approach. However, these changes may result in a number of costs to the organization, such as increased skill requirements, longer training times, and, possibly, higher wages.

Changing jobs to enhance the mechanistic job design dimension is rather unfamiliar to organizational psychologists, but it is still done frequently by industrial engineers. In many cases, this involves a *time and motion study* to assess whether the job in question has been designed efficiently (e.g., Salvendy, 1978). Such a study may reveal, for example, that the way the job is currently designed allows for a number of unnecessary motions and efficiency is being compromised. Elimination of these wasted motions may result in much greater efficiency; hence, productivity may be enhanced. Often, mechanistic redesign also involves redesigning incentive systems so that employees are motivated to use these more efficient work methods and procedures.

Redesign of a job to enhance the biological approach may be initiated by the organization or, in some cases, by an individual employee who is having physical difficulties such as back problems or repetitive-motion injuries (Hollenbeck, Ilgen, & Crampton, 1992; May & Schwoerer, 1994). This type of redesign typically begins with some form of ergonomic assessment of the job(s) in question. This involves an analysis of the job by an individual trained in ergonomics or, in some cases, in occupational health. What such a person would be looking for depends on the particular job being analyzed. However, common problems in ergo-

nomic job design include the existence of repetitive motions or the design of the work station. For many clerical jobs, the height of the desk and the positioning of a worker's computer are key variables that one would assess for possible improvement. Depending on the problem that is identified, there may be a number of ways to enhance ergonomic job design. For example, some jobs can be changed by eliminating some repetitive motions. For other problems, the solution may lie in the redesign or replacement of equipment or work stations. Frequently, the solution to an ergonomic problem may be quite expensive.

If an organization were to enhance a job on the perceptual motor component, this would typically involve some analysis of the job by an expert trained in Human Factors or Engineering Psychology (Wickens & Hollands, 2000). In analyzing the job, such a professional would be largely focusing on the nature of the information the incumbent must work with and how this information is presented. This type of analysis sometimes indicates that the incumbent is simply being required to process too much information; thus, changes may be recommended to reduce information load. Such an analysis may reveal rather straightforward changes that can be made in a job or in the work aids (e.g., computers) associated with the job. However, changes in information presentation may be quite involved and expensive. The problem may not be the amount of information being processed, but the way it is being presented to the incumbent. For example, in the design of automobile instrument panels and computer software, it has been found that information is easier to process when it is presented as icons or symbols, as opposed to text.

Morgeson and Campion (2002) conducted a comprehensive study evaluating

different forms of job redesign among employees in the data analysis division of a large
pharmaceutical company. These authors
compared pre- and post-intervention job satisfaction, training requirements, and work
simplicity. Employees within the organization received one of three interventions: an
intervention geared toward increasing both
the motivational and mechanistic qualities of
the job; an intervention geared toward maximizing only the motivational qualities; or an
intervention geared toward maximizing only
the mechanistic qualities. The motivational
intervention focused on increasing the autonomy, identity, skill variety, and significance of
a job. The mechanistic intervention focused
on integrating fragmented activities and eliminating activities that detracted from the job.

One of the primary purposes for the
authors was to demonstrate that motivational and mechanistic approaches were
not inevitably in conflict with each other.
The authors found significant increases in
job satisfaction from pretest to posttest in
all three redesign groups. In the group
emphasizing both motivational and mechanistic improvement, a measure of job motivation involving autonomy and skill use
increased, but a mechanistic measure of job
motivation did not. In line with expectations,
those receiving only the motivational intervention increased on the motivational measure, and those receiving only the mechanistic
motivation increased on the mechanistic
measure of motivation.

Integrating Approaches to Job Redesign

A recent trend in the job design literature is
the integration of the measures and techniques used to redesign work in ways that
maximize different forms of motivation and
positive outcomes for the employee and the

organization. An example of this integration is
the recent creation of the Work Design Questionnaire (WDQ), a measurement instrument
that assesses job design and the nature of
work through combining measures based on
Job Characteristics Theory (JCT) and the
interdisciplinary approach to job redesign
(Morgeson & Humphrey, 2006). The measure assesses 21 different work characteristics,
including attributes introduced by JCT (e.g.,
autonomy, task variety, task significance, task
identity) and attributes emphasized by the
interdisciplinary approach (e.g., information
processing, complexity, specialization, ergonomics). The authors provide impressive initial evidence for the measure's reliability and
validity.

Another sign of an integrated approach to
work redesign is a recognition of the obstacles
that face any attempt to change an organization in order to enhance employee motivation
and performance. Campion and his colleagues have recently discussed eight such
obstacles, as well as the opportunities that
result from successfully dealing with the
obstacles (Campion, Mumford, Morgeson,
& Nahrgang, 2005). The eight obstacles are
provided in Table 9.1. The first obstacle has
already been discussed in recognizing that
different approaches to work design (e.g.,
motivational versus mechanistic) can affect
different types of outcomes (e.g., satisfaction
versus efficiency). This obstacle can be dealt
with by trying to redesign work in ways that
enhance both satisfaction and efficiency. For
example, a redesign effort in a bank could
simultaneously modify the efficiency of data
processing and allow employees to work on a
complete product.

The second obstacle is related to the first,
and refers to trade-offs between different
approaches to job design being inevitable. For
example, organizational psychologists may
realize that giving workers more autonomy

TABLE 9.1
Eight Obstacles to Using Work Redesign to Increase Employee Motivation and Performance

Obstacle #1:	Work design influences multiple outcomes
Obstacle #2:	Trade-offs between different work-design approaches
Obstacle #3:	Difficulty in choosing an appropriate level of analysis
Obstacle #4:	It is difficult to predict the nature of a job before it exists
Obstacle #5:	Individual differences complicate job redesign
Obstacle #6:	Job enlargement can occur without job enrichment
Obstacle #7:	New jobs need to be created as part of growth or downsizing
Obstacle #8:	Long-term effects may differ from short-term effects

over their jobs will result in additional training, which may result in greater costs for the organization. In such situations those in charge of the redesign need to justify the additional costs in terms of the ultimate benefits in employee attitudes and future performance.

The third obstacle involves difficulties in deciding upon the most appropriate unit of intervention for the redesign effort. Should the jobs of individual employees be modified, or should the tasks that different employees perform be considered separately for redesign? Campion et al. 2005 note that redesign efforts can be attempted at the level of the job, duties involved in a job, tasks that make up jobs, or task clusters that naturally go together. The authors recommend task clusters as especially effective units of analysis in a redesign effort, because task clusters refer to specific activities engaged in by workers, reveal interdependencies between different jobs, and are recognized by employees as representing a *whole* piece of work. Campion et al. further note that most jobs possess between 10 and 15 different tasks. The research described by Morgeson and Campion (2002) with pharmaceutical data analysts used the procedure of designing multiple tasks into clusters before deciding how the work would be redesigned.

The fourth obstacle is that "It is difficult to predict the nature of a job before it exists" (Campion et al., 2005, pg. 375). The authors point out that all attempts to redesign a job are going from a known job to a job that is new and modified. Although organizational psychologists may believe that the newly designed job will be better for the motivation of employees, it is always possible that unexpected issues will arise when the newly redesigned jobs are actually implemented. One way to address this obstacle is to recognize ahead of time the interdependencies that exist between given jobs within an organization and consider how reconstituted jobs will affect each other in the new design. It may also be necessary to make adjustments to the newly designed jobs as unforeseen issues arise.

The fifth obstacle is that "individual differences complicate job redesign" (Campion et al., 2005, pg. 377). It perhaps goes without saying that employees differ and may therefore respond differently to redesign efforts. As described earlier when discussing Job Characteristics Theory, employees differ in their *growth-need strength*, or the importance they attach to challenging and meaningful work. Differences between employees may be especially important when teams are redesigned, as we address in more detail in Chapter 12. After reviewing research on individual and organizational moderators of the effects of work redesign, Campion et al. conclude that, although individual differences may influence reactions to work redesign, they are unlikely to undermine the overall effectiveness of interventions.

The sixth obstacle refers to the problem that results when employees are given greater responsibilities (i.e., their job is enlarged), but the motivational benefit of job enrichment does not occur. This obstacle refers to the critical point that a discrepancy can exist between beliefs of managers and beliefs of employees regarding whether increased duties and/or responsibilities make a job more satisfying and rewarding. Enlargement without enrichment can lead to costs such as decreased satisfaction (Campion & McClelland, 1993). Campion et al. (2005) stress the importance of considering how a job can be enriched and not just enlarged.

The seventh obstacle addresses situations in which an organization is going through a period of rapid growth or downsizing. Under these conditions, the nature of employees' jobs may change dramatically, as fewer employees are available to do the work and must take on additional roles and responsibilities. Campion et al. (2005) discuss numerous options for dealing with the need to combine or separate jobs in the context of these types of transitions. However, the most important recommendation they make is to keep employees informed of the changing roles associated with their jobs and to be clear about how their jobs are being restructured.

The final obstacle addressed by Campion et al. (2005) involves the observation that the long-term effects of a redesign effort may differ from the short-term effects. The authors note that, although efforts to redesign work to increase motivation may result in positive consequences in the short-term, these benefits may decrease or even reverse over a longer period of time. Apparently interventions that enrich employees' jobs are initially met with enthusism and interest, but over the long term employees habituate to the new job and perhaps have mixed feelings about the difficulty of their more complex jobs.

The obstacles and opportunities identified by Campion et al. (2005) illustrate the complexity involved in applying motivational theory to real-world jobs. However, we would argue that this complexity should not deter practitioners from making use of motivational theory and research to enrich the jobs of employees. One of the most important areas of future research on job redesign is investigating the determinants of effective redesign efforts in different types of organizations.

ORGANIZATIONAL DISCIPLINARY PROCEDURES

To this point, we have covered methods by which organizations attempt to motivate employees to engage in productive behaviors. Another use of motivation theory is to discourage employees from engaging in counterproductive behavior. In Chapter 5, on counterproductive behavior, interventions aimed at curbing specific behaviors such as absenteeism, accidents, drug use, and workplace violence were briefly discussed. Therefore, the focus of this section will be on more general organizational disciplinary procedures.

Progressive Discipline

Although specific disciplinary procedures vary widely across organizations, it is quite common for organizations to have what have been described as *progressive disciplinary procedures*. A progressive disciplinary procedure indicates a progression in the severity of the consequences when a work site has continuing or escalating infractions (Arvey & Jones, 1985). For example, such a progressive approach may be applied to safety violations in a manufacturing plant. The first safety-related violation may result in a verbal warning to the offending employee. If more safety-related violations occur, the consequence may increase in severity—a written warning may be followed by a formal written reprimand, a suspension, and eventually, if enough violations occur, dismissal.

What determines the specifics of a progressive disciplinary policy? One obvious factor is the nature of the behavior an organization is attempting to discourage. When counterproductive behaviors are relatively mild, an organization can tolerate a number of infractions before severe consequences are handed out. However, for some behaviors, even one instance cannot be tolerated. For example, most reasonable people would probably agree that an organization cannot tolerate an employee assaulting a coworker or demonstrating blatant forms of sexual harassment. For such behaviors, an organization may opt for a *zero tolerance* policy and terminate an employee at the first infraction.

Another important factor that must be considered when determining a disciplinary policy is the legal environment. Many union contracts contain clauses dealing with employee discipline (Bemmels & Foley, 1996). Some organizations may want to be tough on certain forms of counterproductive behavior, but may be constrained by either the terms of a collective bargaining agreement or a threat of litigation brought by a union. Organizational disciplinary procedures must also be consistent with state and federal laws governing employment. Legislation in some states may constrain an organization from disciplining specific forms of counterpro-

ductive behavior. As an example, alcohol and drug abuse meet the criteria for being disabilities under the terms of the Americans with Disabilities Act of 1990. Organizations are probably much more likely to exhibit tolerance by providing employees with treatment for alcohol and drug abuse problems, even if they would like to adopt more punitive measures.

Unfortunately, relatively little is known about the impact of progressive disciplinary procedures. Despite this lack of empirical evidence, it is likely that the effectiveness of progressive disciplinary procedures depends on a number of factors. One important factor is whether employees are aware of these disciplinary procedures. This may seem like a rather obvious point, but organizations vary widely in their effectiveness in communicating policies to employees. It is possible that an organization could have a progressive disciplinary procedure and its employees are simply unaware of it. If employees don't know about a policy, there is little chance that it will impact their day-to-day behaviors.

When disciplinary policies are applied, those procedures must be fulfilled in a fair manner (Trevino, 1992). Put differently, it is important to have policies applied with a degree of *procedural justice*. It is also important, in the implementation of disciplinary procedures, that employees are treated with respect and dignity. This often involves providing an employee with an opportunity to tell his or her side of the story and rebut any accusations. The term used to describe this form of fairness is *interactional justice* (Colquitt et al., 2001).

In an effort to be fair, some organizations have developed formalized grievance procedures to redress employees' complaints regarding disciplinary procedures. In many cases, grievance procedures are mandated by collective bargaining agreements, although that is not always the case (McCabe, 1988). Some organizations voluntarily create grievance procedures that closely resemble those contained in collective bargaining agreements. Although grievance procedures vary by organization, most typically allow employees to file formal grievances if they feel they have been unfairly disciplined. After such a filing, grievance procedures normally allow for disputes to be settled informally. If this is not possible, more formal procedures are used.

As with disciplinary policies, grievance procedures work best when employees perceive them to be fair and those who utilize them are treated with respect (Bemmels & Foley, 1996). Grievance procedures regarding disciplinary actions can often be avoided if an employee and his or her immediate supervisor can resolve the dispute informally (Cleyman, Jex, & Love, 1995; Klaas, 1989).

CHAPTER SUMMARY

This chapter covered the most common applications of motivation theory in organizations. Without a doubt, the most widely used mechanism that organizations use for motivating behavior is reward systems. Tangible rewards include merit pay, incentive pay, bonuses, fringe benefits, perquisites (perks), and status symbols. Research over the years has shown that tangible rewards such as pay can be very powerful motivators of employee behavior. In many organizations, however, the way in which these reward systems are administered makes it very difficult for employees to make the connection between rewards and performance.

Organizations also motivate employees through the use of a number of intangible rewards such as recognition, praise, and high levels of job autonomy. Compared to the impact of tangible rewards, much less is known about the impact of intangible rewards. Some research and considerable anecdotal evidence, however, suggest that these may often be powerful motivators. It is doubtful that intangible rewards can substitute for low levels of tangible rewards, however.

Compensation of executives was treated as a separate topic, primarily because the manner in which executives are compensated differs greatly from that of rank-and-file employees. Executives' compensations are typically much more dependent on organizational performance than are the compensations of other employees. Research has shown that the size of executive compensation packages is positively related to organizational size and to the amount of discretion executives have in decision making. Thus, it appears that, to a large degree, executives are paid based on the potential impact of their decisions on organizational performance. It was also shown that executives who adopt more of a stewardship approach to their companies appear less motivated by financial compensation.

The most troubling finding in the executive compensation literature is that executive compensation is largely unrelated to organizational performance. This has led to very heated public criticism of what are seen as excess levels of compensation among executives. Despite such criticisms, it is very unlikely that the level of executive compensation will go down appreciably. The procedures that are used to determine these compensation practices appear to be firmly entrenched. Also, to compete for executive talent, organizations often have little choice but to pay these high levels of compensation.

Other than reward systems, the other major method of motivating employees is through the design of work. The basic idea is that the content of people's jobs may have a profound impact on whether they are

RICHARD HACKMAN AND DETOURS IN WORK DESIGN

It's all about discovering and accepting two things about yourself. One, what you are naturally good at. And two, what drives you batty.

My major at MacMurray College was mathematics. I got mostly A's in my math courses but only by working my tail off. Some other math majors, I noticed to my dismay, were getting A's effortlessly. Then I happened to take a social psychology elective. I got an A. Effortlessly. Soon thereafter I made the best decision of my college career: I went ahead and finished up my math major but applied for doctoral study only to psychology programs, hoping against hope that I really did have some natural talent for work in that field. That set my course. Today, I probably would not recognize a differential equation if I tripped over one.

Friends and family tease me that I have higher needs for autonomy and privacy than anyone else they know—and yet I study groups. To them, it seems to be quite a mismatch. It's not. I study groups because, too often, what I most want to do when I'm in one is to escape. Precisely because I find groups so fraught and frustrating I've had plenty of energy for research about how to make them better (to see what we've learned, check out my book *Leading Teams*).

But wait. Why the focus on groups? Isn't Hackman the one who did all that research with Oldham on work design? It's true. But that line of research was a side trail off my main research path. In one of my first small group studies, done while still a doctoral student at the University of Illinois, I used a number of different group tasks to increase the generality of the findings. The attributes of those tasks turned out to shape group performance more powerfully than anything else we measured or manipulated. Then, after I had joined the faculty at Yale University, my colleague Ed Lawler offered me the chance to move beyond the experimental laboratory to assess the impact of task attributes on job behavior in organizations. Once again, task effects were both powerful and provocative, and more research clearly was called for. Greg Oldham, then a doctoral student, joined up and we began the series of studies that eventually resulted in our *Work Redesign* book. Only after that book was published did I return to my main line of research on group behavior and performance. I've been there ever since.

J. Richard Hackman
Department of Psychology
Harvard University

motivated. Approaches to motivation through the design of work have evolved considerably. The oldest was described as the humanistic approach, which was typified by Herzberg's job enrichment. This approach involved primarily building high levels of control and discretion into jobs. Job enrichment was applied successfully, but it eventually gave way to the job characteristics approach. This approach involves changing jobs in order to build in greater levels of the core job dimensions from Job Characteristics Theory (e.g., job autonomy, variety, significance, identity). A recent development relevant to this approach is the importance of illustrating to employees the positive impact their performance has on others.

Campion's interdisciplinary approach to job design has suggested a number of ways that jobs can be changed to enhance a variety of outcomes, some of which are relatively unfamiliar to organizational psychology. The most recent trend in this area is to integrate Job Characteristics Theory with Campion's interdisciplinary approach in order to redesign jobs in an attempt to maximize both motivation and productivity. Regardless of the approach taken, it should always be remembered that job redesign is a complex undertaking that requires careful advance planning and, often, considerable financial resources.

Organizations also use motivation theory to discourage other forms of behavior. The most typical way of doing this is through the use of progressive disciplinary policies. Such policies differ by organization. Their actual content depends on factors such as the behavior being discouraged, collective bargaining agreements, and other legal constraints. Ultimately, the success of a progressive disciplinary policy depends on how well it is communicated and whether it is applied consistently and in a fair manner.

Many organizations often develop grievance procedures to accompany progressive disciplinary measures. These allow for employees to dispute disciplinary actions if they are not considered fair. As with progressive disciplinary procedures, the effectiveness of grievance procedures depends on whether they are seen as fair by employees. In many cases, formal grievance procedures can be avoided if supervisors and subordinates are open to informal problem solving.

SUGGESTED ADDITIONAL READINGS

Campion, M. A., Mumford, T. V., Morgeson, F. P., & Nahrgang, J. D. (2005). Work redesign: Eight obstacles and opportunities. *Human Resource Management, 44,* 367–390.

Mitchell, T. R., & Mickel, A. E. (1999). The meaning of money: An individual difference perspective. *Academy of Management Review, 24,* 568–578.

Mitra, A., Gupta, N., & Jenkins, G. D., Jr. (1997). A drop in the bucket: When is a pay raise a pay raise? *Journal of Organizational Behavior, 18,* 117–137.

Shaw, J. D., Duffy, M. K., Mitra, A., Lockhart, D. E., & Bowler, M. (2003). Reactions to merit pay increases: A longitudinal test of a signal sensitivity perspective. *Journal of Applied Psychology, 88,* 538–544.

Wasserman, N. (2003). Stewards, agents, and the founder discount: Executive compensation in new ventures. *Academy of Management Journal, 49,* 960–976.

Westphal, J. D. (1999). Collaboration in the boardroom: Behavioral and performance consequences of CEO-board social ties. *Academy of Management Journal, 42,* 100–110.

Chapter Ten

Leadership and Influence Processes

Leadership is a topic that has been of interest to organizational psychologists for several decades. Indeed, volumes have been written about leadership, though not all have been products of organizational psychologists. Authors ranging from business executives to collegiate athletic coaches have written books about what it takes to succeed as a leader. Because much of leadership involves getting things done through other people, power and influence represent core activities of leaders. In fact, power and influence are deemed so vital to leaders that some authors have defined leadership largely as a form of influence (Yukl, 1989, 2006).

In this chapter we examine leadership as well as power and influence processes. Coverage of the general approaches to leadership is followed by descriptions of well-known leadership theories. Consistent with recent advances in the study of leadership, the chapter devotes much more attention to *contingency* and process approaches to leadership, in comparison to those that focus exclusively on the traits and behaviors of leaders.

Compared to other treatments of leadership, this chapter is somewhat unique in that power and influence are covered in the same chapter as leadership theories. This was done intentionally to acknowledge that the essence of leadership is influencing other people's behavior. Whether one is leading a church congregation, a Fortune 500 corporation, or a major league soccer team, much of what one does involves influencing others' behaviors. Furthermore, a leader's success in influencing others, as well as the means by

which he or she chooses to do so, will depend heavily on the amount and nature of power held. Power and influence are clearly the "nuts and bolts" of leadership.

DEFINING LEADERSHIP

If you were to pick 10 people at random and ask them to define leadership, there is a good chance that you would get a variety of definitions. According to Yukl and Van Fleet (1992), *leadership* is difficult to define because of the complexity of the leadership process. Because leadership involves interactions between leaders and subordinates (typically, the members of a work group), leadership can be viewed in many ways. For example, we can view leadership as consisting of the behaviors that are enacted by the group leader. These may include organizing the work, obtaining resources for the group, providing encouragement to group members, and ultimately evaluating the group's output (Guzzo & Shea, 1992).

On the other hand, one could just as easily view leadership as a series of functions that need to be carried out in order for a group to be effective. The nature of a group's task may need to be clarified, resources may need to be obtained, the spirits of group members may need lifting, and the group's output must eventually be evaluated. These functions can be but don't necessarily have to be performed by a leader. Any group member with relevant expertise may help to provide task clarification, or someone with an outgoing personality may motivate others. By viewing leadership in this way, we are saying that it resides within groups, and not with one specific individual.

Definitions of leadership often differ in whether they emphasize leadership behaviors or the results of those behaviors. Ideally, when a leader attempts to influence his or her subordinates, these individuals will do what the leader wants, and do it willingly. Sometimes, however, an influence attempt by a leader will result only in grudging compliance or may even be actively resisted by subordinates. According to some definitions of leadership, compliance or resistance does not represent *true* leadership. On the other hand, according to other definitions of leadership, influence attempts that lead only to compliance or resistance still represent leadership, albeit unsuccessful leadership.

Another issue that complicates the task of defining leadership is the frequent distinction between *leadership* and *management*. A leader,

some have argued, is a person who obtains commitment from his or her subordinates and, in some cases, may even inspire them. A manager, on the other hand, is someone who makes sure the "trains run on time" and primarily obtains compliance from his or her subordinates. A manager is someone who doesn't make things worse for his or her work group, but doesn't get them too excited either. Interestingly, the leadership–management distinction is much more of an issue in the popular leadership literature than it is among leadership scholars. This may explain why people have strong feelings about the issue (see Comment 10.1).

Despite all the factors that complicate the meaning of leadership, it is possible to identify some common ground among the numerous definitions. Yukl and Van Fleet (1992) define *leadership* as "a process that includes influencing the task objectives and strategies of an organization, influencing people in the organization to implement the strategies and achieve the objectives, influencing the group maintenance and identification, and influencing the culture of the organization" (p. 149). This definition is summarized in Figure 10.1. Vroom and Jago (2007) have recently defined leadership more succinctly as "a process of motivating people to work together collaboratively to accomplish great things" (pg. 18).

There are several things to note about these definitions. First, leadership involves the influencing of others' behaviors. Second, leadership is viewed as a process and not as an outcome. It is possible, based on this definition, for a leader to engage in unsuccessful influence attempts. Third, these definitions imply that leadership requires a variety of skills. Influencing task objectives and strategy may require strong analytical and conceptual skills; influencing people to implement those strategies and objectives

COMMENT 10.1

MANAGEMENT VERSUS LEADERSHIP

LIKE MANY AREAS in organizational psychology, leadership has had its fair share of problems with definition of important terms and constructs. One issue that often comes up, particularly among those who work in organizations, is the distinction between *management* and *leadership*. A *manager* is typically defined as an individual who engages in traditional administrative behaviors such as planning, helping to organize the work of subordinates, and exerting control over their behavior. A *leader*, on the other hand, is a person who not only fulfills required administrative functions, but also is able to inspire and motivate employees to strive for excellence, and, at times, facilitates meaningful change in organizations.

One of the reasons that we find this "management versus leadership" distinction interesting is that it seems to be more of an issue for employees, and less of an issue for leadership researchers. Although recent theories of charismatic and transformational leadership

address this issue to some degree, leadership researchers have not focused a great deal of effort on the issue. In contrast, I (SMJ) have found that in courses I have taught during the past 10 years, the issue is always raised and discussed with a great deal of enthusiasm. To most people, at least in my experience, managers and leaders are distinct groups.

If people do indeed distinguish between management and leadership, and have strong feelings about it, this suggests two things to me. First, employees in organizations want to work for people who are true leaders and are not there just to perform administrative duties. Second, there is a shortage of real leaders in organizations. There may be many reasons for this; it may be due to the fact that real leaders are often agents of change. If those in positions of authority simply carry out administrative duties, this allows an organization to maintain the status quo, and no pressure for change is created.

---

requires interpersonal and persuasive skills. Finally, leaders are frequently important agents of change in organizations. Changing the culture of an organization is a tall order, although it may be necessary at times if an organization is to survive. Because of the influence they have, leaders are often in the best position to facilitate cultural change.

The Importance of Leadership

What exactly do leaders do that is so important? Leaders are often needed to provide *strategic direction and vision* to groups and, in many cases, to entire organizations (Bass, 1998). Work-group members are often too busy with routine task completion, and with

meeting deadlines, to think about where the group is headed in the future. In many groups, strategic planning and visioning activities are shared among group members, but the leader is typically the focal point of such efforts. In a sense, then, leaders help organizations to channel productive behavior in directions that are beneficial and that meet relevant strategic objectives.

Another important function of leaders, particularly those in small groups, is to engage in *motivation and coaching* behaviors. Even highly experienced employees occasionally need encouragement and, in some cases, help in solving difficult work-related problems. As with strategic planning and visioning, motivation and coaching

FIGURE 10.1
Summary of Yukl and Van Fleet's (1992)
Definition of Leadership

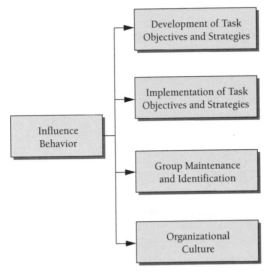

activities could potentially be shared among the members of a group. However, it is often more efficient, as well as less confusing for group members, to have one individual who is primarily responsible for fulfilling these functions. In most cases, that person is the leader.

A third important function of leaders in organizations is *enforcement and interpretation of organizational policies*. For most employees, leaders serve as "linking pins" to people in higher levels of the organization (Likert, 1967). Because of this concept, leaders are often required to interpret and enforce organizational policies. Again, it is certainly possible that a group could informally "police itself," but having a formally designated leader makes it much more likely that organizationally mandated rules and procedures will be followed.

Finally, leaders are important because they are typically responsible for *obtaining resources for groups*. Leaders essentially represent the interests of their work groups within the broader organizational environment. Because of this, groups often rely heavily on the persuasive skills of leaders to obtain resources for task completion. Without a leader, the members of a group may all be trying to obtain resources and, at times, may get in each other's way.

The four leadership functions just mentioned are not meant to be exhaustive, but they make a fairly compelling case for the importance of leadership. Furthermore, with organizations becoming flatter, skilled leadership is even more crucial to the success of organizations. In flatter organizational structures, leaders have a much wider span of control (i.e., they supervise a larger number of employees), and the impact of each leader's behavior is much greater than in organizations with a great many levels. Thus, leadership is very important, if not vital, to the success of an organization.

GENERAL APPROACHES TO LEADERSHIP

Like many of the topics covered in this book, leadership has been of interest for centuries, although much of the early writing on leadership came from philosophers, historians, and political scientists. Only within the past half-century have organizational psychologists become heavily involved in the study of leadership. During this time, distinct approaches to the study of leadership have evolved. In this section, we review three of these approaches: the trait approach, the behavioral approach, and the contingency approach.

The Trait Approach

The basic premise behind the trait approach to leadership is actually quite simple: Those who are effective leaders possess traits that are different from those who are less effective leaders. Leadership research guided by the trait approach is aimed primarily at identifying traits that discriminate between effective and ineffective leaders. Indeed, a good deal of early leadership research was based on the trait approach. More exhaustive summaries of this research can be found in Mann (1959) and Stogdill (1948).

Unfortunately, early trait-based leadership research failed to generate a definitive profile of the traits that characterized "the effective leader," partly because some of the "traits" explored by these early leadership researchers (e.g., physical characteristics, gender) were not based on sound theoretical reasoning. In addition, the aim of most of these early leadership researchers was to use traits to distinguish effective from ineffective leaders. Given that numerous variables influence leaders' effectiveness, it is understandable that using traits alone to predict effectiveness met with only limited success.

Because traits did not predict leader effectiveness well, and because, within psychology, emphasis shifted to environmental influences on behavior, the trait approach to leadership generally fell out of favor in the 1940s and 1950s. Trait-based leadership research was still conducted but was clearly a much less dominant approach to leadership than it previously had been. Over time, however, the trait approach to leadership resurfaced and made important contributions to the study of leadership, primarily due to two factors. First, researchers eventually decreased the emphasis on the prediction of leader effectiveness, in favor of predicting *leader emergence*. In group situations where there is not a formally designated leader, someone within the group eventually assumes the leadership role. Leadership emergence is simply the process by which this occurs.

The trait approach has also made great strides in identifying traits that predict leader emergence (Foti & Rueb, 1990; Zaccaro, Foti, & Kenney, 1991). Those who are more intelligent, have higher needs for dominance, are high self-monitors, and are socially perceptive tend to emerge as leaders when no leader has been formally designated. This profile suggests that emergent leaders are able to (1) accurately "read" the social dynamics of a situation, and (2) adapt their behavior to meet those social demands. Although not yet researched in the trait literature, it is plausible that such individuals are also more likely to end up in leadership positions when formal selection procedures are used. Longitudinal studies of managerial effectiveness would certainly suggest that this is the case.

Second, trait-based leadership research has made a comeback because the traits investigated in more recent research have been more theoretically plausible. According to Yukl and Van Fleet (1992), several traits have been identified that predict managerial effectiveness and advancement within organizations. These include a high energy level, stress tolerance, integrity, emotional maturity, and self-confidence. Given the nature of managerial work, it is easy to see how these traits would be related to success, especially when they are compared to things such as physical characteristics or gender.

Zaccaro (2007) has recently developed an integrative model of how leader traits are related to leader emergence, effectiveness, advancement, and promotion. Zaccaro emphasizes that leader traits include personality traits, cognitive abilities, motives, and values, and that combinations of traits are likely to be better predictors of leader effectiveness than single traits considered in isolation. For example, Kemp, Zaccaro, Jordan, and Flippo (2004) examined the ability of social intelligence, metacognition (awareness of one's thought processes), and tolerance of ambiguity to predict leader effectiveness among military personnel on a 3-day decision-making simulation. The authors found that those leaders with high levels on all three traits performed the most effectively, and that low scores on any one trait harmed performance. This line of research emphasizes the importance of considering how leader traits act in combination rather than in isolation.

In Chapter 4 we talked about the "Big Five" personality traits as predictors of job performance. Recall that personality researchers have identified five major traits: extraversion, neuroticism, conscientiousness, agreeableness, and openness to experience. One new direction in leader traits is to examine the relationships between the Big Five and ratings of leadership and performance. Bono and Judge (2004) found that extraversion was the most consistent predictor of transformational leadership— a type of leadership we will turn to later in the chapter. Transformational leadership refers to the ability of a leader to articulate a clear and important vision that will motivate followers to strive to achieve. The authors noted that, in general, the relationships between the Big Five and leadership were rather weak. The authors suggest that situational variables may influence (i.e., moderate) the relationships between the Big Five and leadership (see also de Hoogh, den Hartog, & Koopman, 2005).

Although much has been done to revive the trait approach to leadership, there are still many questions that trait researchers have yet to answer. For example, what are the practical implications of trait leadership theory? One would assume that the practical value of this approach lies mainly in the area of selection for leadership positions, but that has

not been fully articulated by trait researchers. Another issue that has not been fully addressed by trait researchers is the impact of various combinations of traits within work groups. What happens, for example, if a group consists of several individuals who possess traits indicative of leadership emergence? Do these individuals share leadership functions, or do they compete for this role? Despite these potential shortcomings, the trait approach, particularly in recent years, has advanced our understanding of leadership processes considerably.

The Behavioral Approach

Due largely to shortcomings of early trait research, the focus of leadership research shifted to the behaviors that seem to distinguish effective from ineffective leaders. The best-known taxonomy of leader behavior was developed by Ralph Stogdill and Edwin Fleishman and their colleagues at Ohio State University (e.g., Fleishman, Harris, & Burtt, 1955). According to these researchers, leadership behavior can be broken down into two basic categories: (1) *initiating structure* and (2) *consideration*. Leader behaviors that comprise the initiating structure dimension are aimed at   facilitating the task performance of groups. Examples might include organizing work for subordinates, communicating performance expectations, and making sure that subordinates' behaviors stay focused on the tasks that they are performing.

Consideration is represented by behaviors that are designed to show subordinates that they are valued and that the leader cares about them as people. Examples of this dimension include showing an interest in subordinates' families, "touching base" with subordinates periodically to see how things are going, and being compassionate when problems occur.

During roughly the same time period when the Ohio State leadership studies were conducted, other researchers were involved in efforts to provide meaningful classifications of leader behavior. For instance, Rensis Likert and his colleagues at the University of Michigan made the distinction between *job-centered leadership behavior* and *employee-centered leadership behavior* (Likert, 1961). Blake and Mouton (1964) made a similar distinction between *concern for production* and *concern for people* in the development of their managerial grid. Note that all of these reflect a basic distinction between leader behaviors designed to facilitate task completion, and leader behaviors designed to enhance interpersonal harmony in a group.

Despite the apparent parsimony of classifying leader behaviors into two broad categories, a number of issues were still unresolved. For instance, some argued that these two dimensions were largely independent (e.g., Blake & Mouton, 1964). In other words, a leader could simultaneously exhibit behaviors indicative of initiating structure and consideration. Others argued that these two forms of leader behavior are negatively related (e.g., Likert, 1961). For example, initiating structure behaviors were performed at the expense of consideration, and vice versa.

Another issue was that some leader behaviors were difficult to classify as strictly initiating structure or strictly consideration. For instance, a leader may make a point of talking to each subordinate each day, to see how things are going. This could certainly be viewed as consideration because it provides the leader with an opportunity to express concern for these subordinates. These informal chats may also help to keep subordinates focused on their work-related tasks, and may provide an opportunity to exchange important task-related information with the leader. Thus, the behaviors leaders engage in may be more complex than this two-dimensional classification would suggest.

Although the Ohio State University two-factor approach enjoyed some success initially, a number of authors expressed doubts about the ability of consideration and initiating structure to predict leader effectiveness (Yukl & van Fleet, 1992). Judge, Piccolo, and Ilies (2004) pointed out that these pessimistic assessments were based largely on qualitative reviews of the literature, rather than an objective assessment of the ability of consideration and initiating structure to predict outcomes such as follower satisfaction and leader effectiveness. Judge et al. (2004) conducted meta-analyses of 163 independent correlations between initiating structure, consideration, and these outcomes. The authors found the overall relationship between consideration and key outcomes, controlling for measurement error in the variables, was .48, and that the overall relationship between initiating structure and the key variables was .29. Judge and his colleagues point out that these relationships are rather impressive, and support the validity of the two major categories of leader behavior.

However, one final issue that continues to plague the behavioral approach (and has from the beginning) is that researchers were never able to identify a set of leader behaviors that were consistently associated with effectiveness across all types of situations. This suggests that there is no *universal* set of leader behaviors that will result in leader effectiveness in all situations. Rather, the behaviors that are needed from a leader will vary from situation to situation. This realization led to the contingency approach to leadership, which will be described next.

The Contingency Approach

The contingency approach is based on the assumption that the relationship between leader behaviors and traits and effectiveness depends on characteristics of the particular situation the leader is in. The task of a leader, according to the contingency approach, is to first "read" the situation to determine what behaviors would be most appropriate. Once this is determined, the leader has to adjust his or her behavior to meet the demands of the situation.

To illustrate how the contingency approach works in practice, let's say that a leader has been asked to take charge of a group consisting of five highly skilled and experienced design engineers. In this type of situation, the leader would probably not have to do a great deal of teaching and performance-related coaching. In fact, if the leader tried to do this, the group members might consider him or her an annoyance. Instead, the leader in this situation will be more effective if he or she concentrates on obtaining resources for the group, facilitates professional development activities for group members, and periodically makes an effort to boost the morale of the group.

Now consider a different leader who is in charge of a group of five design engineers who are all recent college graduates. A good deal of this leader's behavior will be focused on task clarification, teaching, and performance-related coaching. In a group like this, these activities would not be considered an annoyance at all; in fact, they would probably be welcomed. To be effective in this situation, a leader would have to be very "hands on" with his or her subordinates. If a leader in this situation spent the bulk of his or her time negotiating for resources within the organization, or remained very distant from the group members, he or she would probably not be successful.

Most leadership theories developed during the past 30 years are contingency theories. Thus, it is accurate to say that the field of leadership has accepted the general premise behind contingency theories. Less consensus, however, has been given to many of the specifics of the contingency approach. For example, there is not a great deal of consensus regarding the specific aspects of the situation that leaders must "read" in order to adjust their behaviors. For example, several contingency theories propose that "subordinates" are one such factor, but there is not a great deal of agreement on what specific aspects of subordinates are the most important.

Another area of disagreement surrounding contingency theories has to do with the behaviors that leaders must exhibit in order to be successful. As readers will see, contingency theories differ in the level of adaptability they ascribe to the leader. In some theories (e.g., Fiedler, 1967), it is proposed that leaders have a predetermined leadership style that is not subject to a great deal of modification. Other contingency theories (e.g., House, 1971), however, propose that leaders are fully capable of adapting their behaviors to different situations. This really speaks to the more basic issue of the malleability of behavior, which was discussed in the previous chapter (e.g., Hellervik, Hazucha, & Schneider, 1992). Based on that literature, the weight of the evidence suggests that leaders are capable of modifying their behaviors to meet situational demands. What is not nearly as clear is what leaders are specifically supposed to do in response to the situations they face.

MODERN THEORIES OF LEADERSHIP

Most leadership theories developed within the past 30 years can be classified as contingency theories. In this section, we examine the contingency leadership theories that have been most influential in the leadership literature. Influence is defined in terms of the research generated by the theories, as well as the impact the theory has had on the practice of leadership within organizations.

Fiedler's Contingency Theory

The basic premise behind Fiedler's contingency theory is actually quite simple. Like all contingency theories, it proposes that the success of a leader depends on the interaction between characteristics of the situation and characteristics of the leader. According to Fiedler, *situation favorability* depends on the three factors illustrated in Figure 10.2. The first of these, leader–member relations, reflects the extent to which a leader gets along well with his or her subordinates. Generally speaking, situations are more favorable for leaders when they get along well with subordinates, and, conversely, less favorable if leader–member relations are poor.

The next situational attribute, task structure, reflects whether the subordinates are working on a task that is very straightforward and structured (e.g., produce 50 cars per day), or whether the task is vague and unstructured (e.g., "Develop innovative products"). Although subordinates may find a lack of structure challenging, from a leader's perspective having a high degree of structure is more favorable than having a low degree. When task structure is high, the leader is required to spend less time clarifying the task

FIGURE 10.2

Determinants of Situation Favorability in Fiedler's Contingency Theory

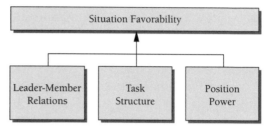

for subordinates, and decisions are typically much easier to make.

The third determinant of situation favorability is the position power of the leader—the amount of formal authority that a leader has over his or her subordinates. Some degree of authority is inherent in all leadership positions, but the amount of authority actually varies considerably. Some leaders are granted the authority to assign subordinates to different jobs, to evaluate their work, and to dismiss those who are not performing well. However, leadership positions do not always carry a great deal of authority. A good example is the chairperson of an academic department. A chairperson is technically "in charge" of an academic department, but this person has very little formal authority beyond that of supervisors in many other types of organization.

From a leader's perspective, a high rather than a low position power is desirable. When position power is high, subordinates will typically do what the leader wants, and the leader does not have to exert a great deal of force over employees. When a leader's position power is low, subordinates may still do what the leader wants, but the leader may have to expend a great deal of effort in order to make that happen. Consider, for example, the chairperson of an academic department who is trying to persuade a tenured faculty member to teach a class that this individual does not want to teach. The chairperson must spend time and effort to persuade this individual to teach the course, and perhaps may have to offer something in return (a course release in the future).

Given these three situational attributes, and the fact that each has two levels, it is possible to come up with eight unique situations (called *octants*) in terms of favorability. These are illustrated in Figure 10.3. The most favorable situations for leaders are those in which leader–member relations are good, task structure is high, and position power is high. In this type of situation, a leader gets along well with his or her subordinates, is directing a group of employees working on a well-defined task, and has a great deal of formal authority. From a leader's perspective, what could be better? A leader can then spend his or her time on activities such as strategic planning, acquiring resources for the group, and perhaps helping subordinates to develop their skills.

At the other end of the spectrum, the least favorable situations for leaders are those in which leader–member relations are poor, task structure is low, and the leader has very low position power. From a leader's perspective, what could be worse? The fact that the leader does not get along well with his or her subordinates is likely to be unpleasant. However, when combined with a very vague and unstructured task and a very low level of authority, this is even worse. A leader in this situation may have to spend the bulk of his or her time trying to influence or negotiate with subordinates in order to get anything accomplished. Furthermore, there is no guarantee that such influence attempts will be successful. The leader will have considerably less time available for things such as

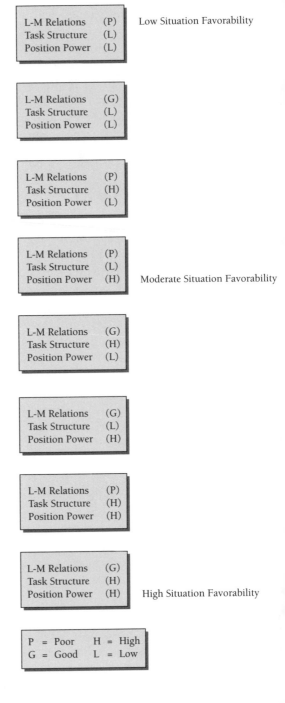

FIGURE 10.3

Summary of the Eight Octants Which Represent Differing Degrees of Situation Favorability

		Low Situation Favorability
L-M Relations	(P)	
Task Structure	(L)	
Position Power	(L)	

L-M Relations	(G)
Task Structure	(L)
Position Power	(L)

L-M Relations	(P)
Task Structure	(H)
Position Power	(L)

		Moderate Situation Favorability
L-M Relations	(P)	
Task Structure	(L)	
Position Power	(H)	

L-M Relations	(G)
Task Structure	(H)
Position Power	(L)

L-M Relations	(G)
Task Structure	(L)
Position Power	(H)

L-M Relations	(P)
Task Structure	(H)
Position Power	(H)

		High Situation Favorability
L-M Relations	(G)	
Task Structure	(H)	
Position Power	(H)	

P	= Poor	H	= High
G	= Good	L	= Low

strategic planning, resource acquisition, or employee development.

In between these extremes are six other situations that Fiedler referred to as having *moderate* favorability for the leader. In the interest of brevity, all of these moderately favorable situations will not be described. However, as an example of a moderately favorable situation, a leader may have good leader–member relations, high task structure, and low position power vis-à-vis his or her subordinates. From the leader's point of view, these situations are inherently more complex than situations of either very high or very low favorability.

The second portion of Fiedler's theory has to do with the characteristics of the leader. According to Fiedler, leaders can be reliably distinguished in terms of whether they are *task-oriented* versus *relationship- oriented*. To measure task versus relationship orientation in leaders, Fiedler and his colleagues developed the *Least Preferred Coworker (LPC) Scale* (Fiedler, 1967). As can be seen in Table 10.1, the LPC Scale consists of 18 pairs of adjectives. Respondents completing this scale are asked to think of a person with whom they currently work or have worked in the past, and with whom they have had the most difficulty in getting work done. A high LPC score indicates that a leader has described his or her least preferred coworker in relatively favorable terms. This indicates that the leader is relationship oriented because he or she is able to rate this coworker favorably, even though the individual is not seen as someone who would facilitate task accomplishment. In contrast, a low LPC score indicates that the least preferred coworker is described in relatively unfavorable terms. This indicates that the leader is task oriented, according to Fiedler, because this coworker's

negative impact on task accomplishment overrides any positive qualities this person may possess.

Fiedler proposed that leaders who are task oriented (herein referred to as Low LPC leaders) are most successful in either highly favorable or highly unfavorable situations. In highly favorable situations, a Low LPC leader will basically leave things alone and not try to introduce major changes. He or she will also not try to "get into people's heads" and become very close to them interpersonally. This type of leader behavior simply is not needed. In contrast, when situations are highly unfavorable, a Low LPC leader is probably the only type that will get anything done. In these situations, a High LPC leader's attempts to develop strong interpersonal ties will likely fall flat and will ultimately reduce the chances of any form of task accomplishment.

When situations are moderately favorable, Fiedler proposed that leaders who are relationship oriented (herein referred to as High LPC leaders) are most effective. The logic here is that moderately favorable situations are not "black and white." Such situations often require some interpersonal finesse, and a High LPC leader has this trait. Let's say, for example, that a leader is in a moderately favorable situation: Leader–member relations are good, but task structure and position power are low. A High LPC leader is needed because the leader may have to rely heavily on his or her relationships with subordinates in order to clarify the task and ultimately get things done. A Low LPC leader would be unsuccessful in this situation, primarily because he or she may not see the complexities in the situation and may simply demand performance. The relationship between LPC and situational favorability is summarized in Figure 10.4.

Considerable research has been done on Fiedler's contingency theory over the years,

TABLE 10.1
Least Preferred Coworker (LPC) Scale (Fiedler, 1967)

Over the course of your life you have probably worked in many groups with other people on your job, in community groups, church groups, athletic teams, etc. Some of your coworkers may have been very easy to work with in attaining the group's goal, while others were less easy to work with.

Think of the person in your life with whom you worked least well. He or she may have been someone you knew in the past or someone you work with now. The person does not have to be the person you like least well, but should be the person with whom you have the most difficulty getting the job done. In this scale you will be describing this person. You do not need to give the person's name.

Following are pairs of words which are opposite in meaning, such as "Very Neat" and "Not Neat." Between each pair of words are eight blanks to form a scale.
EXAMPLE: In describing the person with whom you least like to work, if you ordinarily think of him or her as being "Quite Neat," you would put an "X" in the space marked 7.

If you ordinarily think of this person as being only "Somewhat Neat," you would put your "X" in the space above the 6.

If you think of this person as being "Slightly Untidy," you would mark the space above the 4.

If you would think of this person as being "Very Untidy" (or not neat), you would put your "X" in space 1.

Look at the words at both ends of the line before you mark your "X." Work rapidly, your first answer is likely to be your best one (there are no right or wrong answers, though).
Please do not omit any items, and mark each item only once.

Now use the scale to describe the person with whom you find it hardest to get the job done.

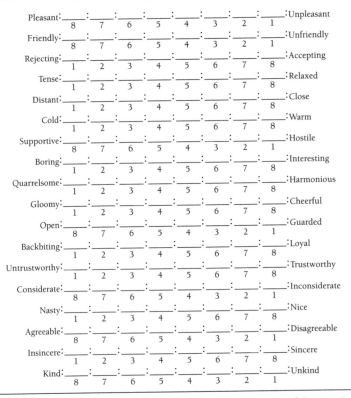

Note: 1 = least descriptive of the Least Preferred Coworker; 8 = most descriptive of the Least Preferred Coworker.
Source: F. E. Fiedler. (1967). *A theory of leadership effectiveness.* New York: McGraw-Hill. Used with permission of the author.
Scores on the LPC Scale can range from 18 to 144. A score of 56 or less indicates that a person is a task-oriented leader; a score of 63 or above indicates that a person is relationship-oriented. Scores between 56 and 63 indicate that a person's leadership style cannot be determined.

FIGURE 10.4

Effectiveness of High versus Low LPC Leaders at Different Levels of Situation Favorability

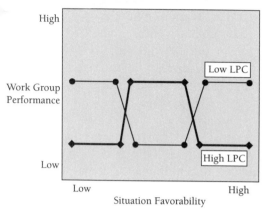

and the evidence is mixed. For example, it has been found that leader LPC scores predict performance in situations of differing favorability in a way that is consistent with the theory (Chemers, 1983; Chemers, Hays, Rhodewalt, & Wysocki, 1985), but other tests have not been supportive (e.g, Schriesheim & Kerr, 1977; Vecchio, 1977). The most comprehensive test of contingency theory to date was a meta-analysis conducted by Schriesheim, Tepper, and Tetrault (1994). This study found that the differences in mean performance levels of High versus Low LPC leaders in different octants generally supported Fiedler's theory. However, in terms of absolute levels of performance, the results were less supportive. For example, in highly favorable situations, it was found, as predicted by Fiedler's theory, that Low LPC leaders out-performed High LPC leaders. However, the performance of High LPC leaders was still above the mean, which is consistent with the idea of "mismatch" proposed by Fiedler. Schriesheim et al. (1994) recommended that "organizations without the ability or interest in situational engineering might consider just trying to make all lead-

ership situations highly favorable (Octant 1)" (p. 571).

Other than the equivocal support, the portion of Fiedler's theory that has been the source of greatest criticism is the LPC Scale. Many researchers have questioned the logic behind the measurement strategy (e.g., McMahon, 1972; Theodory, 1982). In fact, having given the LPC Scale to students for several years, we have noted they are often confused by the instructions. A more serious problem is the lack of support for the construct validity of this scale. Recall from Chapter 2 that construct validity reflects whether a measure is measuring the intended construct or attribute. Strong support for the construct validity of the LPC Scale simply does not exist.

At this point in time, Fiedler's theory no longer represents one of the major theoretical approaches used by leadership researchers. Even so, it is a valuable theory because it has generated a great deal of research on leadership. It has also served as the basis for *Cognitive Resource Theory* (Fiedler & Garcia, 1987), which states that groups draw on the different cognitive resources from the leader, depending on the situation. This is a relatively new approach, and not a great deal of work has been done on it as yet. It does seem to be a promising approach, though, and ultimately may be more useful than Fiedler's original theory.

In addition, Fiedler drew researchers' attention to the importance of considering the role of the situation in understanding the leadership behaviors that are most supportive of effective performance (see Vroom & Jago, 2007). A recent study by Yun, Faraj, and Sims (2005) illustrates the importance of situational factors as determinants of leader effectiveness. These authors examined the effects of leadership in the stressful situation of trauma-resuscitation teams. The authors examined the effects of empowering (delegating responsibility to team members, encouraging initiative) versus directive (expecting team members to follow detailed instructions and guidelines) leadership under situational conditions of high versus low trauma severity and low versus high team experience.

The authors used a scenario approach in which trauma-resuscitation personnel read scenarios describing realistic events varying along leadership style, trauma severity, and team experience. The authors examined how effective participants thought the team would be in the given scenario and how much of a learning opportunity the event would provide. The authors found that empowering leadership was perceived to be most effective when the severity of trauma was low and when the amount of team experience was high. Directive leadership was perceived to be more effective when trauma severity was high or team experience was low. This study showed that the most effective leadership style depended on realistic features of the situation, which is the primary tenet of the contingency approach to leadership.

Path–Goal Theory

Path–Goal Theory represents a very ambitious attempt to blend leadership and employee motivation into one theory (House, 1971; House & Mitchell, 1974). The basic idea behind Path–Goal Theory is that the role of a leader is really to help his or her subordinates become successful. House actually stated this in Expectancy Theory terms (Vroom, 1964); specifically, if a leader is successful, subordinates' level of expectancy (the perception that effort will lead to performance) is raised. Stated differently, the function of leaders is to show subordinates the "path to the goal."

Path–Goal Theory states that a leader must be able to adapt his or her leadership style to the subordinates being supervised and the situation. House proposed that, to be successful, a leader must be capable of utilizing the four different leadership styles: directive leadership, supportive leadership, achievement-oriented leadership, and participative leadership.

Directive leadership focuses on making sure that subordinates know what they are supposed to be doing, and perhaps clarifying task responsibilities. A leader who meets with subordinates once a week to give out work assignments is exhibiting directive leadership. *Supportive leadership* represents behaviors that are aimed at showing concern and caring for subordinates. A leader who makes it a point to ask about a subordinate's sick child is exhibiting supportive leadership.

Achievement-oriented leadership represents behaviors that are aimed at helping employees to improve their performance and ultimately perform better. A leader may exhibit this leadership style in a number of ways, such as providing on-the-job coaching, setting challenging goals, making sure training and development opportunities are available, and seeing to it that subordinates have the resources they need in order to be successful. Finally, *participative leadership* represents behaviors that are aimed at getting the input of subordinates on work-related matters. A leader who regularly seeks the input of subordinates before making important decisions is exhibiting this form of leadership.

Having described the four leadership styles, the next issue is to determine when each of these leadership styles should be used. Path–Goal Theory proposes that leaders should consider two situational factors when they are deciding on the appropriate leadership style (1) characteristics of one's subordinates and (2) characteristics of the work environment. With respect to subordinates, the two key factors that a leader must consider are perceived ability and personality. In considering perceived ability, what would be the most appropriate leadership style for subordinates who perceive themselves as having limited job-related abilities? For these subordinates, a leader would probably need to be quite directive, because these individuals likely would want to know exactly what to do. Participative leadership may not be emphasized because individuals who perceive their abilities to be limited may not have a great deal to contribute. Achievement-oriented and supportive leadership would probably be used to varying degrees, depending on other characteristics of the subordinates.

When subordinates perceive themselves as having a great deal of task-related ability, a leader would probably need to put relatively little emphasis on directing. Instead, the leader may need to strongly emphasize achievement-oriented and participative leadership. Those who perceive their abilities to be high may have a strong desire to further develop those abilities; thus, achievement-oriented behaviors would be called for. These subordinates may also have a great deal to contribute, so it would be in the leader's best interests to solicit input and ideas from these individuals. Supportive leadership would likely be used in varying degrees, depending on other characteristics of subordinates.

The second subordinate characteristic that leaders need to consider when deciding on a leadership style is personality. This is obviously a broad category, but one personality trait that Path–Goal Theory deems important is subordinates' *locus of control*. According to Rotter (1966), locus of control reflects relatively stable individual differences in beliefs regarding control of external reinforcements. A person with an internal locus of control believes that he or she has a great deal of control over reinforcements. Such a person, for example, would believe that working hard would be a good thing to do because it would lead to positive outcomes. Persons with an external locus of control believe that reinforcements in their lives are due to external forces such as luck, fate, or, perhaps, powerful people.

As a leader, managing an individual with an internal locus of control would probably require an emphasis on achievement-oriented and participative leadership, and comparatively less on directive and supportive leadership. An employee with an internal locus of control believes that he or she has control over reinforcements, and hence is also likely to believe that if performance is increased, then positive rewards will result. Facilitating this process requires the use of achievement-oriented leadership. Also, because those with an internal locus of control (*internals*) may also perform well (Spector, 1982), it is often in the best interest of the leader to seek input from such individuals through participative leadership.

Those with an external locus of control will likely need greater direction from the leader; thus, directive leadership behaviors will be needed. Also, it is very likely that those with an external locus of control (*externals*) will need more support from the leader, compared to internals. Having an external locus of control has been shown to be associated with negative mental health outcomes (e.g., Spector, 1982; Storms & Spector, 1987); thus, externals may often be more anxious, frustrated, and dissatisfied than internals.

In addition to the characteristics of subordinates, Path–Goal Theory proposes that leaders must focus on characteristics of the work environment when they are determining the most appropriate leadership style.

One aspect of the situation that is important is the prevailing norms regarding authority and leadership within an organization. This is really an aspect of an organization's culture and reflects, for example, prevailing views on issues such as employee involvement and participation, the extent to which employees should take the initiative to solve work-related problems, and whether managers should get involved in subordinates' personal lives. In an organization that strongly values employee involvement and participation, a participative leadership style would fit much better than in a very autocratic organization. Similarly, in an organization that places a great deal of emphasis on employee self-reliance, a very directive style of leadership would probably not fit very well. On the other hand, achievement oriented and participative styles would be very compatible.

Task structure is a second characteristic of the work environment that is important in determining the most appropriate leadership style. If a leader is directing a group that is working on a highly structured task (e.g., producing a very simple product), there would probably be little need for the leader to adopt a directive or a participative leadership style because members of the group know exactly what they're supposed to do. In contrast, when a task is highly unstructured (e.g., developing a new product), a leader may at times have to be directive, but may also need to be participative in order to help the group figure out how best to approach the task.

The final environmental characteristic proposed by Path–Goal Theory is the nature of the work group one is leading. For example, in some groups, the task of providing direction is done by experienced members of the group rather than the leader. If this is the case, the leader does not need to be directive but could emphasize

other leadership styles. Essentially, this means that the leader's behavior needs to "add value" to the behaviors being performed by members of the group.

House reformulated his theory in 1996 to provide a comprehensive theory that describes 10 different categories of leadership behaviors and identifies which behaviors are appropriate in specific circumstances (House, 1996). The 10 categories cover a large range of behaviors including behaviors designed to clarify the work roles of subordinates to behaviors designed to help subordinates achieve excellence in performance. House derives 22 propositions from his theory that provide guidelines for when a specific type of leader behavior is likely to have positive, negative, or no consequences. The essence of House's theory remains the same: Leaders need to possess a broad repertoire of behaviors that they can strategically call on depending on key aspects of the situation and characteristics of subordinates.

Given the nature of Path–Goal Theory, it is difficult to test in its entirety. However, tests of various parts of the theory have been relatively successful (e.g., Wofford & Liska, 1993). Britt, Davison, Bliese, and Castro (2004) also reviewed a number of studies relevant to the effects of military leadership that supported aspects of House's overall theory. The practical implications of Path–Goal Theory come primarily in the area of management training and development. Specifically, managers need to be trained to recognize meaningful differences among their subordinates, as well as important aspects of the work environment, and they have to learn to use the different leadership styles proposed by Path–Goal Theory. The theory may have implications for selection and placement. For example, if a leader is very good at developing subordinates (i.e., providing achievement-oriented leadership), in organization may wish to place this person in charge of a group consisting of a number of young, high-potential employees. Conversely, if a leader is very adept at participative leadership, an organization may want to place this person in charge of a group that must make many consensus decisions.

Vroom–Yetton–Jago Model

The Vroom–Yetton–Jago model (Vroom & Jago, 1988, 2007; Vroom & Yetton, 1973) is a contingency theory of leadership that focuses on one aspect of leadership: decision making. This model is also more prescriptive than the other theories discussed; that is, this theory is focused on providing leaders with a set of guidelines for which decision-making style to adopt. According to this model, leaders will be more effective to the extent that their decision-making style is compatible with the situations they face.

The first component of the Vroom–Yetton–Jago model to consider is the various styles that a leader could use in making a decision. As can be seen in Table 10.2, in the first decision-making style (AI), the leader makes a decision alone after considering relevant information. The next decision-making style (AII) also involves the leader

making the decision alone, but, in this case, information is obtained from subordinates before making the decision. Decision-making style CI involves sharing the problem with each subordinate individually, and then making the decision alone. Decision-making style CII involves sharing the problem with subordinates as a group and then making the decision alone. The final decision-making style (GII) involves making the decision by group consensus.

According to the model, in order to determine which decision-making style is most appropriate leaders must analyze a situation for the presence or absence of the following attributes: (1) the need for a quality decision; (2) whether the leader has sufficient information to make the decision alone; (3) the degree to which the problem is structured; (4) whether subordinates' acceptance is needed for implementation; (5) whether subordinates will accept the leader's decision; (6) the degree to which subordinates share the organization's goals; (7) whether there will likely be conflict among subordinates as to the most preferred decision; and (8) whether subordinates have enough relevant information to make a decision on their own.

According to the model, these eight situational attributes will determine a "feasibility set" of decision-making strategies. The feasibility set simply represents those decision-making strategies that may be appropriate for a given situation. Figure 10.5 shows how this process works. Notice that these situational questions are asked in a sequential fashion that resembles a flowchart. Specifically, the leader's response to each question narrows the feasibility set until eventually one decision-making style is recommended. For a leader to use this theory, he or she would simply answer each of the questions about the decision to be made,

TABLE 10.2
Decision-Making Styles Proposed by the Vroom–YettonJago Model of Leadership

AI—Leader makes the decision alone after considering the relevant information.

AII—Leader makes the decision alone after obtaining relevant information directly from subordinates.

CI—Leader shares the problem with each subordinate individually and then makes the decision alone.

CII—Leader shares the problem with subordinates as a group and then makes the decision alone.

GII—The decision is made by group consensus.

FIGURE 10.5

The Recommended Decision-Making Sequence Proposed by the Vroom-Yetton-Jago Model

A. Does the problem possess a quality requirement?
B. Do you have sufficient information to make a high-quality decision?
C. Is the problem structured?
D. Is acceptance of decision by subordinates important for effective implementation?
E. If you were to make the decision by yourself, is it reasonably certain that it would be accepted by your subordinates?
F. Do subordinates share the organizational goals to be attained in solving this problem?
G. Is conflict among subordinates over preferred solutions likely?

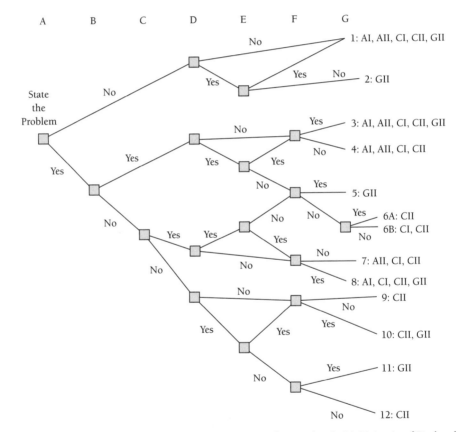

Source: V. H. Vroom and P. W. Yetton. (1973). *Leadership and decision-making* Pittsburgh, PA: University of Pittsburgh Press. Copyright © 1973 by University of Pittsburgh Press. Reprinted with permission.

and, ultimately, a preferred method of decision making would emerge.

Research on the Vroom–Yetton–Jago model has shown that managers are more effective when they adopt decision-making styles that are consistent with the model's prescriptions (Margerison & Glube, 1979; Paul & Ebadi, 1989; Vroom & Jago, 1988,

2007). However, a major methodological limitation of most tests of the model is that they have relied primarily on retrospective descriptions of decisions made by managers. This raises the question of whether managers revise their recollections of decisions in a way that is consistent with the model. More recent research that has not relied on retrospective reports (Field & House, 1990; Parker, 1999) has provided more limited support for the theory.

From a practical point of view, the Vroom–Yetton–Jago model is one of the more useful leadership theories that has been developed. Compared to other theories, this model provides leaders with some specific guidelines for making decisions, rather than merely describing leadership processes. The biggest problem with the Vroom–Yetton–Jago model is that it tends to oversimplify the conditions under which leaders make decisions. For example, in many cases, it is difficult for a leader to provide "Yes–No" answers to the questions posed earlier. Further revisions of this model will be needed to overcome these weaknesses.

Leader–Member Exchange (LMX) Model

Anyone who has been part of a work group, or who has been a leader of one, knows that everyone is not always treated the same. To the contrary, leaders typically develop a unique relationship with each subordinate, and some of these relationships are more positive than others. Based on this idea, Dansereau, Graen, and Haga (1975) developed the *Vertical Dyad Linkage Model* of leadership. The term *Vertical Dyad* was originally used to describe this theory because of its emphasis on the unique relationship between leaders and subordinates. Over time, however, the name of the theory eventually became *Leader–Member Exchange* because this relationship is really one that reflects social exchange between the leader and the subordinate.

According to Dansereau et al. (1975), within work groups there are typically two sets of employees: the *in-group* and the *out-group*. The in-group consists of employees who are trusted confidants of the leader. These are typically individuals who perform well, have a desire to assume greater levels of responsibility, and simply get along well with the leader. Members of the out-group consist of the group of subordinates who have more formal relationships with the leader. Members of the in-group are typically privy to more information from the leader than are members of the out-group, and they are also given more discretion over how to do their jobs. Members of the out-group are typically individuals who may not perform as well, may not desire a great deal of responsibility, or simply may not get along as well with the leader as do members of the in-group.

Gradually, less emphasis has been placed on the in-group/out-group distinction, and more emphasis is on how leader–subordinate relationships develop over time (Graen, 1976). According to Graen (1976), when a subordinate is first assigned to a leader, the leader has relatively limited information as to this person's capabilities. Thus, over time, the leader tests the subordinate by giving him or her assignments of increasing responsibility. To the extent that the subordinate is successful, a positive exchange relationship develops. From the subordinate's point of view, there may be some degree of negotiation as to specific role responsibilities. Other factors that influence the development of this exchange relationship are perceived similarity between subordinates and leaders, as well as the level of interpersonal attraction (Liden, Wayne, & Stilwell, 1993). Exchange relationships are likely to be most positive when subordinates are competent, when they and the leader perceive some degree of mutual similarity, and when subordinates and leaders like each other.

What are the consequences of the exchange relationship that develops between a subordinate and a leader? Gerstner and Day (1997) conducted a meta-analysis of 79 studies that examined correlates of Leader–Member Exchange. They found that LMX was positively related to job performance, job satisfaction, and organizational commitment, and negatively related to outcomes such as turnover and role stressors. One of the most perplexing findings in their meta-analysis was the relatively small correlation between leaders' and subordinates' reports on the quality of the exchange relationship (corrected r = .37). Thus, although leaders and subordinates tend to agree on the quality of the relationship that exists between them, this level of agreement is not great. At present, it is unclear why agreement on the quality of the exchange relationship is not higher, what factors influence agreement, or the impact of disagreements over the quality of the exchange relationship.

LMX Theory is useful for both theoretical and practical reasons. In terms of theory, it presents leadership in a more realistic light, compared to many previous theories. Subordinates are not simply passive recipients of leaders' influence. In terms of practical implications, LMX Theory suggests that it is desirable for leaders to develop positive exchange relationships with their subordinates. This may not be possible 100% of the time, but organizations may be able to facilitate the development of high-quality exchange relationships by training managers in such skills as communicating with subordinates, providing feedback, and engaging in coaching activities.

LMX Theory faces a number of challenges. One of the most important of these is continued refinement of what actually constitutes the *exchange relationship* itself. To measure the exchange relationship, Liden and Maslyn (1998) developed a scale that consisted of four distinct dimensions: (1) affect, which represents the levels of mutual interpersonal attraction between a leader and subordinate; (2) loyalty, which represents the amount of public support provided by each member of the leader–subordinate dyad; (3) contribution, which represents what each member of the leader–subordinate dyad contributes positively to the goals of the organization; and (4) professional respect, which represents the degree to which each member of the leader–subordinate dyad has built a reputation, within and/or outside of work, because he or she excels in his or her line of work. Previous LMX scales have treated it as a one-dimensional construct.

Another challenge for LMX Theory is expansion of its scope. For most people, the unique relationship they develop with their immediate supervisor is one of the most important dimensions of their work experience. As such, it may influence many work outcomes. For example, Kokotovich, Jex, and Adams (2000) found that a high-quality LMX moderated the relationship between role ambiguity and job satisfaction. Employees reporting a high-quality LMX actually reacted positively to role ambiguity. One study also found that LMX was related to the organizational citizenship behavior of altruism (Wayne Andy & Green Hown, 1993). Researchers should further investigate these types of relationships. Recent studies have also suggested that LMX may interact with the cognitive ability of employees to also predict creativity (Tierney, Farmer, & Graen, 1999). More recent studies have also argued that other forms of leadership (e.g., transactional, transformational) influence employee performance through LMX. We now turn to a discussion of these areas of leadership.

Charismatic, Transformational, and Transactional Leadership

These last three leadership theories are the newest to be developed. Although less research has been conducted on these approaches overall, the theories represent where the field of leadership is heading and have become quite influential. Because these approaches to leadership are highly related, they will be discussed together.

The idea of *Charismatic* and *Transformational leadership* is that there are certain leader behaviors and traits that not only influence subordinates but may also inspire them to perform well beyond their capabilities. Another defining characteristic of Charismatic and Transformational leadership is that both have the potential to induce meaningful change in organizations. The terms charismatic and transformational leadership are often used interchangeably, and when a distinction is made between the two forms of leadership, it is noted that charismatic leadership is but one component of transformational leadership.

The term that is sometimes used to describe the opposite of Charismatic and Transformational leadership is *Transactional leadership*. A transactional leader is one who makes sure that subordinates get the job done and follow the rules of the organization. Transactional leaders typically use behavioral principles of reward and punishment to make clear the behaviors that are expected of the employee (Judge & Piccolo, 2004). Transactional leaders, however, do not inspire subordinates or facilitate meaningful change in organizations.

It is important to note, however, that leaders can be capable of engaging in both transactional and transformational leadership depending on the situation. In fact, Bass (1998) has argued forcefully that transactional leadership often forms the base for transformational leadership. The logic here is that a leader must be able to clearly apply rules and contingencies for employees to follow before embarking on the more motivating behaviors involved in transformational leadership.

Judge and Piccolo (2004) have argued that transformational leadership is composed of four primary dimensions. The first dimension is *idealized influence (charisma)*. This component refers to leaders setting the example of exemplary performance and dedication to the organization through conviction and emotional investment. Those who are charismatic tend to have a number of common traits: a captivating tone of voice, direct eye contact with the listener, animated facial expressions, and a powerful, confident, and dynamic communication style. This type of communication style obviously helps a leader to communicate his or her vision and to generate enthusiasm for it. It also helps more generally by increasing the leader's appeal to his or her followers. Charismatic leaders have great "presence" and make a tremendous impression on those around them.

The second dimension is *inspirational motivation*. One task that is often cited in this regard is providing a vision. According to House (1977), a vision is a very generalized ideal state that typically represents shared values and often has moral overtones. An example of a vision for a university might be to enlighten the students; a vision for a military organization might be to uphold freedom around the world; a vision for an auto manufacturer might be to enhance the mobility of society. A vision

COMMENT 10.2

THE VISION THING

ONE OF THE key components of Charismatic and Transformational leadership is vision. A *vision* is essentially an ideal or desirable end state that often has moral overtones. A leader with vision "stands for something" and has a sense of purpose that is communicated to his or her followers.

Vision has become particularly important in the political arena. When candidates run for national office, the vision that they are able to communicate to voters can literally make or break their chances of being elected. In 1980, Ronald Reagan defeated Jimmy Carter for the U.S. Presidency largely based on the vision that he communicated to the American public. Reagan's vision, based heavily on conservative principles, struck a chord with voters who wanted lower taxes and a stronger national defense. Whether or not one agreed with Rea-

gan's "vision," there is no denying that he communicated it well and was quite successful at convincing the public to embrace it.

Just as having a vision propelled Ronald Reagan to victory, a lack of vision may have been one of the major reasons George H. Bush lost the presidency to Bill Clinton in 1992. Although Bush showed excellent crisis-management skills during the Gulf War, he was unable to articulate a coherent vision in the way Reagan did many years earlier. For many voters, it was difficult to tell exactly what Bush stood for. Clinton, in contrast, was very successful at communicating a vision based on economic opportunity, and in many instances seemed to connect with voters much better on a personal level. The end result was that Clinton won a convincing victory over Bush and third-party candidate Ross Perot.

applies to all members of the organization and can thus serve as a general "rallying point" for everyone. Many examples of leaders, particularly in the political arena, can be distinguished on the presence or absence of vision (see Comment 10.2).

The third dimension is *intellectual stimulation*. This dimension refers to the transformational leader's ability to challenge subordinates and encourage them to be creative and take appropriate risks. Leaders may encourage subordinates to think outside the box in order to come up with innovative solutions that will instill a competitive advantage to the organization.

The final dimension is *individualized consideration*. This dimension refers to the leader's ability to attend to the needs of employees and make the employees feel understood and appreciated. In many ways

this dimension incorporates aspects of LMX theory into what it means to be a transformational leader. Transformational leaders tend to have a charismatic communication style.

Research over the years has shown that transformational leadership is related to positive outcomes such as employees' performance, satisfaction, and positive perceptions of leaders (Bass & Avolio, 1993; Shamir, House, & Arthur, 1993). Judge and Piccolo (2004) recently conducted a meta-analysis of over 87 studies examining the correlations between transformational and transactional leadership and various performance outcomes (e.g., follower job satisfaction, follower satisfaction with the leader, leader job performance). The authors found an overall validity coefficient of .44 for transformational leadership and .39 for transactional (contingent reward) leadership. One interesting finding was the rather strong positive correlation (.80) between transformational and transactional leadership in the meta-analysis. This finding strongly suggests that transformational and transactional leadership are not opposing ends of a single dimension of leadership. Bass and his colleagues have also found that both transformational and transactional leadership predict the performance of light infantry platoons in combat-simulation exercises (Bass, Avolio, Jung, & Berson, 2003).

One emerging trend in research on transformational leadership is examining *how* such leadership predicts performance outcomes. Two studies investigating similar determinants were recently conducted by Piccolo and Colquitt (2006) and Purvanova, Bono, and Dzieweczynski (2006). Both papers addressed the idea that transformational leaders cause their employees to be engaged in more meaningful work (e.g., report higher job characteristics such as variety, significance, and autonomy), which then leads their employees to perform better. In support of this hypothesis, Piccolo and Colquitt (2006) found that such job characteristics mediated the relationship between transformational leadership and both task performance and organizational citizenship behavior. Purvanova et al. (2006) also found that perceived job characteristics mediated the relationship between transformational leadership and a different measure of citizenship performance, even when controlling for objective job characteristics. Taken together, the results indicate that transformational leaders produce employees who perform better because the employees take greater ownership of their work and feel their work is more significant.

Other researchers have argued that transformational leadership is related to follower performance through leader-member ex-change (LMX; Wang et al., 2005). The logic here is that transformational leaders end up forming a stronger interpersonal bond with their followers, which leads their followers to perform better. Wang et al. examined leader-follower dyads in organizations across the People's Republic of China. They found that the relationship between transformational leadership and the employee's task performance was completely mediated by a measure of LMX focusing on the quality of the relationship between the employee and supervisor.

Authentic Leadership

One of the most recent approaches to leadership coming from the field of organizational psychology is authentic leadership. Avolio, Gardner, Walumbwa, Luthans, and May (2004) define *authentic leaders* as "those individuals who are deeply aware of how they think and behave and are perceived by others as being aware of their own and others' values/moral perspective, knowledge, and strengths; aware of the context in which they operate; and who are confident, hopeful, optimistic, resilient, and high on moral character" (pp. 802–804). A key aspect of authentic leadership is leaders being "who they are" and harnessing the energy of followers by causing them to connect with the goals of the leader and group.

Avolio et al. (2004) developed a model of authentic leadership illustrating how authentic behavior on the part of the leader results in followers being more likely to personally identify with the leader and collective (i.e., organization), which then leads the followers to experience hope, trust, and positive emotions. These positive emotional states then create the favorable work attitudes of commitment, job satisfaction, meaningfulness, and engagement, which result in the positive

COMMENT 10.3

LEADERSHIP AND CULTURE

CULTURAL DIFFERENCES IN leadership have not been heavily researched by organizational psychologists. One of the few extensive treatises of cultures and leadership was recently completed by House and his colleagues (2003), who examined 17,000 leaders from 951 organizations in 62 societies across the globe. The authors were interested in exploring differences between cultures in how they viewed leadership and the practices that leaders used in the different cultures. The authors also explored value differences across the 62 societies. Six global leader behaviors were identified: charismatic/value-based leadership (leader ability to inspire and motivate others), team-oriented leadership (emphasis on team-building and being diplomatic), participative leadership (involving others in leadership decisions), human-oriented leadership (compassion and consideration toward subordinates), autonomous leadership (individualistic decision making and independence/separation from subordinates), and self-protective leadership (focus behaviors on protecting the individual leader and group through behaviors designed to enhance status and save face).

House and his colleagues found that all cultures believed in the importance of leaders possessing a team orientation and effectively communicating a vision to subordinates. The authors found the most variation in the global leader behaviors of autonomous leadership and self-protective leadership. Autonomous leadership was seen as slightly effective in countries of Eastern Europe (with the exception of Hungary) but was seen as ineffective in most countries of Latin America, the Middle East, and Anglo countries. Self-protective leadership was seen as being slightly effective for the following countries: Albania, Taiwan, Egypt, Iran, and Kuwait. However, this type of leadership was seen as ineffective in other countries, especially in Northern European countries such as France. The book describes the similarities and differences across cultures in perceptions of effective and ineffective leader behaviors, and attempts to link these perceptions to differences in the values of the cultures involved. The research discussed in this book will likely influence future investigations of how leadership differs across cultures.

Source: House, R.J., Hanges, P.J., Javidan, M., Dorfman, P.W., & Gupta, V. (Eds.) (2003). Culture, leadership, and organizations: The GLOBE study of 62 societies. Thousand Oaks, CA: Sage Publications.

outcomes of performance, extra effort, and less withdrawal. The theory of authentic leadership is in its early stages of development, but will likely get much more attention given recent highly publicized incidences of leader corruption and lack of character.

Before ending our discussion of leadership, it is worth noting that, until recently, cross-cultural research on leadership was lacking. However, Comment 10.3 discusses an ambitious project examining conceptions of leadership across 62 different countries. Future research will be addressing the implications of this project for multiple conceptualizations of leadership.

POWER AND INFLUENCE IN ORGANIZATIONS

Regardless of whether one is a chief executive officer of a Fortune 500 company or the supervisor of a janitorial crew, a big part of one's job is influencing others to behave in ways that are consistent with the goals of the organization. Furthermore, the extent to which a leader can influence others depends, to a large extent, on his or her social power over others. In addition, employees other than leaders can use power and influence in either adaptive or dysfunctional ways within organizations. In this section, power will be discussed first, followed by influence tactics.

Defining Power

The term *power* is often used in a negative fashion, even though it is not inherently bad or evil. Power simply represents a person's potential or capacity to influence others (French & Raven, 1959). When one attempts to influence another person's behavior, the outcome of that influence attempt generally takes one of three forms (Kelman, 1958): compliance, identification, or private acceptance. *Compliance* refers to an influence attempt where the target of influence does what is requested, but does not necessarily do it willingly. When a child is told by a parent that he or she cannot have a cookie, the child typically complies with this directive but, if given the choice, would certainly eat the cookie (at least that's the way it works in our houses!). An example of compliance in the workplace might be an employee wearing a piece of safety equipment, even though he or she doesn't want to and does not believe it will necessarily be effective.

The second potential outcome of influence is referred to as *identification*. In this case, the employee does what the leader wants, primarily because he or she likes the leader. As with compliance, when behavior is changed on the basis of identification, there is a change in behavior but not in attitudes; that is, the employee still does not really want to do what the leader wants

done. A work-related example of identification would be employees staying late to help their well-liked leader meet an impending deadline, even though they do not inherently believe in the value of the project.

The third result of influence is referred to as *private acceptance* or *internalization*. In this case, the employee does what the leader wants because he or she believes that it is the right thing to do. Compared to compliance and identification, private acceptance is, in the long run, much more efficient for leaders. Therefore, if subordinates believe that what the leader wants them to do is correct, the leader will need to spend much less time either monitoring to ensure compliance, or making sure that subordinates still like him or her. Keep in mind, however, that it is not always necessary for a leader to obtain private acceptance from subordinates. For example, employees often must comply with safety guidelines, even if they don't agree with them.

The fourth and final outcome of influence that might occur is *resistance*. In this case, the employee simply does not do what the leader asks. Resistance may take the form of an overt refusal, but, more typically, an employee will simply be evasive when the leader inquires about whether the subordinate has carried out the request. This can be a very frustrating situation for a leader, and it is obviously the least desirable outcome from a leader's perspective.

Bases of Power

Leaders are not automatically endowed with an unlimited amount of power over subordinates. Leaders also differ in terms of the sources or bases upon which power over subordinates can be exerted. The most widely cited model of power was proposed by French and Raven (1959) over 40 years ago. According to this model, power rests upon six bases. Some readers may recognize the fact that most treatments of French and Raven's model describe only the first five bases, but the original model did contain six. The first base of power is labeled *coercive power*. The basis of this influence tactic is that one person can punish another. Thus, a subordinate may do what a leader requests because the leader has the power to fire the subordinate. Although the threat of punishment may give a leader considerable power over subordinates, coercive power generally is not a very efficient base of power. If subordinates do what the leader wants only because they are threatened with punishment, the leader's power is diminished considerably if he or she is not around to monitor the ongoing behavior and administer punishment if necessary.

The second power base described by French and Raven is labeled *reward power*. This is essentially the opposite of coercive power. That is, subordinates do what the leader wants because the leader has the ability to reward them in some way. For example, a subordinate may comply with a leader's request that he or she work overtime because the leader has the power to grant this employee a larger pay increase when raises are given out. Unfortunately, as with coercive power, reward power is not a highly efficient power base. It requires the leader to monitor subordinates' behaviors and reward them at the appropriate time. An individual who possesses either coercive or reward power is likely to also possess the corresponding type of power. Leaders differ, however, in the extent to which they ultimately choose to use reward versus coercive power (see Chapter 9).

The third power base is labeled *legitimate power*. This power emanates from the position that one holds in an organization.

In most organizational settings, the fact that one employee is another employee's supervisor means that the supervisor has a legitimate right to make requests of the other person. Note that this legitimate right is independent of the person holding the position. Compared to coercive and reward power, legitimate power is more efficient. It does not require surveillance on the leader's part because, in most organizations, the level of legitimate authority that goes with any given position is typically known. In fact, in many cases, it is even documented in job descriptions and other formal documents. A limitation of legitimate power, however, is that if it is used exclusively, it may elicit only compliance from subordinates and, in the long run, may engender a great deal of resentment among them. People generally do not like to be told to do something simply because "I'm your supervisor."

The fourth power base is *expert power*. This is power based on the fact that an individual is perceived as an expert on something that is important to the target of influence. If the leader of a group of design engineers is also an expert design engineer, this will make subordinates more likely to do what he or she says. One thing that is important to note about expert power is that it is the perception that is important. For this to be a viable power base, subordinates must perceive that the leader is an expert. Regardless of the level of one's true expertise, if this is not perceived, then no expert power exists. It is also possible for nonleaders within a given workgroup or organization to possess expert power. For example, if a certain employee is known as the individual possessing a large amount of knowledge regarding a particular topic or procedure, that employee will have expert power even if he or she is not technically a leader.

The fifth base of power in French and Raven's model is *referent power*. This is power based on subordinates' liking of a leader. Here, as in the identification mode of influence described earlier, subordinates do what the leader wants because they like him or her. Although this form of power does not require surveillance, it is also somewhat more tenuous than expert power because interpersonal attraction is considerably more volatile than expertise. If subordinates no longer have positive feelings toward the leader, then a great deal of his or her power over subordinates is lost.

The sixth and final base of power is referred to as *informational power*. As stated earlier, this is typically not presented as one of the bases of power in the French and Raven model, but it was included in the initial model (Raven, 1993). A leader has informational power to the extent that he or she has high-quality information that will be convincing to subordinates. For example, a person trying to convince someone else to wear a seatbelt would have a great deal of informational power if valid data could be cited showing that the odds of being fatally injured are much lower if a seatbelt is being worn.

After the development of the initial model of power bases, French and Raven made a number of further refinements to the model (Raven, 1993). For example, they differentiated between personal and impersonal forms of reward and coercive power. Rewards and punishments can come in the form of personal approval or disapproval. Conversely, they can also come in more impersonal forms such as a raise or a formal reprimand. French and Raven also refined the concept of legitimate power considerably. They proposed, for example, that legitimate power was based not just on one's formal organizational position, but also on the principle of reciprocity ("I did this for you, so you should feel obligated to do this for me"), equity ("I have worked hard and suffered, so I have the right to ask you to do something to make up for it"), and responsibility or dependence ("I cannot help myself, so you are responsible for helping me").

Expert and referent power were further distinguished in terms of being positive and negative. As originally conceived, both expert and referent power were positive. French and Raven, however, later pointed out that both could be negative as well. Negative expert power represents situations in which a person is seen as having superior knowledge but, at the same time, is seen as using the superior knowledge only in order to further his or her own interests. Negative referent power occurs when a person is seen as someone who is disliked rather than liked. If this person were a leader, subordinates may be inclined to do the opposite of what this individual wants them to do.

Informational power was distinguished in terms of being direct or indirect. When informational power is direct, this means that the leader presents logical arguments to subordinates directly. When it is indirect, the information does not come from the leader directly, but may instead come from another subordinate or another leader. This distinction is important because social psychological research on influence (e.g., Petty & Cacioppo, 1981) has shown that, in some circumstances, information that is conveyed indirectly is given greater weight by the target of influence than information communicated directly.

No competing models of power bases have been proposed, but there has been at least one effort to add to the power bases originally proposed by French and Raven. Finkelstein (1992) examined bases of power within top management teams and, although some of the power bases he proposed corresponded to those in French and Raven's model, there were two that were unique. *Ownership power* represents the extent to which the member of a top management team has an ownership stake in the organization, through either stock ownership or family relations. Within a top management team, an executive who is a significant shareholder or is related to the organizational founder often wields tremendous power.

The other unique power base proposed by Finkelstein (1992) was *prestige power*. This represents the extent to which the member of a top management group has acquired prestige and status outside of the organization. Finkelstein measured this by the number of corporate boards a manager serves on, the level of prestige of those organizations, the number of nonprofit boards one serves on, and, finally, the prestige of the university where the executive received his or her education. Generally speaking, an executive has greater prestige power if he or she serves on the corporate boards of a number of successful organizations, also serves on the boards of nonprofit organizations, and graduated from a prestigious university (e.g., Ivy League).

Influence Tactics

To this point, we have discussed the potential of leaders to influence their subordinates. However, to truly understand the dynamics of power and influence, we must go beyond the potential to influence and examine the specific tactics that leaders use to influence subordinates. According to Yukl and Tracey (1992), nine distinct tactics can be used to influence. These are presented in Table 10.3. As can be seen *rational persuasion* simply involves providing employees a logical explanation of why a given request is

being made. For example, a foreman in a factory may advise a subordinate to wear protective earphones because chronic exposure to loud noises can lead to gradual hearing loss.

When *inspirational appeals* are used, the leader or person doing the influencing attempts to appeal to the target's values or ideals, and to persuade that person that he or she will be able to get something done. As an example of inspirational appeals, a military commander might attempt to encourage his or her troops to continue fighting after they are fatigued. The commander could explain the strategic need to carry on, or could appeal to the troops' sense of patriotism or military duty. As indicated earlier in the chapter, this type of appeal is used frequently by transformational leaders.

In using *consultation*, the leader influences subordinates by seeking their assistance on an activity for which their participation is crucial. This tactic is often used when changes are introduced in organizations. For example, if an organization wants to redesign jobs and must persuade employees to accept these changes, a good way to start is to seek the employees' assistance in the job redesign effort.

By using *ingratiation*, a leader attempts to influence subordinates by putting them in a good mood before making a request. This can be done in a variety of ways such as complimenting the subordinate, agreeing with his or her views or opinions, or doing favors for this person. A supervisor who is getting ready to ask a group of subordinates to work on a weekend may bring the group doughnuts before making the request. Ingratiation must be used carefully, however; it may make people less likely to comply with a request if it is seen as insincere. Some readers may be familiar with the situation comedy "The Office," where the leader often engages

TABLE 10.3
A Summary of Nine Common Influence Tactics Used by Leaders

Tactic	Definition
1. Rational persuasion	The person uses logical arguments and factual evidence to persuade you that a proposal or request is viable and likely to result in the attainment of task objectives.
2. Inspirational appeal	The person makes a request or proposal that arouses your enthusiasm by appealing to your values, ideals, or aspirations or by increasing your confidence that you can do it.
3. Consultation	The person seeks your participation in planning a strategy, activity, or change for which your support and assistance are desired, or the person is willing to modify the proposal to deal with your concerns and suggestions.
4. Ingratiation	The person seeks to get you in a good mood or to think favorably of him or her before asking you to do something.
5. Exchange	The person offers you an exchange of favors, indicates a willingness to reciprocate at a later time, or promises you a share of the benefits if you help to accomplish a task.
6. Personal appeal	The person appeals to your feelings of loyalty and friendship toward him or her before asking you to do something.
7. Coalition	The person seeks the aid of others to persuade you to do something or uses the support of others as a reason for you to agree also.
8. Legitimating	The person seeks to establish the legitimacy of a request by claiming the authority or right to make it or by verifying that it is consistent with organizational policies, rules, practices, or traditions.
9. Pressure	The person uses demands, threats, or persistent reminders to influence you to do what he or she wants.

Source: G. Yukl and J. B. Tracey. (1992). Consequences of influence tactics used with subordinates, peers, and the boss. *Journal of Applied Psychology, 77,* 525–535. Copyright © 1992 by the American Psychological Association. Reprinted with permission.

in blatantly obvious forms of ingratiation that have little effect on employee behavior.

When *exchange* is used as an influence tactic, the leader offers subordinates something in return for complying with a request, or perhaps offers them a share of the benefits that will accrue when a task is accomplished (see Cialdini, 2001). In some companies, forms of exchange are actually mandated by organizational policies. For example, when hourly employees work more than 40 hours per week, they receive overtime pay for doing so. However, this exchange may be strictly between the leader and his or her subordinates. For example, if the manager of a fast-

food restaurant wants employees to come for an early morning crew meeting, one way of getting employees to be there is to provide another incentive, such as an extra 30-minute break.

When a *personal appeal* is used as an influence attempt, the leader appeals to a subordinate's sense of personal loyalty and friendship before making a request. This influence tactic can only be used if two people do in fact share some degree of loyalty and friendship. Prior to making a request of a subordinate, the leader may first state: "We've been friends for a long time, and have been through some tough times together, so I know you're someone I can really count on." After hearing that, most people would find it difficult to turn down the subsequent request.

Forming a *coalition* to influence involves seeking the aid of others to directly persuade a subordinate to comply with a request, or using others as examples of why a request should be honored. A good example: Get a subordinate to comply with a requirement to wear safety equipment by having other subordinates, who are wearing the equipment, persuade this individual that safety equipment is needed. This principle of influence is called *social proof* by Cialdini (2001), and capitalizes on the idea that individuals often determine what is correct or right by noting what other people are doing.

When *legitimating* is used, the leader seeks to establish the legitimacy of his or her request by falling back on his or her authority to make the request or, in some cases, citing organizational policies or rules. In the military, the leader frequently points out that he or she outranks the subordinate; in military organizations, this form of influence tends to work very well because of the emphasis on rank. In other types of organizations, use of legitimating may be less successful and, if used frequently, may ultimately engender animosity among one's subordinates.

The final influence tactic listed in Table 10.3 is *pressure*. This involves the use of demands, threats, or persistent monitoring to make subordinates comply with a request. Suppose a supervisor wants to make sure a subordinate is on time every morning. One way to do this would be to check the person's desk to see if he or she is present by the required time. Although pressure may, at times, get leaders the behavior they desire, this almost always comes in the form of compliance on the part of the employee.

Thus, using pressure typically requires a good deal of energy on the part of the leader because subordinates' behaviors must be frequently monitored.

Although research on influence tactics is still relatively new, there are some reasonably consistent research findings. If a leader wishes to obtain behavior change in the form of *private acceptance*, the most effective way to do so is through inspirational appeals and consultation (Falbe & Yukl, 1992; Yukl, Kim, & Falbe, 1996; Yukl & Tracey, 1992). Tactics such as coalition formation, legitimating, and pressure are unlikely to lead to private acceptance, and, in fact, may even lead to resistance. The reason simply may be that people are generally more enthusiastic about doing things when they feel that they have some freedom of choice in the matter. Brehm (1966) has noted how individuals experience resistance when they experience a threat to their personal freedom, which may lead them to do the opposite of what is requested.

Another consistent finding from this literature is that influence tactics may influence others' behaviors in an additive fashion. For example, Falbe and Yukl (1992) found that the use of combinations of some tactics was more effective at facilitating behavior change than using the tactics alone. For example, an inspirational appeal combined with consultation was more effective than using either of these tactics alone or using single "hard" tactics such as pressure or legitimating. This suggests that, in some cases, the influence process takes time, and the leader must be prepared to use multiple tactics to influence subordinates' behaviors.

The research on influence tactics is still relatively new, but it has produced some very important practical insights for leaders. Perhaps the most important of these is that if leaders want their subordinates to do things willingly, in the long run they are much better off asking them do it rather than simply relying on their position or using more coercive techniques. Although asking may take longer, it will produce more long-lasting behavioral change than will the use of more coercive tactics.

Politics in Organizations

The term *organizational politics* often conjures up images of very negative forms of behavior; therefore, most people want to avoid the politics of an organization. Nevertheless, political behavior is a fact of life and, in many cases, represents an important form of influence within organizations. Organizational politics has been defined as influence behavior, within organizations, that falls outside of the recognized legitimate power system (Yoffie & Bergenstein, 1985). Political behavior is often aimed at benefiting an individual or group at the expense of the organization as a whole and at acquiring more power.

According to Miles (1980), one of the major factors motivating political behavior is uncertainty. For example, when employees are uncertain about the goals of the organization, political behavior often results. Another factor that strongly contributes to political behavior is scarcity of resources. Although technically everyone in the same organization is "on the same team," obtaining scarce resources is a highly competitive process in many organizations. Thus, the manager of a department may have to engage in considerable political behavior in order to obtain even minimally acceptable resources.

Other conditions that motivate political behavior are technological change, ambiguity in decision making, and organizational change. Often, the introduction of new technologies in organizations creates considerable uncertainty with respect to work roles

and lines of authority; both conditions are ripe for political maneuvering. In many organizations, decisions are made with incomplete information; thus, it is not clear which alternative is "correct." When this is the case, political behavior often results because advocates of different positions may attempt to influence the decision-making process. Finally, political behavior is very common during times of organizational change because things are often "up for grabs" and readily amenable to such forms of influence.

Having defined organizational politics, we now turn to specific tactics that people use when they engage in political behavior. Although many tactics could be used to promote one's political agenda, some tactics are more commonly used, and many of these are similar to the general influence tactics discussed in the previous section. According to Allen, Madison, Porter, Renwick, and Mayes (1979), six commonly used political tactics include two that were discussed previously (ingratiation and forming coalitions and networks), and four that are somewhat different from more general influence tactics.

1. *Impression management* represents behaviors that are designed to enhance one's visibility or stature within the organization. Bolino and Turnley (1999) developed a questionnaire to assess five different impression-management strategies employees use based on a classification developed by Jones and Pittman (1982). *Self-promotion* refers to employees discussing their accomplishments and abilities with others to come across as competent (e.g., "Talk proudly about your experience or education"). *Ingratiation* refers to employees doing favors or complimenting others to come across as likeable (e.g., "Compliment your colleagues so they will see you as likeable").

Exemplification refers to people highlighting their moral worthiness by appearing to do more or be more ethical than other employees (e.g., "Try to appear like a hard-working, dedicated employee"). *Intimidation* is where people advertise their power in order to come across as threatening within an organization (e.g., "Be intimidating with co-workers when it will help you get your job done"). Finally, *supplication* is when an employee comes across as weak and needy so that he or she can be protected by others (e.g., "Act like you know less than you do so people will help you out").

2. Another commonly used political tactic is *information management*. In many organizations, "information is power"; thus, one way to advance one's political agenda is to control others' access to information. This may include simply controlling whether others ever receive information and the timing of the information's release. In political campaigns, for example, candidates often withhold negative information about their opponent until just before the election. By doing so, they leave the opposition little time to engage in any form of "damage control" that might save the election.

3. A political tactic that is somewhat counterintuitive, but often highly effective, is *promotion of the opposition*. This may involve eliminating a political rival by helping the person become so successful that he or she is promoted to a higher position in the organization and no longer poses a threat. Using this tactic has a double advantage: The employee appears to be gracious, and an individual who may be a roadblock en route to the desired political objectives is eliminated.

4. A final political tactic used in organizations is an employee's promotion of his or her own agenda by *pursuing line responsibility*—actively seeking a position within the organization that makes it easier to exert one's influence. In most organizations, some positions are crucial to the main business of the organization, and others are considered peripheral. As a general rule, positions that are close to the core technology of an organization (e.g., production, resources acquisition) carry higher levels of influence than positions in departments designed to support that technology (e.g., research and development, human resources).

The political tactics described to this point are relatively benign, but certain tactics reflect the "dark side" of political behavior in organizations. According to DuBrin (1993), more destructive political tactics include the elimination of one's political rivals, use of a "divide and conquer" strategy, and exclusion of one's political adversaries. Political battles in organizations can be brutal. In some cases when members of organizations are competing with each other, the "winner" is able to facilitate the exit of rivals by getting them fired or making their lives so difficult that they leave voluntarily.

The "divide and conquer" strategy may surface in situations in which one individual is at odds with a group of other employees. It is often difficult for an individual to impose his or her will on such a group because of the numerical difference. Thus, one way to overcome this situation is to induce conflict within the group, making it less likely that these individuals will put up a united front. Managers in many types of organizations often bemoan the lack of interpersonal harmony within work groups. However, the irony is that the existence of interpersonal conflict often makes it much easier for managers to control their groups and to advance their personal agendas.

Excluding one's political rivals simply involves making sure that they are "out of the loop" and thus less likely to influence one's agenda. As stated earlier, in many organizations, information is power. Thus, one way to undercut one's rivals is to make sure that they do not receive crucial information that would make it easier for them to exert influence. In practice, this form of influence may involve making sure that one's rivals are not invited to important meetings, or perhaps seeing to it that they receive job assignments in remote areas of the organization.

Unfortunately, not a great deal of empirical research has been devoted to the study of organizational politics. The little research that has been done, however, suggests that political behavior has a negative impact on organizations, particularly when employees lack an understanding of the political landscape (e.g., Ferris, Gilmore, & Kacmar, 1990). When one considers the tactics previously described, this is not surprising. The atmosphere in an organization with a great deal of political behavior is likely to be characterized by tension, mistrust, and, in extreme cases, downright paranoia.

In addition, Vigoda and Cohen (2002) recently conducted a longitudinal study involving employee influence tactics, met expectations on the job, and perceptions of organizational politics. These authors found that greater use of influence tactics at Time 1 was related to lower met expectations of employees (employees feeling the organization did not live up to what they expected) at Time 2, which was then predictive of perception of organizational politics at Time 2. These results illustrate the link between high levels of influence and perception of organizational politics.

It is not realistic to think that political behavior can be (or perhaps even should be) eliminated from organizations. However, there may be ways organizations can decrease the behavior. Political behavior is often the by-product of uncertainty and ambiguity, so being clear about organizational goals and individual employees' job assignments is an important step toward reducing destructive political behavior. Organizations can also reduce political behavior by breaking up obvious cliques or coalitions through transfers or through job rotation. If individuals consistently engage in destructive political behaviors, organizations may be able to reduce these behaviors by confronting the offenders. Often, employees in organizations will "get away with" destructive political behaviors simply because they are never confronted about it.

Perhaps the most important way that managers can decrease political behavior is by setting a good example for subordinates. If a manager is honest and above board in his or her dealings with others in the organization, handles conflicts with others in a constructive manner, and conveys to subordinates that highly destructive political behavior will not be tolerated, this sends a powerful message. Although political behavior in organizations may not be eliminated, it may be possible to decrease it to a nondestructive level.

CHAPTER SUMMARY

This chapter focused on leadership and the closely related topic of influence processes. The study of leadership has been approached from trait, behavioral, and contingency perspectives. Although most modern theories of leadership can be considered contingency

PEOPLE BEHIND THE RESEARCH

STEPHEN ZACCARO AND THE REEMERGENCE OF RESEARCH ON LEADER ATTRIBUTES

My interest in leader attributes and leadership grew from a term paper I wrote for a group dynamics class while in graduate school. In that paper, I had cited an earlier study by Barnlund (1962) that seemed to provide support for the prevailing notion that the particular occupant of the leader role can vary from situation to situation depending upon the set of skills and attributes needed in each situation. David Kenny was my instructor, and he noted in his grading comments that the results of the Barnlund study could be reanalyzed to partition the variance in leader emergence more precisely to different sources. He developed the appropriate statistics for the reanalysis; we applied them to the original study, and found that a large portion of the variance could be attributed to attributes of the leader rather than the situation.

We published the results of this reanalysis in a paper that emphasized trait-based sources of leadership variance. This was in the early 1980s when much of the zeitgeist in leadership research was decidedly in a different direction. However, Robert House had already begun to write about charismatic leadership and about personality and leadership. Then, Robert Lord and his colleagues published their meta-analysis in 1986 supporting a stronger link between leader attributes and emergence. These research lines gave some new impetus to trait-based perspectives of leadership.

In our paper, Kenny and I had speculated that attributes that predicted leader emergence would include qualities that promoted a leader's behavioral flexibility to varying situational demands. I conducted some research with Rose-anne Foti and Dave Kenny to test this notion. We found support linking self-monitoring to leader emergence across different situations. This study sparked for me an ongoing and continuing program of research to identify leader attributes that promote effectiveness in dynamic and multi-faceted organizational domains. We have learned from this work that leadership can likely be explained by complex integrations of leader attributes, residing in a single person or perhaps shared among team members, which foster responsiveness to varying situational demands. We also learned the value of revisiting old ideas, applying more sophisticated methods and approaches to gain new insights.

Stephen J. Zaccaro
Department of Psychology
George Mason University

theories, the trait and behavioral approaches are by no means dead; they still offer some insight into leadership processes.

Fiedler's Contingency Theory proposes that the effectiveness of a leader hinges on the match between situational favorability and whether the leader is task or relationship oriented. This theory has received only mixed support, but it has generated a considerable body of leadership research. It also served as the impetus for other contingency-based leadership theories in subsequent years.

Path–Goal Theory also proposes that leader effectiveness depends on the leader–situation match. It differs from Fiedler's theory, however, in the manner in which effectiveness is defined, and in proposing that leaders are able to adapt different forms of leadership behaviors to different situations. Although Path–Goal Theory still awaits more empirical scrutiny, it serves as a useful guide to the understanding of leadership and may have considerable practical benefits as well.

The Vroom–Yetton–Jago model of leadership is focused on one aspect of leadership behavior: decision making. This theory is somewhat different from the others in that it is largely prescriptive in nature; that is, it provides managers with guidelines for decision making. Support for this model has been strong when managers have been asked to recall decisions, but results have been more equivocal when other sources of data are used.

The Leader–Member Exchange (LMX) Theory proposes that leaders develop a unique relationship with each of their subordinates that is largely based on social exchange. This theory represents a vast departure from previous theories that were based on the rather naïve assumption that

leaders treat all subordinates the same. Research on LMX Theory has yielded very interesting findings on both the determinants and the consequences of differences in exchange relationship quality. Further work, however, appears to be needed to define the dimensions of the exchange relationship and to broaden the scope of LMX research. Some recent research has used LMX processes to explain how transformational leaders produce superior performance in their subordinates.

The most recent heavily researched theory of leadership described was Transformational and Transactional Leadership. To some extent, this approach represents a return to the trait approach that dominated leadership research in the early twentieth century. Transformational leaders not only lead others but inspire them as well. These individuals also are capable of facilitating meaningful change in organizations. Research in this area has been largely descriptive. Transactional leaders emphasize the contingencies necessary for employees to receive rewards and keep track of employee behaviors to deliver contingencies. Recent meta-analyses show that both transformational and transactional leaderships are related to employee performance, and that the two forms of leadership are actually positively related. We briefly introduced a recent theory of authentic leadership that emphasizes leaders acting in ways consistent with their self-concept and showing moral character. Future research is necessary to assess this approach.

Power and influence are at the core of leadership; therefore, both topics were covered in conjunction with leadership theories. Research has shown that leaders typically have multiple bases from which to exert power, and, in some cases, these bases may be situationally specific. Influence tactics represent the various ways in which leaders exert their power in organizations. Research has shown that the most effective tactics are those that give subordinates some freedom of choice, and the least effective tactics are those that involve pressure and appeals to one's formal authority.

Organizational politics represents a distinct form of influence that, in many cases, can be destructive. Political behavior may occur in any organization, but it is typically more prevalent in organizations that have a great deal of uncertainty and scarce resources. Specific political tactics may take a variety of forms—some more negative than others. Although relatively little research on organizational politics exists, there is some evidence that the impact of political behavior is negative. Although political behavior can never be eliminated completely, organizations can reduce it by improving communication and, in some cases, increasing resources. Ultimately, the most effective way for managers to reduce political behavior is to set a positive example in their dealings with subordinates and others in the organization.

SUGGESTED ADDITIONAL READINGS

Graen, G. B., & Uhl-Bien, M. (1995). Development of leader-member exchange (LMX) theory over 25 years: Applying a multi-level multi-domain perspective. *Leadership Quarterly, 6,* 219–246.

Judge, T. A., & Piccolo, R. F. (2004). Transformational and transactional leadership: A meta-analytic test of their relative validity. *Journal of Applied Psychology, 89,* 755–768.

Klein, H. J., & Kim, J. S. (1998). A field study of the influence of situational constraints, leader-member exchange, and goal commitment on performance. *Academy of Management Journal, 41,* 88–95.

Waldman, D. A., & Yammarino, F. J. (1999). CEO charismatic leadership: Levels-of-management and levels-of-analysis effects. *Academy of Management Review, 24,* 266–285.

Zaccaro, S. J. (2007). Trait-based perspectives of leadership. *American Psychologist, 62,* 6–16.

Chapter Eleven

Group Dynamics and Behavior

Most employees belong to some formal work group, and organizations often establish temporary or ad hoc groups to accomplish many important tasks. Furthermore, different groups of people within an organization often work together to accomplish objectives. Thus, a great deal of behavior in organizations takes place within group situations. It is therefore essential to examine behavior in groups in order to obtain a complete understanding of behavior in organizational settings. The prevalence of groups in organizations mirrors their presence in everyday life. For example, most people are part of a family and belong to groups in their communities or churches, or within their professions. It is a good bet that most readers belong to a variety of groups, and that membership in these groups has an important impact on their behaviors and attitudes.

Organizations make frequent use of groups for an obvious reason: A group can accomplish more than an individual. For example, a group of five firefighters can obviously bring a fire under control faster than one firefighter. Groups are also used because the output of several people working on a task may be better—or, in some cases, more creative—than if each person approached the task individually. A third reason that groups are frequently utilized is simply convention. Organizational scholars (e.g., Hackman, 1992) have noted that behavior in organizations is often driven by *social inertia*, or relying on familiar ways of doing things. Because groups have been used in the

past, they are sometimes used without much thought as to whether they are appropriate for a given task.

Given the importance of groups in organizations, two chapters are devoted to this topic. The present chapter serves as an introduction to group behavior through an analysis of the social psychological and organizational psychology literatures. Having a firm foundation of group dynamics and behavior, Chapter 12 focuses specifically on the effectiveness of teams in organizations, and draws largely (though not exclusively) from the organizational psychology literature. After reading these chapters, students should have a firm understanding of the impact of groups in organizational settings.

WHY DO PEOPLE JOIN GROUPS?

People join groups for a multitude of reasons. A major reason is that group membership often results in some form of need satisfaction on the part of the individual. If one takes an evolutionary perspective (e.g., Buss, 1996), group membership may appeal to individuals' basic need for survival. Activities that enhance survival, such as hunting and defense against predators, are often better accomplished collectively than individually. Because of this, some have argued, the tendency to affiliate and form groups has become an adaptive behavior and thus has endured over many centuries.

At the present time, basic survival is not at issue for most people; thus, group membership often allows the fulfillment of other types of needs. One that is typically satisfied by group membership is the need for affiliation. Baumeister and Leary (1995) have forcefully argued that individuals have a strong need to belong to social groups, and that failure to be securely included in desired groups prompts actions to restore group inclusion. Thus, people often join groups simply to be in the company of other people. In fact, when people do not affiliate with others for prolonged periods of time, this may lead to psychological adjustment problems or even more severe forms of psychopathology (see Comment 11.1).

Another need that is often satisfied through group membership is the need for power and control (Schutz, 1958). As was stated in Chapter 10, social power involves the capacity or potential to influence the behavior of others. If one has a strong need to exert power over others, that person needs to be in the company of other people. (It's pretty hard to boss yourself around! Actually, it can be done, but you might get some funny looks!) Thus, people often do join groups so they can hold leadership positions that allow them to exert power and influence over other group members.

Besides providing the opportunity for need satisfaction, group membership often gives people a greater opportunity to achieve goals than they would have if they were acting alone. For example, people often join labor unions because they believe they can achieve higher wages and more favorable working conditions by acting collectively rather than negotiating with their employers as individuals. Other examples of organizations joined for this reason include political parties, criminal organizations, churches, lobbying organizations, and consumer advocacy groups. These organizations seek vastly different goals, but they are similar in their use of the power of collective action to achieve some goal or higher purpose.

A final reason that people often join groups is that being around other people often provides comfort and support (Cohen & Wills, 1985; Smith, Murphy, & Coats, 1999). Particularly when people are anxious, or when they are experiencing stressful periods in their lives, being around other people can offer a great deal of support. This is especially true when the other people comprising a group are experiencing the same difficulties (Schacter, 1959). Examples of group membership can be seen in the numerous support groups for people with certain diseases (e.g., cancer), survivors of tragedies (e.g., loss of a spouse), or people who are going through other major life transitions (e.g., divorce).

PEOPLE NEEDING PEOPLE: THE IMPACT OF SOCIAL ISOLATION

Do PEOPLE HAVE a strong need to be around other people? That is, do people suffer when they are deprived of contact with others? The answer to this question is rather complex, but there are many reasons to believe that social isolation may be detrimental to both mental and physical health. Research in developmental psychology, for example, has shown that children often have severe developmental delays and other long-term difficulties when they are deprived of social contact as infants. Also, studies of individuals such as explorers, scientists working in seclusion, and prisoners document the psychological suffering that often accompanies seclusion from others. This suffering is often greater then the physical hardships these individuals face.

Another indication of the need for social contact (and hence the pain associated with isolation) is the comfort people often find when they are with other people, particularly in times of distress or turmoil. Often, when something traumatic happens in someone's life (e.g., loss of a spouse), the first words of concerned friends or relatives are: "He/She shouldn't be alone." The soothing effect of social contact also explains, at least partially, why many people regularly go to churches, synagogues, and mosques to practice their religious faith. It is certainly possible to practice one's religious faith in isolation; however, doing so with others often provides a great deal of comfort.

Despite the well-documented negative effects, isolation from others can provide people an opportunity for reflection and personal growth. Writers, artists, and others engaged in creative endeavors often find inspiration through solitude and isolation. It is important to note, however, that, for these individuals, the isolation is self-imposed and they are typically able to break their isolation if they want to. This element of choice appears to be a key element in whether social isolation is detrimental.

Source: D. R. Forsyth. (2006). *Group dynamics* (4th ed.). Belmont, CA: Wadsworth/Thompson.

Although organizations typically form groups in order to accomplish work-related tasks, work groups may serve a variety of other purposes for their members, such as affiliation and social support. This point is often overlooked in organizational psychology, but it is important in understanding the behavior of work groups. We now address the defining characteristics of groups, a task more difficult than one might imagine.

DEFINING CHARACTERISTICS OF GROUPS

Psychologists who study group behavior are much more precise in their definition of what constitutes a group, as compared to the way most people use this term in everyday conversation. Although there is no "universal" accepted definition of what constitutes a group (Forsyth, 2006), there is actually a good deal of consensus on the most important defining characteristics. A term that is found in most definitions of a group is *interdependence*. Specifically, to be considered a group, a collection of people must, in some way, be interdependent. This simply means that the outcomes each member of a collective receives depend, to some degree, on the other members of the collective. In work situations, interdependence may be seen when one person may need information from other employees in order to do his or her job. Interdependence may also exist in social situations; that is, people may depend on each other for having fun.

Another key defining characteristic of a group is social interaction. To be considered a group, people must interact with each other in some way. This typically takes the form of verbal and nonverbal communication. If people are not in the same physical location, this interaction may take other forms (e.g., phone, e-mail). On the other hand, people who do not interact are typically not considered to be a group. Consider, for example, five people standing in an elevator. The people in this situation are essentially ignoring each other and would not be considered a group.

A third defining characteristic of a group is the perception of being a group on the part of the actual group members and those external to the group. There may be instances where people interact with each other, and they may even be somewhat interdependent, but do not perceive themselves as a group. Consider, for example, the members of a wedding party. These individuals certainly embody the first two characteristics of a group: They interact and their behavior is somewhat interdependent (e.g., there is usually some predetermined order in which they must walk down the aisle). In most cases, though, these individuals probably perceive themselves as a collection of individuals rather than a group. Furthermore, even if some level of group identity does develop among these individuals, it is very short lived.

Psychologists coined the term *entitativity* to refer to the extent that a collection of individuals is perceived as a whole (Campbell, 1958). Lickel and his colleagues (2000) asked participants to distinguish between a number of different groups in terms of those

that seemed more entitative (*groupy*) than others (Lickel, Hamilton, Wieczorkowska, Lewis, Sherman, & Uhles, 2000). The authors found that intimacy groups such as families and friends were seen as most entitative, followed by work groups, aggregations of people at a location, and broad social categories (e.g., women, lawyers). Groups that perceive themselves as more entitative are likely to have higher levels of cohesion than other groups (e.g., Mullen & Cooper, 1994).

A final key defining characteristic of groups is commonality of purpose. For a collection of people to be a group, they must have some common goal or other reason for existence. Common goals may be quite formal—for example, for a work group—or quite informal, as would be the case for a group of friends who get together simply because they enjoy each other's company. The major point is that for a collection of people to be a group, they must have something they are trying to accomplish collectively.

Based on these defining characteristics of groups, two important points are worth mentioning. First, clearly dividing collections of people into *groups* and *nongroups* is often difficult to do. Some collections of people are more "grouplike" than others. Thus, whether a collection of people constitutes a group is more a matter of degree than it is an absolute judgment. Second, within organizational settings, we often use the term group incorrectly. A formal work *group* may simply be a collection of people who are linked for administrative purposes but exhibit few of the defining characteristics of a group. In universities, for example, academic departments are typically considered groups, even though the work of the *members* (professors) is not usually interdependent. They may interact very infrequently, may not perceive themselves as a group, and may disagree vehemently about departmental goals.

This issue has been addressed somewhat in the organizational psychology literature by using the term *team* to discuss work groups that are configured to accomplish specific tasks (Kozlowski & Bell, 2003). The next chapter deals primary with work groups in an organizational context, and is therefore titled team (rather than group) effectiveness. The other side of this, however, is that, within organizations, informal groups may develop, and the impact of these groups may be powerful. For example, people may develop friendship groups based on their level of seniority within the organization or their common interests (e.g., running, playing golf). These informal groups are important because they may impact employees' attitudes and can ultimately influence whether employees stay with an organization. They are certainly as real as formal groups created by organizational structures.

GROUP STRUCTURE

To understand groups, it is useful to consider group structure, which represents a set of dimensions along which any group can be described. These dimensions also help when we are describing differences between groups. The most important elements of group structure are roles, norms, values, communication patterns, and status differentials. Each of these is discussed next.

Roles

Roles represent prescribed patterns of behavior that are specific to a particular individual, or to the position the individual occupies (King & King, 1990). In organizations,

role-related behaviors are often communicated to employees through formal documents such as job descriptions, but they may also be communicated by more informal means. As an element of group structure, roles are quite relevant. When groups first form, there is a great deal of uncertainty and ambiguity surrounding what individual group members are supposed to do (Levine, Moreland, & Choi, 2001; Tuckman, 1965). Over time, individual group members' roles are defined through the process of role differentiation (Hackman, 1992; Levine et al., 2001). *Role differentiation* simply represents the process by which (1) role-related expectations are communicated to group members, and (2) the various roles within the group take shape. Groups tend to form role structures primarily because this method is much more efficient than having "everyone do everything."

Although the specific roles played by group members may be highly specific and task dependent, more general roles are enacted in all groups. For example, in most groups, a member or members plays what might be described as the *task role*. Behaviors associated with the task role might include clarifying task requirements, providing performance-related coaching and assistance to group members, and, at times, keeping the group focused on the task at hand. In many (but not all) cases, behaviors associated with the task role are performed by a formally designated group leader. It is not unusual, for example, for senior members of a work group to share their expertise with newer members, even when the groups have formally designated leaders.

A second role that is commonly seen in most groups is the socio-emotional role. Behaviors associated with the socio-emotional role are aimed at maintaining the "social fabric" of the group. At various points in the life of any group, there is a need for someone to encourage others, to lighten the atmosphere with a joke, or to diffuse conflicts among group members. Socio-emotional behaviors could obviously be performed by any member of a group, but they often are not performed by a formally designated leader when one is present. Exhibiting socio-emotional behaviors often puts leaders in an awkward position, given that they are also typically responsible for judging the performance of the members of their groups. In professional sports, teams often acquire veteran players because they are able to perform aspects of the socio-emotional role, such as keeping morale high and diffusing personality conflicts among other players.

The third role that is common to most groups is labeled the *individual role*. In all groups, individual members have individual needs and desires that may or may not be compatible with those of the group as a whole. Individual group members pursue these needs to varying degrees, but (hopefully) not to the detriment of the larger group goals. However, these needs could be problematic when they conflict with the goals of the group. In many organizations, for example, employees have incentives that are based purely on individual performance.

A final role that is common in most groups is that of leader. As discussed in our last chapter, leadership comes in many forms and varieties. We bring up the role of leader in our discussion of groups because even small groups will likely designate a leader whose responsibility is to coordinate the activities of the group members and motivate them to perform well. Leaders within groups may be formally designated, or they may emerge as group members determine who can most effectively fill that role (Forsyth, 2006).

Norms

The normative standards (*norms*) that are adopted by the group represent a second important dimension of group structure. Norms are explicit or implicit standards that govern behavior. According to Hackman (1992), groups adopt norms primarily to increase the predictability of group members' behaviors and, more generally, to keep things running smoothly within the group. Groups may adopt norms governing a number of aspects of group behavior, such as the format of meetings, the openness of communication, and even the way people dress. Typically, though, groups adopt norms only for behaviors that are deemed important for the functioning of the group.

Once norms are adopted, group members typically "fall in line" and behave in accordance with those normative standards. In some cases, however, a group member may behave in direct violation of those norms. If such a violation is unintentional, politely bringing it to the person's attention may be all that's needed to correct the behavior. For example, if a new group member arrives at a meeting 15 minutes late because he or she didn't realize the starting time, this type of norm violation can be dealt with simply by bringing it to the person's attention or making light of the infraction.

What happens when norm violation is more intentional and occurs repeatedly? Research suggests that, in these types of situations, group members should try to modify the norm violator's behavior—but only to a point. If repeated attempts fail to bring the norm violator's behavior in line with the prevailing group norms, one of three things can happen. First, the group may eliminate the norm violator. Evidence suggests, however, that this is a fairly drastic step; groups typically expel norm violators only as a last resort. There may even be instances in which a group simply does not have this option. Encouraging group members to assimilate the importance of group norms is a critical component of group socialization (Levine et al., 2001), which we turn to in the next major section of the chapter.

A second option is to allow the norm violator to remain a member of the group—but a very marginal member. Stated differently, the norm-violating group member may become an institutionalized deviant who is essentially ignored by the other members of the group (Dentler & Erikson, 1959). When this happens, the group essentially "gives up" on the norm violator and ignores his or her behavior. In some cases (but not all), being relegated to the role of institutionalized deviant may be enough to prompt a person to leave a group. The negative part of having a person in the role of institutionalized deviant is that the group has essentially lost the contributions of one of its members.

A final possibility is that the norm violator may ultimately change the relevant group norm. One of the positive things about norm violation is that it may force a group to take a critical look at its prevailing norms. Although, in many cases, norms help groups to function more effectively, they may also have negative effects. For example, a group that adopts a norm of never acknowledging internal conflict may function well on the surface but have problems in the long run. Thus, taking a critical look at prevailing group norms may reveal some that are either outdated or dysfunctional for the current group. As Hackman (1992) aptly points out, "Just as it has been said that the unexamined life is not worth living, so it may also be said that an unexamined norm is not worth enforcing" (p. 248).

For a norm violator to actually change prevailing group norms, however, a number of conditions must be present (Moscovici, 1994). Specifically, normative change is much more likely if there is at least one other group member violating the prevailing norm; one group member going against the grain will typically not be enough to change a group norm. It has also been found that the norm violator must be consistent in his or her behavior over time, and that the other members of the group must see this consistency as evidence of the strength of his or her convictions. Normative change is also more likely when the difference between the prevailing norm and the behavior of the norm violator is reasonably consistent with prevailing cultural values. Finally, members of the minority must avoid being cast into the role of institutionalized deviants. All in all, one may conclude that prevailing group norms can be changed by a norm violator, but this is not an easy process.

Values

Schwartz (1994) has defined *values* as "desirable trans-situational goals, varying in importance, that serve as guiding principles in the life of a person or other social entity" (p. 21). In the context of groups, values represent such goals or ideas that the group deems as important (Rokeach, 1973). When new members are socialized into any collective body, the values of that collective body are communicated either explicitly or implicitly. For example, a group producing a product may strongly value quality, a group that deals with customers may strongly value customer satisfaction, and a group that forms for social reasons may strongly value group members' enjoyment.

Regardless of whether a group communicates its values explicitly through written documents or on a more ad hoc basis, new members must accept them in order to remain part of the group. For membership in most groups, new members are not required to become completely committed to all the values of the group. At some level, however, a new group member must accept some of the group's values in order to remain part of the group.

Like norms, values may be functional because they often serve as "rallying points" for a good deal of group members' behaviors. For example, the fact that a group strongly values customer service may motivate group members to "go the extra mile" for customers. Values, however, can also be dysfunctional. A group that values conformity and agreement over all else may, at times, make very poor decisions and ultimately be ineffective (Janis, 1982). Thus, like norms, the values of a group must be periodically made explicit and critically examined.

Communication Patterns

Another way that groups can be described is by the characteristic patterns group members use to communicate with each other. In the group dynamics literature, the most typical distinction regarding communication is between centralized and decentralized communication networks (Leavitt, 1951; Shaw, 1964, 1978). When a centralized communication network is adopted in a group, communication tends to flow from one source to all group members. A typical form of centralized communication, termed the *hub and spokes* model, is depicted in Figure 11.1. Notice that in this type of communication network, one individual (often the group leader) is the focal point. This individual takes in information and disseminates it to the other members of the group. The advantage of this type of centralization is that

it allows information to be standardized; that is, all group members can obtain the same information. This is particularly important when groups are working on tasks that are fairly standardized and routine.

As one looks at Figure 11.1, an obvious disadvantage is that centralized communication tends to restrict and discourage the flow of communication among group members. Depending on the nature of the task, this may ultimately have a negative impact on the performance of individual group members and the group as a whole. For example, it has been shown that performance on highly complex tasks is hindered by highly centralized communication flow (Hackman, 1990; Leavitt, 1951). For example, if a group of researchers is working on developing a new product, communicating only through a supervisor would be highly inefficient.

Highly centralized communication also has a less obvious problem: It puts a great deal of reliance on one person; that is, the "hub" of any centralized communication network must take in and disseminate a great deal of information and may simply overload the person with too much information. This form of communication network is also

FIGURE 11.1
The Hub-and-Spokes Communication Network

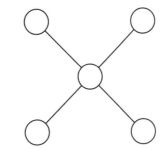

The lines with no arrows indicate that communication flows in a bidirectional manner.
Adapted from: M. E. Shaw. (1964). Communication networks. *Advances in Experimental Social Psychology, 1,* 111–147.

based on the premise that the information that is disseminated by the person occupying the focal point will be accurate and consistent. In a highly centralized communication network, there is a great deal of potential for the person occupying the focal point to disseminate information in a way that enhances his or her political agenda without enhancing the productivity of the group.

In direct contrast to centralized communication networks, in a decentralized network communication flows freely within the group. The network depicted in Figure 11.2, which is referred to as a *Comcon*, depicts decentralized communication quite clearly. Note that everyone in this five-person group communicates with everyone else. Compared to a centralized network, a clear advantage of decentralization is that it allows communication to flow wider and faster. If two members of a group need to communicate with each other about an important issue, they can do so without having to go though an immediate supervisor. Research has shown that this type of free-flowing communication is an asset, especially when a group is working on a highly complex interdependent task (Leavitt, 1951). The primary disadvantage of decentralization is the sheer amount of information that is communicated. This is particularly true with the widespread use of electronic communication. Groups using highly decentralized communication must develop ways of managing the flow of information that do not restrict it, but that do, at the same time, introduce some level of consistency.

Other than their degree of centralization, groups can often be distinguished according to whether group members communicate with each other (Moreno, 1953). In some groups, members communicate a great deal of information. However, in other groups, communication is very restricted and group

FIGURE 11.2
The "Comcon" Communication Network

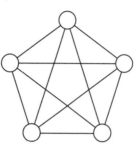

The lines with no arrows indicate that communication flows in a bidirectional manner.
Adapted from: M. E. Shaw. (1964). Communication networks. *Advances in Experimental Social Psychology, 1,* 111–147.

members often find themselves "out of the loop" on important issues. A low level of communication among group members is often (but not always) symptomatic of an inability or unwillingness of a leader to grapple with the issue of communication. It may also be symptomatic of more serious problems within a group (Hackman, 1990).

Another aspect of communication can be seen in groups: the differences between formal and informal communication patterns. Formal communication methods include things such as written memos and directives, formal statements of policy, and information provided at group meetings. Virtually all engage in some formal communication, although the degree to which they stay in touch varies considerably. Formal communication is often necessary for dissemination of important information and policies to group members.

Communication within groups may also be quite informal. Group members may engage in small talk before beginning their workday, or may discuss work-related matters while socializing after work. Organizations obviously have less control over informal communication than they do over more formal modes of communication. Indeed, the "grapevine" can be a very important source of communication for group members. A key issue, however, is the accuracy of information that is communicated within informal communication networks. When the information is accurate, informal communication networks can be a highly efficient way to communicate information. On the other hand, when it is inaccurate, this can create big problems within groups or even within entire organizations (see Comment 11.2).

Status Differentials

As groups develop, there are typically differences in status among the various group members. The reasons for such status differences are generally classified into two general categories: diffuse status characteristics and task-specific status characteristics. Diffuse status characteristics are those that are not directly related to the task the group is performing but are still seen as legitimate bases on which to attribute status. In many societies, status is based on one's occupation. In American society, those employed in professional occupations, such as medicine, law, and engineering, are typically accorded higher status than individuals in occupations such as sales or manual labor. Many societies also attribute status based on demographic variables such as age, gender, and ethnic origin. Evidence of the impact of diffuse status characteristics can clearly be seen in studies of jury deliberations (e.g., Schneider & Cook, 1995).

COMMENT 11.2

INFORMAL COMMUNICATION NETWORKS: THE "GRAPEVINE"

MOST OF THE research on communication in groups and organizations deals with formal systems of communication, but we know that much of the communication that takes place in groups and organizations is informal. The term *grapevine* is often used to describe such informal communication networks. Anyone who has worked in an organization has probably acquired or distributed information through the grapevine.

Managers in organizations are often leery of grapevine communication; they fear that such information is often inaccurate. Are managers justified in their distrust of the grapevine? Not a great deal of research has been done on this form of communication, so the evidence is somewhat mixed. Some research has shown that managers' distrust of the grapevine is justified; information communicated through the grapevine is often inaccurate. Other research, however, has shown that the accuracy of grapevine communication is quite high, especially when the information being communicated is not controversial.

We know one thing for sure about the grapevine: It is much quicker than more formal communication channels. News often travels fast in organizations. Thus, rather than completely avoid it, managers can sometimes use the grapevine as a way to quickly communicate information. This obviously must be done carefully, but it may be a very useful way to work around more cumbersome formal communication channels when information must be communicated rapidly.

Sources: R. Hershey. (1966). The grapevine—Here to stay but not beyond control. *Personnel, 20,* 64; and B. Smith. (1996). Care and feeding of the office grapevine. *Management Review, 85,* 6.

Groups may also attribute status based on differences in group members' relative contributions to the task the group is performing. As one would expect, an individual who has contributed a great deal to the group's task performance, or who is capable of doing so in the future, is typically accorded higher status than a group member whose contributions are more limited (Strodtbeck & Lipinski, 1985). For example, in a military combat team, prior combat experience would be seen as a relevant basis on which to attribute status.

In work situations, one obvious and very tangible consequence of status differentials is that higher-status group members are typically paid more than those with a lower status. Whether such differentials are based on diffuse or task-specific status characteristics, they are typically reflected in employees' paychecks and, in some cases, these differences are quite dramatic. For example, in professional sports, star players are often paid several million dollars more than players of lower status.

A somewhat less tangible consequence of status differentials is that they typically impact a group's level of tolerance for norm violation. Put simply, compared to lower-status group members, high-status group members are given greater latitude in violating group norms. Hollander (1971) introduced the concept of idiosyncrasy credits to explain this process. Idiosyncrasy credits are akin to financial currency that group members "bank" and may use in the event that they must violate a group norm. The more idiosyncrasy credits one has accrued, the more latitude one is given in violating a group norm. In most group situations, high-status members have considerably more idiosyncrasy credits than lower-status members do and thus are able to violate group norms with fewer repercussions.

One important point to note about idiosyncrasy credits is that even high-status group members do not have an infinite supply. Each time a high-status group member violates a norm, his or her idiosyncrasy credits are reduced by an amount proportionate to the importance of the norm. Thus, even high-status group members may eventually run out of idiosyncrasy credits and risk being sanctioned by the group for norm violations. This often occurs in professional sports, when teams initially accept unconventional behavior on the part of talented players, but ultimately reach a point where such behavior is not tolerated and the player is released or traded.

In addition to running the risk of depleting their supply of idiosyncrasy credits, high-status group members must be careful that their norm violations do not negatively influence the group. Research has shown that when a norm violation on the part of a high-status group member negatively impacts a group, this behavior is viewed more negatively than similar behavior on the part of a low-status group member (Forsyth, 2006). This is most likely due to the fact that high-status group members have much greater potential than lower-status members to positively impact a group. Thus, a norm violation on the part of a high-status group member that negatively impacts the group is much more visible and salient than similar behavior coming from low-status members.

STAGES OF GROUP DEVELOPMENT

Now that the basic dimensions of group structure have been described, we turn to the issue of how groups develop and change over time. All groups are somewhat unique in the way they are formed and the manner in which they may change over time. Despite this uniqueness, group dynamics researchers and theorists have identified a great deal of commonality in the way group behavior unfolds over time. Three of the most popular theoretical models describing the process of group development are described in the following paragraphs.

Tuckman's (1965) Stage Model

Tuckman (1965) reviewed 50 articles dealing with development processes in a variety of groups (e.g., therapy groups, sensitivity training groups, naturally occurring groups, laboratory groups) and concluded that there was a good deal of commonality in the processes by which these groups developed over time. Based on these findings, he proposed a stage model of group development that ultimately became quite popular and has endured very well over time (see Forsyth, 2006; Kozlowski & Bell, 2003). The stages in this model are presented in Figure 11.3, and reflect the major issues that a group must grapple with at various points in its development.

As can be seen, the first stage in the model is *forming*. This is the beginning point in the life of a group and is typically characterized by a great deal of uncertainty, or even anxiety, on the part of group members. This occurs because members of a group may be unfamiliar with each other and may have vastly different expectations about what to expect from membership in the group. At this point in the life of a group, members may deal with such uncertainties by depending heavily on the group leader for information and direction. Ultimately, though, the uncertainties that accompany membership in a new group gradually dissipate over time as group members acquire information and feel more comfortable being part of the group.

FIGURE 11.3
Tuckman's (1965) Model of Group Development

After issues associated with being in a new group are resolved, the next stage in group development is labeled *storming*. As one might guess from its name, this stage is characterized by conflict over a number of issues. For example, group members may disagree over important group norms, or perhaps over who should assume leadership responsibilities. This stage may be rather unpleasant, but it is also necessary if the groups hope to ultimately function effectively. If group members never acknowledge their disagreements, these may ultimately come out in subtler ways and prevent the group from ever performing effectively. It should be noted, however, that it is also possible for group members to be too vigorous in airing their differences. If conflicts are too intense and personal, group members may simply be unable to work together and never move past this stage. It is perhaps not surprising that groups containing people with agreeable personalities experience less conflict than groups with people prone to be disagreeable (Graziano, Jenson-Campbell, & Hair, 1996).

Assuming that the conflicts identified during the storming stage can be resolved, the group next moves into the *norming* stage. In a very real sense, this is the point where a "collection of people" becomes a "group." Some level of role differentiation in group members' behavior occurs, and the behavior of the group develops some consistent patterns. For example, different group members may serve different functions, and the group may develop norms with regard to meetings, modes of communication, and, perhaps, the way group members are expected to dress. Once the norming stage is reached, the group is capable of functioning as a collective body, rather than simply as a collection of individuals.

After a group has reached the norming stage and is capable of working as an integrated unit, the next stage in group development is *performing*. This is the point at which a group accomplishes the major task or tasks for which it was formed. For example, if a group was formed to develop a strategic plan for an organization, this would be the point at which the group would actually come up with that plan. As Tuckman (1965) and others (e.g., Hackman, 1990, 1992) point out, not all groups reach this stage in group development. Problems during the earlier stages of group development (e.g., unresolved conflicts) may prevent a group from accomplishing its major tasks. All groups, however, have the potential to reach this stage.

What happens when a group ultimately performs the task for which it was formed? A group may simply keep on performing this same task or move on to another one. In many other cases, a group is disbanded and the individuals move on to other activities. In recognition of this fact, Tuckman and Jensen (1977) added a fifth stage, *adjourning*, to the

original model. In some cases, particularly when groups are formed for a very short duration, the adjourning phase is relatively mundane. That is, group members simply move on. However, when group members are together for a long period or the group experience is very intense, this can be a difficult time. Group members may genuinely miss each other and have feelings of loss or abandonment. Over time, group members will usually overcome these feelings, but initially it may be very difficult.

During the adjourning stage, the group members may reflect on their experiences in the group. Did they feel that the group was successful? Was working in the group a rewarding experience? Did they enjoy working with the other members of the group? These types of reflections are important, for two reasons. First, they may influence members' general views about working in groups. People who have negative experiences may be hesitant to work in groups in the future. Second, such reflections may strongly influence whether the members of a particular group can work together in the future. In organizations, ad hoc groups often have to form and adjourn several times. If the members of a group have very negative reflections of being in a group, they may be unable to reconvene the group and function effectively in the future.

Tuckman's (1965) model is certainly useful in describing developmental processes in a great many groups. However, there are instances in which groups do not strictly adhere to the sequence described in the model. For example, a group of individuals may have to come together and perform immediately, and address other issues later. There may also be cases in which a group of individuals immediately adheres to a strong set of norms, and deals with other issues later. The important point for readers to understand is that this model explains group development in general.

A second and related point is that Tuckman's (1965) model is best thought of as cyclical. For example, a group may progress all the way to the performing stage, but may have to digress to storming if important conflicts among group members arise. Also, in many instances, the composition of a group may change over time. Each time a new member joins a group, certain elements of the forming stage are replayed. For the new member, this period may be fraught with uncertainty and anxiety. However, longer-tenured group members may also have apprehensions about the new group member(s), and thus may experience a good deal of uncertainty of their own. The important point here is that real groups in organizations do not develop in a lock-step fashion. Over time, they cycle back and forth between different stages.

Moreland and Levine's (1982) Model

Group development can also be viewed in terms of the manner in which new group members are socialized into—and ultimately out of—a group. Moreland and Levine (1982) proposed a model to explain this socialization process (see also Levine et al., 2001). Although not a model of group development per se, this model is useful in helping to understand many of the important transitions that occur in groups over time.

The major premise underlying Moreland and Levine's (1982) model is that the socialization of group members occurs in five unique stages. These stages are demarcated by the transitions an individual makes progressing from first being an outsider, then a group member, and, ultimately, an ex-member. The other important portion of Moreland

and Levine's model, especially with respect to group development, is that each stage in the model is characterized by unique processes on the part of the individual seeking group membership and the group itself.

The full model is depicted in Figure 11.4. As can be seen, the first stage in the model is *investigation*. At this point in time, an individual is only a prospective member of a group. From the individual's point of view, this period is focused on gathering information about the group because information of this sort will help the individual decide whether he or she will ultimately seek membership in the group. The group, at this point, is trying to recruit or attract prospective members. To do this, the group may provide prospective members with information and, in most cases, emphasize the positive aspects of group membership and downplay the negative ones. The recruitment process was described in some detail in Chapter 3.

FIGURE 11.4
Moreland and Levine's (1982) Model of Group Socialization

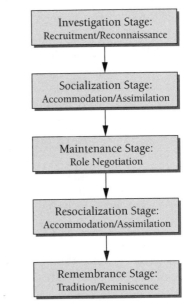

If a prospective member decides that membership in a group is attractive, he or she may decide to seek membership. Assuming that the individual is allowed by the group to do so, the individual moves on to the next stage in the model, which is *socialization*. At this point, the individual enters the group and makes the important transition from being an outsider to being a new member. The major task for the new member at this point is trying to fit in with the group and assimilate its norms and values. The major task for the group at this point is to facilitate this assimilation process by educating the new group member. This may also be a time of adjustment for the group, however, because they may have to accommodate or adjust to some of the unique characteristics of new group members. New members will not give up all of their individuality. Thus, the major issue at this point is balancing conformity to group norms with new members' individuality.

Assuming that such a balance can be achieved, the individual is accepted into the group as a full member. This is represented by the *maintenance* stage in the model. The major issue at this stage is for the group member to carve out his or her niche through the process of role negotiation. Through this give-and-take process, the individual ultimately settles into a comfortable pattern of behavior as a group member. Depending on the nature of the group, this stage may last for a short or long period of time. An individual may remain a member of a group for several years, although the specific roles he or she plays may vary over time, depending on this role-negotiation process.

Eventually, an individual's views may diverge from those of the group, and the individual may become a marginal group member. This is represented by the *resocial-*

ization stage. This is a critical period because it represents a point at which the individual diverges from the group in important ways. If such divergence cannot be resolved through the same assimilation and accommodation processes that were operating during the initial socialization, the individual may ultimately leave the group. On the other hand, if the individual can be successfully resocialized, he or she will again become a full member of the group.

If resocialization is not successful and the individual ultimately decides to leave the group, this leads to the final stage in the model: *remembrance*. At this point, the individual assumes the role of an ex-member and reflects on his or her experience in the group. Such reflections may be positive or negative, but they will undoubtedly have an impact on the individual's subsequent behavior in group settings. From a group's perspective, the major task at this point is to maintain some level of stability or tradition, even though the exit of a member represents an important change (see Comment 11.3).

Although Moreland and Levine's (1982) model is designed primarily to explain the process of group member socialization, it is also useful in helping to understand how groups develop over time. Most groups go through this cyclical process of bringing in new members, socializing them, and ultimately seeing them leave. Thus, this model provides useful insight into the processes that groups engage in, at least relative to the entry and exit of specific group members.

Gersick's Punctuated Equilibrium Model

In the group dynamics literature, the idea that groups strive to maintain an equilibrium point between task accomplishment and the interpersonal needs of group members has

COMMENT 11.3

GROUPS THAT LIVE ON: DAVE, SAMMY, GARY, . . . AND DAVE?

STUDENTS ARE OFTEN surprised to find that college professors enjoy listening to music other than Mozart, Bach, or some other titan of refined classical music. Both authors enjoy Van Halen, and one (SMJ) even listens to the group when writing manuscripts. The other author's (TWB) claim to fame is seeing Van Halen perform in support of the album titled "1984," which was the group's last concert with lead singer David Lee Roth.

In terms of group dynamics, one of the things that is interesting about Van Halen is how they have been able to remain highly successful, despite having to replace a key member of the group three times. When the group started in the 1970s, David Lee Roth was the lead vocalist. He remained with the group until the mid-1980s, when he left to pursue a solo career. After Roth's exit, the group hired Sammy Hagar, who remained with the group until the mid-1990s. Like Roth, Hagar left the group to pursue a solo career. Following Hagar's departure, the group turned to Gary Cherone. Cherone had the shortest tenure with the group; he recorded only one album. Since Cherone has left, the group remains without a lead singer. However, in a somewhat odd twist of fate, Van Halen has recently announced that David Lee Roth will once again be fronting the group for a tour in the fall of 2007.

Throughout these key personnel changes, the group has still managed to be highly successful. Why? One of the reasons is that, despite having three lead vocalists, the other members of the group have remained constant. Eddie Van Halen, Alex Valen, and Mike Anthony have been members of the group from the start (although note that Mike Anthony has been replaced in the recent incarnation of Van Halen by Eddie Van Halen's 15-year-old son, Wolfgang). They have provided the group with stability and a distinctive sound that is independent of the lead vocalist. Another key to the group's success is that, along with stability, they have had the ability to adapt. The style and lyrics of the group's music have changed somewhat with each of the changes in the lead vocalist.

Perhaps the lesson here is that, in order for a group to be successful over time, its members need to have some level of stability in their membership. This serves to maintain continuity and perhaps reinforces important norms and values. However, when groups have changes in personnel, they must be flexible and willing to utilize the unique talents of these new group members.

Source: http://www.van-halen.com.

---

been proposed for some time (e.g., Bales, 1965). Building on this general principle, Gersick (1988) proposed that groups might go through periods of relative inertia versus rapid change depending on group members' awareness of time and deadlines. For example, if a task force has 2 months to develop a strategic plan for an organization, Gersick's (1988) model proposes that this group may spend a good portion of the first month

"spinning its wheels" in an attempt to define the task, decide on how best to approach the task, and possibly deal with internal conflicts. However, once the halfway point is reached, the model predicts that group members will recognize that their time is limited, and a great deal of progress will be made in a relatively short period of time.

Gersick's (1988) model is well suited to organizational settings because groups in organizations are typically formed to accomplish meaningful tasks and often have to do so within a specific time frame. In contrast, groups in laboratory settings often do not have meaningful tasks to perform, and deadlines have little relevance because the duration of their activity is very limited. Furthermore, this model has received support using a variety of methodological approaches (e.g., Gersick, 1989; Hackman, 1990; Page, Davis, Berkow, & O'Leary, 1989).

The major practical implication of Gersick's (1988) Punctuated Equilibrium Model is that managers should be patient with groups when they are beginning to work on a task. This model also suggests that it is desirable for the members of task-performing groups to be aware of deadlines. Based on Gersick's model, one would assume that if group members are not made aware of deadlines, this will increase the probability that the group will flounder indefinitely and, ultimately, will never become productive.

Thus far, the models and issues we have discussed have emphasized *intragroup* dynamics. The focus has been on processes that occur within groups and between group members. The remainder of this chapter focuses on *intergroup* dynamics, where the emphasis is on how groups interact with one another. We will see that groups can work together to accomplish joint tasks or can compete with one another in escalating spirals of conflict. Understanding group behavior in organizations requires an analysis of both intragroup and intergroup processes.

INTERGROUP DYNAMICS AND BEHAVIOR

To highlight the importance of intergroup behavior, consider an example of a fairly typical organizational activity: hiring a new employee. In most organizations, a decision to hire a new employee typically begins in the department or unit that is doing the hiring. For example, in a university setting, if a psychology department wants to hire a new organizational psychologist, that department would typically send a hiring request to a university or college committee that is set up to handle faculty staffing issues. Assuming that the request to hire is approved, the psychology department would then work with the human resources department, and perhaps the college dean's office, throughout the hiring process. Notice that throughout this process a great deal of intergroup cooperation is needed to successfully complete the task of hiring a new faculty member.

In discussing the determinants and consequences of intergroup behavior, we first describe the various forms of intergroup transactions that typically occur in organizations. We then address the factors that influence both the frequency and the quality of intergroup interactions. From there, we address the issue of intergroup conflict and strategies that can be used to keep intergroup conflict to manageable levels.

TYPES OF INTERGROUP INTERACTIONS

Given the vast array of organizational tasks that may require interactions among two or more groups, intergroup behavior might take a variety of forms. According to Thomas (1976), the nature of intergroup interactions depends largely on the degree to which groups must interact in order to achieve their goals (i.e., their interdependence), and the degree of compatibility between the goals of different groups. Crossing these two factors yields the matrix in Figure 11.5.

As can be seen at the bottom of the matrix, there are some instances in which groups simply do not have to interact in order to achieve their goals. Groups can accomplish some goals by acting more or less autonomously. If this is the case, and if the goals of two groups are reasonably compatible, interaction between these two groups can best be described as accommodation. This means that there is some cordial give and take between the two groups. An example of accommodation might be two baseball teams deciding the order in which they are going to use the field for pregame practice. This is obviously not a crucial issue, so the coaches of the two teams might have a cordial discussion and make a decision.

Where interaction is not crucial and the goals of two groups are incompatible, the typical interaction is best described as avoidance; the groups can simply avoid interacting with each other. In many organizations, there are groups or departments that are pursuing vastly different and, to a large extent, conflicting goals. A group of researchers working on new product development is pursuing a goal that is far different

from that of a group of engineers attempting to streamline current production processes. Such groups obviously have different goals, and these goals are largely independent. Thus, in many organizations, these types of groups can avoid interacting with each other.

Given the level of complexity in today's organizations, and the interdependence of many tasks, the reality is that groups often must interact with other groups in order to accomplish their goals. This state of affairs is reflected in the top portion of the matrix in Figure 11.5. As can be seen, when interaction is crucial to goal accomplishment and the goals of two groups are largely compatible, the interactions between groups can best be described as collaboration. An example of this might be two research groups that are researching the same phenomenon. One group may possess expertise that the other does not have. Thus, by working together collaboratively, these two research groups accomplish more than they would if each was to work independently.

Where interaction is crucial to goal attainment, yet the goals of groups are incompatible, the interactions are typically characterized by competition. Two top collegiate football teams that are striving for a national championship are interdependent in the sense that they must play each other in order to achieve their goals. However, their goals are obviously diametrically opposed—there can only be one national champion. Thus, when these two teams play, there is a very high level of competition. There may also be instances in organizations when groups compete with each other. Sales groups may compete for awards, different academic departments may compete for scarce resources, and different political parties may compete for the right to govern. One negative aspect of competition is that it may lead to destructive conflict among groups.

FIGURE 11.5

Conceptual Map of the Various forms of intergroup Behavior

On the other hand, if approached in a positive manner, competition has the potential to bring out the best in a group (see Comment 11.4).

The final form of intergroup interaction depicted in Figure 11.5 is compromise. This form occurs when interaction is moderately important to goal attainment and there is also a moderate degree of goal compatibility between groups. Probably the best example of this form of interaction is that which occurs between unions and management within unionized organizations. It is not crucial for these groups to interact frequently in order for each to achieve their goals. However, there obviously must be a certain degree of interaction in order to produce a collective bargaining agreement and to periodically resolve disputes. With regard to goal compatibility, there is probably what could be described as a modest level. A union's goal of obtaining higher wages and benefits for its membership would appear to be incompatible with an organization's goal of controlling personnel costs. However, a union has a vested interest in an organization's staying in business and, for that reason, may at times compromise on issues. Conversely, an organization may make concessions to a union at times because its employees are needed to produce a product or perform a service for customers.

COMMENT 11.4

THE PROS AND CONS OF INTERGROUP COMPETITION

As with individuals, groups in an organization often find themselves in competition. This is often due to a scarcity of organizational resources, but it may also be due to incompatible goals between the groups. For example, if one work group gains approval from upper management, this often means that others do not. Thus, groups in organizations are often in a position of competing against each other and, typically, are keenly aware of this competition.

Is competition between groups a bad thing? Not necessarily. When groups are competing, this may serve as an important source of motivation to group members. They may work harder, come up with more innovative ideas, and behave more cooperatively toward each other when they are competing with other groups. These types of behaviors, if widely prevalent, have the potential for enhancing organizational effectiveness. There are, however, some negative aspects of intergroup competition. For example, members of competing groups may communicate very little and develop distorted perceptions of each other (Forsyth, 2006). It is also not unusual for groups in competition to actively try to thwart each others' efforts in order to "win."

Can organizations foster some level of intergroup competition, but not let it escalate to destructive levels? This is a difficult question to answer (and one that has not been addressed empirically). The most likely way to accomplish this is by focusing competition primarily on the tasks that groups are performing, rather than on the personalities of individual group members. People should be able to compete without having to dislike each other. Competition can also be more positive when organizations move away from a "winner takes all" mentality. When groups perform better by competing with each other, there may in fact be many "winners." Ultimately, the question really revolves around how organizations manage intergroup competition.

PREDICTORS OF INTERGROUP INTERACTION PATTERNS

Although interactions between groups in organizations are obviously influenced by the goals being pursued, many other factors influence the quality and frequency of inter-group interactions. In the intergroup litera-ture, those factors shown to have the most consistent effects are interdependence, orga-nizational culture, past history, and the social networks that evolve within organiza-tions. Each of these is reviewed in the follow-ing paragraphs.

Interdependence

A relatively consistent theme in reviews of the intergroup literature (see Alderfer & Smith, 1982, and Brett & Rognes, 1986) is that a major factor influencing the interac-tions between groups is interdependence. The degree to which groups depend on each other increases the frequency of interaction and, in some cases, heightens the potential for conflict. There are, however, different forms of interdependence and these may have very different consequences for group interactions. According to Thomas (1976), pooled interdependence exists when groups are relatively independent of each other but their combined outputs contribute to the organization as a whole (see also Mathieu & Day, 1997). A good example of pooled interdependence is the organizational struc-ture of automotive manufacturers such as General Motors. Divisions such as Chevrolet, Buick, and Pontiac operate relatively independent of each other, yet they combine to determine the profitability of the corpo-ration as a whole. To some extent, it is a misnomer to call this arrangement interde-pendence because these divisions run fairly autonomously. Keep in mind, however, that

even when there is pooled interdependence, groups are not completely independent of each other. For example, if the Pontiac Division of General Motors is performing poorly, the other divisions may be negatively impacted.

A second common form of interdepend-ence in organizations is referred to as *sequen-tial interdependence*. In this form, the outputs of one group serve as the inputs to another. In many organizations, a good example of sequential interdependence can be seen when new products are developed. For instance, the market research department may conduct a study and determine that consumers desire a product that the organi-zation currently does not offer. This infor-mation may then be passed on to the research and development department, which is responsible for the actual develop-ment of this new product. Once the new product has been developed and tested, the information from research and development may be passed on to the production engi-neers who will determine how this new product will be manufactured.

Reciprocal interdependence is commonly found among groups in organizations. This form of interdependence involves a series of continuous mutual exchanges among groups. As one might guess, reciprocal interdependence is highly complex and requires the most interaction among groups. In many organizations, reciprocal interdependence commonly exists between groups involved in manufacturing and maintenance. A manufacturing department depends on maintenance to repair equip-ment in order to minimize production delays and machine downtime. Conversely, a maintenance department relies heavily on the cooperation of those on the manufac-turing side when repairs must be made and when preventative maintenance measures are taken. Note that one of the hallmarks of reciprocal interdependence is that there is a relatively equal status among the groups. Thus, with this form of interdependence, it is less likely that one group can gain the upper hand on another. The dependence is mutual.

What determines the type of interdependence that exists between any two groups? One obvious determinant is the nature of the task(s) that different groups are performing. Different tasks, by their very nature, require different levels and forms of interaction between groups. Generally speaking, groups that perform relatively complex tasks will often require higher levels of interaction compared to groups performing simpler tasks. Complex tasks may have greater information requirements that can only be satisfied through interaction with other groups.

Another important determinant of the form of interdependence between groups is organizational structure. As will be shown in Chapter 13, an organization can be structured in a variety of ways, ranging from very hierarchical and bureaucratic to structures that revolve primarily around important organizational projects. Often, when organizations are very formal and there are rigid boundaries around groups, the need and desire for intergroup interaction may be decreased. Hence, groups can operate fairly autonomously. Conversely, when such boundaries are more permeable, a great deal more intergroup interaction may be required, and, consequently, higher levels of interdependence will result.

A final potential determinant of interdependence is the authority system that predominates within an organization. Meyer and Allen (1997) draw a distinction between control and commitment organizations. In control organizations, the primary authority mechanisms center on formal rules and monitoring mechanisms. In such an environment, interdependence may be discouraged because it makes control more difficult. In commitment organizations, much more authority rests with individual employees, and there is less emphasis on formal rules and monitoring. In this type of environment, communication may flow very freely among groups, and there is a great deal more potential for interdependence.

Organizational Culture

Organizational culture essentially represents the set of implicitly shared norms and values that predominate within a given organization (Schein, 1990). With respect to intergroup relations, some organizations may develop cultures that encourage and value positive intergroup interactions. For example, some universities have cultures that encourage and facilitate interdepartmental cooperation. Individuals in such a culture may engage in a great deal of interdisciplinary work without even thinking about it, because it is so ingrained in the culture of the institution. Conversely, in other organizations, the culture may discourage most forms of intergroup interaction. For example, in some universities, the culture makes academic departments very "compartmentalized." Communication with other academic departments is infrequent, and they are viewed with suspicion. In this type of culture, it is doubtful that productive cross-departmental collaboration will occur.

The effects of culture may be particularly salient during the socialization of new employees. The newcomers are informed very quickly about group customs regarding expected behaviors toward other groups. If a new employee mistakenly behaves the wrong way in this regard, he or she is quickly "brought into line" and reminded of the prevailing norms regarding interaction with other groups. Given the power of norms to shape behavior (e.g., Hackman, 1992), such messages will typically have a very important effect on the general quality of intergroup relations.

Past History with Intergroup Relations

Another important factor that influences the quality of relations between pairs of groups is past history. If the members of two groups have generally had positive experiences working together, they are likely to approach future interactions in a positive manner. Conversely, if interactions have been contentious, groups will tend to approach future interactions with a great deal of apprehen-

sion and suspicion. Unfortunately, apprehension and suspicion on the part of one group tend to evoke similar feelings in members of other groups (see Comment 11.5).

Readers may wonder whether the influence of history tends to decay over time as new members, who do not have the "baggage" associated with past interactions, are brought into groups. As noted in Chapter 3, one of the major dimensions of socialization into organizations is being "educated" about the past history of the organization and, in many cases, of the specific work group that a new employee joins (Van Maanen & Schein, 1979). This education often includes a detailed history of events that have involved other organizational groups. Thus, in many cases, new employees are expected to "carry the baggage" associated with past conflicts and adjust their behavior accordingly. Employees who resist such pressures may encounter very negative sanctions

COMMENT 11.5

THE IMPACT OF PAST HISTORY: A NEGLECTED TOPIC

BECAUSE A GREAT deal of research on intergroup behavior has been carried out in laboratory settings, there is very little empirical evidence of the impact of past history on intergroup relations. However, anyone who has joined an established group in an organization would likely attest to the powerful impact that past history has on intergroup relations. As with individuals, groups in organizations often have histories of dealing with each other that may even transcend the tenure of individual group members.

If groups have had a positive history of working together to get things done, interactions will be approached positively by the members of both groups. Furthermore, these positive interactions will likely be mutually reinforcing and the positive relations between

groups will continue. In contrast, when two groups have a negative history, it may be difficult for them to work productively in the future. Members of each group may be taught to view each other with a great deal of suspicion and mistrust. Unfortunately, when people are treated with suspicion and mistrust, this evokes similar feelings and a negative spiral may begin.

Future research is needed on the mechanisms that are involved in communicating the "past history" of intergroup relations to new group members. The greatest need, however, is future research that examines how groups that have negative histories can reverse this negative spiral and develop positive working relations.

from their more experienced coworkers, or, perhaps, may never become fully integrated into the group.

Social Networks in Organizations

When all is said and done, much of the quality of intergroup interaction depends on the nature of the relationships (i.e., the social network) that develop between individual members of groups. To the extent that individual members of a group develop cordial relationships with individual members of another group, this should enhance the quality of intergroup relationships. Evidence of this principle can often be seen in the area of international relations. For example, when leaders of nations get along well and have

rewarding interpersonal relationships, this compatibility often positively influences diplomatic relations (see Comment 11.6).

Although not a great deal of research has linked personal relationships within organizations to the quality of intergroup relations, there is some evidence that the two variables are related. For example, LaBianca, Brass, and Gray (1998) examined the social networks within a large health care facility and found that negative relations among individual members of different groups had an impact on the quality of intergroup relations. When one member of a group had a negative encounter with a member of another group, this negatively impacted the quality of the relations between the two groups. Interestingly, positive social ties between

---

COMMENT 11.6

THE IMPACT OF PERSONAL RELATIONSHIPS ON INTERGROUP RELATIONS

PEOPLE OFTEN THINK of international relations as being governed by highly formal mechanisms such as treaties and collective alliances such as NATO. Such formal mechanisms do exist and do influence the transactions between nations. We also know, however, that international relations are influenced by highly personal relationships that develop between national leaders.

A good example of this is the relationship that ultimately developed between U.S. President George H. W. Bush and Soviet leader Mikhail Gorbachev during the first term of Bush's presidency. Interestingly, the first meeting between these two men, which occurred in 1988 when Bush was president-elect, did not go very well. Despite getting off on the wrong foot initially, Bush and Gorbachev ultimately developed a genuine friendship. Furthermore, the friendship that developed between these two world leaders may have been one of the

reasons that the United States supported Gorbachev, even when it became obvious that he was losing his grip on power. Complementing this strong relationship between Bush and Gorbachev was an equal, if not stronger, relationship between U.S. Secretary of State James Baker and Soviet Foreign Minister Eduard Shevardnadze.

Although events in most organizations are not as dramatic as those that occurred between the United States and the former Soviet Union, it is true that relations between groups in any setting are strongly impacted by the interpersonal relations that develop between group leaders or members. When all is said and done, intergroup relations, like most forms of social behavior, are a "relationship business."

Source: G. H. W. Bush and B. Skowcroft. (1999). *A world transformed.* New York: Knopf.

individuals from different groups had no impact on intergroup relations. These findings suggest that when group members form impressions of other groups, they utilize information that is derived from the direct experience of their own group members. This may be much easier than approaching encounters with other group members objectively and, on that basis, forming an impression of the other group. These findings also suggest that individuals weigh negative information more heavily than positive information in forming their impressions of other groups. One reason for this may simply be that negative information is more distinctive and thus is more "attention getting" than positive information (Fiske, 2004; Taylor, 1991). Another related reason may be that most people generally approach interpersonal interactions in a positive manner. Thus, negative interactions run counter to our expectations and thus receive more weight in the impression-formation process.

INTERGROUP CONFLICT

Even a cursory perusal of the intergroup literature reveals that much of it is focused on conflict between groups. That is not to say that all intergroup encounters are negative. However, as we will see in this section, many conditions surrounding intergroup transactions in organizations greatly increase the potential for relations between groups to be highly contentious. In this section, we focus on the conditions that lead to intergroup conflict, describe the potential effects of intergroup conflict, and finally explore ways to diffuse or reduce it.

Causes of Intergroup Conflict

An impressive program of research in social psychology has shown that groups may be inherently more prone to conflict and competition in comparison to individuals, a finding termed the *interpersonal-intergroup discontinuity effect* (Schopler & Insko, 1992). Studies demonstrating this effect typically use mixed-motive games, where either individuals or groups have to choose between cooperative moves where both parties obtain a small reward, versus competitive moves where one party obtains a large reward and the other party receives nothing. In multiple studies, groups playing the game are more likely to make competitive choices than when individuals are playing against each other (Schopler et al., 2001; Wildschut, Insko, & Gaertner, 2002).

As one might imagine, conflict between groups in organizations may be caused by a number of different factors. Thus, pinning down the causes of conflict to a manageable number is no easy task. However, within organizations, a small number of factors seem to contribute disproportionately to intergroup conflict. These include competition for resources, goal incompatibility, time incompatibility, and contentious influence tactics. Each is discussed briefly in the following paragraphs.

One of the realities of life in most organizations is that resources are scarce. Most organizations cannot provide groups with lavish support in the form of budgets, personnel, or even physical space. As a result, groups are often in the position of competing very hard with each other for these scarce resources. Like any competitive situation, there are often "winners" and "losers" in the resource game. Furthermore, the fact that there are winners and losers in the competition for resources has the potential to create very intense and long-standing conflicts between groups.

To a certain extent, the fact that groups must compete for resources is unavoidable.

If members of groups understand and accept this, conflicts may be kept from escalating to destructive levels. However, another way that organizations can help to prevent such competition from escalating to destructive levels is to make sure that the resource-allocation process is fair (Colquitt et al., 2001). When resource-allocation procedures are fair, groups will not always be pleased with the resources allocated to them; however, at least they will be satisfied with the procedures used to allocate the resources. Ways of doing this may include making sure that all groups have equal access to the resources-allocation process, and that political considerations are minimized as much as possible. However, the reality is that, in most organizations, resources will never be in abundance, and competition for them will always be an issue that organizations must face.

A second common cause of intergroup conflict is goal incompatibility. At the most general level, goal incompatibility exists when the goals of two or more groups are in direct opposition—that is, one group accomplishes its goals at the direct expense of another group's achieving its goals (Brown, Maras, Massar, Vivian, & Hewstone, 2001). For example, in a democratic system of government, the goal of each political party is to assume control over various branches of government, but this can only be done by thwarting the same goal of other political parties. In an organizational setting, a common example of goal incompatibility often exists between marketing and production. The primary goal of the marketing function is to satisfy customers by giving them what they want, when they want it. The production function, however, attempts to achieve efficiency and economies of scale—both of which are tough to do if products are tailored to individual customers and delivered very quickly.

One important point to consider about goal incompatibility is the distinction between real goal incompatibility versus perceived goal incompatibility (Brown et al., 2001). In many instances, such as the one previously described, there are real incompatibilities in the goals of different groups. In many other cases, however, the extent of incompatibility is much more a matter of perception. For example, in colleges and universities, many people believe that educating students and encouraging faculty research are completely incompatible goals. In contrast, a good number of people in higher education believe that educating students and encouraging faculty research may actually be highly compatible goals. It is obviously beyond the scope of this chapter to decide which of these two positions is correct. The more important point is that this, along with many other forms of goal incompatibility, is largely a matter of perceptions and opinions.

A third cause of intergroup conflict, which is actually closely related to goal incompatibility, is time incompatibility. Due to the pursuit of different goals and the performance of different tasks, work groups may work under very different time frames. In a research and development department, for example, current product development projects ultimately may not come to fruition for a decade or longer. As a result, those who work in research and development may take their time and accumulate considerable data before making important decisions.

In contrast to research and development, those whose jobs revolve around the production of products typically work under a much different time frame. Production schedules are typically made in a very short time span, and the major concern is what is happening at the moment rather than what may occur 10 years hence. Because of this short time frame, those in production may need information very quickly and may not have the luxury of taking the time needed to consider every possible alternative before they make a decision.

The issue of time incompatibility is often dealt with by making sure that there is little interdependence between groups that operate under very different time frames. This can be done in a number of ways, but it is most typically accomplished through physical separation. For example, the Xerox research and development center in Palo Alto, California, is credited with groundbreaking advances in computer technology and is located far from the company's East Coast corporate headquarters.

In some cases, it is not possible for organizations to create such "buffer zones" between groups with differing time frames. For example, a sales group must deal frequently with a market research group to gauge customers' needs, or a production group may need crucial information from a research and development group to plan future production processes. Where such groups depend on each other, the potential for conflict is quite evident. Groups that operate on a very short time frame may see the other group as being indecisive and overanalyzing problems. In contrast, groups operating under a long-term perspective may see the other group as reckless and not caring about the quality of the information it is issuing.

Disputes like these are often difficult to resolve because they may have been going on for many years and, in some cases, may even be part of an individual's professional socialization before entering the organization. For example, people trained in production management may be taught to be leery of "R & D types." Conversely, those likely to enter research and development fields may be socialized to assume that those in areas such as marketing do not appreciate the scientific value of their work.

A final factor that may lead to conflict between groups is the use of contentious influence tactics by members of one group toward members of another. The term *contentious influence tactics* simply means trying to influence another individual or other individuals through the use of threats, demands, or other negative methods.

Recall from Chapter 5 that the use of contentious influence tactics is a general determinant of conflict in organizations, and the fact that they may lead to intergroup conflict may come as no surprise.

One obvious reason that contentious influence tactics heighten the potential for intergroup conflict is that they tend to invite retaliation. When someone requests something in a rude or abrasive manner, the natural response of the person on the receiving end is to respond to the request in a rude or abrasive manner, or to simply refuse to comply (Falbe & Yukl, 1992). This can lead to a negative cycle of escalation and, ultimately, bitter conflict. In some cases, status differences may prevent direct retaliation (e.g., a subordinate cannot directly retaliate when a supervisor is rude), but retaliation may occur nonetheless. One of the authors (SMJ) can recall an instance in which a former faculty colleague was very demanding (and, at times, rude) about his clerical work requests. The clerical person assigned to him accepted such requests without being rude, but his clerical requests typically went to "the bottom of the pile" when she was prioritizing her work.

Another reason that such influence tactics lead to intergroup conflict has to do with the social networks that exist in groups (LaBianca et al., 1998). Employees in organizations obviously do not work in a social vacuum. Thus, when a person from one group attempts to influence a member of another group in a contentious manner, this individual will often relay news of a bad experience to members of his or her own group. As a result, some individuals may develop "bad reputations" before ever having any direct contact with members of another group. Unfortunately, when this is the case, the potential for conflict is greatly heightened.

Consequences of Intergroup Conflict

Most organizations would prefer to have different groups work well together because the alternative is unpleasant. However, to merely say that intergroup conflict is "unpleasant" begs the question: What really happens within a group when it is in conflict with another group? Fortunately, a fair amount of social psychological research has examined this very issue, although some of the research has not been conducted in formal organizational settings (e.g., Sherif, 1966).

One thing we know very clearly is that conflict changes group members' perceptions of each other (Roccas & Schwartz, 1993). As one might expect, members of groups in conflict view each other in a negative manner. It is also clear from the intergroup literature that members of groups in conflict tend to adopt an "us versus them" mentality (Castano, Yzerbyt, Paldini, & Sacchi, 2002; Depret & Fiske, 1999). Members of the other group are viewed as being very different, but very similar to each other (e.g., "They're all alike in accounting"). Conversely, members of one's own group are viewed as positive and as having a much greater degree of individuality than the "out-group." Making

this "in-group" versus "out-group" distinction may not actually reflect the complexity of situations, but it is cognitively much easier for the members of groups embroiled in conflict (Linville, Fischer, & Salovey, 1989).

Another thing that typically happens when groups are in conflict is that, within groups, members often become more cohesive—that is, when groups see a threat from an outside group, they may pull together and become highly cohesive (Castano et al., 2002). A good example of this is the intense social bond that often develops between soldiers who are involved in combat. It is not unusual for such individuals to develop friendships that far outlast their military service (see Siebold, 2006). This "common enemy" effect also occurs in organizations; the members of a group band together when faced with an outside threat.

Beyond the perceptual changes that have been discussed to this point, intergroup conflict may also have tangible negative effects in organizations. If groups are completely independent and have little need to interact, conflict will have little tangible impact other than perhaps a bit of discomfort here and there. However, in most organizations, it is unlikely that any one group could be completely independent of other groups. Thus, in most cases where there is intergroup conflict, the groups involved in such conflict must interact. What, then, does intergroup conflict do to the quality of intergroup interactions?

One point most of us know from experience is that when two groups are embroiled in a conflict, the interaction between members of these groups is certainly strained and often unpleasant. Because of this, members of groups in conflict may actively try to avoid each other, even if they are highly interdependent. The quality of work may then be compromised. For example, it is not unusual for students in universities to ask faculty from more than one academic department to serve on thesis or dissertation committees. If different academic departments represented in a committee are in conflict, this may greatly decrease the communication between faculty and ultimately make it more difficult for students. Put differently, the student may be caught in the middle of such a conflict.

The other outcome that may occur when groups are in conflict is that members of each group may go out of their way to make things as difficult as possible for the other group. Phone calls from members of the other group may be returned late, or requests for information may be ignored. The most troubling aspect of this is that contentious behavior tends to breed contentious behavior. As a result, groups (like individuals) may get caught up in a vicious cycle of conflict that is difficult to break. Thus, the conflict may take on a life of its own, often to the detriment of customers or the quality of the work in general.

Another troubling aspect of intergroup conflict is that groups often pass on these conflicts to newcomers. That is, when a new member enters a group, he or she is "educated" about the history of the conflict and is expected to adjust his or her behavior accordingly. If the newcomer is seen fraternizing with members of the "other" group, or expresses positive views toward them, his or her own group members may react very sternly in order to bring the newcomer "back into line." In very extreme cases, a newcomer who refuses to embrace the group's conflicts and act accordingly may be forced to leave the group or may do so voluntarily.

A final problem caused by intergroup conflict is that, when groups are in conflict with each other, their goals focus primarily inward and less toward the organization as a whole (Sherif, 1966). Put differently, what happens in the group may become more important than what happens in the organization as a whole. This may not be a problem if the goals of a group are perfectly aligned with the goals of the organization. However, it could be a major problem if the goals of a group are unrelated to or are in conflict with the major goals of the organization. For example, a group that has a primary goal of maintaining intergroup harmony and stability may be a liability to an organization that places a strong emphasis on quickly adapting to change in the environment.

IMPROVING THE QUALITY OF INTERGROUP RELATIONS

Given the potentially dysfunctional effects of intergroup conflict, organizations have a vested interest in keeping it to a manageable level. In fact, organizations would ideally like to create conditions that foster positive intergroup relations so that destructive conflicts do not occur in the first place. In this section, we examine some of the most commonly used methods for improving intergroup relations. These include superordinate goals, negotiation, group member exchanges, intergroup team development, and, finally, decreasing the interdependence among groups.

Superordinate Goals

One of the dangers of intergroup conflict is that groups will focus inward and become more focused on their own goals than on those of the organization as a whole. Thus, one way of improving relations between groups is to introduce *superordinate goals*— goals that both groups endorse and that often require cooperative intergroup behavior to be achieved. The notion of superordinate goals comes from the Robbers Cave study, which was conducted over 40 years ago by Muzafer and Carol Sherif and their colleagues at the University of Oklahoma (Sherif, Harvey, White, Hood, & Sherif, 1961). In this study, groups of boys believed they were participating in a summer camp at Robbers Cave in Oklahoma, but they were actually participating in a study of intergroup conflict. The researchers assigned these boys to two groups and created all the conditions that would likely foster intergroup conflict. For example, the two groups had different names ("Eagles" and "Rattlers"), were physically separated, and competed against each other in a variety of athletic contests. These manipulations were largely successful at creating a good deal of intergroup conflict.

After creating this state of intergroup conflict, the researchers then set about testing various methods of reducing it. One approach, which was largely unsuccessful, was simply to get the two groups together for a meal. The groups' reaction to this intervention was rather messy: They engaged in a food fight! This finding has also been supported in subsequent research (e.g., Brown, Condor, Matthews, Wade, & Williams, 1986) and thus suggests that simply getting groups together will not diffuse conflict.

The other approach employed by the researchers, however, met with much greater success. They staged a series of "incidents" that required the cooperation of both groups in order to solve a problem. For example, when both groups were being transported to a certain area of the camp, the bus they were riding in broke down and required the combined efforts of both groups to fix it. The groups were also forced to cooperate to fix a staged plumbing problem in the cabin in which they both ate. In both incidents, the groups were forced to work together to solve a problem that negatively impacted both groups.

What lessons can organizations learn about managing intergroup conflict from groups of boys at a summer camp? One is that simply getting conflicting groups to interact with each other will probably not reduce the conflict. In fact, the findings from the Robbers Cave study, and subsequent research, suggest that such efforts may actually intensify conflicts (although it's unlikely, in organizations, that food fights would break out!). The more practical implication, for example, is that simply locating conflicting groups in close physical proximity will probably not successfully diffuse conflicts (Allport, 1954).

The other important lesson from this study is that conflict can be reduced if members of groups must cooperate in order to achieve superordinate goals. Thus, for example, if two groups must cooperate to produce a product or prepare an important report, this may go a long way toward diffusing conflict. Furthermore, what makes this very feasible in organizational settings is that opportunities to introduce superordinate goals typically abound. For example, an organization can always point out the fact that the "superordinate goal" is the success of the organization.

It is also possible in many organizations to evoke the concept of superordinate goals through the introduction of a "common enemy" that the groups must band together to fight. In professional sports, coaches often build team unity by focusing on opponents or, in some cases, on criticism of the team by the news media. In organizations, this "common enemy" approach could obviously target a competitor, but could also focus on the poor economic environment, or perhaps on government regulators. Organizations, however, need to be careful in using this approach. If an organization becomes too internally focused and adopts an extreme "us versus them" mentality, important external cues may be missed, which may ultimately reduce the effectiveness of the organization as a whole.

Negotiation

In any type of conflict, one of the problems is that the parties involved avoid each other and, as a result, do not communicate. The irony, of course, is that conflicts can often be resolved if the parties sit down and communicate rationally about their differences. One way of doing this is through some form of negotiation, typically between the leaders of the groups in conflict (Brett & Rognes, 1986).

Negotiation involves a discussion of the issues causing conflict between the groups and, ultimately, a resolution of those issues in a manner that is acceptable to both groups. Why is negotiation a potential mechanism for reducing intergroup conflict? First, negotiation facilitates communication. Negotiation is a bilateral influence technique; it involves a mutual exchange between parties (Kipnis, 1984). During this mutual exchange, it is possible for misunderstandings and misperceptions to be corrected.

Another reason that negotiation can be successful is that it is generally seen as a fair method of dispute resolution, especially when all parties abide by the resolution (Fiske, 2004). Often, when groups are in conflict in organizations, the managers of the conflicting groups will make their cases to someone at a higher level, and a decision will be made that favors one group or the other. In another common way of handling disputes between groups, a higher-level manager serves as a mediator, much in the way mediators help to resolve labor disputes. In the first method, the dispute is resolved but there is often a "winner" and a "loser." Thus, members of one of the two groups involved in the dispute may feel that they have been treated unfairly. In the second scenario, where a higher-level manager mediates disputes, the problem that caused the dispute may never be resolved. There is also a chance, in this scenario, that a higher-level manager may favor one group over the other and effectively "force" a resolution that is unfavorable to one of the groups.

Although negotiation can be used effectively to resolve intergroup disputes, not all forms of negotiation are equally effective. Fischer and Ury (1981) coined the term *principled negotiation* to refer to a style of negotiating whereby parties strive to achieve resolution to problems, rather than to stake out positions. This "problem-solving" approach to negotiating is likely to result in creative resolutions to problems that may in fact be quite palatable to both groups. In contrast, when groups in conflict approach a negotiation with a mentality that states "This is my position, and I'm not going to compromise," they are doing little to resolve the dispute and may even be heightening the conflict. Unfortunately, according to Brett and Rognes (1986), many managers of groups are not trained in principled negotiation techniques and may lack more general negotiation skills. Thus, organizations that want to encourage managers to resolve intergroup conflict through negotiation should provide managers with training in negotiation.

Member Exchanges

As we've seen, one of the things that happens when groups are in conflict is that group members distort their perceptions. Members of their own group are seen positively, and members of the other group are seen negatively (Tajfel, 1981). One way to combat such biased perceptions is for groups to periodically engage in member exchanges: For a stated period of time, members of the conflicting groups will switch and reverse roles. This type of intervention may initially be uncomfortable for those working in the "enemy camp," but it can also be very instrumental in reducing intergroup conflict. As an example, at a university where one of the authors (SMJ) once worked, there was a program whereby faculty could become "administrative interns" for 1 year. These individuals essentially worked as administrators for 1 year, although they were still responsible for a small portion of their other faculty duties. The program was designed primarily for faculty considering administrative careers, but it also helped to educate the faculty "interns" about some of the challenges faced by administrators. Although not a member-exchange program, per se, it did help the participants to increase their understanding and therefore may have had the effect of reducing conflict between faculty and the university's administration.

There are obviously some situations in which member exchanges cannot occur. If the tasks performed by groups require vastly different skills, or if large geographic differences exist, exchanges may be impractical. There may also be some cases where conflict is so bad that the individual being exchanged may have a very difficult time or may even be harassed. However, when they are possible, member exchanges can be an excellent way of correcting misperceptions and, ultimately, diffusing conflict.

Intergroup Team Development

Team development (an approach discussed in more detail in Chapter 12) is an intervention that has been used to improve performance within groups. Team-development approaches have also been designed to facilitate or improve relations between different groups (Dyer, 1987; French & Bell, 1995). Team development will also be described in greater detail in Chapter 16, but two specific intergroup team-development interventions are relevant here.

One intervention, which was developed by Blake, Shephard, and Mouton (1964), is a structured way of highlighting possible areas of misperception and encouraging groups to work through their misperceptions. Figure 11.6 provides a summary of the basic steps involved in this intervention. The first step is to have the members of both groups generate two lists. The first list is designed to reflect how each group views the other group. This includes perceptions of the other group, what the other group does that "gets in our way," and so on. The second list reflects each group's prediction of what the other group will say about them; that is, each group is trying to anticipate what the other group dislikes about them, or how they are perceived.

FIGURE 11.6

Summary of the Steps Involved in a Typical Intergroup Team Development Intervention

After each group generates these two lists separately, they reconvene to "compare notes" on their perceptions. This can be a quite revealing exercise because it highlights important issues and problems that are preventing the groups from working together, and it can serve as the basis for concrete actions designed to improve relations between the groups. As an example, let's say that the members of one group see the other group as unresponsive and unwilling to provide service to them, and the other group has similar perceptions. Discussing these perceptions may allow both groups to develop a greater understanding of the pressures faced by the other group. It may also lead to concrete action plans designed to improve the situation.

A variation of this intervention, the *organizational mirror technique*, can also be used very effectively for correcting the misperceptions of conflicting groups. With this technique, one group forms a circle around the perimeter of the other group. The group "inside the fishbowl" is instructed to discuss its self-perceptions and its perceptions of the other group. During this time, the group observing is instructed not to interrupt, even if they feel that the perceptions of the group are not correct. The groups then may reverse roles; the group seeking feedback may discuss what they have heard and may possibly seek clarification. Following this step, the groups reconvene and ultimately generate a master list of action plans for improving the relations between the two groups.

As with the previous intervention, the organizational mirror may provide unique opportunities for members of groups in conflict to correct misperceptions and resolve misunderstandings. The advantages of the organizational mirror technique, however, are that it may be less time consuming and

more adaptable. A consultant may be able to employ this technique at several points during a day-long intergroup team-development intervention. A potential disadvantage of the fishbowl technique is that it is potentially very confrontational. Therefore, this method should only be used in conjunction with a consultant who is well trained in group facilitation and conflict management. The technique probably should not be used when groups are embroiled in highly intense, personalized conflicts.

Reducing the Need for Intergroup Interaction

Despite well-intentioned efforts to improve intergroup relations, there may be times when groups simply cannot work well together. This may be due to irreconcilable personality conflicts or the nature of the work that groups perform being too different. One way of dealing with intergroup conflict is creating conditions in which two groups have little or no need to interact. This can generally be done in one of two ways. The first approach is to change the structure of an organization, or the flow of work, so that the level of interdependence between two groups is greatly reduced. A way of doing this is to create a "coordinating group" to manage the interactions between groups. In this type of structure, each group needs to communicate only with the coordinating group. This eliminates the need to interact with the other group. To decrease interdependence, organizations frequently *outsource* products or services that are currently being performed internally. The auto industry has relied heavily on outsourcing for many of the parts that they used to produce internally. This has proved to be cost effective and undoubtedly has reduced the level of interdependence among internal groups.

A second general way to reduce interdependence among groups, particularly in sequential production systems, is to build some level of "slack" into the system. If one group supplies parts to a second group, for example, maintaining a reserve inventory of these parts will decrease the interdependence of the groups. Creating slack resources of this type results in somewhat less sequential interdependence. This decrease in interdependence may ultimately decrease tensions between the two groups, because one is not so dependent on the other.

The Resource-Allocation Process

A final way that organizations can potentially reduce conflict between groups is through the resource-allocation process. As was noted earlier in the chapter, a very common cause of intergroup conflict is that groups are often in competition for scarce organizational resources. Thus, one way to reduce conflict is to reexamine the resource-allocation process to make sure that groups have the resources they need to be effective.

At first glance, the suggestion that organizations "give groups more resources" may seem to be a rather simplistic and naïve way of decreasing intergroup conflict. After all, the vast majority of organizations operate under conditions whereby resources are scarce. This may be true, but organizations do have control over where those scarce resources are allocated and the process by which resource-allocation decisions are made. Thus, organizations can choose to allocate resources in a manner that is commensurate with group needs, or they can do so on the basis of political gamesmanship and "back-room dealing." Similarly, organizations can make the choice to allocate resources in a fair, rational manner, or they can do so in a highly secretive, clandestine fashion.

When organizations allocate resources in a fair, rational, and open manner, this will not necessarily eliminate the problem of resource scarcity. However, based on what is known about procedural justice (e.g., Folger & Cropanzano, 1998), it is certainly possible that even when groups come up short on resources, they will still see the resource-allocation process as fair. Another more general benefit of fair resource-allocation procedures is that these may simply foster a more positive organizational climate. When people feel they are being treated fairly by the organization, this will tend to foster a climate of openness and trust as opposed to mistrust and paranoia. Such a climate certainly does not guarantee positive intergroup relations, but it certainly makes them more likely.

CHAPTER SUMMARY

The purpose of this chapter was to provide an overview of group dynamics of behavior by drawing on contributions from both social and organizational psychology. We began by examining the defining characteristics of a group. Despite the numerous definitions proposed over the years, most maintain that the key features are interdependence, interaction, perception of being a group, and some commonality of purpose among group members.

Group structure represents a number of dimensions that can be described. The most common dimensions of group structure include roles, norms, values, status differentials, and communication patterns. Group members' behaviors come to be differentiated; normative behavior patterns develop; behaviors that are consistent with certain values are emphasized; status hierarchies emerge; and, finally, consistent modes of communication are adopted.

DONELSON FORSYTH AND THE DYNAMICS OF GROUPS

My interest in groups and their processes can be traced—as it should be—to the many influential groups that I have joined over the years. Some of these groups, such as high school cliques that sharply differentiated between those thought to have social value and those considered unworthy, teams that failed miserably or succeeded unexpectedly, peer groups that contributed to my delinquency more than my rectitude, and work groups that rarely did any work, piqued my interest in social, rather than purely psychological, causes of behavior. Growing up in an American society that stressed the values of individualism and self-reliance over team-work and interdependence, I wondered how people manage to combine their individual motivations and actions in the pursuit of shared goals.

I continue to be intrigued by all aspects of groups and interpersonal relations: why networks of relationships form; how groups sustain their members; when people conform to the standards set by others; why and when groups perform to their full potential or fall short of their goals and fail; how leaders can motivate those around them. When I examine any one of these topics, I often find that group-level processes offer members the means to reach goals that would have eluded them as individuals. Yet, my own experiences in groups—and the research data as well—remind us that many groups fail to reach their goals; for every high performing team we find ones that blunder through their tasks and never search for ways to improve. As I'm obsessed with avoiding failure on a personal level, and have therefore found many ways to bolster my sense of self-worth each time I do misstep, I continue to be intrigued by the intricacies of responsibility allocation in groups. In a number of studies I have examined how people working in groups react to group-level setbacks and failures as well as achievements and successes. That research suggests that groups provide members with the perfect habitat to mask their own inadequacies, for rarely is a single member of a group held responsible for any group's failure. Whereas the lone worker who performs poorly will be easily evaluated as inadequate, when submerged in a group the loafing, distracted, or the incompetent member may escape detection—except when appraisals are provided by co-workers whose own outcomes are undermined by an inferior other. Moreover, because the relative contributions of each person to a group activity are difficult to pinpoint precisely, the group microcosm provides members with the opportunity to take more credit for their group's work than they actually deserve. Hence, when I total the responsibility claims of each member of a group, I usually find that members feel they are more responsible than the average other group member—particularly if they are the leader of the group.

These findings suggest that groups in organizational settings, to maximize their productivity, should monitor their responsibility allocation mechanisms, but they also suggest that the natural tendency for individuals to use the group context to maximize or minimize their personal responsibility may be functional: Some undertakings may seem so risky that people would not undertake them if they knew they would bear the brunt of the blame should they fail, and individuals may be less motivated to expend effort in pursuit of shared goals if they could not take a bit of extra credit when the group succeeds.

Donelson R. Forsyth
Jepson School of Leadership Studies
University of Richmond

A number of models have been developed to describe the manner in which groups develop over time. The best known of these is Tuckman's (1965) model, which is based on the issues that must be dealt with at various points in the life of a group. Moreland and Levine's (1982) model approaches group development from the perspective of the socialization of new group members. Gersick's (1988) Punctuated Equilibrium Model focuses specifically on task groups. Each of these provides somewhat different and unique insights into group development.

After discussing within-group dynamics and behavior, we then examined a relatively neglected topic in the group literature: intergroup relations. In most organizations groups must work together collaboratively to accomplish many important tasks. We discussed the various types of interactions that may occur between groups, ranging from avoidance to collaboration depending on the compatibility of goals and the level of interdependence that exists between two groups. Other factors that determine the nature of intergroup interactions include the type of interdependence, task-related demands, the culture of the organization, past events that have transpired between groups, and the nature of the individuals that comprise each of the groups.

Given that different groups in organizations may have different goals, operate on different time frames, and employ different types of people, the potential for intergroup conflict is often high. Thus, it is not surprising that a great deal of the intergroup literature has focused on conflict. Conflict between groups—due to biases in perceptions and a tendency to adopt an "us versus them" mentality—clearly has a negative impact on relations between groups. While negative in and of themselves, biases may ultimately have a negative impact on organizational effectiveness. Thus, organizations have a vested interest in keeping intergroup conflict at manageable levels.

From the social psychological literature, a method that has been shown to reduce intergroup conflict is the adoption of *superordinate goals*. These are goals that transcend the interests of individual groups and often require collaborative efforts in order to achieve them. Among other methods of reducing intergroup conflict, the chapter discussed member exchanges, intergroup team-development interventions, decreasing interdependence among groups, and improvement of the resource-allocation process. Given the realities of organizational life, it is doubtful that intergroup conflict can ever be completely eliminated. However, it is certainly possible for organizations to keep it to manageable levels.

SUGGESTED ADDITIONAL READINGS

Brett, J. M., Goldberg, S. B., & Ury, W. L. (1990). Designing systems for resolving disputes in organizations. *American Psychologist, 45,* 162–170.

Forsyth, D. R. (2006). *Group dynamics* (4th Ed.). Belmont, CA: Wadsworth/Thompson.

Johnson, D. W., & Johnson, F. P. (2000). *Joining together: Group theory and group skills* (7th ed.). Boston: Allyn and Bacon.

Levine, J. M., & Moreland, R. L. (1998). Small groups. In D. T. Gilbert, S. T. Fiske, & G. Lindzey (Eds.), *The handbook of social psychology* (Vol. 2, pp. 415–469). New York: McGraw-Hill.

Nelson, R. E. (1989). The strength of strong ties: Social networks and intergroup conflict in organizations. *Academy of Management Journal, 32,* 377–401.

Chapter Twelve

Team Effectiveness

In Chapter 11, we provided an overview of research on group and intergroup behavior, focusing primarily on how groups come to exist and develop and how they get along with each other. These are certainly important processes in organizations. Thus, the field of organizational psychology has benefited greatly from the work of social psychologists who were the early pioneers of group dynamics research. However, two characteristics of early social psychological group dynamics research place limitations on its usefulness to organizational psychologists. First, very little social psychological group dynamics research directly examined the determinants of group effectiveness. Rather, the dependent variables examined in this research have typically been attributes of individuals rather than of performance groups. Research that directly examines team effectiveness is inherently more useful to organizational psychologists.

Second, the overwhelming majority of social psychological group studies have been conducted in laboratory settings. As was pointed out in Chapter 2, organizational phenomena are often replicated quite well in laboratory settings; thus, generalizability is often robust (Locke, 1986). Team effectiveness, however, may be one organizational variable for which generalizing from laboratory to field settings may be problematic because the environmental context in which a team performs is an important key to understanding team effectiveness. In laboratory settings, groups are formed randomly, and they perform tasks in relatively standardized settings. In fact, proper exper-

imental methodology dictates that the environmental conditions under which different groups perform must be as similar as possible (Cook & Campbell, 1979).

In real organizations, however, there are important differences in the environmental context in which various teams perform. For example, even within the same organization, there are important differences among work teams in staffing levels, the manner in which rewards are distributed, the way leaders set goals with team members, and the way teams interface with other teams. Also, in real organizations, members often have known each other prior to their present team assignments, and those prior relationships may promote collegiality or lead to conflict. These contextual factors are difficult to simulate in laboratory research, yet there is little denying that they influence the effectiveness of teams.

Due to the importance of organizational context, what has been described as an *organizational psychology* team literature has developed relatively recently. In fact, many have come to the conclusion that when it comes to the study of team effectiveness, "the torch has been passed" from social to organizational psychology. Levine and Moreland (1990)—who, incidentally, are both social psychologists—make the point by stating: "Despite all the excellent research on small groups within social psychology, that discipline has already lost its dominance in this field. The torch has effectively been passed to (or, more accurately, picked up by) colleagues in other disciplines, particularly organizational psychology. They have no doubts about the importance of small groups and are often in the forefront of group research. So, rather than lamenting the decline of interest in group, we should all be celebrating the resurgence, albeit in a different locale" (p. 620). This point has also been made by other researchers (see Ilgen, Hollenbeck, Johnson, & Jundt, 2005).

The purpose of this chapter is to discuss the voluminous amount of recent work, primarily by organizational psychologists, on the factors that contribute to team effectiveness. We purposefully use the term *team* rather than *group* because so much of the work done by organizational psychologists uses teams within organizations performing their normal work or being placed in realistic simulations to provide a more controlled assessment of team dynamics and performance. Kozlowski and Bell (2003) provide a detailed definition of what constitutes a team. They define *work teams* as "composed of two or more individuals who (a) exist to perform organizationally relevant tasks, (b) share one or more common goals, (c) interact socially, (d) exhibit task interdependencies, (e) maintain and manage boundaries, and (f) are embedded in an organizational context that sets boundaries, constrains the team, and influences exchanges with other units in the broader entity" (p. 334).

We begin the chapter by examining a basic question: What constitutes team effectiveness? The focus then shifts to examining several influential models of team effectiveness. These models have helped to guide much of the organizational research on team effectiveness and have served as a foundation for many organizational efforts to improve the performance of teams.

Across these models, several variables seem to pop up repeatedly as determinants of team effectiveness. These include team composition, task design, organizational resources, organizational rewards, team goals, and team processes (e.g., shared mental models, transactive memory). Each of these will be examined individually, and some of the most common methods organizations use to improve the performance of teams will be described. The chapter concludes with a brief discussion of the role that teams are likely to play in organizations in the future.

DEFINING TEAM EFFECTIVENESS

To say that teams now represent an important part of organizational life is certainly an understatement. Nearly all organizations use small teams to accomplish at least some tasks, and it has become increasingly popular for small teams to be the basic foundations upon which organizations are built (Guzzo & Shea, 1992; Kozlowski & Bell, 2003; Peters & Waterman, 1982).

Despite the importance of team effectiveness, it is not necessarily easy to define what is meant by an *effective* team. Steiner (1972) proposed one of the earliest theoretical propositions bearing on team effectiveness:

Actual productivity = Potential productivity − Process losses

The potential productivity of a team represents the highest level of performance that is attainable by a team. Consider the following example. If each of the five starting players on a basketball team is capable of scoring 20 points per game, those players collectively should be able to score at least 100 points per game. The term *process losses* represents less-than-optimal ways of combining the inputs of team members into a team product. Process losses generally occur because of a lack of coordination among team members, or because the motivation of individuals may change when they are performing in a team setting (Latane, Williams, & Harkins, 1979). The team previously described may not reach its scoring *potential* because the styles of the individual players do not mesh well, or because individual players may not feel a great deal of personal responsibility for the team's performance and, as a result, may reduce their effort.

Steiner's (1972) basic model is certainly useful in helping us to understand, in a very general sense, what determines team performance, but it also has some serious limitations. The most serious flaw is that this model doesn't specify which aspect(s) of the team, or the organizational context, can be used to enhance the coordination of team members or to prevent process losses. The other problem with this model is that it is based on the rather naïve assumption that organizational goals and team goals are perfectly aligned (Hackman, 1992). For example, if a team's goal is to produce a high-quality product, and the organization's goal is for the team to produce a large quantity, the team may appear to suffer from process loss, but in fact it may be quite successful; the team is simply succeeding on its own terms.

The definition of *team effectiveness* that has been used most often by researchers was put forth by Hackman (1987) in a comprehensive review of the work-team design literature. According to Hackman, team effectiveness is a multidimensional construct consisting of three interrelated dimensions. The first of these dimensions is related to the output of the team, the second has to do with the long-term viability of the team as a performing unit, and the third has to do with the impact of the team experience on individual team members. Each of these will be discussed in the following paragraphs.

The vast majority of teams in organizations are formed to fulfill some specific charge or purpose; that is, they are formed to do something. For example, a top management team may be formed to create a long-range strategic plan, a surgical team may be assembled to perform a delicate cardiac bypass operation, and a rescue team may be formed to evacuate hurricane victims from their homes. Thus, one way to measure the effectiveness of a team is to judge whether its *output* is satisfactory. As Hackman (1987) states, for a team to be judged successful, "The productive output of the work team should meet or exceed the performance standards of the people who receive and/or review the output" (p. 323). In the previous examples, the top management team would hardly be considered a success if it failed to produce a viable strategic plan, the surgical team would be unsuccessful if the patient's arteries remain blocked, and the rescue team would be unsuccessful if the hurricane victims are not evacuated. Task accomplishment is thus an important component of team effectiveness.

Vince Lombardi, the legendary football coach of the Green Bay Packers, told his team: "Winning isn't everything, it's the only thing." In many organizations, a variant of this attitude prevails in that the quality of a team's output is seen as the only indicator of its effectiveness. According to Hackman (1987), a second indication of the effectiveness of a team is whether the social processes used in performing the task maintain or enhance the capability of the team members to work together in the future. In some cases, teams accomplish their assigned tasks, but they do so in such a contentious manner that they are incapable of working together in the future. According to Hackman, a team would hardly be considered effective if it essentially burns itself up while performing its assigned task, even if that task is performed successfully. In some cases, a team comes together only once to perform a task (e.g., a search committee is selecting a new college president). In most organizations, however, this is more the exception than the rule.

Working as part of a team can be an extremely rewarding experience. Often, a great deal of satisfaction goes with collective accomplishment, and the social relationships that often develop in teams can be extremely rewarding. Unfortunately, there is also a downside to working in teams. Depending on others to get things done can be extremely frustrating, high-performing individuals may not receive their full share of the credit for a team's performance, and relationships with other team members may go sour. According to Hackman (1987), if the experiences of team members are largely negative and frustrating, this is an indication that the team is unsuccessful. Thus, the third

dimension of team effectiveness is team member satisfaction. This is really related to the second point about viability, but goes somewhat further. Specifically, those who are largely negative about teamwork may be loath to work in any team within the organization in the future. When a team performs its task well, while completely ignoring the needs of team members, it can hardly be considered effective (see Comment 12.1).

MODELS OF TEAM EFFECTIVENESS

As with many of the topics covered in this book, there have been a number of attempts to model the factors that contribute to team effectiveness. Like any theoretical models, the models of team effectiveness are incomplete; that is, they do not include every possible factor that contributes to team effectiveness. They are useful, however, in highlighting the general factors that differentiate successful and unsuccessful teams. They also help us to understand the processes by which these general factors work together to influence team effectiveness. This aids in organizing research findings and may also guide organizational efforts toward improving the performance of teams. In this section, we examine five of the most influential models in the team-effectiveness literature.

McGrath's (1964) Model

McGrath (1964) proposed that team effectiveness is determined by a basic input–process–output sequence; that is, certain inputs lead to differences in team process, which eventually lead to differences in team output. This basic idea is expanded in Figure 12.1 as a model of team effectiveness. Notice that McGrath included Individual-

COMMENT 12.1

WINNING ISN'T EVERYTHING: A BROADER VIEW OF GROUP EFFECTIVENESS

DESCRIBING HACKMAN'S (1987) multidimensional view of group effectiveness frequently generates a great deal of discussion and, at times, vigorous debate. Typically, these discussions center around one question: "If a group performs its task well, does it really matter if people can work together in the future, or whether they have enjoyed working as part of the group?" After all, most organizations exist primarily to make a profit, not to provide psychological gratification to their employees.

This point of view is certainly compelling, but it is also rather shortsighted, and it ignores some of the realities of organizational life. There may be crisis situations in which individuals must come together, perform very quickly, and disband immediately after their task is finished. For example, an international crisis may require that a number of national security officials come together to decide whether military intervention is warranted. In such a case, one could argue that making the correct decision is far more important than the satisfaction of the group members or the viability of the group.

In most organizations, however, group membership is more stable; thus, long-term viability and member satisfaction are important issues. Groups that repeatedly accomplish their primary tasks, but create a great deal of dissatisfaction among their members, often cannot survive over the long haul. Furthermore, when employees have bad experiences in a work group, these incidents will often carry over to other situations. The employees may even be reluctant to work in groups in the future. Thus, a group leader who is concerned about the psychological needs of the group members may appear to be compromising task performance, at least in the short term. Ultimately, though, groups under this type of direction are often much more successful than those governed by a "win-at-all-costs" philosophy.

Source: J. R. Hackman. (1987). The design of work teams. In J. W. Lorsch (Ed.), *Handbook of organizational behavior* (pp. 315–342). Englewood Cliffs, NJ: Prentice-Hall.

Level Factors, Team-Level Factors, and Environment-Level Factors in the input column. Individual-Level Factors include characteristics of team members that may have an impact on team effectiveness, such as their level and mix of skills, attitudes, and personality characteristics.

Team-Level Factors are essentially structural properties of teams themselves. These may include elements of team structure (e.g., roles, authority structure, norms), the level of cohesiveness within the team, and the number of individuals within the team. McGrath (1964) emphasized that all teams are not created equal, and some are designed in a more optimal fashion than others. Thus, some teams are more "primed" for success than others.

Environment-Level Factors represent aspects of the organizational context under which the team works. Perhaps the most important of these is the task that the team is performing. The nature of the task will dictate, to a large degree, the most appropriate strategies to be used by the team. The task may also be important for motivational reasons. One of the problems inherent in teamwork is *social loafing*, where team members

FIGURE 12.1
McGrath's Model of Group Effectiveness

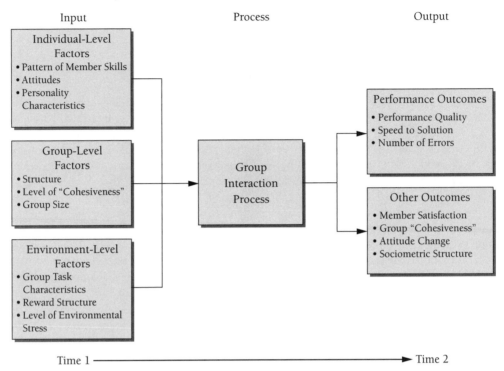

Input   Process   Output

Individual-Level Factors
• Pattern of Member Skills
• Attitudes
• Personality Characteristics

Group-Level Factors
• Structure
• Level of "Cohesiveness"
• Group Size

Environment-Level Factors
• Group Task Characteristics
• Reward Structure
• Level of Environmental Stress

Group Interaction Process

Performance Outcomes
• Performance Quality
• Speed to Solution
• Number of Errors

Other Outcomes
• Member Satisfaction
• Group "Cohesiveness"
• Attitude Change
• Sociometric Structure

Time 1 ⟶ Time 2

Adapted from: J. E. McGrath. (1964). Social psychology: *A brief introduction.* New York: Holt. Reprinted by permission of the author.

do not exert as much effort in a group as they would alone (Latane et al., 1979). Social loafing is probably less likely to occur when a team is performing a complex and stimulating task. More will be said about task characteristics later in the chapter.

Two other important aspects of the environment are the Reward Structure and the level of Environmental Stress under which the team performs. Rewards are important in shaping individual performance, so it makes sense that they would also be a determinant of team performance as well. The most important consideration is whether the performance of the team is rewarded, rather than simply the performance of individual team members. The level of environmental

stress may be determined by a number of factors, such as the criticality of work the team is performing and the time pressure under which it must be performed. A high level of environmental stress may lead to problems in a team's decision-making processes (e.g., Janis, 1982) or to conflicts surrounding the distribution of authority within the team (e.g., Driskell & Salas, 1991). Furthermore, individuals become less effective team members when under environmental stressors such as heavy workload or time pressure (Driskell, Salas, & Johnston, 1999).

Given all of these input factors, the model proposes that they combine to determine Team Interaction Process, which represents the manner in which a team performs its task. Obviously, this may cover a good deal of territory, but the most crucial aspects of the team process are likely to be things such as the performance strategies adopted by the team, the level of interpersonal harmony within the team, and the ability of the team to have a shared understanding of the task and coordinate the necessary responses (Salas, Sims, & Burke, 2005). Recent research on team effectiveness has emphasized the importance of team processes for team effectiveness. These processes will be detailed as we describe other models and determinants of team effectiveness.

McGrath's model then proposes that Team Interaction Process will have a direct effect on the output of teams. The *Output* of a team can be viewed in two ways. First and foremost, a team's output can be viewed in terms of the level of performance. This would include factors such as the judged quality of the team's output, the time it takes for the team to make a decision or develop a solution to a problem, or, possibly, the number of errors that are made in performing the task. The category titled *Other Outcomes* represents social aspects of the team experience, such as the satisfaction of team members, the level of cohesiveness within the team after the task is performed, the attitudes of team members, and, finally, the pattern of relationships following the team's performance. Although these do not represent team performance per se (Hackman [1987] would later argue that they are part of it), they are still important outcomes.

It is difficult to overemphasize the impact that McGrath's model had on team research. Ilgen et al., (2005) recently noted that most team research has been either explicitly or implicitly guided by the input–process–outcome model. The likely reason for the success of the model is its breadth and simplicity. Most of the factors influencing teams

can be categorized either as Inputs, Processes, or Outcomes. However, other organizational researchers have attempted to add to these basic concepts, including additional components in the prediction of team effectiveness.

Gladstein's (1984) Model

Gladstein (1984) proposed a model of team effectiveness that, in many ways, is quite similar to McGrath's (1964). As can be seen in Figure 12.2, this model follows the same general input–process–output sequence. The inputs in this model are also very similar to those proposed by McGrath. Notice that, at the team level, these include characteristics of individual team members as well as elements of team structure. At the organizational level, however, the model differs somewhat from McGrath's. The critical factors proposed by Gladstein include the resources available to teams (training and technical consultation are available to teams and to the markets of customers they serve) as well as aspects of organizational structure (rewards and supervisory control).

Gladstein (1984) proposed that all of these inputs contribute directly to the team process. The critical elements of the team process include communication, level of support, handling of conflict, discussion of performance strategies, weighing of individuals' outputs, and *boundary management*, or the manner in which the team interfaces with other units both inside and outside of the organization. Team process is then proposed to lead to team effectiveness (indicated by performance and satisfaction), as it does in McGrath's model.

This model differs from McGrath's in two important ways. First, Gladstein proposes that inputs have a direct impact on team effectiveness, in addition to the effect that

FIGURE 12.2
Gladstein's Model of Group Effectiveness

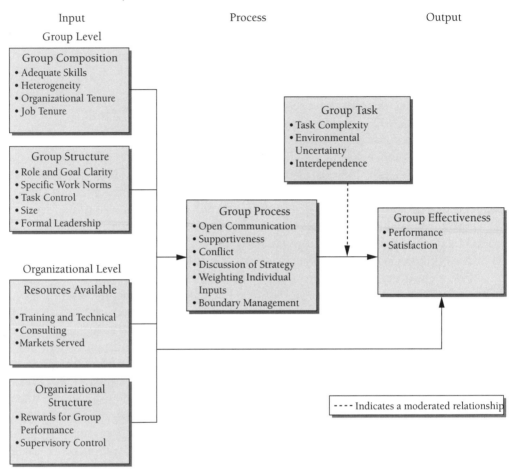

Adapted from: D. Gladstein. (1984). Groups in context: A model of task group effectiveness. *Administrative Science Quarterly, 29,* 499–517. Copyright © 1984, Cornell University Press. Reprinted by permission.

is mediated by team process. For example, a team with extraordinary levels of skill may be effective, regardless of the quality of team process. A second important difference is that Gladstein proposed that a team's task moderates the relationship between team process and team effectiveness. For example, a very unstructured, freewheeling style of interaction may be useful for a team creating a new product, but inappropriate for a team that is merely required to follow directions. This suggests that some forms of team proc-

ess will be more or less effective, depending on the complexity, uncertainty, and interdependence present in the team's task. Recall that McGrath (1964) proposed that the nature of the task represented an input that contributed directly to team process and, subsequently, to effectiveness.

When Gladstein (1984) tested her model of team effectiveness, she used a sample of sales teams from the marketing division of an organization in the communications industry and found mixed support. The model received the strongest support for the prediction of team members' perceptions of effectiveness, but support was much weaker when predicting actual sales revenue. This suggests that perhaps the model is more reflective of individuals' "implicit theories" of the determinants of team effectiveness than of actual team effectiveness. Another important finding from this study was that task characteristics did not moderate the relations between team process and effectiveness (perceived or sales revenue). This finding is difficult to interpret, given that the study was cross-sectional and there was not a great deal of variation in the nature of the tasks that these teams performed.

Hackman's (1987) Model

Building again on the general input–process–output framework, Hackman (1987) developed what he termed a *normative* model of team effectiveness. The term *normative* was used because Hackman's intent was clearly to develop a model that explicitly revealed the most important *performance levers* that organizations could use to enhance team effectiveness. Stated differently, Hackman's purpose in developing this model was more to serve as a guide to improving team performance rather than merely facilitating an understanding of why a team fails.

As can be seen in Figure 12.3, the two "input" factors in the model are organizational context and team design. Under organizational context, the most important factor proposed by Hackman is the reward system under which teams work. One important aspect of an organizational reward system, with respect to teams, is whether challenging and specific performance objectives exist. The failure to provide performance objectives often plagues individual-level reward systems but is partic-

ularly problematic with teams simply because most organizational performance–management systems are designed with individuals, not teams, in mind.

A second important aspect of organizational reward systems is that they must be designed so that teams receive positive consequences for excellent performance. The reinforcement value of positive consequences on individual behavior is well known (e.g., Luthans & Kreitner, 1985; Weiss, 1990). According to Hackman (1987), this same principle applies to teams, even though individual team members must ultimately see the connection between the performance of the team and the potential rewards it may obtain. If there are few positive consequences for excellent team performance, this will have an adverse motivational effect on teams.

The third aspect of organizational reward systems that is important is that rewards and objectives must focus on team, not individual, behavior. This is admittedly a tricky route for organizations to navigate because most organizational reward systems are designed for individuals, and many employees may be averse to completely giving up the possibility of having their performance rewarded. However, it is also true that, in some cases, individual and team-level reward systems work at cross-purposes. For example, in professional sports, it is becoming increasingly popular for teams to put incentive clauses, based purely on individual performance, into players' contracts. Unfortunately, in some cases, the behaviors reinforced by these incentive clauses do not support team performance.

In the organizational context, two other factors that contribute to team effectiveness are the educational and informational systems present in the organization. People do

FIGURE 12.3
Hackman's Normative Model of Group Effectiveness

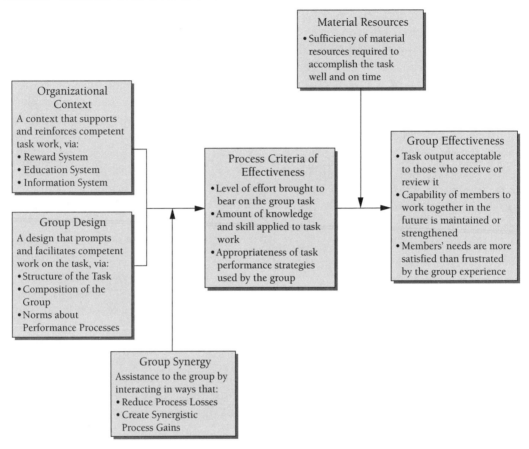

Adapted from: J. R. Hackman. (1987). The design of work teams. In J. W. Lorsch (Ed.), *Handbook of organizational behavior* (pp. 315–342). Englewood Cliffs, NJ: Prentice-Hall.

not automatically know how to work as part of a team; thus, teams often need educational and training assistance. In addition, teams need valid information so that they can competently make decisions and carry out tasks. To the extent that either of these is lacking or is of poor quality, it will undermine team effectiveness.

The team-design component has to do largely with the structural features of the work team. Chief among these factors is the structure of the task that the team is performing. According to Hackman (1987), the design of a team's task has important impli-

cations for motivation (e.g., Hackman & Oldham, 1980), but it may also be important for other reasons. Some tasks simply do not lend themselves well to teamwork (e.g., solving a highly technical problem); thus, an organization may have to face the fact that a given task may not be appropriate for teams.

The other features of the team-design component are the composition of the team and the team's performance-related norms. Teams obviously need individuals who possess the skills and abilities necessary to do the work. They also need individuals who possess at least a minimal level of compatibility in terms of personality and temperament. As was shown in Chapter 11, norms can have a powerful impact on behavior within teams. Most critical is whether teams develop norms that favor a high level of performance and effort.

As can be seen in Figure 12.3, the model proposes that both organizational context and team design contribute to what is termed the *process criteria of effectiveness*. These criteria are represented by the level of effort the team members exert, the amount of knowledge and skill they apply to the task, and the appropriateness of task-performance strategies. Hackman (1987), in effect, turned what is team process in other models into an intermediate or proximal criterion of effectiveness. For example, the fact that team members are working hard on a task is an intermediate indicator that they will be successful.

Notice, however, that the impact of both organizational context and team design on the process criteria of effectiveness depends on team synergy. According to Hackman (1987), team synergy relates to the extent to which a team avoids process losses (e.g., wasting or misdirecting time), or whether the team takes the initiative to create innovative strategic plans. Specifically, the team may create synergistic process gains by building on each other's ideas. By putting this concept into his theory, Hackman (1987) reminds us that teams may squander a favorable performance situation, or, conversely, they may do great things with only average conditions.

The next step in the model is from process criteria of effectiveness to actual team effectiveness, which was defined previously. This represents the familiar link between team process and team effectiveness, which is part of the previous two models. Hackman (1987) adds a somewhat different wrinkle,

however, by proposing that material resources moderate the relation between the process criteria of effectiveness and team effectiveness. A team can operate in a very favorable organizational context, have favorable design features, translate these favorable conditions into positive team processes, and, ultimately, not be successful. For example, a production team will not be successful if it does not have the tools necessary to produce the required products (see also Peters & O-Conner, 1985).

Shea and Guzzo's (1987) Model

Shea and Guzzo (1987) proposed a model of team effectiveness that is much less extensive than those previously described but nonetheless highlights some important determinants of team effectiveness. According to their model, team effectiveness is a consequence of three key factors: (1) outcome interdependence, (2) task interdependence, and (3) potency. Outcome interdependence reflects the extent to which members of a team share a common fate. An example of high outcome interdependence would occur if all of the members of a team were to receive a cash bonus because the team performed well. As one might expect, outcome interdependence is influenced, to a large extent, by organizational compensation practices. According to Shea and Guzzo (1987), a high degree of outcome interdependence will foster many of the behaviors necessary for teams to be effective—for example, cooperation, workload sharing, and so on. On the other hand, if team members' outcomes are largely independent, the chances that team members will act cooperatively are reduced, thereby reducing overall team effectiveness.

Task interdependence involves the degree to which members of a team have to depend on each other to get their work done.

Interdependence is typically cited as one of the crucial characteristics that define teams. Thus, task interdependence can be seen more as a test of the appropriateness of teams than as a direct determinant of effectiveness per se. As one might expect, teams will generally be more effective when the tasks they are performing require a certain amount of interdependence. If there is very little interdependence, this is a sign that a team may not be appropriate or that the task may need to be redesigned (see Comment 12.2).

Potency reflects the collective belief among team members that the team can be effective (Guzzo, Yost, Campbell, & Shea, 1993). It is analogous to the individual-level construct of self-efficacy, which represents individuals' beliefs that they can carry out various courses of action (Bandura, 1997). According to Shea and Guzzo (1987), potency is the most proximal determinant of team effectiveness—a proposition that has received some empirical support (e.g., Riggs & Knight, 1994). Presumably, potency positively impacts team effectiveness because it fosters persistence and may also lead to greater cooperation and cohesion among team members (see Jex & Bliese, 1999). A recent meta-analysis found a relatively strong relationship between collective efficacy and team performance (Gully, Joshi, Incalcaterra, & Beaubein, 2002). Team members who have a collective belief in their ability

---

COMMENT 12.2

TO TEAM OR NOT TO TEAM?: A CRUCIAL QUESTION

ALTHOUGH ORGANIZATIONS ARE often quite rational, they are also subject to fads and fashion. After all, decisions in organizations are made by people, and people are certainly persuaded by fad and fashion to make a variety of personal choices. (What else could possibly explain the popularity of leisure suits in the 1970s?!)

The use of teams in organizations has literally skyrocketed in the past 20 years, and there is no sign that this trend will be reversed. A positive aspect of the trend is that teams are highly appropriate for many organizational tasks. That is, much of the work performed in today's organizations requires a high degree of coordination and interdependence. Furthermore, the speed at which the competitive environment changes often makes it unlikely that one person can keep up with everything; thus, knowledge sharing among team members is often critical.

Despite all of the positive aspects of teams, they are certainly not appropriate for every task, nor do they fit well with the culture of every organization. Generally speaking, teams tend not to work well when tasks require highly independent work, or in organizations that do not encourage and value participation among their employees. The author (SMJ) has seen many cases, both as an employee and an external consultant, in which teams are formed with very little consideration as to whether they are appropriate. It is as if managers often form teams as a "reflex action," which suggests that, in some instances, the use of teams is due to fad or fashion ("Everybody uses teams") rather than serious task-related considerations. This is unfortunate because, in such instances, teams may actually create more problems than they solve.

Does this mean that organizations should not use teams? Not at all. It does mean, however, that organizations need to think very carefully about task-related demands, and realistically appraise their culture before they create teams to perform tasks.

to perform their mission will likely better coordinate their actions and communicate during episodes of team performance.

Shea and Guzzo (1987) proposed that three key variables contribute to team potency: (1) resources, (2) rewards, and (3) goals. As one would expect, when a team has access to numerous resources, their availability will reinforce team members' perceptions that they are capable of performing any task and responding to any challenge. Rewards are an important determinant of potency because they signal that performance means something, and this signal provides a team with an incentive to develop the internal capabilities necessary to perform well. To the extent that teams have challenging, specific goals, effort and persistence are enhanced, as well as performance-strategy development. All of these, in turn, should enhance potency. The contribution of rewards, resources, and goals to potency, and ultimately to effectiveness, has been supported empirically (Guzzo & Campbell, 1990), although clearly more work needs to be done.

Campion's Synthesis of Team-Effectiveness Models

Campion, Medsker, and Higgs (1993) provided an extensive review of the team-effectiveness literature and, based on that review, a model of team effectiveness that represents a synthesis of all of the models covered up to this point (as well as some others). Thus, what is presented in this section is not a new model, but rather a *meta* model of team effectiveness that emphasizes the common features underlying other models.

This synthesis of team-effectiveness models is presented in Figure 12.4. Notice that this model is clearly simpler than the first three that were described. Only factors that directly

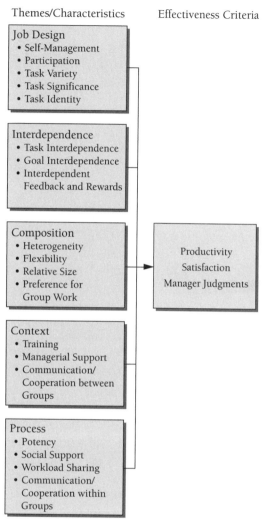

Source: M. A. Campion, G. J. Medsker, and A. C. Higgs. (1993). Relations between work group characteristics and effectiveness: Implications for designing effective work groups. *Personnel Psychology, 46,* 823–850. Reprinted by permission.

influence team effectiveness are proposed; thus, many of the intermediate linkages and moderator variables described in previous models are not included. The column labeled "Themes/Characteristics" indicates that there are essentially five general direct determinants of team effectiveness. The first of these, job design, centers around the nature of the task that the team is performing. According to Campion et al. (1993), the key aspects of a team's task environment include the degree of self-management and participation among team members, as well as the level of variety, significance, identity, and opportunity for feedback that is built into a team's task. High levels of effectiveness are associated with high degrees of all of these factors, although for different reasons. Self-management and participation enhance the team's sense of ownership of their work, and the task characteristics are likely to have their effects through enhanced intrinsic motivation.

The second determinant of effectiveness is labeled interdependence. This represents the degree to which team members are interdependent in terms of the tasks that they perform, the goals that the team adopts, the feedback they receive, and the rewards they strive for. As with Shea and Guzzo's (1987) model, Campion et al. (1993) proposed that higher levels of interdependence in all of these areas should enhance effectiveness. This is proposed primarily because a high level of interdependence will tend to foster cooperation and will also lead team members to coordinate their efforts.

The third determinant, labeled composition, largely involves the characteristics of the team members themselves. One key aspect of this is the degree to which teams are composed of members who possess heterogeneous skills and are flexible enough to cover for each other when required. Another important factor here is the relative size of the team. Although there is no magic number that is recognized as the "correct" team size, the general rule of thumb is that teams should be large enough to do the work, but not too large (i.e., more is not better). Finally, the variable preference for teamwork

is somewhat unique because it is not contained in the previous models. Some people simply like or dislike working in some teams more than others.

The third category, labeled context, is comprised of factors in the organizational environment in which the team performs. These include the training available to teams, the degree to which managers support teams, and the extent to which there is cooperation and communication among different teams. Teams will be most effective when the organizational context provides plentiful training opportunities, when managers support teams, and when there is a high degree of cooperation and communication among teams.

The last determinant of team effectiveness in this model is process. This represents potency, or team members' collective perceptions of the team's capabilities, as well as the levels of social support, workload sharing, and communication/cooperation within the team. As with previous models of team effectiveness, Campion et al. (1993) proposed that a positive team process directly facilitates team effectiveness. That is, teams are more successful when there are high levels of potency (i.e., members believe in the team's capabilities), social support, workload sharing, and communication/cooperation among members.

The final notable feature of the Campion et al. (1993) model is the category of "effectiveness criteria." These criteria are largely based on Hackman's (1987) definition of team effectiveness; however, notice that the one component of Hackman's definition that is missing is viability, or the likelihood that members of a team will work together in the future.

The Campion et al. (1993) model provides a comprehensive account of the major factors that influence team effectiveness and has received empirical support. Specifically, Campion et al. and Campion, Papper, and Medsker (1995) showed that many of the characteristics proposed to be related to team effectiveness were related to effectiveness criteria among employees in a large insurance company. Thus, like Gladstein (1984), Campion et al. not only proposed a model but tested it as well. The most obvious weakness in the Campion et al. model is that it proposed direct relations only between themes/characteristics and effectiveness criteria.

A Summary of the Team-Effectiveness Models

In this section, we examined four of the most widely cited models of team effectiveness and one attempt to synthesize these models. The common characteristic in all of these models is they follow the familiar input–process–output sequence—that is, they propose that aspects of the organizational context (e.g., rewards, interdependence, task design) directly impact the way a team works, and this, in turn, impacts effectiveness. These models are valuable because they highlight a number of organizational and team factors that influence team performance. Furthermore, there appears to be a good deal of consensus on what these contextual factors are. For example, most models highlight the composition of the team, the reward systems under which teams work, the design of the task that the team is working on, the resources available to the team, the goals that are set for a team (or those that it sets for itself), and internal processes such as cohesiveness, communication, and conflict management. Organizations have some degree of control over all of these variables and thus may be able to change them in order to improve team effectiveness. Given their

importance, each of these factors is examined in greater detail in the following section.

Although models based on the input–process–output approach have served team researchers well over the years, authors have recently recognized some limitations in these models. Ilgen et al. (2005) point out that many of the team-level variables found to influence the relationships between inputs and outputs are not necessarily processes, but rather emergent states such as a sense of collective efficacy. In addition, the authors note "the I-P-O framework limits research by implying a single-cycle linear path from inputs through outcomes" (p. 520). Rigid adherence to this type of framework prevents researchers from examining the consequences of various outputs (e.g., performance) for characteristics of the teams or processes engaged in by the team members. Finally, Marks, Mathieu, and Zaccaro (2001) noted that existing input–process–output models fail to consider the importance of temporal factors in how teams function. These authors noted that teams go through different phases (planning their performance, implementing goal-directed activities) as they do their work, and these phases need to be incorporated into models of team effectiveness. Therefore, future modeling of team effectiveness will need to consider bidirectional influences between components of input–process–output models and the importance of temporal phases in team performance.

DETERMINANTS OF TEAM EFFECTIVENESS

Although models of team effectiveness are useful in highlighting important variables that contribute to team effectiveness and in mapping out the processes by which they have such an impact, they are often short on detail. In this section, we take a closer look at several of the most common determinants of team effectiveness.

Team Composition

Perhaps one of the most robust findings in the team-effectiveness literature is that teams staffed with more highly skilled members are more effective than teams possessing lower absolute skill levels (Guzzo & Shea, 1992; Hackman, 1987). The average cognitive ability of a team has been found to be a predictor of performance in different types of teams, including military tank crews (Tziner & Eden, 1985). This finding is consistent with the literature on individual-level performance that has shown a very robust relation between cognitive ability and performance (Schmidt & Hunter, 1988). Devine and Phillips (2000) conducted a meta-analysis across all of the studies investigating the relationship between cognitive ability and team performance, and found the relationship was strongest when the teams were performing an unfamiliar task.

Given that team members' skill/ability is positively related to team effectiveness, does this mean that organizations need only hire talented people in order to make teams effective? Probably not. Another relatively consistent finding in the literature is that, although the absolute level of skill/ability in a team is important, organizations must also consider the mix of skills/abilities within teams (Campion et al., 1995). For example, if a basketball team is to be effective, it is certainly necessary to have players who are capable of scoring a lot of points. On the other hand, it is also important to have players who rebound well and others who are defensive specialists. A team composed only of scorers would probably not do very well. In fact, it has been shown that diversity of team

skills is positively related to team performance (Guzzo & Shea, 1992).

Despite the importance of team members' skill/ability, there are instances in which even teams composed of highly talented members are ineffective. In addition to cognitive ability, team personality has also been found to predict team performance. The most reliable personality predictor is team conscientiousness, which at the individual level reflects someone who is reliable, orderly, and follows through with different types of tasks (Barrick & Mount, 2005). Van Vianen and De Dreu (2001) found that team-level agreeableness and conscientiousness were both related to team performance. In addition, a recent meta-analysis revealed that team agreeableness and conscientiousness were both related to superior team performance across a number of published studies (Peeters, Van Tuijl, Rutte, & Reymen, 2006). Another interesting finding in the meta-analysis was that variability among team members in both agreeableness and conscientiousness was negatively related to team performance. That is, controlling for the overall level of agreeableness or conscientiousness, teams that varied widely on agreeableness or conscientiousness tended to perform poorer.

Researchers have also examined whether the relationship between personality and team performance may depend on the type of team task being performed. LePine, Colquitt, and Erez (2000) found that conscientiousness was negatively related to team decision-making effectiveness when the decision rules presented to the team required adaptability. The need for order possessed by conscientious individuals may make adapting to changing circumstances more difficult.

Another reason that team members' personalities may be important is that they may influence the climate within the team. George (1990), for example, found that teams could be distinguished in terms of their *affective tone*, which was determined by the personalities of individual team members. Teams with more positive affective tones were found to provide higher levels of service to customers—an important aspect of performance for these teams, who were employed in a retail environment. The fact that personality influences the climate of teams should not be surprising, given that the climates of entire organizations are influenced by the personalities of individual employees (Schneider, 1987).

In addition to the direct impact of team members' personalities, as well as the impact on team climate, the particular mix of personalities within a team may also have an important effect on team effectiveness. Within team settings, individual team members may have personalities that "clash," thus leading to negative conflict. It is also possible that one team member who possesses a very negative personality trait can have a negative impact on the processes within a team and may ultimately have a negative impact on performance. For example, in a study by Barrick et al. (1998), teams that had at least one member with a very low level of emotional stability reported lower levels of social cohesion, flexibility, communication, and workload sharing, and higher levels of conflict compared to teams that did not have such a member. Interestingly, though, having at least one team member with low emotional stability did not have a negative impact on team performance.

A final aspect of team composition that may contribute to team effectiveness is the attitudes of team members. The impact of team members' attitudes can be seen in one of two ways. The most direct way is what Campion et al. (1993) termed "preference for team work (p. 828)," which reflects whether people like working in team settings. Despite the proliferation of teams in organizations, it is still likely that not everyone enjoys working in team settings. Despite the camaraderie that is often found in collective work, teamwork can be frustrating because of social loafing, conflict, and other difficulties. Campion et al. (1993) found that where the average level of preference for teamwork was low, teams performed lower on several performance criteria (see also Driskell, Goodwin, Salas, & O'Shea, 2006).

Another way that attitudes may come into play involves the similarity of team members' attitudes. Social psychological research has shown conclusively that people tend to like people who are perceived as being similar to themselves (Byrne, 1971). Thus, teams are likely to function more effectively when there is at least a moderate level of similarity in their attitudes toward important issues such as the effectiveness of the team leader or the supportiveness of the organization (Bliese & Britt, 2001). Despite the potential value of agreement, it is also possible that agreement may be too high. When the members of a team agree on everything, they may suppress needed debate and cause the team to become extremely resistant to change. Janis (1982) referred to such a dynamic as *groupthink*, which he defined as " . . . a mode of thinking that people engage in when they are deeply involved in a cohesive in-group, when the members' striving for unanimity overrides their motivation to realistically appraise alternative courses of action. . . . Groupthink refers to a deterioration of mental efficiency, reality testing, and moral judgment that results from in-group pressures" (p. 9; see also Whyte, 1998).

Task Design

Another consistent theme among the models reviewed is that the design of a team's task is a key variable that influences team effectiveness. The exact manner in which task design is proposed to influence team effectiveness varies considerably between models, however. At the most basic level, task design is important because it speaks to the issue of whether the task a team is performing is appropriate for teams. Generally speaking, tasks involving a high level of interdependence are best accomplished by teams. Conversely, tasks that require primarily independent work are best performed by individuals. The zeal to use teams may blind organizations to the fact that some tasks are best accomplished by individuals.

Assuming for the moment that the task a team is performing is appropriate for teams, in what other ways does task design influence team effectiveness? One way is through its motivational impact. Individuals' motivation can be increased by redesigning jobs to enhance features such as autonomy, feedback, skill variety, task significance, and task identity (Hackman & Oldham, 1980). This same basic logic applies to teams; thus, members of teams that are performing tasks that are challenging, interesting, and engaging are likely to be more motivated than members of teams performing more mundane tasks.

The design of a team's task is also important. Even tasks that are well suited for teams can be approached in a variety of ways; thus, some task-related strategies will be more effective than others. Therefore, an important determinant of team effectiveness is the extent to which strategies and approaches are appropriate for the task(s) it is performing. It has been shown that teams (a) tend not to allocate much of their time to discus-

sions of task-related strategies (Hackman & Morris, 1975), and (b) tend to be more effective when they do, especially when they are performing complex tasks (Hackman Brousseau, & Weiss, 1976; Mathieu et al., 2000).

Beyond the important impact it has on effectiveness, the nature of a team's task is often a key to understanding team interactions and processes. Many of the behavioral dynamics that occur within teams can be understood only within the context of the work that a team performs. For example, Denison and Sutton (1990) describe many of the dynamics (e.g., loud music, joking) that occur in an operating room. To a large extent, these behaviors represent team members' mechanism for reducing tension because the work they do often has life-and-death consequences.

Organizational Resources

Just as individuals need organizational resources to perform well, so do teams. Given this need for organizational resources, an important question is: "What specific organizational resources do teams need in order to be effective?" To a certain degree, teams need many of the same resources that individuals need. Consider, for example, Peters and O'Connor's (1988) classification of organizational conditions that constrain individual performance. Many of these conditions also apply to teams. For example, teams often need equipment, information, budgetary resources, and time in order to accomplish their assigned tasks.

Teams may also have important and unique resource needs. Chief among these are training and consultation on how to work as a team. Members of teams may need training and assistance in learning how to work cooperatively with others, understanding how to coordinate their efforts with other team members, and, perhaps, training in how to resolve task-related disputes (Driskell, Salas, & Johnston, 2001). In the authors' experience, many organizations form work teams and instruct team members to "work out the details" with respect to task completion, but the organizations ignore issues associated with the internal dynamics of the team. Such an approach is based on the rather naïve assumption that teamwork comes naturally to people and they will be able to adapt to it naturally. Even a collection of highly intelligent, reasonable individuals may perform very poorly as a team.

Another resource need that is unique to teams is meeting space/time. For a team to be successful, the members need to be more than a collection of individuals working on their own. To be a collective entity, teams need to come together face-to-face, communicate with each other about task-related matters, and develop some level of cohesion. If an organization provides no meeting space, or very limited time, a team may never fully develop into a mature performing unit.

A final resource to consider is leadership. Just as individuals often rely on leaders in order to be successful, teams need leadership in order to be effective. Leaders of teams, however, must strike a delicate balance between being too detached and unavailable and being too directive, particularly in "self-managed" or autonomous work teams. Hackman (1990) likens the leadership of teams to being on a balance beam to show how leaders must often strike this delicate balance. What, then, is the appropriate balance? The answer depends, to a large extent, on the nature of the team one is leading and the organization in which the team resides. For teams that are largely self-directed, Hackman suggests that leaders essentially need to provide the team with an engaging

sense of direction," provide task-related assistance and consultation as needed, and work within the organization to obtain resources for the team. For anyone who has filled this role, these are demanding activities that are quite different from more traditional forms of supervision. DeChurch and Marks (2006) recently found that quality of leader coordination and strategizing were positively related to team performance in an F-22 battle simulation task.

Rewards

One of the most consistent findings with respect to individual-level performance is that rewards tend to enhance effort and, as a result, often lead to high levels of performance (Luthans & Kreitner, 1985). Rewards are also an important determinant of team performance, although the issues organizations face in designing team-level reward systems are vastly different from those faced when designing rewards for individuals. Many organizations make the mistake of espousing the value of "teamwork" while rewarding employees solely on the basis of their individual accomplishments. Under such conditions, it is unlikely that teams will perform very effectively. Recognizing this, more and more organizations have been developing team-based compensation plans (Lawler, Mohrman, & Ledford, 1995), and there is some empirical evidence to suggest that team-based rewards are associated with team effectiveness (Hertel, Konradt, & Orlikowski, 2004).

One of the most fundamental issues organizations face in designing reward systems for teams is the extent to which the work they do is truly interdependent. If the work that teams do is truly interdependent, then rewarding teams rather than individuals is appropriate (Wageman & Baker, 1997). But what if a team performs a task that is not highly interdependent? Team-level reward systems are then less appropriate and, in fact, may be downright unfair. Consider, for example, a team of five individuals who perform independently. If rewards are based on team performance and the team performs well, less competent team members are rewarded because they are lucky enough to be in a team with others who are highly competent. On the other hand, if the team performs poorly, highly competent individuals are penalized because they happen to be in a team with fellow employees who are much less competent than they are.

Another important issue that organizations must consider in the design of team-level reward systems is the interplay between individual- and team-level rewards. It is rare to find organizations in which employees are rewarded solely on the basis of team-level performance. In most organizations that have team-level reward systems, these must coexist with individual-level reward systems (DeMatteo, Eby, & Sundstrom, 1998). Furthermore, in most cases, individual-level reward systems are better established than those based on team performance. In the authors' opinion, it is unrealistic to think that individual-level reward systems can be eliminated, even in organizations that depend heavily on the performance of teams.

It is important to not have individual- and team-level reward systems work against each other. If a team-level reward system is going to be effective, it is important to not have behaviors encouraged by the individual-level reward system undermine team performance, and vice versa. This may seem to be a rather obvious proposition, but it is actually quite common in organizations. For example, in sales organizations, individuals are typically rewarded largely on the basis of the dollar value of their own sales. Thus, individuals are highly motivated to make as many sales as possible, and will likely allocate their time accordingly.

On the other hand, when one considers the performance of a sales team, each individual's effort to maximize his or her sales volume may not necessarily maximize the team effort. In the long run, the team may be better served if individual salespeople devote at least some of their time to servicing existing accounts, providing training and guidance to less-experienced salespeople, and making sure they keep current on emerging product lines. Unfortunately, the prospect of earning high sales commissions may induce a form of "tunnel vision" in employees that ultimately undermines team performance. Furthermore, organizations are often quite naïve about this conflict between employees' maximizing their own rewards and contributing to the performance of the team or of the organization as a whole.

A third consideration in the design of team-level reward systems is the degree to which teams have control over their own performance. This is an issue in the design of individual-level reward systems, but it is especially salient with team-level reward systems because the performance of teams may be highly dependent on the efficiency and reliability of the technologies they employ (Goodman, 1986), or it may be limited by organizational resource constraints (Shea & Guzzo, 1987). Holding teams to high performance standards while, at the same time, providing them with faulty technology or very limited resources is unfair and counterproductive. Teams may be able to overcome such performance barriers (Tesluk & Mathieu, 1999), but it is questionable whether this can be done in the long run without having adverse motivational effects on team members and ultimately undermining the team's viability (Hackman, 1987).

One final issue to consider in examining the consequences of team reward systems is the attitudes of employees toward team-based rewards. Haines and Taggar (2006) recently examined the predictors of positive attitudes toward team reward structures. The authors found that the most direct predictors of a positive attitude were belief in the value of teamwork and the employee's job performance. Interestingly, believing in the value of teamwork was positively related to a favorable attitude to team-based reward structures, but individual performance was negatively related to such a favorable attitude. Individuals who performed well as individuals were less inclined to want team-based reward systems, which may reflect a concern that their individual efforts will go unnoticed by their supervisors.

Team Goals

In many ways, the impact of goals on team performance mirrors the impact of goals on individual-level performance. For example, O'Leary-Kelly, Martocchio, and Frink (1994) conducted a meta-analysis of the team goal-setting literature and found strong support for the impact of goals on team performance. This finding has been reinforced by individual studies that have been conducted subsequent to this review (e.g., Whitney, 1994). Given such findings, it is tempting to conclude that there is a perfect correspondence between team and individual goal setting.

There are, however, some important differences in the dynamics associated with individual- and team-level goal setting. For example, an important consideration in setting goals for teams is the interplay between team goals and individual-level goals. This is analogous to the dilemma organizations face in developing team-level reward systems. It has been found, for example, that team-level goals are much more effective when individuals either do not have goals or have goals that are compatible with team goals (Mitchell & Silver, 1990). Thus, organizations must be cognizant of the overall goal system when they are developing performance-related goals for teams (DeShon et al., 2004).

Another important divergence between the individual and team goal-setting literatures has to do with the intervening mechanisms between goals and performance. Because the impact of goals is so well established, goal-setting researchers have recently focused the majority of their attention on explaining why goal setting works (see Chapter 8). Most explanations for the effects of goal setting have centered on the fact that goals serve as an important focal point for self-regulation (Klein, 1989), and goal commitment is a crucial intervening step between goals and performance (Ambrose & Kulik, 1999).

Although comparatively less research has examined the processes responsible for team goal-setting effects, there is some evidence that the mechanisms responsible for these effects are quite different from those responsible at the individual level. For example, there is some evidence that *collective efficacy* may be an important intervening mechanism between team goals and performance. Whitney (1994) found that teams that were assigned difficult goals reported higher levels of collective efficacy, compared to teams with easier or "do your best" goals. Thus, teams given difficult goals may take this as a sign that the organization considers them more capable than other teams (e.g., "We have a difficult goal, therefore we must be good."). These enhanced feelings of competence may then subsequently lead to a high level of performance through many of the same mechanisms by which goals enhance individual-level performance (e.g., increased effort, commitment, strategy development).

Another important difference between individual- and team-level goal processes is that difficult goals may enhance members' attraction to the team or team cohesion (Whitney, 1994); that is, a difficult goal may serve to "draw team members together" in a way that enhances attraction to the team and ultimately enhances performance. Supporting this idea, Aube and Rousseau (2005) examined the relationship between team goal commitment and multiple indicators of team effectiveness (e.g., team performance, team viability) among intact teams working in Canadian organizations. The authors found a positive relationship between team goal commitment and indexes of effectiveness. The authors also found that this relationship was completely a function of supportive team behaviors. That is, teams committed to attaining a group goal were more likely to help each other out when needed, which resulted in superior team performance. It is important to point out, however, that for enhanced cohesiveness and attraction to facilitate team performance, a team must have norms that support high levels of performance (Seashore, 1954).

Within-Team Processes

Organizational psychologists have been very active in identifying key team processes that connect inputs to indicators of effectiveness. However, although team processes are seen as central to understanding the effectiveness of teams, Kozlowski and Bell (2003) note " . . . there is little convergence on a core set of processes" (p. 346). Numerous taxonomies of team processes have been offered by different researchers (Dickinson & McIntyre, 1997; Hallam & Campbell, 1997; Mathieu & Day, 1997; Kozlowski & Bell,

2003; Salas et al., 2005). Despite lack of complete agreement in the processes that influence team performance, most of these taxonomies highlight a handful of processes that have been empirically found to predict team performance in both laboratory and applied settings. The purpose of this section is to focus on certain elements of team process that seem to be more important than others.

In the most general sense, team process represents the way in which teams accomplish their tasks. Team process is not concerned with what a team produces, but rather how a team does its work. Given this general definition, a number of different elements of team process may be important to team effectiveness. For the present chapter we highlight the team processes presented in Table 12.1. Table 12.1 also divides these processes into those that are behavioral and cognitive/affective in nature.

BEHAVIORAL PROCESSES

Many of these processes are self-explanatory and make intuitive sense. Considering the behavioral team processes, *communication* among team members would appear to be a necessary requirement for effective performance, and research supports this prediction (Ancona & Caldwell, 1992a, 1992b). Communication within a team reflects both the amount of information flow and the manner in which information is disseminated. Teams in which members share little information with each other and communicate very infrequently tend to perform more poorly than teams with more free-flowing communication (Hackman, 1987). The size of this difference, however, depends to a large extent on the nature of the task that a team is performing. Highly interdependent and complex tasks have much greater information requirements

TABLE 12.1
Behavioral and Cognitive/Affective Team Processes

Category	Description
Behavioral	
Communication:	"Exchange of information between two or more team members" (p. 25; Dickinson & McIntyre, 1997)
Coordination:	"Team members executing their activities in a timely and integrated manner" Performance of team members influenced by others (Dickinson & McIntyre, 1997)
Cooperation:	Team members helping one another to complete interdependent tasks (Wagner, 1995). Seen as the opposite of conflict (Kozlowski & Bell, 2003)
Cognitive/Affective	
Team Cohesion	
Task:	"The group's shared commitment or attraction to the group task or goal" (p. 349, Kozlowski & Bell, 2003)
Interpersonal:	The extent to which group members like each other and are attracted to each other (Siebold, 2006)
Team Efficacy:	"A team's belief that it can successfully perform a specific task" (p.820, Gully et al., 2002)
Team Empower.:	Task motivation that is due to team members' collective, positive assessments of their organizational tasks (Kirkman et al., 2004)
Shared Mental Mod.:	Shared knowledge structures about team tasks, goals, and activities (Salas et al., 2005)
Team Conflict:	Conflict over tasks or emotional issues within a team (Jehn, 1994)

than tasks that are simple or require very low levels of interdependence. In addition, researchers have also distinguished between task-related and task-unrelated communication, with the latter type of communication being related to poor team performance (Toquam, Macauley, Westra, Fujita, & Murphy, 1997).

Another aspect of communication, which was discussed in the previous chapter, is the extent to which a team's style of communication is either highly centralized or highly decentralized. Recall that centralized forms of communication have been found to be effective when teams are performing tasks that are relatively simple and have few coordination requirements. Decentralization, however, tends to facilitate performance when a team is working on highly complex tasks or tasks that have high coordination requirements.

A manifestation of this issue (centralization versus decentralization) that the authors have observed over the years when conducting team-development activities is the extent to which all members of a team participate. Although no data can be presented to back this up, one of the most common attributes of teams that appeared to be performing well has been that all members tended to participate and voice their opinions. On the other hand, in more dysfunctional teams, it was common to find participation very uneven among team members. Typically, one or two highly vocal team members dominated a great deal of the team's deliberations. This may lead a team to become dysfunctional because those who are the most vociferous may not always have the best ideas (in fact, in the author's experience, the opposite is often the case). Thus, many potentially good ideas never see the light of day.

With respect to communication, a final issue that has only recently become important is teams' use of electronic communication (e.g., e-mail). Employees in many organizations rely heavily on electronic communication, and there has been some research on this form of communication. For example, although electronic communication is highly efficient for transmitting factual information (Carey & Kacmar, 1997), it is much less effective when a team's task is highly interdependent, or the information to be communicated is emotive in nature (Straus & McGrath, 1994). Also, because users of electronic communication may feel a certain degree of anonymity that is not possible in face-to-face encounters, electronic communications may be more blunt and less tactful (Dubrovsky, Keisler, & Sethna, 1991).

Research on electronic communication within teams is still relatively new, but some consistent findings are beginning to emerge. For example, it has been found that members of teams generally prefer not to use electronic communication media when important, task-related information must be communicated (Straus & McGrath, 1994). The reason: Electronic communication is a rather limited communication medium. It is not possible to use physical gestures and other forms of nonverbal communication, so it may take longer for a person to get a point across (McGrath, 1990).

Despite this somewhat negative assessment of electronic communication, there are some instances when it may be superior to have over face-to-face communication. For example, if the purpose of the communication is simply to disseminate information, electronic communication is much more efficient than a face-to-face meeting. Some readers have probably had the experience of attending a meeting that was merely an "information dump" and could have been accomplished by other means (e.g., electronic transmission of information).

Another instance in which electronic communication may be effective is when teams are working on brainstorming tasks. *Brainstorming* is often used when teams need to come up with creative or novel ideas. The major ground rules of brainstorming are that participants should be encouraged to generate as many ideas as possible (e.g., quantity is more important than quality), ideas should not be evaluated as they are generated, and participants should try to build on the ideas of others. Certainly, under the right conditions, brainstorming can be done very well face-to-face. However, in many cases, participants may experience evaluation apprehension or become hesitant at the prospect of sharing novel ideas in front of others. There is some evidence that when brainstorming is done through electronic communication, participants may overcome such apprehension (Gallupe et al., 1992). This is due largely to the anonymity that electronic communication allows.

The research on electronic communication, although still fairly new, is important. As more and more organizations make use of teams in which members are geographically dispersed (e.g., "virtual" teams; Kirkman & Mathieu, 2005), it will become crucial to understand the limitations of such arrangements. The little research done so far suggests that teams may lose something if they are allowed to communicate only electronically. Clearly, more research is needed to strengthen these findings and communicate other limitations of various communication media.

Coordination has been defined as "activities required to manage interdependencies with the team work flow" (p. 352; Kozlowski & Bell, 2003, and coordination has been measured through observer ratings of team member interactions or through the actual monitoring of exchanges between team members as a task is completed (Brannick, Roach, & Salas, 1993; Stout, Salas, & Carson, 1994). *Cooperation*, also referred to as *"backup-behavior,"* refers to the extent to which employees help each other and give each other needed information in completing tasks (Wagner, 1995). Cooperation can be assessed either by surveying team members (Hallam & Campbell, 1997) or by examining the number of exchanges that occur between team members (Seers, Petty, & Cashman, 1995). Communication, coordination, and cooperation all represent team processes that are conducive to effective team performance.

Affective/Cognitive Processes

The remainder of team processes described in Table 12.1 deal with either cognitive issues related to how team members think about one another and their tasks or affective variables related to how team members feel about each other and the work they are doing as a team. Team cohesiveness is another variable that is measured in most team-effectiveness models, but not all models consider it to be an aspect of team process. Although cohesiveness has been defined in a variety of ways, most team researchers see it as the degree to which the members of a team are attracted to the team and place a high value on team membership (Mudrack, 1989). In everyday language, cohesiveness is often described as the level of "team spirit" or "espirit de corps" that we see within teams.

It has been demonstrated that highly cohesive teams tend to be more effective when prevailing norms support high performance (Seashore, 1954). However, we also know that it may be possible for teams to be too cohesive. As was noted earlier, Janis (1982) believed that "groupthink" is likely to occur when teams are so cohesive that they lose the capacity to realistically appraise their capabilities. In terms of team process, this is manifested in the suppression of dissent and inaccurate appraisals of the environment.

More recent research suggests that team cohesiveness may be multidimensional, and that this may have an impact on team effectiveness. According to Hackman (1992), it is possible to distinguish between *interpersonal-based cohesiveness* and *task-based cohesiveness* (see also Mullen & Cooper, 1994; Siebold, 2006). When cohesiveness is interpersonal, members' attraction to the team is based largely on how much they like the other team members and enjoy their company. Members of a college fraternity are likely to be cohesive for largely interpersonal reasons. The same would apply to more informal teams and friendship cliques. When cohesiveness is task based, members' attraction to the team is largely based on their attraction to the task that the team is performing (see Table 12.1). The members of a presidential campaign staff may develop a high level of cohesiveness because of their mutual support for the candidate they are supporting. Members of professional sports teams may also develop this form of cohesiveness as they strive to win a championship.

Distinguishing between interpersonal and task-based cohesiveness may have important consequences for team effectiveness. Mullen and Cooper (1994) conducted a meta-analysis of the team cohesion literature and concluded that task cohesion was a stronger predictor of team performance than interpersonal cohesion (see also Siebold, 2006). This suggests that just because people like each other and enjoy being together, they will not necessarily be an effective team. In fact, it would not be hard to imagine a scenario in which a very high level of interpersonal cohesiveness could even be counterproductive. Members of a team may enjoy each other so much that they allocate very little time to their task.

According to Hackman (1992), this distinction in forms of cohesiveness highlights very clearly the importance of a team's task design. If tasks are designed so that they are interesting, challenging, and psychologically engaging, the chances are increased that team members will develop high task-based cohesiveness that will ultimately enhance a team's performance. On the other hand, if a team's task is very mundane and uninteresting, there is less chance that high levels of task-based cohesiveness will develop. Ultimately, team members may be very "lukewarm" about what they are doing, and this may be reflected in the team's performance. In the future, more research on the dimensionality of cohesiveness, and the implications of this, is needed.

In addition to team cohesion, earlier in the chapter we discussed the importance of team efficacy, sometimes also referred to as *collective efficacy*. As indicated in Table 12.1, collective efficacy refers "a sense of collective competence shared among members when allocating, coordinating, and integrating their resources as a successful, concerted response to specific situational demands" (Zaccaro, Blair, Peterson, & Zazanis, 1995, p. 309). In many ways collective efficacy can be seen as the team members' beliefs that they can accomplish the team's objectives under different operational conditions. Not surprisingly, collective efficacy has been found to predict better team performance on a variety of tasks (Gully et al., 2002). Team members who have a collective belief in their ability to perform their mission will

likely better coordinate their actions and communicate during episodes of team performance.

A variable related to collective efficacy is *team empowerment*. Kirkman, Rosen, Tesluk, and Gibson (2004) defined team empowerment as increased task motivation that is due to team members' collective, positive assessments of their organizational tasks. Whereas collective efficacy is focused on team members' beliefs about their ability to perform team tasks, team empowerment refers to the team members' beliefs in the meaningfulness of their tasks. According to Kirkman et al., team empowerment is based on the strength of the team (potency), the perceived meaningfulness of team tasks, a sense of autonomy in being able to perform as a team, and a sense that the team is having a positive impact on broader organizational goals. These four variables are additive and subject to change over time. Kirkman et al. found that team empowerment predicted the performance of virtual teams as indexed by ratings of customer satisfaction and improvement in the time it took to process tasks. Furthermore, the relationship between team empowerment and process improvement was especially strong when teams had fewer face-to-face meetings. This research suggests that team empowerment may be especially important when team members are less able to interact and communicate.

The next cognitive/affective team-level process presented in Table 12.1 is shared mental models. *Shared mental models* allow team members to organize information that deals with team goals, member tasks, and even how to coordinate efforts. Salas et al. argue there are two forms of mental models: *team related* and *task related*. Team-related mental models deal with team functioning. Task-related models deal with materials that are needed or information on how certain equipment is used. It has been posited that these shared mental models can allow teams to work more effectively and efficiently. Mathieu, Heffner, Goodwin, Salas, and Cannon-Bowers (2000) found that team-related mental models were significantly related to team performance, and task-related models were indirectly related to team performance through team processes.

The final important component of team process that can influence team effectiveness is the manner in which teams handle conflicts. Any time people come together to accomplish a task collectively, some level of conflict is inevitable. Members of a team may disagree over a variety of issues, such as who should play a leadership role in the team or how the task should be approached. Some individuals may simply not like each other because of fundamental personality and value differences. In addition to the sources of conflict, the level of conflict may vary from very minor friendly disagreement all the way to physical aggression.

Although conflict is consistently negatively associated with team member attitudes, it is not always negatively associated with lower levels of team performance. According to Jehn (1994), conflict within teams can be characterized as being task related and emotion related. When conflict is task related, team members have differences over task-related issues. For example, they may disagree on the way a team should prioritize its work, which work methods are most appropriate, or which team members should be performing which tasks. Jehn states that task-based conflict does not detract from team effectiveness and, in many cases, can actually enhance it. When team members' disagreements center on task-related issues, this may facilitate communication about these issues and ultimately generate innovative ideas that enhance effectiveness.

In contrast, when conflict is emotion related, team members have differences over more personal issues. Even reasonable people may "see the world differently" because of fundamental value differences, and thus not get along well. According to Jehn (1994), emotion-related conflict can and often does detract from team performance. In fact, if such conflicts are allowed to escalate to extremely high levels, they may ultimately lead to the abolishment of a team. Why is this form of conflict so destructive? One reason is that it is simply unpleasant for all team members. Being in a heated conflict with another person is unpleasant, and it is also unpleasant to watch such conflicts unfold. Thus, in many cases, team members may simply withdraw from such unpleasant situations.

Perhaps a more important reason that emotion-related conflicts reduce effectiveness is that they distract team members' attention away from important task-related matters. When two people in a team become bitter enemies, they may become so focused on "one-upping" each other that they pay little attention to the task that they are supposed to be performing.

Between-Team Processes

Although most of the research on processes in the team-performance literature has focused on within-team dynamics, some recent research has also emphasized the importance of examining processes that occur between teams as predictors of organization-level performance (Marks et al., 2005; Mathieu & Day, 1997). Mathieu and Day point out that organizational success is frequently predicated on effective between-team communication, coordination, and cooperation, and that researchers examining organizational effectiveness need to map out critical team-to-team interfaces and assess the quality of the interactions between these teams. These authors identified five important processes that occurred between teams in a nuclear power plant. *Formalization* was defined as the extent to which there are rules, procedures, and standard methods for team members to coordinate their activities. *Coordination* refers to the sequencing and spacing of activities between departments to accomplish a common goal. *Cooperation* refers to the extent to which employees from different departments maintain a positive interpersonal relationship. *Goal priority* refers to the extent to which employees from different departments agree about the priority of organizational goals. Finally, *interdependence* refers to the extent to which the actions of one department affect the operations of another department.

Mathieu and Day (1997) examined the interactions between teams within a nuclear plant and were able to uncover that some teams shared a high level of interdependence with many other teams (e.g., operations, radiological control), whereas other teams operated in relative isolation from each other. Importantly, there was variability in which teams within the plant scored high versus low on the team processes that were assessed. Some teams were judged higher on coordination and cooperation, whereas other teams scored higher on goal priority. Mathieu and Day used this information to develop targeted recommendations for individual teams. Given the amount of cross-team interaction necessary in modern organizations, research on between-team processes is likely to increase in the future.

ENHANCING THE EFFECTIVENESS OF TEAMS

Assuming for the moment that an organization has identified tasks that are appropriate for teams, what specific steps can organizations take to increase the odds that teams will be effective? In this section, we examine three general approaches that organizations can take to enhance team effectiveness. As readers will note, these steps correspond to activities that are typically conducted by Human Resources departments in organizations. This was done intentionally, to emphasize that they are not just general concepts; they are concrete, "actionable" steps.

Selection

Based on research by Barrick et al. (1998), it appears that one way of improving team effectiveness is to simply use some of the same factors that have been found to be robust predictors of individual performance (Barrick & Mount, 1991; Schmidt & Hunter, 1998). Specifically, they found that average levels of general mental ability within teams were positively related to performance. In addition, it was found that average levels of conscientiousness were also positively related. Thus, to some degree, organizations can use selection to improve team performance in much the same way that they enhance individual performance.

Although much less research has accumulated on team performance as compared to individual performance, individual characteristics such as general mental ability and personality appear to explain much less variance in team than in individual performance. For example, Schmidt and Hunter (1998) found that general mental ability explained approximately 31% of the variance in individual performance. In comparison, Barrick et al. (1998) found that average general mental ability explained approximately 5% of the variance in team performance. Therefore, there are probably other team composition factors that need to be considered when selecting people for teamwork.

Recall that Campion et al. (1993) proposed and found evidence for a positive relation between *preference for teamwork* and several team-level performance criteria. Thus, organizations selecting people for teams might be wise to consider whether these individuals prefer working in team settings. In Campion et al.'s study, there was a reasonable amount of variance in preference for teamwork, suggesting that people do indeed vary in the degree to which they enjoy working as part of a team. However, a potential problem with using such a measure, particularly with job applicants, is that they may not be truthful in reporting their preferences. That is, if they know that a job requires teamwork, they may report that they enjoy working in teams (even if they do not) to enhance their chances of being hired. Although little research to date has addressed this issue, Nagel (1999) found evidence, in a laboratory simulation, for this type of distortion. One way to deal with this issue might be to use other selection methods, such as personal history, to measure applicants' affinity for working in team situations.

Instead of considering individuals' preferences, selection efforts might be aimed at assessing the knowledge, skills, and abilities (KSAs) needed in order to work in teams. Stevens and Campion (1999) used this approach to develop a selection instrument that they labeled the Teamwork Test. The specific KSAs measured by this instrument are presented in Table 12.2. As can be seen, these are teamed into two general categories: Interpersonal KSAs and Self-Management KSAs. In the Interpersonal category, the KSAs deemed most important have to do with conflict resolution, collaborative problem solving, and communication. The Self-Management KSAs have to do with goal setting/time management and planning/task coordination.

Stevens and Campion (1999) also attempted to provide predictive validity evidence for this instrument in two organizations. Overall, their findings provided support for the predictive validity of this instrument. More specifically, their instrument explained variance in team performance beyond that explained by the general mental ability of team members. This suggests that this instrument may ultimately be a useful tool for organizations, although some further development may be needed. These findings are also interesting because they suggest that working in teams may require certain unique skills and abilities that may not be assessed by traditional selection instruments.

Hirschfeld and his colleagues (2006) recently examined knowledge of teamwork principles as a predictor of effective teamwork. These authors assessed how well employees performed on a test designed to assess their knowledge of multiple teamwork concepts and found that the average team score on the objective test was related to expert ratings of how effective the employees worked together as a team. This research suggests that knowledge of teamwork principles may be another criterion for selection.

Organizational Reward Systems

Nearly all of the models of team effectiveness covered earlier in this chapter mentioned rewards as being an important factor contributing to team effectiveness. Quite simply, teams tend to be more effective when organizations reward their efforts. Unfortunately, in many organizations where teams are utilized, the rewards are focused almost

TABLE 12.2
Dimensions Comprising the Stevens and Campion (1999) Teamwork Test

I. Interpersonal KSAs
  A. Conflict Resolution KSAs
    1. The KSA to recognize and encourage desirable, but discourage undesirable team conflict.
    2. The KSA to recognize the type and source of conflict confronting the team and implement and appropriate resolution strategy.
    3. The KSA to implement an integrative (win-win) negotiation strategy, rather than the traditional distributive (win-lose) strategy.
  B. Collaborative Problem Solving KSAs
    4. The KSA to identify situations requiring participative problem solving and to utilize the proper degree and type of participation.
    5. The KSA to recognize the obstacles to collaborative group problem solving and implement proper corrective actions.
  C. Communication KSAs
    6. The KSA to understand communication networks, and to utilize decentralized networks to enhance communication where possible.
    7. The KSA to communicate openly and supportively; that is, to send messages that are (a) behavior- or event-oriented, (b) congruent, (c) validating, (d) conjunctive, and (e) owned.
    8. The KSA to listen nonevaluatively and to appropriately use active listening techniques.
    9. The KSA to maximize the consonance between nonverbal and verbal messages and to recognize and interpret the nonverbal messages of others.
    10. The KSA to engage in small talk and ritual greetings as a recognition of their importance.
II. Self-Management KSAs
  D. Goal Setting and Performance Management KSAs
    11. The KSA to establish specific, challenging, and accepted team goals.
    12. The KSA to monitor, evaluate, and provide feedback on both overall team performance and individual team-member performance.
  E. Planning and Task Coordination KSAs
    13. The KSA to coordinate and synchronize activities, information, and tasks among team members.
    14. The KSA to help establish task and role assignments for individual team members and ensure proper balancing of workload.

Source: M. J. Stevens and M. A. Campion. (1999). Staffing work teams: Development and validation of a selection test for teamwork settings. *Journal of Management, 25,* 207–228. Copyright © 1999. Reprinted with permission from Elsevier Science.

exclusively at the individual level. In fact, even in organizations that do have team-level rewards, these must coexist with individual-level reward systems. How then do organizations make sure that individual- and team-level reward systems complement each other?

According to Wageman and Baker (1997), two important considerations in the design of team-level reward systems are task interdependence and outcome interdependence. As defined earlier, task interdependence reflects the extent to which team members must work collaboratively in order to get their work done. Outcome interdependence reflects the extent to which the members of a team share a "common fate"; that is, do they all receive the same positive or negative outcome if the team performs well or poorly? For a team-level reward system to work well, there must be alignment between task and outcome interdependence. Team-level reward systems work best when both task and outcome interdependence are high. If a great deal of interdependence is required to perform a task, it stands to reason that the outcomes team members receive should be similar.

As Wageman (1996) points out, however, team reward systems are often ineffective because these two forms of interdependence are misaligned. Consider, for example, a situation in which the work performed by team members is highly interdependent, but the outcomes they receive are not. This will likely create disincentives for the members of a team to work cooperatively because those who receive the highest rewards will be seen as being over-rewarded. On the other hand, what if there is very little task interdependence, but a great deal of outcome interdependence? In a case like this, those who perform well may resent sharing a common fate with those whose performance is far below theirs. The major point is that organizations often fail to consider these two forms of interdependence when rewarding teams, and thus may inadvertently create a disincentive for people to work as a team.

In Chapter 9 we discussed specific ways in which organizations may reward the performance of teams, so they will be mentioned only briefly here. The most common of these include profit sharing and gain sharing, although Employee Stock Ownership Plans may also be used for this purpose. The specifics of all of these compensation plans differ, but they all share one common characteristic: They are appropriate primarily in situations where employees in teams work on highly interdependent tasks. Thus, when they are designing team reward systems, organizations must pay particular attention to the nature of the work that teams are performing.

Organizations can also attempt to enhance the performance of teams through non-monetary rewards such as awards and recognition. Again, as with monetary compensation, it is important that the awards and recognition that are provided to individuals do not negate the effects of those at the team level. In professional team sports, individual-level honors and recognition are often viewed as more important than collective achievement. After all, individuals are inducted to sports halls of fame, not teams. Thus, organizations not only need to reward team performance, but they must also create a climate in which collective achievement is viewed as being at least as important as individual accomplishments.

Team-Development Interventions

A final way that organizations may enhance the effectiveness of teams is through training or team-development activities. Team development will be discussed in much more detail in Chapter 16, so only a brief overview will be provided here. According to Dyer (1987), team development represents a variety of team-based training interventions that are aimed at one or more crucial aspects of team functioning. For example, team-development activities may be aimed at clarifying roles within a team, establishing goals and priorities, and tackling more sensitive interpersonal issues (Beer, 1976; French & Bell, 1995).

Specific forms of team development may be carried out quite differently, but most involve some common generic steps. For example, in most cases, teams participate in team-development activities with the assistance of an outside consultant or facilitator; *outside*, in this case, means someone from outside the team (this can be either someone who is external to the organization, or someone who is an organizational member). Compared to a team member, an individual from outside the team can be much more objective about the team and its process.

Another characteristic common to most team-development activities is that they are data based; that is, some data about the function of the team are collected prior to the actual intervention. Typically, pre-intervention data are collected through surveys and interviews of team members, although other methods may also be used (e.g., archival data, observations). After data are collected and summarized, they are usually used as the basis for choosing the specific team-development intervention. For example, if data indicate a lack of role clarity among team members, the focus of team development would typically be on role clarification (for an example, see Schaubroeck et al., 1993).

While not a great deal of research has examined the impact of team development on team performance, there is some indication that it may improve team effectiveness. For example, in a review of the work-team literature, Sundstrom, DeMeuse, and Futrell (1990) found that team-development activities, particularly those focused on task-related issues, have a positive effect on team performance. In contrast, when team-development activities are focused on interpersonal issues, the results are much less positive. This may be due to the fact that the underlying causes of interpersonal problems within teams (e.g., personality and value differences) are much less amenable to changes, as compared to the causes of task-related problems.

THE FUTURE OF TEAMS IN ORGANIZATIONS

Given the challenges associated with designing and managing teams, it might be tempting to conclude that teams are just another fad that will pass with time. In the authors' opinion, this is not the case; teams are now a permanent part of organizational life and will continue to be in the foreseeable future. One reason for this is that more and more of the work being performed in organizations is becoming complex and mentally demanding (i.e., "knowledge work"). Often, teams can be much more effective in tackling such complex tasks because they offer variety in the skills and knowledge of team members.

Another reason that teams will continue to flourish in organizations of the future is that they are highly compatible with the changing nature of employee–employer relationships. Organizations are becoming leaner; they are relying less and less on formal job descriptions and more and more on temporary employees. In this type of environment, it is very convenient for organizations to retain a small *core staff* of permanent employees and bring in temporary employees on an as-needed basis. Furthermore, when temporary employees are brought into an organization, it is often advantageous to create project teams to accomplish tasks.

Given this trend, a future challenge for organizations is their ability to assemble teams and have them working effectively within a very short time frame. This may involve many of the factors discussed in this chapter, but those likely to be most important in the future are the characteristics of the individuals comprising teams. More specifically, in the future, it may be especially crucial for individuals to have a set of generic knowledge, skills, and abilities (Driskell et al., 2006; Stevens & Campion, 1999) that facilitates team effectiveness. This obviously raises the issue of where individuals will acquire these generic KSAs. They might be trained by organizations, but it is unlikely that this would be effective if temporary employees are being used. Perhaps, in schools of the future, *teamwork* will be as common as reading, writing, and arithmetic.

CHAPTER SUMMARY

In this chapter, we focused specifically on the issue of team effectiveness. In doing so, the relative emphasis shifted from predominantly laboratory-based social psychological research to the organizational psychology team literature. Although many definitions of team effectiveness have been proposed, Hackman's (1987) is the most well-accepted. This defines *team effectiveness* in terms of task performance, team viability, and the satisfaction of team members. We also gave a more elaborate definition of teams offered by Kozlowski and Bell (2003).

There have also been a number of team-effectiveness models; several were reviewed in the chapter. We began by examining McGrath's model (1964) and ended up with Campion's attempt to synthesize many team-effectiveness models. Although the specifics of the models described are different, a common characteristic of most is the idea that team process is a key mediating variable. Nevertheless, the importance of team process has not been supported well empirically, and it is possible that causal sequences other than the familiar input–process–output may explain team effectiveness.

From the team-effectiveness models described, several specific determinants of team effectiveness were chosen for further review. These included team composition, task design, reward systems, and team process. As with individual performance, teams need members with relevant skills/abilities in order to be successful. However, research has also shown that it is important to have the right mixture of abilities/skills, and that personality and attitudes are important as well.

Task design is an important determinant of team effectiveness, for several reasons. Teams are often ineffective because they are performing tasks that are not well suited for teams; organizations often overlook this fact in their zeal to utilize teams. Task design is important in determining the most important strategies for teams to use, and it may also have motivational effects on team members.

As with individual performance, rewards are a very important determinant of team performance. Simply put, if organizations want teams to perform well, reward systems must be designed so that the teams' accomplishments are rewarded. In designing team reward systems, however, organizations must consider the level of both task and outcome interdependence. It is also crucial that the individual and team reward systems do not work against each other.

Team process is ubiquitous in the team-effectiveness literature. Ironically, despite its importance, there is a lack of consensus on what actually constitutes the most important dimensions of team process. No attempt is made to resolve this issue here. Instead we discussed a number of behavioral and cognitive/affective processes that have been linked to team effectiveness. These included communication, coordination, collaboration, cohesion, team efficacy, empowerment, and conflict.

Based on the determinants of team effectiveness, three general approaches to enhancing team effectiveness were offered: (a) selection, (b) reward system administration, and (c) team-development activities. As with individual performance, organizations can enhance the performance of teams by selecting highly skilled individuals. Selection for teamwork, however, may require a consideration of individuals' preferences as well as specific team-related skills. The most fundamental issue with regard to reward administration is simply to make sure that teams are rewarded for their performance. Organizations must also make sure that team-level reward systems fit the tasks that teams

PEOPLE BEHIND THE RESEARCH

EDUARDO SALAS AND HIS TEAMMATES ALONG THE WAY

Studying work teams takes a team. I've been fortunate to have had (and continue to do so) great teammates along my career. These teammates supported and encouraged each other; promoted creativity, innovation and could resolve conflicts; cooperated and communicated well (most of the time); took leadership roles when needed; "shared a mental model" of what, how, why, and when to do required research tasks. I've had teammates that were interested in applying the best industrial/organizational and human factors science possible to solve team performance problems and who had a passion for thinking and doing team research, but we all ultimately were driven to have impact—impact on how to compose, manage, train, develop or assess aviation, medical, financial, military, oil, engineering and industry teams.

All began at Old Dominion University in the early 80's when two of my advisors (Ben B. Morgan, Jr. and Albert S. Glickman) got interested in seeking funds to study teams over time. They got me interested in work teams. And the race began. As soon as I left graduate school, I was hired by the U.S. Navy in Orlando (then

the Naval Training Systems Center; now NAV-AIR Orlando). My first assignment was to develop a research program aimed at understanding, measuring and improving team performance. We worked first, with gunfire and submarine teams, then aviation.[1] We began to look at aircrews and their coordination demands. We outlined and tested a number of principles on how to design and deliver Crew Resource Management (CRM) training (now a popular strategy used in commercial aviation and medical settings). We developed a set of CRM training guidelines for the Navy to implement across all aviation platforms. These early successes gave us momentum. We were also interested in getting information out—to other work team scientists, team training developers and practitioners. So, we sought to publish our work widely and in different forums.

In the late 80's we had our biggest opportunity and challenge. The "TADMUS Program" came along.[2] The Tactical Decision Making under Stress research program funded by the Office of Naval Research launched a new era in team research. It was an era of theory building; of developing expert teams; of studying teams in complex and "natural" settings; of developing process and outcome metrics; and of designing team training strategies. So concepts like shared mental models; mutual performance monitoring, back-up behavior, interpositional knowledge, anticipation rater, team leader training, team self-correction training, cross-training and many others surfaced in the literature done to this program. This program made contributions to theory, measurement, and training of work teams. This was quite a ride—where we, I believe, changed how people in the Navy (and maybe beyond) looked at work teams. It was a ride with ups and downs; with joy and moments of not much joy; with growth and intellectual stimulation, and great personal satisfaction.

As I left the Navy in 1999[3], a new world opened up to me. And now I spend my time thinking and researching about shared cognition, multicultural teamwork, simulation-based team training, and team performance measurement and diagnosis. I still work with real work teams like coalition forces, in medical settings, at NASA, the oil and financial teams. It is a new ride.

So to study teams it takes a team—a team of good, passionate, motivated, fun, and engaging colleagues. And by the way, I've learned that effective teamwork is complex, dynamic, elusive, and difficult to maintain; that maintaining shared mental models is not trivial, but possible; the importance of theory and of robust metrics; the value of translating what we know

into practical terms and of working closer with the customer; and that you need great set of teammates to study working teams; and that you need to have fun practicing our science. And I've had some great ones along the way . . .

Eduardo Salas
Department of Psychology
University of Central Florida

[1]My teammates were Carolyn Prince, Randy Oser, Renee Stout, David Baker, Clint Bowers, Florian Jentsch and more . . .

[2]My teammates were Jan Cannon-Bowers, Joan Johnston, Kim Smith-Jentsch, Carol Paris, Scott Tannenbaum, Marvin Cohen, Bob McIntyre, Daniel Serfaty, Nancy Cooke, Steve Koslowski and more . . .

[3]My teammates were Shawn Burke, Steve Fiore, and my students Katherine Wilson, Heather Priest, Kevin Stagl, Dana Sims, Cameron Klein, Mike Rosen and more . . .

perform, and that they are aligned with individual-level reward systems.

In this chapter, the final method of enhancing team effectiveness was team development. Team-development activities represent training interventions that are designed to improve various aspects of team functioning (e.g., definition of roles, setting goals). Most team-development interventions utilize the services of an outside consultant/facilitator, and most are data based. Research has shown that team-development activities may enhance team effectiveness. It appears, however, that interventions focused on task-related issues are more successful than those focused on interpersonal issues.

SUGGESTED ADDITIONAL READINGS

Alper, S., Tjosvold, D., & Law, K. S. (2000). Conflict management, efficacy, and performance in organizational teams. *Personnel Psychology, 53,* 625–642.

Ilgen, D. R., Hollenbeck, J. R., Johnson, M., & Jundt, D. (2005). Teams in organizations: From input–process–output models to IMOI models. *Annual Review of Psychology, 56,* 517–543.

Kozlowski, S. W. J. & Bell, B. S., (2003). Work groups and teams in organization. In W. C. Borman, D. R. Ilgen, & R. J. Klimoski (Eds.), *Handbook of psychology: Industrial and organizational psychology* (pp. 333–375). Hoboken, NJ: Wiley.

Marks, M. A., DeChurch, L. A., Mathieu, J. E., Panzer, F. J., & Alonso, A. (2005). Teamwork in multi-team systems. *Journal of Applied Psychology, 90*(5), 964–971.

Salas, E., Sims, D. E., & Burke, C. S. (2005). Is there a "big five" in teamwork? *Small Group Research, 36*(5), 555–599.

Simons, T. L., & Peterson, R. S. (2000). Task conflict and relationship conflict in top management teams: The pivotal role of intrateam trust. *Journal of Applied Psychology, 85,* 102–111.

Chapter Thirteen

Organizational Theory and Design

A major theme throughout this book has been that the primary focus of organizational psychology is individual behavior. Consistent with this theme, we have explored a number of factors that impact the behavior of individual employees in organizations. Some of these (e.g., compensation programs) are aimed directly at individuals; others (e.g., groupthink) reside primarily at the group level. In this chapter, we raise the level of analysis one step higher and explore the impact of organizational design on employee behavior and overall organizational effectiveness.

For the most part organizational psychologists have tended to shy away from *macro-level* issues such as organizational theory and design. As a result, much of the work in this area has been done by sociologists, as well as those trained directly in organizational theory and other areas of management (e.g., strategic management). In recent years, there has also been work done by those in operations research who mathematically model organizational scenarios (Kujacic & Bujovic, 2003).

The reluctance of organizational psychologists to tackle macro-level issues such as organizational design is unfortunate for two reasons. First, anyone who has worked in an organization knows that organizational structure does impact individual employees, although such influences are admittedly often indirect. For example, in a university setting, the manner in which academic departments are grouped often has implications for resource allocations and the extent to which faculty in different departments

collaborate. Thus, to ignore organizational design is to ignore a very important impact on employee behavior (Bourrier, 2005; Hornstein & de Guerre, 2006), and ultimately the effectiveness of an organization (Russo & Harrison, 2005).

A second reason organizational psychologists should not avoid macro-level issues is that those trained in fields such as sociology, organizational theory, and strategic management often provide an incomplete picture of the impact of organizational design. Just as organizational psychologists tend to focus (or, some would say, overfocus) on individual behavior, the analyses provided by those trained in other fields often exclude individual behavior. To say that the design of an organization contributes to its effectiveness begs the question: How, specifically, does the design of an organization impact the behavior of those in the organization, and does it make the organization more, or less, effective? Therefore, an interdisciplinary approach to organizational design that includes the contributions of sociology, organizational theory, strategic management, and organizational psychology will be taken in the present chapter.

The chapter will begin by discussing the broad field of organizational theory. Organizational theories are simply different approaches to organizing human endeavors such as work. Organizational theories are important because they form the basis for concrete organizational designs. The focus of the chapter then shifts to a discussion of the major factors that impact the decisions organizations make with respect to organizational design. The chapter will then examine recent innovations in the design of organizations; these designs depart widely from traditional organizational theories. The chapter concludes with a summary of empirical research on the impact of organizational design and a description of factors that will likely impact the design of organizations of the future.

WHAT IS AN ORGANIZATIONAL THEORY?

In the organizational sciences (e.g., organizational behavior, organizational psychology), one of the more misunderstood terms is *organizational theory*. To some, organizational theory is a field of study; to others, it is the process of using metaphorical language to describe organizational processes (e.g., McKenna & Wright, 1992; Morgan, 1986), or it represents an attempt to determine the best way to organize work organizations. The

term is used to indicate all of these things, but an *organizational theory* is really just a way of organizing purposeful human action. Given the diversity of purposeful human endeavors, there are numerous ways to organize them, and, hence, a great many organizational theories.

The academic discipline that really has taken the lead in theorizing about the organization of purposeful human behavior is sociology. Sociology is essentially the study of macro-level forces (e.g., social stratification, social institutions) on human behavior (e.g., Merton, 1968; Parsons, 1951). A classic illustration of this was sociologist Emil Durkheim's classic study of the determinants of suicide (Durkheim, 1951). Durkheim proposed and found support for the idea that some forms of social structure result in alienation and a sense of hopelessness (called *anomie*), which ultimately leads to higher rates of suicide. Given this historical backdrop, it is natural that sociologists would be more interested in the impact of the structure and design of organizations than psychologists would be. In fact, the Hawthorne studies, which are considered one of the most important historical events contributing to the development of organizational psychology, were conducted under the direction of sociologist Elton Mayo.

Given that organizational theory deals with different ways of organizing human activity, how does one *theorize* about organizations? In most scientific disciplines, if one wants to theorize about something and ultimately study it, the most common approach is to bring it into a laboratory for closer inspection. Unfortunately, organizational theorists cannot do this because organizations are largely abstractions, and thus cannot easily be subjected to laboratory investigations. Although we can draw elegant organization charts to represent reporting relationships, and so on, what keeps an organization together is the fact that an organization's employees understand its design and adapt their behavior accordingly (Katz & Kahn, 1978).

Given these constraints, organizational theorists have been forced to adopt more indirect methods of investigation. Perhaps the most common of these methods has been the use of metaphors to describe and understand organizational structures (McKenna & Wright, 1992). A metaphor is simply a type of figurative language; that is, using words or phrases to communicate anything other than their literal meaning. For example, if a person were to look out the window and say that it is "raining cats and dogs," that person would be using a metaphor.

The most common metaphor used in the organizational theory literature has been to liken organizations to biological organisms and apply general systems theory to describe them (Katz & Kahn, 1978; von Bertalanffy, 1956). If we liken organizations to biological organisms, this leads to several important conclusions that may have important implications for organizational functioning. Perhaps the most important of these is that organizations are in constant interaction with the environment around them, just as any biological system must interact with the larger ecosystem in which it is embedded. Like biological systems that ignore the larger ecosystem, organizations that ignore their larger environment (e.g., customers, public opinion) may risk extinction. Because of this, organizations often spend considerable time and financial resources attempting to understand (and sometimes control) their external environments.

A second major implication of the biological organism metaphor is that an organization consists of a series of subsystems that must work together in order for the organization to function optimally. As an analogy, the human body, which is a highly complex biological system, consists of a number of organ systems that control physiological activities such as circulation, digestion, and respiration. Most of the coordination among these systems is controlled by a complex array of chemical messengers that are released by the brain. In organizations, coordination among subsystems is often achieved through the structural arrangements themselves, but, in some cases, special mechanisms (e.g., coordinating committees) are established for it.

Another metaphor that is quite common in organizational theory is that of the organization as a machine. Like machines, organizations take environmental input, transform the input in some fashion, and return that input, in an altered form, back into the environment. Many of the implications of the *organization as machine* metaphor are quite similar to the *organization as biological organism* metaphor. That is, organizations must pay attention to the external environment and to the coordination of its internal components. An additional implication of the machine metaphor, however, is the importance of making sure that the *components* of the machine (i.e., people and processes) are performing properly. This is typically accomplished in a number of ways, including selection, performance appraisal, performance coaching, and, in some cases, redesign of jobs in order to maximize the unique capabilities of individuals.

Although the biological organism and machine metaphors have the longest histories in organizational theory, McKenna and Wright (1992) point out that other metaphors may also be useful to organizational theorists. For example, they point out that organizations can be likened to the brain—with all its complex interconnections—and to families—with their complex relationships—and to political arenas—with all of their influence and power dynamics. While these metaphors have yet to be used extensively by organizational theorists, they probably reflect the realities of many organizations today. As we will see later in the chapter, the design of many organizations today is highly complex so these new metaphors are needed.

MAJOR ORGANIZATIONAL THEORIES

Having provided a brief overview of the field of organizational theory, we now move on to a consideration of the major organizational theories themselves. Organizational theories simply represent ideas or models of the form in which human activity can be organized. Obviously, there could be an almost infinite number of ideas about organizing human activity; however, over the years, three general types of organizational theories have been developed. These three types are described next.

Classical Organizational Theories

Historically, the term *classical organizational theory* has been used to denote models of organizing that were developed from approximately the early twentieth century until the mid-1940s. The best known of these classical theories were scientific management (Taylor, 1911), ideal bureaucracy (Weber, 1947), and administrative management (Fayol, 1984). Each is discussed briefly in the following paragraphs.

The term *scientific management* was first introduced in describing the history of organizational psychology (see Chapter 1) and was examined further in our discussion of job design (see Chapter 9). We resurrect this

term yet again because it also has implications for the ways organizations are designed. As might be remembered from our earlier discussion, a fundamental principle of scientific management was that those who design the work should be separate from those who actually perform the work. The implications of this approach for organizing work are quite important. For example, it implies that there should be distinct status or hierarchical differences among employees. In Taylor's writings, it is fairly obvious that those who design the work occupy a higher status than those who perform it. An organization that is designed from a scientific management perspective thus has many levels and many ways to distinguish among those levels.

Recall that another fundamental principle of scientific management is that work should be broken down into the smallest and simplest components possible. For example, the various steps involved in the production of an automobile would be broken down into the simplest possible instructions. The implication of this emphasis on simplification is that an organization should be structured such that employees performing very similar tasks should be grouped together. Furthermore, in most cases, the best way to manage these groups of employees is to create departmental structures that are based on these highly specialized activities. Thus, an organization that is designed according to scientific management will consist of a large number of departments, with each performing a highly specialized function.

Beyond these more concrete organizational design implications of scientific management, there are also a number of less tangible implications. Perhaps one of the most important of these is that a scientifically managed organization will have a great number of rules and procedures for employees to follow. Frederick Taylor became famous for using empirical research to determine the most efficient way to carry out work tasks. The underlying assumption behind this quest for efficiency was that there is "one best way" to do any job or accomplish any task. The trick is to find it. This tendency is likely to be generalized to other organizational tasks; thus, such organizations are likely to have thick *policies and procedures* manuals that have scripted procedures for employees to follow in the event of any contingency.

The term *ideal bureaucracy* may strike some as an oxymoron because the term *bureaucracy* is often used as a codeword for organizational inefficiency and administrative inflexibility. In reality ideal bureaucracy simply represents one idea or theory of how human activity should be organized. Most attribute the development of ideal bureaucracy to Max Weber, who is generally credited with being one of the pioneers of the macro side of organizational psychology. Weber, as you may recall, wore many intellectual hats and made contributions to history, economics, political science, and sociology during his lifetime. In Weber's time, there were few organizations in the form that we see them today. Instead, a great many "organizations" of his era were loosely run family businesses, or they consisted of an individual craftsman who worked independently. Given these organizational forms, there was not a great need for organizing, per se.

With the advent of the Industrial Revolution, however, there arose a great need to organize large numbers of people who had left rural areas to work in factories located in large cities. Furthermore, the organizational models that were predominant in the late nineteenth and early twentieth centuries were not adequate for handling these large

organizations. For example, at that time, a great deal of one's success was based on social connections or the nature of one's family bloodline—not surprising, given that a good number of organizations of that era were family run. The problem with this model being implemented in industrial settings was that those who possessed the best social or family connections were not always capable of performing the tasks required by the work.

Weber proposed ideal bureaucracy as an alternative that would result in more efficient operations and more effective use of talent in organizations. One of the primary assumptions behind ideal bureaucracy (and one that many people forget) is a noble one: Rewards should be based on one's contributions to the organizations, as opposed to social or familial connections. Unfortunately, many of the more negative assumptions underlying bureaucracy have tended to overshadow this one.

As in scientific management, there is, in ideal bureaucracy, a strong reliance on previously developed rules and procedures to guide behavior. In a truly efficient ideal bureaucracy, there should be a rule or procedure covering almost any situation that employees may encounter. This may often explain why bureaucracies have so much difficulty when there is a highly novel situation, and, in many cases, why people have a negative view of this organizational form.

Another hallmark of ideal bureaucracy is very close supervision of employees. Bureaucratic organizations typically are characterized by very narrow spans of control; that is, each supervisor does not supervise a large number of employees. One thing is accomplished by a narrow span of control: It is easier for a supervisor to meet the needs of his or her subordinates. Answering questions and helping to train 4 employees is obviously much easier than doing the same tasks with 40. A narrow span of control also makes it far easier for supervisors to monitor the behaviors of their subordinates. This has led many to conclude that bureaucracy is based on the assumption that employees will not work unless their behaviors are tightly monitored—not a particularly positive view of human nature.

Another important principle of ideal bureaucracy is unity of command. In a bureaucratic structure, each employee should ideally have one (and only one) direct supervisor. For anyone prone to cynicism, a logical conclusion would be that this principle, like the narrow span of control, would make it easier for an organization to control its employees. Unity of command, however, may have some tangible positive benefits for employees as well. If an employee reports to only one supervisor, this reduces the odds that he or she would have to meet the combined and potentially conflicting expectations of more than one individual. As will be discussed later in this chapter, one of the problems with some modern organizational designs that violate this principle is that they increase role conflict among employees (e.g., Joyce, 1986).

A third important principle of ideal bureaucracy is unity of direction. This means that information within a bureaucratic organization flows in one direction—typically, from the top of the organization down to lower levels. The primary benefit of information flowing in one direction is that it increases predictability and stability. This makes everyone's lives easier when vast amounts of information must be processed and also makes it much easier for the top management of an organization to control employees' access to information. Top managers can make sure that employees "know only what they need to know," and nothing

more. This principle, like the others previously discussed, makes it far easier for employees to be controlled than would be the case if information within an organization flowed freely.

Ultimately, like any other organizational theory, ideal bureaucracy is neither good nor bad. The extent to which it enhances or detracts from organizational effectiveness depends to a large extent on how it is implemented, and whether it is appropriate for the organization's environment. As will be shown later in the section on contingency theories, there are some situations in which bureaucracy is very appropriate. In other situations, however, organizations that use it are highly prone to failure.

The term *administrative management* was first coined by Henri Fayol, who was an engineer by training and eventually became the chief executive of a French mining company. Fayol (1984) sought to develop a relatively universal set of organizing principles for managers to apply in organizations. To give these principles meaning, however, Fayol presented them in the context of the activities of managers, or behaviors he called *management functions*. According to Fayol, the major functions of managers included planning, organizing, commanding, coordination, and controlling. The principles that Fayol proposed were designed to assist managers in carrying out these essential functions.

Table 13.1 presents Fayol's 14 organizing principles. As can be seen, many items on this list are similar to the principles of ideal bureaucracy that were described earlier. For example, Fayol advocated, among other bureaucratic principles, the division of work, having a well-defined authority structure, unity of command, unity of direction, order, and equity in the way individuals are rewarded. Among the unique principles that

TABLE 13.1
Fayol's Classic Principles of Organizing

Principle	Fayol's Comments
1. Division of work	Individuals and managers work on the same part or task.
2. Authority and responsibility	Authority: right to give orders; power to exact obedience; goes with responsibility for reward and punishment.
3. Discipline	Obedience, application, energy, behavior. Agreement between firm and individual.
4. Unity of command	Orders received from one supervisor.
5. Unity of direction	One head and one plan for activities with the same objective.
6. Subordination of individual interest to general interest	Organizational objectives come before the objectives of the individual.
7. Remuneration of personnel	Fairness of pay to the organization and the individual; discussed various forms.
8. Centralization	Amount of discretion held by the manager compared to that allowed to subordinates.
9. Scalar chain	Line of authority from lowest to top.
10. Order	A place for everyone, and everyone in his or her place.
11. Equity	Emphasis on kindness and justice.
12. Stability of tenure of personnel	Ability in managerial ranges; time to adapt to work.
13. Initiative	Power of thinking out and executing a plan.
14. Esprit de corps	Harmony and union among personnel is strength.

Adapted from: From H. Fayol. (1984). *General and industrial management.* Belmont, CA: Lake Publishing.

Fayol added were stability of personnel, encouraging people to take initiative, and having a high level of cohesion and camaraderie among employees. These three additions are interesting, simply because they do not seem to be in line with those of ideal bureaucracy. In fact, they seem more compatible with organizational theories that were developed due to perceived limitations of bureaucracy.

Although many of Fayol's principles are useful, and in fact put into practice in many organizations even today, they have also been widely criticized on a number of counts. Perhaps the most vigorous criticism of these principles, and classical theories in general, is that they ignore the "human element" in organizations (e.g., McGregor, 1960). That is, these principles paint a picture of employees in organizations as being interchangeable

cogs in a grand machine, rather than humans with emotions, desires, and creative talents. The other major criticism of Fayol's principles has been that they are simply too general. To take one example, Fayol advocates fairness in the remuneration of employees, which most managers would likely agree is a desirable principle. However, even though he does offer some suggestions on how to accomplish this goal (Fayol, 1984), these suggestions are rather vague. The same problem plagues many of the other principles as well.

Humanistic Organizational Theories

Recall from Chapter 1 that the Human Relations movement began in the 1940s, largely as a response to organizations being designed according to the classical theories described in the previous section. According to those at the forefront of the Human Relations movement, most notably Douglas McGregor and Rensis Likert, classically designed organizations dehumanized the workplace and vastly underutilized the creativity and initiative of employees. The primary reason for this negative impact of classical theory can be traced largely to its underlying assumptions about human nature. With their strong emphasis on order and control, classical organizational theories are based on the assumption that employees will not work unless they are prodded to do so, and they lack the creativity and initiative to define their roles on their own. The best known of these humanistic organizational theories were McGregor's Theory X/Y Leadership Distinction and Likert's concept of The Human Organization.

In his 1960 book, *The Human Side of Enterprise*, McGregor made a distinction between two types of managers: Theory X and Theory Y. Managers characterized as Theory X operate under the assumption that most people have an inherent dislike for work and, as a result, need to be coerced and supervised very closely if they are to work toward the goals of the organization. Another fundamental assumption of the Theory X manager is that people have little ambition, are not self-directed, and value security over all else. This again suggests the need for high levels of managerial control and close supervision of employees.

In direct contrast to the Theory X manager, the Theory Y manager operates under the assumption that work is a natural part of peoples' lives, and rather than avoid it, most people seek greater meaning in it. As a result, individuals are capable of some degree of self-control and will work toward the goals of the organization to the extent that they find doing so to be personally reward-ing. Another fundamental Theory Y assumption is that, under the right conditions, many people will seek out responsibility and will creatively solve organizational problems if they are allowed to do so. A final key assumption of Theory Y is that most organizations are designed in a way that results in the underutilization of employees' skills and talents. Given that classical organizational designs were still dominant at the time McGregor wrote this book, this was an obvious criticism of classical organizational theory.

Although the Theory X/Y distinction is made at the individual manager level and thus is not technically a theory of organizing, it is not difficult to extend these ideas to the organizational level. An organization that is populated with Theory X managers is likely to have very narrow spans of control, strict lines of authority, and a vast number of rules and procedures—in short, the design would be based largely on classical organizational design principles. The Theory Y organization, in contrast, would include wider spans of control, more flexible lines of authority, and rules only for very important issues. These are logical design features if one assumes that employees are capable of doing their work without close supervision, and that they are bright enough to engage in creative problem solving when novel problems occur.

The primary benefit of the Theory Y organization is that it is inherently more humane and potentially more psychologically fulfilling for employees than Theory X organizations. Within such organizations, work can be a source of personal growth rather than a "necessary evil" that one must endure in order to make a living. There are, however, potential downsides to the Theory Y organization. Specifically, many have argued that it is rather naïve to assume that all employees want to achieve personal growth through their work experiences (e.g., Hackman & Oldham, 1980), and that everyone can work productively with only minimal supervision. Another potential drawback associated with the Theory Y organization is that because lines of authority are not as clear as in classically designed organizations, there is greater potential for confusion and conflict regarding employees' roles and responsibilities.

The other organizational theory that has come to be seen as highly representative of the humanistic perspective is Likert's idea of the *human organization*. In his 1961 book, *New Patterns of Management*, Likert proposed that organizations could be classified into four different types, which corresponded to System 1 through System 4. A System 1 organization was described by Likert as an *exploitive authoritarian type*. This type of organization is very similar to Theory X because it is characterized as having very little trust in employees, little communication between employees and management, very centralized decision making, and control achieved in a very "top-down" manner. This type of organization, according to Likert, would result in largely dissatisfied employees and, ultimately, a low level of organizational performance.

The System 2 organization, which was labeled *benevolent authoritative*, was proposed to be much like the System 1 organization, although some notable differences were present. For example, in this type of organization, there is some level of trust in employees and, at times, management uses their ideas. There is also more communication in this type of organization and, on occasion, employees have an opportunity to communicate their ideas to upper management. To sum up this type, employees are still treated in a largely authoritative manner, but the organization is a bit nicer to them. According to Likert, employees in this type of organization may derive some moderate level of satisfaction toward their work and organizational performance may be "fair to good."

The System 3 organization was labeled *consultative* by Likert. This type of organization is very different from System 1 in that there is substantially greater trust in employees and their ideas are used a great deal more. In addition, there is more overall communication in such an organization and, compared to the other organizational forms, much more of it flows from the bottom up. Decision making is still primarily in the hands of those at higher organizational levels, but the manner in which this authority is exerted is different than in the System 1 and System 2 organizations. In System 3 organizations those at the top of the organization set broad policies, and more specific operational decisions are made by those at lower levels. Employees in the consultative organization work on goals that they adopt after some discussion, and, at times, they may resist organizational goals. Some level of control resides at lower organizational levels and the information that flows within the organization is accurate. According to Likert, the consultative organization is capable of "good" performance, although it may never reach a level of extremely high excellence.

System 4, the final type of organization in Likert's typology, is labeled *participative group*. This type of organization is essentially the complete opposite of the System 1 or exploitive authoritarian organization. For example, in this type of organization, managers have complete trust in subordinates and, as a result, are always seeking their input before making decisions. Communication in this type of organization is free-flowing in all directions, and there is often a great reliance on teamwork. As might be expected, decision making occurs at all organizational levels and with a high level of involvement. Employees in the participative group organization work on goals that they have a say in developing and, as a result, there is a great deal of acceptance of them. Control mechanisms are applied at all levels of the organization, and the information available to employees is complete and accurate. According to Likert, the participative group organization is the only one of the four that is truly capable of "excellent" performance. Therefore, it is probably not a coincidence that highly successful organizations (e.g., Peters & Waterman, 1982) often have much in common with Likert's System 4 organization.

Likert (1961) originally proposed four organizational types. More recently, J. Likert and Araki (1986) proposed that there is also a System 5. The System 5 organization is essentially identical to System 4, but differs in one important respect. Specifically, in a System 5 organization, leadership is truly a shared enterprise. Essentially, the organization has no "bosses." This model is common in universities where academic departments are essentially self-managed. Outside of academia this model is rare, although it may eventually become more prevalent in the future.

Although many would agree that the System 4 or 5 organizations are most likely to be successful, it is questionable whether this would always be the case. For example, having completely free-flowing information may be an advantage in some ways, but it also may lead to problems such as information overflow or distortion. Similarly, having complete trust in employees may be a good policy, provided people are in fact trustworthy. Furthermore, in the more recently developed System 5 organization, although the absence of bosses may contribute to an egalitarian atmosphere, it may also be problematic at times when someone needs to take charge.

The overall point is that there is much about McGregor's Theory Y or Likert's System 4 or 5 organizations that can lead to organizational effectiveness. However, the major weakness in these organizational theories is the notion that there is one most effective way to run an organization. That was essentially the problem with classical organizational theories. This dissatisfaction with the "one best way" approach to organizations led to the development of contingency theories of organization.

Contingency Organizational Theories

Recall from Chapter 10 that contingency theories of leadership developed largely because leadership theorists recognized that there is no singular set of personal traits or one set of behaviors that will always distinguish good leaders from poor ones. Similarly, organizational theorists gradually came to the realization that neither a classic nor a humanistic organizational form was appropriate all of the time. Thus, the basic premise of contingency organizational theories is that design of an organization must be consistent with the situation (Lawrence & Lorsch, 1967).

More recently organizational scholars labeled this the *congruence* perspective (Nadler & Tuchman 1992; 1997). The idea, much like the early contingency approach, is that organizations should be designed in ways that are congruent not only with an organization's strategy, but with other factors as well, including the work that an organization does, characteristics of the individuals within the organization, and the informal processes within the organization. Given this perspective, the obvious question then becomes: What specific internal and external factors do organizations need to pay most attention to when making organizational design decisions? In the following section, we discuss five factors that have most often been cited as driving organizational design decisions.

DETERMINANTS OF ORGANIZATIONAL DESIGN

Organizational design decisions should be made on some rational basis; that is, the design of an organization should serve some purpose. Keeping this in mind, there are many purposes that organizational design decisions can serve. Most commonly, design decisions are made to support an organization's strategy, to help it cope with environmental uncertainty, to reflect the beliefs and assumptions of those in power, and to support its core technology—in some cases, however, design is essentially preordained because of the size of an organization. Each of these factors is discussed next.

Strategy

An organization's strategy consists of its long-range goals and the tactics it uses to reach those goals. Strategic differences in organizations have a number of implications for organizational issues such as staffing, compensation and reward systems, and performance appraisals. According to Galbraith (1995), the aspects of organizational structure that tend to have the greatest impact on strategy implementation include the level of specialization, the shape of the organization, the distribution of power within the organization, and the departmental structure. *Specialization* refers simply to the types and numbers of specialties that an organization uses in performing its work. When organizations have a high degree of specialization,

this tends to improve the performance of various subtasks—excellence in engineering is more likely when there is a high concentration of engineers. Unfortunately, high specialization also makes it more difficult to integrate all of the different specialties. If an organization's strategy is to produce a highly specialized product—and produce it very consistently over time—then high specialization is preferred. On the other hand, if an organization pursues a strategy that involves changing products quickly in response to consumer demand, then a high level of specialization is a liability because it does not allow an organization to react quickly to the market. For many organizations the trend in recent years has been to veer away from specialization, largely because more and more organizations are pursuing strategies that require quick responses to changes in market conditions, and because many highly specialized tasks can be automated.

A second organizational design factor impacting strategy implementation is the shape of the organization. According to Galbraith (1995), the shape of an organization is reflected by the number of people who form departments at each hierarchical level. A narrow organization is one that has a relatively large number of levels but relatively few individuals at each level. In contrast, a very flat organization is one that has a relatively few number of levels, but each level is comprised of a large number of employees. Figure 13.1 highlights this distinction.

From a strategic point of view, the shape of an organization has some important consequences. When organizations are narrow, a great deal of time and energy is typically invested in communication, supervision, and, especially, decision making. Stated differently, a narrow organization expends a great deal of resources on "running itself."

<u>**FIGURE 13.1**</u>
Contrast between a Flat and Narrow Organizational Structure

This time spent on internal issues obviously takes time away from externally focused activities such as interfacing with customers or determining trends in the competitive market. As a result, a narrow organization is most appropriate for an organization pursuing a strategy that involves producing highly specialized products or services in markets where the demand is fairly consistent.

A very flat organization, in contrast, spends far less time on internal processes such as supervision and decision making. With such large spans of control, these types of organizations often rely on teams or coordinating committees to provide typical supervisory functions. Also, with a flatter organizational structure, decisions can be made without having to go through many organizational layers. Flatter organizational structures thus allow much quicker responses to consumer demand or the penetration of highly volatile market segments.

This is likely the reason why organizations in new or emerging sectors of the economy (e.g., Internet-based commerce) often have flat organizational structures (Sine, Mitsuhashui, & Kirsch, 2006).

A third organizational design principle that impacts strategy implementation is distribution of power within an organization. As Galbraith (1995) notes, the distribution of power in organizations is typically reflected in the manner in which decisions are made. This can be seen both vertically and horizontally. Vertical distribution of decision-making power reflects the extent to which the decision making in an organization is centralized versus decentralized. Centralization would be present if the headquarters of an organization made all important decisions; decentralization would be present if decision making was pushed down to the level of those who either produce the product or directly interact with the customers.

Horizontal distribution of power is reflected in whether managers shift decision-making power to the department or unit that has the best information or is in the best position to make a decision. An example of horizontal decision-making power that is becoming increasingly common is organizations' shift of decision making to units that have the most customer contact, particular in highly volatile customer-driven industries.

An organization that concentrates power in the hands of a few top managers is likely to have difficulty implementing a strategy that involves quick responses to market conditions. When decisions need to be made very quickly—often, by those who are close to consumers (e.g., salespeople, customer service employees)—this type of organizational structure is simply inefficient. Similarly, an organization that is very hesitant to share power horizontally is often unable to take advantage of cost-saving opportunities associated with contracting out aspects of their business. They simply lack the knowledge to take advantage of such opportunities.

The final aspect of structure that will impact strategy implementation is an organization's departmental structure. According to Galbraith (1995), departments may be formed according to a number of criteria, including function, product line, customer segments, geographical areas, or work-flow processes. Traditionally, departmentalization by function (e.g., marketing, production, human resources) has been the most common form in organizations (see Fig. 13.2). The primary advantage of this form of departmentalization is that it promotes a high level of specialization and, as a result, a high level of excellence in each particular function. This type of structure, for example, makes it is easier for groups of product engineers to exchange ideas that will potentially

FIGURE 13.2
Example of a Functional Department Structure

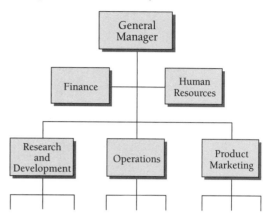

Source: J. R. Galbraith. (1995). *Designing organizations: An executive briefing on strategy, structure, and process.* San Francisco: Jossey-Bass. Copyright © 1995 Jossey-Bass. Reprinted by permission of John Wiley & Sons, Inc.

lead to new and creative products (Damanpour, 1991).

Despite this benefit, a departmental structure based on functional specialization has two primary weaknesses. First, this type of organizational structure is very good if an organization produces a single product or a very limited number of products or services. However, as the number of products or services increases, managers who lead functional teams can easily become overwhelmed because of the complexity that is introduced. A second disadvantage of this type of structure is that it does not promote a great deal of cross-fertilization of ideas among functional groups. In this type of structure employees may become very compartmentalized and thus not take advantage of the ideas of other specialties in the development of new products or services. This is often the reason that universities, most of which have departmental structures based on academic disciplines, tend not to have a great deal of collaboration across departments.

FIGURE 13.3
Example of a Product-Based Structure

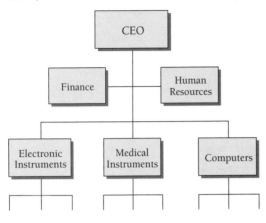

Source: J. R. Galbraith. (1995). *Designing organizations: An executive briefing on strategy, structure, and process.* San Francisco: Jossey-Bass. Copyright © 1995 Jossey-Bass. Reprinted by permission of John Wiley & Sons, Inc.

In terms of strategy, a functional structure is likely to work best in a relatively stable environment—one in which technological change is not rapid. Organizations with functional structures have a difficult time in industries where competitive advantage is determined largely by the speed with which organizations are able to respond to market demands.

A second basis on which many current organizations create departmental structures is the products or services offered. Figure 13.3 provides an illustration of how such an organization might look. Notice that immediately below the CEO are the finance and human resources departments. The departments at the next level, however, correspond to the various products or services in which this organization specializes (e.g., electronic instruments, medical instruments, computers). In this type of structure, the functional specialties that were described earlier are included under each of the product groupings. That is, there would be a

marketing group for electronic instruments, another for medical instruments, and so on.

A product-based departmental structure is an advantage if an organization's strategy is to penetrate many markets or to have a highly diverse set of products. As stated earlier, a functional departmental structure would be quickly overwhelmed if an organization pursued this type of strategy. According to Galbraith (1995), however, there are two principal disadvantages associated with a product-based departmental structure. First, general product managers often tend to think of themselves as entrepreneurs and thus want considerable autonomy and independence. Although this may be a way to foster innovation (e.g., Puranam, Singh, & Zollo, 2006), it also can result in an organization's consistently "reinventing the wheel" because these individuals act independently of each other.

A second and related problem is that it is difficult to achieve functional "economies of scale" that benefit the organization as a whole in product-based structures. Note in Figure 13.3 that there is a marketing department for each of this organization's three product lines. While beneficial in some ways, this can also be wasteful because it precludes the organization's taking advantage of complimentary approaches to marketing or advertising. In effect, each marketing department focuses on its own product and may not have the larger interests of the organization as its first priority.

A third departmental structure proposed by Galbraith (1995) is based on the various markets that an organization serves. This may lead to a departmental structure based on the customers the organization serves or the various industries in which the organization operates. Market-driven departmental structures are becoming increasingly popular, given the decline in large-scale heavy manufacturing and the increasing number of firms in the service sector. This type of structure is particularly advantageous in the service sector because it enables the organization to react very quickly when, for some reason, customers' preferences change. The primary concern, as with the product-based structure, is that organizations may waste a considerable amount of time duplicating functional activities within each market.

A fourth type of departmental structure is based on geographic location. For example, an organization may create a "Northeast" division that is responsible for all operations in the New England states and a "Midwest" division that is concerned with all business in the Great Lakes region. Most typically, geographical structures are found in industries where service is provided on-site and regional differences may be important to the business. Fast-food companies such as McDonald's or Burger King are organized in this fashion. The primary service is provided on-site (you can't e-mail someone a Big Mac!), and there may be important regional differences in food preferences.

The primary advantage of a geographic structure is that organizations can more easily provide personal services to customers and make adjustments to those services based on regional preferences. A potential disadvantage of this structure again, however, is duplication of functional activities. Also, geographical dispersion makes it more difficult to maintain consistency and company-wide quality standards. Recent advances in communication technology have made consistent quality somewhat less of a concern, but it still remains an issue for many products and services.

A final way that organizations may structure their departments is according to major work-flow processes. According to Galbraith

FIGURE 13.4

Example of a Work-Flow Process Structure

Source: J. R. Galbraith. (1995). *Designing organizations: An executive briefing on strategy, structure, and process.* San Francisco: Jossey-Bass. Copyright © 1995 Jossey-Bass. Reprinted by permission of John Wiley & Sons, Inc.

(1995), this is the newest type of departmental structure. Figure 13.4 shows an example of a departmental structure that is process based. Notice that the three departments in this organizational structure correspond to the processes of new product development, order fulfillment, and customer acquisition/maintenance. Functional groups would reside within each of these process-related departments.

When compared to the functional organizational structure, the process-based structure has one advantage: There is potentially a lower amount of duplication of effort because there is less need to duplicate functions across departments responsible for different processes. For example, customer service personnel would reside exclusively in the customer acquisition and maintenance department, so these efforts would not be duplicated across departments. This structure may also force an organization to take a hard look at its major work-flow process; in fact, this type of structure cannot be created unless an organization does so. By looking at its major processes, an organization may gain valuable insights into how to become more effective and efficient. For example, by developing a greater understanding of its distribution systems, a consumer product company may be able to adopt a strategy of reducing costs by maintaining smaller inventories.

Level of Environmental Uncertainty

Organizations differ greatly in the degree of environmental uncertainty they must face. One obvious factor that impacts environmental uncertainty is the number of years an organization has been in existence. New or start-up organizations typically face a highly uncertain environment as they try to survive (Aldrich, 1999). Conversely, organizations that have been in existence for many years have an established track record and consequently a higher level of certainty.

Another important factor impacting uncertainty is the level of competition an organization faces. An organization operating in an industry with few competitors will face a far more certain environment compared to one operating in an industry with many competitors. A related factor impacting uncertainty is the degree of stability in an organization's competitive environment. Some organizations produce goods and services that have rather stable demand; for others, the demand may fluctuate very widely. A third factor impacting an organization is the extent to which its markets are affected by external factors such as government regulations. Examples of very stable environments would include government and regulated utilities. Examples of very uncertain market sectors would include high technology, consumer products, and transportation.

Uncertainty is related to organizational design because the degree of uncertainty often impacts the speed at which organizations must adapt to external conditions. A computer software company, for example, must be constantly prepared to bring new products to market and to satisfy the rapid changes in technology. A regulated utility, on the other hand, typically does not have to adapt nearly as quickly because it has much less volatility in its environment. Given this consideration, as a general rule organizations that operate in highly uncertain environments need organizational structures that allow them to act quickly when change occurs (Burns & Stalker, 1961).

Based on the organizational theories that have been discussed up to this point, it seems fairly clear that highly bureaucratic organizational structures are not very adaptable in highly uncertain environments (O'Toole & Meier, 2003). Having a large number of rules and procedures, clear lines of authority, and small spans of control may keep things humming along very smoothly in stable environments. When things change, however, it is very difficult for highly bureaucratic organizations to change course quickly. More humanistic organizations fare much better in uncertain environments. In these types of organizations, power is shifted to lower levels, and employees at these levels are empowered to make decisions without first having lengthy deliberations with superiors.

Recent research, however, has shown that the relationship between organizational structure and environmental uncertainty may be more complicated than Burns and Stalker (1961) originally proposed. Since, Mitsuhashui, and Kirsch (2006) found that having a more humanistic (or organic) organizational structure was not beneficial for *all* organizations operating in highly turbulent emerging segments of the economy. Specifically, they found that new organizations working in highly turbulent environments benefited from many attributes of bureaucratic organizing (e.g., rules, administrative control). This suggests that start-up organizations, which are typically formed by entrepreneurs not professional managers, still need to pay close attention to organizational and administrative issues.

Beliefs and Assumptions of Those in Power

Organizations are created by people; therefore, at some level organizations typically reflect the beliefs and assumptions of people who hold positions of power. In some cases this would be the organizational founder, but it could also be those in high-level positions. What specific beliefs of such individuals would impact organizational design? One of the fundamental judgments that managers in organizations must make is whether their employees can be trusted (Dansereau, Graen, & Haga, 1975). Organizations that are run by managers who place little trust in their employees will likely favor organizational designs that allow for high levels of managerial control. These designs offer very small spans of control, limited and highly centralized communication, and other mechanisms that discourage independent action on the part of employees.

A related issue is the extent to which managers respect their employees' job-related skills or believe in their competence (Liden & Maslyn, 1998). This is obviously related to trust but is not the same thing. For example, a manager may believe that his or her employees are trustworthy people, yet he or she may have little confidence in their skills. Managers may also see some employees as highly competent, yet have little trust

in them. Organizations run by managers who have little confidence in their employees will probably be designed to resemble organizations where there is low trust. The similar designs achieve the same goal: a high level of control over employees. Conversely, when managers in organizations have a great deal of confidence in employees, it is more likely that the organizational design will allow employees to use their unique skills and abilities. Organizational arrangements may allow employees to exercise independent judgment and decision making, and to communicate freely with each other. Furthermore, in some cases, organizations create designs that specifically facilitate creativity (Galbraith, 1995). An organization with a long history of doing this is 3M (see Comment 13.1).

A final belief or assumption of those in power that may impact organizational design is the level of organizational performance that is expected or desired. As we saw earlier, Likert (1961) proposed that there is a strong connection between the desire to maintain managerial control and organizational performance. In the System 1 organization, managers maintain very high levels of control, yet the price they pay for this control is high—such organizations will likely only be mediocre. In contrast, in the System 4 and System 5 organizations, managers give up a good deal of control, which is risky. However, the rewards that go along with doing so are potentially very high because theses organizations are capable of truly excellent performance.

Although it seems illogical, there may be reasons why managers in an organization would be comfortable with minimal performance. For example, managerial compensation packages often provide disincentives for taking steps to create long-term organizational excellence. Specifically, stock option plans often reward managers for taking steps

THE 3M PATH TO INNOVATION

THE MINNESOTA MINING and Manufacturing Company, more commonly known as 3M, was founded in 1902 by five businessmen whose original intent was to mine the mineral corundum and sell it to grinding-wheel manufacturers. The manufacturers needed this mineral to make abrasive materials such as sandpaper. Unfortunately, the mineral found in the mine they purchased in Crystal Bay, Minnesota, contained another material that was not suitable for abrasives; thus, they were not able to carry out their original plan. The company ultimately decided to manufacture abrasives themselves and, after several years of struggle, expanded into the production of adhesives. Ultimately, as most readers are well aware, 3M became the leader in both industries. Today, 3M is one of the most successful corporations in existence. Annual sales are approximately $15 billion, half of which comes from outside the United States.

By any measure, 3M's credentials as an innovative company are impressive. For example, 30% of the company's sales come from products that have been introduced within the past 4 years. In 1998 alone, 3M gained 611 patents, and it consistently ranks in the top 10 U.S. companies in patents granted. How do they do it? One obvious factor is their recruit-

ment and hiring of top scientific talent. Another factor that has been widely cited is 3M's long-standing "15% rule" among its research personnel. More specifically, researchers are encouraged to spend up to 15% of their time on projects that are based purely on their own interests. The most visible outcome of the 15% rule is the ubiquitous "post-it"® note. Many other product innovations have resulted from this policy as well.

Another major factor in 3M's success as an innovator is its organizational structure. Research personnel are organized into Corporate Laboratories, Divisional Laboratories, and Technology Centers. Researchers in each of these areas are focused on somewhat different activities (e.g., "basic" research, modification of existing products and technologies), but they are encouraged to communicate freely with each other and with customers. This type of structure facilitates the sense of scientific community that is needed for innovation and the probability that innovations have market potential.

Source: E. Gundling. (2000). *The 3M way to innovation: Balancing people and profit.* Tokyo: Kodansha International.

to boost short-term stock prices (e.g., layoffs, cuts in research and development expenditures) at the expense of long-term excellence (Gomez-Mejia, 1994). Thus, managers may sacrifice long-term success for short-term gains.

Another potential reason has to do with the culture of the organization. According to Peters and O'Connor (1988), over time, many

organizations develop a "culture of justification": Employees' primary concern becomes justifying minimal levels of performance. In such an organizational culture, high levels of performance are not rewarded; in fact, they may actually be punished. As a result, over time, those who strive for excellence either leave the organization or simply retreat to a minimal level of performance themselves. A logical corollary to this sequence is that managers who demand excellence typically do not fare well in such an environment.

Organizational Size

As a general rule, organizational design increases in importance as organizations increase in size. An organization consisting of five family members has no need for formal departmental or divisional structures. In such situations a highly informal organizational structure will probably suffice. As organizations grow in size, however, coordinating the efforts of individuals with a highly informal organizational structure becomes increasingly difficult. Thus, as organizations grow in size, the level of formalization in organizational structure needs to increase. The ability and/or willingness to adopt a more formal organizational structure often distinguish new businesses that succeed from those that fail (Since, Haverman, & Tolbert, 2005).

Empirical research has supported the relationship between organizational size and structure. Perhaps the best-known research was conducted by the Aston research group in Great Britain (Hickson, Pugh, & Pheysey, 1969). These researchers found that organizational size, along with major organizational technology (which will be described next), were both associated with organizational structure. Organizations that were large (as measured by number of employees) tended to exhibit the characteristics of bureaucracy, or what has also been labeled *mechanistic* organizational structure (Burns & Stalker, 1961). In contrast, smaller organizations tended to resemble characteristics of humanistic organizations, or what has been labeled *organic* organizational structure.

Larger organizations gravitate toward more bureaucratic designs because this helps them cope with the complexities that are inevitable when large numbers of people are involved. For example, having free-flowing communication in a large organization could potentially lead to information overload and, ultimately, chaos. Unfortunately, many organizations face a competitive environment that is not well served by having a highly bureaucratic organizational structure. Thus, many organizations deal with this issue by creating what may be described as a *hybrid* type of organizational structure, in which the organization as a whole might be described as a bureaucracy. However, within smaller organizational units, the structure and culture are more like those of a humanistic organization.

Small organizations obviously have less need for coordination and thus are able to adopt a purer version of humanistic organizational structure. For example, in these organizations, communication is more free-flowing, roles are less well defined, and employees are consulted on a regular basis. Highly organic structures often work very well, but there may be a point at which more formalization is necessary. As an example, many successful high-technology companies are started by technical experts who have little, if any, formal managerial experience. As a result, most of these companies tend to adopt highly informal organizational structures and cultures. As their sales revenues increase, these types of organizations are often acquired by larger organizations wishing to capitalize on their technical innovations. When these acquisitions occur, a major dilemma for the parent company is how much structure to impose on these small innovative organizations (see Comment 13.2).

COMMENT 13.2

THE COORDINATION-AUTONOMY DILEMMA

FOR MOST ORGANIZATIONS one of the biggest challenges is to come up with highly innovative products or services for their customers. Many organizations respond to this challenge by spending large amounts of money on research and development. Other organizations, however, take a different approach—they acquire highly innovative small organizations and use this innovation to their advantage.

According to Puranam, Singh, and Zollo (2006) the major dilemma large organizations face when they acquire a small, innovative company is striking the optimal balance between coordination and autonomy. In other words, do they completely absorb the new company into their structure, or do they allow their new acquisition to operate autonomously? Too much coordination and control could potentially decrease the very quality that they were seeking in the acquired company—namely, innovation and creativity. On the other hand, allowing the new company to operate with complete independence may prevent it from using the resources the larger company has to offer. So what is the optimal balance?

Based on a study of large manufacturing organizations that had acquired small, technology-based firms, Puranam et al. (2006) concluded that a high level of coordination and control is probably *not* advisable if the acquired organization does not have a great deal of experience in developing new products; in these cases a high level of autonomy is better. On the other hand, acquired organizations that have a longer track record of product development are not adversely affected by coordination.

The overall conclusion one might draw from this research is that organizations acquiring very young companies with creative "potential" must be prepared to give these organizations the autonomy and freedom to reach that potential.

Source. Puranam, P., Singh, H., & Zollo, M (2006). Organizing for innovation: Managing the coordination-autonomy dilemma in technology acquisitions. *Academy of Management Journal, 49,* 268–280.

Major Technologies

The word *technology* typically conjures up images of complex machinery and manufacturing processes. Although this applies to some, technology need not be highly complex. *Technology* is defined simply as the primary means by which inputs from the environment are converted into something tangible that can be returned to the environment (Katz & Kahn, 1978; Scott, 1990). For an organization that makes paper products, for example, technology represents the processes used to convert wood to products such as paper napkins and tissue paper. The "technology" of a drug treatment center represents the therapeutic methods and interventions that are used to "convert" people from being addicted to alcohol and drugs to being free from these addictions.

An organization's primary technology is related to organizational design in several ways. At the most general level, the two must be compatible. Since an organization's technology is typically established prior to its structure, the structure is typically created to support technology rather than the reverse. One of the most widely cited studies that relates structure and technology was conducted by Woodward (1965). In this study, a number of organizations were classified as having one of three primary technologies. Large-batch technology organizations were those that used traditional assembly-line production processes; that is, products were mass produced, and this was done in a sequential fashion. The second type of organization was described as having small-batch technology. This type of organization produced products that were essentially custom made, and thus it was not possible to obtain the economies of scale that are possible with mass production. The third type of technology in this study was described as continuous-process technology. Organizations using this type of technology are not mass-producing a product; they are converting material from one state to another.

Based on this classification of technology types, Woodward (1965) found a distinct relationship between technology and organizational design. The largest difference in organizational design was found between organizations that used large-batch and those that used small-batch technology. Organizations that used large-batch technology tended to have bureaucratic or mechanistic organizational structures. Presumably, the need to maintain control and certainty during the production process would be responsible for this finding. Organizations using small-batch technology tended to have more humanistic or organic structures. One would assume that this would be due to the fact that custom-made products require a high level of adaptability and flexibility in an organization—both of which are hard to achieve in a typical bureaucratic organization. The third type of organization, the one using continuous-process technology, was found to be a hybrid between bureaucratic and humanistic structures.

Although Woodward's (1965) findings have been widely cited over the years, they have also been criticized. The major criticism of her study was that organizational technology and organizational size were confounded. Because technology tends to covary quite strongly with organizational size, it has been asserted that her findings are due primarily to organizational size. Researchers in the previously mentioned Aston project empirically tested this idea and found that, although size was a predictor of organizational design, it was not completely confounded with technology (Hickson et al., 1969)—that is, technology and organizational design had independent effects on the design of organizations.

Another potential limitation of Woodward's (1965) research is that many organizations do not rely on only one technology; rather, they utilize multiple technologies. Universities, for example, often use quite different instructional methodologies for undergraduate education than they do for graduate programs. This leads to a question: What type of organizational structure would be present in an organization that utilizes very different technologies at the same time? At present, there are no definite answers to this question. However, it is probably logical to assume that organizations often deal with this issue by having several structures.

A final limitation is that the classification developed by Woodward over 40 years ago may not be as applicable today. For example, because of changes in manufacturing technology, organizations are now capable of producing customized versions of products that were mass-produced at the time of Woodward's study (e.g., Zammuto & O'Connor, 1992). In addition, many tasks that were once performed by assembly-line workers have now been automated. Thus, employees involved in mass production today are much more likely to be involved in monitoring tasks as opposed to repetitive tasks. As a result, the organizational structure needed for mass production may be quite different today than it was 40 years ago; for example, it may be more similar to structures that support continuous-process technology.

RECENT INNOVATIONS IN ORGANIZATIONAL DESIGN

While the distinction between classical and humanistic organizations is useful, many organizations today have adopted organizational designs that resemble neither of these. These different organizational designs have evolved for a number of reasons. One is that many organizations have found that purely bureaucratic or purely humanistic organizational designs have not allowed them to meet the challenges of their competitive environment. Also, different organizational designs have developed as a way to better leverage both employee skills and organizational resources. Finally, evolution of these different organizational forms has corresponded to recent changes in managerial philosophy. In this section, we examine three of the most common recent innovations in organizational design: (1) the team-based organization, (2) the matrix organization, and (3) the virtual organization.

The Team-Based Organization

In the past 20 years, research on group or team effectiveness within organizational psychology has grown rapidly (Guzzo & Shea, 1992). Along with this increasing interest, organizations have dramatically increased their use of teams. Most organizations utilize teams under the assumption that teams represent a much more effective way to utilize

FIGURE 13.5
Example of a Team-Based Organization

and combine employees' skills rather than simply having employees work as individuals. Teams can be very effective tools in organizations, yet they are certainly not the answer to all problems. In fact, teams may create problems of their own.

A team-based organization is one that goes beyond the occasional ad hoc use of teams and uses them as the basis for their organizational structure. Figure 13.5 illustrates an organizational design that is based entirely on teams. As can be seen, this small organization consists of four cross-functional teams that correspond to the organization's four primary product lines. According to Mohrman and Quam (2000), in a team-based organization, teams are used to "carry out their core work, to develop and deliver the products and services that provide value to customers" (p. 20). In this type of organization, teams have responsibility for activities such as planning work, staffing, and compensating team members.

According to Galbraith (1995), a number of important issues must be addressed for even a simple team-based organizational structure to work effectively. One of the most important of these is coordination of the activities of the different teams comprising the structure. This is important because the activities of one team often impact the activities of others. As an example, let's say the marketing efforts of each of the teams in Figure 13.5 are not coordinated well. This could, for example, result in sales representatives from each team calling on the same customers at the same time; this decreases the chances of any sale being made and is embarrassing to the organization. One of the most common ways to achieve coordination is to create what is essentially an *executive committee* consisting of the leaders of each of the teams. That is, the leader of each team belongs to a higher-level team that meets periodically to consider issues of coordination between teams. Given the size and complexity of an organization, there may be several such executive or coordinating committees at various levels of the organization. A variant of this method would be to create various coordinating committees from different organizational levels.

Many academic departments in universities utilize this mechanism by having an executive committee comprised of the chairperson, the director of the undergraduate program, and the directors of the graduate programs. These individuals are often responsible for setting overall departmental policy in a way that balances the needs of the various programs offered by the department. Such a committee might also be charged with creating long-term strategic plans. A secondary benefit of this type of committee is that it can be an excellent mechanism for training members of an academic department to assume leadership positions in the future.

Another crucial issue in implementing a team-based organizational structure is creating a compatible reward system. As was stated in Chapter 12, a common problem with the use of teams in general is that organizational reward systems are often aimed primarily at individual-level performance. As a result, individuals often have little incentive to put the interests of the team ahead of their own. This issue becomes even more important with a team-based structure because overall organizational performance is intimately tied to the performance of individual teams.

One way to align reward systems with a team-based structure is to base rewards primarily on the team performance or even the organizational performance. Compensation methods such as profit sharing and gain sharing are common ways of accomplishing this objective. This is not to say that organizations should completely ignore individual performance. However, if organizational performance depends primarily on team performance, this should be the focal point of the reward system.

Organizations implementing team-based organizational structures must also consider the nature of the work being performed by the teams. One obvious question must be asked before implementing a team-based organizational structure: Does the work lend itself to a team-based structure? This may seem like a rather obvious point, yet many organizations overlook it. In their zeal to reap the benefits of teamwork, many organizations overlook the fact that the work being performed does not lend itself to a team-based structure. If the work does not lend itself to a team-based structure, an organization can either abandon this structure or redesign the work.

Finally, organizations committed to implementing a team-based organizational structure must take a hard look at their selection procedures. As with any organization, employees must be selected based on whether they are able to perform important job-related tasks.

However, as discussed in Chapter 12, team-based organizations must also confront the fact that not all individuals want to work within a team-based structure. Some individuals are more comfortable than others working in a team-based environment (Campion et al., 1993). There is also evidence that some individuals possess better team-based skills than others do (e.g., Stevens & Campion, 1999).

The Matrix Organization

In a matrix organization there are essentially two separate organizational structures at the same time (Davis & Lawrence, 1977). One of these structures is often represented by traditional functional departments such as marketing, engineering, accounting, and so on. At the same time, a second structure is superimposed on this traditional departmental structure. Most typically, this second structure is based on organizational projects, although there are many other bases for creating this second structure. Consumer product companies often have secondary structures based on brands or, in some cases, different markets that they serve.

In a typical matrix structure managers in charge of different projects draw employees from each of the functional departments until a project is completed. Figure 13.6 provides a simple illustration of how this might work in practice. Notice that project A draws employees from all three functional departments, project B draws employees from both marketing and engineering, and project C draws employees from both marketing and accounting. Projects in matrix organizations may be of limited duration, but in some cases they are relatively permanent. For example, in consumer product companies that have matrix structures based on brands, these structural arrange-

FIGURE 13.6
Example of a Matrix Organizational Structure

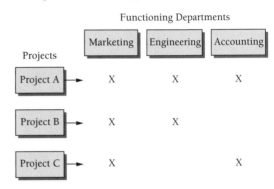

ments are more or less permanent. It is highly likely, however, that the specific needs of each of the brands may change over time, and thus the specific functional resources devoted to each brand may also fluctuate over time.

The primary advantage of a matrix structure is that it allows an organization to quickly shift the focus of its design to the most important parts of its business. For example, the lifeblood of an organization that is a major defense contractor is obviously defense contracts. Therefore, if such an organization receives a large contract to develop an advanced weapons system, a matrix structure allows it to quickly shift a great deal of its internal resources to that project. When the project is completed, resources can then be quickly reallocated to other projects as needed.

Matrix structures are used frequently by consumer product companies because they allow an organization to use a unique approach in the way it handles different products or product lines. For example, a well-established product line may require a vastly different advertising approach than a product that has just emerged on the scene. In the consumer product environment, matrix structures also help to guard against complacency. Having people assigned to products (e.g., brand managers) makes it more likely that the organization will continue trying to improve them through research and development efforts and through the use of consumer data.

Beyond these more obvious benefits, there are also intangible benefits. For example, being a project or brand manager can be a highly developmental experience for managers. In fact, Procter and Gamble—one of the largest consumer product companies in the world—is known to use brand management positions explicitly for developmental purposes. Brand managers not only learn a great deal about a particular product or product line, they also learn a great deal about the organization as a whole as they draw resources for their brand. Project or brand managers in any organization also learn a great deal about negotiation and compromise because, in many cases, they are not simply handed resources; instead, they must negotiate with functional managers in order to get them.

Matrix structures also pose a number of challenges. One of the biggest challenges is that matrix structures often end up pitting project or brand managers against functional managers. This can result in a great deal of dysfunctional conflict and political gamesmanship (e.g., de Laat, 1994). Some organizations address this issue by establishing clear priorities; for example, the needs of projects take priority over the needs of functional departments. While this might be helpful, it introduces some dysfunctional effects of its own. Functional managers may come to see themselves as "second-class citizens" in comparison to project or brand managers. As a result, functional management is often seen as an undesirable position,

particularly if one wants to be promoted to upper management.

Matrix structures can also have a negative impact on employees working in functional departments. In a large organization with a matrix structure, employees working in a functional department often have to juggle the demands of several projects at once. This may result in work overload and can often impose conflicting demands on employees (Joyce, 1986). Beyond these workload issues, a by-product of matrix structure is that employees may have to work for several "bosses" at the same time. Furthermore, these different bosses may have very different performance standards and interpersonal styles. Thus, from an employee's point of view, working under a matrix structure could be highly stressful. Functional managers must communicate frequently with project managers to ensure that they are not overworking employees.

The Virtual Organization

According to Galbraith (1995), an example of a virtual organization is one that decides to produce a product or service but contracts with other firms to provide a key part of that product or service. The major automotive manufacturers have, to a large extent, become virtual organizations. Although they continue to assemble automobiles, most of the parts that were once produced internally are now produced by external suppliers.

The primary motivation for forming virtual organizations is cost reduction. In the case of the auto companies, the capital and other internal resources needed to produce automotive parts have simply increased to a level that is prohibitive. It is therefore much cheaper to simply buy the parts from external

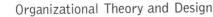

suppliers. A second motivation is that contracting out more peripheral functions allows an organization to concentrate all of its energy on its core business. In college athletics, for example, many universities hire outside companies to make travel arrangements when they play road games. Since this used to be a task performed by coaches, contracting this out allows coaches to focus on other more important aspects of their jobs (e.g., recruiting, developing game plans).

Despite the potential advantages of virtual organizations, this type of organizational design also has its drawbacks. When an organization enters into a partnership with a supplier, there is some degree of risk. For example, when auto companies do not produce their own parts, ensuring that those parts meet quality standards is obviously more difficult. Organizations have some leverage in this regard because suppliers obviously want to maintain the relationship. According to Galbraith (1995), organizations typically deal with this uncertainty by thoroughly investigating potential business partners before entering into relationships. Another way is to build "escape clauses" into business partnerships, as consultants often do.

Employing a virtual organizational structure makes it difficult for an organization to maintain a coherent culture. In the extreme, an organization that contracts out nearly everything ceases to become a distinct organizational entity; instead, it becomes a rather large conglomeration of different organizational cultures. This status may make it very difficult to instill a sense of commitment and loyalty in employees. This may also explain why some organizations have stayed away from the virtual organization concept. As the virtual organization becomes more prevalent, though, organizations will probably find effective ways to deal with this issue.

RESEARCH ON ORGANIZATIONAL DESIGN

Perhaps one of the clearest themes in the organizational design literature over the years is that organizational designs can be viewed as adaptive responses to the environment. For example, the designs of organizations differ as a function of environmental uncertainty (Burns & Stalker, 1961), technology (Scott, 1990; Woodward, 1965), strategy (Galbraith, 1995), and sheer organizational size (Hickson et al., 1969). Thus, one thing that empirical research has shown is that organizational designs do not just appear; rather, they typically come about as a response to an organization's environment. Interestingly, though, it has also been proposed that organizational design may at times reflect the personality quirks of individual managers (Kets de Vries & Miller, 1986). Therefore, organizational design decisions may not always have a rational or functional basis.

Another clear theme in organizational design research is that there is no one best way to design an organization. Research has shown that organizational designs come about as a result of environmental factors. However, there is not as much evidence that organizations with designs matching their environments are always successful. If anything, organizational design research has shown, with respect to design, that there are many paths to organizational success. It appears, though, that a key factor in whether a given organizational design leads to success is whether internal policies and procedures are congruent with the design. Perhaps the best example of this is the literature on team-based organizations, which has shown that organizations using this type of design are much more successful if their compensation practices are congruent with it (Mohrman & Quam, 2000).

A third major theme is clearly evident in organizational design research: The design of organizations has tangible effects on employee behavior. It has been shown, for example, that the design of an organization may impact employees' willingness to contribute ideas (Boode, 2005), managers' attention to environmental issues (Russo & Harrison, 2006), and employees' use of safe work practices (Bourrier, 2005). It has also been found that organizational structure has an impact on individual employees' perceptions of fairness (Schminke, Ambrose, & Cropanzano, 2000), which in turn may have an impact on many subsequent behaviors.

Findings of this sort are important because they suggest that the design of an organization makes a difference. They also suggest possible mediating mechanisms (e.g., fairness perceptions) by which organizational designs—or any other organizational intervention, for that matter—impact organizational effectiveness. Perhaps most importantly, they force us to shift our thinking from viewing organizational designs as "boxes and arrows" to seeing them for what they really are—purposeful interventions designed to shape and influence human behavior in a particular direction. For those in the field of psychology, this is important because it drives home the point that macro-level factors such as organizational design are important. Conversely, for those trained in organizational theory or strategy, it suggests that something very important is in the "black box" between macro-level variables such as design and organizational effectiveness.

THE FUTURE OF ORGANIZATIONAL DESIGN

How will organizations be designed in the future? This question obviously cannot be answered with complete certainty. We do know, however, that a number of trends will clearly shape organizations in the future. One trend that has impacted many aspects of organizational functioning is the ever-increasing sophistication of information technology. Business transactions that used to take weeks to accomplish can now be completed in a matter of seconds. This increased sophistication of information technology has been a double-edged sword for organizations. On the positive side, it has resulted in a level of efficiency and speed that is unprecedented. At the same time, however, it has contributed to a highly volatile environment in many business sectors that were previously much more stable.

With respect to organizational design, information technology has led organizations to place a premium on speed and flexibility. Thus, based on the organizational designs that were discussed in this chapter, there will likely continue to be an increasing trend toward designs that resemble Likert's System 4 and System 5, as well as the team-based structures. The reason for this is that speed often demands that lower-level employees must be empowered to make many decisions that were once reserved for management. Organizations simply will not have time to go up through a large chain of command to make every decision.

The other implication of information technology is that it will likely increase the use of more flexible organizational designs. It will become increasingly more common for organizations to consist of individuals who spend some or all of their time "off site" through telecommuting. This will also make virtual organizations much more appealing, and therefore more likely to be used. For example, through videoconferencing, regular meetings can take place between those at organizational headquarters and suppliers in different parts of the country, or even the world. Thus, in the future, we may need to seriously rethink what an *organization* actually is.

A second trend, which is actually somewhat related to the first, is the globalization of the economy. With the fall of communism in the early 1990s, coupled with free trade agreements and a trend toward standardization of currency, the world has increasingly embraced free-market capitalism. Furthermore, countries that were at one time essentially closed to Western society (e.g., China) are now becoming active trading partners with the West. Obviously, the extent to which this globalization of the economy will lead to global prosperity depends on a number of factors (e.g., maintaining world peace, stabilizing new free-market economies). However, it will have a major impact on organizations.

With respect to organizational design, globalization will clearly increase the incentive of organizations to expand their markets beyond national borders. Thus, an increasing number of organizations will add foreign subsidiaries to their existing structures. How these foreign subsidiaries are managed and integrated with the existing structure will be the major issue these organizations will face. Organizational design issues will focus primarily on determining the appropriate combination of direction and autonomy to give these foreign subsidiaries (Boode, 2005).

A third trend that will likely impact organizational design is the growing contingent workforce (Beard & Edwards, 1995). Recall from Chapter 1 that this is an important trend that was predicted to have an impact on many areas of organizational psychology. In the realm of organizational design, the increasing availability of a contingent workforce, combined with the previously discussed trends, will make the virtual organization much more prevalent in the future. Having contingent employees readily

available makes it much easier for organizations to quickly reconfigure themselves in order to take advantage of market opportunities. In the past, more permanent bureaucratic structures made this type of flexibility nearly impossible. Of course, along with these new opportunities come a number of challenges, such as maintaining consistent performance standards and instilling a coherent sense of organizational culture in these transient employees.

CHAPTER SUMMARY

In this chapter, we shifted the focus from individual- and group-level phenomena to a broader level. This shift is important because a complete understanding of behavior in organizations requires that we look at it from all three vantage points. The chapter began with a discussion of the field of organizational theory, primarily focusing on its intellectual roots and its linkage to the closely related field of organizational design. The focus then shifted to a description of the three most general types of organizational designs. Classical organizational designs are represented by Scientific Management, Ideal Bureaucracy, and Administrative Management. Humanistic organizational designs are best represented by McGregor's Theory X/Y and Likert's System 4 organization. Classical and humanistic organizational designs have both advantages and disadvantages. Furthermore, the appropriateness of each of these organizational types depends largely on situational factors, and this leads to the third type of organizational design: contingency organizational design.

Based on the premise that contingency theory is the dominant paradigm in organizational design today, the chapter then shifted to the major factors that are taken

DAVID NADLER AND MULTIPLE APPROACHES TO UNDERSTANDING HUMAN ORGANIZATIONS

When I was in college, I had summer jobs, and in two successive summers I worked in one of the best jobs I ever had, and subsequently one of the worst. I was puzzled by how two organizations could be so radically different—one extremely effective with motivated staff, and one very bureaucratic with disaffected staff. That began my interest in organizations, and as I read, I got very interested in the whole area of change, leadership, and interpersonal relations.

When I went to business school at Harvard, I was exposed, however, to a whole new set of ideas. I was lucky enough to have classes with Jay Lorsch and Paul Lawrence, who were working on ideas of systems, environment, and structure. At the same time, I was taking a seminar in psychoanalytic theory and organizations, which stretched me in other directions. Much of this came together in my doctoral work at Michigan. People there were thinking about systems theory and organizations. In a course with Ed Lawler, he asked us, as a mid-term assignment, to "develop a framework to explain the behavior of organizations." My mid-term paper was the beginning of work on developing an integrated theory of organizations, which ultimately became the Congruence Model that Michael Tushman and I developed and have used for several decades.

I ended up with a strong view of organizations as both social and technical systems. You need to think about both the "software" (people, behavior, culture, etc.) and the "hardware" (structure, systems, processes) in the context of strategy, to understand what's going on.

After seven years in academia, I left to create a consulting firm. I used the same approach in working with clients, but have tried to always be open to new ideas, new models, and the value of scientific inquiry in solving real problems. On reflection, no one theory, approach, or framework explains everything. Each concept or model gives us a different set of lenses to understand this very complex creation we call the human organization. Academics and leaders alike need to be ready to use different tools and approaches.

David A. Nadler
Senior Partner, Delta
  Organization & Leadership
Vice Chairman,
  Marsh & McLennan Companies, Inc.

into consideration when organizations make design decisions. These included strategy, level of environmental uncertainty, beliefs and assumptions of those in power, organizational size, and the dominant technology. Given this number of factors, there will obviously be a variety of organizational designs. Furthermore, it is very likely that different organizational designs may coexist within the same organization.

The chapter then shifted to focus on three relatively recent trends in the design of organizations: (1) team-based organizational structure, (2) matrix organizational structure, and (3) the virtual organization. Although each of these organizational designs is different, they all allow organizations to respond more quickly to market opportunities and to make better uses of their internal resources. Furthermore, all three of these organizational designs require that other organizational subsystems must be properly aligned in order for them to work well.

There has been considerable research on the impact of organizational design, and this was summarized according to the dominant themes. One of these themes is that designs appear to be at least partially traceable to adaptive responses to the environments in which organizations operate. Research has also shown that there is no "right way" to design an organization; however, organizations that tend to align their various subsystems with their structure tend to be the most effective. A third theme is that organizational designs do influence the behavior of employees. This serves as an important linkage between micro- and macro-level organizational behavior.

The chapter concluded with a brief discussion of factors that are likely to influence organizational designs of the future. These include information technology, globaliza-tion of the economy, and the increasing number of contingent employees. These trends may have many influences on organizations, but their most likely impact on design will be to increase the use of virtual organizational designs. Organizations will then be better able to expand and contract quickly, and to move much more quickly into previously untapped global markets.

SUGGESTED ADDITIONAL READINGS

Boode, G. (2005). Boundaries on the move: The impact of cultural values and language on organizational design and communication within an organization in Thailand. *Asian Pacific Business Review, 11, 519–533.*

Bourrier, M. (2005). The contribution of organizational design to safety. *European Management Journal, 23,* 98–104.

Russo, M. V., & Harrison, N. S. (2005). Organizational design and environmental performance: Clues from the electronics industry. *Academy of Management Journal, 48,* 582–583.

Since, W. D., Mitsuhashi, H., & Kirsch, D. (2006). Revisiting Burns and Salker: Formal structure and new venture performance in emerging economic sectors. *Academy of Management Journal, 49,* 121–132.

Chapter Fourteen

erhaps the best way to appreciate organizational culture is to imagine entering an unfamiliar organization for the very first time—either as a new employee or a customer. In some ways, this experience is similar to entering a foreign country. For example, members of the organization may use words and phrases that are not fully understood; they may engage in behaviors that they take quite seriously but have little meaning to outsiders; and they may tell jokes and stories that only they can fully understand. If we were to stay in the organization long enough to make the transition to full-fledged organizational members, or interact with members of the organization frequently enough, many of the unfamiliar things that we initially observed would become much more meaningful.

While the study of culture has a long tradition in anthropology and sociology, the study of organizational culture is actually very new. In fact, most researchers have traced its beginning to the late 1970s (Pettigrew, 1979). However, the fact that organizational psychologists have studied organizational culture for only a short period of time does not decrease its importance. To the contrary, culture is an extremely important key to understanding many behavior patterns in organizations. In fact, all behavior in organizations occurs in a cultural context. This may explain why some things (e.g., incentive pay) work well in some organizations yet fail miserably in others. Culture may also help us to understand why some organizations are successful and why others are not (e.g., Mason, 2004).

Organizational Culture

This chapter provides an overview of organizational culture and many of its implications. We begin by defining what is meant by organizational culture—no small feat, considering that this concept comes not only from psychology, but also from cultural anthropology and sociology. We then describe two recent attempts to describe the dimensions underlying organizational culture. The chapter then shifts to an explanation of the various ways in which culture is reflected in organizations. As we'll see, some of these are rather obvious, but culture is often reflected in very subtle ways. We then explore the factors that shape the culture of an organization. The chapter will then focus on the various methods that can be used to study organizational culture. The chapter then shifts to a discussion of organizational culture change, and concludes with an examination of the impact of organizational culture, both on the success of the organization as a whole and on individual organizational members.

DEFINING ORGANIZATIONAL CULTURE

There are many definitions of organizational culture in the organizational psychology literature (e.g., Louis, 1983; Martin, 2002). Fortunately, however, most of these have a great deal in common. In an effort to integrate these various definitions, Ravisi and Schultz (2006) state that *organizational culture* is "a set of shared mental assumptions that guide interpretation and action in organizations by defining appropriate behavior for various situations" (p. 437). There are two important aspects of this definition. First, this definition implies that culture is the "view of the world" that the members of an organization share. By "view of the world," we mean that culture essentially represents the "lens" through which employees of an organization learn to interpret the environment. Secondly, and perhaps most important, this definition also implies that culture guides the behavior of employees in an organization. For example, culture impacts how employees treat each other, the quality of decisions that are made, and ultimately whether or not an organization is successful.

According to Schein (1985, 1992), there are three levels of an organization's culture, and each succeeding level is more difficult for outsiders to decipher. The most visible level of organizational culture is reflected in artifacts, technology, and behavior patterns. Artifacts, which will be discussed in more depth later, are aspects of the physical environment that communicate cultural meaning. Technology represents the means by which organizations transform input from the outside environment. Behavior patterns, of course, simply represent what employees in the organization do.

The next level of culture, according to Schein (1992), is represented by the shared values within the organization. Values simply represent individuals' broad tendencies to prefer certain things, or states of affairs, over others (Hofstede, 1980). The values that might be salient within an organization could be a number of things: loyalty, customer service, collegiality, and self-preservation, to name a few. According to Schein, values are less accessible to an outsider than are things such as behavior patterns, and, typically, they must be inferred by the outsider through symbolic means. For example, if an organization rewards and promotes employees largely on the basis of seniority, one might infer that the organization tends to place a high value on loyalty and retention.

In considering values in organizations, it is important to distinguish between the values that are espoused by the organization, and those that are actually in operation (e.g., the "true" values). In many organizations, there is a strong relationship between the espoused and the true values. For example, innovation has always been an espoused value at 3M, and studies of this organization (e.g., Gundling, 2000) have shown that generally company practices are consistent with it. In some organizations, however, there is a disconnect between what an organization claims to value, and the values that appear to be guiding overt behavior. As an example, many organizations claim to place a high value on diversity, yet have few minority employees in management positions; many organizations claim to place a high value on performance, yet tolerate consistently poor performance from employees; and many organizations claim that customer service is one of their core values, yet customers are treated rudely. The important implication of this is that in many cases researchers must go beyond espoused values in order to truly understand organizational culture.

The third layer of culture, according to Schein (1992), is represented by the basic beliefs and assumptions held by the members of an organization. These beliefs and assumptions are so deeply ingrained that people take them for granted; they are important, however, because they impact the more visible aspects of culture (Denison & Mishra, 1995). To better understand basic beliefs and assumptions, let's consider a basic assumption that we operate under in our daily lives, at least in Western society. For example, when people greet each other, it is common for one or both persons involved in such an encounter to ask the other, "How are you doing?" or "How's it going?" Most people understand that these questions, particularly when people do not know each other very well, are merely forms of greeting, and appropriate responses might be "Fine, thanks" or "Not bad; how are you?" On the other hand, most people would be uncomfortable if a person responded to this question with a detailed 30-minute explanation of all of the challenges they have faced in the past month.

What are the basic beliefs and assumptions that people hold in organizational settings? This is a difficult question to answer because organizations, and the people in them, differ so widely. However, if one thinks about it, there are probably some beliefs and assumptions that may be salient, regardless of the situation. For example, employees in organizations have basic beliefs and assumptions about things such as whether the organization can be trusted, whether the organization supports them, whether the psychological environment is threatening or supportive, or whether hard work and dedication pay off. There are obviously other basic assumptions that are quite specific to a given organizational setting. For example, members of an accounting firm may have basic assumptions about the ethics surrounding the tax deductions they seek for their clients, or the teachers in an elementary school may hold common basic assumptions regarding the benefits of parental involvement in children's education.

Compared to the other two levels of culture discussed, basic beliefs and assumptions are difficult to study because they are so ingrained; in fact, Schein (1992) argued that they are not at a conscious level. Because of this, it is extremely difficult for a naïve organizational outsider to determine what these beliefs and assumptions are. It is also difficult for employees, particularly those who have been around for a long time, to articulate the basic beliefs and assumptions of their organization because they are so ingrained. Most typically, basic beliefs and assumptions are determined only through painstaking research processes such as field observation, use of informants, and careful study of organizational archives. More will be said about studying organizational culture later in the chapter.

Having defined organizational culture and described its various levels, an important issue to consider is that, even though most organizations have what could be described as an "organization-wide" culture, they also contain a number of identifiable *subcultures*. Janson (1994) proposed that, in most organizations, there are six subcultures; these are presented in Table 14.1. As can be seen, the first subculture is labeled "Elite culture/

TABLE 14.1
Possible Subcultures within an Organization Proposed by Janson (1994)

Elite culture/corporate culture—"For your eyes only" or "For public consumption"
Departmental culture—Horizontal slice; for example, sales department
Divisional culture—Vertical slice; for example, a division
Local culture—Within a geographical location/unit
Issue-related culture—Metaphorical, related to an important issue throughout the
    organization; for example, safety culture or quality culture
Professional culture—On the basis of professional background and training

Source: J. V. Mbijen. (1998). Organizational culture. In P. J. Drenth and H. Thierry (Eds.), *Handbook of work and organizational psychology* (2nd ed., Vol. 4, pp. 113–131). Hove, England: Psychology Press. Reprinted with permission of publisher.

corporate culture" and is essentially represented by those at the highest levels of the organization. The subculture in which the chief executive and the top executive group of an organization live is much different than most other employees. These individuals typically have more pleasant surroundings than other employees, and they have a great deal of control over information dissemination in the wider organization.

The next form of subculture described by Janson is labeled "Departmental." Individuals within the same department work very closely together, face many of the same challenges, and collectively experience success and failure. Because of this, individuals within departments may develop many of the same views and thus have many of the same basic assumptions about the organization. In universities, this is very evident when one looks at the different cultures that develop in academic departments (see Comment 14.1).

The next level of subculture development is at the "division" level. In a business organization, for example, the marketing division may consist of the sales, market research, and advertising departments. In a university, the equivalent of a division is a *college* that is composed of several academic departments.

Divisional subcultures develop for essentially the same reasons as departmental subcultures. Employees in the same division may work under many of the same policies and may experience many of the same challenges. As a result, individuals within the same division may begin to develop many of the same basic assumptions, and hence a subculture develops.

The next level of subculture that may develop is labeled "Local culture" and is based on geographic regions. Local subcultures may be identical to divisional subcultures when an organization's structure is based on geographic region. However, this is not always the case. Local subcultures develop largely based on local customs and norms of the region in which a unit works. For example, as a graduate student, the first author worked as a contractor in the Florida division of a large telecommunications company. Based on conversations with others in that organization, it became evident that there were distinct regional differences between this division and other regional divisions of the company. Due to the warm weather in Florida, the dress code was a bit more relaxed, and the manner in which people dealt with each other was a bit more informal than in other parts of the organization.

COMMENT 14.1

ACADEMIC DEPARTMENT CULTURES AND SUBCULTURES

AS MOST READERS have probably noted in taking courses in a variety of departments, there tends to be a great deal of variation in the cultures of various academic departments. For example, the cultures of academic departments in the arts and humanities tend to be more "laid back" and relaxed in comparison to academic departments in engineering and the hard sciences.

Academic departments in business schools also tend to be distinct in their own way. For example, many business school faculty dress formally (many business schools require that faculty wear business attire when teaching), and many of their offices resembled those in corporations. Considering that most faculty members in business schools are trained in business schools, and that their primary mission is to train students for business careers, it is understandable that a businesslike culture would develop.

Psychology departments tend to have very interesting cultures because of the dominance of subcultures. Particularly in large psychology departments with several doctoral programs, the subcultures that develop in each of the areas may be quite different. For example, the culture of a clinical psychology faculty might be very different from the culture of an industrial/organizational psychology faculty. The cultures of both groups, in turn, may be very different than the culture of a social psychology faculty.

The next time you're in an academic department, look around and see if you can find any clues about the culture of that department. Better yet, do this with two or more departments and see what the differences are. You might be surprised and fascinated by what you find!

Subcultures may also develop due to some important issues faced throughout the organization. Recently, much work has been done on the construct of "safety culture" in organizations (Hofmann & Stetzer, 1998). In reality, in most organizations, there are probably many safety "subcultures"; that is, safety is likely to be viewed and practiced quite differently in many different parts of an organization. Other important issues that may be the basis for subculture development may include affirmative action, whether pay should be based on performance, and views of the trustworthiness of management, to name a few.

The final basis for subculture development proposed by Janson is the professional training of employees. In some organizations, this could be the basis for the wider organizational culture (e.g., accounting firms, law firms, consulting firms); but, in many other cases, organizations employ groups of individuals who have obtained very different forms of professional training. For example, an organization that hires groups of chemical engineers may find that these individuals constitute a distinct subculture within the organization. In fact, in some cases, employees may have a much greater identification with their professional subculture than with the organization or division in which they work. Physicians, for example, often identify more strongly with the medical profession than they do with the hospitals or clinics in which they are employed.

Given that subcultures coexist with the overall organizational culture, a logical question is which of these has the strongest impact on employees? Adkins and Caldwell (2004) examined this issue with employees in a large consulting firm that was comprised of four distinct subcultures based on type of service provided (Strategic Consulting, Technology Consulting, Process Reengineering, and Change Management Consulting). What these researchers found was that job satisfaction was positively associated with the degree to which employees fit into *both* the overall culture and the subculture in which they worked. This suggests that while subcultures are important to employees, they also do not completely negate the importance of the overall culture of the organization.

MODELS OF ORGANIZATIONAL CULTURE

Having defined what organizational culture is, we will now discuss common dimensions along which organizational cultures can be described. Anyone who has worked in several different organizations knows that, to a large extent, no two organizational cultures are completely alike. Therefore, it is probably futile to develop a finite typology of all organizational culture types or dimensions. Over the years, however, researchers have discovered what they have considered to be clusters of cultural attributes that are common to most organizations. In this section, we examine two of these common models of organizational culture.

The O'Reilly, Chatman, and Caldwell Model

O'Reilly, Chatman, and Caldwell (1991) developed a self-report measure of organizational culture, the Organizational Culture Profile (OCP). While the specifics of the OCP will be discussed later in the chapter,

the substantive model underlying the OCP will be described briefly here. The substantive model behind the OCP is simply that cultures can be distinguished based on the predominant values that are reinforced within a particular organization. According to O'Reilly et al., most organizational cultures can be distinguished according to the seven values that are presented and defined in Table 14.2. According to this model, what makes each culture unique is its "profile" on these seven cultural dimensions. For example, the culture of one organization might place a high value on innovation, respect for people, and it may have a strong team orientation. In contrast, the culture of another organization might place a high value on stability, attention to detail, and it may place a low value on innovation.

Unlike other models of organizational culture that have sought to link cultural dimensions to organizational performance, much of the research on the O'Reilly et al. (1991) model has been focused on the fit between organizational culture and personalities of individual employees (e.g., Judge & Cable, 1997). One might imagine, though, that in certain circumstances some of these cultural dimensions would likely be associated with organizational performance. It is hard to imagine, for example, a successful high-techology company with a culture that places a low value on O'Reilly, Chatman, and Caldwell model – " . . . innovation and a very high value on stability. It is also likely that an organization providing a service to consumers would need to place a high value on respect for people and attention to detail in order to be successful.

The Denison Model

A second model of organizational culture, which also served as the basis for a culture

TABLE 14.2
O'Reilly et al. (1991) Seven Organizational Values

Value	Definition
Innovation	The extent to which an organization encourages employees to be innovative, seek out new opportunities, and take risks
Stability	The extent to which an organization emphasizes rules and values predictability
Respect for people	The extent to which an organization emphasizes mutual respect, fairness, and tolerance of differences among employees
Outcome orientation	The extent to which an organization encourages employees to take action and to strive for excellence in their work
Attention to detail	The extent to which an organization encourages employees to be precise and detail-oriented in doing their work
Team orientation	The extent to which an organization emphasizes collaboration and teamwork among employees
Aggressiveness	The extent to which an organization encourages competition and aggressiveness among employees

Source: Q'Reilly, C.A, Chatman, J., & Caldwell, D.F. (1991). People and organizational culture: A profile comparison approach to assessing person-environment fit. *Academy of Management Journal, 34,* 487–516.

measure, was proposed by Daniel Denison and colleagues (Denison, 1990; Denison & Mishra, 1995). The model, which is presented in Figure 14.1, is much more complex than that proposed by O'Reilly et al. (1991). The basic idea is that organizational culture can be described according to the four general dimensions of Adaptability, Mission, Involvement, and Consistency. Each of these general dimensions, in turn, can be described in terms of three subdimensions. For example, the general dimension of Mission is subdivided into Strategic Direction and Intent, Goals and Objectives, and Vision. Adaptability is subdivided into Creating Change, Customer Focus, and Organizational Learning. Involvement is subdivided into Empowerment, Team Orien-tation, and Capability Development. Finally, Consistency is subdivided into Core Values, Agreement, and Coordination/Integration. Readers will also note that this model allows the cultures of organizations to be described along two broad dimensions (External versus Internal Focus; Flexible versus Stable) based on where they score on the various subdimensions.

While the Denison model is relatively new, it has been subject to a great deal of empirical scrutiny and been used in many organizations to facilitate diagnosis of cultural problems (Denison, Haaland, & Goelzer, 2004). In the future this model will likely be the focus of continued research.

MANIFESTATIONS OF ORGANIZATIONAL CULTURE

Given that organizational culture can be described along a common set of dimensions, what makes these cultural dimensions visible to both employees and organizational outsiders? In other words, what exactly contributes to differences in the "feel" of different organizations? This is an important question because culture cannot be studied, diagnosed, or in some cases changed if we do not understand the various ways that culture is communicated. Fortunately, organizational culture researchers have come up with

FIGURE 14.1

The denison organizational culture model

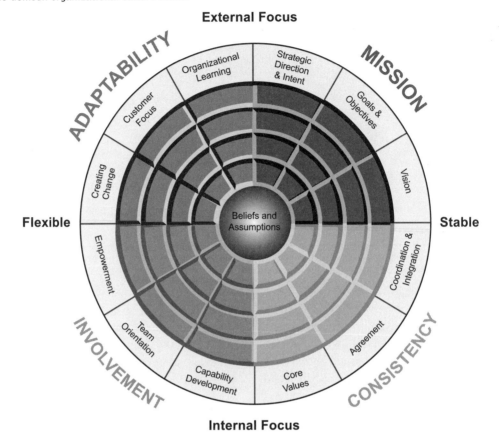

External Focus

ADAPTABILITY

MISSION

Organizational Learning

Strategic Direction & Intent

Customer Focus

Goals & Objectives

Creating Change

Vision

Flexible

Beliefs and Assumptions

Stable

Empowerment

Coordination & Integration

Team Orientation

Agreement

Capability Development

Core Values

INVOLVEMENT

CONSISTENCY

Internal Focus

a number of ways, and they are described in this section.

Symbols and Artifacts

According to Cohen (1974), symbols are "objects, acts, relationships, or linguistic formations that stand ambiguously for a multiplicity of meanings, evoke emotions, and impel men to action" (p. 23). In most organizations, symbols provide us with information on the nature of the culture. Perhaps one of the most revealing symbols in an organization is the physical layout in which employees work. In some organizations, employees' offices are located in large open areas; in others, however, employees are given a great deal more privacy by having their offices placed in more remote locations. In the former setting, the office layout may be symbolic of a culture that places a high value on sociability and openness of communication and, in fact, employees may engage in these types of behaviors. In the latter, the layout may be symbolic of a culture characterized by a high degree of secrecy, or perhaps just a great deal of respect for privacy; employees in such a culture may tend to provide information to each other only on a "need to know" basis.

According to Schein (1983) an artifact is very similar to a symbol; the only difference is that artifacts represent a more direct attempt to convey cultural meaning, whereas symbols are more indirect. As with symbols, artifacts are most easily found in the physical environment of organizations. One of the most typical cultural artifacts in organizations is the physical manifestation of the major technology that is used. In educational settings, for example, classrooms are artifacts in that they convey the fact that students are to be reasonably obedient recipients of the knowledge that is passed down to them. In the Army, the uniform is a powerful artifact to remind everyone that they are all soldiers regardless of the setting in which they work and the job they perform.

Rites and Rituals

Rites represent "relatively elaborate, dramatic, planned sets of activities that consolidate various forms of cultural expressions into one event, which is carried out through social interactions, usually for the benefit of an audience" (Trice & Beyer, 1984, p. 655). The most common rites carried out in organizations are summarized in Table 14.3. As can be seen, rites of passage are often used to symbolize the

socialization from organizational outsiders to full-fledged organizational members. The military's use of basic training is probably the most dramatic organizational rite of passage, but other organizations have these as well. For example, a familiar rite of passage in academic settings is the oral defense of one's master's thesis or doctoral dissertation.

In some cases, rites are designed to sanction or, in a more general sense, to convey negative information to employees. Rites of degradation often occur when there is a problem in the organization or when there must be a change in personnel. A recent and highly publicized example of this was the execution of former Iraqi dictator Saddam Hussein. When someone is denied tenure in a university there is no public event, but the year following the denial of tenure is a type of degradation ceremony. During this year, a faculty member must face his or her peers each day, knowing that he or she has failed to meet tenure standards and thus will not be employed there the following year.

In direct contrast, rites of enhancement are designed to convey positive information. This can be positive information about the organization or public recognition of individuals for exceptional levels of performance. To illustrate this type of rite, Trice and Beyer

TABLE 14.3
A Summary of Organizational Rites

Type of Rites	Example
Rites of passage	Induction and basic training in the U.S. Army
Rites of degradation	Firing and replacing top executives
Rites of enhancement	Mary Kay seminars
Rites of renewal	Organizational development activities
Rites of conflict reduction	Collective bargaining
Rites of integration	Office Christmas party

Source: H. M. Trice and J. M. Beyer. (1984). Studying organizational culture through rites and ceremonials. *Academy of Management Review, 9,* 653–669. Reprinted with permission of the Copyright Clearance Center.

COMMENT 14.2

PROFESSIONAL MEETINGS: GOING TO SIOP?

For nearly 20 years, a yearly spring ritual for many industrial/organizational psychologists has been attendance at the annual conference of the Society for Industrial and Organizational Psychology (SIOP). The most recent (2007) SIOP conference was held in New York City; this conference has also taken place in Boston, Miami, St. Louis, Montreal, San Francisco, San Diego, Nashville, New Orleans, Dallas, Atlanta, and Orlando.

Why do so many industrial/organizational psychologists make the SIOP conference a regular event? One reason is that going to the conference allows them to keep up on the latest developments in both the science and practice of industrial/organizational psychology. Each year, the conference program includes symposia and poster sessions that allow researchers and practitioners to discuss their findings and exchange ideas. This is particularly important for researchers, because much of what appears in academic journals is often 1 or 2 years old!

Another important (and perhaps less understood) function of the SIOP conference is that it serves a socialization function. Each year, many graduate students attend this conference for the first time and receive their first taste of what it is like to be in this profession. They learn who the important people in the profession are and how to conduct themselves as professionals. They are also educated about the major issues facing the profession. These things are obviously important in transmitting a professional culture that will live on far longer than any individual. Furthermore, graduate students attending this conference for the first time leave feeling very enthused about the profession they have chosen and eager to attend the next year.

(1984) provide the example of the employee seminars conducted by the Mary Kay cosmetics company. During these seminars, the company legacy is celebrated, and individual employees are recognized for outstanding sales performance—all of which is done with a great deal of fanfare and glamour. Many of the activities at the annual meetings of professional organizations often serve this purpose as well (see Comment 14.2).

In most organizations, there are times when problems need to be addressed and employees need to renew their sense of purpose within the organization. Rites of renewal serve this purpose. Trice and Beyer (1984) cite the use of organizational-development interventions as a prime example of rites of renewal in organizations. For example, interventions such as team building, survey feedback, and Management by Objectives (MBO), which are often part of organizational development programs, can be seen as ritualistic activities that ultimately serve to renew employees' sense of purpose. While such activities provide employees with reassurance that something is being done about the problems in the organization, they may also mask the real causes of problems. By doing this, they may reinforce the existing power structure and social arrangements within the organization.

This view of organizational development proposed by Trice and Beyer (1984) is certainly provocative, although many organizational-development professionals would probably disagree with it. In fact, there is some empirical evidence that organizational-development interventions can facilitate positive change in organizations (e.g., French & Bell, 1995), and thus are more than expensive "feel good" rituals. On the other hand, it is possible for organizational development to be applied in a somewhat ritualistic fashion—an employee opinion survey is conducted, a report is written and filed away. While everyone may feel good about the process, the reality is that after this process is completed none of the substantive problems within the organization are even addressed, much less solved.

Rites of conflict reduction are often conducted in organizations when potentially debilitating conflict needs to be addressed. Perhaps the best example of this type of rite in unionized organizations is the collective bargaining process. According to Trice and Beyer (1984), this activity is a rite because, in most cases, each side knows that an agreement is ultimately going to be reached. However, on the way to getting there, each side must "play a game" that is consistent with its role. For example, representatives of the company must initially present an unacceptable contractual offer in order to show that they are good stewards of organizational resources. The union representatives, in turn, must reject that offer and make contractual demands that they know the organization cannot agree to, just to show that they are protecting the interests of the union membership. Ultimately, this give-and-take process will produce a contract that is acceptable, if not ideal, to both sides.

The final type of rites described by Trice and Beyer (1984) are rites of integration. The major purpose behind rites of integration is to encourage and revive common feelings that serve to bind members of the organization together. In most organizations, the common example of this form of rite is the annual holiday office party. At most holiday gatherings employees typically suspend normal rules

of protocol and simply have fun together. This experience of having fun together presumably serves to make the social ties that bind these people together that much stronger, even if it is only for an afternoon or evening.

Rituals are closely related to rites because they are also enacted through behavior patterns. Trice and Beyer (1984) define a *ritual* as "a standard, detailed set of techniques and behaviors that manage anxieties, but seldom produce intended, technical consequences of practical importance" (p. 655). Perhaps the most visible examples of ritualistic behavior come from the world of sports—in particular, from baseball. Many baseball players, for example, believe that it is bad luck to step on the chalk lines when running onto the field, and often make a visible effort to avoid doing so (just watch closely sometime!). Perhaps the most elaborate rituals ever seen in baseball came from former major league baseball player and hall of famer Wade Boggs. Boggs would eat only chicken on the day of a game, and he had to field the same number of ground balls prior to each game. In Boggs's case, however, these might not be considered rituals because they evidently did him some good—he won several American League batting titles and ended his career with over 3,000 hits!

Employees in most organizations do not engage in ritualistic behaviors similar to those of professional athletes. Organizational rituals, however, do exist and they do convey information about the organizational culture. For example, employees in many organizations develop nearly ritualistic behavior that centers on daily breaks and lunch time. Each day, employees may congregate in the same location or eat at the same restaurant at precisely the same time. In contrast, in some organizations, individuals may spend these times eating at their desks or perhaps reading a book. In the former case, such rituals convey strong social bonds within the organization; in the latter case, they may suggest a culture that values individuals' privacy and solitude.

Other common ritualistic behaviors in organizations can be seen at the beginning and end of the workday. Employees, for example, may congregate around the coffee machine and exchange pleasantries, or perhaps talk about sports or current events. In other organizations, each employee may begin the day by quickly going to his or her desk and immediately beginning to work. In the former case, one might again presume that the social ties are a bit stronger; in fact, they reach to the point where employees may feel that such daily activities are highly vital to their work, even though the information exchanged may actually be quite trivial. In the latter case, this behavior, at least on the surface, may convey a high level of diligence and a desire to accomplish tasks. It may also be indicative of a high level of conflict and suspicion among the employees of an organization.

Another ritual that can be very revealing about the culture of organizations—or, in many cases, subcultures—is the type of socializing after work hours. In some academic departments a common ritual on Friday afternoons is socializing over drinks at a local bar. In contrast, in some academic departments, faculty rarely, if ever, socialize outside of work hours. In the former case, this weekly ritual conveys that members of a department see themselves as more than just coworkers, and they wish to extend the social bonds beyond the confines of the work environment. A lack of socializing outside of work could mean that coworkers do not find each other's company appealing; it may also signify an organizational culture in which employees get along quite well, but place a very high value on spending time with their families.

Stories, Legends, and Dramas

It is certainly well documented, from fields such as cultural anthropology (e.g., Geertz, 1973) and communication theory (Pacanowsky & O'Donnell-Trujillo, 1983), that story telling and passing on legends are very important ways of passing on information about a culture. In organizational settings, *stories* are defined as "narratives based on true events—often a combination of truth and fiction" (Trice & Beyer, 1984, p. 655). Employees in organizations tell many stories, some of which may be completely irrelevant to cultural transmission. What makes a story a vehicle for cultural transmission is that it is intentionally meant to convey something important about the culture of the organization—in many cases, to organizational newcomers. A good example of this can be seen in a brief story contained in Derek Jeter's 2001 book *The Life You Imagine: Life Lessons for Achieving Your Dreams*. In this book Jeter describes an instance during his rookie year when he and Don Mattingly (former Yankee great and current bench coach) are leaving the field at the end of a workout during spring training. Even though the two players were alone and could leisurely walk off the field, Jeter states that Mattingly suggests they sprint off the field (which they do) because "you never know whose watching." This story obviously says something about the integrity of Mattingly, but more importantly, about the culture of the team. More specifically, hard work and effort are not just for show, but are important all the time.

A *legend* is a "handed-down narrative of some wonderful event that is based on history, but is embellished with fictional details" (Trice & Beyer, 1984, p. 655). In schools throughout the United States, children learn about how the founding fathers, such as Thomas Jefferson, Benjamin Franklin, and Alexander Hamilton, cooperated to produce the Constitution, and what this signifies about our national culture. As historical analysis has shown, however, the processes surrounding the development of the U.S. Constitution were anything but cooperative (Tolson, 2001, February 26). Many of the framers of the Constitution were highly political and very self-interested. In fact, the partisan politics seen today is relatively tame in comparison. Notice, however, that teaching this slightly inaccurate version of history does serve to transmit cultural values that are important in a democracy such as the United States.

Legends are also used in organizations to convey important cultural details. The specific legends passed on typically focus on important milestones such as the founding of the organization, a critical organizational crisis, or an important innovation that has had a great impact on the organization. Within 3M, the details surrounding many product innovations, such as a Post-it® note, take on a legendary status, and the individuals responsible for these innovations are seen as almost larger than life (Gundling, 2000). Passing on these legends to new employees within 3M serves the purpose of communicating the fact that innovation and creativity are important parts of the culture.

A final mechanism for the transmission of culture is through what Pettigrew (1979) termed organizational *dramas*. An organizational drama is simply a significant or defining event in the history of an organization. The occurrences of organizational dramas provide researchers with a window into the culture of an organization; relating these dramas to new organizational members also provides a way for organizations to transmit organizational culture to newcomers. According to Pettigrew, the most typical orga-

nizational dramas are the entry and exit of organizational leaders, changes in the structure of an organization, and noteworthy successes or failures.

Language and Communication

Language is one of the key things that distinguish humans from other species. It stands to reason, then, that the culture of an organization would be reflected in the language of organizational employees; in fact, each organization typically has its own unique vernacular. Similarly, the manner in which employees in an organization communicate with each other may also reveal important information about an organization's culture. Each of these is discussed in the following paragraphs.

With respect to spoken language, organizational terminology can be quite revealing. Several years ago one of the authors conducted a brief training seminar in an organization in which virtually all employees referred to their various departments as *worlds* rather than by more standard terms such as *departments* or *units*. Although use of this terminology may have been completely coincidental, it also could have been indicative of a great deal of "turf battles" and compartmentalization within the organization. Another example of this, which may be familiar to many readers, is Disney's long-standing practice of referring to park visitors as *guests* rather than customers (Van Maanen, 1991). This signifies that people who pay to visit the Disney theme parks should be treated by employees as though they were visitors in their homes. Disney has also traditionally used theatrical terminology (e.g., employees are *cast members*) to reinforce the point that they are in the business of providing entertainment.

The mode of communication used by employees in organizations can also provide insights into organizational culture. Employees in some organizations favor highly impersonal one-way modes of communication such as written messages, voice mail, and e-mail. What does reliance on these forms of communication suggest about organizational culture? It may simply mean that people want to save time. However, it could also mean that people really do not want to communicate with each other. While impersonal modes of communication such as e-mail are very efficient, they also get employees into the habit of "issuing directives" and making "declarations" to their fellow employees rather than engaging in two-way communication and meaningful dialogue. As a result, this may be indicative of a culture characterized by high suspicion and conflict.

In contrast, the preferred mode of communication in some organizations is much different. Employees may favor highly personal, face-to-face communication rather than more impersonal modes such as e-mail or written memos. In terms of organizational culture, this may indicate that there is a great deal of emphasis on interpersonal harmony and on making sure that others' feelings are considered when making decisions. This may also indicate a highly participative culture in which a great deal of consultation must take place prior to decisions being made.

THE DEVELOPMENT OF ORGANIZATIONAL CULTURE

According to Schein (1992), the two major functions of organizational culture are external adaptation and internal integration. The notion of external adaptation reflects an anthropological, or even an evolutionary, approach to organizational culture. To cultural anthropologists, the totality of a culture reflects behaviors and beliefs that have survived over time because they have helped a group of people adapt more successfully to their environment. This obviously has evolutionary overtones because adaptation is a central part of the evolutionary process.

When we apply the concept of external adaptation, we come up with the proposition that organizational cultures develop and persist because they help an organization to survive and flourish. This concept is quite easy to illustrate if one looks at organizations that possess cultural attributes that most observers would consider very positive. For example, developing a culture that emphasizes innovation kept 3M from going out of business, and this continues to help it remain one of the most successful corporations in the world. Similarly, developing a culture that puts customer service and comfort above all else helped Disney make the transition from a small film-animation company to a large entertainment conglomerate.

External adaptation can also explain why some organizations ultimately develop cultures that possess what some would consider negative attributes. According to Mason 2004, the organizational culture of NASA changed from one that strongly emphasized safety and technical excellence, to one primarily concerned with cost efficiency and meeting schedules. When one considers the pressures faced by this organization over the years (e.g., decreased congressional funding, pressure to meet launch deadlines), this change in culture is understandable. However, as Mason points out, the price of this emphasis on efficiency has been less vigilance about safety issues; in fact, this may have contributed to some of its failures such as the *Challanger* and *Columbia* space shuttle accidents.

In addition to facilitating external adaptation, Schein (1992) proposed that organizational culture facilitates internal integration. Consider for a moment how an organization could function if it had no identifiable culture. In such a scenario, how would new members be integrated into the organization and taught how to assume their new roles? Thus, culture can be thought of as a sort of "glue" that bonds the social structure of a larger organization together. This is critical because, when all is said and done, organizations are ultimately social constructions and, without social integration, they would cease to exist (Katz & Kahn, 1978).

This integrative function can be seen at various levels of an organization, and thus serves as an explanation for the development of organizational subcultures. Furthermore, some of these subcultures may result from individuals in a particular department or function sharing common experiences or similar academic training. Because of this, the various areas that are represented by graduate programs (e.g., Clinical, I/O, Social, Experimental) within large psychology departments often develop very distinct subcultures based on commonality of academic training and experiences. The development of these subcultures, provided they aren't at odds with each other, increases social cohesion within these areas and enhances the professional socialization of graduate students. The existence of subcultures does not mean, however, that there is no overall departmental culture. Regardless of the area, all faculty typically have had at least some overlap in their training as doctoral-level psychologists.

A final factor that often shapes an organization's culture is its founder or its chief executive. How do influential founders and high-level executives put their own "personal stamp" on the culture of an organization? This question has not achieved a great deal of empirical attention, but several mech-

anisms are possible. One is that these individuals have a great deal of control over who is hired, particularly at the highest levels. Because people generally like to be in the company of others whom they perceive to be similar to them (Byrne, 1971), it is highly likely that employees hand-picked by a founder or chief executive have similar values. Furthermore, because those who really didn't share his or her values either declined to join the company or ultimately left (Schneider, 1987), those remaining probably shaped a culture that was very similar to his or her personality.

Founders and influential executives also have a great deal of influence over the strategy an organization decides to pursue (Finkelstein, 1992). Choice of strategy, in turn, may ultimately impact the culture that develops in the organization. For example, an organization that chooses to pursue a strategy of offering a very limited number of highly specialized products will likely develop a very different culture, compared to an organization where the primary source of competitive advantage is high-quality customer service. In the former case, the culture that develops may place a premium on technical expertise. In contrast, in the latter case, a culture may develop that places a much higher value on social skills and the reduction of conflict.

A final issue to consider, particularly with respect to founders, is whether they continue to impact the culture of an organization when they are no longer involved with it on a day-to-day basis (e.g., after retirement or death). Again, little empirical research has examined this issue. However, based on what we do know about culture, the legacy of an organizational founder may be reflected in the culture for quite some time. That is, through processes of cultural transmission (e.g., rites, stories), cultures will typically perpetuate themselves, and thus outlive the founding member of the organization. This is particularly true if the original culture of the organization has led to success and is thus seen as having some adaptive value. Disney is a good example of an organization that has worked hard to preserve the legacy of the founder, Walt Disney, and it has been very successful in doing so.

MEASURING ORGANIZATIONAL CULTURE

To scientifically determine the effect of organizational culture, we need to be able to measure it and to do so with a great deal of precision. Like many variables in organizational psychology, organizational culture is very complex and thus very difficult to measure. In this section, we examine common approaches to measuring organizational culture.

Self-Report Assessments of Culture

The most direct way to measure the culture of an organization is to create some type of self-report measure, administer this measure to a sample of organizational employees, and then create a numerical index to describe the culture. The most popular self-report measure of organizational culture over the years has been the Organizational Culture Profile (OCP), which is based on the previously described model of organizational culture proposed by O'Reilly, Chatman, and Caldwell (1991). The OCP measures employee perceptions of the predominate values within an organization, which are summarized in Table 14.2. Because the OCP provides measures of organizations and not individuals, the scores for each of these values are typically formed by averaging individual employees' ratings.

Another relatively common self-report measure of organizational culture is Hofstede's

(1980) measure of organizational values. This self-report instrument, which is based on Hofstede's work on differences in national cultures, assesses the following potential organizational values: process-oriented versus results-oriented; employee-oriented versus job-oriented; parochial versus professional; open system versus closed system; loose control versus tight control; normative control versus tight control. As with the OCP, individual employees' scores are aggregated to come up with the scores for the organization. The organization's unique culture is then determined by examining the pattern of the scores on this instrument.

The most recent self-report measure of culture is the *Denison Organizational Culture Survey* (Denison, Cho, & Young, 2000). This measure consists of 60 items that are designed to measure the 12 dimensions of the previously described Denison model of organizational culture (see Fig. 14.1). Like the other measures described, responses of employees in an organization are averaged. While this measure is still relatively new, compared to the OCI and Hofstede's measure, Denison and colleagues have shown it to be a useful diagnostic tool in many types of organizations.

Self-report measures of organizational culture are relatively easy to administer, and they provide quantitative indexes that researchers can use to describe and compare organizational cultures. Unfortunately there are also some serious limitations associated with self-report assessments of organizational culture. Recall that the essence of organizational culture is the basic assumptions shared by the employees in an organization. Because these basic assumptions are rarely questioned by employees, they are, to a large extent, unconscious. Thus, employees who are immersed in the culture of an organization are probably going to be able to report only the surface aspects of that culture, such as values, which are exactly assessed by self-report measures.

Self-report measures of culture may also be problematic because they impose a somewhat arbitrary structure on the respondent. Although researchers have found that certain values or dimensions of organizational culture are important to assess, there may be others that are more specific to a given organization and contribute greatly to its culture. For example, compared to a business organization the culture of an educational institution may be heavily influenced by highly unique external factors such as the level of educational funding that is provided by the state government. These highly specific factors are typically not measured in standard self-report culture measures.

A more serious problem with self-report is that there is no way of assessing whether respondents are describing the *actual* culture of the organization or the *idealized* culture of the organization. In many organizations, there is a great deal of difference between what employees would like the culture to be and what it actually is. Employees completing self-report measures may very well report, essentially, an idealized version, and not the reality, of the culture. This occurs simply because of the many weaknesses inherent in self-report measurement (e.g., Spector, 1994) and the fact that employees, particularly those at higher organizational levels, may have "blind spots" regarding the culture.

Ethnographic Methods of Culture Assessment

Ethnography is the use of qualitative, observational methods of assessing behavior. Researchers conducting ethnographic assessment of organizational culture (herein referred to as *ethnographers*) typically observe and record behavior in an organization for an extended period of time. In some cases, ethnographers present themselves as outside researchers. In other cases, however, ethnographers may actually become members of the organizations they are trying to analyze. The most notable example of this type of research in the organizational literature was Van Maanen's analysis of police culture (Van Maanen, 1975). In order to study this organization, Van Maanen actually went through a police academy as a recruit and recorded his observations.

Other than direct observation, another tool often used by ethnographers is interviewing informants (Johnson, 1990). An informant is a member of the organization to whom ethnographers can go for information. In many cases, informants help ethnographers make sense out of what they have observed in the organization. According to Johnson, there is no ideal informant in any ethnographic study; however, it is obviously important that any informant should possess a detailed knowledge of the organization being studied.

When choosing an organizational informant, ethnographers often seek out long-tenured employees. Indeed, these individuals may be very helpful because they are able to provide a historical context for understanding much of what goes on in an organization. A potential drawback of long-tenured employees, though, is that they may be so immersed in the culture that they are unable to describe it accurately. The "first impressions" of a relatively new employee may ultimately provide as much (or more) insight into an organization's true culture. The best course of action for ethnographers, if possible, is to seek organizational informants who represent a variety of tenure levels.

The obvious benefit of ethnographic assessment of organizational culture is that it does not require the researcher to directly ask employees about the culture of the organization. If we accept the notion that organizational culture represents the shared "basic assumptions" of employees, then qualitative methods are more likely than self-report measures to capture these assumptions, simply because basic assumptions are at a level of consciousness that is very difficult for employees to access. Thus, more information about culture can probably be gleaned from observing employees' behaviors, rather than directly asking them questions. Unfortunately, ethnography is a labor-intensive and, at times, painstaking process. Many researchers do not have the time to observe an organization for long periods or the capability of coding all of those observations. There is also a potential for observer bias in ethnographic research. There are ways that ethnographers can address this issue (e.g., via informants or multiple observers), but observation ultimately involves a good deal of subjectivity.

Other Methods of Cultural Assessment

By far, the most common methods of culture assessment are self-report surveys and ethnography. Given the vast methodological tool-kit available to organizational psychologists, however, there are certainly other ways culture could be assessed. One method, which is not used very often in organizational culture research, is the use of archival information from the organization. Most organizations produce a good deal of archival information, and some of this may provide clues about culture. For example, an organization's annual report could be analyzed through content analysis to provide information about culture. If a good portion of the text of the annual report

deals with customer service, this is a sign that customer service is a major part of an organization's culture. Similarly, if all of an organization's top executives are long-tenured employees, this may be a sign that, in the organization, a strong value is placed on experience.

Another method, which has not been used frequently, is to assess culture through measuring employees' cognitive maps of the organizations (see Silvester, Anderson, & Patterson, 1999). Cognitive mapping is simply a way of determining the underlying heuristics that employees use to process information about the organization. To construct cognitive maps, employees are interviewed, and the information from these interviews is subjected to a standardized coding process. Although this is a relatively new process, it certainly holds great promise for future researchers as a method of culture assessment.

CHANGING ORGANIZATIONAL CULTURE

So far, in defining organizational culture, we have emphasized the values and basic assumptions that have been passed down through many generations and, as a result, are shared among employees. Another key point in the previous discussion is that organizational cultures do not develop in a random fashion; rather, they develop and are sustained over time because they help an organization adapt to its competitive environment. However, what happens when that competitive environment changes? The attributes of an organization's culture that helped it compete in the previous competitive environment may be irrelevant, or perhaps even counterproductive, in the new environment. Thus, at times organizations have to change their cultures in order to survive.

Even if their competitive environment is relatively stable, organizations may attempt to change their cultures for other reasons. Often, the desire for culture change accompanies significant changes in the top management team of an organization. In such cases change is driven more by the desires of those in top management than by necessity. Cultures also change because the people in an organization change over time. Although it is often argued that this process favors cultural stability (e.g., Kristof (1996); Schneider, 1987), it may not always be the case. When different people come into an organization, they may gradually change its interpersonal dynamics and, ultimately, its culture.

Many of the organizational development interventions that will be described in Chapter 15 are ultimately aimed at changing the culture of an organization, so the topic will not be covered in great depth here. In this section, however, two important questions about culture change are addressed:

1. Why is changing the culture of an organization so difficult?
2. What are some of the common mechanisms by which organizational cultures change?

Why Is Culture Change Difficult?

In almost any comprehensive treatment of organizational culture it is concluded that organizational culture is hard to change once it has been established (Denison, 1990; Hatch, 1993; Schein, 1985, 1992). That's not to say that organizational culture is completely intractable; in fact, over a long period of time most organizational cultures evolve and change, due to a number of factors that will be covered in the next section. What is difficult, however, is for organizations to change their cultures very quickly. A

manager cannot simply write a memo to employees on a Friday informing them that, as of Monday, the culture will be different (though some organizations may naïvely think this is possible).

One reason that it is difficult to change the culture of an organization has to do with the definition of culture that was presented at the beginning of the chapter. As was pointed out, the essence of organizational culture resides in the basic assumptions shared by employees. Recall that basic assumptions can be about anything, but those relevant to organizational culture typically have something to do with the organization and its major activities. What makes these assumptions "basic" is that they are shared among employees and, as such, are rarely if ever questioned or put under objective scrutiny.

Because of this, "basic assumptions" are highly resistant to change. Furthermore, in those cases when basic assumptions are challenged in organizations, the challenge may actually serve to strengthen employees' beliefs in those basic assumptions. For example if a new employee refuses to accept the basic assumptions that are inherent in an organization's culture, this will typically force other employees to "bring that person into line." In the process of doing so, the core values and assumptions may be strengthened, regardless of whether that person eventually accepts them, actively resists them, or ultimately leaves the organization. Although basic assumptions are viewed by most organizational culture experts as being highly resistant to change, it should be noted that this view is not shared by all (see Comment 14.3).

Another reason organizational culture is difficult to change is because there are typically those who stand to benefit if the culture remains static. A logical corollary

COMMENT 14.3

IS ORGANIZATIONAL CULTURE REALLY SO DIFFICULT TO CHANGE?

IN NEARLY ALL reviews of organizational culture, one of the common assertions is that once the culture of an organization is established it is extremely difficult to change. This is because, by definition, *culture* represents beliefs and assumptions that are so rarely questioned that they are not even conscious. Thus, it takes a lot of effort to get people to question basic assumptions and, in the process, change culture.

Although this is by far the dominant viewpoint, there are some organizational culture researchers that disagree. Wilkins and Ouchi (1983), for example, point out that the idea of organizational culture being difficult to change comes from cultural anthropology. Cultural anthropologists, as many readers know, are primarily interested in societal cultures. Societal cultures are obviously very difficult to change because most people become totally immersed in their societal culture.

In the case of organizational culture, however, there is a great deal of variation in the degree of "enculturation." Some employees do become "true believers" and faithfully espouse the values and assumptions of their organization. On the other hand, employees may be very much opposed to the values and assumptions of their organization. Most employees are probably somewhere between these two extremes. Given this variation in employee enculturation, it is probably easier to change the culture of an organization than an entire society.

Source: A. L. Wilkins and W. G. Ouchi. (1983). Efficient cultures: Exploring the relationship between culture and organizational performance. *Administrative Science Quarterly, 28,* 468–481.

to this is: There are often some who stand to lose (or perceive this to be the case) if the culture is changed. Perhaps the best way to illustrate this is through one of the most fundamental assumptions shaping organizational culture: how employees should be rewarded. Let's say that one of the most basic assumptions of an organization's culture is that rewards should be based primarily on seniority. Further assume that a new organizational president is hired and is determined to change the culture to one in which rewards are instead based primarily on performance.

Given this scenario, consider first the issue of who benefits from the present culture of this organization. It is very clear that the primary beneficiaries of the present culture are those who have been employed in the organization for a long period of time, assuming of course that the organization's reward policies actually reflect the culture. Now consider who stands to lose if the culture of the organization changes and performance is then valued above all else. Not all long-tenured employees will be hurt by this change, because some of these individuals may be among the organization's best performers. Rather, employees who perform their jobs poorly, regardless of tenure, stand to lose the most from such a culture change.

Among those actively resisting such a change, however, long-tenured poor-performing employees would probably be the most vigorous. These individuals may resist such a culture change by actively arguing against it, or even failing to follow policies that are based on it. These individuals not only must give something up (rewards based on seniority), but they may also be hurt again (based on their performance, they will not be highly rewarded) by the culture change. Regardless of how bad or dysfunctional an organizational culture may appear, there are typically those who benefit from having it remain that way, and those who stand to lose by changing it. Many attempts to change organizational culture end up in failure because those initiating the change haven't recognized this.

A final reason that organizational culture cannot be easily changed goes back to the factors that shape culture in the first place. Recall that the most important of these is adaptation. Cultures develop and flourish over time because they serve some purpose or help some group adapt more effectively to its environment. That's not to say that maladaptive cultures never develop. For the most part, though, cultures remain stable because they serve some adaptive function (Mason, 2004). It follows, then, that superficial or misguided attempts to change organizational culture would probably encounter resistance.

The Nature of Organizational Culture Change

According to Schein (1992), organizations are like individuals in that they pass through distinct "life" stages. These stages are important because they help us to understand how organizations change and evolve over time. During the *Birth and Early Growth* phase, the organization is founded and is beginning to develop a distinct culture. As one might imagine, during this phase, organizational culture is strongly impacted by the organizational founder(s) or the family of the founder. Such individuals can often literally hire or fire at will and are in a position to

demand a great deal of loyalty. Furthermore, just to survive, organizations at this stage may demand a great deal of commitment on the part of employees. Also, at this stage, when the organization is most vulnerable, external events can potentially have great effects on the organization and, in fact, become part of organizational folklore.

In the second stage, *Organizational Midlife*, an organization typically becomes "bigger" structurally. This may also be a time of growth and expansion, as organizations decide to explore new markets or product lines. With respect to organizational culture, the great structural complexity that often accompanies this stage may result in a number of organizational "subcultures." These subcultures may be based on a number of things, such as geographic location, product lines or divisions, or even functional specialties. The obvious danger at this stage is that the subcultures may become so distinct that the organization begins to lose its more general, overarching culture.

The third and final stage in this model is *Organizational Maturity*. This is essentially the "crossroads" in the life of an organization. At this point, an organization is often faced with the choice of renewal (e.g., continuing on indefinitely) or stagnation and, ultimately, death. In this sense, organizations have an advantage over people—they can live on indefinitely whereas people cannot. Organizational culture is a key factor in determining this choice between renewal and stagnation. Organizations that fail to change any aspect of their cultures stand a good chance of failure. On the other hand, organizations that live on indefinitely must decide which aspects of their cultures need to be changed and which ones need to be preserved over time.

Schein (1985, 1992) proposed a number of mechanisms by which organizational cultures change over time within the context of these organizational life stages. These are summarized in Table 14.4. During the Birth and Early Growth phase, organizational culture may change through any of four primary mechanisms. The mechanism of natural evolution represents the processes that shape an organizational culture when it attempts to adapt to its environment. When viewed in a general sense, this simply represents those aspects of organizational culture that contribute to its survival. For example, during the early life of an organization, changing from a highly autocratic to a highly collaborative culture is adaptive, and this may become part of the organization's permanent culture.

A second mechanism that frequently leads to culture change in the early stages of an organization is referred to by Schein as "self-guided evolution through organizational therapy" (2003). In other words, there is a deliberate attempt or intervention conducted to change the organizational culture. The term *organizational therapy* is used to refer to a variety of interventions (some of which will be described in Chapter 15) that are designed to facilitate culture change. As an example, the top management of a relatively new organization may decide that the culture of the organization should be very team oriented. In this case, the *therapy* used to achieve this culture change might be in the form of training on topics such as team decision making or resolving interpersonal conflict in teams. In other cases, organizations use reorganization or restructuring in order to change a culture (Hannan, Polos, & Carroll, 2003).

Another mechanism used for culture change is referred to by Schein as "managed evolution through hybrids." In this case, culture change is also initiated intentionally, although the mechanism is much different from the one in the previous example. In this case, the mechanism is through the appointment of "hybrids" in key positions within the organization. A *hybrid* is an individual who has grown up in the present organizational culture but, at the same time, may not accept all of the underlying assumptions on which it is based. By putting these types of individuals

TABLE 14.4
Culture Change Mechanisms at Different Stages of the Organizational Lifecycle

Stage	Change Mechanisms
1. Birth and Early growth	1. Natural evolution
	2. Self-guided evolution through organizational therapy
	3. Managed evolution through hybrids
	4. Managed "revolution" through outsiders
2. Organizational midlife	1. Planned change and organizational development
	2. Technological seduction
	3. Change through scandal and explosion of myths
	4. Incrementalism
3. Organizational maturity	1. Coercive persuasion
	2. Turnaround
	3. Reorganization, destruction, and rebirth

Source: E. H. Schein. (1985). *Organizational culture and leadership: A dynamic view.* San Francisco: Jossey-Bass. Copyright 1985, Jossey-Bass. Reprinted by permission of John Wiley & Sons.

in key positions, the culture may not change radically, but it may shift in a way that is ultimately more adaptive for the organization.

The final mechanism used for culture change during the early life of an organization is referred to as "managed revolution through outsiders." This mechanism is like the one just described, except that the "agents of change" are individuals from outside of the organization who are much less familiar with the organizational culture than organizational insiders. Bringing these types of individuals into an organization can potentially initiate a great deal of culture change because they are likely to question many of the basic assumptions on which the current culture is based. While this may be a difficult process, for both current employees and the outsiders that are brought in, it may help an organization rethink outdated or dysfunctional aspects of its culture and ultimately lead to culture change.

By the time an organization reaches the midlife stage, the culture is relatively well established and different mechanisms may be needed to facilitate change. The first of these, in Table 14.4, is referred to as *planned change and organizational development*. This represents a deliberate attempt to guide and facilitate the change process. This is a sign of organizational maturity because it shows recognition that adaptation is necessary for success. While all organizational-development programs have somewhat different goals, the fundamental purpose of most is to change the culture of the organization, or at least provide an organization with the capability to do so. Organizations using this type of strategy typically bring in outside consultants, although, in some large organizations, an organizational-development function may be established.

The second change mechanism in organizational midlife is referred to as *technolog-*

ical seduction. This refers to the use of technology as a lever for organizational culture change, and it may occur in two different ways. Technology may drive organizational change because of the technologies that emerge within the organization. For example, a "high-tech" culture may develop in a computer company, due to the types of employees needed to fill many of the positions in such an organization. In addition, organizations can sometimes induce culture change by introducing new and unfamiliar technology. The idea that technology can shape the social environment is well known and can be traced back to the sociotechnical systems perspective and the Tavistock studies of coal mining (Trist & Bamforth, 1951).

A third mechanism of culture change during organizational midlife is through scandal and the explosion of myths. For example, a scandal involving an organization may force organizational members to rethink some of their basic assumptions, which may ultimately lead to culture change. This may occur, for example, when a charismatic leader in an organization is caught engaging in illegal behavior. On a societal level, one could certainly argue that the Watergate scandal in the early 1970s led many to rethink their assumptions about government officials. Ultimately, this has led to a great deal of mistrust and skepticism toward these people.

The explosion of myths occurs when one of the generally accepted organizational myths is publicly proven to be false. As an example, a myth commonly held in many organizations is that employees' jobs are secure. If layoffs do occur, this results in an explosion of this myth and the culture of an organization may change as a result. At the social level, a myth that persisted among Americans was that there was little possibility of terrorism being carried out on our own soil. Most thought that terrorism was something that occurred only in the Middle East. The events on September 11, 2001, obviously shattered this myth, and it is probably one of the reasons that people were so shocked by these acts.

The final mechanism for change during organizational midlife is referred to as *incrementalism*. This means that change does occur, but it occurs very slowly. For example, most organizations in the midlife stage have employees who represent a variety of tenure levels. Some have been with the organization for a long time, others have been around for a few years, and others are new. Over time, as new employees come into an organization and others either retire or leave, the organization will undoubtedly change, although in subtle ways. As an example, academic departments in many universities are changing because a large number of faculty hired during the early 1970s are now retiring. These changes are incremental, however, because all of these individuals are unlikely to retire at once. New faculty are brought in gradually, and the change is often very subtle and hard to detect.

During the final stage, organizational maturity, an organization is really faced with the choice of stagnation/decline or changing in ways that will facilitate its renewal. Thus, a change in organizational culture may be a very critical issue. One way that change may be achieved at this point is through what Schein (1985) described as *coercive persuasion*. In this case, organizations use a variety of coercive tactics to facilitate changes in individuals, which will ultimately lead to changes in the culture. A common way that organizations use this mechanism is by providing long-tenured employees with the option of early retirement. Another way that organizations may facilitate change in this manner is through the threat of undesirable work assignments or by altering working conditions in ways that are undesirable to any employees who will not change.

The second change mechanism during Organizational Maturing is described by Schein (1985) as *turnaround*. To a large extent, turnaround embodies many of the change mechanisms that were previously described. During turnaround, the organization recognizes the need for a cultural change and takes the steps necessary for the change to occur. In many cases, this may be through the application of organizational-development methods, but it could also be through a change in personnel. As Schein (1985, 1992) points out, for turnaround to be successful, it must be a comprehensive effort and involve all members of the organization.

The final change mechanism in organizational maturing is referred to as *reorganization, destruction, and rebirth*. This is probably the most extreme form of culture change because it essentially involves destroying the present culture and instituting a new one. Given the extremity of this method, it is typically reserved for times of crisis or times when the only alternative to culture change is failure. An example of this change mechanism can often be seen in the federal government when the U.S. president is reelected to a second term in office. Specifically, many of the cabinet members and key members of the administration from the first term resign or are replaced with new appointees. The impact of such changes, one would assume, is to change the culture surrounding the administration, and hence enhance its effectiveness.

THE IMPACT OF ORGANIZATIONAL CULTURE

So far, we have examined a variety of issues pertaining to organizational culture—how it is defined, how it is measured, how it changes—and two models that provide a comparison of different organizational cultures. However, some important questions have yet to be examined: Does organizational culture make a difference in important organizational outcomes? Do organizations with certain cultural attributes tend to be more successful than organizations without such attributes? Do organizations with cultural attributes tend to attract, hire, and retain better employees than organizations without such attributes? Do employees in organizations with certain cultural attributes tend to be more satisfied and to have a better quality of work life than employees in organizations without such attributes? In this section, a brief summary of research evidence bearing on each of these questions will be provided.

Culture and Organizational Performance

The issue of linking organizational culture with organizational performance has certainly received some attention (e.g., Denison, 1984; Denison & Mishra, 1995; Peters & Waterman, 1995; Wilkins & Ouchi, 1983). Early attempts to do this, as in Peters and Waterman's 1982 best-selling book *In Search of Excellence*, were focused primarily on qualitative comparisons of successful and unsuccessful companies. While such an approach can provide useful insights, it is certainly limited from a methodological perspective. Thus, more recent research has attempted to correlate dimensions of organizational culture with organizational performance.

Kotter and Heskett (1992) conducted what is perhaps the most comprehensive empirical study. They investigated 207 U.S. organizations spread among 25 different industries. They measured the strength of organizational culture and examined how this related to a number of

performance indexes, such as revenues, stock price, expansion of the work force, and net income. The fact that culture and performance were measured using different sources is important because it decreases the possibility that culture and performance were related simply because of a common-method bias.

The results of this study suggest that organizational culture does make a difference in bottom-line organizational performance. For example, organizations with cultures that these authors labeled *adaptive* performed much better than organizations with cultures labeled *unadaptive*. The major differences between adaptive and unadaptive cultures are highlighted in Table 14.5. When one looks at these differences, it becomes fairly clear that an organization with an adaptive culture would be a much more enjoyable place to work, compared to an organization that is unadaptive. Furthermore, from the results of this study, it appears an adaptive culture translates into organizational success.

Denison and colleagues have conducted research that is very similar to Kotter and Heskett (1992), where they correlate dimensions of culture with organizational performance. Table 14.6 contains correlations between the 12 culture dimensions from the Denison model and overall effectiveness from Denison, Haaland, and Goelzer (2004). These correlations are based on responses from 36,820 individuals from 210 organizations in three regions of the world (North America, Asia, and Europe). As can be seen, all culture dimensions are positively correlated with organizational effectiveness, but not to the same degree. For example, in North American organizations the three strongest predictors of effectiveness were Capability Development, Coordination, and Empowerment. The weakest were Customer Focus and Creating Change. In Asian organizations

TABLE 14.5
Key Differences between Adaptive and Unadaptive Corporate Cultures

	Adaptive Corporate Cultures	*Unadaptive Corporate Cultures*
Core values	Managers care deeply about customers, stockholders, and employees. They place a high value on people and processes that create useful change.	Managers care about themselves, their immediate work group, or some product or technology. They value the orderly and risk-reducing management processes.
Common behavior	Managers pay close attention to all their constituencies, especially customers; initiate change when needed; take risks.	Managers behave politically and bureaucratically. They do not change their strategies quickly to adjust to or take advantage of changes in their business environments.

Source: J. P. Kotter and J. L. Heskett. (1992). *Corporate culture and performance.* New York: Free Press. Reprinted with the permission of The Free Press, a division of Simon & Schuster, Inc. Copyright © 1992 by Kotter Associates Inc. and James L. Heskett.

none of the dimensions were significantly correlated with overall effectiveness because so few (n = 7) were included in the study. However, based on the magnitude of the correlations it appears that the best predictors were Creating Change, Organizational Learning, and Team Orientation. The weakest were Customer Focus and Capability Development. Finally, in European organizations the three strongest predictors of organizational performance were Strategic Direction and Intent, Coordination and Integration, and Agreement. The weakest were Capability Development and Organizational Learning.

Like Kotter and Heskett's (1992) study, Denison's results suggest that culture does contribute to the success of an organization, though not all dimensions contribute the same. Denison's data also suggest that the impact of organizational culture is impacted by national culture. This is often overlooked in organizational culture research, but it is very important given that many organizations have global operations.

Probably the most important issue in future research in this area will be an attempt to explain the mediating linkages between culture and organizational performance. It has been proposed, for example, that organizational culture may impact the level of employee creativity (Tesluk, Farr, & Klein,

TABLE 14.6
Correlation between dimensions from Denison's Organizational Culture Model and Overall Effectiveness by Region

Dimension	North America	Asia	Europe
Empowerment	.65*	.57	.60*
Team orientation	.61*	.71	.53*
Capability development	.70*	.48	.50*
Core values	.58*	.62	.73*
Coordination and integration	.69*	.62	.74*
Creating change	.48*	.87	.68*
Customer focus	.36*	.19	.62*
Organizational learning	.50*	.82	.52*
Strategic direction/intent	.55*	.66	.79*
Goals and objectives	.60*	.54	.62*
Vision	.53*	.71	.67*
Number of organizations	169	7	34

Note: *p < .05
Source: Denison, D.R., Haaland, S., & Goelzer, P. (2004). Corporate culture and effectiveness: Is Asia different than the rest of the world? *Organizational Dynamics, 33,* 98–109.

1997), the strength of employee motivation (Weiner & Vardi, 1990), and the reporting of unethical behavior (Ellis & Arieli, 1999). Much more work is needed, however, to explain why culture makes a difference in organizational performance.

The Impact of Culture on Recruitment and Retention

Compared to the literature on organizational culture and performance, much more empirical research has investigated the impact that organizational culture has on attracting, recruiting, and retaining employees. (This issue was examined in some detail in Chapter 3 and will not be covered extensively here.) The basic finding in both of these areas is that individuals tend to be attracted to organizations that possess cultures that they perceive to be compatible. Furthermore, once people are in organizations, they will tend to remain in organizations that they perceive to be compatible.

In terms of retention, fit is probably also important but far less theoretical and empirical work has been done compared to the work on attraction. One of the reasons for this lack of information is that theoretical models of turnover (e.g., Mobley, 1977) have typically focused on characteristics of the job rather than organizational-level variables such as culture. Furthermore, we know that turnover is a complex process and is affected by variables (e.g., economic conditions, family considerations) that have little to do with the job or the organization (e.g., Carsten & Spector, 1987; Lee & Mitchell, 1994). It seems plausible, though, that if an employee perceives that the culture is incompatible with his or her values or personality, this would certainly prompt a search for a new job. High turnover may be one mediating factor in the relationship between culture

and organizational performance (Kotter & Heskett, 1992). Further research needs to be done to address these issues.

Culture and Employee Satisfaction/ Well-Being

Given the pervasiveness of organizational culture, to say that it impacts employee satisfaction and well-being seems to be stating the obvious. Surprisingly, there is not a great deal of empirical evidence bearing on this issue—perhaps because of the difficulty of conducting the multiorganizational studies necessary to test such hypotheses. What little evidence exists, however, suggests that culture makes a difference in the quality of employees' work lives. For example, Hatton et al. (1999) found that a mismatch between the actual culture of the organization and what employees felt that culture should be was associated with a number of negative outcomes. For example, perceived mismatch was associated with lower job satisfaction, higher job strain, general stress, and turnover intent. These findings suggest that there is no universally appropriate culture. Rather, the key again appears to be whether the culture meets employees' expectations. It has also been shown that safety climate, which is certainly an aspect of an organization's culture, is related to an organization's safety record (Clarke, 2006), which ultimately impacts health.

To provide more explanation of the impact of organizational culture on employees' quality of life, Peterson and Wilson (1998) proposed the model presented in Figure 14.2. Note that the key mediating factor in the relation between culture and employee health is business and management systems. Culture directly impacts the business and management systems that are deployed by the organization. These, in turn,

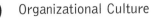

<u>**FIGURE 14.2**</u>
Model of the Relation between Culture, Work, and Health

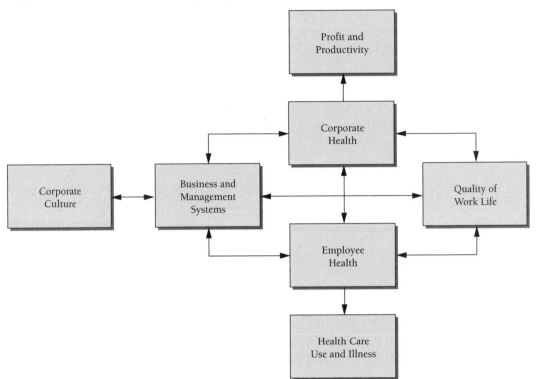

Source: M. Peterson and J. Wilson. (1998). A culture-work-health model: A theoretical conceptualization. *American Journal of Public Health, 22,* 378–390. Reprinted by permission of PNG Publications.

may then impact employee health. As an example, an organization with a very controlling culture may have a human resources system that requires employees to account very carefully for their time. There is, in fact, evidence that culture does impact organizational choices of human resources systems (Aycan, Kanungo, & Sinha, 1999). This high level of control, in turn, may detract from quality of life and ultimately detract from employees' health.

Although it clearly needs empirical assessment, the connection between organizational culture and employee well-being has certainly been recognized (e.g., Monroy, Jonas, Mathey, & Murphy, 1998; Murphy, 1996). More specifically, there has been

increasing emphasis on examining the characteristics of "healthy organizations"—those that are economically successful and possess healthy employees. Extensive models of organizational health await development, and a key factor in that development is likely to be organizational culture. In the future, linking macro-level variables such as organizational culture to employee health and well-being will likely become a major focus of the employee health literature (e.g., Bliese & Jex, 1999).

CHAPTER SUMMARY

This chapter examined the important topic of organizational culture. Although *culture* has been defined in a variety of ways, the essence of culture lies in the basic assumptions and values held by the members of an organization. This definition is widely accepted in organizational psychology, and it reflects the impact that cultural anthropology and sociology have had on the study of organizational culture.

All organizational cultures are unique to some degree, but there have been efforts to develop "models" of organizational culture. O'Reilly et al. (1991) developed a model of eight dimensions of organizational culture that are based on employees' perceptions of underlying values. Denison and colleagues contend that organizational culture can be described according to four broad dimensions and that each of these four can be broken down into more specific subdimensions. Both of these models have been very useful in both research and organizational diagnosis.

The culture of an organization is reflected in a variety of ways; some are understandable to outsiders and others are more difficult to comprehend. Symbols and artifacts represent the major physical manifestations of culture; rites and rituals represent behavioral manifestations. Language and stories can also be an important window into culture, both directly and for more symbolic reasons. Ultimately, culture is difficult to comprehend and an outsider needs a long time to decipher it.

The culture of an organization may be shaped by a number of factors. For most organizations, the organizational founder(s) is the most important factor in initially shaping the organization. Over time, however, culture will also be impacted and shaped by the extent to which it facilitates organizational adaptation and survival. Cultures tend to develop and ultimately persist over time because they have adaptive value for the organization.

Studying organizational culture can be challenging, but it is necessary in order to fully understand it. There are certainly instances of the use of self-report measures of culture, although many organizational culture researchers are wary of this method. As a result, the most typical method of studying organizational culture has been ethnography. Using a qualitative assessment of a culture is consistent with the notion that members of a culture are not good at reporting their basic assumptions. This methodology is also consistent with the anthropological roots of this field. In the future, other methods will probably be available for studying culture as well.

Changing the culture of an organization is difficult, given that culture is reflected in basic assumptions. Nevertheless, organizational cultures do change over time, and, in most cases, the mechanisms responsible for change depend on the life stage of the organization. Clearly, though, organizational culture change is not something that occurs quickly or easily in organizations. True organizational culture change usually occurs only in response to extreme environmental conditions.

A final factor to consider in examining organizational culture is its impact on important outcomes. Not a great deal of empirical research has been done on the effects of organizational culture, most likely because multiple organizations are needed to do such research. Nevertheless, empirical research has shown that organizational culture may impact a number of important outcomes such as performance, attraction and recruitment of employees, employee retention, and employee satisfaction and well-being. Although a great deal of research is yet to be done in this area, it appears that there is no one type of culture that is ideal. The most important factor

PEOPLE BEHIND THE RESEARCH

JENNIFER CHATMAN AND MATCHING PEOPLE WITH ORGANIZATIONS

As a graduate student watching all my friends go out and find their first "real jobs," I became intrigued with the idea that some people were much more committed, that is, willing to go the extra mile, on their jobs than others. What could account for this difference? I didn't think it was a personality issue because all my friends were smart (of course) and hard working. I decided that it must be something about the way the companies they worked for treated them, or the match between the organization's culture and their own preferences. To study this issue, I decided to look into the public accounting industry because with very few firms, I could capture nearly the entire industry (they were called "The Big Eight" back in the late '80's when I did my first study; after many mergers and Arthur Andersen's demise with Enron, they are often referred to as "The Final Four!"). I also chose this industry because the firms are so similar in structure, size, and tech-

nology so that any differences in people's level of commitment would have to be due to differences in the organization's *culture*, that is, their values and behavioral norms.

Even within this very homogeneous industry, there were striking differences in organizational culture. One firm valued detail orientation above all else, another valued initiative, and a third cared most about developing a single culture across the entire, global firm. These striking differences played out in a number of important ways for employees. For example, those who fit well with the culture stayed longer, were promoted faster, and demonstrated greater commitment to the firm. Interestingly, these outcomes of *person-culture fit* mattered more for performance than did the more typical *person-job fit* we think of which is how well people's knowledge, skills, and abilities fit the specific job. What this implies is that, as a job seeker, it may be more important to find an organization whose culture matches your own preferences (e.g., are you a team player or do you like to focus more on individual achievement?) than to find the perfect job regardless of the organization. That is, job selection is more effectively viewed as *organization selection* because, if you resonate with the culture of the organization you join, chances are you'll be very successful there and hold many different jobs over time.

Jennifer A. Chatman
Haas School of Business
University of California, Berkeley

appears to be a match between organizational culture and characteristics of employees rather than what is considered to be the *idealized* culture.

SUGGESTED ADDITIONAL READINGS

Adkins, B., & Caldwell, D. (2004). Firm or subgroup culture: Where does fitting matter most? *Journal of Organizational Behavior, 25,* 969–978.

Denison, D. R., & Mishra, A. K. (1995). Toward a theory of organizational culture and effectiveness. *Organization Science, 6,* 204–223.

Mason, R. O. (2004). Lessons in organizational ethics from the Columbia disaster: Can culture be leathal? *Organizational Dynamics, 33,* 128–142.

VanVianen, A. E. M. (2000). Person-organization fit: The match between newcomers' and recruiters' preferences for organizational cultures. *Personnel Psychology, 53,* 113–150.

Chapter Fifteen

Organizational Change and Development

I t is often said that change is one of the few constants in today's organizations. In this final chapter, we cover the various ways in which organizations seek to change through the use of organizational development. Organizational development is a process by which organizations use the theories and technology of the behavioral sciences to facilitate changes that enhance their effectiveness. Since organizational development draws on many of the theories and research findings that have been covered in previous chapters, it is fitting that organizational development is the focus of this final chapter.

The chapter will begin by defining organizational development and then focus on why organizations seek to change. Many organizations seek to change simply to be able to survive. If they don't change, they'll go out of business. Organizations, however, may also change for more proactive reasons. We will then discuss the theoretical models that have been most influential in guiding the work of organizational-development practitioners. The discussion will be followed by descriptions of the most popular organizational-development interventions.

After describing organizational-development interventions, the focus of the chapter will shift to a more general discussion of process issues in organizational development. Perhaps the most important of these issues is the conditions necessary to sustain meaningful organizational change, as well as conditions that often stand in the way of change. This will be followed by a discussion of the evaluation of organizational-development interventions—an important topic,

considering the cost of organizational change. The chapter will conclude with an exploration of some of the most common ethical issues faced by organizational-development professionals.

WHAT IS ORGANIZATIONAL DEVELOPMENT AND WHY IS IT USED?

Organizational development has been defined in a variety of ways, by a number of authors (French & Bell, 1995; Porras &

Robertson, 1992). Porras and Robertson, however, integrated the numerous definitions of organizational development and stated that: "Organizational development is a set of behavioral science–based theories, values, strategies, and technologies aimed at planned change of the organizational work setting for the purpose of enhancing individual development and improving organizational performance, through the alteration of organizational members' on-the-job behaviors" (p. 722).

Several aspects of this definition are noteworthy. First, the focus of organizational development is facilitating organizational changes that enhance both organizational performance *and* individual development. This distinguishes organizational development from organizational interventions that focus exclusively on enhancing either organizational performance or individual development. Second, organizational development is rooted in the theories and methodology of the behavioral sciences. Therefore, organizational development is different from approaches to organizational change, which are based solely on changes in manufacturing technology or, perhaps, information systems. It is true, however, that organizational development can assist in the implementation of changes in manufacturing or information technology (e.g., Barrett, Grant, & Wailes, 2005; Davidson, 2006). Finally, this definition makes it very clear that the key to organizational change is changing the behavior of employees.

Now that organizational development has been defined, the next issue to explore is why organizational development is used. One of the most common motivating factors behind organizational-development programs can best be described as *survival*. Organizational decision makers may realize (hopefully, not too late) that change is necessary if the organization is to remain competitive. Consider the following example. One of the authors once worked for a large telecommunications company that was engaged in a fairly comprehensive organizational-development program. The motivating force behind this program was actually quite simple. Prior to the program, this organization (like others in that industry) operated in a very stable, regulated environment. When this industry was deregulated, top management recognized that if the organization did not become more marketing oriented and customer focused, they would not remain competitive.

Another powerful motivator of change is poor organizational performance. When an organization fails to show a profit over an extended period of time, or sees its market share being steadily eroded, it will often facilitate organizational change. This factor was undoubtedly at work at the Chrysler Corporation in the late 1970s. During that period, Chrysler had lost market share and was literally in danger of going out of business. The fact that Chrysler was performing so poorly made it easier for Lee Iaccoca to institute a number of organizational changes that ultimately turned the company around (Iaccoca, 1984).

The desire for survival is often the motivating factor behind many organizational-development programs, but there are certainly other factors as well. In some cases, relatively effective organizations will engage in programs of planned change, and they could do so for a variety of reasons. For example, an effective organization may engage in change for strategic reasons (e.g., Buller, 1988). A manufacturing organization that decides to enter the consumer products business, perhaps through an acquisition, may have to institute a number of organizational changes in order to make this strategy work effectively. An organization that competes primarily on the basis of product quality may decide that it wants to put greater emphasis on customer service. Again, organizational changes may very well be necessary if this strategy is successful.

Some organizations may simply anticipate changes in the external environment and proactively respond to those changes. For example, many fast-food restaurants anticipated demographic changes in the population, which led to greater utilization of retirees as employees. As another example, several years ago, some universities put considerable resources into long-distance education programs because they anticipated changes in computer technology and an increase in the number of working adults who would want to attend college. In both instances, organizational development was the tool of choice for facilitating these changes.

A final reason for organizations' engaging in programs of planned change can simply be described as self-improvement; that is, no external pressure for change exists, and there are no concrete strategic reasons for changing. Instead, a well-functioning organization may just want to improve itself in some way. An example of this motivation for change occurs when a major league baseball team wins the World Series and then is very active, during the off-season, acquiring new players and making changes in the coaching staff. This response may be due to the fact that, despite its success, the team recognizes that it still has some weaknesses that need to be addressed. Organizations that are always striving to get better will remain competitive longer than organizations in which success leads to complacency (Ferrier, Smith, & Grimm, 1999).

A BRIEF HISTORY OF ORGANIZATIONAL DEVELOPMENT

While there is no recognized "father of organizational development," the person who would probably be most deserving of that title would be Kurt Lewin, whose contributions to the broader field of organizational psychology were described in Chapter 1. With respect to organizational development, Lewin made a number of contributions, but two stand out as being most important. First, Lewin was the first psychologist to provide the field of organizational development with a theoretical base. His Three-Step Model of Change and Action Research continues to serve as an important theoretical guide to organizational-development practitioners. Second, Lewin played a key role in the establishment of both the Center for the Study of Group Dynamics, at Massachusetts Institute of Technology (MIT), and the National Training Laboratories (NTL), in Bethel, Maine.

The Center for the Study of Group Dynamics was a fertile site for the study of many group processes that are important to organizations. It also served as the training ground for many individuals who played important roles in shaping the emerging field of organizational development (French & Bell, 1995). Although Lewin died before the establishment of the National Training Laboratories (NTL), he was instrumental in their development. The major purpose of the NTL was to provide laboratory or T-group training to managers and educators. T-groups are essentially unstructured groups in which participants learn both through their interactions and through the evolving group dynamics. Although there has been considerable criticism of T-groups over the years (e.g., Campbell & Dunnette, 1968), the purported goals of T-group training—enhancement of interpersonal skills and awareness of group dynamics—are certainly worthwhile. In the early 1950s, T-groups were synonymous with organizational development, and nearly all of the early practitioners of organizational development were either laboratory trainers, or they had gone through such training.

Along with Lewin and the development of T-groups, a major factor in the history of organizational development was the application of survey research methods in organizations. This was begun in 1946 when the Survey Research Center (SRC) was established at the University of Michigan under the direction of Rensis Likert. Likert, along with individuals such as Floyd Mann, devoted considerable attention to the development and refinement of survey research methodology. This technique became part of the field of organizational development in 1947, when Likert was able to interest Detroit Edison in conducting a survey on employee attitudes, perceptions, reactions, and behaviors.

What made this project at Detroit Edison unique, however, was that the SRC staff not only conducted the survey and compiled the results, but they also helped the company present the results back to the employees. The approach taken by the SRC researchers, which is now commonplace, was to use what was termed an *interlocking chain of conferences* to feed the data back. The top management team would first receive the survey results. Each individual in this group would then present the results back to his or her own group, with the assistance of a consultant. This process would then be repeated until the results of the survey were filtered down to everyone in all levels of the organization. From these beginnings, survey feedback

has become one of the most common and most effective (Bowers, 1973) organizational development interventions.

A third major historical foundation of organizational development was the development and use of action research methods. Action research, as mentioned earlier, is attributed to Kurt Lewin and is often used to describe the more general process by which organizations change. Action research also has an applied side and, during the mid-1940s and early 1950s, many action research projects were conducted not only in business organizations but also in educational institutions and community settings. In addition to the general process of action research, one of the important principles that came out of the action research movement was the idea that research is a collaborative effort between the researcher and the members of an organization. Indeed, organizational-development practitioners today stress the importance of participation of members of the client system in the organizational-development process (Halbesleben, Osburn, & Mumford, 2006).

The final historical foundation of organizational development was the sociotechnical systems and socioclinical work that emerged in Great Britian. The center of this activity was the Tavistock Clinic, which was established in 1920 to provide psychotherapy and to treat the battle neuroses resulting from World War I. The work at Tavistock that contributed the most to the field of organizational development was a series of experiments, by Trist and Bamforth (1951), in the redesign of work in coal mines. These researchers found a strong link between the design of work and the social structure and group dynamics within the mines. This research was important on its own merits, and it served as one of the first applications, in an actual industrial setting, of the ongoing U.S.

work on group dynamics. Trist conducted many subsequent investigations of the interaction between the design of work and the social environment. The Tavistock work has served as a foundation for many work-redesign interventions, and it has helped to provide more general insight into the relationship between the technological and social environments.

As will be evident throughout this chapter, many of the interventions and approaches in organizational development can be traced to the historical foundations discussed previously. Like any field, however, organizational development is not static; thus, a number of more recent trends in the field will shape the future. One clear recent trend in organizational development is the increased interest in interventions aimed at improving team functioning. Small teams represent the building blocks of many organizations today, and the success of entire organizations depends heavily on the success of individual teams. It is no surprise, then, that team building has become by far one of the most popular organizational-development interventions.

A second recent trend is the increased use of large-scale, broad-based organizational-change interventions (Mirvis, 2005; Steil & Gibbons-Carr, 2005). This trend toward more large-scale change efforts is probably due to a number of factors. For example, because of the volatile competitive environments many organizations face, change often needs to be comprehensive and must occur quickly. Thus, organizations often cannot wait for individual- or team-focused interventions to facilitate wider organizational change. This trend also reflects, to some degree, a maturing of the field of organizational development. Over time, the accumulated wisdom of organizational-development researchers and practitioners has shown that, for real change to occur in an organization, the entire system must be involved (e.g., Beckhard, 1967). What better way to get total system involvement than to make the whole organization the focus of an intervention?

Another current trend in organizational development is that the extent of application has grown widely. Organizational development is used in a wide variety of organizations (see, e.g., Athey & Hautaluoma, 1988) and has become truly international in scope (e.g., Perlaki, 1994; Rao & Vijayalakshmi, 2000). Perhaps the only negative fact associated with the growth of organizational development is that it makes the establishment of common ethical and professional standards quite difficult. Although many organizational-development practitioners are trained specifically in organizational development and in closely related fields, such as industrial/organizational psychology, organizational behavior, and human resources management, there is no specific "credential" that one must have as a practitioner of organizational development. As a result, few safeguards exist to protect organizations against incompetent or unethical organizational-development practitioners. However, in recent years, organizational-development professionals have taken some steps to establish firm standards of professional practice (see Comment 15.1).

THE THEORY BASE OF ORGANIZATIONAL DEVELOPMENT

In most comprehensive treatments of organizational development, the author(s) inevitably point out that organizational development is a field without a strong theoretical base (e.g., Beer, 1976; Burke, 1994; Porras & Robertson, 1992; Porras & Silvers,

COMMENT 15.1

THE ORGANIZATIONAL-DEVELOPMENT PROFESSION

ORGANIZATIONAL DEVELOPMENT HAS come a long way as a profession during the past 50 years. When the field was first developing, organizational development was seen primarily as a technology that was applied by those with training in psychology and other behavioral sciences. Over time, however, this field has developed an identity that is distinct from psychology and other behavioral sciences. For example, many organizational-development practitioners now belong to professional associations that are designed to advance the interests of the profession and provide some guidelines for its practice. The two largest associations are the Organizational Development Network (http://www.odnetowrk.org/) and the Organizational Development and Change Division of the Academy of Management (http://www.aom.pace.edu/odc/).

Another indication of the growth of the organizational-development profession can be found in the number of its academic programs. According to the most recent estimates from the Organizational Development and Change Division of the Academy of Management, there are now eight stand-alone doctoral programs in organizational development. If one adds to this the 14 masters' programs and six certificate programs, it is now quite possible for a person interested in organizational development to obtain advanced and specific training in this field. In years past, those interested in organizational development were forced to obtain academic training in related fields (e.g., psychology, sociology, communications) and learn the specifics of organizational development primarily through work experience.

The emergence of professional associations representing organizational-development professionals is positive, for two reasons. First, greater organization of the profession will lead to higher professional standards, which will ultimately lead to better practice. Second, given the growth in academic programs in organizational development, there will undoubtedly be more empirical research and theorizing. These will be crucial if organizational development is truly going to be both a science and a technology.

1991). Often, consultants apply organizational-development interventions based much more on empiricism, or even trial-and-error, than on solid theoretical grounding. This has led some observers to view organizational development more as a technology than as a legitimate subtopic within organizational psychology. Such views are certainly provocative and may have some merit, but organizational-development practitioners do in fact have a theory base that practitioners can look to for guidance. In this section, we review that theory base.

Lewin's Three-Step Model

The oldest theory of the organizational-change process is referred to as *Lewin's Three-Step Model* (Lewin, 1947). Lewin used a physical metaphor to explain the process by which social systems change. The use of metaphor in theory development was introduced in Chapter 13 on organizational design (e.g., McKenna & Wright, 1992) and is also quite useful in describing organizational change. Like organizational design, organizational change is a highly abstract

FIGURE 15.1

Lewin's Three-Step Model of the Organizational
Change Process

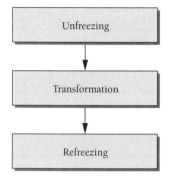

process that cannot be readily simulated or modeled in a laboratory setting.

The three steps in Lewin's model are presented in Figure 15.1. In the first step in the change process, the stage labeled *unfreezing*, an organization begins to recognize the need for change. This is a crucial step in the change process, according to Lewin (1947), because an organization cannot, and will not change unless there is some recognition of the need for change. Many factors described earlier as motivators of organizational change (e.g., loss in profits, major environmental changes) would qualify as *unfreezing events*. That is, if an organization is unprofitable or faces dramatic changes in its operating environment, this *could* make its employees recognize the need for change. The word *could* is italicized because it is certainly possible for an organization to recognize these unfreezing events, yet not connect them to the need for organizational change. Mirvis (2005) describes the case of a Dutch food company that wanted to place more emphasis on quality control. In order to begin the change process, this company took all of its employees to a warehouse that was completely filled with wasted products. These employees then watched as these

defective products were destroyed. By doing this the company was emphasizing, in dramatic fashion, the need for all employees to have higher quality standards.

Assuming that a sufficient level of organizational unfreezing has occurred, the second step in Lewin's model is change or transformation. This is also a crucial step in the process because it represents tangible changes in the way an organization operates. For example, an organization may convert to a team-based structure, or redesign jobs to enhance customer satisfaction, or engage in any number of other changes. In addition to being a crucial step, this is also a very difficult step. Changes introduced at this point may require that employees do things very differently than in the past. For some, this may be invigorating; for most people, however, changing the way they have done things in the past is a very difficult process.

When an organization changes or transforms itself in some way, the next step is refreezing. The changes that are enacted during the second step in the model become a relatively permanent part of an organization's behavioral repertoire. Refreezing may also be a difficult step because employees may be resistant to the organizational changes. For example, it is quite common for employees to initially be very enthused about enacting organizational changes. However, after their initial enthusiasm wears off, employees may revert to old ways of doing things. For true refreezing to occur, employees must see that it is in their best interests to maintain the organizational changes that are carried out in the transformation phase.

Perhaps the greatest strength of Lewin's Three-Step model is its simplicity. This model is easy to understand and, in fact, provides an organization with some useful guidance in carrying out organizational changes. For example, an organization must consider the need to prepare its employees prior to introducing changes (e.g., unfreezing), and must anticipate some degree of resistance before these changes become a permanent part of the culture (e.g., refreezing). Organizations that do not pay attention to these factors are unlikely to have successful change efforts.

Ironically, simplicity is also one of the primary weaknesses of Lewin's model. More specifically, the model has been criticized for having an overly simplistic view of the change process (Purser & Petranker, 2005). Another problem with this model is that it does not provide a great deal of insight into how, for example, the process of unfreezing actually works; for that matter, it provides little insight into how organizations can actually facilitate the processes of change or refreezing. Thus, although Lewin's model is good as a description of organizational change, it falls somewhat short as a comprehensive model of the organizational-change process because it lacks explanatory power.

The Action Research Model

A second general theoretical model of the organizational change process, also attributed to Kurt Lewin, is the Action Research Model. The general idea behind action research is that organizational change is likened to a cyclical research process. Action research also emphasizes that throughout all phases of the research process, there is active collaboration between the researcher and the members of the client system. The major steps in the action research process, as delineated by Lewin (1951), are presented in Figure 15.2.

As can be seen, the first step in the action research process is problem identification. For any research to be undertaken, or any change to occur, there has to be some recognition of a problem that people care about. In

FIGURE 15.2
Lewin's Action Research Model

the most general sense, a problem exists any time there is a difference between the current state of affairs and the desired state of affairs. For example, an organization's profits may be lower than they should be; the level of employee turnover may be higher than the organization feels is desirable; or the number of workers' compensation claims filed by employees may be higher than the organization feels it should be.

The second step in the Action Research Model is development of hypotheses. Obviously, for any particular problem, there could be a multitude of causes. Fortunately, based on prior theory and, perhaps, the experience of organizational members, it is often possible to focus heavily on some causes and pay less attention to others. For example, if the problem area identified is employee turnover, many years of research on turnover has shown that factors such as employees' job attitudes and the economic environment are important contributing factors (Hulin, 1991). Based on this knowledge, it may be useful to examine employee attitudes and, possibly, explore the external job market to develop some hypotheses about turnover.

After hypotheses have been specified, the next step in the action research process is data collection. This is an important step because it distinguishes action research from less scientific forms of inquiry. For example, the previously described hypotheses could be tested by asking experts or perhaps even through introspective methods. When action research is used, however, the scientific method is used, and it requires that hypotheses be tested by gathering empirical data.

After empirical data are collected, the next step in the action research process is data interpretation. The critical question the action researcher is trying to answer at this point is: Do the empirical data support, or fail to support, the proposed hypotheses? The biggest dilemma for the researcher at this point is essentially "deciding how to decide" whether the data support the hypotheses. Fortunately, inferential statistical methods are available (e.g., Hays, 1988) to assist the action researcher in making such decisions.

After the data are interpreted and a decision is made about whether the hypotheses are supported, is the action research sequence complete? The researcher may possibly lose interest in a particular problem; but, more typically, the action research cycle will repeat itself. For example, if the researcher collects data and finds that job satisfaction is inversely related to turnover (as suspected), this raises other important questions. What measures could the organization take toward raising employees' levels of job satisfaction and, by inference, reducing turnover? Are certain facets of job satisfaction more important than others in determining turnover? These are empirical questions that could certainly be tested

through further research projects. Put differently, the action research cycle can be repeated once again in order to answer these questions.

Thus, according to the Action Research Model, the process of organizational change can be characterized as a continuing cyclical process of hypothesis generation, data collection, data evaluation, and, ultimately, intervention. Another important aspect of the Action Research Model was alluded to earlier: The research process is a collaborative effort between the researchers and members of the client system. In a more traditional research project, there is a distinct power or status differential between researchers and the "subjects" of studies. Although researcher–participant collaboration can pose some difficult dilemmas at times (e.g., Mirvis & Seashore, 1979), its positive benefit is that the client system assumes ownership of the organizational-change process—an important ingredient in maintaining organizational change over time.

To a certain extent, the advantages and disadvantages associated with the Action Research Model are similar to those associated with Lewin's Three-Step Model. That is, the action research provides a very useful guide to understanding organizational change. Furthermore, there is empirical evidence that action research can be a useful approach to solving problems in organizations (e.g., Halbesleben et al., 2006). However, like the Three-Step Model, it also does not directly explain the most important factors that are involved in the change process. For example: Does change begin with the leadership of an organization or with lower-level employees? What are the factors that lead to resistance to change? How does an organization sustain organizational change over the long term? In fairness to Lewin, the

Action Research Model was never really intended to be a theory of organizational change. Rather, it is probably most appropriate to think of the Action Research Model more as a general "theory of intervention" than as a theory of organizational change.

General Systems Theory

A third general theoretical base upon which much of organizational development rests is General Systems Theory. General Systems Theory, which was briefly covered in Chapter 13, was developed by von Bartalanffy in 1950 and made its way into organizational psychology in 1966, through the work of Katz and Kahn. The basic idea of general systems, as applied to organizations, is that organizations import material from the environment, transform that input, and ultimately return it to the environment in some altered form. As a result, organizations are constantly in a dynamic interaction with their external environments. More often than not, organizations change in reaction to, or in anticipation of, changes in the external environment. If organizations were "closed systems" and therefore could ignore the external environment, there would be little need to engage in organizational change and development activities.

Another aspect of General Systems Theory that has greatly influenced the field of organizational development is the idea that any system is comprised of a series of smaller "subsystems." As an analogy, the human body is composed of a number of "subsystems" that guide functions such as circulation, digestion, and so on. Katz and Kahn (1966) pointed out that organizations also consist of a number of interrelated subsystems that guide such functions as importing materials from the environment (e.g., purchasing), transforming those materials

(e.g., production), and making sure that the transformed materials are returned to the external environment (e.g., marketing).

The idea of interrelated subsystems is relevant to organizational development because whenever a change is introduced in one part of an organization, those guiding the change must be on the lookout for the "system-wide" ramifications of that change. If an organization decided to change to a team-based structure (a change that is, in fact, becoming increasingly popular), there would be many system-wide implications of this change. Within a team-based structure, supervisors become more like "advisers" or "consultants" rather than bosses. It is also quite likely that working in teams may require fundamentally different skills and abilities than are found in more traditional structures. Finally, for a team-based structure to be effective, a vastly different compensation system is needed. Thus, one change may require changes in the way that leaders and other employees are selected and trained, as well as changes in the organization's compensation system.

Theories of Organizational Change

The theories covered to this point are useful and provide some insight into the general processes involved in organizational change and development, but they do not describe the specific organizational factors that are involved in the change process. One of the major reasons there are so few specific theories of organizational change is that organizations are so diverse. As a result, it is quite difficult to create a model that serves as a generalized guide to change in all organizations. Fortunately, some theories of this type have been developed, and two are reviewed in this section.

FIGURE 15.3
Burke's Theory of Organizational Change

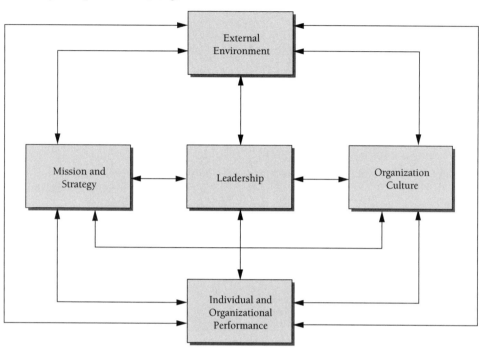

Burke (1994) developed a theory of the organizational-transformation process that is general enough to apply to a great variety of organizational types. As can be seen in Figure 15.3, the model proposes that organizational transformation is the result of interrelated factors. Starting at the top of the model, the external environment is often a key factor in initiating organizational transformation because change is often motivated by survival or by the desire to capitalize on a new opportunity. The model proposes that the external environment has a direct impact on leadership, the mission and strategy of an organization, and organizational culture. Note, however, that in each of the three cases, these effects are reciprocal. For example, the external environment impacts leadership, but leadership could also shape the

external environment. The same could be said for mission and strategy and for organizational culture. Note that all three of these organizational factors are interrelated.

The model further proposes that mission and strategy, leadership, and organizational culture have a direct impact on individual and organizational performance. Note, however, that, as in the first portion of the model, all relations are reciprocal. That is, mission and strategy, leadership, and organizational culture impact performance but are also impacted by the performance of individuals and the organization as a whole. The other notable feature of the model is the dynamic feedback loop between performance and the external environment. It is possible for the external environment to have a direct impact on individual and organizational performance. Also, the performance of individuals and the organization as a whole impacts the external environment.

Burke's (1994) model tells us several important things about the process of organizational change. First, it clearly shows that the external environment plays a key role in the organizational-change process. This is certainly consistent with General Systems Theory, and it reinforces the point that organizations cannot afford to ignore the external environment. The model also suggests that there are three key "levers of change" that organizations can use if they want to sustain meaningful change over time. These levers are the interrelated factors of mission and strategy, leadership, and organizational culture. Let's consider each of these factors.

Mission and strategy dictate what an organization's purpose is, and how it plans to achieve this purpose. It follows, then, that a change in mission and strategy will serve as a powerful catalyst for broader organizational change. Furthermore, at the individual employee level, mission and strategy are important because they help to provide individuals with a sense of purpose and coherence. Therefore, if mission and strategy are changed, this will serve as a powerful message to employees that their behaviors must also change in some way.

The leadership within an organization is important for a number of reasons. Organizational leaders play a key role in developing organizational mission and strategy, as well as shaping the culture. They also make key contributions to the development of internal policies and procedures and the representation of the organization to the external environment. Thus, it should come as no surprise that organizations are only as effective as their leaders and that the involvement of top management is a key factor in sustaining successful organizational change.

Organizational culture, as discussed in the previous chapter, represents the underlying values and basic assumptions that are present in an organization. Culture can have powerful effects, both positive and negative, on the performance of individuals and entire organizations. It follows, then, that culture would play a key role in organizational change. This might occur very directly; that is, organizational change might be viewed as culture change.

Culture may also play a more indirect role in organizational change. It is much more likely that changes will be sustained or will "take hold" if they are at least somewhat compatible with an organization's prevailing culture. For example, an organization that decides to redesign jobs to enhance employee autonomy yet retains a highly authoritarian culture will probably not be successful in sustaining this form of organizational change. In this case, the organization may have the option of implementing less dramatic organizational change, or attempting to change to a more participative culture prior to implementing the job design intervention.

Porras and Robertson (1992) have proposed a theoretical framework from which to view the organizational change and development process. This model, presented in Figure 15.4, is a bit more detailed than Burke's (1994), although there are some similarities. For example, Porras and Robertson (1992) propose that the external environment is an important factor in driving organizational change. They also propose that the overall purpose of the organization (represented by vision) drives many of the tangible interventions that are designed to facilitate organizational change. Based on the vision that is being carried out, several interrelated variables proposed in the model may be used as levers of change for an organization. These include organizational arrangements, social factors,

FIGURE 15.4
Porras and Robertson's Model of the Organizational Change Process

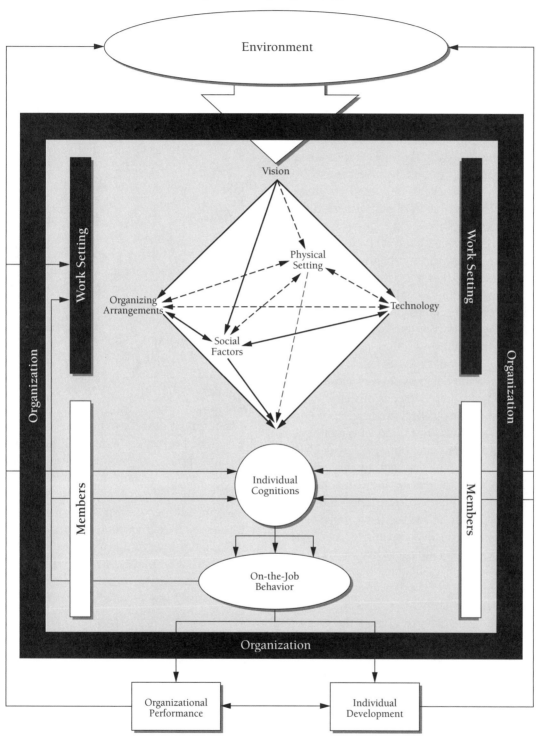

Source: J. I. Porras and P. J. Robertson. (1992). Organizational development: Theory, practice, and research. In M. D. Dunnette and L. M. Hough (Eds.), *Handbook of industrial and organizational psychology* (2nd ed., Vol. 3, pp. 719–822). Palo Alto, CA: Consulting Psychologists Press, Inc. Reprinted by permission.

the physical setting, and the organization's technology.

Changes in these aspects of the work setting should ultimately lead to improved organizational performance and enhanced individual development. Notice, in the model, that these changes are fully mediated by individual cognitions and the behavior of employees. This is clearly the most important and fundamental proposition in Porras and Robertson's model: Behavior change is the key mediating variable in organizational change. At first glance, this would appear to be a rather obvious statement, but it is also a very important one. Many times, when we speak of the *organizational-change process*, we tend to forget that organizations are collections of people. An organization becomes more innovative only if its individuals come up with new product designs and creative solutions to problems; an organization becomes more customer-service oriented if individual employees place high priority on serving customers.

The major practical implication of Porras and Robertson's (1992) model is that organizations must pay attention to behavior change when instituting organizational change. Often, failure to consider individual behavior change amounts to organizational decision makers' failure to see the perspective of employees, which is "What's in it for me?" There are cases when employees may stand to gain very little by changing their behaviors, even if organizational decision makers believe that the associated changes are needed.

The organizational-change theories presented in this section are still quite general. However, compared to the more general models of the change process presented earlier, they tell us a great deal more about specific things that an organization can do to facilitate and sustain change. With that in mind, we now shift the focus to specific organizational-development interventions.

ORGANIZATIONAL-CHANGE INTERVENTIONS

Generally speaking, organizational-change interventions differ in terms of (1) the level in the organization at which they are aimed and (2) the process(es) they are designed to impact. Organizational-development interventions are typically aimed at individuals, groups, or the organization as a whole. Of these, the most popular level of intervention is groups, largely because most organizations have realized how important groups are to the success of organizations. Despite the popularity of group-level interventions, another trend is occurring in organizational development: the use of broad, system-wide interventions (French & Bell, 1999; Mirvis, 2005). Individual-level interventions are also used frequently—although, in many organizations, these are presented simply as training programs rather than as organizational-development interventions.

In terms of processes that interventions are designed to impact, essentially anything that can impact the performance of individuals, or the organization as a whole, could be the focus of an organizational-development intervention. Common examples of processes on which organizational-development interventions are focused are the roles that employees are asked to play; the goals that drive individual employees and organizations as a whole; group and intergroup processes; organizational structure; and organizational strategy.

Individual-Level Interventions

In reviewing the history of organizational development, one of the first organizational-development interventions was sensitivity training, also known as T-group training. Although T-group training is carried out in groups, it is an intervention aimed at the individual. This is because the primary goals of T-group training are enhancement of interpersonal skills and competence, enhanced awareness of the impact of one's behavior on others, and a greater general understanding of group dynamics (Forsyth, 1999).

Although T-group training was at one time the most popular intervention in organizational development, it is rarely used by organizational-development practitioners today. Probably the major reason is that the effectiveness of T-groups is doubtful (Campbell & Dunnette, 1968). It is also difficult to transfer back to the workplace what one has learned in the T-group. The total honesty and authenticity that are the hallmarks of the T-group movement may not play well in most real-world work settings. Also, some ethical questions surround the use of T-groups—in particular, requiring that employees participate.

Despite the fact that T-groups are rarely used now as an organizational-development intervention, it's the impact of this intervention on the field of organizational development that cannot be overestimated. Many organizational-development interventions that are popular today (e.g., process consultation, team building) are rooted in the T-group movement. Although team-building sessions typically do not focus on interpersonal issues, the ground rules that govern team-building meetings quite often parallel those of T-group sessions—for example, participant candor is encouraged, and efforts are made to maintain a sense of "psychological safety."

Another common individual-level organizational-development intervention is job redesign (Hackman & Oldham, 1980; Parker & Wall, 1998). Job redesign was discussed in some detail in Chapter 9, so it will not be covered in depth here. Job redesign

can be a powerful individual-level organizational-development intervention because employees typically spend more time working on their job tasks than on any other activity in the workplace. Thus, job redesign can be a very powerful and efficient way to change the behavior of employees. The primary limitation of job redesign is that it does not typically address more "macro" issues in the work environment; that is, even if jobs in an organization are successfully redesigned this will not compensate for a culture of mistrust and hostility. Another drawback of job redesign is that it is costly. The expense necessary to diagnose and change jobs may be prohibitive for some organizations, and the system-wide effects of job redesign may be far reaching.

Another commonly used organizational-development intervention that is focused on individual employees is Management by Objectives (MBO) (Carroll & Tosi, 1973). Although the specifics of MBO programs vary widely among different organizations, certain features are common to most. Specifically, most involve some level of joint goal setting between employees and their supervisors. In addition, in most MBO programs, the performance of individual employees is assessed in relation to their progress in accomplishing these objectives. In general, empirical research has shown that MBO programs have a positive effect on employee performance (Rodgers & Hunter, 1991), particularly when they are supported by top management. There is, however, evidence that the effects of MBO could be negative if objectives are not clearly stated (Dahlsten, Styhre, & Willander, 2005).

Group-Level Interventions

As stated earlier, the most common level at which organizational development-interventions are focused is the group or team. This is because more and more organizations are adopting team-based structures (Gordon, 1992). It may also reflect the key role that T-groups played in the history of organizational development. By far the most common group-level organizational-development intervention is team building (Covin & Kilman, 1991). According to Liebowitz and DeMeuse (1982), *team building* is defined as "a long-term, data-based intervention in which intact work teams experientially learn, by examining their structures, purposes, norms, values, and interpersonal dynamics, to increase their skills for effective teamwork. It is a direct attempt to assist the group in becoming more adept at *identifying, diagnosing, and solving its own problems*, usually with the aid of a behavioral science consultant" (p. 2, italics added). This is obviously a very general definition, and research has shown that there is a great deal of variation in the way team building is carried out in organizations (Offermann & Spiros, 2001).

The italicized portion of this definition—*identifying, diagnosing, and solving its own problems*—really captures the essence of the team-building process. A work group that successfully engages in a team-building intervention is not necessarily going to be problem free. Rather, this group will be capable of recognizing when things are not going well, diagnosing the root causes of the problem(s), and taking steps to solve the problem(s).

Although team-building interventions do vary considerably from organization to organization, Liebowitz and DeMeuse (1982) describe a series of eight steps that are common to most. These steps are presented in Figure 15.5. The first step in the team-building process is labeled scouting. Scouting is a preliminary step that involves an exchange of information between a consul-

FIGURE 15.5
Major Steps in the Team-Building Process

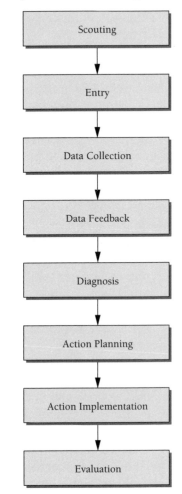

tant and a potential client organization. The consultant would typically describe his or her expertise, values, and style of operation. The organization, in turn, would normally describe the nature of its problem(s) as well as its views regarding the potential causes of these problem(s). If it is determined that team building is an appropriate intervention, the process would move ahead to the next step. If team building is inappropriate, the consulting relationship may be terminated, unless the consultant can offer other needed services.

Assuming that team building is appropriate, the process then moves on to the next step: entry. This is the point at which the client–consultant relationship begins to be formalized. Although this is typically done through written contracts, there is considerable variation in the way consulting contracts are drawn up. Some consultants prefer contracts that are very specific about the nature of the work the consultant will perform; others prefer contracting to be more open ended (e.g., Schein, 1987). Regardless of how the actual contract is worded, what is important at this point is that the consultant and the client organization forge a common understanding on the major dimensions of the consulting relationship (e.g., activities of the consultant, fees, time frame of the work, method of billing). It is also important at this point that the consultant establishes credibility with the client organization, and that there is enough managerial support to sustain the project.

When the preliminary steps of scouting and entry have been completed, the consultant begins the process of data collection. This simply involves collecting information, from a variety of sources, on the current functioning of the work groups in an organization. This may also involve personal interviews of group members, although consultants often obtain data from a variety of other sources, such as surveys, observations, and archival records (e.g., minutes of meetings, performance records). Surveys are probably the most common form of data collection since there are many measures of team functioning available (see Wageman, Hackman, & Lehman, 2005). Regardless of the data-collection method(s) used, the major objective here is to get as complete a picture of the functioning of groups as possible. Thus, the more methods and sources of information that can be used, the better.

After data on group functioning are collected, the next steps are to summarize these data and then engage in some form of data feedback. This typically involves holding meetings with each of the work groups in the client organization and presenting the data that have been collected. Although at first glance this may appear to be just "telling people what they already know," this may not always be the case. For example, some group members may have a much more positive picture of their group's functioning than is indicated by the data. Ideally, such discrepancies serve as "unfreezing experiences" for the group members and prompt a desire for a closer examination of the team's functioning. Group members may deny these discrepancies by questioning the accuracy of the data, or they may even turn hostile toward the process or the consultant.

During data feedback, certain themes or areas of concern often surface. For example, group members may be dissatisfied with the level of communication or with the way decisions are made within their group. Unfortunately, data are simply numbers; typically, they do not tell a group why a particular issue continues to surface. Thus, at this point, the group needs to engage in diagnosis, which represents the group's attempt to explain why the data came out the way they did. This is a very crucial step in the team-building process because, for many groups, it may be the first time they have ever taken a serious look at their work methods and internal processes (Hackman & Morris, 1975).

Ultimately during the diagnosis stage groups identify things that are preventing them from performing up to their full capabilities. One could also think of these as *barriers to performance*. Developing a list of performance barriers is an important first step in the team-building process because once these are identified the group can begin to address them. This is the purpose of the next step: action planning. During this phase, one or more action plans are developed for each of the important problems or performance barriers identified. For example, if one of the problems identified in the diagnosis stage is "Poor communication among group members," a corresponding action plan might be "Increase the number of group meetings from once a month to once every 2 weeks."

Action plans are very important because they represent the most tangible products of a team-building meeting—particularly, what a group has committed to do (often in writing) to make it function more effectively. One thing is important to consider, however: Not all action plans are of equal value. Action plans are much more useful if they are specific and measurable, have an identifiable time frame associated with them, and hold an individual or individuals responsible for implementing them. Typically, when one or more of these attributes is missing, the action plan will be forgotten soon after the team-building meeting adjourns.

After the team-building meeting is over, the group goes back to its normal routine and thus enters the next phase: action implementation. This involves implementing the action plans that were agreed upon during the team-building meeting. This is the most challenging part of the team-building process because even if the group's action plans are very good (e.g., specific, measurable), they often require group members to give up old habits and engage in new behaviors. For example, it may be easy for a leader to talk about letting group members have more input into decisions, but it's quite another thing to actually relinquish a portion of his or her control over decision making.

The final stage in the team-building process is evaluation, which normally takes place after some period of time has passed since the team-building meeting. Evaluation involves the assessment of the group's progress on the implementation of the action plans. This step is important because it makes the group accountable for implementing its action plans. If there is no follow-up, groups will either fail to implement action plans or will begin to implement them but lose interest. Often, the evaluation portion of the process comes in the form of a follow-up meeting in which the groups, with the assistance of a consultant, review progress on each of the action plans generated during the initial team-building meeting. Ideally, this meeting will reveal that the group is implementing the action plans as written. In some cases, though, it may reveal that the action plans need to be revised, or that there are external factors preventing the group from implementing them as written.

As with many organizational-development interventions described in this chapter, not a great deal of empirical research exists on the effectiveness of team-building interventions. The little empirical research that has been done provides mixed support for the effectiveness of team building. Some empirical data have failed to support the effectiveness of team building (e.g., Eden, 1985), but there is also evidence that team building can be a very effective method of improving a number of group processes (e.g., Cohen & Bailey, 1997). A key factor in determining the success of team building is whether there is a need for it in the first place. If a team is functioning very well, or works under conditions of very low interdependence, team building may have little effect on group processes or outcomes.

A second organizational-development intervention that may also be aimed at the group level is process consultation (Schein, 1969, 1987). Process consultation is actually both a philosophy of consulting and an organizational-development intervention. As a consulting philosophy, process consultation emphasizes that the role of a consultant is to guide an organization through the process of discovering what its problems are and help in finding solutions to those problems. In doing so, the emphasis is on *how* things are done (e.g., process issues) rather than *what* is actually done. Readers eager to learn more about process consultation as a consulting philosophy are strongly urged to read Edgar Schein's various works on the topic (Schein, 1987).

Process consultation also represents a set of interventions that may be used by a consultant. Although these interventions are not exclusive to group settings, this is the context in which they are often used. Schein (1987) classified interventions on a continuum, based on how confrontational they are vis-à-vis the client. The least confrontational type of intervention that a process consultant can use is an exploratory inquiry. For example, a process consultant may ask a group: "How have things been going the past few months?" or "Tell me a little bit about things that are important to the group's success."

The second general type of intervention described by Schein (1987) is a diagnostic intervention. In this case the process consultant does not tell the client what to do, although the questions he or she may ask are more focused than in the exploratory inquiry stage. If a group decides that its primary problem is poor communication among group members, a diagnostic inquiry might be: "What do you think contributes to this poor communication within your group?" or "What can I do to help you improve communication?" It is doubtful that members of such a group would perceive either of these questions as being confrontational. On the other hand, they do focus on a specific aspect of group functioning, both in terms of isolating the problem and in determining whether the consultant will be able to help them solve it.

The third level proposed by Schein (1987) is action alternative interventions. While this type of intervention does not involve telling the client what to do, it is potentially more confrontational than the first two types of interventions because the process consultant is asking the group: "What have you done about the problem?" So, for example, if a group feels that internal communication is a problem and that the nature of their work roles contributes to this problem, the process consultant might ask, as an action alternative intervention, "What have you done to improve the situation?" or "If roles are the problem, have you done anything to change the roles of group members in a way that would facilitate communication?"

Why does Schein (1987) consider these questions to be potentially confrontational? The key to answering this question really lies in the difference between the roles of client and consultant. According to Schein, consulting is really all about helping, and therefore consultants are really professional helpers. If one accepts this notion, a logical corollary is that the client organization is in the position of seeking help, primarily because it cannot solve a particular problem on its own. The idea that an organization needs help potentially puts it in a dependent or lower status position vis-à-vis the consultant. Therefore, when the process consultant asks—"What have you done about this problem?"—the client organization risks embarrassment by saying that it has done the wrong thing or, worse yet, it has done nothing to solve the problem.

The final type of intervention described by Schein (1987) is labeled confrontive interventions. In interventions of this type, the process consultant makes recommendations as to how to solve the problem. For example, a process consultant may say: "Why don't you try_____as a way to solve the problem?" or "I would recommend trying_____." These statements are clearly more directive than the previous three. They are also potentially more confrontational, because the client may assume that the way he or she had been doing things is incorrect. Intervening in this way also tends to reinforce the status differences between the client and the process consultant that were previously described.

According to Schein (1987), a key issue in process consultation is how far and how quickly one moves along this intervention from exploratory inquiries to confrontive interventions. Many consultants begin with confrontive interventions or move to that point very quickly, often because the client expects or even demands it. Many organizations see consultants as bright experts to whom they can essentially "hand off" their problems. Unfortunately, handing off problems is often counterproductive because even extremely bright consultants rarely have enough information to immediately make concrete recommendations to an organization. Most problems in organizations are too complex and are embedded in a cultural context that an outside consultant cannot completely understand.

Another reason problems are handed off is simply because it is reinforcing to a consultant. Both authors have experienced the positive feelings associated with being seen as an expert by employees of an organization and having one's advice taken seriously. When members of an organization ask for advice, consultants are often compelled to offer something more concrete than "What

do you think the problem is?" The irony, of course, is that, in the long run, a consultant is often much more helpful to the client organization by keeping his or her interventions at the exploratory or diagnostic levels. By doing so, the consultant ultimately obtains much more information about the organization and its problems than he or she would by immediately being confrontational. Therefore, if the consultant needs to make recommendations in the future, these will be based on much more solid information.

Staying at the exploratory or diagnostic levels is also beneficial because these interventions force members of a client organization to think. As a result, these types of interventions help to sharpen employees' analytical and diagnostic skills so that they ultimately develop the capacity to solve some of the problems on their own. It also increases the chances that, although the members of the client organization are being helped by the process consultant, they will ultimately come up with the solution to whatever problem(s) are identified. This is important because members of the client organization are typically in a much better position than the consultant to judge what will and what will not work in that organization.

In addition to this general typology of interventions, Schein (1987) proposed a number of more specific interventions that fit into this typology. These are presented in Table 15.1. To reiterate a point made earlier, these interventions were not specifically designed to be applied to groups, but they are often used to improve group functioning. Notice that many of these interventions are so simple, and are used so frequently, that we don't really think of them as being organizational-development interventions. Terms such as *active interested listening, forcing historical reconstruction, forcing concretization, forcing process emphasis,* and *diagnostic*

TABLE 15.1

A Listing and Categorization of Process Consulting Interventions

Intervention	Category
1. Active, interested listening	Exploratory
2. Forcing historical reconstruction	Diagnostic
3. Forcing concretization	Diagnostic
4. Forcing process emphasis	Diagnostic
5. Diagnostic questions and probes	Diagnostic, action oriented
6. Process management and agenda setting	Confrontive
7. Feedback	Confrontive
8. Content suggestions and recommendations	Confrontive
9. Structure management	Confrontive
10. Conceptual inputs	Potentially confrontive

Adapted from: E. H. Schein. (1987). *Process consultation: Lessons for managers and consultants* (Vol. II). Reading, MA: Addison-Wesley.

questions and probes are used all the time as a way to help people figure out what their problems are.

Items 6 through 10 in Table 15.1 are more specific to group settings and require a bit more explanation. With process management and agenda setting, the process consultant might provide suggestions as to how group meetings should be conducted or how the agenda might be structured. While potentially confrontational, these interventions may also be very helpful. For example, one of the problems that the authors have observed in group meetings over the years is poor management of the group's time—that is, the group may consistently get through only one or two agenda items during its meetings. One way to deal with this problem is to be very structured in setting the meeting agenda and allocating a certain number of minutes to each agenda item.

Providing feedback is also a potentially confrontational intervention, yet it may also be quite useful to a group. A process consultant sitting in a group meeting can observe many things about the group's functioning. Probably the most visible thing is the manner in which the group communicates. Is communication very formal, or do group members feel free to jump in at any time? Do all members of the group communicate, or do one or two group members dominate the discussions? If a group's discussions are dominated by a small number of vocal employees, having a consultant point this out could be highly confrontational. This is particularly true if this behavior pattern is indicative of other problems in the group. Despite being potentially confrontational, this type of feedback may be highly useful because a group may not even be aware that this is happening.

When a consultant makes content suggestions and recommendations, he or she is being even more directive and potentially "confrontive." A process consultant, for example, may recommend that a work group allot time at the end of a meeting for group members to discuss concerns they have with the way the group functions. Recommendations could also be made about the frequency of team meetings—a process consultant may suggest that a group that meets only once a month should start meeting twice a month.

This type of intervention is potentially confrontational because, although the process consultant is not explicitly saying that things have been done wrong, the recommendations given to the work group may convey that opinion.

With structure management, the process consultant may make recommendations regarding the design of a group's task, or perhaps the manner in which a group carries out its tasks. For example, in a group where each group member performs a highly specialized task, a consultant may recommend combining tasks in order to increase the meaningfulness of the work. This is again potentially confrontational because the process consultant is directing the client to accept a solution to a problem that he or she, rather than the client, has proposed.

The final intervention listed in Table 15.1 is labeled conceptual inputs. It is common for process consultants to present relevant conceptual material during group-related interventions. For example, a consultant who is helping a group improve its effectiveness may provide the group with a 20 minute "lecturette" in which models of group effectiveness are described. Although conceptual inputs can certainly be useful, they can also be counterproductive, particularly if they are overused. As Schein (1987) points out, conceptual inputs may be confrontational if they highlight weaknesses in a group's processes. For example, a group that does not encourage a great deal of debate and open communication when decisions are made may become quite uneasy if a process consultant were to provide a brief lecture on Groupthink. Recall from Chapter 11 that a lack of open debate and communication are two of the primary symptoms of Groupthink.

Given the generality of process consultation, there is little empirical evidence as to whether this approach is effective. It would seem, however, that there would be a number of advantages in using this method, as opposed to more traditional forms of consultation. As Schein (1987) points out, organizations often know that something is "not right," but they are not sure where the problems lie. Thus, more often than not organizations and work groups need help and guidance in discovering what those problems are and how best to solve them. Process consultation is ideal in this type of situation because the primary assumption behind this model is that the client owns the problem and is ultimately the one who knows the organization well enough to figure out the problems—and the solutions to the problems.

Organization-Wide Interventions

Interventions that target the organization as a whole are becoming increasingly popular, for a number of reasons. For example, organizational change is most likely to occur and be sustained when the entire organization is involved in the change effort (Burke, 1994). Also, given the rapid rate of change in the business environment today, many organizations do not have the luxury of intervening with groups or individuals and then waiting for these interventions to facilitate organization-wide change.

The most widely used organization-wide intervention is survey feedback. In a typical survey feedback program, a survey is administered to all employees. It may address issues such as attitudes, perceptions of organizational climate, perceptions of management, and perceived level of organizational effectiveness, among other things. After the survey is administered and returned, the results are tabulated and then presented back to employees, typically within their own work groups.

As with most organizational-development interventions, the exact manner in which survey feedback interventions are carried out varies depending on the organization and consultant involved. A common practice, though, is for consultants to first conduct personal interviews or focus groups with at least a random sample of employees. Based on the themes that emerge from this initial stage, survey items are then developed (e.g., Gavin, 1984). In other cases consultants may have a standardized instrument that they administer to employees. An advantage of using a standardized approach is that an organization's results can be compared with those of other organizations in the same industry or the same geographical location. A disadvantage of this type of survey instrument is that the items are not specific to the particular organization, so many issues that are important to employees may be missed.

Although survey development is important, the feedback process is the key part of survey feedback, and thus it will be discussed in a bit more detail. In a model survey feedback program, the data are fed back to every employee in the organization, in a trickle down procedure. That is, the top management team of an organization first reviews the survey results. Each member of the top management team then shares the data with his or her subordinates. This process is repeated until everyone in the organization has had an opportunity to review the data. The feedback process is what makes it an organization-wide intervention, and it distinguishes true survey feedback from many employee opinion surveys conducted in organizational settings. For example, if a consultant conducts a survey of organizational employees and prepares a written summary report for top management, but the process essentially ends at this point, this is not true survey feedback.

Research has shown that survey feedback is an effective organizational-change intervention. In fact, Bowers (1973) compared several organizational-development interventions and found that survey feedback was the most effective. Other evidence has also shown that survey feedback is an effective intervention (Neuman, Edwards, & Raju, 1989). Research has also investigated more specific factors that impact the feedback process. For example, Klein, Kraut, and Wolfson (1971) found that employees are most responsive to feedback when it comes from their managers and is perceived as relevant to their actual work groups. Because of this, in many survey feedback interventions, two types of data are presented back to employees: (1) data that represent the opinions of the entire organization and (2) data that represent the opinions of the department in which the work group may reside.

A second organization-wide intervention is changing the structure of an organization. As discussed in Chapter 13, organizations have numerous options when it comes to organizational structures. The rationale behind structural change is quite simple. If all of the departments in an organization are restructured, employees have no choice but to engage in at least some form of change. Unfortunately, though, the changes that are brought about by structural changes may ultimately be only "pseudo" changes. Unless a change in structure is accompanied by changes in employees' behaviors, this is a relatively ineffective method of organizational change. For example, if an organization changes to a team-based structure, this will not result in meaningful organizational change if individual employees continue to act primarily in their own self-interests.

Other common methods of facilitating broad-based organizational change are through strategic planning and visioning interventions. Strategic planning is simply an organization's plan for what it is going to accomplish and the mechanisms that will be used to accomplish it. Strategic planning is an important function in an organization because it drives important activities, such as human resources planning and compensation, and it influences key decisions such as acquisitions. Given this importance, one obvious way for an organization to effect change would be to change its strategic objectives. For example, the top management of an organization that had once relied primarily on getting its products to market quickly may decide that it wants to be seen as a technological innovator. This type of strategic decision is highly significant, and an organization would likely have to change in a variety of ways in order to carry out this new strategy. For example, this organization might decide to hire the best technical talent available, or perhaps acquire a small but highly innovative competitor. It may also require a fundamental change in organizational culture, or perhaps even in structure.

The process of visioning simply requires the members of an organization (usually top management) to decide (1) what the organization would look like if it were ideal, (2) what the organization currently looks like, and (3) what strategic steps need to be taken in order to get the organization from where it is to where it could begin an ideal state. An example of this visioning process is depicted in Figure 15.6. This type of activity can be very useful, particularly prior to strategic planning, because it forces organizational decision makers to think about where they

FIGURE 15.6
Example of the Visioning Process

are headed and, perhaps more importantly, how to get there.

Most typically, strategic planning and visioning processes will represent the beginning of a long-term, large-scale organizational-change process. These two macro-level interventions will necessitate many other interventions at many other organizational levels. At Harley-Davidson, for example, a long-term process of organizational change essentially began with a simple visioning exercise (Teerlink & Ozley, 2000) and then branched out to a variety of other interventions needed to help that organization get from where it was to where it ultimately wanted to be (see Comment 15.2). When looked at in this way, it is probably more accurate to think of very global interventions (such as visioning) as precursors to organizational change rather than interventions themselves.

A form of visioning that may be used in conjunction with strategic planning is referred to as *scenario planning* (Schwartz & Ogilvy, 1998). In scenario planning, members of an organization come together and use multiple scenarios of the future environment in order to facilitate discussion, and they develop plans for responding to these scenarios. Steil and Gibbons-Carr (2005) describe how scenario planning was used at a large conference of faculty from dental schools. Using this method, conference participants planned potential responses to future challenges in dental education.

COMMENT 15.2

ORGANIZATIONAL CHANGE AT HARLEY-DAVIDSON

IN TERMS OF brand loyalty and identification, few organizations have been as successful as motorcycle manufacturer Harley-Davidson. Its products not only provide transportation, but they have really come to symbolize a lifestyle as well. Harley-Davidson endured some very tough times in the early 1980s due to Japanese competition and labor problems. Remarkably, the company pulled together, weathered this crisis, and by the late 1980s was again very profitable. Unfortunately, to get through this crisis, the organization adopted a very rigid "command and control" culture in which employees obeyed orders but took little personal initiative. This culture helped save the company; but, unfortunately, changes were needed if the company was to continue to grow in the absence of an external crisis.

In the book *More than a Motorcycle: The Leadership Journey at Harley-Davidson*, Rich Teerlink and Lee Ozley describe the difficult, long-term process of moving from a "command and control" culture to one in which employees are empowered and feel a sense of ownership. What's striking about this process is that it began with a very simple visioning exercise. Specifically, the top executives at Harley-Davidson, with the assistance of a consultant, discussed how the company was currently functioning and how the company ideally should be functioning. An examination of the differences between these two (current versus ideal) began a process that has gone on for over 10 years and has led to significant changes in organizational structure, performance appraisal, compensation practices, and labor relations.

A number of important lessons about organizational change can be learned from this book. Perhaps most important is: For organizational change to be meaningful, it must be comprehensive. Another important lesson is that organizational change must be supported by top management in order to succeed. Rich Teerlink, one of the authors, was the chief executive officer of Harley-Davidson through most of this change process, and he strongly supported it. Without his support, it is doubtful that this process would have survived. Finally, in reading this book, it becomes very obvious that this change process did not always go smoothly. There were times when union support of the change process was low and other times in which more immediate crises took higher priority. Ultimately, though, the organization kept at it and produced meaningful, positive organizational changes.

Source: R. Teerlink and L. Ozley. (2000). *More than a motorcycle: The leadership journey at Harley-Davidson.* Boston, MA: Harvard Business School Press.

CONDITIONS NECESSARY FOR SUCCESSFUL ORGANIZATIONAL CHANGE

Up to this point, we have defined organizational development, covered the theoretical base of this field, and described some of the more commonly used organizational-development interventions. In this section, we shift the focus to the organizational-development process. More specifically, we examine organizational factors that impact whether or not organizational change and development interventions are successful. These include top management support, the consultant who guides the organization through the change process, general resistance to change, and organizational ownership of the change and development process.

Top Management Support

For most initiatives in organizational settings to succeed, support from top management personnel is crucial; in fact, a lack of top management support is almost a guarantee of failure. Thus, it should come as no surprise that top management support is a key factor in determining whether or not organizational-development programs are successful. In this section, we examine why top management support is so important to the success of organizational change.

A very practical reason that top management support is crucial is that top management personnel have a great deal of control over organizational resources. This is important because organizational change and development programs are very expensive. Not only does an organization typically have to pay the fees of outside consultants; in most cases, organizational change and development programs require a great deal of employees' time. Employees' time is a finite resource; therefore, during the time that employees are engaged in organizational-development activities, they are not producing products, serving customers, or doing other things that directly support the mission of the organization. If top management personnel do not commit these types of resources to an organizational development effort, it will likely fail.

Top management support is also crucial because, in most organizations, top management personnel provide an organization with its strategic direction. Organizations

do not change in a random fashion—rather, they typically change for some logical reason. Top management's involvement and support are essential in order to give an organizational-change effort proper direction. If an organizational-change effort were to be conducted without this involvement, it is quite possible that change might occur, but the change might be counterproductive.

A final reason that top management's support is so crucial is that it has symbolic value. Although it is unlikely that most employees in organizations feel a strong personal connection to members of their top management team, they do look to these individuals for guidance. If members of the top management team are indifferent toward an organizational-development effort, this signals to employees that the program is unimportant. Conversely, if top managers enthusiastically support it, this communicates to employees that the organizational effort is important and that they should be committed to it.

The Consultant Guiding the Process

Many students see organizational-development consulting as a glamorous profession characterized by high earnings, interesting work, and exciting travel opportunities. While there is certainly some truth to this, it is also true that organizational-development consulting is very hard work. Facilitating day-long meetings, traveling to confer with clients, and summarizing interview and survey data can all be physically and mentally draining. Consultants must also constantly be aware of the ethical implications of their behaviors.

Organizational-development consultants have a very strong impact on whether an organizational-change program is successful. A highly skilled organizational-development consultant will greatly enhance the odds that an organizational-change program will be successful, even if the organization may initially be vague about what it is trying to accomplish. On the other hand, a poorly trained organizational-development consultant who is lacking in skill will most certainly increase the odds that an organizational-change program will fail.

Given the importance of the organizational-development consultant, a question that naturally arises is: "What are the attributes of an effective organizational-development consultant?" This is a difficult question to answer because the success of a consultant largely depends on the fit between his or her skills and personality, and the attributes of the client organization. A consultant may be a smashing success in one organization but a miserable failure in another. Despite this situational specificity, it is possible to come up with a set of general attributes that tend to characterize successful consultants.

One attribute that may seem obvious to readers is that consultants need to have a well-developed knowledge of organizational development and, more generally, behavior in organizations. This is important because consultants observe behavioral processes in organizations and, based on these observations, make recommendations about organizational-development interventions. Such knowledge often (but not always) comes from graduate study in the behavioral sciences or related fields (e.g., organizational behavior, industrial relations, human resources management). A consultant, however, may also acquire such knowledge through several years of working in a corporate training and development department, or through continuing education.

In addition to knowledge, several skills are needed in order to develop a successful consulting relationship with an organization. Probably the most basic skill consultants

need to have is listening. Particularly when a consultant first makes contact with an organization, it is important that he or she gathers as much information about that organization as is possible. The only way to do that is for the consultant to actively listen as members of the organization explain why they want to embark on a program of organizational change. Consultants must also listen to members of an organization describe the history and culture of the organization, since problems (and solutions to problems) occur in a historical and cultural context.

It is also important for consultants to possess very well-developed communication skills. Consulting involves a great deal of verbal communication with the members of a client organization, but it also requires that the consultant can communicate effectively in other ways (e.g., in writing, nonverbally). Consultants must be highly skilled communicators because much of their communication with the client organization comes in the form of feedback about problems and process issues. If an organization is going to change successfully, the consultant's feedback must be frequent and easy for members of an organization to understand.

Organizational-development consultants also need to have a solid grasp of research methodology and data analysis. Organizational-development consulting almost always involves the collection of empirical data about the client organization, analysis of those data, and a summary of the data in a form that members of the client organization can readily understand. Consultants who do not possess at least minimal skills in data collection and analysis, and who are unable to summarize data for nontechnical audiences, are at a distinct disadvantage compared to those who can. Consultants who lack these skills may rely on less rigorous methods of data gathering and ultimately may compromise the quality of an organizational-change effort.

In addition to knowledge and skill, some intangible qualities are important for organizational-development consultants to possess. For example, any type of consulting demands a very strong sense of ethics. Inevitably, consultants are told things "in confidence," and they may even detect that organizational members are attempting to use their services for political purposes. These are difficult situations that require the highest ethical standards. It is also important that consultants clearly communicate these standards to clients before accepting a consulting assignment.

Another highly important, yet intangible, quality necessary for organizational-development consulting is flexibility. Effective consultants are flexible enough to see an organization and its problems as they really are, not as they are seen through the lens of a particular theory or their favorite intervention. This type of flexibility may at times lead a consultant to conclude that an organization's problems do not fit his or her skill set; thus, a particular consulting assignment may not be appropriate. In the short term, this may result in lost consulting revenue; in the long run, however, it helps to build a consultant's credibility. Flexibility also requires a willingness to see multiple sides of an issue, and occasionally to admit that one is wrong. If a consultant offers advice or an assessment of a problem that ultimately turns out to be wrong, he or she needs to be flexible enough to admit the error and learn from it.

A final intangible characteristic that is crucial in effective consulting is credibility. How does a consultant establish and maintain credibility with an organization? When consultants initially come into contact with organizations, they are often sought out because of their academic credentials, prior work they have done, or an influential book they have written. In such cases, the organization certainly has a positive view of the consultant, and positive expectations about his or her capabilities, but the consultant does not yet have credibility. This is because credibility is an earned commodity, not a professional entitlement. Credibility is earned over time as the consultant interacts with the organization.

Perhaps the most important factor in determining credibility is whether the consultant keeps his or her word. When the consultant tells an employee that what he or she says will be held in confidence, is this information really held in confidence? When the consultant tells an organization that a report summarizing an employee attitude survey will be completed by a certain date, is the report delivered on or before that date? When a client organization is told that a project will cost a certain amount, does the consultant bill for that amount? These are obviously hypothetical examples, but they serve to underscore the point that credibility is something that consultants accrue each time they meet (or, ideally, exceed) the expectations of the client organization.

General Resistance to Change

Humans are basically creatures of habit and, as such, they find a great deal of comfort in routine and familiarity. Consequently, even considering a change often evokes a great deal of apprehension and anxiety. This general principle certainly applies in the workplace as well. As was shown in Chapter 14, people in organizations develop routines and rituals surrounding many behaviors and these become highly ingrained in an organization's culture. Once behaviors become highly ingrained, it is very difficult to change them, even if such changes are positive. Fear of change often comes from a belief that changes will have a negative impact, or from just general fear of the unknown.

It is unlikely that organizations can ever completely eliminate resistance to change. What can be done, though, is to introduce organizational changes in a way that decreases the potential for resistance. One way of doing this is to provide the opportunity for employee participation in the implementation of the organizational changes. As was shown over 50 years ago by Coch and French (1948), employees are much more receptive to changes when they have the opportunity to participate in their implementation. Autocratic methods of organizational change may appear to be much quicker and easier than participative methods, but, in the long run, organizations stand a much greater chance of encountering employee resistance if changes are imposed on employees. Research over the years has certainly affirmed the value of allowing employees to participate in organizational changes that may impact them (e.g., Piderit, 2000).

Change can also be made less threatening to employees if organizations maintain a high level of communication with employees throughout the change process. This is important for two reasons. First, a high level of communication is likely to increase employee perceptions of procedural justice with respect to an organizational change. More specifically, employees will feel as though the organizational changes will be handled in a way that is fair to all employees. Communication is also important because it provides employees with a rational basis to assess the costs and benefits of the change. Research has shown that employees are less likely to resist organizational changes if they see that the benefits outweigh the costs (Giangreco & Peccei, 2005), so clearly communicating these provides employees with the information necessary to make this judgment.

A final thought to consider is that in some cases strong resistance to change among employees may be a sign that an organizational change should be reconsidered. While resistance to change is typically treated by researchers as something that must be "overcome" (Piderit, 2000), employee reactions to proposed changes may at times be a valuable "reality check" for an organization. This is especially true in organizations where top management has sought out little input from rank-and-file employees prior to going ahead with organizational-change programs.

Organizational Ownership of the Change and Development Process

It is often tempting for organizations to abdicate responsibility for organizational change and development programs to outside consultants. The primary reason for this is quite simple: Changing an organization is very hard work. Developing a new vision for an organization, participating in team-building activities, or conducting survey feedback meetings are all mentally and physically draining activities. Given this difficulty, it is tempting for members of an organization to sit back and let a consultant take care of these chores and submit a report to the organization. Ultimately, though, the solutions that come strictly from consultants with no involvement from members of an organization may not mesh well with the realities of an organization's culture (Schein, 1987). Employees may also have little enthusiasm for implementing changes recommended by a consultant.

Organizations may also resist ownership because organizational development can be very threatening. During the course of an organizational-development program, employees are often faced with some harsh realities. For example, they may realize that their organization is not as effective as it could be, or that it is not as ideal a place to work as they once thought it was. Even more threatening for employees is the possibility that they may bear some of the responsibility for some of the organization's problems. Viewing an organizational-development program as "something the consultant does" may be a way of sparing employees the difficult task of confronting the organization's (and, by implication, their own) shortcomings.

One thing consultants can do to increase ownership is to stress its importance at the beginning of the organizational-development process. Often, in an effort to win a consulting contract with an organization, a consultant is tempted to portray the role of the organization as being very minimal (e.g., the consultant will take care of everything). However, in the long run, this model is often counterproductive because the change process rarely works without the participation of members of the client organization.

Consultants can also increase organizational ownership by striving to make the client a true partner in the change process. It is often tempting for consultants to give organizations advice in a very top-down or authoritative manner, particularly when they see things being done in the organization that are obviously counterproductive. If consultants can resist this temptation, however, and explore such counterproductive practices in a collaborative manner, this will ultimately be of greater help to the organization. It is also much more empowering to the client organization, because when problems occur in the future, the organization will be able to solve them.

EVALUATION OF ORGANIZATIONAL-DEVELOPMENT PROGRAMS

At this point in the chapter, some readers may find the organizational-development process, and the various interventions used by organizational-development consultants, quite interesting. More skeptical readers, however, may be asking themselves: "Does any of this stuff actually *work*?" This is certainly an important question, given the large amount of resources that are required to implement an organizational-development program.

In this section, we tackle the difficult question of whether organizational development actually "works" and, perhaps just as important, why it works. We do this by first examining the issue of evaluative criteria. One of the problems in evaluating anything is that we are often vague in specifying the criteria by which we judge effectiveness. We then discuss the most common research designs that are used in the evaluation of organizational-development programs and the difficulty of measuring change. Finally, a brief review of the published literature on the effectiveness of various organizational-development interventions is provided.

The Problem of Evaluative Criteria

Within the broader field of industrial/organizational psychology, "the criterion problem" is typically associated with personnel selection (e.g., Campbell, 1990). To be sure, when organizations attempt to systematically validate selection procedures, deciding on appropriate criteria is a major challenge. What measures indicate whether or not an employee is effective? How do we assess the contribution of an employee to an organization's success? Both of these questions need to be answered if one is to truly assess the value of employee-selection procedures.

The criterion problem is also an important issue when evaluating organizational-development programs. If an organizational-development program is viewed in a holistic manner (e.g., the diagnosis, interventions, follow-up), the criterion problem becomes particularly acute. This is because the primary goals of most, if not all, organizational-development programs are the same: enhanced organizational effectiveness and employee well-being (Porras & Robertson, 1992; Kohler & Munz, 2006). How, then, can we show that an organization is more effective and employee well-being has improved after the implementation of an organizational-development program? One way this could be done is through standard financial measures such as stock price, sales revenues, return on assets, market share, health care costs, or any number of other measures that have been developed through cost-accounting procedures.

Financial data are appealing because they have the feel of objectivity. When an organization improves its financial performance or employee health care costs are reduced following the implementation of an organizational-development program, it is hard to argue that such results were due to methodological artifacts. A disadvantage of the financial indexes mentioned previously is that they represent a fairly narrow view of organizational effectiveness and employee well-being. For example, is an organization truly effective if its stock price goes up, but it lays off 30% of its workforce? Are an organization's employees better off if health care utilization goes down 20%, yet its rate of turnover is one of the highest in its industry?

Another way to assess organizational effectiveness and employee well-being, which can be equally as narrow, is to do so primarily in terms of employee behaviors and attitudes. For example, organizations might use the results of employee opinion surveys, rates of turnover, or number of grievances filed to indicate in a general sense how well the organization is performing. These effectiveness criteria may be much more relevant to the aims of an organizational-development program than financial data alone. Unfortunately, though, these criterion measures may be as narrow as the financial indexes described previously. Is an organization effective if its employees are highly satisfied with their jobs, yet its stock price declines steadily over a 3-year period? Is an organization effective if its employees report low levels of stress, yet it continues to lose market share to its competitors?

The best approach to measuring overall organizational effectiveness or employee well-being is to utilize multiple criteria measures. This provides the most complete picture of organizational effectiveness and, in fact, yields the most comprehensive view of the impact of organizational-development programs. Also, if such data are collected over a relatively long period of time, they may be particularly revealing. For example, in some cases, the initial impact of organizational-development programs on traditional financial measures is actually negative (e.g., Griffin, 1991), but, over time, may ultimately end up being positive. Conversely, with measures of employee attitudes and well-being, employees' initial reactions to organizational development may be very positive. Over time, however, the novelty of an organizational-development program may wear off, and such measures may return to baseline levels.

Deciding on the proper criterion measure is a bit easier if evaluation efforts are focused on specific organizational-development interventions, as opposed to a general program of organizational change. For example, evaluating an organizational-development program that features team building would logically call for some assessment of group or team effectiveness as the criterion. Furthermore, within the group-effectiveness literature, there exists some excellent guidance as to the criteria that define group effectiveness (e.g., Guzzo & Shea, 1992; Hackman, 1987). Even with such guidance, however, coming up with the actual criterion measures may be more easily said than done.

Evaluation Research Designs

A research design is simply a plan for data collection (Cook, Campbell, & Perrachio, 1990). When any organizational intervention is evaluated, some type of research design is needed because some data needs to be collected in order to assess the impact of that intervention. In organizational settings, researchers typically have much less control over data collection than do laboratory researchers. As a result, when conducting evaluation research, a number of methodological "compromises" usually have to be made in order to obtain any data showing the effectiveness of interventions. For example, in organizational settings it is rare to be able to randomly assign research participants to conditions, and researchers have little control over either the implementation of the intervention or extraneous variables that may impact the intervention. That's not to say that this is always the case (see Shperling & Shirom, 2005), but it is typical of field settings.

The most typical way that organizational-development practitioners deal with challenges in data collection is simply not to conduct any form of systematic evaluation at all (Porras & Robertson, 1992). Often, if an organizational-development intervention seems like it might be helping, this may be good enough for upper management. For those trained in the behavioral sciences, this apparent disregard for rigorous evaluation of organizational-development programs is troubling. However, when one considers that evaluation can be a very human and often a political process, this disregard for evaluation is often quite rational (see Comment 15.3).

One of the most common designs used in evaluation research—and, unfortunately, one of the least powerful—is the One Group, Posttest Only design. In this type of design, participants in an organizational-development intervention would simply indicate whether or not they felt the intervention was useful or effective. This is obviously a very easy design to implement. However, a major disadvantage of this design is that there is no baseline from which to evaluate the impact of the intervention. Also, because there is no control group there is no way of knowing whether there would have been a positive change in the criterion measure if the organizational-development intervention had not been implemented. Due to these weaknesses, Cook and Campbell (1979) refer to this design as generally *uninterpretable*.

Another commonly used design is the One Group, Pretest–Posttest design. In this case, a baseline measure is obtained both prior to and after an organizational-development intervention or program is implemented. For example, measures of group process may be obtained prior to and 3 months after the implementation of a team-building intervention. The advantage of this design is that there is a baseline measure. However, because there is still no control group, it is impossible to tell whether the observed effects would be obtained in the absence of the intervention. With the team-building example, it is possible that, as team members get to know each other better over time, their interactions and subsequent group processes would improve

COMMENT 15.3

THE POLITICS OF EVALUATION

IN MOST DISCUSSIONS of evaluation, including the one in this chapter, the bulk of the material deals with technical issues such as evaluative criteria and research designs. Furthermore, these technical issues are important to consider if organizational interventions are to be evaluated properly. Unfortunately, however, in focusing on the technical aspects of evaluation, we often overlook the politics of the evaluation process.

Why is evaluation often a political process? The key to answering this question is to understand what is actually occurring when an evaluation takes place. When we evaluate something, we are literally determining its value. For example, if we are evaluating a team-building program, what we are really doing is determining whether this program has any value to the organization. One of the reasons that organizations often do not want to know the true value of organizational-development interventions is that they're afraid of what they might find out. Obviously, if an intervention is evaluated and found to be very effective, everyone's happy.

However, what happens when an intervention is evaluated and found to be very ineffective? In this case, everyone is unhappy, particularly if the organization has invested considerable resources in the intervention. There may also be cases in which a particular individual (e.g., a Human Resources director) initiates an intervention. If this is the case, such an individual has a great deal riding on the success or failure of that intervention. Thus, for political reasons, it may not be in this person's best interests to conduct a thorough, methodologically rigorous evaluation.

The major point is that, even though evaluation is a technical process, it is also a very human process. Useful evaluation can only take place in organizations in which people are willing to accept negative outcomes, to learn from them, and ultimately to improve the implementation of future interventions. Unfortunately, based on my own experience and the low prevalence of rigorous evaluation, such organizations are probably more the exception than the rule.

even in the absence of a team-building intervention.

To address this issue, the researcher actually has several options. One is to add a control group and thus create a Pretest–Posttest with Control Group design. By doing this, the effects of the intervention can be compared against those of a group that does not take part in the intervention, thus providing the researcher with a firmer base for judging the effectiveness of the intervention. Unfortunately, in most organizational settings, control groups are hard to come by because of a limited number of

employees, and in many cases the unwillingness of management to withhold a potentially valuable intervention.

If a control group cannot be obtained, researchers can use the Pretest–Posttest with Multiple Dependent Measures design. This design is similar to the previously described One Group, Pretest–Posttest design except that the researcher measures two sets of dependent measures: one set that should be impacted by the intervention and another set that should not be. If, for example, a team-building intervention has a positive impact on group-process measures, yet it has no impact on participants' satisfaction with fringe benefits, this suggests that the intervention was effective.

A second option is a One Group, Interrupted Time Series design. This is similar to the One Group, Pretest–Posttest design except that several measures of a dependent variable are obtained prior to and after the intervention. By obtaining these multiple measures, the researcher is able to statistically model the behavior of the dependent measure over time and, more importantly, determine whether the intervention has any impact on that measure. This design is also useful because it allows the researcher some assessment of whether the effects that are observed persist over time.

The research designs briefly described in this section represent only a small sample of those available for the evaluation of organizational-development interventions or entire programs. Readers seeking more information about research designs are urged to consult Cook and Campbell (1979) or Cook et al. (1990). More specific information about evaluation research can be found in Shaw, Greene, and Mark (2006) and Bamberger (2006). Given the large number of research designs available, in most cases it is possible to conduct some form of evaluation of organizational-development programs even in the most challenging of field situations.

The Challenge of Measuring Change

The primary aim of evaluation research is to measure change. Although much has been written about the statistical issues surrounding the measurement of change (e.g., Cronbach & Furby, 1970), conceptual issues surrounding the meaning of change also impact the evaluation of organizational-development programs. In this section, we focus on the conceptual meaning of change in organizational-development research.

Golembiewski, Billingsley, and Yeager (1976) proposed that *change* in response to organizational-development interventions and programs can come in three varieties, which they labeled as Alpha, Beta, and Gamma change, respectively. Alpha change represents what we typically think of as *true* change; that is, an organization truly improves in some way after the organizational-development intervention. The meaning of the dependent measures used, as well as the manner in which participants perceive the measures, remain the same both prior to and after an organizational-development intervention. As an example, an organization may implement a survey feedback program and find that the levels of job satisfaction of employees truly increase as a result of this program.

Beta change represents a situation in which the participants' frames of reference change with respect to the dependent measure being assessed. Thus, beta change can be thought of as a methodological artifact rather than a true form of change. As an example, suppose an organization implemented a team-building intervention designed to improve communication within work groups. To evaluate this intervention, group members' perceptions of communication may be measured prior to and following the intervention. In this case the researcher might find that scores on the communication measure indicate that levels of communication have improved following the intervention. However, an alternative explanation is that, by going through this intervention, participants develop a greater awareness of the various ways in which people in groups communicate. Thus, what seemed to participants like a "small" amount of communication prior to the intervention, may seem like an "above-average" amount following the intervention. Note that in this example the actual level of communication has not really changed. What has changed, however, is participants' definition of the various points on the scale measuring communication.

Gamma change represents a situation in which participants essentially redefine or reconceptualize key dependent or outcome variables. Like beta change, this can also be thought of as a methodological artifact. Golembiewski et al. (1976), however, argued that because one of the goals of organizational development is to change employee perspectives, this may actually be a legitimate form of change. As an example of beta change, an organization may implement an intervention designed to increase employee input into organizational decision making. To evaluate this intervention, the level of participation may be assessed prior to and after the program has been implemented. Prior to the intervention, employees may conceptualize participation as being somewhat narrow and something that is not part of their role. As a result, they may rate this very low. After the intervention, however, they may view participation in a much broader sense, see it as something that is part of their job, and, consequently, rate it much higher than they did in the pretest. Note that in this example the *actual* level of participation has not changed. Rather, employees have changed the way they define participation.

How does the researcher distinguish among alpha, beta, and gamma change when evaluating an organization program? One way is obviously to decrease reliance on self-report criterion measures, or at least supplement self-reports with other criterion measures (e.g., Liu, Spector, Jex, 2004; Spector & Jex, 1991). Both beta and gamma change effects are due to cognitive processes. Thus, these artifacts can be avoided by utilizing at least some nonself-report measures in the evaluation process. For example, archival measures of performance could be used in conjunction with survey measures of employee attitudes when evaluating the impact of an organizational-development intervention.

To assess whether gamma change has occurred, one recommendation has been to compare the dimensionality of scales used to measure key dependent measures at pretest and posttest (Armenakis, Bedeian, & Pond, 1983; Armenakis & Zmud, 1979). Recall that gamma change represents a change in respondents' conceptualization of key dependent measures. Given this change in conceptualization, it is possible that the dimensionality of scales may change from pretest to posttest measurement. While this is certainly logical, at least from a statistical point of view, in practice it is often difficult to apply. Individual scale items contain a good deal of measurement error (Nunnally & Bernstein, 1994), and evaluation studies often have sample sizes that severely limit the usefulness of such analyses.

Evidence on the Effectiveness of Organizational Development

As was stated earlier, many organizational-development programs are conducted without the benefit of any formal evaluation. Fortunately, enough empirical evaluations of organizational-development programs have been conducted over the years and they have yielded several summaries, using both qualitative and quantitative methods. The most widely cited qualitative summary of the effectiveness of a number of organizational-development interventions was conducted by Bowers (1973). The most important finding from this review was that when a number of organizational-development interventions were compared, survey feedback appeared to be the most effective.

Another widely cited qualitative review of organizational-development studies was conducted by Terpstra (1981), who summarized 52 published organizational-development studies. Compared to Bowers' (1973) review, Terpstra's was more systematic because he coded each study reviewed, in terms of whether the effects of the organizational-development program were positive, neutral, or negative. Based on this classification, his conclusion was that the effects of organizational development are generally positive. This effect, however, was found to be moderated by methodological rigor; positive findings were most likely to be found in studies that were lacking in methodological rigor. Subsequent studies, however, have not supported Terpstra's claim of a pervasive "positive findings" bias in organizational-development evaluation (e.g., Bullock & Svyantek, 1983; Woodman & Wayne, 1985).

In more recent years, researchers have applied meta-analytic methods to the evaluation of organizational-development interventions. For example, meta-analytic reviews have supported the effectiveness of MBO (Rodgers & Hunter, 1991), as well as a number of other organizational-development interventions (e.g., Guzzo, Jette, & Katzell, 1985; Neuman et al., 1989). For the most part, these quantitative reviews suggest that many organizational-development interventions have a positive impact on a number of employee attitudes and behaviors. It is also true, however, that in all of these meta-analyses, a portion of variance in the effects is left unexplained after accounting for statistical artifacts such as sampling error, unreliability, range restriction, and so on.

This suggests that, while organizational-development interventions often have positive effects, these effects may vary considerably across organizations. Such variability also probably reflects the fact that many organizational programs, as well as interventions within programs, fail. Relying on the published literature may slightly overestimate the effectiveness of organizational-development programs and interventions because studies that show positive effects stand a much better chance of being published than those that show no effects or even negative effects (see Dahlsten, Styhre, & Willander, 2005).

SPECIAL ISSUES IN CLIENT–CONSULTANT RELATIONSHIPS

At this point, a relatively comprehensive coverage of organizational development has been provided. However, one aspect of the organizational-development process that has not been covered is the relationship between the organizational-development consultant and the organization. This is an important topic because some readers may ultimately assume the role of organizational-development consultant at some point in their careers. Therefore, in this final section, we briefly examine some of the important issues that a consultant faces in facilitating organizational-development programs.

Balancing the Needs of Multiple Clients

When providing consulting services to an organization, the first client an organizational-development consultant encounters is typically a member of the top management team or, in some cases, a human resources executive. Individuals at these levels often initiate organizational-development activities because they tend to focus on "big picture" issues such as overall organizational effectiveness and change. In addition, individuals at these levels are typically able to authorize the budgetary resources needed for consulting services.

Once a consultant is in an organization, however, the list of "clients" begins to grow very quickly. For example, depending on the size of the organization, a consultant may very well come into contact with employees ranging from division heads to hourly workers. One of the challenges that consultants often face, particularly as they deal with employees at lower levels of the organization, is the perception that they are only serving the interests of those in upper management. This is a difficult challenge, especially because consultants are typically brought into organizations by upper-management employees.

Probably the most effective way to balance the needs of multiple clients is to address the issue in the earliest stages of the consulting relationship. That is, when a consultant first enters an organization, he or she needs to make his or her initial contact aware that there will likely be multiple, and often competing, interests among various employees in the organization. After making the client aware of this, the next issue that needs to be confronted is how the consultant will handle such competing interests.

In the authors' opinion, consultants are best served by maintaining a neutral stance when faced with such situations. If a consultant appears to be too "pro-management," he or she risks losing credibility with lower-level employees and may then find it very difficult to obtain their cooperation in carrying out the organizational-development program. Conversely, becoming too aligned with lower-level employees may put a consultant in the awkward position of going against the individual(s) who facilitated his or her entry into the organization. Ultimately, consultants are best served by assuming that conflicts of interests will occur and making it clear to all parties involved that the consultants will not take sides.

Maintaining Confidentiality

A very simple rule of thumb for consultants regarding confidentiality: If you assure someone that the information he or she is giving you is confidential, honor that commitment. In actuality, though, maintaining confidentiality in consulting relationships can be a very complex issue that poses some serious ethical dilemmas. One of the reasons is that consultants are often tempted to violate it. For example, a member of upper management may want to know what a particular vice president said about her leadership style during a focus-group session. A group of hourly employees may want to know what upper management is planning to do with regard to a rumored merger. In both of these hypothetical cases, the consultant may be tempted to reveal confidential information, primarily because it would please the party receiving the information and is reinforcing to the consultant.

Confidentiality may also be compromised due to carelessness on the part of the consultant or those working for the consultant (e.g., Gavin, 1984). For example, a consultant may provide the top management group with written comments from a survey and forget to first delete the names of the respondents. A consultant may unknowingly leave the notes from an interview with an employee in a place where anyone can see them. Obviously, in both cases, the violation of confidentiality is completely unintentional. However, regardless of the intent, such lapses are embarrassing to the consultant and could severely damage a consulting relationship.

Perhaps the most typical reason for consultants' being pressured to reveal confidential information is because of misunderstandings regarding the limits of confidentiality. For example, the organization's top echelon may feel that they will be able to view completed questionnaires that employees have filled out, but the consultant plans to provide them with only summary data. Or, perhaps the manager of a group plans to find out "who said what" during the personal interviews of group members prior to a team-building session, but the consultant plans to report only the general themes that emerged during these interviews. In both of these cases, the problem is a lack of clarity regarding the confidentiality of the information being collected by the consultant.

The best way to avoid such misunderstandings is for the consultant to clarify all issues surrounding confidentiality prior to formally entering into the consulting relationship. Often, when consultants begin working with an organization, there is a temptation to "dive right in" and simply deal with issues such as confidentiality as they arise. In the long run, though, consultants and organizations are much better served by taking the time to thoroughly address issues such as confidentiality prior to beginning a project.

Terminating a Consulting Relationship

Some consulting assignments are short-term in nature, so there are clear starting and ending points. However, consultants also develop relationships with organizations that are more long term, and the services provided are less well defined in scope. A consultant may essentially be "on retainer" and be utilized by an organization in a variety of ways. This is helpful to an organization because, over time, the consultant may develop considerable knowledge of the organization and its problems. Long-term relationships with organizations can also be very advantageous for a consultant. They may be quite lucrative and may also result in the development of some very satisfying relationships with members of the organization. However, what happens if relationships like these go sour?

Deciding when to terminate a consulting relationship is obviously one of the most difficult issues a consultant faces, and there are no easy solutions. A common criterion that consultants use for making this decision is whether the consulting relationship is professionally satisfying. Particularly for part-time consultants, providing consulting services is done more out of interest in the activity than for financial gain. Therefore, some consultants will decide to terminate a consulting relationship when the consulting activity is no longer of interest.

Another common basis on which a consultant may decide to terminate a consulting relationship is whether he or she is helping an organization. Recall from the discussion of process consultation (Schein, 1987) that consulting is essentially a form of professional helping. Given this definition, a consultant may conclude that, although he or she is trying to be helpful, the services being provided are not really doing the client organization any good. This may be due to the fact that different services may be needed, or perhaps the organization has improved to a certain level and further improvement is unlikely.

Finally, a consultant may decide to terminate a consulting relationship due to philosophical or value differences with the client organization. A consultant may terminate a relationship upon discovering that the organization condones sexual harassment of its female employees, or that it "looks the other way" in response to other unethical behaviors. Making the decision to terminate an otherwise satisfying consulting relationship for these types of reasons is obviously difficult. However, in the long run, a consultant is probably better off terminating such a relationship and working with organizations where such conflicts do not exist.

CHAPTER SUMMARY

In this chapter, we examined the important area of organizational change and development. We began by defining organizational development and describing the typical reasons that organizations engage in programs of planned change. The focus of the chapter then shifted to a discussion of the historical roots of organizational development. As was shown, this field has a rich history and benefited from the contributions of many organizational psychologists.

The chapter then shifted to a discussion of the theoretical foundations of organizational development. Some theories focus on the general phenomenon of organizational change, and others serve as a foundation for more specific interventions. Although theories can be useful guides in the implementation of organizational-development programs, organizational-development practitioners must be careful not to depend too heavily on theory.

The next section of the chapter focused on organizational-development interventions. Given the number of interventions, this was not intended to be a comprehensive coverage; rather, the goal was to highlight for readers the most widely used organizational-development interventions. Typically, inter-ventions focus on the individual, the group, or broad organizational levels. Of these three, interventions at the group level are presently the most popular, although broad organizational interventions are being used more frequently in recent years. Regardless of the level at which interventions take place, however, some level of behavior change has to occur if these interventions are to enhance organizational effectiveness.

A number of factors were discussed that impact the success of organizational-development programs. These included top management support, consultant competence, and organizational ownership of the change process. Top management personnel typically have the power to authorize the resources needed for an organizational-change effort to occur, and employees often look to top management in deciding what is and what is not important. The competence level of the consultant is a crucial factor because even a useful intervention will not be effective if it is applied incompetently. Finally, if an organization does not take ownership of the organizational-development process, then such efforts are reduced to being passing fads rather than catalysts for change.

Evaluation of organizational-development programs is challenging, for a number of reasons. Specifically, it is often difficult to come up with appropriate criteria; a good deal of creativity may be needed to produce appropriate research designs; and it may be difficult to assess whether the changes observed are caused by the organizational-development program rather than artifacts. Despite these challenges, considerable evaluation research has been conducted in the field of organizational development. Generally speaking, the results of organizational development have been shown to be positive, although there is considerable organization-to-organization variation.

PHILIP MURVIS AND LESSONS FROM STUDYING ORGANIZATIONAL CHANGE

Two factors shaped my intellectual interest and emotional energy for organization development (OD). My college and doctoral years were during an era of social change: the civil and women's rights movement, anti-Vietnam war protests, Watergate, and such. Early on I saw myself as an activist and believed, like so many, that knowledge from psychology could be used to redress wrongs and make things right.

One issue that caught my attention concerned the frustrations of younger people entering the workforce in the 1970s. They were what Daniel Yankelovich called the "new breed" worker with higher education levels than their predecessors and more "anti-authority" attitudes. And they were not well suited to the routinized industrial and service job designs of that era nor to the conformist, strictly hierarchical business cultures of the time. As a result, the '70s was an era of the 'blue collar blues' and 'white collar woes' and when the quality of American-made goods began to decline and then pale versus imports from Japan.

I had studied OD in college, from the vantage of scholarly Chris Argyris and also radical Saul Alinsky. At the University of Michigan, in the org. psych. program, I was involved in several action research projects with Ed Lawler to, in my mind, "save the worker." This was stimulating because I got the chance to do OD research in many different kinds of organizations and to work with lot of different kinds of people. It was also sobering because I learned that my ideas on work reform weren't always matched by the interests of many workers and managers and that even when they were it was damnably difficult to effect organization change.

My first book on OD was called, aptly, *Failures in Organization Development and Change*, and included case studies by many leaders in the field describing their failures and what they learned from them. Since then, I've studied OD and applied it to corporate mergers and acquisitions, the global transformation of companies, and, most recently, in the advance of corporate citizenship.

A few things to take away from my life and work: (1) Get out in the field early and often—book learning is fine but nothing teaches like experience, then reflecting on it, and comparing what you find with the field's rich knowledge-base; (2) Look for the new—find what's emerging in organizations, such as "bottom of the pyramid" markets, new ways of managing employee diversity, new forms of customer engagement—and see how OD can engage those trends; and (3) Go global—travel, connect virtually to students in Asia and elsewhere, engage fellow students from foreign lands, go to international conferences and so on. It's challenging to discover that what you know to be true takes different twists and turns in other lands.

Philip H. Murvis
Bethesda, MD

The final section of the chapter discussed some of the common challenges in client–consultant relationships. These include balancing the needs of various clients within an organization, maintaining confidentiality of information, and deciding when to terminate a consulting relationship. As with most other difficult issues, there are no formulas or easy solutions. In most cases, though, taking the time to address these issues prior to formally beginning the consulting process is the best way to ensure that they do not become major problems down the road.

SUGGESTED ADDITIONAL READINGS

Detert, J. R., Schroeder, R. G., & Mauriel, J. J. (2000). A framework for linking culture and improvement initiatives in organizations. *Academy of Management Review, 25,* 850–963.

Dyer, W. (1994). *Team building: Current issues and new alternatives* (3rd ed.). Reading, MA: Addison-Wesley.

Mirvis, P. H. (2005). Large group interventions: Change as theater. *The Journal of Applied Behavioral Science, 41,* 122–138.

Ryan, A. M., Chan, D., Ployhart, R. E., & Slade, L. A. (1999). Employee attitude surveys in a multinational organization: Considering language and culture in assessing measurement equivalence. *Personnel Psychology, 52,* 37–58.

Wageman, R., Hackman, J. R., & Lehman, E. (2005). Team Diagnostic Survey: Development of an instrument. *The Journal of Applied Behavioral Science, 41,* 373–398.

References

Abelson, M. A., & Baysinger, B. D. (1984). Optimal and dysfunctional turnover: Toward an organizational level model. *Academy of Management Review, 9*, 331–341.

Abramis, D. J. (1994). Work role ambiguity, job satisfaction, and job performance: Meta-analysis and review. *Psychological Reports, 75*, 1411–1433.

Ackerman, P. L. (1989). Within-task correlations of skilled performance: Implications for predicting individual differences? (Comment on Henry & Hulin, 1987). *Journal of Applied Psychology, 74*, 360–364.

Adams, G. A., & Beehr, T. A. (1998). Turnover and retirement: A comparison of their similarities and differences. *Personnel Psychology, 51*, 641–665.

Adams, G. A., King, L. A., & King, D. W. (1996). Relationship of job and family involvement, family social support, and work-family conflict with job and life satisfaction. *Journal of Applied Psychology, 81*, 411–420.

Adams, J. S. (1965). Inequity in social exchange. In L. Berkowitz (Ed.), *Advances in Experimental Social Psychology* (Vol. 2, pp. 267–299). San Diego, CA: Academic Press.

Adkins, B., & Caldwell, D. (2004). Firm or subgroup culture: Where does fitting matter most? *Journal of Organizational Behavior, 25*, 969–978.

Adler, S., Skov, R. B., & Salvemini, N. J. (1985). Job characteristics and job satisfaction: When cause becomes consequence. *Organizational Behavior and Human Decision Processes, 35*, 266–278.

Aguinis, H., & Stone-Romero, E. F. (1997). Methodological artifacts in moderated multiple regression and their effects on statistical power. *Journal of Applied Psychology, 82,* 192–206.

Aiello, J. R., & Kolb, K. J. (1995). Electronic performance monitoring: A risk factor for workplace stress. In S. L. Sauter & L. R. Murphy (Eds.) *Organizational risk factors for job stress* (pp. 163–179). Washington, DC: American Psychological Association.

Ajzen, I. (1988). *Attitudes, personality, and behavior.* Chicago: Dorsey.

Ajzen, I. (2001). Nature and functions of attitudes. *Annual Review of Psychology, 52,* 27–58.

Albanese, R., & Van Fleet, D. D. (1985). Rational behavior in groups: The free riding tendency. *Academy of Management Review, 10,* 244–255.

Alderfer, C. P. (1969). An empirical test of a new theory of human needs. *Organizational Behavior and Human Performance, 4,* 142–175.

Alderfer, C. P., & Smith, K. K. (1982). Studying intergroup relations embedded in organizations. *Administrative Science Quarterly, 27,* 35–65.

Aldred, C. (1994). U.K. ruling focuses attention to job stress. *Business Insurance, Dec., 5,* 55–56.

Aldrich, H. (1999). *Organizations evolving.* London: Sage.

Allen, D. G. (2006). Do organizational socialization tactics influence newcomer embeddedness and turnover? *Journal of Management, 32*(2), 237–256.

Allen, N. J., & Meyer, J. P. (1990). The measurement and antecedents of affective, continuance, and normative commitment to the organization. *Journal of Occupational Psychology, 63,* 1–18.

Allen, N. J., & Meyer, J. P. (1996). Affective, continuance, and normative commitment to the organization: An examination of construct validity. *Journal of Vocational Behavior, 49,* 252–276.

Allen, R. W., Madison, L. W., Porter, L. W., Renwick, P. A., & Mayes, B. T. (1979). Organizational politics: Tactics and characteristics of its actors. *California Management Review, 12,* 77–83.

Allport, G. W. (1954). *The nature of prejudice.* Reading, MA: Addison-Wesley.

Amabile, T. M. (1983). The social psychology of creativity: A componential conceptualization. *Journal of Personality and Social Psychology, 45,* 357–376.

Amabile, T. M., & Conti, R. (1999). Changes in the work environment for creativity during downsizing. *Academy of Management Journal, 42,* 630–640.

Ambrose, M. L., & Kulik, C. T. (1999). Old friends, new faces: Motivation research in the 1990s. *Journal of Management, 25,* 142–175, 231–292.

Ambrose, M. L., Seabright, M. A., & Schminke, M. (2002). Sabotage in the workplace: The role of organizational justice. *Organizational Behavior and Human Decision Processes, 89,* 803–812.

Americans with Disabilities Act of 1990, Publ. L. No. 101–336, 104 Stat. 328 (1990). Codified at U.S.C.A. § 12101 et seq.

Andersson, L., & Pearson, C. M. (1999). Tit for tat? The spiraling effect of incivility in the workplace. *Academy of Management Review, 24,* 452–471.

Armenakis, A., Bedeian, A. G., & Pond, S. (1983). Research issues in OD evaluation: Past, present, and future. *Academy of Management Review, 8,* 320–328.

Armenakis, A., & Zmud, R. W. (1979). Interpreting the measurement of change in organizational research. *Personnel Psychology, 32,* 709–723.

Arvey, R. D., Bhagat, R. S., & Salas, E. (1991). Cross-cultural and cross-national issues in personnel and human resources management: Where do we go from here? In G. R. Ferris & K. M. Rowland (Eds.), *Research in personnel and human resources management* (Vol. 9, pp. 367–407). Greenwich, CT: JAI Press.

Arvey, R. D., Bouchard, T. J., Segal, N. L., & Abraham, L. M. (1989). Job satisfaction: Environmental and genetic components. *Journal of Applied Psychology, 74,* 187–192.

Arvey, R. D., & Jones, A. P. (1985). The use of discipline in organizational settings. In B. M. Staw & L. L. Cummings (Eds.), *Research in organizational behavior* (pp. 367–408). Greenwich, CT: JAI Press.

Ashford, S. J., & Black, J. S. (1996). Proactivity during organizational entry: The role of desire for control. *Journal of Applied Psychology, 81,* 199–214.

Ashforth, B. E., & Humphrey, R. H. (1993). Emotional labor in service roles: The influence of identity. *Academy of Management Review, 18,* 88–115.

Athey, T. R., & Hautaluoma, J. E. (1988). Team building in religious organizations. *Organization Development Journal, 62–65.*

Atkinson, J. W. (1964). *An introduction to motivation.* Princeton, NJ: Van Nostrand.

Aube, C., & Rousseau, V. (2005). Team goal commitment and team effectiveness: The role of task interdependence and supportive behaviors. *Group Dynamics: Theory, Research, and Practice, 9,* 189–204.

Aust, B., & Ducki, A. (2004). Comprehensive health promotion interventions at the workplace: Experiences with health circles in Germany. *Journal of Occupational Health Psychology, 9,* 258–270.

Austin, J. T., Humphreys, L. G., & Hulin, C. L. (1989). Another view of dynamic criteria: A critical reanalysis of Barrett, Caldwell, and Alexander. *Personnel Psychology, 42,* 583–596.

Austin, J. T., & Vancouver, J. B. (1996). Goal constructs in psychology: Structure, process, and content. *Psychological Bulletin, 120,* 338–375.

Averill, J. E. (1973). Personal control over aversive stimuli and its relationship to stress. *Psychological Bulletin, 80,* 286–303.

Avolio, B. J., Gardner, W. L., Walumbwa, F. O., Luthans, F., & May, D. R. (2004). Unlocking the mask: A look at the process by which authentic leaders impact follower attitudes and behavior. *The Leadership Quarterly, 15,* 801–823.

Aycan, Z., Kanungo, R. N., & Sinha, J. B. (1999). Organizational culture and human resource management practices: The model of culture fit. *Journal of Cross-Cultural Psychology, 30,* 501–526.

Bachrach, D. G., Bendoly, E., & Podsakoff, P. M. (2001). Attributions of the "causes" or group performance as an explanation of the organizational citizenship behavior/organizational performance relationship. *Journal of Applied Psychology, 86,* 1285–1293.

Bachrach, D. G., & Jex, S. M. (2000). Organizational citizenship and mood: An experimental test of perceived job breadth. *Journal of Applied Social Psychology, 30,* 641–663.

Bagozzi, R. P., & Yi, Y. (1990). Assessing method variance in multitrait-multimethod matrices: The case of self-reported affect and perceptions at work. *Journal of Applied Psychology, 75,* 547–560.

Bales, R.F. (1965). *The equilibrium problem in small groups.* In A. P. Hare, E. F.

Bamberger, J. (2006). Current views on creativity research. *Psyccritiques,*

Bandura, A. (1986). *Social foundations of thought and action: A social-cognitive theory.* Englewood Cliffs, NJ: Prentice-Hall.

Bandura, A. (1997). *Self-efficacy: The exercise of control.* New York: Freeman.

Bandura, A. (2001). Social cognitive theory: An agentic perspective. *Annual Review of Psychology, 52,* 1–26.

Barkema, H. G., & Gomez-Mejia, L. R. (1998). Managerial compensation and firm performance: A general research framework. *Academy of Management Journal, 41,* 135–145.

Barling, J. (1996). The prediction, experience, and consequences of workplace violence. In G. R. VandenBos & E. Q. Bulatad (Eds.), *Violence on the job: Identifying risks and developing solutions* (pp. 29–49). Washington, DC: American Psychological Association.

Barling, J., Dupre, K. E., & Hepburn, C. G. (1998). Effects of parents' job insecurity on children's work beliefs and attitudes. *Journal of Applied Psychology, 83,* 112–118.

Barling, J., & Griffiths, A. (2003). A history of occupational health psychology. In J. C. Quick & L. E. Tetrick (Eds.), *Handbook of occupational health psychology* (pp. 19–31). Washington DC: American Psychological Association.

Baron, R. A., & Bell, P. A. (1976). Aggression and heat: The influence of ambient temperature, negative affect, and a cooling drink on physical aggression. *Journal of Personality and Social Psychology, 33,* 245–255.

Baron, R., Handley, R., & Fund, S. (2006). The impact of emotional intelligence on performance. In V. U. Druskat, F. Sala, & G. Mount (Eds.), *Linking emotional intelligence and performance at work: Current research evidence with individuals and groups* (pp. 3–19). Mahwah, NJ: Lawrence Erlbaum Associates.

Baron, R. M., & Kenny, D. A. (1986). The moderator-mediator variable distinction in social psychological research: Conceptual, strategic and statistical considerations. *Journal of Personal and Social Psychology, 51,* 1173–1182.

Barrett, G. V., Caldwell, M., & Alexander, R. (1985). The concept of dynamic criteria: A critical reanalysis. *Personnel Psychology, 38,* 41–56.

Barrett, M., Grant, D., & Wailes, N. (2005). ICT and organizational change: Introduction to the special issue. *Journal of Applied Behavior Science, 42*(1), 6–22.

Barrick, M. R., & Mount, M. K. (1991). The big five personality dimensions and job performance: A meta-analysis. *Personnel Psychology, 44,* 1–26.

Barrick, M. R., & Mount, M. K. (2005). Yes, personality matters: Moving on to more important matters. *Human Performance, 18,* 359–372.

Barrick, M. R., Mount, M. K., & Strauss, J. P. (1993). Conscientiousness and performance of sales representatives: Test of the mediating effects of goal setting. *Journal of Applied Psychology, 78,* 715–722.

Barrick, M. R., Stewart, S. L., Neubert, M. J., & Mount, M. K. (1998). Relating member ability and personality to work-team processes and team effectiveness. *Journal of Applied Psychology, 83,* 377–391.

Barrick, M. R., Stewart, G. L., & Piotrowski, M. (2002). Personality and job performance: Test of the mediating effects of motivation among sales representatives. *Journal of Applied Psychology, 87,* 43–51.

Bass, B. M. (1998). *Transformational leadership: Industrial, military, and educational impact.* Mahwah, NJ: Erlbaum.

Bass, B. M., & Avolio, B. J. (1993). Transformational leadership: A response to critiques. In M. M. Chemers & R. Ayman (Eds.), *Leadership theory and research: Perspectives and directions* (pp. 49–80). San Diego, CA: Academic Press.

Bates, C. A., Bow Bass, B. M., Avolio, B. J., Jung, D. I., & Berson, Y. (2003). Predicting unit performance by assessing transformational and transactional leadership. *Journal of Applied Psychology, 88,* 207–218.

Bauer, T. N., & Green, S. G. (1998). Testing the combined effects of newcomer information seeking and manager behavior on socialization. *Journal of Applied Psychology, 83,* 72–83.

Baugh, S. G., & Roberts, R. M. (1994). Professional and organizational commitment among professional engineers: Conflicting or complementing? *IEEE Transactions on Engineering Management, 41,* 108–114.

Baumeister, R. F., & Leary, M. R. (1995). The need to belong: Desire for interpersonal attachments as a fundamental human motivation. *Psychological Bulletin, 117,* 497–529.

Beach, L. R. (1993). *Making the right decision.* Englewood Cliffs, NJ: Prentice-Hall.

Beard, K. M., & Edwards, J. R. (1995). Employees at risk: Contingent work and the psychological experience of contingent workers. In C. L. Cooper & D. M. Rousseau (Eds.), *Trends in organizational behavior* (Vol. 2., pp. 109–126). Chichester, England: Wiley.

Becker, H. S. (1960). A note on the concept of commitment. *American Journal of Sociology, 66,* 32–42.

Becker, T. E. (1992). Foci and bases of commitment: Are they distinctions worth making? *Academy of Management Journal, 35,* 232–244.

Beckhard, R. (1967). The confrontation meeting. *Harvard Business Review, 45,* 149–153.

Beehr, T. A. (1986). The process of retirement: A review and recommendations for future investigation. *Personnel Psychology, 39,* 31–55.

Beehr, T. A. (1995). *Psychological stress in the workplace.* London: Routledge.

Beehr, T. A. (1998). Research on occupational stress: An unfinished enterprise. *Personnel Psychology, 51,* 835–844.

Beehr, T. A., & Franz, T. M. (1987). The current debate about the meaning of job stress. In J. M. Ivancevich & D. C. Ganster (Eds.), *Job stress: From theory to suggestion* (pp. 5–18). New York: Haworth Press.

Beehr, T. A., Jex, S. M., & Ghosh, P. (2001). The management of occupational stress. In C. M. Johnson, W. K. Redmon, & T. C. Mawhinney (Eds.), *Handbook of organizational performance: Behavior analysis and management* (pp. 225–254). New York: Haworth Press.

Beehr T. A., Jex, S. M., Stacy, B. A., & Murray, M. A. (2000). Work stress and co-worker support as predictors of individual strains and performance. *Journal of Organizational Behavior, 21,* 391–405.

Beehr, T. A., & Newman, J. E. (1978). Job stress, employee health, and organizational effectiveness: A facet analysis, model, and literature review. *Personnel Psychology, 31,* 665–699.

Beehr, T. A., Walsh, J. T., & Taber, T. D. (1980). Relationship of stress to individually and organizationally valued states: Higher order needs as a moderator. *Journal of Applied Psychology, 61,* 35–40.

Beer, M. (1976). The technology of organization development. In M. D. Dunnette (Ed.), *Handbook of industrial and organizational psychology* (pp. 937–993). Chicago: Rand McNally.

Bellarosa, C., & Chen, P. Y. (1997). The effectiveness and practicality of stress management interventions. *Journal of Occupational Health Psychology, 2,* 247–262.

Bem, D. J. (1972). Self-perception theory. In L. Berkowitz (Ed.), *Advances in experimental social psychology* (Vol. 6, pp. 1–62). New York: Academic Press.

Bemmels, B., & Foley, J. R. (1996). Grievance procedure research: A review and theoretical recommendations. *Journal of Management, 22,* 359–384.

Bennett, J. B., & Lehman, W. E. K. (1998). Workplace drinking climate, stress, and problem indicators: Assessing the influence of teamwork (group cohesion). *Journal of Studies on Alcohol, 59,* 608–618.

Bennett, R. J., & Robinson, S. L. (2000). Development of a measure of workplace deviance. *Journal of Applied Psychology, 85*(3), 349–360.

Bentler, P. M. (1990). Comparative fit indices in structural models. *Psychological Bulletin, 107,* 238–246.

Berdahl, J. L., & Moore, C. (2006). Workplace harassment: Double jeopardy for minority women. *Journal of Applied Psychology, 91,* 426–436.

Berkowitz, L., & Donnerstein, E. (1982). External validity is more than skin deep. *American Psychologist, 37,* 245–257.

Bernichon, T., Cook, K. E., & Brown, J. D. (2003). Seeking self-evaluative feedback: The interactive role of global self-esteem and specific self-views. *Journal of Personality and Social Psychology, 84,* 194–204.

Bertua, C., Anderson, N., & Salgado, J. F. (2005). The predictive validity of cognitive ability tests: A UK meta-analysis. *Journal of Organizational and Occupational Psychology, 78,* 387–409.

Bettencourt, L. A., Gwinner, K. P., & Meuter, M. L. (2001). A comparison of attitude, personality, and knowledge predictors of service-oriented organizational citizenship behaviors. *Journal of Applied Psychology, 86,* 29–41.

Bialek, H., Zapf, D., & McGuire, W. (1977). *Personnel turbulence and time utilization in an infantry division* (Hum RRO FR-WD-CA 77–11). Alexandria, VA: Human Resources Research Organization.

Blake, R. R., & Mouton, J. (1964). *The managerial grid.* Houston, TX: Gulf.

Blake, R. R., Shephard, H. A., & Mouton, J. S. (1964). *Managing intergroup conflict in industry.* Houston, TX: Gulf.

Blakely, G. L., Andrews, M. C., & Moorman, R. H. (2005). The moderating effects of equity sensitivity on the relationship between organizational justice and organizational citizenship behaviors. *Journal of Business and Psychology, 20,* 259–273.

Blau, G., & Andersson, L. (2005). Testing a measure of instigated workplace incivility. *Journal of Occupational and Organizational Psychology, 78*(4), 595–614.

Bliese, P. D. (2000). Within-group agreement, non-independence, and reliability: Implications for data aggregation and analysis. In K. J. Klien & S. W. Kozlowski (Eds.), *Multilevel theory, research, and methods in organizations* (pp. 349–381). San Fransisco: Jossey-Bass.

Bliese, P. D., & Britt, T. W. (2001). Social support, group consensus, and stressor-strain relationships: Social context matters. *Journal of Organizational Behavior, 22,* 425–436.

Bliese, P. D., & Jex, S. M. (1999). Incorporating multiple levels of analysis into occupational stress research. *Work and Stress, 13,* 1–6.

Bliese, P. D., & Jex, S. M. (2002). Incorporating a mulitilevel perspective into occupational stress research: Theoretical, methodological, and practical implications. *Journal of Occupational Health Psychology,* 7(3), 265–276.

Bobko, P. (1995). Editorial. *Journal of Applied Psychology, 80,* 3–5.

Bolino, M. C. (1999). Citizenship and impression management: Good soldiers or good actors? *Academy of Management Review, 24,* 82–98.

Bolino, M. C., & Turnley, W. H. (1999). Measuring impression management in organizations: A scale development based on the Jones and Pittman taxonomy. *Organizational Research Methods, 2,* 187–206.

Bond, J. T., Galinsky, E., & Swanberg, J. (1998). *The 1997 National Study of The Changing Workforce.* New York: Families and Work Institute.

Bono, J. E., & Judge, T. A. (2003). Core self-evaluations: A review of the trait and its role in job satisfaction and job performance. *European Journal of Personality, 17,* S5–S18.

Bono, J. E., & Judge, T. A. (2004). Personality and transformational and transactional leadership: A meta-analysis. *Journal of Applied Psychology, 89,* 901–910.

Boode, G. (2005). Boundaries on the move: The impact of cultural values and language on organizational design and communication within an organization in Thailand. *Asian Pacific Business Review, 11,* 519–533.

Borman, W. C. (1991). Job behavior, performance, and effectiveness. In M. D. Dunnette & L. M. Hough (Eds.), *Handbook of industrial and organizational psychology* (2nd ed., Vol. 2, pp. 271–398). Palo Alto, CA: Consulting Psychologists Press.

Borman, W. C., & Motowidlo, S. J. (1993). Expanding the criterion domain to include elements of contextual performance. In N. Schmitt & W. C. Borman (Eds.), *Personnel selection in organizations* (pp. 71–98). San Francisco: Jossey-Bass.

Bouchard, T. D., Jr. (1976). Field research methods: Interviewing, questionnaires, participant observation, systematic observation, unobtrusive measures. In M. D. Dunnette (Ed.), *Handbook of industrial and organizational psychology* (pp. 363–413). Chicago: Rand McNally.

Bourrier, M. (2005). The contribution of organizational design to safety. *European Management Journal, 23,* 98–104.

Bowen, D. E., Ledford, G. E., & Nathan, B. R. (1991). Hiring for the organization, not the job. *Executive, 4*, 35–51.

Bowers, D. G. (1973). OD techniques and their results in 23 organizations: The Michigan ICL study. *Journal of Applied Behavioral Science, 9*, 21–43.

Bowling, N. A., & Beehr, T. A. (2006). Workplace harassment from the victim's perspective: A theoretical model and meta-analysis. *Journal of Applied Psychology, 91*(8), 998–1012.

Braddy, P. W., Meade, A. W., & Kroustalis, C. M. (2006). Organizational recruitment website effects on viewers' perceptions of organizational culture. *Journal of Business and Psychology, 20*(4), 525–543.

Bramel, D., & Friend, R. (1981). Hawthorne, the myth of the docile worker, and class bias in psychology. *American Psychologist, 36*, 867–878.

Brannick, M. T., Roach, R. M., & Salas, E. (1993). Understanding team performance: A multimethod study. *Human Performance, 6*(4), 287–308.

Brannick, M. T., & Spector, P. E. (1990). Estimation problems in the block diagonal model of the multitrait-multimethod matrix. *Applied Psychological Measurement. 14*, 325–339.

Breaugh, J. A., & Colihan, J. P. (1994). Measuring facets of job ambiguity: Construct validity evidence. *Journal of Applied Psychology, 79*, 191–202.

Brehm, J. W. (1966). *A theory of psychological reactance*. Oxford, England: Academic Press.

Brett, J. M., & Rognes, J. K. (1986). Intergroup relations in organizations. In P. S. Goodman (Ed.), *Designing effective work groups* (pp. 202–236). San Francisco: Jossey-Bass.

Bridges, W. (1994). *JobShift: How to prosper in a workplace without jobs*. Reading, MA: Addison-Wesley.

Britt, T. W., Adler, A. B., & Bartone, P. T. (2001). Deriving benefits from stressful events: The role of engagement in meaningful work and hardiness. *Journal of Occupational Health Psychology, 6*(1), 53–63.

Britt, T. W., Castro, C. A., & Adler, A. B. (2005). Self-engagement, stressors, and health: A longitudinal study. *Personality and Social Psychology Bulletin, 31*(11), 1475–1486.

Britt, T. W., Davison, J. M., Bliese, P. D., & Castro, C. A. (2004). How leaders can influence the health consequences of stressors. *Military Medicine, 169*, 541–545.

Britt, T. W., Dickinson, J. M., Moore, D. M., Castro, C. A., & Adler, A. B. (2007). Correlates and consequences of morale versus depression under stressful conditions. *Journal of Occupational Health Psychology, 12*, 34–47.

Britt, T. W., Thomas, J. L., & Dawson, C. R. (2006). Self-engagement magnifies the relationship between qualitative overload and performance in a training setting. *Journal of Applied Social Psychology, 36*(9), 2100–2114.

Broadbent, D. E. (1985). The clinical impact of job design. *British Journal of Clinical Psychology, 24,* 33–44.

Brockner, J., Grover, S., Reed, T. F., & DeWitt, R. L. (1992). Layoffs, job insecurity, and survivors' work effort: Evidence of an inverted-U relationship. *Academy of Management Journal, 35,* 413–425.

Brockner, J., Grover, S., Reed, T. F., DeWitt, R. L., O'Malley, M. (1987). Survivors' reactions to layoffs: We get by with a little help from our friends. *Administrative Science Quarterly, 32,* 526–542.

Brotheridge, C., & Grandey, A. (2002). Emotional labor and burnout: Comparing two perspectives of "people work." *Journal of Vocational Behavior, 60,* 17–39.

Brown, R., Condor, S., Matthews, A., Wade, G., & Williams, J. A. (1986). Explaining intergroup differentiation in industrial organization. *Journal of Occupational Psychology, 59,* 273–286.

Brown, R., Maras, P., Massar, B., Vivian, J., & Hewstone, M. (2001). Life on the ocean wave: Testing some intergroup hypotheses in a naturalistic setting. *Group Processes and Intergroup Relations, 4,* 81–97.

Bryant, H. (2005). *Juicing the game: Drugs, power, and the fight for the soul of major league baseball.* New York: Viking.

Buch, K., & Aldrich, J. (1991). O. D. under conditions of organizational decline. *Organizational, Development Journal, 9,* 1–5.

Buckley, M. R., Fedor, D. B., Veres, J. G., Weise, D. S., & Carraher, S. M. (1998). Investigating newcomer expectations and job-related outcomes. *Journal of Applied Psychology, 83,* 452–461.

Buell, P., & Breslow, L. (1960). Mortality from coronary heart disease in California men who work long hours. *Journal of Chronic Diseases, 11,* 615–626.

Buller, P. F. (1988). For successful strategic organizational change: Blend OD practices with strategic management. *Organizational Dynamics, 16,* 42–55.

Bullock, R. J., & Svyantek, D. J. (1983). Positive-findings bias in positive-findings bias research: An unsuccessful replication. *Academy of Management Proceedings,* 221–224.

Buono, A. F., & Bowditch, J. L. (1989). *The human side of mergers and acquisitions: Managing collision between people, cultures, and organizations.* San Francisco: Jossey-Bass.

Burke, W. W. (1994). *Organization development* (2nd ed.). Reading, MA: Addison-Wesley.

Burns, T., & Stalker, G. M. (1961). *The management of innovation.* London: Tavistock.

Buss, D. M. (1996). The evolutionary psychology of human social strategies. In E.

T. Higgins & A. W. Kruglanski (Eds.), *Social psychology: Handbook of basic principles* (pp. 3–38). New York: Guilford.

Bussing, A., & Hoge, T. (2004). Aggression and violence against home care workers. *Journal of Occupational Health Psychology, 9*(3), 206–219.

Byrk, A., & Raudenbush, S. (1992). *Hierarchical linear models: Applications and data analysis methods.* Newbury Park, CA: Sage.

Byrne, D. (1971). *The attraction paradigm.* New York: Academic Press.

Byrne, J. E. (1988). Caught in the middle. *Business Week, Sept., 12,* 80–88.

Cable, D. M., & Parsons, C. K. (2001). Socialization tactics and person-organization fit. *Personnel Psychology, 54*(1), 1–23.

Cable, D. M. & Turban, D. (2001). Recruitment Image Equity: Establishing the dimensions, sources and value of job seekers' organizational beliefs. In G. Ferris (Ed.), *Research in personnel/human resource management* (Vol. 20), pp. 115–163 Greenwich, CT: JAI Press.

Cable, D. M., & Yu, K. Y. T. (2006). Managing job-seekers organizational image beliefs: The role of media richness and media credibility. *Journal of Applied Psychology, 91*(4), 828–840.

Caldwell, D. E., & O-Reilly, C. A. (2003). The determinants of team-based innovation in organizations: The role of social influence. *Small Group Research, 34,* 497–517.

Campbell, D. T. (1958). Common fate, similarity, and other indices of the status of aggregates of persons as social entities. *Behavioral Science, 3,* 14–25.

Campbell, D. T., (1999). Innovative strategies to thrive in today's health care environment. *ADVANCE for Speech-Language Pathologists and Audiologists, 9,* 9–10.

Campbell, D. T., & Fiske, D. W. (1959). Convergent and discriminant validation by the multi-trait-multimethod matrix. *Psychological Bulletin, 56,* 81–105.

Campbell, J. P. (1990). Modeling the performance prediction problem in industrial and organizational psychology. In M. D. Dunnette & L. M. Hough (Eds.), *Handbook of industrial and organizational psychology* (2nd ed., Vol. 1, pp. 687–732). Palo Alto, CA: Consulting Psychologists Press.

Campbell, J. P. (1994). Alternative models of job performance and their implications for selection and classification. In M. G. Rumsey, C. B. Walker, & J. H. Harris (Eds.), *Personnel selection and classification* (pp. 33–51). Hillsdale, NJ: Erlbaum.

Campbell, J. P., & Dunnette, M. D. (1968). Effectiveness of t-group experiences in managerial training. *Psychological Bulletin, 70,* 73–104.

Campion, M. A. (1993). Editorial. Article review checklist: A criterion checklist for reviewing research articles in applied psychology. *Personnel Psychology, 46,* 705–718.

Campion, M. A. (1996). A message from your president: How to publish the results of applied projects (or how two needles can find each other in a haystack). *Industrial-Organizational Psychologist, 33,* 9–10.

Campion, M. A., & Berger, C. J. (1990). Conceptual integration and empirical test of job design and compensation relationships. *Personnel Psychology, 43,* 525–554.

Campion, M. A., Cheraskin, L., & Stevens, M. J. (1994). Career-related antecedents and outcomes of job rotation. *Academy of Management Journal, 37,* 1518–1542.

Campion, M. A., & McClelland, C. L. (1991). Interdisciplinary examination of the costs and benefits of enlarged jobs: A job design quasi-experiment. *Journal of Applied Psychology, 76,* 186–198.

Campion, M. A., & McClelland, C. L. (1993). Follow-up and extension of the interdisciplinary costs and benefits of enlarged design. *Journal of Applied Psychology, 70,* 29–43.

Campion, M. A., Medsker, G. J., & Higgs, A. C. (1993). Relations between work group characteristics and effectiveness: Implications for designing effective work groups. *Personnel Psychology, 46,* 823–850.

Campion, M. A., Mumford, T. V., Morgeson, F. P., & Nahrhang, J. D. (2005). Work redesign: Eight obstacles and opportunities. *Human Resource Management, 44,* 367–390.

Campion, M. A., Papper, E. M., & Medsker, G. J. (1995). Relations between work team characteristics and effectiveness: Replication and extension. *Personnel Psychology, 49,* 429–452.

Campion, M. A., & Thayer, P. W. (1985). Development and field evaluation of an interdisciplinary measure of job design. *Journal of Applied Psychology, 70,* 29–43.

Cannon, W. B. (1914). The interrelations of emotions as suggested by recent physiological researches. *American Journal of Psychology, 25,* 256–282.

Caplan, R. D. (1987). Person-environment fit in organizations: Theories, facts, and values. In A. W. Riley & S. J. Zaccaro (Eds.), *Occupational stress and organizational effectiveness* (pp. 103–140). New York: Praeger Press.

Caplan, R. D., Cobb, S., French, J. R. P., Jr., Harrison, R. V., & Pinneau, S. R. (1975). *Job demands and worker health: Main effects and occupational differences.* Washington, DC: U.S. Government Printing Office.

Caplan, R. D., & Jones, K. W. (1975). Effects of workload, role ambiguity, and Type A personality on anxiety, depression, and heart rate. *Journal of Applied Psychology, 60,* 713–719.

Carey, A. (1967). The Hawthorne studies: A radical criticism. *American Sociological Review, June,* 403–417.

Carey, J. M., & Kacmar, C. J. (1997). The impact of communication mode and task complexity on small group performance and member satisfaction. *Computers in Human Behavior, 13,* 23–49.

Carroll, S. J., & Tosi, H. L. (1973). *Management by objectives.* New York: Macmillan.

Carsten, J. M., & Spector, P. E. (1987). Unemployment, job satisfaction, and employee turnover: A meta-analytic test of the Muchinsky model. *Journal of Applied Psychology, 72,* 374–381.

Cartwright, S., & Cooper, C. L. (1997). *Managing workplace stress.* Thousand Oaks, CA: Sage.

Carver, C. S., & Scheier, M. F. (1981). *Attention and self-regulation: A control theory approach to human behavior.* New York: Springer.

Cascio, W. F. (1998). *Applied psychology in human resource management* (5th ed.). Upper Saddle River, NJ: Prentice-Hall.

Casper, W. J., Fox, K. E., Sitzmann, T. M., & Landy, A. L. (2004). Supervisor referrals to work-family programs. *Journal of Occupational Health Psychology, 9*(2), 136–151.

Castano, E., Yzerbyt, V., Paladino, M. P., & Sacchi, S. (2002). I belong, therefore, I exist: Ingroup identification, ingroup entitativity, and ingroup bias. *Personality and Social Psychology Bulletin, 28,* 135–143.

Chadwick-Jones, J., Nicholson, N., & Brown, C. (1982). *Social psychology of absenteeism.* New York: Praeger.

Champoux, J. E. (1991). A multivariate test of the job characteristics theory of work behavior. *Journal of Occupational Behavior, 12,* 431–446.

Chan, D. (1998). Functional relations among constructs in the same content domain at different levels of analysis: A typology of composition models. *Journal of Applied Psychology, 83,* 234–246.

Chao, G. T., O'Leary-Kelly, A. M., Wolf, S., Klein, H. J., & Gardner, P. D. (1994). Organizational socialization: Its content and consequences. *Journal of Applied Psychology, 79,* 730–749.

Chapman, D. S., & Webster, J. (2003). The use of technologies in recruiting, screening, and selection process for job candidates. *International Journal of Selection and Assessment, 11,* 113–120.

Chatman, J. (1991). Matching people and organizations: Selection and socialization in public accounting firms. *Administrative Science Quarterly, 36,* 459–484.

Chattopadhyay, P. (1998). Beyond direct and symmetric effects: The influence of demographic dissimilarity on organizational citizenship behavior. *Academy of Management Journal, 42,* 273–287.

Chemers, M. M. (1983). Leadership theory and research: A systems/process integration. In R. R. Paulus (Ed.), *Group process* (pp. 9–39). New York: Springer-Verlag.

Chemers, M. M., Hays, R. B., Rhodewalt, F., & Wysocki, J. (1985). A person-environment analysis of job stress: A contingency model explanation. *Journal of Personality and Social Psychology, 49,* 628–635.

Chen, G. (2005). Newcomer adaptation in teams: Multilevel antecedents and outcomes. *Academy of Management Journal, 48,* 101–116.

Chen, P. Y., & Spector, P. E. (1992). Relationships of work stressors with aggression, withdrawal, theft, and substance use: An exploratory study. *Journal of Occupational and Organizational Psychology, 65,* 177–184.

Cialdini, R. B. (2001). *Influence: Science and practice.* Needham Heights, MA: Allyn & Bacon.

Clarke, S. (2006). Workplace harassment from the victim's perspective: A theoretical model and meta-analysis. *Journal of Occupational Health Psychology, 11,* 315–327.

Cleyman, K. L., Jex, S. M., & Love, K. G. (1995). Employee grievances: An application of the leader-member exchange model. *International Journal of Organizational Analysis, 3,* 156–174.

Cober, R. T., Brown, D. J., Levy, P. E., Cober, A. B., & Keeping, L. M. (2003). Organizational web sites: Web site content and style as determinants of organizational attraction. *International Journal of Selection and Assessment, 11*(2–3), 158–169.

Coch, L., & French, J. R. P., Jr. (1948). Overcoming resistance to change. *Human Relations, 1,* 512–532.

Cohen, A. (1974). *Two dimensional man: An essay on the anthropology of power and symbolism in complex society.* London: Routledge and Kegan Paul.

Cohen, J. (1992). A power primer. *Psychological Bulletin, 112,* 155–159.

Cohen, J., & Cohen, P. (1983). *Applied multiple regression/correlation for the behavioral sciences.* Hillsdale, NJ: Erlbaum.

Cohen, S., & Wills, T. A. (1985). Stress, social support, and the buffering hypothesis. *Psychological Bulletin, 98,* 310–357.

Cohen, S. G., & Bailey, D. E. (1997). What makes teams work: Groups effectiveness research from the shop floor to the executive suite. *Journal of Management, 20,* 239–290.

Cohen-Charash, Y., & Spector, P. E. (2000). The role of justice in organizations: A meta-analysis. *Organizational Behavior and Human Decision Processes, 86,* 287–321.

Colarelli, S. M., Dean, R. A., & Konstans, C. (1987). Comparative effects of personal and situational influences on job outcomes of new professionals. *Journal of Applied Psychology, 72,* 558–566.

Collins, J. M., & Schmidt, F. L. (1993). Personality, integrity, and white collar crime: A construct validity study. *Personnel Psychology, 46*(2), 295–311.

Colquitt, J. A., Conlon, D. E., Wesson, M. J., Porter, C., & Ng, K. Y. (2001). Justice at the millennium: A meta-analysis of 25 years of organizational justice research. *Journal of Applied Psychology, 85,* 678–707.

Connolly, J. J., & Viswesvaran, C. (2000). The role of affectivity in job satisfaction: A meta-analysis. *Personality and Individual Differences, 29,* 265–281.

Conway, J. M. (1999). Distinguishing contextual performance from task performance for managerial jobs. *Journal of Applied Psychology, 84,* 3–13.

Cook, T. D., & Campbell, D. T. (1979). *Quasi-experimentation: Design and analysis issues for field settings.* Chicago: Rand McNally.

Cook, T. D., Campbell, D. T., & Perrachio, L. (1990). Quasi experimentation. In M. D. Dunnette & L. M. Hough (Eds.), *Handbook of industrial and organizational psychology* (2nd ed., Vol. 1, pp. 491–576). Palo Alto, CA: Consulting Psychologists Press.

Cooper, C. L., & Dewe, P. (2004). *Stress: A brief history.* Malden, MA: Blackwell Publishing.

Cooper, C. L., Dewe, P., & O'Driscoll, M. (2003). Employee assistance programs. In J. C. Quick & L. E. Tetrick (Eds.), *Handbook of occupational health psychology* (pp. 289–304). Washington, DC: American Psychological Association.

Cooper, M. L., Russell, M., & Frone, M. R. (1990). Work stress and alcohol effects: A test of stress-induced drinking. *Journal of Health and Social Behavior, 31,* 260–276.

Cooper-Hakim, A., & Viswesvaran, C. (2005). The construct of work commitment: Testing an integrative framework. *Psychological Bulletin, 131,* 241–259.

Cotton, J. L. (1995). Participation's effect of performance and satisfaction: A reconsideration of Wagner. *Academy of Management Review, 20,* 276–278.

Covin, T., & Kilman, R. (1991). Profiling large scale change efforts. *Organizational Development Journal, 9,* 1–8.

Cox, M. H., Shephard, R. J., & Corey, P. (1981). Influence of employee fitness, productivity and absenteeism. *Ergonomics, 24,* 795–806.

Crampton, S. M., & Wagner, J. A., III. (1994). Percept-percept inflation in micro organizational research: An investigation of prevalence and effect. *Journal of Applied Psychology, 79,* 67–76.

Cronbach, L. J., & Furby, L. (1970). How should we measure "change"—or should we? *Psychological Bulletin, 74,* 68–80.

Cropanzano, R., & James, K. (1990). Some methodological considerations for the behavioral genetic analysis of work attitudes. *Journal of Applied Psychology, 75,* 433–439.

Crowne, D. P., & Marlowe, D. (1964). *The approval motive: Studies in evaluative dependency.* New York: Wiley.

Crystal, G. S. (1991). *In search of excess.* New York: Norton.

Crystal, G. S. (1995). *Turner's compensation stirs executive pay criticism.* CompFlash, Dec 3.

Cunningham, C. J. L. (2005). *New applicant decision making: Understanding the influence of salary, family-friendly/life-friendly policies, and culture as influential organizational attributes.* Unpublished master's thesis, Bowling Green State University, Bowling Green, OH.

Daily, C. M., Johnson, J. L., Ellstrand, A. E., & Dalton, D. R. (1998). Compensation committee composition as a determinant of CEO compensation. *Academy of Management Journal, 41,* 209–220.

Dahlsten, F., Styhre, A., & Willander, M. (2005). The unintended consequences of management by objectives: The volume growth target at Volvo Cars. *Leadership & Organization Development Journal, 26*(7), 529–541.

Damanpour, F. (1991). Organizational innovation: A meta-analysis of effects of determinants and moderators. *Academy of Management Journal, 34,* 555–590.

Dane, F. C. (1990). *Research methods.* Pacific Grove, CA: Brooks-Cole.

Dansereau, F., Alutto, J. A., & Yammarino, F. J. (1984). *Theory testing in organizational behavior: The variant approach.* Englewood Cliffs, NJ: Prentice-Hall.

Dansereau, F., Graen, G., & Haga, W. (1975). A vertical dyad approach to leadership within formal organizations. *Organizational Behavior and Human Performance, 13,* 46–78.

Davidson, E. (2006). A technology frames perspective on information technology and organizational change. *The Journal of Applied Behavioral Science, 42,* 23–39.

Davis, S. M., & Lawrence, P. R. (1977). *Matrix.* Reading, MA: Addison-Wesley.

Davis-Blake, A., & Pfeffer, J. (1989). Just a mirage: The search for dispositional effects in organizational research. *Academy of Management Review, 14,* 385–400.

Dawis, R. V. (1990). Vocational interests, values, and preferences. In M. D. Dunnette & L. M. Hough (Eds.), *Handbook of industrial and organizational psychology* (2nd ed., Vol. 1, pp. 833–871). Palo Alto, CA: Consulting Psychologists Press.

Day, A. L., & Catano, V. M. (2006). Screening and selecting out violent employees. In K. E. Kelloway, J. Barling, & J. J. Hurrell (Eds.), *Hankbook of workplace violence* (pp. 549–577). St. Mary's University: Sage Publications, Inc.

Day, D. V., & Bedeian, A. G. (1991). Predicting job performance across organizations: The interaction of work orientation and psychological climate. *Journal of Management, 17,* 589–600.

Day, D.V., Sin, H-P., & Chen, T.T. (2004). Assessing the burdens of leadership: Effects of formal leadership roles on individual performance over time. *Personnel Psychology, 57,* 573–605.

Deadrick, D. L., & Madigan, R. (1990). Dynamic criteria revisited: A longitudinal study of performance stability and predictive validity. *Personnel Psychology, 43,* 717–744.

DeChurch, L. A., & Marks, M. A. (2006). Leadership in multi-system teams. *Journal of Applied Psychology, 91,* 311–329.

Deci, E. L. (1975). *Intrinsic motivation.* New York: Plenum Press.

Deci, E. L., & Ryan, R. M. (1985). *Intrinsic motivation and self-determination in human behavior.* New York: Plenum.

DeFrank, R. S. & Ivancevich, J. M. (1998). Stress on the job: An executive update. *Academy of Management Update, 12*(3), 55–66.

De Hoogh, A. H. B., Den Hartog, D. N., & Koopman, P. L. (2005). Linking the Big Five-Factors of personality to charismatic and transactional leadership; perceived work environment as a moderator. *Journal of Organizational Psychology, 26,* 839–865.

de Laat, P. B. (1994). Matrix management of projects and power struggles: A case study of an R&D laboratory. *Human Relations, 47,* 1089–1119.

De La Rose, G. M. (2006). *Towards an understanding of individual ratings of cohesion within work units: A multilevel study.* Unpublished master's thesis. Bowling Green State University, Bowling Green, OH.

DeMatteo, J. S., Eby, L. T., & Sundstrom, E. (1998). Team-based rewards: Current empirical evidence and directions for future research. *Research in Organizational Behavior, 20,* 141–183.

Denison, D. R. (1984). Bringing corporate culture to the bottom line. *Organizational Dynamics, 13,* 5–22.

Denison, D. R. (1990). *Corporate culture and organizational effectiveness.* New York: Wiley.

Denison, D. R., Cho, H. J., & Young, J. (2000). *Diagnosing organizational culture: Validating a model and method.* Working paper, International Institute for Management Development, Lausanne, Switzerland.

Denison, D. R., Haaland, S., & Goelzer, P. (2004). Corporate culture and organizational effectiveness: Is Asia different from the rest of the world? *Organizational Dynamics, 33*(1), 98–109.

Denison, D. R., & Mishra, A. K. (1995). Toward a theory of organizational culture and effectiveness. *Organization Science, 6,* 204–223.

Denison, D. R., & Sutton, R. I. (1990). Operating room nurses. In J. R. Hackman (Ed.), *Groups that work (and those that don't)* (pp. 293–308). San Francisco: Jossey-Bass.

Dentler, R. A., & Erikson, K. T. (1959). The functions of deviance in groups. *Social Problems, 7,* 98–107.

Depret, E. F., & Fiske, S. T. (1999). Perceiving the powerful: Intriguing individuals versus threatening groups. *Journal of Experimental Social Psychology, 35,* 461–480.

DeShon, R. P., Kozlowski, S. W. J., Schmidt, A. M., Milner, K. R., & Wiechmann, D. (2004). A multiple-goal, multilevel model of feedback on the regulation of individual and team performance in training. *Journal of Applied Psychology, 89,* 1035–1056.

Devine, D. J., & Phillips, J. L. (2000, April). *Do smarter teams do better? A meta-analysis of team-level cognitive ability and team performance.* Paper presented at the 15th annual conference of the Society for Industrial-Organizational Psychology, New Orleans, LA.

Dickinson, T. L. & McIntyre, R. M. (1997). A conceptual framework for teamwork measurement. In M. T. Brannick, E. Salas, & C. Prince (Eds.), *Team performance assessment and measurement* (pp. 19–43). Mahwah, NJ: Lawrence Erlbaum Associates.

Dickter, D. N., Roznowski, M., & Harrison, D. A. (1996). Temporal tempering: An event history analysis of the process of voluntary turnover. *Journal of Applied Psychology, 81,* 705–716.

Diefendorff, J. M., Brown, D. J., & Kamin, A. M. (2002). Examining the roles of job involvement and work centrality in predicting organizational citizenship behaviors and job performance. *Journal of Organizational Behavior, 23,* 93–108.

Dillman, D. A. (2000). *Mail and Internet surveys: The tailored design method* (2nd ed.). New York: Wiley.

Dipboye, R. L., & Flanagan, M. F. (1979). Research settings in industrial and organizational psychology: Are findings in the field more generalizable than in the laboratory? *American Psychologist, 34,* 141–151.

Driskell, J. E., Goodwin, G. F., Salas, E., & O'Shea, P. G. (2006). What makes a good team player? Personality and team effectiveness. *Group Dynamics: Theory, Research, and Practice, 10,* 249–271.

Driskell, J. E., & Salas, E. (1991). Group decision making under stress. *Journal of Applied Psychology, 76,* 473–478.

Driskell, J. E., Salas, E., & Johnston, J. (1999). Does stress lead to a loss of team perspective? *Group Dynamics: Theory, Research, and Practice, 3*(4), 291–302.

Driskell, J. E., Salas, E., & Johnston, J. (2001). Stress management: Individual and team training. In E. Salas, C. A. Bowers, & E. Edens (Eds.), *Improving teamwork in organizations: Applications of resource management training* (pp. 55–72). Mahwah, NJ: Erlbaum.

Driskell, J. E., Salas, E., & Johnston, J. H. (2006). Decision making and performance under stress. In T. W. Britt, C. A. Castro, & A. B. Adler (Eds.), *Military life: The psychology of serving in peace and combat* (pp. 128–154). Westport, CT: Praeger Security International.

DuBrin, A. J. (1993, Fall). Deadly political sins. *National Business Employment Weekly,* 11–13.

Dubrovsky, V. J., Keisler, S., & Sethna, B. N. (1991). The equalization phenomenon: Status effects in computer-mediated and face-to-face decision making groups. *Human-Computer Interaction, 6,* 119–146.

Dudley, N. M., Orvis, K. A., Lebiecki, J. E., & Cortina, J. M. (2006). A meta-analytic investigation of conscientiousness in the prediction of job performance: Examining the intercorrelations and the incremental validity of narrow traits. *Journal of Applied Psychology, 91,* 40–57.

Durkheim, E. (1951). *Suicide* (J. A. Spaulding & G. Simpson, Trans.). Glencoe, IL: Free Press.

Dyer, W. G. (1987). *Team building: Issues and alternatives* (2nd ed.). Reading, MA: Addison-Wesley.

Eagly, A. H., & Chaiken, S. (1993). *The psychology of attitudes.* Fort Worth, TX: Harcourt, Brace, & Jovanovich.

Eastman, K. K. (1994). In the eyes of the beholder: An attributional approach to ingratiation and organizational citizenship behavior. *Academy of Management Journal, 37,* 1379–1391.

Eden, D. (1985). Team development: A true field experiment at three levels of rigor. *Journal of Applied Psychology, 70,* 94–100.

Eden, D., & Aviram, A. (1993). Self-efficacy training to speed reemployment: Helping people help themselves. *Journal of Applied Psychology, 78,* 352–360.

Edwards, J. R. (1992). A cybernetic theory of stress, coping, and well-being in organizations. *Academy of Management Review, 17,* 238–274.

Edwards, J. R. (1994). The study of congruence in organizational behavior research: Critique and a proposed alternative. *Organizational Behavior and Human Decision Processes, 58,* 51–100.

Edwards, J. R., & Parry, M. E. (1993). On the use of polynomial regression equations as an alternative to difference scores in organizational research. *Academy of Management Journal, 36,* 1577–1613.

Edwards, J. R., Scully, J. A., & Brtek, M. D. (1999). The measurement of work: Hierarchical representation of the multimethod job design questionnaire. *Personnel Psychology, 52,* 305–334.

Ekman, P. (1973). Cross-cultural studies of facial expression. In P. Ekman (Ed.), *Darwin and facial expression: A century of research in review* (pp. 169–222). New York: Academic Press.

Ellickson, M. C. (2002). Determinants of job satisfaction of municipal government employees. *Public Personnel Management, 31,* 343–358.

Ellis, S., & Arieli, S. (1999). Predicting intentions to report administrative and disciplinary infractions: Applying the reasoned action model. *Human Relations, 52,* 947–967.

Elsayed-Ekhouly, S. M., & Buda, R. (1996). Organizational conflict: A comparative analysis of conflict styles across cultures. *International Journal of Conflict Management, 7*(1), 71–80.

Enchautegui-de-Jesus, N., Hughes, D., Johnston, K. E., & Hyun, J. O. (2006). Well-being in the context of workplace ethnic diversity. *Journal of Community Psychology, 34*(2), 211–223.

Equal Employment Opportunity Commission. (1980). *Guidelines on sexual harassment in the workplace* [No. 45 FR 74676–74677]. Washington, DC: Author.

Erez, A., & Judge, T. A. (2001). Relationship of core self-evaluations to goal setting, motivation, and performance. *Journal of Applied Psychology, 86,* 1270–1279.

Eskew, D., & Hennemen, R. L. (1996). Survey of merit pay plan effectiveness: End of the line for merit pay or hope for improvement. *Human Resource Planning, 19,* 12–19.

Evans, M. G., & Ondrack, D. A. (1991). The motivational potential of jobs: Is a multiplicative model necessary? *Psychological Reports, 69,* 659–672.

Fahr, J. L., Dobbins, G. H., & Cheng, B. S. (1991). Cultural relativity in action: A comparison of self-ratings made by Chinese and U.S. workers. *Personnel Psychology, 44,* 129–147.

Falbe, C. M., & Yukl, G. (1992). Consequences for managers of using single influence tactics and combinations of tactics. *Academy of Management Journal, 35,* 638–652.

Falkenberg, L. W. (1987). Employee fitness programs: Their impact on the employee and organization. *Academy of Management Review, 12,* 511–522.

Farrell, D., & Stamm, C. L. (1988). Meta-analysis of the correlates of employee absence. *Human Relations, 41,* 211–227.

Fayol, H. (1984). *General and industrial management.* Belmont, CA: Lake Publishing.

Feldman, D. C. (1976). A contingency theory of socialization. *Administrative Science Quarterly, 21,* 433–452.

Feldman, D. C. (1981). The multiple socialization of organizational members. *Academy of Management Review, 6,* 309–318.

Ferrier, W., Smith, K., & Grimm, C. (1999). The role of competitive action in market share erosion and industry dethronement: A study of industry leaders and challengers. *Academy of Management Journal, 42,* 372–388.

Ferris, G. R., Gilmore, D. C., & Kacmar, K. M. (1990, April). *Potential moderators of the organizational politics-job anxiety relationship.* Paper presented at the annual Society for Industrial and Organizational Psychology Convention, Miami, FL.

Festinger, L. (1954). A theory of social comparison processes. *Human Relations, 7,* 114–140.

Fiedler, F. E. (1967). *A theory of leader effectiveness*. New York: McGraw-Hill.

Fiedler, F. E., & Garcia, J. E. (1987). *New approaches to leadership: Cognitive resources and organizational performance*. New York: Wiley.

Field, R. H. G., & House, R. J. (1990). A test of the Vroom-Yetton model using manager and subordinate reports. *Journal of Applied Psychology, 75*, 362–366.

Finkelstein, M. A., & Penner, L. A. (2004). Predicting organizational citizenship behavior: Integrating the functional and role identity approaches. *Social Behavior and Personality, 32*, 383–398.

Finkelstein, S. (1992). Power in top management teams: Dimensions, measurement, and validation. *Academy of Management Journal, 35*, 505–538.

Finkelstein, S., & Boyd, B. K. (1998). How much does the CEO matter? The role of managerial discretion in setting of CEO compensation. *Academy of Management Journal, 41*, 179–199.

Finkelstein, S., & Hambrick, D. C. (1988). Chief executive compensation: A synthesis and reconciliation. *Strategic Management Journal, 9*, 543–558.

Fischer, R. & Ury, W. (with B. Patton, Ed.) (1981). *Getting to YES: Negotiating agreement without giving in*. Boston: Houghton-Mifflin.

Fishbein, M. (1979). A theory of reasoned action: Some applications and implications. In H. Howe & M. Page (Eds.), *Nebraska symposium on motivation* (pp. 65–116). Lincoln: University of Nebraska.

Fisher, C. D., & Gitelson, R. R. (1983). A meta-analysis of the correlates of role conflict and role ambiguity. *Journal of Applied Psychology, 68*, 320–333.

Fiske, S. T. (2004). *Social beings: A core motives approach to social psychology*. Hoboken, NJ: Wiley.

Fitzgerald, L. F. (1993). Sexual harassment: Violence against women in the workplace. *American Psychologist, 48*, 1070–1076.

Fitzgerald, L. F., Drasgow, F., Hulin, C. L., Gelfand, M. J., & Magley, V. J. (1997). Antecedents and consequences of sexual harassment in organizations: A test of an integrated model. *Journal of Applied Psychology, 82*, 359–378.

Flannery, T. P., Hofrichter, D. A., & Platten, P. E. (1996). *People, performance, and pay: Dynamic compensation for changing organizations*. New York: Free Press.

Fleishman, E., Harris, E. F., & Burtt, H. E. (1955). *Leadership and supervision in industry*. Columbus, OH: Bureau of Educational Research, Ohio State University.

Florkowski, G. W. (1987). The organizational impact of profit sharing. *Academy of Management Review, 12*, 622–636.

Florkowski, G. W., & Schuster, M. H. (1992). Support for profit sharing and commitment: A path analysis. *Human Relations, 45,* 507–523.

Folger, R., & Cropanzano, R. (1998). *Organizational justice and human resource management.* Thousand Oaks, CA: Sage.

Ford, R. N. (1973). Job enrichment lessons from AT&T. *Harvard Business Review,* Sept/Oct, 96–106.

Forsyth, D. R. (1999). *Group dynamics* (3rd ed.). Belmont, CA: Brooks/Cole-Wadsworth.

Forsyth, D. R. (2006). *Group dynamics* (4th ed.). Belmont, CA: Wadsworth/Thompson.

Foti, R. J., & Rueb, J. (1990, April). *Self-monitoring, traits, and leadership emergence.* Paper presented at the annual meeting of the Society for Industrial and Organizational Psychology, Miami, FL.

Fowler, F. J., Jr. (1984). *Survey research methods.* Beverly Hills, CA: Sage.

Fox, M. L., Dwyer, D. J., & Ganster, D. C. (1993). Effects of stressful demands and control on physiological and attitudinal outcomes in a hospital setting. *Academy of Management Journal, 36,* 289–318.

Fox, S., & Spector, P. E. (1999). A model of work frustration-aggression. *Journal of Organizational Behavior, 20*(6), 915–931.

Frambach, R. T., & Schillewaert, N. (2002). Organizational innovation adoption: A multi-level framework of determinants and opportunities for future research. *Journal of Business Research, 55,* 163–176.

Frank, L. L., & Hackman, J. R. (1975). A failure of job enrichment: The case of the change that wasn't. *Journal of Applied Behavioral Science, 11,* 413–436.

Frankenhaeuser, M. (1979). Psychoneuroendocrine approaches to the study of emotion as related to stress and coping. In H. E. Howe & R. A. Diensbier (Eds.), *Nebraska symposium on motivation* (pp. 123–161). Lincoln, NE: University of Nebraska Press.

French, J. R. P., Caplan, R. D., & Harrison, R. V. (1982). *The mechanisms of job stress and strain.* Chichester, England: Wiley.

French, J. R. P., Jr., & Kahn, R. L. (1962). A programmatic approach to studying the industrial environment and mental health. *Journal of Social Issues, 18,* 1–47.

French, J. R. P., Jr., & Raven, B. H. (1959). The bases of social power. In D. Cartwright (Ed.), *Studies in social power* (pp. 150–167). Ann Arbor, MI: Institute for Social Research.

French, W. L., & Bell, C. H. (1995). *Organization development: Behavioral science interventions for organization improvement* (5th ed.). Englewood Cliffs, NJ: Prentice-Hall.

Frese, M. (1985). Stress at work and psychosomatic complaints: A causal interpretation. *Journal of Applied Psychology, 70,* 314–328.

Frese, M., Kring, W., Soose, A., & Zempel, J. (1996). Personal initiative at work: Differences between East and West Germany. *Academy of Management Journal, 39,* 37–63.

Fried, Y., & Ferris, G. R. (1987). The validity of the job characteristics model: A review and meta-analysis. *Personnel Psychology, 40,* 287–322.

Fried, Y., Rowland, K. M., & Ferris, G. R. (1984). The physiological measurement of work stress: A critique. *Personnel Psychology, 37,* 583–615.

Friedland, N., Keinan, G., & Regev, Y. (1992). Controlling the uncontrollable: Effects of stress on illusory perceptions of controllability. *Journal of Personality and Social Psychology, 63,* 923–931.

Frone, M. R. (2003). Predictors of overall and on-the-job substance use among young workers. *Journal of Occupational Health Psychology, 8*(1), 39–54.

Frone, M. R. (2004). Alcohol, drugs, and workplace safety outcomes: A view from a general model of employee substance use and productivity. In J. Barling, & M. R. Frone (Eds.), *The psychology of workplace safety* (pp. 127–156). Washington, DC: American Psychological Association.

Frone, M. R. (2006). Prevalence and distribution of alcohol use and impairment in the workplace: A U.S. national survey. *Journal of Studies on Alcohol, 67*(1), 147–156.

Fuller, J. A., Stanton, J. M., Fisher, G. G., Spitzmuller, C., Russel, S. S., & Smith, P. C. (2003). A lengthy look at the daily grind: Time series analysis of events, mood, stress, and satisfaction. *Journal of Applied Psychology, 88*(6), 1019–1033.

Galbraith, J. R. (1995). *Designing organizations: An executive briefing on strategy, structure, and process.* San Francisco: Jossey-Bass.

Gallagher, D. G. (2005). Part-time and contingent employment. In J. Barling, E. K. Kelloway, & M. R. Frone (Eds.), *Handbook of work stress* (pp. 517–541). Thousand Oaks, CA: Sage.

Gallupe, R. B., Dennis, A. R., Cooper, W. H., Valacich, J. S., Bastianutti, L. M., & Nunamaker, J. F., Jr. (1992). Electronic brainstorming and group size. *Academy of Management Journal, 35,* 350–369.

Gangreco, A., & Pecccie, R. (2005). The nature and antecedents of middle manager resistance to change: Evidence from an Italian context. *International Journal of Human Resources Management, 16*(10), 1812–1829.

Gannon, M. J. (1971). Sources of referral and employee turnover. *Journal of Applied Psychology, 55,* 226–228.

Ganster, D. C., & Schaubroeck, J. (1991). Work stress and employee health. *Journal of Management, 17,* 235–271.

Gavin, J. F. (1984). Survey feedback: The perspectives of science and practice. *Group and Organization Studies, 9,* 29–70.

Geertz, C. (1973). *The interpretation of cultures.* New York: Basic Books.

Gelade, G. A., Dobson, P., & Gilbert, P. (2006). National differences in organizational commitment: Effect of economy, product of personality, or consequence of culture? *Journal of Cross-Cultural Psychology, 37,* 542–556.

George, J. M. (1990). Personality, affect, and behavior in groups. *Journal of Applied Psychology, 75,* 107–116.

George, J. M., & Bettenhausen, K. (1990). Understanding prosocial behavior, sales performance, and turnover: A group-level analysis. *Journal of Applied Psychology, 75,* 689–709.

George, J. M., & Brief, A. P. (1992). Feeling good-doing good: A conceptual analysis of the mood at work-organizational spontaneity relationship. *Psychological Bulletin, 112,* 310–329.

Gerhart, B. (1987). How important are dispositional factors as determinants of job satisfaction? Implications for job design and other personnel programs. *Journal of Applied Psychology, 72,* 366–373.

Gerhart, B. (1990). Voluntary turnover and alternative job opportunities. *Journal of Applied Psychology, 75,* 467–476.

Gerhart, B., & Milkovich, G. T. (1990). Organizational differences in compensation and financial performance. *Academy of Management Journal, 33,* 663–691.

Gerhart, B., & Milkovich, G. T. (1992). Employee compensation: Research and practice. In M. D. Dunnette & L. M. Hough (Eds.), *Handbook of industrial and organizational psychology* (2nd ed., Vol. 3, pp. 481–569). Palo Alto, CA: Consulting Psychologists Press.

Gersick, C. J. G. (1988). Time and transition in work teams: Toward a new model of group development. *Academy of Management Journal, 31,* 9–41.

Gersick, C. J. G. (1989). Marking time: Predictable transitions in task groups. *Academy of Management Journal, 32,* 274–309.

Gerstner, C. R., & Day, D. V. (1997). Meta-analytic review of leader-member exchange theory: Correlates and construct issues. *Journal of Applied Psychology, 82,* 827–844.

Gilliland, S. W., & Landis, R. S. (1992). Quality and quantity goals in a complex decision task: Strategies and outcomes. *Journal of Applied Psychology, 77,* 672–681.

Gladstein, D. (1984). Groups in context: A model of task group effectiveness. *Administrative Science Quarterly, 29,* 499–517.

Glick, W. H., Jenkins, G. D., Jr. & Gupta, N. (1986). Method versus substance: How strong are underlying relationships, between job characteristics and attitudinal outcomes? *Academy of Management Journal, 29,* 441–464.

Goff, S. J., Mount, M. K., & Jamison, R. L. (1990). Employer supported childcare, work/family conflict, and absenteeism: A field study. *Personnel Psychology, 43,* 793–810.

Golden, T. D., Veiga, J. F., & Simsek, Z. (2006). Telecommuting's differential impact on work-family conflict: Is there no place like home? *Journal of Applied Psychology, 91*(6), 1340–1350.

Goldstein, I. L. (1993). *Training in organizations* (3rd ed.). Pacific Grove, CA: Brooks/Cole.

Goldstein, I. L., & Ford, J. K. (2002). *Training in organizations: Needs assessment, development, and evaluation* (4th ed.). Belmont, CA: Wadsworth.

Golembiewski, R. T., Billingsley, K., & Yeager, S. (1976). Measuring change and persistence in human affairs: Types of change generated by OD designs. *Journal of Applied Behavioral Science, 23,* 295–313.

Gomez-Mejia, L. R. (1994). Executive compensation: A reassessment and future research agenda. In G. R. Ferris (Ed.), *Research in personnel and human resource management* (Vol. 12, pp. 161–222). Greenwich, CT: JAI Press.

Gomez-Mejia, L. R., & Welbourne, T. M. (1989). The strategic design of executive compensation programs. In L. R. Gomez-Mejia (Ed.), *Compensation and benefits* (pp. 216–260). Washington, DC: Bureau of National Affairs.

Goodale, J. G., & Aagaard, A. K. (1975). Factors relating to varying reactions to the four-day work week. *Journal of Applied Psychology, 60,* 33–35.

Goodman, P. S. (1986). The impact of task and technology on group performance. In P. S. Goodman (Ed.), *Designing effective work groups* (pp. 120–167). San Francisco: Jossey-Bass.

Gordon, J. (1992). Work teams: How far have they come? *Training, 29,* 59–65.

Graen, G. (1976). Role making process within complex organizations. In M. D. Dunnette (Ed.), *Handbook of industrial and organizational psychology* (pp. 1201–1245). Chicago: Rand McNally.

Grandey, A. A. (2000). Emotional regulation in the workplace: A new way to conceptualize emotional labor. *Journal of Occupational Health Psychology, 5*(1), 95–110.

Grandey, A. A. (2003). Managing emotions in the workplace. *Personnel Psychology, 56*(2), 563–566.

Grandey, A. A., Fisk, G. M., & Steiner, D. D. (2005). Must "service with a smile" be stressful? The moderating role of personal control for American and French employees. *Journal of Applied Psychology, 90*(5), 893–904.

Grant, A. M. (2007). Relational job design and the motivation to make a prosocial difference. *Academy of Management Review, 32*(2), 393–417.

Grant, A. M., Campbell, E. M., Chen, G., Cottone, K., Lapedis, D., & Lee, K. (2007). Impact and the art of motivation maintenance: The effects of contact with beneficiaries on persistence behavior. *Organizational Behavior and Human Decision Processes, 103*(1) 53–67.

Graziano, W. G., Jensen-Campbell, L. A., & Hair, E. C. (1996). Perceiving interpersonal conflict and reacting to it: The case for agreeableness. *Journal of Personality and Social Psychology, 70,* 820–835.

Greenberg, J. (1990). Employee theft as a reaction to underpayment inequity: The hidden cost of pay cuts. *Journal of Applied Psychology, 5,* 561–568.

Greenberg, J. (2002). Who stole the money, and when? Individual and situational determinants of employee theft. *Organizational Behavior and Human Decision Processes, 89,* 985–1003.

Greenhalgh, T., Robert, G., & MacFarlane, F. (2004). Diffusion of innovations in service organizations: Systematic review and recommendations. *Milbank Quarterly, 82,* 581–629.

Greenhaus, J., & Buetell, N. (1985). Source of conflict between work and family roles. *Academy of Management Review, 10,* 76–88.

Griffeth, R. W., & Hom, P. W. (1987). Some multivariate comparisons of multinational managers. *Multivariate Behavioral Research, 22,* 173–191.

Griffeth, R. W., Hom, P. W., & Gaertner, S. (2000). A meta-analysis of antecedents and correlates of employee turnover: Update, moderator tests, and research implications for the next millennium. *Journal of Management, 26*(3), 463–488.

Griffin, M. A., & Neal, A. (2000). Perceptions of safety at work: A framework for linking safety climate to safety performance, knowledge, and motivation. *Journal of Occupational Health Psychology, 5*(3), 347–358.

Griffin, R. W. (1991). Effects of work redesign on employee perceptions, attitudes, and behavior: A long-term investigation. *Academy of Management Journal, 34,* 425–435.

Griffin, R. W., & McMahan, G. C. (1994). Motivation through job design. In J. Greenberg (Ed.), *Organizational behavior: State of the science* (pp. 23–44). New York: Erlbaum and Associates.

Gruber, J. E. (1998). The impact of male work environments and organizational policies on women's experiences of sexual harassment. *Gender and Society, 12,* 301–320.

Gruman, J. A., Saks, A. M., & Zweig, D. I. (2006). Organizational socialization tactics and newcomer proactive behaviors: An integrative study. *Journal of Vocational Behavior, 69*(1), 90–104.

Guion, R. M., & Highhouse, S. (2004). *Essentials of personnel assessment and selection.* New Jersey: Lawrence Erlbaum Associates Publishers.

Gully, S. M., Incalcaterra, K. A., Joshi, A., & Beaubien, J. M. (2002). A meta-analysis of team-efficacy, potency, and performance: Interdependence and level of analysis as moderators of observed relationships. *Journal of Applied Psychology, 87,* 819–832.

Gundling, E. (2000). *The 3M way to innovation: Balancing people and profit.* Tokyo: Kodansha International.

Gupta, N., & Jenkins, D. G. (1985). Dual career couples: Stress, stressors, strains, and strategies. In T. A. Beehr, & R. S. Bhagat (Eds.), *Human stress and cognition in organizations* (pp. 141–176). New York: Wiley.

Gutek, B., Cohen, A., & Konrad, A. (1990). Predicting social-sexual behavior at work: A contact hypothesis. *Academy of Management Journal, 33,* 560–577.

Guzzo, R. A., & Campbell, R. J. (1990, August). *Conditions for team effectiveness in management.* Paper presented at the annual meeting of the Academy of Management, San Francisco.

Guzzo, R. A., Jette, R. D., & Katzell, R. A. (1985). The effects of psychologically based intervention programs on worker productivity: A metaanalysis. *Personnel Psychology, 38,* 275–291.

Guzzo, R. A., & Shea, G. P. (1992). Group performance and intergroup relations in organizations. In M. D. Dunnette & L. M. Hough (Eds.), *Handbook of industrial and*

organizational psychology (2nd ed., Vol. 3, pp. 269–313). Palo Alto, CA: Consulting Psychologists Press.

Guzzo, R. A., Yost, P. R., Campbell, R. J., & Shea, G. P. (1993). Potency in groups: Articulating a construct. *British Journal of Social Psychology, 32,* 87–106.

Hackett, R. D. (1989). Work attitudes and employee absenteeism: A synthesis of the literature. *Journal of Occupational Psychology, 62,* 235–248.

Hackett, R. D., & Guion, R. M. (1985). A reevaluation of the absenteeism-job satisfaction relationship. *Organizational Behavior and Human Decision Processes, 35,* 340–381.

Hackman, J. R. (1987). The design of work teams. In J. W. Lorsch (Ed.), *Handbook of organizational behavior* (pp. 315–342). Englewood Cliffs, NJ: Prentice-Hall.

Hackman, J. R. (Ed.). (1990). *Groups that work (and those that don't): Creating the conditions for effective teamwork.* San Francisco: Jossey-Bass.

Hackman, J. R. (1992). Group influences on individuals in organizations. In M. D. Dunnette & L. M. Hough (Eds.), *Handbook of industrial and organizational psychology* (2nd ed., Vol. 3, pp. 199–267). Palo Alto, CA: Consulting Psychologists Press.

Hackman, J. R., Brousseau, K. R., & Weiss, J. A. (1976). The interaction of task design and group performance strategies in determining group effectiveness.

Organizational Behavior and Human Performance, 16, 350–365.

Hackman, J. R., & Lawler, E. E. (1971). Employee reactions to job characteristics. *Journal of Applied Psychology, 55,* 259–286.

Hackman, J. R., & Morris, C. G. (1975). Group tasks, group interaction process, and group performance effectiveness: A review and proposed integration. In L. Berkowitz (Ed.), *Advances in experimental social psychology* (Vol. 9, pp. 47–87). New York: Academic Press.

Hackman, J. R., & Oldham, G. R. (1975). Development of the Job Diagnostic Survey. *Journal of Applied Psychology, 60,* 159–170.

Hackman, J. R., & Oldham, G. R. (1976). Motivation through the design of work: Test of a theory. *Organizational Behavior and Human Performance, 16,* 250–279.

Hackman, J. R., & Oldham, G. R. (1980). *Work redesign.* Reading, MA: Addison-Wesley.

Haines, V. Y., & Taggar, S. (2006). Antecedents of team reward attitude. *Group Dynamics: Theory, Research, and Practice, 10,* 194–205.

Halbesleben, J. R. B., Osburn, H. K., & Mumford, M. D. (2006). Action research as a burnout intervention: reducing burnout in the federal fire service. *Journal of Applied Behavioral Science, 42*(2), 244–266.

Hall, D. T., & Nougaim, K. E. (1968). An examination of Maslow's need hierarchy in an organizational setting. *Organizational Behavior and Human Performance, 3,* 12–35.

Hallam, G., & Campbell, D. (1997). The measurement of team performance with a standardized survey. In M. T. Brannick, E. Salas, & C. Prince (Eds.), *Team performance assessment and measurement* (pp. 155–171). Mahwah, NJ: Lawrence Erlbaum Associates.

Hallock, D. E., Salazar, R. J., & Venneman, S. (2004). Demographic and attitudinal correlates of employee satisfaction with an ESOP. *British Journal of Management, 15,* 321–333.

Hammer, T. H., & Landau, J. (1981). Methodological issues in the use of absence data. *Journal of Applied Psychology, 66,* 574–581.

Hannan, M. T., Polos, L., & Carroll, G. R. (2003). The fog of change: Opacity and asperity in organizations. *Administrative Science Quarterly, 48*(3), 399–432.

Hansen, C. P. (1988). Personality characteristics of the accident involved employee. *Journal of Business and Psychology, 2,* 346–365.

Hansen, C. P. (1989). A causal model of the relationships among accidents, biodata, personality, and cognitive factors. *Journal of Applied Psychology, 74,* 81–90.

Harrison, D. A., Newman, D. A., & Roth, P. L. (2006). How important are job attitudes? Meta-analytic comparisons of integrative behavioral outcomes and time sequences. *Academy of Management Journal, 49,* 305–325.

Hatch, M. J. (1993). The dynamics of organizational culture. *Academy of Management Review, 18,* 657–693.

Hatcher, L., & Ross, T. L. (1991). From individual incentives to an organization-wide gain sharing plan: Effects on teamwork and product quality. *Journal of Organizational Behavior, 12,* 169–183.

Hatton, C., Rivers, M., Mason, H., Mason, L., Emerson, E., Kiernan, C., et al. (1999). Organizational culture and staff outcomes in services for people with intellectual disabilities. *Journal of Intellectual Disability Research, 43,* 206–218.

Hays, W. L. (1988). *Statistics* (4th ed.). New York: Holt, Rinehart and Winston.

Heinisch, D. A., & Jex, S. M. (1997). Negative affectivity and gender as moderators of the relationship between work-related stressors and depressed mood at work. *Work and Stress, 11,* 46–57.

Hellervik, L. W., Hazucha, J. F., & Schneider, R. J. (1992). Behavior change: Models, methods, and a review of evidence. In M. D. Dunnette & L. M. Hough (Eds.), *Handbook of industrial and organizational psychology* (2nd ed., Vol. 3, pp. 823–895). Palo Alto, CA: Consulting Psychologists Press.

Hellstrom, C., & Hellstrom, T. (2002). Highways, alleys, and by-lanes: Charting the pathways for ideas and innovation in organizations. *Creativity and Innovation Management, 11,* 107–114.

Henkoff, R. (1990). Cost cutting: How to do it right. *Fortune, Apr, 9,* 40–46.

Henry, R., & Hulin, C. L. (1987). Stability of skilled performance across time: Some generalizations and limitations on utilities. *Journal of Applied Psychology, 72,* 457–462.

Henry, R., & Hulin, C. L. (1989). Changing validities: Ability-performance relations and utilities. *Journal of Applied Psychology, 74,* 365–367.

Hertel, G., Konradt, U., & Orlikowski, B. (2004). Managing distance by interdependence: Goal setting, task interdependence, and team-based rewards in virtual teams. *European Journal of Work and Organizational Psychology, 13,* 1–28.

Herzberg, F. (1968). One more time: How do you motivate employees? *Harvard Business Review, Jan/Feb,* 52–62.

Herzberg, F., Mausner, B., & Snyderman, B. (1959). *The motivation to work.* New York: Wiley.

Hickson, D. J., Pugh, D. S., & Pheysey, D. (1969). Operations technology and organization structure: An empirical reappraisal. *Administrative Science Quarterly, 14,* 378–397.

Highhouse, S., & Hoffman, J. R. (2001). Organizational attraction and job choice. In C. L. Cooper & I. T. Robertson (Eds.), *International Review of Industrial and Organizational Psychology 2001* (Vol. 16, pp. 37–64). Chichester, England: Wiley.

Hirschfeld, R. R., Jordan, M. H., Field, H. S., Giles, W. F., & Armenakis, A. A. (2006). Becoming team players: Team members' mastery of teamwork knowledge as a predictor of team task proficiency and observed teamwork effectiveness. *Journal of Applied Psychology, 91,* 467–474.

Hochschild, A. R. (1979). Emotion work, feeling rules, and social structure. *American Journal of Sociology, 85,* 551–575.

Hochschild, A. R. (1983). *The managed heart: Commercialization of human feeling.* Berkeley: University of California Press.

Hochschild, A. R. (1989). *The second shift: Working parents and the revolution at home.* New York: Viking.

Hofmann, D. A., & Morgeson, F. P. (1999). Safety-related behavior as a social exchange: The role of perceived organizational support and leader-member exchange. *Journal of Applied Psychology, 84,* 286–296.

Hofmann, D. A., & Stetzer, A. (1998). The role of safety climate and communication in accident interpretation: Implication from negative events. *Academy of Management Journal, 41,* 644–657.

Hofmann, D. A., & Tetrick, L. E. (2003). The etiology of the concept of health: Implications for "organizing" individual and organizational health. In D. A. Hofmann and L. E. Tetrick (Eds.), *Health and safety in organizations: A multilevel perspective* (pp. 1–28). San Francisco: Jossey-Bass.

Hofstede, G. (1980). *Culture's consequences: International differences in work-related values.* Beverly Hills, CA: Sage.

Hofstede, G. (1984). *Culture's consequences: International differences in work-related values (Abridged ed.).* Newbury Park, CA: Sage.

Hogan, E. A., & Overmeyer-Day, L. (1994). The psychology of mergers and acquisitions. In C. L. Cooper & I. T. Robertson (Eds.), *International review of industrial and organizational psychology 1994* (Vol. 9, pp. 247–280). Chichester, England: Wiley.

Hogan, J., & Hogan, R. (1989). How to measure employee reliability. *Journal of Applied Psychology, 74,* 273–279.

Hollander, E. P. (1971). *Principles and methods of social psychology* (2nd ed.). New York: Oxford University Press.

Hollenbeck, J. R., Ilgen, D. R., & Crampton, S. M. (1992). Lower back disability in occupational settings: A review of the literature from a human resource management view. *Personnel Psychology, 45,* 247–278.

Holtom, B. C., Mitchell, T. R., Lee, T. W., & Interrieden, E. J. (2005). Shocks as causes of turnover: What they are and how organizations can manage them. *Human Resources Management, 44*(3), 337–352.

Hom, P. W., Caranikas-Walker, F., Prussia, G. E., & Griffeth, R. W. (1992). A meta-analytic structural equations analysis of a model of employee turnover. *Journal of Applied Psychology, 77,* 890–909.

Homans, G. C. (1958). Social behavior as exchange. *American Journal of Sociology, 63,* 597–606.

Hornstein, H. A., & deGuerre, D. W. (2006). Bureaucratic organizations are bad for our health. *Ivey Business Journal, March/April,* 1–4.

House, R. J. (1971). A path-goal theory of leader effectiveness. *Administrative Science Quarterly, 16,* 321–339.

House, R. J. (1977). A 1976 theory of charismatic leadership. In J. G. Hunt & L. L. Larson (Eds.), *Leadership: The cutting edge.* Carbondale: Southern Illinois University Press.

House, R. J. (1996). Path-goal theory of leadership: Lessons, legacy, and a reformulated theory. *Leadership Quarterly, 7,* 323–352.

House, R. J., Hanges, P. J., Javidan, M., Dorfman, P. W., & Gupta, V. (Eds.). (2004). *Culture, leadership, and organizations: The GLOBE study of 62 societies.* Thousand Oaks, CA: Sage Publications.

House, R. J., & Mitchell, T. R. (1974). Path-goal theory of leadership. *Contemporary Business, 3,* 81–98.

Hovorka-Mead, A. D., Ross, W. H., Whipple, T., & Renchin, M. B. (2002). Watching the detectives: Seasonal student employee reactions to electronic monitoring with and without advance notification. *Personnel Psychology, 55*(2), 329–362.

Huang, X., & Van de Vliert, E. (2003). Where intrinsic job satisfaction fails to work: National moderators of intrinsic motivation. *Journal of Organizational Behavior, 24,* 159–179.

Huang, X., & Van de Vliert, E. (2004). Job level and national culture as roots of job satisfaction. *Applied Psychology: An International Review, 53,* 329–348.

Hugick, L., & Leonard, J. (1991). Job dissatisfaction grows; "moonlighting" on the rise. *Gallop Poll News Service, 56,* 1–11.

Hulin, C. L. (1991). Adaptation, commitment, and persistence in organizations. In M. D. Dunnette, & L. M. Hough (Eds.), *Handbook of industrial and organizational psychology* (2nd ed., Vol. 2, pp. 445–505). Palo Alto, CA: Consulting Psychologists Press.

Hunter, J. E., Schmidt, F. L., & Huy, L. (2006). Implications of direct and indirect range restriction for meta-analyis methods and findings. *Journal of Applied Psychology, 91,* 594–612.

Hunter, J. E., Schmidt, F. L., & Judiesch, M. K. (1990). Individual differences in output variability as a function of job complexity. *Journal of Applied Psychology, 75,* 28–42.

Hurrell, J. J., Jr. (1995). Commentary: Police work, occupational stress, and individual coping. *Journal of Organizational Behavior, 16,* 27–28.

Iacocca, L. (1984). *Iacocca: An autobiography.* New York: Bantam Books.

Iaffaldano, M. T., & Muchinsky, P. M. (1985). Job satisfaction and job performance:

A meta-analysis. *Psychological Bulletin, 97,* 251–273.

Ilgen, D. R., & Davis, C. A. (2000). Bearing bad news: Reaction to negative performance feedback. *Applied Psychology: An International Review, 49,* 550–565.

Ilgen, D. R., Hollenbeck, J. R., Johnson, M., & Jundt, D. (2005). Teams in organizations: From input-process-output models to IMOI models. *Annual Review of Psychology, 56,* 517–543.

Ilgen, D. R., Mitchell, T. R., & Frederickson, J. W. (1981). Poor performers: Supervisors' and subordinates' responses. *Organizational Behavior and Human Performance, 27,* 386–410.

Ilies, R., & Judge, T. A. (2003). On the heritability of job satisfaction: The mediating role of personality. *Journal of Applied Psychology, 88,* 750–759.

International Telework Association and Council. (2001). Telework America report. Retrieved November 20, 2007, from http://www.workingfromanywhere.org/telework/twa2001.htm.

Ironson, G. H., Smith, P. C., Brannick, M. T., Gibson, W. M., & Paul, K. B. (1989). Constitution of a job in general scale: A comparison of global, composite, and specific measures. *Journal of Applied Psychology, 74,* 193–200.

Ivancevich, J. M., & Matteson, M. T. (1980). *Stress and work: A managerial perspective.* Glenview, IL: Scott, Foresman.

Ivancevich, J. M., Schweiger, D. M., & Power, F. R. (1987). Strategies for managing human resources during mergers and acquisitions. *Human Resource Planning, 10,* 19–35.

Jackofsky, E. F. (1984). Turnover and performance: An integrated process model. *Academy of Management Review, 9,* 74–83.

Jackson, S. E., & Schuler, R. S. (1985). A meta-analysis and conceptual critique of research on role ambiguity and role conflict in work settings. *Organizational Behavior and Human Decision Processes, 36,* 16–78.

Jackson, S. E., Stone, V. A., & Alvarez, E. B. (1992). Socialization amidst diversity: The impact of demographics on work team oldtimers and newcomers. In L. L. Cummings & B. M. Staw (Eds.), *Research in organizational behavior* (Vol. 15, pp. 45–109). Greenwich, CT: JAI Press.

James, L. R., & Brett, J. (1984). Mediators, moderators, and tests for mediation. *Journal of Applied Psychology, 69,* 307–321.

James, L. R., Demaree, R. G., & Wolf, G. (1984). Estimating within-group interrater reliability with and without response bias. *Journal of Applied Psychology, 69,* 85–98.

James, L. R., & Jones, A. P. (1974). Organizational climate: A review of theory and research. *Psychological Bulletin, 81,* 1096–1112.

James, L. R., Mulaik, S., & Brett, J. (1982). *Causal analysis: Assumptions, models, and data.* Beverly Hills, CA: Sage.

Janis, I. L. (1982). *Groupthink: Psychological studies of policy decisions and fiascos* (2nd ed.). Boston: Houghton Mifflin.

Janson, N. (1994). *Safety culture: A study of permanent way staff at British Rail*. Amsterdam: Vrije University.

Jarzabkowski, P., & Searle, R. H. (2004). Harnessing diversity and collective action in the top management team. *Long Range Planning, 37,* 399–419.

Jaskyte, K. (2005). The impact of organizational socialization tactics on role ambiguity and role conflict of newly hired social workers. *Administration in Social Work, 29*(4), 69–87.

Jeanneret, P. R. (1991). Growth trends in I/O psychology. *Industrial-Organizational Psychologist, 29,* 47–52.

Jehn, K. A. (1994). Enhancing effectiveness: An investigation of advantages and disadvantages of value-based intragroup conflict. *International Journal of Conflict Management, 5,* 223–238.

Jenkins, G. D., Jr., Mitra, A., Gupta, N., & Shaw, J. D. (1998). Are financial incentives related to performance? A meta-analytic review of empirical research. *Journal of Applied Psychology, 83,* 777–787.

Jex, S. M. (1991). The psychological benefit of exercise in work settings: A review, critique, and alternative model. *Work and Stress, 5,* 133–147.

Jex, S. M. (1998). *Stress and job performance: Theory, research, and implications for managerial practice*. Thousand Oaks, CA: Sage.

Jex, S. M., Adams, G. A., Bachrach, D. G., & Sorenson, S. (2003). The impact of situational constraints, role stressors, and commitment on employee altruism. *Journal of Occupational Health Psychology, 8*(3), 171–180.

Jex, S. M., Adams, G. A., Elacqua, T. C., & Bachrach, D. J. (1998, May). *Type A as a moderator: An examination using component measures*. Paper presented at the 1998 annual conference of the American Psychological Society, Washington, DC.

Jex, S. M., & Beehr, T. A. (1991). Emerging theoretical and methodological issues in the study of work-related stress. In G. R. Ferris & K. M. Rowland (Eds.), *Research in personnel and human resources management* (Vol. 9, pp. 311–364). Greenwich, CT: JAI Press.

Jex, S. M., Beehr, T. A., & Roberts, C. K. (1992). The meaning of occupational "stress" items to survey respondents. *Journal of Applied Psychology, 77,* 623–628.

Jex, S. M., & Bliese, P. D. (1999). Efficacy beliefs as a moderator of the impact of work-related stressors: A multilevel study. *Journal of Applied Psychology, 84,* 349–361.

Jex, S. M., & Elacqua, T. C. (1999). Self-esteem as a moderator: A comparison of global and organization-based measures. *Journal of Occupational and Organizational Psychology, 72,* 71–81.

Jex, S. M., & Heinisch, D. A. (1996). Assessing the relationship between exercise and employee mental health: Some methodological concerns. In J. Kerr, A. Griffiths, & T. Cox (Eds.), *Workplace health: Employee fitness and exercise* (pp. 55–67). London: Taylor & Francis.

Jex, S. M., & Spector, P. E. (1988, April). *Is social information processing a laboratory phenomenon?* Paper presented in M. Deselles (Chair), Job attitude measurement: Variations on a theme. Symposium presented at the 1988 Society for Industrial and Organizational Psychology Convention, Dallas, TX.

Jex, S. M., & Spector, P. E. (1989). The generalizability of social information processing to organizational settings: A summary of two field experiments. *Perceptual and Motor Skills, 69,* 883–893.

Jex, S. M., & Spector, P. E. (1996). The impact of negative affectivity on stressor-strain relations: A replication and extension. *Work and Stress, 10,* 36–45.

Johns, G. (1991). Substantive and methodological constraints on behavior and attitudes in organizational research. *Organizational Behavior and Human Decision Processes, 49,* 80–104.

Johns, G., & Xie, J. L. (1998). Perceptions of absence from work: People's Republic of China versus Canada. *Journal of Applied Psychology, 83,* 515–530.

Johns, G., Xie, J. L., & Fang, Y. (1992). Mediating and moderating effects in job design. *Journal of Management, 18,* 657–676.

Johnson, J. G. (1990). *Selecting ethnographic informants.* Newbury Park, CA: Sage.

Johnson, W. B., & Packer, A. H. (1987). *Workforce 2000: Work and workers for the 21st century.* Indianapolis, IN: Hudson Institute.

Jones, B., Flynn, D. M. & Kelloway, E. K. (1995). Perception of support from the organization in relation to work stress, satisfaction, and commitment. In S. L. Sauter & L. R. Murphy (Eds.), *Organizational risk factors for job stress* (pp. 41–52). Washington, DC: American Psychological Association.

Jones, E. E., & Pittman, T. S. (1982). Toward a general theory of strategic self-presentation. In J. Suls (Ed.), *Psychological perspectives on the self* (pp. 231–261). Hillsdale, NJ: Lawrence Erlbaum.

Jones, J. W., & Boye, M. W. (1992). Job stress and employee counterproductivity. In J. C. Quick, J. J. Hurrell, & L. R. Murphy (Eds.), *Stress and well-being at work* (pp. 239–251). Washington, DC: American Psychological Association.

Jonsson, D., Rosengren, A., Dotevall, A., Lappas, G., & och Wilhelmensen, L. (1999). Job control, job demands, and social support at work in relation to cardiovascular disease risk factors in MONICA 1995, Goteborg. *Journal of Cardiovascular Risk, 6,* 379–385.

Jordan, M., Herriot, P., & Chalmers, C. (1991). Testing Schneider's ASA theory.

Applied Psychology: An International Review. 40, 47–54.

Joshi, A., Liao, H., & Jackson, S. E. (2006). Cross-level effects of workplace diversity on sales performance and pay. *Academy of Management, 49*(3), 459–481.

Joyce, W. F. (1986). Matrix organization: A social experiment. *Academy of Management Journal, 29,* 536–561.

Judge, T. A., Bono, J. E., Eriz, A., & Locke, E. A. (2005). Core self-evaluations and job and life satisfaction: The role of self-concordance and goal attainment. *Journal of Applied Psychology, 90,* 257–268.

Judge, T. A., & Cable, D. M. (1997). Applicant personality, organizational culture, and organizational attraction. *Personnel Psychology, 50,* 359–394.

Judge, T. A., & Colquitt, J. A. (2004). Organizational justice and stress: The mediating role of work-family conflict. *Journal of Applied Psychology, 89*(3), 395–404.

Judge, T. A., Heller, D., & Mount, M. K. (2002). Five-factor model of personality and job satisfaction: A meta-analysis. *Journal of Applied Psychology, 3,* 530–541.

Judge, T. A., & Piccolo, R. F. (2004). Transformational and transactional leadership: A meta-analytic test of their relative validity. *Journal of Applied Psychology, 89,* 755–768.

Judge, T. A., Piccolo, R. F., & Ilies, R. (2004). The forgotten ones? The validity of consideration and initiating structure in leadership research. *Journal of Applied Psychology, 89,* 36–51.

Judge, T. A., Scott, B. A., & Ilies, R. (2006). Hostility, job attitudes, and workplace deviance: Test of a multilevel model. *Journal of Applied Psychology, 91*(1), 126–138.

Judge, T. A., Thoresen, C. J., Bono, J. E., & Patton, G. K. (2001). The job satisfaction-job performance relationship: A qualitative and quantitative review. *Psychological Bulletin, 127,* 376–407.

Judge, T. A., Van Vianen, A. E. M., & De Pater, I. E. (2004). Emotional stability, core self-evaluations, and job outcomes: A review of the evidence and an agenda for future research. *Human Performance, 17,* 325–346.

Kahn, R. L. & Byosiere, P. (1992). Stress in organizations. In M. D. Dunnette & L. M. Hough (Eds.), *Handbook of industrial and organizational psychology* (2nd ed., Vol. 2, pp. 571–650). Palo Alto, CA: Consulting Psychologists Press.

Kahn, R. L., Wolfe, D. M., Quinn, R. P., Snoek, J. D., & Rosenthal, R. A. (1964). *Organizational stress: Studies in role conflict and ambiguity.* New York: Wiley.

Kammeyer-Mueller, J. D., Wanberg, C. R., Glomb, T. M., & Ahlburg, D. (2005). The role of temporal shifts in the turnover process: It's about time. *Journal of Applied Psychology, 90,* 644–658.

Kanfer, R. (1990). Motivation theory and industrial/organizational psychology. In

M. D. Dunnette & L. M. Hough (Eds.), *Handbook of industrial and organizational psychology* (2nd ed., Vol. 1, pp. 75–170). Palo Alto, CA: Consulting Psychologists Press.

Kanfer, R., Ackerman, P. L., Murtha, T. C., Dugdale, B., & Nelson, L. (1994). Goal setting, conditions of practice, and task performance: A resource allocation perspective. *Journal of Applied Psychology, 79,* 826–835.

Kanigel, R. (1997). *The one best way: Frederick Winslow Taylor and the enigma of efficiency.* New York: Viking.

Karambayya, R. (1989). *Contexts for organizational citizenship behavior: Do high performing and satisfying units have better "citizens"?* York University Working Paper, North York, Ontario, Canada.

Karasek, R. A. (1979). Job demands, job decision latitude, and mental strain: Implications for job redesign. *Administrative Science Quarterly, 24,* 285–308.

Karasek, R. A., Baker, D., Marxer, F., Ahlbom, A., & Theorell, T. (1981). Job decision latitude, job demands, and cardiovascular disease: A prospective study of Swedish men. *American Journal of Public Health, 71,* 694–705.

Katz, D., & Kahn, R. L. (1966). *The social psychology of organizations.* New York: Wiley.

Katz, D., & Kahn, R. L. (1978). *The social psychology of organizations* (2nd ed.). New York: Wiley.

Katzell, R. A., & Austin, J. T. (1992). From then to now: The development of industrial-organizational psychology in the United States. *Journal of Applied Psychology, 77,* 803–835.

Kauffeld, S., Jonas, E., & Grote, S. (2004). Climate for innovation: Creation and first psychometric validation of an instrument for measuring the climate for innovation in organizations. *Diagnostica, 50,* 153–164.

Keenan, A., & Newton, T. J. (1985). Stressful events, stressors and psychological strains in young professional engineers. *Journal of Occupational Behavior, 6,* 151–156.

Kelley, H. H. (1973). The process of causal attribution. *American Psychologist, 28,* 107–128.

Kelley, H. H., & Thibaut, J. W. (1978). *Interpersonal relations: A theory of interdependence.* New York: Wiley.

Kelman, H. C. (1958). Compliance, identification, and internalization: Three processes of attitude change. *Journal of Conflict Resolution, 2,* 51–60.

Kemp, C. F., Zaccaro, S. J., Jordan, M., & Flippo, S. (2004, April). *Cognitive, social, and dispositional influences on leader adaptability.* Poster presented at the 19th annual meeting of the Society for Industrial and Organizational Psychology, Dallas, TX.

Keppel, G. (1982). *Design and analysis: A researcher's handbook* (2nd ed.). Englewood Cliffs, NJ: Prentice-Hall.

Keppel, G., & Zedeck, S. (1989). *Data analysis for research designs: Analysis of variance and multiple regression/correlation approaches.* New York: Henry Holt & Company.

Kerr, J. H. (1975). On the folly of rewarding A, while hoping for B. *Academy of Management Journal, 18,* 769–783.

Kerr, J. H., & Vos, M. C. (1993). Employee fitness programs, absenteeism, and general well-being. *Work and Stress, 7,* 179–190.

Kets de Vries, M. F. R., & Miller, D. (1986). Personality, culture, and organization. *Academy of Management Review, 11,* 266–279.

Kim, T. Y., Cable, D. M., Kim, S. P. (2005). Socialization tactics, employee productivity, and person-organization fit. *Journal of Applied Psychology, 90*(2), 232–241.

King, L. A., & King, D. W. (1990). Role conflict and role ambiguity: A critical assessment of construct validity. *Psychological Bulletin, 107,* 48–64.

Kipnis, D. (1984). The use of power in organizations and interpersonal settings. *Applied Social Psychology Annual, 5,* 179–210.

Kirkman, B. L., Rosen, B., Tesluk, P. E., & Gibson, C. B. (2004). The impact of team empowerment on virtual team performance: The moderating role of face-to-face interaction. *Academy of Management Journal, 47*(2), 175–192.

Kirsch, I. (2006). Medication and suggestion in the treatment of depression. In M. D. Yapko (Ed.), *Hypnosis and treating depression: Applications in clinical practice* (pp. 271–280). New York: Routledge/Taylor & Francis Group.

Klaas, B. S. (1989). Determinants of grievance activity and the grievance system's impact on employee behavior: An integrated perspective. *Academy of Management Review, 14,* 445–458.

Klein, H. J. (1989). An integrated control theory model of work motivation. *Academy of Management Review, 14,* 150–172.

Klein, K. J. (1987). Employee stock ownership and employee attitudes: A test of three models [Monograph]. *Journal of Applied Psychology, 72,* 319–332.

Klein, K. J., Dansereau, F. J., & Hall, R. J. (1994). Levels issues in theory development, data collection, and analysis. *Academy of Management Review, 19,* 195–229.

Klein, S. M., Kraut, A. I., & Wolfson, A. (1971). Employee reactions to attitude survey feedback: A study of the impact of structure and process. *Administrative Science Quarterly, 16,* 497–514.

Koestner, R., Zuckerman, M., & Olsson, J. (1990). Attributional style, comparison focus of praise, and intrinsic motivation. *Journal of Research in Personality, 24,* 87–100.

Kohler, J. M., & Munz, D. C. (2006). Combining individual and organizational stress interventions: An organizational development approach. *Consulting Psychology Journal: Research and Practice, 58*(1), 1–12.

Kohler, S. S., & Mathieu, J. E. (1993). Individual characteristics, work perceptions, and affective reactions influences on differentiated absence criteria. *Journal of Organizational Behavior, 14,* 515–530.

Kokotovich, M., Jex, S. M., & Adams, G. A. (2000, April). *Leader-member exchange: A moderator of the stressor-satisfaction relationship.* Paper presented at the annual meeting of the Society for Industrial and Organizational Psychology, New Orleans, LA.

Komaki, J., Barwick, K. D., & Scott, L. R. (1978). A behavioral approach to occupational safety: Pinpointing and reinforcing safe performance in a food manufacturing plant. *Journal of Applied Psychology, 63,* 434–445.

Komaki, J., Heinzmann, A. T., & Lawson, L. (1980). Effective training and feedback: Component analysis of a behavioral safety program. *Journal of Applied Psychology, 65,* 261–270.

Konovsky, M. A., & Cropanzano, R. (1991). Perceived fairness of employee drug testing as a predictor of employee attitudes and health. *Journal of Applied Psychology, 76,* 698–707.

Konovsky, M. A., & Pugh, S. D. (1990). Citizenship behavior and social exchange. *Academy of Management Journal, 37,* 656–669.

Kossek, E. E., & Ozeki, C. (1998). Work-family conflict, policies, and the job-life satisfaction relationship: A review and directions for organizational behavior-human resources research. *Journal of Applied Psychology, 83,* 139–149.

Kotter, J. P., & Heskett, J. L. (1992). *Corporate culture and performance.* New York: Free Press.

Kozlowski, S. W. J. & Bell, B. S. (2003). Work groups and teams in organization. In W. C. Borman, D. R. Ilgen, & R. J. Klimoski (Eds.), *Handbook of psychology: Industrial and organizational psychology* (pp. 333–375). Hoboken, NJ: Wiley.

Kozlowski, S. W. J., Chao, G. T., Smith, E. M., & Hedlund, J. (1993). Organizational downsizing: Strategies, interventions, and research implications. In C. L. Cooper & I. T. Robertson (Eds.), *International review of industrial and organizational psychology* (Vol. 8, pp. 263–332). London: Wiley.

Kraizberg, E., Tziner, A., & Weisberg, J. (2002). Employee stock options: Are they indeed superior to other incentive compensation schemes? *Journal of Business and Psychology, 16,* 383–390.

Kraus, S. J. (1995). Attitudes and the prediction of behavior: A meta-analysis of the empirical literature. *Personality and Social Psychology Bulletin, 21,* 58–75.

Kristof, A. L. (1996). Person-organization fit: An integrative review of its conceptualization, measurement, and implications. *Personnel Psychology, 49,* 1–50.

Kuhn, R. (1988). Psychological tests reduce counterproductive acts by employees. *Assets Protection, 9,* 9–12.

Kujacic, M., & Bojovic, N. (2003). Organizational design of post corporation structure using fuzzy multicriteria decision making. *Computation & Mathematical Organizational Theory, 9,* 5–18.

Kunin, T. (1955). The construction of a new type of attitude measure. *Personnel Psychology, 8,* 65–67.

LaBianca, G., Brass, D. J., & Gray, B. (1998). Social networks and perceptions of intergroup conflict: The role of negative relationships and third parties. *Academy of Management Journal, 41,* 55–67.

Landy, F. J., & Farr, J. L. (1980). Performance rating. *Psychological Bulletin, 87,* 72–107.

Lapierre, L. M., & Allen, T. D. (2006). Work-supportive family, family-supportive supervision, use of organizational benefits, and problem-focused coping: Implications for work-family conflict and employee well-being. *Journal of Occupational Health Psychology, 11*(2), 169–181.

Latack, J. C., & Foster, L. W. (1985). Implementation of compressed work schedules: Participation and job redesign as critical factors. *Personnel Psychology, 38,* 75–92.

Latack, J. C., & Halvovic, S. J. (1992). Coping with job stress: A conceptual evaluation framework for coping measures. *Journal of Organizational Behavior, 13*(5), 479–508.

Latane, B., Williams, K., & Harkins, S. (1979). Many hands make light the work: The causes and consequences of social loafing. *Journal of Personality and Social Psychology, 37,* 822–832.

Latham, G. P., & Huber, V. L. (1992). Schedules of reinforcement: Lessons from the past and issues for the future. *Journal of Organizational Behavior Management, 12,* 125–149.

Latham, G. P., & Locke, E. A. (1991). Self-regulation through goal setting. *Organizational Behavior and Human Decision Processes, 50,* 212–247.

Latham, G. P., & Pinder, C. G. (2005). Work motivation and research at the dawn of the twenty-first century. *Annual Review of Psychology, 56,* 485–516.

Lawler, E. E. (1990). *Strategic pay: Aligning organizational strategies and pay systems.* San Francisco: Jossey-Bass.

Lawler, E. E., & Jenkins, D. G. (1992). Strategic reward systems. In M. D. Dunnette & L. M. Hough (Eds.), *Handbook of industrial and organizational psychology* (2nd ed., Vol. 3, pp. 1009–1035). Palo Alto, CA: Consulting Psychologists Press.

Lawler, E. E., Koplin, C. A., Young, T. F., & Fadem, J. A. (1968). Inequity reduction over time in an overpayment situation. *Organizational Behavior and Human Performance, 3,* 253–268.

Lawler, E. E., Mohrman, S., & Ledford, G. (1995). *Creating high performance organizations: Practices and results of, employee involvement and TQM in Fortune 1000 companies*. San Francisco: Jossey-Bass.

Lawrence, P. R., & Lorsch, J. W. (1967). *Organization and environment: Managing differentiation and integration*. Boston: Harvard Business School, Division of Research.

Lazarus, R. S. (1966). *Psychological stress and the coping process*. New York: McGraw-Hill.

Leana, C. R., & Feldman, D. D. (1992). *Coping with job loss*. New York: Lexington Books.

Leavitt, H. J. (1951). Some effects of certain communication patterns on group performance. *Journal of Abnormal and Social Psychology, 46,* 38–50.

Lee, K., Allen, N. J., Meyer, J. P., & Rhee, K. (2001). The three-component model of organizational commitment: An application to South Korea. *Applied Psychology: An International Review, 50,* 596–614.

Lee, T. W., & Mitchell, T. R. (1994). An alternative approach: The unfolding model of voluntary employee turnover. *Academy of Management Review, 19,* 51–89.

Lee, T. W., Mitchell, T. R., Holtom, B. C., McDaniel, L. S., & Hill, J. W. (1999). The unfolding model of voluntary turnover: A replication and extension. *Academy of Management Journal, 42,* 450–462.

Lee, T. W., Mitchell, T. R., Wise, L., & Fireman, S. (1996). An unfolding model of employee turnover. *Academy of Management Journal, 39,* 5–36.

Lee, T. W., Mitchell, T. R., Sablynski, C. J., Burton, J. P., & Holto, B. C. (2004). The effects of job embeddedness on organizational citizenship, job performance, volitional absences, and voluntary turnover. *Academy of Management Journal, 47,* 711–722.

Lehman, W. E., Farabee, D. J., Holcom, M. L., & Simpson, D. D. (1995). Prediction of substance use in the workplace: Unique contributions of personal background and work environment variables. *Journal of Drug Issues, 25,* 253–274.

LePine, J. A., Colquitt, J. A., & Erez, A. (2000). Adaptability to changing task contexts: Effects of general cognitive ability, conscientiousness, and openness to experience. *Personnel Psychology, 53,* 563–593.

Levin, I., & Stokes, J. P. (1989). Dispositional approach to job satisfaction: Role of negative affectivity. *Journal of Applied Psychology, 74,* 752–758.

Levine, J. M., & Moreland, R. L. (1990). Progress in small group research. In M. R. Rosenzweig & L. W. Porter (Eds.), *Annual Review of Psychology, 41,* 585–634.

Levine, J. M., Moreland, R. L., & Choi, H. S. (2001). Group socialization and newcomer innovation. In M. A. Hogg & R. S. Tindale (Eds.), *Blackwell handbook of social psychology: Group processes* (pp. 86–106). Malden, MA: Blackwell.

Levy, P. E., Cober, A. B., & Keeping, L. M. (2003). Organizational web sites: Web site style and content and determinants of organizational attraction. *International Journal of Selection and Assessment, 11,* 158–169.

Lewin, K. (1947). Frontiers in group dynamics. *Human Relations, 1,* 26–41.

Lewin, K. (1951). *Field theory in social science.* New York: Harper.

Lewis, M. (2004). *Moneyball: The art of winning an unfair game.* New York: W. W. Norton & Company.

Lickel, B., Hamilton, D. L., Wieczorkowska, G., Lewis, A., Sherman, S. J., & Uhles, A. N. (2000). Varieties of groups and the perception of group entitativity. *Journal of Personality and Social Psychology, 78,* 223–246.

Liden, R. C., & Maslyn, J. M. (1998). Multidimensionality of leader-member exchange: An empirical assessment through scale development. *Journal of Management, 24,* 43–72.

Liden, R. C., Wayne, S. J., Stilwell, D. (1993). A longitudinal study on the early development of leader-member exchanges. *Journal of Applied Psychology, 78,* 662–674.

Liebowitz, S. J., & DeMeuse, K. P. (1982). The application of team building. *Human Relations, 35,* 1–18.

Likert, R. (1961). *New patterns of management.* New York: McGraw-Hill.

Likert, R. (1967). *The human organization.* New York: McGraw-Hill.

Likert, J. G., & Araki, C. T. (1986). Managing without a boss: System 5. *LODJ, 7,* 17–20.

Lim, S., & Cortina, L. M. (2005). Interpersonal mistreatment in the workplace: The interface and impact of general incivility and sexual harassment. *Journal of Applied Psychology, 90*(3), 483–496.

Linville, P. W., Fischer, G. W., & Salovey, P. (1989). Perceived distributions of the characteristics of ingroup and outgroup members: Empirical evidence and a computer simulation. *Journal of Personality and Social Psychology, 38,* 689–703.

Liu, C. (2003). *A comparison of job stressors and job strains among employees holding comparable jobs in Western and Eastern societies.* Unpublished doctoral dissertation, University of South Florida, Tampa, FL.

Liu, C., & Spector, P. E. (2005). International and cross-cultural issues. In J. Barling, E. K. Kelloway, & M. R. Frone (Eds.), *Handbook of occupational health psychology* (pp. 487–516). Thousand Oaks, CA: Sage.

Liu, C., Spector, P. E., & Jex, S. M. (2005). The relation of job control with job strains: A comparison of multiple data sources. *Journal of Occupational and Organizational Psychology, 78*(3), 325–336.

Lievens, F., & Highhouse, S. (2003). A relation of instrumental and symbolic attributes to a company's attractiveness as an employer. *Personnel Psychology, 56,* 75–102.

Locke, E. A. (1968). Toward a theory of task motivation and incentive. *Organizational Behavior and Human Performance, 3,* 157–189.

Locke, E. A. (1976). The nature and causes of job satisfaction. In M. D. Dunnette (Ed.), *Handbook of industrial and organizational psychology* (pp. 1297–1349). Chicago: Rand McNally.

Locke, E. A. (1982). The ideas of Frederick W. Taylor: An evaluation. *Academy of Management Review, 7,* 14–24.

Locke, E. A. (1986). Generalizing from laboratory to field settings: Ecological validity or abstraction of essential elements. In E. A. Locke (Ed.), *Generalizing from laboratory to field studies* (pp. 3–9). Lexington, MA: Heath.

Locke, E. A., & Henne, D. (1986). Work motivation theories. In C. L. Cooper & I. T. Robertson (Eds.), *International review of industrial and organizational psychology 1986* (pp. 1–35). Chichester, England: Wiley.

Locke, E. A., & Latham, G. P. (1990a). *A theory of goal setting and task performance.* Englewood Cliffs, NJ: Prentice-Hall.

Locke, E. A., & Latham, G. P. (1990b). Work motivation and satisfaction: Light at the end of the tunnel. *Psychological Science, 4,* 240–246.

Locke, E. A., & Latham, G. P. (2004). What should we do about motivation theory? Six recommendations for the twenty-first century. *Academy of Management Review, 29,* 388–404.

Locke, E. A., & Latham, G. P. (2006). New directions in goal-setting theory. *Current Directions in Psychological Science, 15,* 265–268.

Lok, P., & Crawford, J. (2001). Antecedents of organizational commitment and the mediating role of job satisfaction. *Journal of Managerial Psychology, 16,* 594–613.

Long, R. G., Bowers, W. P., Barnett, T., & White, M. C. (1998). Research productivity in graduates in management: Effects of academic origin and academy affiliation. *Academy of Management Journal, 41,* 704–714.

Lord, R. G., & Hanges, P. J. (1987). A control system model of organizational motivation: Theoretical development and applied implications. *Behavioral Science, 32,* 161–178.

Lord, R. G., & Hohenfeld, J. A. (1979). Longitudinal field assessment of equity aspects on the performance of major league baseball players. *Journal of Applied Psychology, 64,* 19–26.

Louis, M. R. (1983). Organizations as culture-bearing milieux. In L. R. Pondy, P. J. Frost, G. Morgan, & T. Dandridge (Eds.),

Organizational symbolism (pp. 39–54). Greenwich, CT: JAI Press.

Louis, M. R. (1990). Acculturation in the workplace: Newcomers as lay ethnographers. In B. Schneider (Ed.), *Organizational climate and culture* (pp. 85–129). San Francisco: Jossey-Bass.

Lowin, A. (1968). Participative decision making: A model, literature critique, and prescriptions for research. *Organizational Behavior and Human Performance, 3,* 68–106.

Luthans, F., & Kreitner, R. (1985). *Organizational behavior modification and beyond: An operant and social learning approach* (2nd ed.). Glenview, IL: Scott, Foresman.

Maidani, E. A. (1991). Comparative study of Herzberg's two-factor theory of job satisfaction among public and private sectors. *Public Personnel Management, 20,* 441–448.

Majchrzak, A. (1987). Effects of management policies on unauthorized absence behavior. *Journal of Applied Behavioral Science, 23,* 501–523.

Mann, R. D. (1959). A review of the relationships between personality and performance in small groups. *Psychological Bulletin, 56,* 241–270.

Margerison, C., & Glube, R. (1979). Leadership decision-making: An empirical test of the Vroom-Yetton model. *Journal of Management Studies, 16,* 45–55.

Marks, M. A., DeChurch, L. A., Mathieu, J. E., Panzer, F. J., & Alonso, A. (2005). Teamwork in multi-team systems. *Journal of Applied Psychology, 90*(5), 964–971.

Marks, M. A., Mathieu, J. E., & Zaccaro, S. J. (2001). A temporally based framework and taxonomy of team processes. *Academy of Management Review, 26,* 356–376.

Marrow, A. J. (1969). *The practical theorist: The life and work of Kurt Lewin.* New York: Basic Books.

Martin, J. (2002). *Organizational culture: Mapping the terrain.* Thousand Oaks, CA: Sage.

Martocchio, J. J. (1994). The effects of absence culture on individual absence. *Human Relations, 47,* 243–262.

Martocchio, J. J., & Harrison, D. A. (1993). To be there or not to be there: Questions, theories, and methods in absenteeism research. *Research in Personnel and Human Resources Research, 11,* 259–329.

Maslow, A. H. (1943). A theory of human motivation. *Psychological Review, 50,* 370–396.

Mason, R. O. (2004). Lessons in organizational ethics from the Columbia disaster: Can culture be lethal? *Organizational Dynamics, 33,* 128–142.

Mathieu, J. E., & Kohler, S. S. (1990). A cross-level examination of group absence influences on individual absence. *Journal of Applied Psychology, 75,* 217–220.

Mathieu, J. E., & Zajac, D. M. (1990). A review and meta-analysis of the antecedents, correlates, and consequences of organizational commitment. *Psychological Bulletin, 108,* 171–194.

Matteson, M. T., & Ivancevich, J. M. (1987). *Controlling work stress.* San Francisco: Jossey-Bass.

May, D. R., Reed, K., Schwoerer, C. E., & Potter, P. (2004). Ergonomic office design and aging: A quasi-experimental field study of employee reactions to an ergonomics intervention program. *Journal of Occupational Health Psychology, 9*(2), 123–135.

May, D. R., & Schwoerer, C. E. (1994). Employee health by design: Using employee involvement teams in ergonomic job design. *Personnel Psychology, 47,* 861–876.

Mayo, E. (1933). *The human problems of an industrial civilization.* New York: Macmillan.

McCabe, D. M. (1988). *Corporate nonunion complaint procedures and systems: A strategic human resources management analysis.* Westport, CT: Praeger.

McCall, M. W., Jr., & Bobko, P. (1990). Research methods in the service of discovery. In M. D. Dunnette & L. M. Hough (Eds.), *Handbook of industrial and organizational psychology* (2nd ed., Vol 1, pp. 381–418). Palo Alto, CA: Consulting Psychologists Press.

McClelland, D. (1961). *The achieving society.* Princeton, NJ: Van Nostrand.

McClelland, D. (1965). Toward a theory of motive acquisition. *American Psychologist, 20,* 321–333.

McCloy, R. A., Campbell, J. P., & Cudeck, R. (1994). A confirmatory test of a model of performance determinants. *Journal of Applied Psychology, 79,* 493–505.

McDaniel, M. A., Schmidt, F. L., & Hunter, J. E. (1988). Job experience correlates of job performance. *Journal of Applied Psychology, 73,* 327–330.

McEvoy, G. M., & Cascio, W. F. (1985). Strategies for reducing employee turnover: A meta-analysis. *Journal of Applied Psychology, 70,* 342–353.

McEvoy, G. M., & Cascio, W. F. (1987). Do good or poor performers leave? A meta-analysis of the relationship between performance and turnover. *Academy of Management Journal, 30,* 744–762.

McGrath, J. E. (1964). *Social psychology: A brief introduction.* New York: Holt.

McGrath, J. E. (1990). Time matters in groups. In J. Galegher, R. E. Kraut, & C. Egido (Eds.), *Intellectual teamwork: Social and technological foundations of cooperative work* (pp. 23–61). Hillsdale, NJ: Erlbaum.

McGrath, J. E., & Beehr, T. A. (1990). Time and the stress process: Some temporal issues in the conceptualization and measurement of stress. *Stress Medicine, 6,* 93–104.

McGregor, D. (1960). *The human side of enterprise.* New York: McGraw-Hill.

McKee-Ryan, F., Song, Z., Wanberg, C. R., & Kinicki, A. J. (2005). Psychological and physical well-being during unemployment: A meta-analytic study. *Journal of Applied Psychology, 90*(1), 53–76.

McKenna, D. D., & Wright, P. M. (1992). Alternative metaphors for organizational design. In M. D. Dunnette & L. M. Hough (Eds.), *Handbook of industrial and organizational psychology* (2nd ed., Vol. 3, pp. 901–960). Palo Alto, CA: Consulting Psychologists Press.

McMahon, J. (1972). The contingency theory: Logic and method revisited. *Personnel Psychology, 25,* 697–710.

McMillan-Capehart, A. (2005). A configurational framework for diversity: Socialization and culture. *Personnel Review, 34*(4), 488–503.

McMullen, T. J. (1991). *Personality correlates of on-the-job substance use: Exploring an alternative to urinalysis.* Unpublished master's thesis, Central Michigan University, Mount Pleasant.

McNamara, R. S., Blight, J., Brigham, S., Biersteker, T., & Schandler, H. (1999). *Argument without end: In search of answers to the Vietnam tragedy.* New York: Public Affairs.

McNeely, B. L., & Meglino, B. M. (1994). The role of dispositional and situational antecedents in prosocial organizational behavior: An examination of the intended beneficiaries of prosocial behavior. *Journal of Applied Psychology, 79,* 836–844.

Meichenbaum, D. (1977). *Cognitive-behavior modification: An integrated approach.* New York: Plenum Press.

Merton, R. K. (1968). *Social theory and social structure.* New York: Free Press.

Meyer, H. H., Kay, E., & French, J. R. P., Jr. (1965). Split roles in performance appraisal. *Harvard Business Review, 43,* 123–129.

Meyer, J. P., & Allen, N. J. (1991). A three-component conceptualization of organizational commitment. *Human Resource Management Review, 1,* 61–89.

Meyer, J. P., & Allen, N. J. (1997). *Commitment in the workplace: Theory, research, and application.* Thousand Oaks, CA: Sage.

Michaels, C. E., & Spector, P. E. (1982). Causes of employee turnover: A test of the Mobley, Griffeth, Hand, and Meglino model. *Journal of Applied Psychology, 67,* 53–59.

Miles, R. H. (1980). *Macro organizational behavior.* Glenview, IL: Scott, Foresman.

Milgram, S. (1974). *Obedience to authority.* New York: Harper & Row.

Milkovich, G. T., & Newman, J. (1990). *Compensation.* Homewood, IL: Irwin.

Miller, V. D., & Jablin, F. M. (1991). Information seeking during organizational entry: Influences, tactics, and a model of the process. *Academy of Management Review, 16,* 92–120.

Milliken, F. J., Martins, L. L., & Morgan, H. (1998). Explaining organizational responsiveness to work-family issues: The role of human resource executives as interpreters. *Academy of Management Journal, 41*, 580–596.

Mirvis, P., & Seashore, S. (1979). Being ethical in organizational research. *American Psychologist, 34*, 766–780.

Mirvis, P. H. (2005). Large group interventions: Change as theater. *Journal of Applied Behavioral Science, 41*(1), 122–138.

Mitchell, T. R. (1974). Expectancy models of job satisfaction, occupational preferences and effort: A theoretical, methodological, and empirical appraisal. *Psychological Bulletin, 81*, 1053–1077.

Mitchell, T. R., Holtom, B. C., Lee, T. W., Sablynski, C. J., & Erez, M. (2001). Why people stay: Using job embeddedness to predict voluntary turnover. *Academy of Management Journal, 44*(6), 1102–1121.

Mitchell, T. R., & Kalb, L. S. (1982). Effects of job experience on supervisor attributions for a subordinate's poor performance. *Journal of Applied Psychology, 67*, 181–188.

Mitchell, T. R., & Silver, W. R. (1990). Individual and group goals when workers are interdependent: Effects on task strategy and performance. *Journal of Applied Psychology, 75*, 185–193.

Mobley, W. H. (1977). Intermediate linkages in the relationship between job satisfaction and employee turnover. *Journal of Applied Psychology, 62*, 237–240.

Mobley, W. H., Griffeth, R. W., Hand, H. H., & Meglino, B. M. (1979). Review and conceptual analysis of the employee turnover process. *Psychological Bulletin, 86*, 493–522.

Mohamed, M. A. K. (2002). Assessing determinants of departmental innovation. *Personnel Review, 31*, 620–641.

Mohrman, S. A., & Quam, K. (2000). Consulting to team-based organizations: An organizational design and learning approach. *Consulting Psychology Journal: Practice and Research, 52*, 20–35.

Mone, M. A., Mueller, G. C., & Mauland, W. (1996). The perceptions and usage of statistical power in applied psychology and management research. *Personnel Psychology, 49*, 103–120.

Mone, M. A., & Shalley, C. E. (1995). Effects of task complexity and goal specificity on change in strategy and performance over time. *Human Performance, 8*, 243–252.

Monroy, J., Jonas, H., Mathey, J., & Murphy, L. (1998). Holistic stress management at Corning, Incorporated. In M. K. Gowing, J. D. Kraft, & J. C. Quick (Eds.), *The new organizational reality: Downsizing, restructuring, and revitalization.* Washington, DC: American Psychological Association.

Moorhead, G., & Griffin, R. W. (1998). *Organizational behavior: Managing people and organizations* (5th ed.). Boston: Houghton Mifflin.

Moorman, R. H. (1991). Relationship between organizational justice and organizational citizenship behaviors: Do fairness perceptions influence employee citizenship? *Journal of Applied Psychology, 76,* 845–855.

Moreland, R. L., & Levine, J. M. (1982). Socialization in small groups: Temporal changes in individual-group relations. *Advances in Experimental Social Psychology, 15,* 137–192.

Moreno, J. L. (1953). *Who shall survive? A new approach to the problem of human inter-relations* (revised ed). Washington, DC: Nervous and Mental Disease Publishing Co.

Morgan, G. (1986). *Images of organization.* Beverly Hills, CA: Sage.

Morgeson, F. P., & Campion, M. A. (2002). Minimizing tradeoffs when redesigning work: Evidence from a longitudinal quasi-experiment. *Personnel Psychology, 55,* 589–612.

Morgeson, F. P., & Humphrey, S. E. (2006). The work design questionnaire (WDQ): Developing and validating a comprehensive measure for assessing job design and the nature of work. *Journal of Applied Psychology, 91,* 1321–1339.

Morrison, E. W. (1993). Longitudinal study of the effects of information seeking on newcomer socialization. *Journal of Applied Psychology, 78,* 173–183.

Morrison, E. W. (1994). Role definitions and organizational citizenship behavior: The importance of the employee's perspective. *Academy of Management Journal, 37,* 1543–1567.

Morrison, E. W. (2002). Newcomers' relationships: The role of social network ties during socialization. *Academy of Management Journal, 45,* 1149–1160.

Morrison, E. W., & Robinson, S. L. (1997). When employees feel betrayed: A model of how psychological contract violation develops. *Academy of Management Review, 22,* 226–256.

Moscovici, S. (1994). Three concepts: Minority, conflict, and behavioral styles. In S. Moscovici, A. Mucchi-Faina, & A. Maas (Eds.), *Minority influence* (pp. 233–251). Chicago: Nelson-Hall.

Motowidlo, S. J., Packard, J. S., & Manning, M. R. (1986). Occupational stress: Its causes and consequences for job performance. *Journal of Applied Psychology, 71,* 618–629.

Mowday, R. T., Porter, L. W., & Steers, R. M. (1982). *Organizational linkages: The psychology of commitment, absenteeism, and turnover.* San Diego, CA: Academic Press.

Mowday, R. T., Steers, R. M., & Porter, L. W. (1979). The measurement of organizational commitment. *Journal of Vocational Behavior, 14,* 224–247.

Muchinsky, P. M. (1977). A comparison of within- and across-subjects analyses of the expectancy-value model for predicting effort. *Academy of Management Journal, 20,* 154–158.

Muchinsky, P. M., & Morrow, P. C. (1980). A multidisciplinary model of employee turnover. *Journal of Vocational Behavior, 17,* 263–290.

Mudrack, P. E. (1989). Defining group cohesiveness: A legacy of confusion. *Small Group Behavior, 20,* 37–49.

Mulcahy, C. (1991). Workplace stress reaches "epidemic" proportion. *National Underwriter, 4,* 20.

Mullen, B., & Cooper, C. (1994). The relation between group cohesion and performance: An integration. *Psychological Bulletin, 115,* 210–227.

Mumford, M. D., & Licuanan, B. (2004). Leading for innovation: Conclusions, issues, and directions. *The Leadership Quarterly, 15,* 163–171.

Murphy, K. R. (1989a). Dimensions of job performance. In R. Dillion & J. W. Pelligrino (Eds.), *Testing: Theoretical and applied perspectives* (pp. 218–247). New York: Praeger.

Murphy, K. R. (1989b). Is the relationship between cognitive ability and performance stable over time? *Human Performance, 2,* 183–200.

Murphy, K. R. (1994). Toward a broad conceptualization of jobs and job performance: Impact of changes in the military environment on the structure, assessment, and prediction of job performance. In M. G. Rumsey, C. B. Walker, & J. H. Har-

ris (Eds.), *Personnel selection and classification* (pp. 85–102). Hillsdale, NJ: Erlbaum.

Murphy, K. R. (2004). Assessment in work settings. In S. N. Haynes & E. M. Heiby (Eds.), *Comprehensive handbook of psychological assessment, Vol. 3: Behavioral Assessment* (pp. 346–364). Hoboken, NJ: Wiley Publishers.

Murphy, K. R., & Cleveland, J. N. (1990). *Performance appraisal: An organizational perspective.* Boston: Allyn & Bacon.

Murphy, K. R., Thornton, G. C., III., & Reynolds, D. H. (1990). College students' attitudes toward employee drug testing programs. *Personnel Psychology, 43,* 615–631.

Murphy, L. R. (1984). Occupational stress management: A review and appraisal. *Journal of Occupational Psychology, 57,* 1–15.

Murphy, L. R. (1996). *Future directions for job stress research and practice: Expanding the focus from worker health to organizational health.* Opening keynote speech at the 2nd National Occupational Stress, Conference 1996, Brisbane, Queensland, Australia.

Murray, H. A. (1938). *Explorations in personality.* New York: Oxford University Press.

Nadler, D. A., & Tushman, M. L. (1992). Designing organizations that have good fit: A framework for understanding new architectures. In D. A. Nadler, M. Gerstein, & R. B. Shaw (Eds.), *Organizational architecture* (pp. 39–56). San Francisco: Jossey-Bass.

Nadler, D. A., & Tushman, M. L. (1997). *Competing by design: The power of organizational architecture.* New York: Oxford University Press.

Nagel, C. M. (1999). *The perception of fit within the interview process.* Unpublished master's thesis, University of Wisconsin, Oshkosh.

National Council on Compensation Insurance. (1988). *Emotional stress in the workplace: New legal rights in the eighties.* New York: Author.

National Council on Compensation Insurance. (1991). *Issues report, 1991.* Boca Raton, FL: Author.

Neal, A., & Griffin, M. A. (2006). A study of the lagged relationships among safety climate, safety motivation, safety behavior, and accidents at the individual and group levels. *Journal of Applied Psychology, 91*(4), 946–953.

Nelson, D. L., & Simmons, B. L. (2003). Deriving benefits from stressful events: The role of engagement in meaningful work and hardiness. In J. C. Quick & L. E. Tetrick (Eds.), *Handbook of occupational health psychology* (pp. 97–119). Washington, DC: American Psychological Association.

Nelson, T. D. (1993). The hierarchical organization of behavior: A useful feedback model of self-regulation. *Current Directions in Psychological Science, 2,* 121–126.

Neuman, G. A., Edwards, J. E., & Raju, N. S. (1989). Organizational development interventions: A meta-analysis of their effects on satisfaction and other attitudes. *Personnel Psychology, 42,* 461–483.

Ng, E. S. W., & Burke, R. J. (2005). Person-organization fit and the war for talent: Does diversity management make a difference. *International Journal of Human Resources Management, 16*(7), 1195–1210.

Nielsen, I. K., Jex, S. M., & Adams, G. A. (2000). Development and validation of scores on a two-dimensional workplace friendship scale. *Educational and Psychological Measurement, 60,* 628–643.

Nunnally, J. C., & Bernstein, I. H. (1994). *Psychometric theory* (3rd ed.). New York: McGraw-Hill.

O'Donnell, M. P. (1986). Definition of health promotion. Part II: Levels of programs. *American Journal of Health Promotion, 1,* 6–9.

Offermann, L. R., & Spiros, R. K. (2001). The science and practice of team development: Improving the link. *Academy of Management Journal, 44,* 376–392.

Oh, H., Chung, M. H., & Labianca, G. (2004). Group social capital and group effectiveness: The role of informal socializing ties. *Academy of Management Journal, 47*(6), 860–875.

O'Leary-Kelly, A. M., Griffin, R. W., Glew, D. J. (1996). Organization-motivated aggression: A research framework. *Academy of Management Review, 21,* 225–253.

O'Leary-Kelly, A. M., Martocchio, J. J., & Frink, D. D. (1994). A review of the influence of group goals on group performance. *Academy of Management Journal, 37,* 1285–1301.

Ones, D. S., & Viswesvaran, C. (2000). Most published authors in Journal of Applied Psychology and Personnel Psychology during the 1990s. *Industrial-Organizational Psychologist, 37,* 26–35.

Ones, D. S., Viswesvaran, C., & Schmidt, F. L. (1993). Comprehensive meta-analysis of integrity test validities: Findings and implications for personnel selection and theories of job performance. *Journal of Applied Psychology Monograph, 78,* 679–703.

O'Reilly, C. A., & Caldwell, D. (1979). Information influences as a determinant of task characteristics and job satisfaction. *Journal of Applied Psychology, 64,* 157–165.

O'Reilly, C. A., Chatman, J., & Caldwell, D. (1991). People and organizational culture: A profile comparison approach to assessing person-organization fit. *Academy of Management Journal, 34*(3), 487–516.

Organ, D. W. (1977). A reappraisal and reinterpretation of the satisfaction-causes-performance hypothesis. *Academy of Management Review, 2,* 46–53.

Organ, D. W. (1994). Organizational citizenship behavior and the good soldier. In M. G. Rumsey, C. B. Walker, & J. H. Harris (Eds.), *Personnel selection and classification* (pp. 53–67). Hillsdale, NJ: Erlbaum.

Organ, D. W., & Konovsky, M. (1989). Cognitive versus affective determinants of organizational citizenship behavior. *Journal of Applied Psychology, 74,* 157–164.

Organ, D. W., & Ryan, K. (1995). A meta-analytic review of attitudinal and dispositional predictors of organizational citizenship behavior. *Personnel Psychology, 48,* 775–802.

Ostroff, C. (1992). The relationship between satisfaction, attitudes, and performance: An organizational level analysis. *Journal of Applied Psychology, 77,* 963–974.

Ostroff, C., & Kozlowski, S. W. J. (1992). Organizational socialization as a learning process: The role of information acquisition. *Personnel Psychology, 45,* 849–874.

O'Toole, L. J., & Meier, K. J. (2003). Bureaucracy and uncertainty. In B. C. Burden (Ed.), *Uncertainty in American politics* (pp. 98–117). Cambridge, UK: Cambridge University Press.

Pacanowsky, M. E., & O'Donnell-Trujillo, N. (1983). Organizational communication as cultural performance. *Communication Monographs, 50,* 126–147.

Page, R. C., Davis, K. C., Berkow, D. N., O'Leary, E. (1989). Analysis of group process in marathon group therapy with users of illicit drugs. *Small Group Behavior, 20,* 220–227.

Parker, C. P. (1999). The impact of leaders' implicit theories of employee participation on tests of the Vroom-Yetton model. *Journal of Social Behavior and Personality, 4,* 45–61.

Parker, S., & Wall, T. (1998). *Job and work redesign: Organizing work to promote well-being and effectiveness.* Thousand Oaks, CA: Sage.

Parsons, T. (1951). *The social system.* New York: Free Press.

Paul, R. J., & Ebadi, Y. M. (1989). Leadership decision-making in a service organization: A field test of the Vroom-Yetton model. *Journal of Occupational Psychology, 62,* 201–211.

Pearlman, J. (2006). *Love me, hate me: Barry Bonds and the making of an antihero.* HarperCollins.

Peeters, M. A. G., Van Tuijl, H. F. J. M., Rutte, C. G., & Reymen, I. M. M. J. (2006). Personality and team performance: A meta-analysis. *European Journal of Personality, 20,* 377–396.

Pelletier, K. R. (1991). A review and analysis of the health and cost effective outcome studies of comprehensive health promotion and disease preventive programs. *American Journal of Health Promotion, 5,* 311–315.

Perkins, L. A., Thomas, K. M., & Taylor, G. A. (2000). Advertising and recruitment: Marketing to minorities. *Psychology & Marketing, 17*(3), 235–255.

Perlaki, I. (1994). Organizational development in Eastern Europe: Learning to build culture-specific OD theories. *Journal of Applied Behavioral Science, 30,* 297–312.

Perlman, B., McCann, L. I., & McFadden, S. H. (1999). How to land that first teaching job. In B. Perlman, L. I. McCann, and S. H. McFadden (Eds.), *Lessons learned: Practical advice for the teaching of psychology* (Vol 1. pp. 3–6). Washington, DC: The American Psychological Association.

Perrewe, P. L., & Ganster, D. C. (1989). The impact of job demands and behavioral control on experienced job stress. *Journal of Organizational Behavior, 10,* 213–229.

Peter, R., Geissler, H., & Siegrist, J. (1998). Associations of effort-reward imbalance at work and reported symptoms in difference groups of male and female public transport workers. *Stress Medicine, 14,* 175–182.

Peters, L. H., & O'Connor, E. J. (1980). Situational constraints and work outcomes: The influences of a frequently overlooked construct. *Academy of Management Review, 5,* 391–397.

Peters, L. H., & O'Connor, E. J. (1988). Measuring work obstacles: Procedures, issues, and implications. In F. D. Schoorman & B. Schneider (Eds.), *Facilitating work group effectiveness* (pp. 105–123). Lexington, MA: Lexington Books.

Peters, T. J., & Waterman, R. H. (1982). *In search of excellence: Lessons from America's best-run companies.* New York: Harper & Row.

Peterson, M., & Wilson, J. (1998). A culture-work-health model. *American Journal of Health Behavior, 22,* 378–390.

Peterson, M. F., Smith, P. B., Akande, A., Ayestaran, S., Bocher, S., Callan, V., et al. (1995). Role conflict, ambiguity, and overload: A 21-nation study. *Academy Management Journal, 38,* 429–452.

Peterson, S. J., & Luthans, F. (2006). The impact of financial and nonfinancial incentives on business-unit outcomes over time. *Journal of Applied Psychology, 91,* 156–165.

Pettigrew, A. M. (1979). On studying organizational cultures. *Administrative Science Quarterly, 24,* 570–581.

Petty, M. M., Singleton, B., & Connell, D. W. (1992). An experimental evaluation of an organizational incentive plan in the electrical utility industry. *Journal of Applied Psychology, 77,* 427–436.

Petty, R. E., & Cacioppo, J. T. (1981). *Attitudes and persuasion: Classic and contemporary approaches.* Dubuque, IA: Brown.

Piccolo, R. F., & Colquitt, J. A. (2006). Transformational leadership and job behaviors: The mediating role of core job characteristics. *Academy of Management Journal, 49,* 327–340.

Piderit, S. K. (2005). Rethinking resistance and recognizing ambivalence: A multidimensional view of attitudes toward an organizational change. *Academy of Management Review, 25*(4), 783–794.

Pierce, J. L., & Dunham, R. B. (1992). The 12-hour work day: A 48-hour, eight day week. *Academy of Management Journal, 35,* 1086–1098.

Pierce, J. L., & Newstrom, J. W. (1982). Employee responses to flexible work schedules: An inter-organization, intersystem comparison. *Journal of Management, 8,* 9–25.

Pierce, J. L., Newstrom, J. W., Dunham, R. B., & Barber, A. E. (1989). *Alternative work schedules.* Needham Heights, MA: Allyn & Bacon.

Pinder, C. C. (1998). *Work motivation in organizational behavior.* Upper Saddle River, NJ: Prentice-Hall.

Ployhart, R. E., & Hakel, M. D. (1998). The substantive nature of performance variability: Predicting interindividual differences in intraindividual performance. *Personnel Psychology, 51,* 859–901.

Ployhart, R. E., Weekly, J. A., & Baughman, K. (2006). The structure and function of human capital emergence: A multilevel examination of the attraction-selection-attrition model. *Academy of Management, 49,* 661–677.

Podsakoff, P. M. (1982). Determinants of a supervisor's use of rewards and punishments: A literature review and suggestions for further research. *Organizational Behavior and Human Performance, 29,* 58–83.

Podsakoff, P. M., Ahearne, M., & MacKenzie, S. B. (1997). Organizational citizenship behavior and the quantity and quality of work group performance. *Journal of Applied Psychology, 82,* 262–270.

Podsakoff, P. M., MacKenzie, S. B., Lee, J. Y., & Podsakoff, N. M. (2003). Common method biases in behavioral research: A critical review of the literature and recommended remedies. *Journal of Applied Psychology, 88*(5), 879–903.

Podsakoff, P. M., & Williams, L. J. (1986). The relationship between job performance and job satisfaction. In E. A. Locke (Ed.), *Generalizing from laboratory to field settings* (pp. 207–253). Lexington, MA: Heath.

Porras, J. I., & Robertson, P. J. (1992). Organizational development: Theory, practice, and research. In M. D. Dunnette & L. M. Hough (Eds.), *Handbook of industrial and organizational psychology* (2nd ed., Vol. 3, pp. 719–822). Palo Alto, CA: Consulting Psychologists Press.

Porras J. I., & Silvers, R. C. (1991). Organization development and transformation. *Annual Review of Psychology, 42,* 51–78.

Powell, C. L. (1995). *My American journey.* New York: Ballantine Books.

Powers, W. T. (1973a). Feedback: Beyond behaviorism. *Science, 179,* 351–356.

Powers, W. T. (1973b). *Behavior: The control of perception.* Chicago: Aldine.

Powers, W. T. (1978). Quantitative analysis of purposive systems: Some spadework at the foundations of scientific psychology. *Psychological Review, 85,* 417–435.

Pritchard, R. D. (1969). Equity theory as a predictor of productivity and work quality. *Psychological Bulletin, 70,* 596–610.

Pritchard, R. D. (1992). Organizational productivity. In M. D. Dunnette & L. M. Hough (Eds.), *Handbook of industrial and organizational psychology* (2nd ed., Vol. 3, pp. 443–471). Palo Alto, CA: Consulting Psychologists Press.

Puffer, S. M. (1999). Global statesman: Mikhail Gorbachev on globalization. *Academy of Management Executive, 13,* 8–14.

Pulakos, E. D. (1984). A comparison of rater training programs: Error training and accuracy training. *Journal of Applied Psychology, 69,* 581–588.

Puranam, P., Singh, H., & Zollo, M. (2006). Organizing for innovation: Managing the coordination-autonomy dilemma in technology acquisitions. *Academy of Management Journal, 49,* 268–280.

Purser, R. E., & Petranker, J. (2005). Unfreezing the future: Exploring the dynamic of time in organizational change. *Journal of Applied Behavioral Science, 41,* 182–203.

Purvanova, R. K., Bono, J. E., & Dzieweczynski, A. (2006). Transformational leadership, job characteristics, and organizational citizenship performance. *Human Performance, 19,* 1–22.

Quinones, M. A., Ford, J. K., & Teachout, M. S. (1995). The relationship between work experience and job performance: A conceptual and meta-analytic review. *Personnel Psychology, 48,* 887–910.

Rao, T. V., & Vijayalakshmi, M. (2000). Organization development in India. *Organization Development Journal, 18*, 51–63.

Rau, R. (2004). Job strain or healthy work: A question of task design. *Journal of Occupational Health Psychology, 9*(4), 322–338.

Raven, B. H. (1993). The bases of power: Origins and recent developments. *Human Relations, 49*, 227–251.

Ravisi, D., & Schultz, M. (2006). Responding to organizational identity threats: Exploring the role of organizational culture. *Academy of Management Journal, 49*, 433–458.

Reid, G. L. (1972). Job search and the effectiveness of job-finding methods. *Industrial and Labor Relations Review, 25*, 479–495.

Reilly, R. R., Brown, B., Blood, M. R., & Malatesta, C. (1981). The effect of realistic previews: A study and discussion of the literature. *Personnel Psychology, 34*, 823–834.

Renn, R. W., & Vandenberg, R. J. (1995). The critical psychological states: An underrepresented component in job characteristics model research. *Journal of Management, 21*, 279–303.

Rentsch, J. R., & Schneider, B. (1991). Expectations for postcombination organizational life: A study of responses to merger and acquisition scenarios. *Journal of Applied Social Psychology, 21*, 233–252.

Riggs, M. L., & Knight, P. A. (1994). The impact of perceived group success-failure on motivational beliefs and attitudes: A causal model. *Journal of Applied Psychology, 79*, 755–766.

Riordan, C. M., & Griffeth, R. W. (1995). The opportunity for friendship in the workplace: An underexplored construct. *Journal of Business and Psychology, 10*, 141–154.

Roberts, C. K. (1995). The role of personality in perceived free riding. Unpublished doctoral dissertation, Central Michigan University, Mount Pleasant.

Roccas, S., & Schwartz, S. H. (1993). Effects of intergroup similarity on intergroup relations. *European Journal of Social Psychology, 23*, 581–595.

Rodgers, R., & Hunter, J. E. (1991). Impact of management by objectives on organizational productivity. *Journal of Applied Psychology, 76*, 322–336.

Rokeach, M. (1973). *The nature of human values*. New York: Free Press.

Roman, P. M., & Blum, T. C. (1995). Employers. In R. H. Coombs & D. M. Ziedonis (Eds.), *Handbook on drug abuse prevention* (pp. 139–158). Boston: Allyn & Bacon.

Ronen, S. (2001). Self-actualization versus collectualization: Implications for motivation theories. In M. Erez, U. Kleinbeck, & H. Thierry (Eds.), *Work motivation in the context of a globalized economy*. Mahwah, NJ: Erlbaum.

Rosen, C., Klein, K. J., & Young, K. M. (1986). *Employee ownership in America: The equity solution*. Lexington, MA: Lexington.

Rosen, T. H. (1987). Identification of substance abusers in the workplace. *Public Personnel Management, 16*, 197–205.

Rosenthal, R. (1991). *Meta-analytic techniques for social research* (Rev. ed.). Newbury Park, CA: Sage.

Ross, L. (1977). The intuitive psychologist and his shortcomings: Distortions in the attribution process. In L. Berkowitz (Ed.), *Advances in experimental social psychology*. New York: Academic Press.

Rotter, J. B. (1966). Generalized expectancies for internal versus external control of reinforcement. *Psychological Monographs* (Entire issue, No. 609).

Rousseau, D. (1985). Issues of level in organizational research: Multi-level and cross-level perspectives. In L. L. Cummings & B. M. Staw (Eds.), *Research in organizational behavior* (Vol. 7, pp. 1–38). Greenwich, CT: JAI Press.

Runkel, P. J., & McGrath, J. E. (1972). *Research on human behavior*. New York: Holt, Reinhart and Winston.

Russo, M. V., & Harrison, N. S. (2005). Organizational design and environmental performance: Clues from the electronics industry. *Academy of Management Journal, 48,* 582–583.

Ryan, A. M., Chan, D., Ployhart, R. E., & Slade, L. A. (1999). Employee attitude surveys in a multinational organization: Considering language and culture in assessing measurement equivalence. *Personnel Psychology, 52,* 37–58.

Ryan, R. M., & Deci, E. L. (2000). Self-determination theory and the facilitation of intrinsic motivation. *American Psychologist, 55,* 68–78.

Ryan, R. M., & Deci, E. L. (2001). On happiness and human potentials: A review of research on hedonic and eudaimonic well-being. *Annual Review of Psychology, 52,* 141–166.

Rynes, S. L. (1991). Recruitment, job choice, and post hire consequences: A call for new research directions. In M. D. Dunnette & L. M. Hough (Eds.), *Handbook of industrial and organizational psychology* (2nd ed., Vol. 2, pp. 399–444). Palo Alto, CA: Consulting Psychologists Press.

Rynes S. L., Bretz, R. D., Jr. & Gerhart, B. (1991). The importance of recruitment in job choice: A different way of looking. *Personnel Psychology, 44,* 487–522.

Sackett, P. R., & Larsen, J. R., Jr. (1990). Research strategies and tactics in industrial and organizational psychology. In M. D. Dunnette & L. M. Hough (Eds.), *Handbook of industrial and organizational psychology* (2nd ed., Vol.1, pp. 419–490). Palo Alto, CA: Consulting Psychologists Press.

Salancik, G. R., & Pfeffer, J. (1977). An examination of need satisfaction models of job attitudes. *Administrative Science Quarterly, 22,* 427–456.

Salancik, G. R., & Pfeffer, J. (1978). A social information processing approach to job attitudes and task design. *Administrative Science Quarterly, 23,* 224–253.

Salas, E., Sims, D. E., & Burke, C. S. (2005). Is there a "big five" in teamwork? *Small Group Research, 36*(5), 555–599.

Sales, S. M., & House, J. (1971). Job dissatisfaction as a possible risk factor in coronary heart disease. *Journal of Chronic Diseases, 23,* 189–194.

Salvendy, G. (1978). An industrial engineering dilemma: Simplified versus enlarged jobs. In R. Muramatsu & N. A. Dudley (Eds.),. *Production and industrial systems* (pp. 965–975). London: Taylor & Francis.

Scandura T. A., & Williams, E. A. (2000). Research methodology in management: Current practices, trends, and implications for future research. *Academy of Management Journal, 43,* 1248–1264.

Scarpello, V., & Jones, F. F. (1996). Why justice matters in compensation decision making. *Journal of Organizational Behavior, 17,* 285–299.

Schacter, S. (1959). *The psychology of affiliation.* Stanford, CA: Stanford University Press.

Schaffer, B. S., & Riordan, C. M. (2003). A review of cross-cultural methodologies for organizational research: A best practice approach. *Organizational Research Methods, 6*(2), 169–215.

Schat, A. C. H., & Kelloway, K. E. (2005). Reducing the adverse consequences of workplace aggression and violence: The buffering effects of organizational support. *Journal of Occupational Health Psychology, 8*(2), 110–122.

Schaubroeck, J., Ganster, D. C., & Jones, J. R. (1998). Organization and occupation influences in the attraction-selection-attrition process. *Journal of Applied Psychology, 83,* 869–891.

Schaubroeck, J., Ganster, D. C., & Kemmerer, B. E. (1994). Job complexity, Type A behavior, and cardiovascular disorder: A prospective study. *Academy of Management Journal, 34,* 966–975.

Schaubroeck, J., Ganster, D. C., Sime, W. E., & Ditman, D. (1993). A field experiment testing supervisory role clarification. *Personnel Psychology, 46,* 1–25.

Schaubroeck, J. & Keuhn, K. (1992). Research design in industrial and organizational psychology. In C. L. Cooper and I. T. Robertson (Eds.), *International review of industrial and organizational psychology 1991* (pp. 99–121). Chichester, England: Wiley.

Schaubroeck, J., & Merritt, D. E. (1997). Divergent effects of job control on coping with work stressors: The key role of self-efficacy. *Academy of Management Journal, 40,* 738–754.

Schein, E. H. (1969). *Process consultation: Its role in organization development.* Reading, MA: Addison-Wesley.

Schein, E. H. (1983). The role of the founder in creating organizational culture. *Organizational Dynamics, Summer,* 13–28.

Schein, E. H. (1985). *Organizational culture and leadership: A dynamic view.* San Francisco: Jossey-Bass.

Schein, E. H. (1987). *Process consultation: Lessons for managers and consultants* (Vol. 2). Reading, MA: Addison-Wesley.

Schein, E. H. (1990). Organizational culture. *American Psychologist, 45,* 109–119.

Schein, E. H. (1992). *Organizational culture and leadership: A dynamic view* (2nd ed.). San Francisco: Jossey-Bass.

Schleicher, D. J., Watt, J. D., & Greguras, G. J. (2004). Reexamining the job satisfaction-performance relationship. *Journal of Applied Psychology, 89,* 165–177.

Schmidt, F. L., & Hunter, J. E. (1998). The validity and utility of selection methods in personnel psychology: Practical and theoretical implications of 85 years of research findings. *Psychological Bulletin, 124,* 262–274.

Schmidt, F. L., Hunter, J. E., & Outerbridge, A. N. (1986). The impact of job experience and ability on job knowledge, work sample performance, and supervisory ratings of performance. *Journal of Applied Psychology, 71,* 432–439.

Schminke, M., Ambrose, M. L., & Cropanzano, R. S. (2000). The effect of organizational structure on perceptions of procedural fairness. *Journal of Applied Psychology, 85,* 294–304.

Schmitt, N. S. (2004). Beyond the Big Five: In creases in understanding and practical utility. *Human Performance, 17,* 347–357.

Schneider, B. (1987). The people make the place. *Personnel Psychology, 40,* 437–454.

Schneider, B., Smith, D. B., Taylor, S., & Fleenor, J. (1998). Personality and organizations: A test of the homogeneity of personality hypothesis. *Journal of Applied Psychology, 83,* 462–470.

Schneider, B., Hanges, P. J., Smith, D. B., & Salvaggio, A. N. (2003). Which comes first: Employee attitudes or organizational financial and market performance? *Journal of Applied Psychology, 88,* 836–851.

Schneider, J., & Cook, K. (1995). Status inconsistency and gender: Combining revisited. *Special issue: Extending interaction theory. Small Group Research, 26,* 372–399.

Schopler, J., Insko, C. A., Wieselquist, J., Pemberton, M., Witcher, B., Kozar, R., Roddenberry, C., & Wildschut, T. (2001). When groups are more competitive than individuals: The domain of the discontinuity effect. *Journal of Personality and Social Psychology, 80,* 632–644.

Schriesheim, C. A., & Kerr, S. (1977). Theories and measures of leadership: A critical appraisal of current and future directions. In J. G. Hunt & L. L. Larson (Eds.), *Leadership: The cutting edge* (pp. 9–45). Carbondale: Southern Illinois University Press.

Schriescheim C. A., Tepper, B. J., & Tetrault, L. A. (1994). Least preferred coworker score, situational control, and leadership effectiveness: A meta-analysis of contingency model performance predictions. *Journal of Applied Psychology, 79,* 561–573.

Schuler, M. (2004). Management of the organizational image: A method for organizational image configuration. *Corporate Reputation Review, 7*(1), 37–53.

Schutz, W. C. (1958). *FIRO: A three-dimensional theory of interpersonal behavior.* New York: Rinehart.

Schwab, D. P. (1991). Contextual variables in employer performance-turnover relationships. *Academy of Management Journal, 34,* 966–975.

Schwartz, S. H. (1994). Are there universal aspects in the structure and content of human values?, *Journal of Social Issues, 50,* 19–45.

Schwartz, P., & Ogilvy, J. (1998). Plotting your scenarios. In L. Fahey & R. Tandall (Eds.), *Learning from the future* (pp. 57–80). New York: John Wiley.

Schweiger, D. M., & DeNisi, A. S. (1991). Communication with employees following a merger: A longitudinal field experiment. *Academy of Management Journal, 34,* 110–135.

Scott, W. R. (1990). Technology and structure: An organizational-level perspective. In P. S. Goodman & L. S. Sproull (Eds.), *Technology and organizations* (pp. 109–143). San Francisco: Jossey-Bass.

Sears, W. (1986). Winning the productivity battle: Roles and responsibilities for HRD practitioners. *Leadership & Organizational Development Journal, 7*(1), 17–20.

Seashore, S. E. (1954). *Group cohesiveness in the industrial work group.* Ann Arbor: University of Michigan Press.

Seers, A., Petty, M. M., Cashman, J. F. (1995). Team-member exchange under team and traditional management: A naturally occurring quasi-experiment. *Group and Organization Management, 20,* 18–38.

Selye, H. (1956). *The stress of life.* New York: McGraw-Hill.

Shamir, B., House, R. J., & Arthur, M. B. (1993). The motivational effect of charismatic leadership: A self-concept based theory. *Organization Science, 4,* 577–594.

Shaw, J. D., Duffy, M. K., Mitra, A., Lockhart, D. E., & Bowler, M. (2003). Reactions to merit pay increases: A longitudinal test of a signal sensitivity perspective. *Journal of Applied Psychology, 88,* 538–544.

Shaw, M. E. (1964). Communication networks. *Advances in Experimental Social Psychology, 1,* 111–147.

Shaw, M. E. (1978). Communication networks fourteen years later. In L. Berkowitz (Ed.), *Group processes.* New York: Academic Press.

Shaw, I. F., Greene, J. C., & Mark, M. M. (Eds.). (2006). *The sage handbook of evaluation.* Beverly Hills, CA: Sage.

Shea, G. P., & Guzzo, R. A. (1987). Groups as human resources. In K. M. Rowland & G. R. Ferris (Eds.), *Research in personnel and human resources management* (Vol. 5, pp. 323–356). Greenwich, CT: JAI Press.

Sheldon, K. M., & Elliot, A. J. (1998). Not all personal goals are personal: Comparing autonomous and controlled reasons for goals as predictors of effort and attainment. *Personality and Social Psychology Bulletin, 24,* 546–557.

Sheldon, K. M., & Houser-Marko, L. (2001). Self-concordance, goal attainment, and the pursuit of happiness: Can there be an upward spiral? *Journal of Personality and Social Psychology, 80,* 152–165.

Sheldon, K. M., Turban, D. B., Brown, K. G., Barrick, M. R., & Judge, T. A. (2003). Apply self-determination theory to organizational research. *Research in Personnel and Human Resources Management, 22,* 357–393.

Sherif, M. (1966). *In common predicament: Social psychology of intergroup conflict and cooperation.* Boston: Houghton Mifflin.

Sherif, M., Harvey, O. J., White, B. J., Hood, W. R., & Sherif, C. W. (1961). *Intergroup conflict and cooperation: The Robbers Cave experiment.* Norman, OK: Institute of Group Relations.

Shim, W., & Steers, R. M. (1994). *Mediating influences on the employee commitment-job performance relationship.* Unpublished manuscript.

Shperling, Z. & Shirom, A. (2005). A field experiment assessing the impact of the focused diagnosis intervention on job autonomy. *Journal of Applied Behavioral Science, 41*(2), 222–240.

Si, S. X., & Hitt, M. A. (2004). A study of organizational image resulting from international joint ventures in transitional economies. *Journal of Business Research, 57,* 1370–1377.

Siebold, G. (2006). Military group cohesion. In T. W. Britt, C. A. Castro, & A. B. Adler (Eds.), *Military life: The psychology of serving in peace and combat. Vol. 1: Military performance* (pp. 185–201). Westport, CT: Praeger Security International.

Siegrist, J. (1996). Adverse health effects of high-effort/low-reward conditions. *Journal of Occupational Health Psychology, 1,* 27–41.

Siegrist, J. (2002). Effort-reward imbalance at work and health. In P. L. Perrewe & D. C. Ganster (Eds.), *Historical and current perspectives on stress and health* (pp. 261–291). Amsterdam: JAI Elsevier.

Siegrist, J., Starke, D., Chandola, T., Godin, I., Marmot, M., Niedhammer, I., & Richard, P. (2004). The measurement of effort-reward imbalance at work: European comparisons. *Social Science & Medicine, 58,* 1483–1499.

Silvester, J., Anderson, N. R., & Patterson, F. (1999). Organizational culture change: An inter-group attributional analysis. *Journal of Occupational and Organizational Psychology, 72,* 1–23.

Since, W. D., Mitsuhashi, H., & Kirsch, D. (2006). Revisiting Burns and Salker: Formal structure and new venture performance in emerging economic sectors. *Academy of Management Journal, 49,* 121–132.

Sinclair, R. R., Tucker, J. S., Cullen, J. C., & Wright, C. (2005). Performance differences among four organizational commitment profiles. *Journal of Applied Psychology, 90,* 1280–1287.

Skibba, J. S., & Tan, J. A. (2004). Personality predictors of firefighter job performance and job satisfaction. *Applied H. R. M. Research, 9,* 39–40.

Skinner, B. F. (1971). *Beyond freedom and dignity.* New York: Knopf.

Skogstad, A., Einarsen, S., Torsheim, T., Aasland, M. S., & Hetland, H. (2007). The destructiveness of laissez-faire leadership behavior. *Journal of Occupational Health Psychology, 12,* 80–92.

Slaughter, J. E., & Zickar, M. J. (2006). A new look at the roles of insiders in the newcomer socialization process. *Group and Organization Management, 31*(2), 264–290.

Small, M. (1999). *The presidency of Richard Nixon.* Lawrence: University of Kansas Press.

Smith, B. (1996). Care and feeding of the office grapevine. *Management Review, 85,* 6.

Smith, E. R., Murphy, J., & Coats, S. (1999). Attachment to groups: Theory and measurement. *Journal of Personality and Social Psychology, 77,* 94–110.

Smith, J. C. (1993). *Understanding stress and coping.* New York: Macmillan.

Smith, P. C., Kendall, L. M., & Hulin, C. L. (1969). *Measurement of satisfaction in work and retirement.* Chicago: Rand McNally.

Soupata, L. (2005). Engaging employees in company success: The UPS approach to a winning team. *Human Resource Management, 44,* 95–98.

Sparks, K., Cooper, C., Fried, Y., & Shirom, A. (1997). The effect of hours of work on health: A meta-analytic review. *Journal of Occupational and Organizational Psychology, 70,* 391–408.

Spector, P. E. (1982). Behavior in organizations as a function of employees' locus of control. *Psychological Bulletin, 91,* 482–497.

Spector, P. E. (1985). Measurement of human service staff satisfaction: Development of Job Satisfaction Survey. *American Journal of Community Psychology, 13,* 693–713.

Spector, P. E. (1986). Perceived control by employees: A meta-analysis of studies concerning autonomy and participation at work. *Human Relations, 11,* 1005–1016.

Spector, P. E. (1987a). Interactive effects of perceived control and job stressors on affective reactions and health outcomes for clerical workers. *Work and Stress, 1,* 155–162.

Spector, P. E. (1987b). Method variance as an artifact in self-reported affect and perceptions at work: Myth or significant problem? *Journal of Applied Psychology, 72,* 438–443.

Spector, P. E. (1994). Using self-report questionnaires in OB research: A comment on the use of a controversial method. *Journal of Organizational Behavior, 15,* 385–392.

Spector, P. E. (1997a). *Job satisfaction: Application, assessment, causes, and consequences.* Thousand Oaks, CA: Sage.

Spector, P. E. (1997b). The role of frustration in anti-social behavior at work. In R. A. Giacalone & J. Greenberg (Eds.), *Anti-social behavior in the workplace* (pp. 1–17). Thousand Oaks, CA: Sage.

Spector, P. E. (2006). *Industrial and organizational psychology: Research and practice.* Australia: Wiley.

Spector, P. E., Dwyer, D. J., & Jex, S. M. (1988). Relations of job stressors to affective, health, and performance outcomes: A comparison of multiple data sources. *Journal of Applied Psychology, 73,* 11–19.

Spector, P. E., & Jex, S. M. (1991). Relations of job characteristics from multiple data sources with employee affect, absence, turnover intentions, and health. *Journal of Applied Psychology, 76,* 46–53.

Spector, P. E., & Jex, S. M. (1998). Development of four self-report measures of job stressors and strain: Interpersonal conflict at work scale, organizational constraints scale, quantitative workload inventory, and physical symptoms inventory. *Journal of Occupational Health Psychology, 3,* 356–367.

Spector, P. E. & O'Connell, B. J. (1994). The contribution of individual dispositions to the subsequent perceptions of job stressors and job strains. *Journal of Occupational and Organizational Psychology, 67,* 1–11.

Spector, P. E, Sanchez, J. I., Siu, L. O., Selgado, J., & Ma, J. (2004). Eastern versus Western control beliefs at work: An investigation of secondary control, socioinstrumental control, and work locus of control in China and the US. *Applied Psychology, 53(1),* 38–50.

Spielberger, C. D. (1979). *Preliminary manual for the state-trait personality inventory (STPI).* Unpublished paper, University of South Florida, Tampa.

Staber, U. (2004). Networking beyond organizational boundaries: The case of project organizations. *Creativity and Innovation Management, 13,* 30–40.

Stajkovic, A. D., & Luthans, F. (1997). A meta-analysis of the effects of organizational behavior modification on task performance, 1975–1995. *Academy of Management Journal, 40,* 1122–1149.

Stajkovic, A. D., & Luthans, F. (1998). Self-efficacy and work-related performance: A meta-analysis. *Psychological Bulletin, 124,* 240–261.

Stajkovic, A. D., & Luthans, F. (2003). Behavioral management and task performance in organizations: Conceptual background, meta-analysis, and test of alternative models. *Personnel Psychology, 56,* 155–194.

Staw, B. M. (1975). Attribution of the "causes" of performance: A general alternative interpretation of cross-sectional research on organizations. *Organizational Behavior and Human Performance, 13,* 414–432.

Staw, B. M., Bell, N. E., & Clausen, J. A. (1986). The dispositional approach to job attitudes: A lifetime longitudinal test. *Administrative Science Quarterly, 31,* 56–77.

Staw, B. M., & Boettger, R. D. (1990). Task revision: A neglected form of work performance. *Academy of Management Journal, 33,* 534–559.

Staw, B. M., & Ross, J. (1985). Stability in the midst of change: A dispositional approach to job attitudes. *Journal of Applied Psychology, 70,* 469–480.

Steel, R. P. (1996). Labor market dimensions as predictors of the reenlistment decisions of military personnel. *Journal of Applied Psychology, 81,* 421–428.

Steel, R. P., & Griffeth, R. W. (1989). The elusive relationship between perceived employment opportunity and turnover behavior: A methodological or conceptual artifact? *Journal of Applied Psychology, 74,* 846–854.

Steel, R. P., & Rentsch, J. R. (1995). Influence of cumulation strategies on the long-range prediction of absenteeism. *Academy of Management Journal, 6,* 1616–1634.

Steers, R. M., Mowday, R. T., & Shapiro, D. L. (2004). The future of work motivation theory. *Academy of Management Review, 29,* 379–387.

Steers, R. M., & Rhodes, S. R. (1978). Major influences on employee attendance: A process model. *Journal of Applied Psychology, 63,* 391–407.

Steil, G., & Gibbons-Carr, M. (2005). Large group scenario planning: Scenario planning with the whole system in the room. *Journal of Applied Behavioral Science, 41*(1), 15–29.

Steiner, I. D. (1972). *Group process and productivity.* New York: Academic Press.

Stevens, M. J., & Campion, M. A. (1999). Staffing work teams: Development and validation of a selection test for teamwork settings. *Journal of Management, 25,* 207–228.

Stogdill, R. M. (1948). Personal factors associated with leadership: A survey of the literature. *Journal of Psychology, 25,* 35–71.

Stone, D. L., & Kotch, D. A. (1989). Individuals' attitudes toward organizational drug testing policies and practices. *Journal of Applied Psychology, 74,* 518–521.

Storms, P. L., & Spector, P. E. (1987). Relationships of organizational frustration with reported behavioral reactions: The moderating effect of locus of control. *Journal of Occupational Psychology, 60,* 227–234.

Straus, S. G., & McGrath, J. E. (1994). Does the medium matter? The interaction of task type and technology on group performance and member reactions. *Journal of Applied Psychology, 79,* 87–97.

Strodtbeck, F. L., & Lipinski, R. M. (1985). Becoming first among equals: Moral considerations in jury foreman selection. *Journal of Personality and Social Psychology, 49,* 927–936.

Stroh, L. K., & Dennis, L. E. (1994). An interview with Madame Nguyen Minh Hoa: Vietnam's move to a market economy and the impact on women in the workplace. *Industrial-Organizational Psychologist, 31,* 37–42.

Sturman, M. C., Cheramie, R. A., & Cashen, L. H. (2005). The impact of job complexity and performance measurement on the temporal consistency, stability, and test-retest reliability of employee job performance ratings. *Journal of Applied Psychology, 90,* 269–283.

Sullivan, S. E., & Bhagat, R. S. (1992). Organizational stress, job satisfaction, and job performance: Where do we go from here? *Journal of Management, 18,* 353–374.

Sulsky, L., & Smith, C. (2005). *Work Stress.* Belmont, CA: Thomson Wadsworth.

Sundstrom, E., DeMeuse, K. P., & Futrell, D. (1990). Work teams: Applications and effectiveness. *American Psychologist, 45,* 120–133.

Sverke, M., Hellgren, J., & Naswall, K. (2002). No security: A meta-analysis and review of job insecurity and its consequences. *Journal of Occupational Health Psychology, 7*(3), 242–264.

Swanson, N. G., & Murphy, L. R. (1991). Mental health counseling in industry. In C. L. Cooper & I. T. Robertson (Eds.), *International review of industrial and organizational psychology* (pp. 265–282). New York & London: Wiley.

Sweeney, P. D., & McFarlin, D. B. (1997). Process and outcome: Gender differences in the assessment of justice. *Journal of Organizational Behavior, 18,* 83–98.

Tabachnick, B. G., & Fidell, L. S. (1983). *Using multivariate statistics.* New York: Harper & Row.

Tabachnick, B. G., & Fidell, L. S. (1996). *Using multivariate statistics* (3rd ed.). New York: Harper & Row.

Tajfel, H. (1981). *Human groups and social categories.* New York: Cambridge University Press.

Taylor, F. W. (1911). *Principles of scientific management.* New York: Harper.

Taylor, S. E. (1991). Asymmetrical effects of positive and negative events: The mobilization-minimization hypothesis. *Psychological Bulletin, 110,* 67–85.

Taylor, S. E., Klein, L. C., Lewis, B. P., Gruenewald, T. L., Gurung, R. A. R., & Updegraff, J. A. (2000). Biobehavioral responses to stress in females: Tend-and-befriend, not fight-or-flight. *Psychological Review, 107*(3), 411–429.

Teerlink, R., & Ozley, L. (2000). *More than a motorcycle: The leadership journey at*

Harley-Davidson. Boston: Harvard Business School Press.

Terpstra, D. E. (1981). Relationship between methodological rigor and reported outcomes in organization development evaluation research. *Journal of Applied Psychology, 66,* 541–543.

Tesluk, P. E., Farr, J. L., Klein, S. R. (1997). Influences of organizational culture and climate on individual creativity. *Journal of Creative Behavior, 31,* 27–41.

Tesluk, P. E., & Jacobs, R. R. (1998). Toward an integrated model of work experience. *Personnel Psychology, 51,* 321–355.

Tesluk, P. E., & Mathieu, J. E. (1999). Overcoming roadblocks to effectiveness: Incorporating management of performance barriers into models of work group effectiveness. *Journal of Applied Psychology, 84,* 200–217.

Tetrick, L. E., & Quick, J. C. (2003). Prevention at work: Public health in occupational settings. In J. C. Quick & L. E. Tetrick (Eds.). *Handbook of occupational health psychology* (pp. 3–18). Washington, DC: American Psychological Association

Tett, R. P., Jackson, D. N., Rothstein, M. (1991). Personality measures as predictors of job performance: A meta-analytic review. *Personnel Psychology, 44,* 703–742.

Tett, R. P., & Meyer, J. P. (1993). Job satisfaction, organizational commitment, turnover intention, and turnover: Path analyses based on meta-analytic findings. *Personnel Psychology, 46,* 259–293.

Theodory, G. C. (1982). The validity of Fiedler's contingency logic. *Journal of Psychology, 110,* 115–120.

Thomas, J. L., & Castro, C. A. (2003). Organizational behavior and the U.S. peacekeeper. In T. W. Britt & A. B. Adler (Eds.), *The psychology of the peacekeeper: Lessons from the field* (pp. 127–146). Westport, CT: Praeger Publishers.

Thomas, K. (1976). Conflict and conflict management. In M. D. Dunnette (Ed.), *Handbook of industrial and organizational psychology* (pp. 889–935). Chicago: Rand McNally.

Thomas, L. T., & Ganster, D. C. (1995). Impact of family-supportive work variables on work-family conflict and strain: A control theory perspective. *Journal of Applied Psychology, 80,* 6–15.

Thomas, P., McDonnell, J., McCulloch, J., While, A., Bosanquet, N., & Ferlie, E. (2005). Increasing capacity for innovation in bureaucratic primary care organizations: A whole system participatory action research project. *Annals of Family Medicine, 3,* 312–317.

Thoreson, C. J., Bradley, J. C., Bliese, P. D., & Thoreson, J. D. (2004). The big five personality traits and individual job performance growth strategies in maintenance and transitional job stages. *Journal of Applied Psychology, 89,* 835–853.

Tiegs, R. B., Tetrick, L. E., & Fried, Y. (1992). Growth need strength and context satisfaction as moderators of the relations of the job characteristics model. *Journal of Management, 18,* 575–593.

Tierney, P., Farmer, S. M., & Graen, G. B. (1999). An examination of leadership and employee creativity: The relevance of traits and relationships. *Personnel Psychology, 52,* 591–620.

Tolson, J. (2001, February 26). Founding rivalries: More like squabbling brothers than "fathers," how did they succeed. *U.S. News and World Report,* 50–55.

Tombaugh, J. R., & White, L. P. (1990). Downsizing: An empirical assessment of survivors' perceptions of a postlayoff environment. *Organization Development Journal, 8,* 32–43.

Toquam, J. L., Macaulay, J. L., Westra, C. D., Fujita, Y., & Murphy, S. E. (1997). Assessment of nuclear power plant crew performance variability. In M. T. Brannick, E. Salas, & C. Prince (Eds.), *Team performance assessment and measurement* (pp. 253–287). Mahwah, NJ: Lawrence Erlbaum Associates.

Trevino, L. K. (1992). The social effects of punishment in organizations: A justice perspective. *Academy of Management Review, 17,* 647–676.

Trevor, C. O., Gerhart, B., Boudreau, J. W. (1997). Voluntary turnover and job performance: Curvilinearity and the moderating influences of salary growth and promotions. *Journal of Applied Psychology, 82,* 44–61.

Trice, H. M., & Beyer, J. M. (1984). Studying organizational culture through rites and ceremonials. *Academy of Management Review, 9,* 653–669.

Trip, T. M., Bies, R. J., & Aquino, K. (2002). Poetic justice or petty jealousy? The aesthetics of revenge. *Organizational Behavior and Human Decision Processes, 89,* 966–984.

Trist, E. L., & Bamforth, K. W. (1951). Some social and psychological consequences of the long-wall method of coal-getting. *Human Relations, 4,* 3–38.

Trubisky, P., Ting-Toomey, S., & Lin, S. (1991). The influence of individualism collectivism and self-monitoring on conflict styles. *International Journal of Intercultural Relations, 15*(1), 65–84.

Tubre, T. C., Sifferman, J. J., & Collins, J. M. (1996, April). *Jackson and Schuler (1985) revisited: A meta-analytic review of the relationship between role stress and job performance.* Paper presented at the annual meeting of the Society for Industrial and, Organizational Psychology, San Diego, CA.

Tucker, L. A., Aldana, S., & Friedman, F. M. (1990). Cardiovascular fitness and absenteeism in 8,301 employed adults. *American Journal of Health Promotion, 5,* 140–145.

Tuckman, B. W. (1965). Developmental sequences in small groups. *Psychological Bulletin, 63,* 384–399.

Tuckman, B. W., & Jensen, M. A. C. (1977). Stages of small group development revisited. *Group and Organization Studies, 2,* 419–427.

Turner, A. N., & Lawrence, P. R. (1965). *Industrial jobs and the worker.* Cambridge, MA: Harvard University, Graduate School of Business.

Tziner, A., & Eden, D. (1985). Effects of crew composition on crew performance: does the whole equal the sum of its parts? *Journal of Applied Psychology, 70*(1), 85–93.

U.S. Bureau of Labor Statistics. (1999). *National census of fatal occupational injuries 1998.* Washington, DC: Author.

U.S. Bureau of Labor Statistics. (2004). [Online] Available at http://www.bls.gov/iif/home.html/ Accessed January 25, 2007.

U.S. Department of Health and Human Services. (2002). *National occupational research agenda: Update 2001.* Washington, DC: Author

VandenHeuvel, A., & Wooden, M. (1995). Do explanations of absenteeism differ for men and women? *Human, Relations, 48,* 1309–1329.

Van De Vliert, E., & Van Yperen, N. W. (1996). Why cross-national differences in role overload? Don't overlook ambient, temperature! *Academy of Management Journal, 39,* 986–1004.

Van Dyne, L., & LePine, J. A. (1998). Helping and voice extra-role behaviors: Evidence of construct and predictive validity. *Academy of Management Journal, 41,* 108–119.

Van Eerde, W., & Thierry, H. (1996). Vroom's expectancy models and work-related criteria: A meta-analysis. *Journal of Applied Psychology, 81,* 575–586.

Van Maanen, J. (1975). Police socialization: A longitudinal examination of job attitudes in an urban police department. *Administrative Science Quarterly, 20,* 207–228.

Van Maanen, J. (1991). The smile factory: Work at Disneyland. In P. J. Frost, L. F. Moore, M. R. Louis, C. C. Lundberg, & J. Martin (Eds.), *Reframing organizational culture* (pp. 58–76). Newbury Park, CA: Sage.

Van Maanen, J., & Schein, E. H. (1979). Toward a theory of organizational socialization. In B. M. Staw (Ed.), *Research in organizational behavior* (Vol. 1, pp. 209–264). Greenwich, CT: JAI Press.

Van Rooy, D. L., Dilchert, S., & Viswesvaran, C. (2006). Multiplying intelligences: Are general, emotional, and practical intelligences equal? In K. R. Murphy (Ed.), *A critique of emotional intelligence: What are the problems and how can they be fixed* (pp. 235–262). Mahwah, NJ: Lawrence Erlbaum Associates.

Van Rooy, D. L., & Viswesvaran, C. (2004). Emotional intelligence: A meta-analytic investigation of predictive validity and nomological net. *Journal of Vocational Behavior, 65,* 71–95.

Van Scotter, J. R., & Motowidlo, S. J. (1996). Interpersonal facilitation and job dedication as separate facets of contextual performance. *Journal of Applied Psychology, 81,* 525–531.

Van Vianen, A. E. M. (2000). Person-organization fit: The match between new-comers' and recruiters' preferences for organizational cultures. *Personnel Psychology, 53,* 113–150.

Van Vianen, A. E. M., & De Dreu, C. K. W. (2001). Personality in teams: Its relationship to social cohesion, task cohesion, and team performance. *European Journal of Work and Organizational Psychology, 10*(2), 97–120.

Vecchio, R. P. (1977). An empirical examination of the validity of Fiedler's model of leadership effectiveness. *Organizational Behavior and Human Performance, 19,* 180–206.

Vigoda-Gadot, E., & Ben-Zion, E. (2004). Bright shining stars: The mediating effect of organizational image on the relationship between work variables and army officers' intention to leave the service for a job in high-tech industry. *Public Personnel Management, 33*(2), 201–224.

Vigoda, E., & Cohen, A. (2002). Influence tactics and perceptions of organizational politics: A longitudinal study. *Journal of Business Research, 55,* 311–324.

Vigoda-Gadot, E., Vinarski-Peretz, H., Ben-Zion, E. (2003). Politics and image in the organizational landscape: An empirical examination among public sector employees. *Journal of Managerial Psychology, 18*(8), 764–787.

Villanova, P., & Roman, M. A. (1993). A meta-analytic review of situational constraints and work-related outcomes: Alternative approaches to conceptualization. *Human Resource Management Review, 3,* 147–175.

Vinokur, A. D., van Ryn, M., Gramlich, E. M., Price, R. H. (1991). Long-term follow-up and benefit-cost analysis of the Jobs program: A preventive intervention for the unemployed. *Journal of Applied Psychology, 76,* 213–219.

Visweswaran, C. (2002). Assessment of individual performance: A review of the past century and a look ahead. In N. Anderson, D. S. Ones, H. K. Sinangil, & C. Visweswaran (Eds.), *Handbook of industrial, work, and organizational psychology* (pp. 110–126). Thousand Oaks, CA: Sage.

Viteles, M. S. (1932). *Industrial psychology.* New York: Norton.

Viteles, M. S. (1953). *Motivation and morale in industry.* New York: Norton.

Vizquel, O.(with Bob Dyer). (2002). *Omar! My life on and off the field.* Cleveland, OH; Gray & Company Publishers.

von Bertalanffy, L. (1956). General systems theory. *General systems Yearbook of the Society for General Systems Theory, 1,* 1–10.

Vroom, V. H. (1964). *Work and motivation.* New York: Wiley.

Vroom, V. H. (1995). *Work and motivation* (2nd ed.). New York: Wiley.

Vroom, V. H., & Jago, A. C. (1988). *The new leadership: Managing participation in organizations.* Englewood Cliffs, NJ: Prentice-Hall.

Vroom, V. H., & Jago, A. G. (2007). The role of the situation in leadership. *American Psychologist, 62,* 17–24.

Vroom, V. H., & Yetton, P. W. (1973). *Leadership and decision making.* Pittsburgh, PA: University of Pittsburgh Press.

Wageman, R. (1996). Interdependence and group effectiveness. *Administrative Science Quarterly, 40,* 145–180.

Wageman, R., & Baker, G. (1997). Incentives and cooperation: The joint effects of task and reward interdependence on group performance. *Journal of Organizational Behavior, 18,* 139–158.

Wagman, R., Hackman, R. J., & Lehman, E. (2005). Team Diagnostic Survey: Development of an Instrument. *Journal of Applied Behavioral Science, 41*(4), 373–398.

Wagner, J. A. (1994). Participation's effect on performance and satisfaction: A reconsideration of research evidence. *Academy of Management Review, 19,* 312–330.

Wagner, J. A. (1995). Studies of individualism-collectivism: Effects on cooperation in groups. *Academy of Management Journal, 38,* 152–172.

Wagner, J. A., & Gooding, R. Z. (1987). Shared influence and organizational behavior: A meta-analysis of situational variables expected to moderate participation-outcome relationships. *Academy of Management Journal, 30,* 524–541.

Waldman, D. A., & Spangler, W. D. (1989). Putting together the pieces: A closer look at the determinants of job performance. *Human Performance, 2,* 29–59.

Wanberg, C. R. (1997). Antecedents and outcomes of coping behaviors among unemployed and reemployed individuals. *Journal of Applied Psychology, 82,* 731–744.

Wang, H., Law, K. S., Hackett, R. D., Wang, D., & Chen, Z. X (2005). Leader-member exchange as a mediator of the relationship between transformational leadership and followers' performance and organizational citizenship behavior. *Academy of Management Journal, 48,* 420–432.

Wanous, J. P. (1989). Installing realistic job previews: Ten tough choices. *Personnel Psychology, 42,* 117–134.

Wanous, J. P., Poland, T. D., Premack, S. L., Davis, K. S. (1992). The effects of met expectations on newcomer attitudes and behaviors: A review and meta-analysis. *Journal of Applied Psychology, 77,* 288–297.

Wanous, J. P., & Zwany, A. (1977). A cross-sectional test of the need hierarchy. *Organizational Behavior and Human Performance, 18,* 78–97.

Wasserman, N. (2006). Stewards, agents, and the founder discount: Executive compensation in new ventures. *Academy of Management Journal, 49,* 960–976.

Watson, D., & Clark, L. (1984). Negative affectivity: The disposition to experience aversive emotional states. *Psychological Bulletin, 96,* 465–490.

Wayne-andy, S. J., & Green-hawn, S. A. (Dec 1993). The effects of leader-member exchange on employee citizenship and impression management behavior. *Human Relations,* Vol 46(12), pp. 1431–1440.

Webb, E. J., Campbell, D. T., Schwartz, R. D., Sechrest, L., & Grove, J. B. (1981). *Nonreactive measures in the social sciences* (2nd ed.). Boston: Houghton Mifflin.

Weber, M. (1947). *The theory of social and economic organization* (A. M. Henderson & T. Parsons. Trans.). New York: Free Press.

Webster's New World Dictionary (1984). (2nd College ed.). New York: Simon & Schuster.

Weed, E. D. (1971). Job enrichment "Cleans up" at Texas Instruments. In J. R. Maher (Ed.), *Perspectives in job enrichment.* New York: Van, Nostrand.

Weiner, Y., & Vardi, Y. (1990). Relationships between organizational culture and individual motivation–A conceptual integration. *Psychological Reports, 67,* 295–306.

Weiss, D. J., Dawis, R. V., England, G. W., & Lofquist, L. H. (1967). *Manual for the Minnesota Satisfaction Questionnaire*

(Minnesota Studies in Vocational Rehabilitation. No. 22). Minneapolis: University of Minnesota.

Weiss, H. M. (1990). Learning theory and industrial and organizational psychology. In M. D. Dunnette & L. M. Hough (Eds.), *Handbook of industrial and organizational psychology* (2nd ed., Vol.1, pp. 171–222). Palo Alto, CA: Consulting Psychologists Press.

Weiss, H. M., & Shaw, J. (1979). Social influences on judgments about tasks. *Organizational Behavior and Human Performance, 24,* 126–140.

Weitz, J. (1952). A neglected concept in the study of job satisfaction. *Personnel Psychology, 5,* 201–205.

White, S., & Mitchell, T. (1979). Job enrichment versus social cues: A comparison and competitive test. *Journal of Applied Psychology, 64,* 1–9.

Whitehead, T. N. (1935). Social relationships in the factory: A study of an industrial group. *Human Factor, 9,* 381–394.

Whitehead, T. N. (1938). *The industrial worker.* Cambridge, MA: Harvard University Press.

Whitney, K. (1994). Improving group task performance: The role of group goals and group efficacy. *Human Performance, 7,* 55–78.

Whyte, G. (1998). Recasting Janis's Groupthink Model: The key role of collective efficacy in decision making fiascoes.

Organizational Behavior and Human Decision Processes, 73, 185–209.

Wickens, C. D., & Hollands, J. G. (2000). *Engineering psychology and human performance,* (3rd ed.). Upper Saddle River, NJ: Prentice-Hall.

Wildschut, T., Insko, C. A., & Gaertner, L. (2002). Intragroup social influence and intergroup competition. *Journal of Personality and Social Psychology, 82,* 975–992.

Wilkins, A. L., & Ouchi, W. G. (1983). Efficient cultures: Exploring the relationship between culture and organizational performance. *Administrative Science Quarterly, 28,* 468–481.

Williams, C. R., & Livingstone, L. P. (1994). Another look at the relationship between performance and voluntary turnover. *Academy of Management Journal, 37,* 269–298.

Williams, L. J., & Anderson, S. E. (1991). Job satisfaction and organizational commitment as predictors of organizational citizenship and in-role behavior. *Journal of Management, 17,* 601–617.

Williams, L. J., & Anderson, S. E. (1994). An alternate approach to method effects using latent variable models: Applications in organizational behavior research. *Journal of Applied Psychology, 79,* 323–331.

Williams, L. J., Cote, J. A., & Buckley, M. R. (1989). Lack of method variance in self-reported affect and perceptions at work: Reality of artifact? *Journal of Applied Psychology, 74,* 462–468.

Williams, M. L., McDaniel, M. A., & Nguyen, N. T. (2006). A meta-analysis of the antecedents and consequences of pay level satisfaction. *Journal of Applied Psychology, 91,* 392–413.

Wilson, M., Northcraft, G. B., & Neale, M. A. (1985). The perceived value of fringe benefits. *Personnel Psychology, 38,* 309–320.

Wilson, T. B. (1995). *Innovative reward systems for the changing workplace.* New York: McGraw-Hill.

Wofford, J. C., & Liska, L. Z. (1993). Path-goal theories of leadership: A meta-analysis. *Journal of Management, 19,* 857–876.

Wood, R. E. (1986). Task complexity: Definition of the construct. *Organizational Behavior and Human Decision Processes, 37,* 60–82.

Woodman, R. W., & Wayne, S. J. (1985). An investigation of positive findings bias in evaluation of organization development interventions. *Academy of Management Journal, 28,* 889–913.

Woodward, J. (1965). *Industrial organization: Theory and practice.* London: Oxford University Press.

Worchel, S., Cooper, J., Goethals, G. R., & Olson, J. M. (2000). *Social psychology.* Belmont, CA: Wadsworth.

Wright, K. B. (2005). Researching Internet-based populations: Advantages and disadvantages of online survey research, online questionnaire authoring software packages, and web survey services. *Journal of Computer-Mediated Communication, 10*(3), http://jcmc.indiana.edu/vol10/issue3/wright.html.

Wright, P. M. (1992). An examination of the relationships among monetary incentives, goal level, goal commitment, and performance. *Journal of Management, 18,* 677–693.

Wright, P. M., George, J. M., Farnsworth, S. R., & McMahan, G. (1993). Productivity and extra-role behavior: The effects of goals on spontaneous helping. *Journal of Applied Psychology, 78,* 374–381.

Xie, J. L. (1996). Karasek's model in the People's Republic of China: Effects of job demands, control, and individual differences. *Academy of Management Journal, 39,* 1594–1618.

Yen, H. R., & Niehoff, B. P. (2004). Organizational citizenship behaviors and organizational effectiveness: Examining relationships in Taiwanese banks. *Journal of Applied Social Psychology, 34,* 1617–1637.

Yoffie, D., & Bergenstein, S. (1985). Creating political advantage: The rise of corporate enterpreneurs. *California Management Review, Fall,* 124–139.

Yukl, G. (1989). *Leadership in organizations.* Englewood Cliffs, NJ: Prentice-Hall.

Yukl, G. A. (2006). *Leadership in organizations* (6th Ed.). Upper Saddle River. NJ: Pearson Prentice Hall.

Yukl, G., Kim, H., Falbe, C. M. (1996). Antecedents of influence outcomes. *Journal of Applied Psychology, 81,* 309–317.

Yukl, G., & Tracey, J. B. (1992). Consequences of influence tactics used with subordinates, peers, and the boss. *Journal of Applied Psychology, 77,* 525–535.

Yukl, G., & Van Fleet, D. D. (1992). Theory and research on leadership in organizations. In M. D. Dunnette & L. M. Hough (Eds.), *Handbook of industrial and organizational psychology* (2nd ed., Vol.2, pp. 147–197). Palo Alto, CA: Consulting Psychologists Press.

Yun, S., Faraj, S., & Sims, H. P. (2005). Contingent leadership and effectiveness of trauma resuscitation teams. *Journal of Applied Psychology, 90,* 1288–1296.

Zaccaro, S. J. (2007). Trait-based perspectives on leadership. *American Psychologist, 62,* 6–16.

Zaccaro, S. J., Blair, V., Peterson, C., & Zazanis, M. (1995). Collective efficacy. In J. E. Maddux (Ed.), *Self-efficacy, adaptation, and adjustment: Theory, research, and application* (pp. 305–328). New York: Plenum Press.

Zaccaro, S. J., Foti, R. J., & Kenney, D. A. (1991). Self-monitoring and trait-based variance in leadership: An investigation of leader flexibility across multiple group situations. *Journal of Applied Psychology, 76,* 308–315.

Zammuto, R. F. & O'Connor, E. J. (1992). Gaining advanced manufacturing technologies benefits: The role of organization design and culture. *Academy of Management Review, 17,* 701–728.

Zapf, D., Dormann, C., Frese, M. (1996). Longitudinal studies in organizational stress research: A review of the literature with reference to methodological issues. *Journal of Occupational Health Psychology, 2,* 145–169.

Zickar, M. J. (2001). Using personality inventories to identify thugs and agitators: Applied psychology's contribution to the war against labor. *Journal of Vocational Behavior, 58,* 149–164.

Zickar, M. J. (2003). Remembering Arthur Kornhauser: Industrial psychology's advocate for worker well-being. *Journal of Applied Psychology, 88,* 363–369.

Zohar, D. (2000). A group-level model of safety climate: Testing the effect of group climate on microaccidents in manufacturing jobs. *Journal of Applied Psychology, 85*(4), 587–596.

Zohar, D. (2003). Safety climate: Conceptual and measurement issues. In J. C. Quick & L. E. Tetrick (Eds.), *Handbook of occupational health psychology* (pp. 123–142). Washington, DC: American Psychological, Association.

Zweig, D., & Webster, J. (2002). Where is the line between benign and invasive?: An examination of psychological barriers to the acceptance of awareness monitoring systems. *Journal of Organizational Behavior, 23*(5), 605–633.

Author Index

A

Aagaard, A. K., 224
Aasland, M. S., 189, 190
Abelson, M. A., 179
Abraham, L. M., 141
Abramis, D. J., 211
Ackerman, P. L., 211, 248
Adams, G. A., 6, 16, 212, 213, 322
Adams, J. S., 118, 240, 242
Adkins, B., 446
Adler, A. B., 29, 205, 282
Adler, S., 139
Aguinis, H., 51
Ahearne, M., 116, 119
Ahlbom, A., 208
Ahlburg, D., 149, 159
Aiello, J. R., 171
Ajzen, I., 146, 160
Akande, A., 227, 228

Albanese, R., 213
Aldana, S., 226
Alderfer, C. P., 238, 260
Aldred, C., 199
Aldrich, H., 426
Aldrich, J., 219
Alexander, R., 107
Allen, D. G., 74, 76, 78
Allen, N. J., 89, 153, 154, 155, 156, 157, 158, 159, 160, 161, 162, 165, 182, 281, 359
Allen, R. W., 333
Allen, T. D., 224, 225
Allport, G. W., 367
Alonso, A., 401
Alutto, J. A., 16
Alvarez, E. B., 90
Amabile, T. M., 122, 124
Ambrose, M. L., 237, 243, 247, 395, 437

Anderson, N., 112
Anderson, N. R., 458
Anderson, S. E., 35, 118
Andersson, L., 190, 191, 213
Andrews, M. C., 118
Aquino, K., 243
Araki, C. T., 420
Arieli, S., 467
Armenakis, A. A., 403, 507
Arthur, M. B., 324
Arvey, R. D., 141, 299
Ashford, S. J., 247
Ashforth, B. E., 221
Athey, T. R., 477
Atkinson, J. W., 238
Aube, C., 396
Aust, B., 223
Austin, J. T., 9, 106, 237, 246
Averill, J. E., 215
Aviram, A., 219
Avolio, B. J., 194, 324, 325
Aycan, Z., 468
Ayestaran, S., 227, 228

B
Bachrach, D. G., 118, 119, 120,
    212, 215
Bagozzi, R. P., 35
Bailey, D. E., 490
Baker, D., 208
Baker, G., 393, 404, 405
Bales, R. F., 354
Bamberger, J., 506
Bamforth, K. W., 463, 476
Bandura, A. , 249, 250, 283, 386

Barber, A. E., 224
Barkema, H. G., 285
Barling, J., 188, 202, 220
Barnett, T., 124
Baron, R., 113
Baron, R. A., 37
Baron, R. M., 260
Barrett, G. V., 107
Barrett, M., 474
Barrick, M. R., 114, 115, 116, 174, 186, 254,
    255, 390, 391, 402
Bartone, P. T., 205
Barwick, K. D., 186
Bass, B. M., 305, 323, 324, 325
Bastianutti, L. M., 398
Bates, C. A., 194
Bauer, T. N., 86
Baughman, K., 106, 107, 108, 140
Baumeister, R. F., 236, 237, 340
Baysinger, B. D., 179
Beach, L. R., 183
Beard, K. M., 438
Beaubien, J. M., 386, 397, 400
Becker, H. S., 39
Becker, T. E., 155, 156
Beckhard, R., 477
Bedeian, A. G., 116, 507
Beehr, T. A., 16, 190, 199, 201, 202, 206,
    207, 209, 211, 212, 213, 222
Beer, M., 405, 477
Bell, B. S., 89, 343, 350, 376, 396, 397, 398,
    407
Bell, C. H., 223, 405, 451, 473, 475, 486
Bell, N. E., 141
Bell, P. A., 37

Bellarosa, C., 222

Bem, D. J., 139

Bemmels, B., 299

Bendoly, E., 119

Bennett, J. B., 192

Bennett, R. J., 187

Bentler, P. M., 53

Berdahl, J. L., 195

Bergenstein, S., 333

Berger, C. J., 173, 263

Berkow, D. N., 355

Berkowitz, L., 38

Bernichon, T., 247

Bernstein, I. H., 43, 133, 507

Berson, Y., 194

Bertua, C., 112

Bettencourt, L. A., 117

Bettenhausen, K., 116

Beyer, J. M., 449, 450, 451, 452

Bhagat, R. S., 201

Bialek, H., 96

Biersteker, T., 124

Bies, R. J., 243

Billingsley, K., 506, 507

Black, J. S., 247

Blair, V., 400

Blake, R. R., 369

Blakely, G. L., 118

Blau, G., 190

Bliese, P. D., 21, 51, 54, 55, 114, 318, 386, 391, 468

Blight, J., 124

Blood, M. R., 87

Blum, T. C., 191

Bobko, P., 43

Bocher, S., 227, 228

Boettger, R. D., 247

Bojovic, N., 411

Bolino, M. C., 120, 333

Bond, J. T., 217

Bono, J. E., 141, 151, 255, 256, 308, 325

Boode, G., 437, 438

Borman, W. C., 98, 171

Bosanquet, N., 127

Bouchard, T. D., Jr., 22

Bouchard, T. J., 141

Boudreau, J. W., 181

Bourrier, M., 411

Bow Bass, B. M., 194

Bowditch, J. L., 218

Bowen, D. E., 5

Bowers, D. G., 476, 495, 507, 508

Bowers, W. P., 124

Bowler, M., 276

Bowling, N. A., 190

Boyd, B. K., 286

Boye, M. W., 187

Braddy, P. W., 62, 88

Bradley, J. C., 114

Bramel, D., 13

Brannick, M. T., 35, 135, 399

Brass, D. J., 361, 365

Breaugh, J. A., 211

Brehm, J. W., 332

Breslow, L., 212

Brett, J., 50, 52

Brett, J. M., 358, 368

Bretz, R. D., Jr., 64

Bridges, W., 16, 121, 247

Brief, A. P., 117
Brigham, S., 124
Britt, T. W., 29, 205, 212, 282, 318, 391
Brockner, J., 219
Brotheridge, C., 221
Brousseau, K. R., 392
Brown, B., 87
Brown, C., 177
Brown, D. J., 65, 88, 118
Brown, J. D., 247
Brown, K. G., 254, 255
Brown, R., 363, 367
Brtek, M. D., 294
Bryant, H., 193
Buch, K., 219
Buckley, M. R., 35
Buckley, M. R., 87, 87
Buda, R., 228
Buell, P., 212
Buetell, N., 16
Buller, P. F., 474
Bullock, R. J., 508
Buono, A. F., 218
Burke, C. S., 381, 396, 397
Burke, R. J., 90
Burke, W. W., 477, 483, 484
Burns, T., 426, 429, 436
Burtt, H. E., 308
Buss, D. M., 340
Bussing, A., 189
Byosiere, P., 201
Byrk, A., 55
Byrne, D., 90, 391, 455
Byrne, J. E., 219

C
Cable, D. M., 63, 65, 78, 89, 446
Cacioppo, J. T., 329
Caldwell, D. E., 127
Caldwell, D., 139, 446, 447, 456, 469
Caldwell, M., 107
Callan, V., 227, 228
Campbell, D., 396, 399
Campbell, D. T., 23, 30, 31, 133, 342, 375, 504, 506
Campbell, J. P., 97, 98, 99, 100, 101, 103, 104, 108, 109, 110, 117, 159, 204, 476, 502
Campbell, R. J., 386
Campion, M. A., 39, 50, 138, 173, 261, 263, 289, 291, 294, 295, 296, 297, 298, 387, 388, 389, 390, 391, 403, 404, 406, 434
Cannon, W. B., 200
Caplan, R. D., 201, 208, 212
Caranikas-Walker, F., 149
Carey, A., 13
Carey, J. M., 398
Carraher, S. M., 87, 88
Carroll, G. R., 462
Carroll, S. J., 487
Carsten, J. M., 71, 149, 467
Cartwright, S., 201
Carver, C. S., 248
Cascio, W. F., 5, 60, 62, 87, 170, 180, 215
Cashen, L. H., 109
Cashman, J. F., 399
Casper, W. J., 225
Castano, E., 365
Castro, C. A., 29, 282, 318
Catano, V. M., 189

Chadwick-Jones, J., 177

Chaiken, S., 132

Chalmers, C., 65

Champoux, J. E., 261

Chan, D., 54

Chandola, T., 209

Chao, G. T., 68, 69, 85, 161

Chapman, D. S., 62, 63

Chatman, J., 66, 446, 447, 456, 469

Chattopadhyay, P., 118

Chemers, M. M., 315

Chen, G., 89

Chen, P. Y., 188, 222

Chen, T. T., 24

Chen, Z. X., 118, 325

Cheng, B. S., 41

Cheramie, R. A., 109

Cheraskin, L., 289

Cho, H. J., 456

Choi, H. S., 345, 352

Chung, M. H., 89

Cialdini, R. B., 331, 332

Clark, L., 16, 141

Clarke, S., 185, 467

Clausen, J. A., 141

Cleveland, J. N., 104, 171

Coats, S., 340

Cobb, S., 201, 212

Cober, A. B., 65, 88

Cober, R. T., 65, 88

Coch, L., 501

Cohen, A., 194, 448

Cohen, A., 335

Cohen, J., 48, 50

Cohen, P., 50

Cohen, S. G., 490

Cohen, S., 237, 340

Cohen-Charash, Y., 243

Colarelli, S. M., 116, 175

Colihan, J. P., 211

Collins, J. M., 187, 211

Colquitt, J. A., 218, 243, 299, 325, 363, 390

Condor, S., 367

Conlon, D. E., 243, 299, 363

Connell, D. W., 280

Connolly, J. J., 141

Conti, R., 122, 124

Conway, J. M., 98

Cook, K., 348

Cook, K. E., 247

Cook, T. D., 30, 31, 375, 504, 506

Cooper, C., 202, 212, 217, 342, 399

Cooper, C. L., 174, 201

Cooper, J., 189

Cooper, M. L., 192

Cooper, W. H., 398

Cooper-Hakim, A., 158, 159

Corey, P., 226

Cortina, J. M., 114

Cortina, L. M., 194

Cote, J. A., 35

Cotton, J. L., 216

Council, 224

Covin, T., 488

Cox, M. H., 226

Crampton, S. M., 35, 295

Crawford, J., 155

Cronbach, L. J., 406

Cropanzano, R., 141, 159, 193, 243, 371, 437

Crowne, D. P., 35
Crystal, G. S., 284, 285, 286, 287
Cudeck, R., 110
Cullen, J. C., 160
Cunningham, C. J. L., 67, 225

D
Dahlsten, F., 487, 508
Daily, C. M., 285
Dalton, D. R., 285
Damanpour, F., 122, 126, 423
Dansereau, F., 16, 54, 321, 427
Davidson, E., 474
Davis, C. A., 247
Davis, K. C., 355
Davis, K. S., 87
Davis, S. M., 434
Davis-Blake, A., 118, 141
Davison, J. M., 318
Dawis, R. V., 66, 135, 136
Dawson, C. R., 212
Day, A. L., 189
Day, D. V., 24, 116, 322
De Dreu, C. K. W., 390
De Hoogh, A. H. B., 308
De La Rosa, G. M., 41
de Laat, P. B., 435
De Pater, I. E., 116
Deadrick, D. L., 107
Dean, R. A., 116, 175
DeChurch, L. A., 393, 401
Deci, E. L., 254, 255
DeFrank, R. S., 199
deGuerre, D. W., 411
Demaree, R. G., 16, 55

DeMatteo, J. S., 394
DeMeuse, K. P., 488
Den Hartog, D. N., 308
DeNisi, A. S., 218
Denison, D. R., 392, 443, 447, 456, 459, 465, 466
Dennis, A. R., 398
Dennis, L. E., 16
Dentler, R. A., 345
Depret, E. F., 365
Devine, D. J., 390
Dewe, P., 174, 201
DeWitt, R. L., 219
Dickinson, J. M., 282
Dickinson, T. L., 396, 397
Dickter, D. N., 182
Diefendorff, J. M., 118
Dilchert, S., 112
Dillman, D. A., 27, 28
Dipboye, R. L., 38
Ditman, D., 23, 223, 406
Dobbins, G. H., 41
Dobson, P., 157
Donnerstein, E., 38
Dorfman, P. W., 326
Dormann, C., 156
Dotevall, A., 208
Drasgow, F., 194
Driskell, J. E., 222, 380, 391, 393, 406
DuBrin, A. J., 334
Dubrovsky, V. J., 398
Ducki, A., 223
Dudley, N. M., 114
Duffy, M. K., 276
Dugdale, B., 248

Dunham, R., 224

Dunnette, M. D., 476

Dupre, K. E., 220

Durkheim, E., 412

Dwyer, D. J., 35, 102, 137, 206, 208, 210, 284

Dyer, W. G., 369, 405

Dzieweczynski, A., 325

E

Eagly, A. H., 132

Eastman, K. K., 120

Ebadi, Y. M., 320

Eby, L. T., 394

Eden, D., 219, 390, 490

Edwards, J. E., 495, 508

Edwards, J. R., 209, 249, 294, 438

Einarsen, S., 189, 190

Ekman, P., 221

Elacqua, T. C., 51, 212

Ellickson, M. C., 138

Elliot, A. J., 255

Ellis, S., 467

Ellstrand, A. E., 285

Elsayed-Ekhouly, S. M., 228

Emerson, E., 467

England, G. W., 135, 136

Equal Employment Opportunity Commission, 194

Erez, A., 115, 116, 390

Erez, M., 72, 76, 184

Erikson, K. T., 345

Eriz, A., 255, 256

Eskew, D., 275

Evans, M. G., 261

F

Fadem, J. A., 243

Fahr, J. L., 41

Falbe, C. M., 213, 332, 364

Falkenberg, L. W., 226

Fang, Y., 261

Farabee, D. J., 192

Faraj, S., 315

Farmer, S. M., 322

Farnsworth, S. R., 247

Farr, J. L., 104, 466

Farrell, D., 177

Fayol, H., 414, 415, 416

Fedor, D. B., 87, 88

Feldman, D. C., 69, 70, 71, 72, 78, 87

Feldman, D. D., 219

Ferlie, E., 127

Ferrier, W., 475

Ferris, G. R., 138, 146, 206, 260, 284, 335

Festinger, L., 139

Fidell, L. S., 47

Fiedler, F. E., 310, 313, 314, 315

Field, H. S., 403

Field, R. H. G., 321

Finkelstein, M. A., 118

Finkelstein, S., 286, 329, 330, 455

Fireman, S., 184

Fischer, G. W., 365

Fischer, R., 368

Fishbein, M., 132

Fisher, C. D., 211

Fisher, G. G., 30

Fisk, G. M., 221

Fiske, D. W., 133

Fiske, S. T., 362, 365

Fitzgerald, L. F., 194

Flanagan, M. F., 38

Flannery, T. P., 273

Fleishman, E., 308

Flippo, S., 307

Florkowski, G. W., 279

Flynn, D. M., 211

Foley, J. R., 299

Folger, R., 243, 371

Ford, J. K., 113, 114, 173

Ford, R. N., 289

Forsyth, D. R., 213, 341, 344, 349, 350, 357, 487

Foster, L. W., 224

Foti, R. J., 307

Fowler, F. J., Jr., 27

Fox, K. E., 225

Fox, M. L., 208, 210

Fox, S., 168

Frambach, R. T., 122

Frank, L. L., 293

Frankenhaeuser, M., 202, 212

Franz, T. M., 201, 202

Frederickson, J. W., 172

French, J. R. P., 208

French, J. R. P., Jr., 170, 171, 174, 201, 205, 212, 327, 329, 501

French, W. L., 223, 405, 451, 473, 475, 486

Frese, M., 156, 204

Fried, Y., 138, 146, 202, 204, 206, 212, 217, 260, 261, 284

Friedland, N., 213

Friedman, F. M., 226

Friend, R., 13

Frink, D. D., 395

Frone, M. R., 185, 190, 191, 192

Fujita, Y., 397

Fuller, J. A., 30

Fund, S., 113

Furby, L., 406

G

Gaertner, L., 362

Gaertner, S., 6

Galbraith, J. R., 421, 422, 423, 424, 425, 427, 432, 435, 436

Galinsky, E., 217

Gallagher, D. G., 17

Gallupe, R. B., 398

Gannon, M. J., 62

Ganster, D. C., 23, 65, 204, 208, 210, 223, 225, 406

Garcia, J. E., 315

Gardner, P. D., 68, 69, 85, 161

Gardner, W. L., 325

Gavin, J. F., 495, 509

Geertz, C., 452

Geissler, H., 209

Gelade, G. A., 157

Gelfand, M. J., 194

George, J. M., 65, 116, 117, 247, 391

Gerhart, B., 64, 181, 142, 273, 274, 280, 286

Gersick, C. J. G., 354, 355, 373

Gerstner, C. R., 322

Ghosh, P., 202, 222

Gibbons-Carr, M., 477, 496

Gibson, C. B., 397, 400

Gibson, W. M., 135

Gilbert, P., 157

Giles, W. F., 403

Gilliland, S. W., 247

Gilmore, D. C., 335

Gitelson, R. R., 211

Gladstein, D., 381, 382, 389

Glew, D. J., 213

Glick, W. H., 36

Glomb, T. M., 149, 159

Glube, R., 320

Godin, I., 209

Goelzer, P., 147, 465, 466

Goethals, G. R., 189

Goff, S. J., 225

Golden, T. D., 225

Goldstein, I. L., 31, 173

Golembiewski, R. T., 506, 507

Gomez-Mejia, L. R., 285, 286, 428

Goodale, J. G., 224

Gooding, R. Z., 216

Goodman, P. S., 394

Goodwin, G. F., 391

Gordon, J., 488

Graen, G., 321, 322, 427

Gramlich, E. M., 219

Grandey, A. A., 221

Grant, D., 474

Gray, B., 361, 365

Graziano, W. G., 351

Green Hown, S. A., 322

Green, S. G., 86

Greenberg, J., 187, 189, 243

Greene, J. C., 506

Greenhalgh, T., 122

Greenhaus, J., 16

Greguras, G. J., 151

Griffeth, R. W., 3,181, 213

Griffeth, R. W., 6, 143, 149, 467

Griffin, M. A., 185

Griffin, R. W., 4, 138, 213, 223, 288, 289, 293

Griffiths, A., 202

Grimm, C., 475

Grote, S., 125

Grove, J. B., 23

Grover, S., 219

Gruber, J. E., 194

Gruenewald, T. L., 200

Gruman, J. A., 77, 89

Guion, R. M., 146, 158, 172, 173, 176

Gully, S. M., 386, 397, 400

Gundling, E., 428, 442, 453

Gupta, N., 11, 36, 220, 246, 247

Gupta, V., 326

Gurung, R. A. R., 200

Gutek, B., 194

Guzzo, R. A., 5, 277, 304, 376, 385, 386, 387, 390, 394, 432, 504, 508

Gwinner, K. P., 117

H

Haaland, S., 147, 465, 466

Hackett, R. D., 118, 146, 158, 176, 325

Hackman, J. R., 138, 177, 223, 258, 260, 263, 288, 290, 293, 294, 339, 343, 345, 346, 347, 351, 355, 360, 378, 379, 381, 383, 384, 385, 388, 390, 392, 393, 394, 396, 399, 400, 407, 419, 487, 489, 504

Hackman, R. J., 489

Haga, W., 321, 427

Haines, V. Y., 395

Hair, E. C., 351

Halbesleben, J. R. B., 476, 481

Hall, D. T., 237

Hall, R. J., 54

Hallam, G., 396, 399

Hallock, D. E., 278, 279

Halvovic, S. J., 228

Hambrick, D. C., 286

Hamilton, D. L., 342

Hammer, T. H., 175, 176

Hand, H. H., 149, 467

Handley, R., 113

Hanges, P. J., 152, 249, 326

Hannan, M. T., 462

Hansen, C. P., 185, 186

Harkins, S., 377, 380

Harris, E. F., 308

Harrison, D. A., 152, 160, 178, 182

Harrison, N. S., 411, 437

Harrison, R. V., 201, 208, 212

Harvey, O. J., 365, 367

Hatch, M. J., 459

Hatcher, L., 280

Hatton, C., 467

Hautaluoma, J. E., 477

Hays, R. B., 315

Hays, W. L., 481

Hazucha, J. F., 270, 271, 310

Hedlund, J., 219

Heinisch, D. A., 204, 206, 226

Heinzmann, A. T., 186

Heller, D., 141

Hellervik, L. W., 270, 271, 310

Hellgren, J., 219

Hellstrom, C., 122

Hellstrom, T., 122

Henkoff, R., 219

Henne, D., 237

Hennemen, R. L., 275

Henry, R., 107

Hepburn, C. G., 220

Herriot, P., 65

Hertel, G., 393

Herzberg, F., 256, 257

Heskett, J. L., 465, 466, 467

Hetland, H., 189, 190

Hewstone, M., 363

Hickson, D. J., 429, 431, 436

Higgs, A. C., 387, 388, 391, 403

Highhouse, S., 64, 65, 88, 172, 173

Hill, J. W., 184

Hirschfeld, R. R., 403

Hochschild, A. R., 177, 218, 220

Hofmann, D. A., 186, 199, 445

Hofrichter, D. A., 273

Hofstede, G., 41, 143, 442, 456

Hogan, E. A., 218

Hogan, J., 191, 192

Hogan, R., 191, 192

Hoge, T., 189

Hohenfeld, J. A., 24, 25, 243

Holcom, M. L., 192

Hollander, E. P., 349

Hollands, J. G., 184, 295

Hollenbeck, J. R., 295, 376, 381, 389

Holtom, B. C., 72, 76, 183, 184

Hom, P. W., 6, 149

Homans, G. C., 239

Hood, W. R., 365, 367
Hornstein, H. A., 411
House, J., 204
House, R. J., 310, 316, 318, 321, 323, 326
House, R. J., 324
Houser-Marko, L., 255
Hovorka-Mead, A. D., 171
Huang, X., 145, 261
Huber, V. L., 283
Hugick, L., 273
Hulin, C. L., 106, 107, 134, 137, 139, 142, 146, 180, 194, 480
Humphrey, R. H., 221
Humphrey, S. E., 296
Humphreys, L. G., 106
Hunter, J. E., 106, 112, 113, 115, 174, 182, 390, 402, 487, 508
Hurrell, J. J., Jr., 223
Huy, L., 112

I
Iacocca, L., 474
Iaffaldano, M. T., 150, 152
Ilgen, D. R., 172, 247, 295, 376, 381, 389
Ilies, R., 47, 141, 142
Incalcaterra, K. A., 386, 397, 400
Insko, C. A., 362
International Telework Association and
Interrieden, E. J., 183
Ironson, G. H., 135
Ivancevich, J. M., 199

J
Jablin, F. M., 78, 79, 81, 82, 84, 86, 161
Jackofsky, E. F., 180

Jackson, D. N., 186
Jackson, S. E., 82, 90, 145, 146, 211, 212
Jacobs, R. R., 466
Jago, A. C., 304, 315, 316, 319, 320
James, K., 141
James, L. R., 16, 50, 52, 54, 55
Jamison, R. L., 225
Janis, I. L., 346, 380, 391, 399
Janson, N., 443
Jaskyte, K., 74, 76
Javidan, M, 326
Jeanneret, P. R., 15
Jehn, K. A., 397, 401
Jenkins, D. G., 162, 220, 246, 274, 276, 278
Jenkins, G. D., Jr., 11, 36, 246, 247
Jensen, M. A. C., 351, 352
Jensen-Campbell, L. A., 351
Jette, R. D., 277, 508
Jex, S. M., 21, 24, 35, 40, 41, 51, 54, 55, 80, 102,118, 120, 137,139, 141, 145, 199, 201, 202, 204, 206, 212, 213, 215,222, 226, 284, 322, 386, 468, 507
Johns, G., 47, 106, 178, 180, 261
Johnson, J. G., 457
Johnson, J. L., 285
Johnson, M., 376, 381, 389
Johnson, W. B., 224
Johnston, J., 380, 393, 406
Jonas, E., 125
Jonas, H., 468
Jones, A. P., 16, 54, 299
Jones, B., 211
Jones, E. E., 333
Jones, F. F., 275
Jones, J. R., 65

Jones, J. W., 187
Jones, K. W., 212
Jonsson, D., 208
Jordan, M., 65, 307
Jordan, M. H., 403
Joshi, A., 386, 397, 400
Joyce, W. F., 416
Judge, T. A., 47, 65, 115, 116, 141, 142, 151, 218, 254, 255, 256, 308, 309, 323, 324, 446
Judiesch, M. K., 112
Jundt, D., 376, 381, 389
Jung, D. I., 194

K
Kacmar, C. J., 398
Kacmar, K. M., 335
Kahn, R. L., 2, 116, 119, 201, 205, 210, 211, 413, 430, 455, 482
Kalb, L. S., 172
Kamin, A. M., 118
Kammeyer-Mueller, J. D., 149, 159
Kanfer, R., 234, 237, 248
Kanungo, R. N., 468
Karambayya, R., 119
Karasek, R. A., 208, 210, 226
Katz, D., 2, 116, 119, 205, 210, 413, 430, 455, 482
Katzell, R. A., 9, 277, 508
Kauffeld, S., 125
Kay, E., 170, 171, 174
Keenan, A., 213
Keeping, L. M., 65, 88
Keinan, G., 213
Keisler, S., 398

Kelley, H. H., 171, 240
Kelloway, E. K., 211
Kelloway, K. E., 168
Kemmerer, B. E., 65
Kemp, C. F., 307
Kendall, L. M., 134
Kenney, D. A., 307
Kenny, D. A., 260
Keppel, G., 46
Kerr, J. H., 226, 272
Kerr, S., 315
Kets de Vries, M. F. R., 436
Kiernan, C., 467
Kilman, R., 488
Kim, H., 332
Kim, S. P., 89
Kim, T. Y., 89
King, D. W., 6, 211, 343
King, L. A., 6, 211, 343
Kinicki, A. J., 219
Kipnis, D., 368
Kirkman, B. L., 397, 400
Kirsch, D., 422, 426
Klein, H. J., 68, 69, 85, 161, 248, 249
Klein, K. J., 54, 278
Klein, L. C., 200
Klein, S. M., 495
Klein, S. R., 466
Knight, P. A., 386
Koestner, R., 283
Kohler, J. M., 503
Kohler, S. S., 175
Kokotovich, M., 322
Kolb, K. J., 171
Komaki, J., 186

Konovsky, M. A., 118, 159, 193

Konrad, A., 194

Konradt, U., 393

Konstans, C., 116, 175

Koopman, P. L., 308

Koplin, C. A., 243

Kossek, E. E., 6, 225

Kotch, D. A., 193

Kotter, J. P., 465, 466, 467

Kozar, R., 362

Kozlowski, S. W. J., 82, 84, 85, 86, 89, 91,
    117, 161, 219, 343, 350, 376, 396, 397,
    398, 407

Kraizberg, E., 279

Kraus, S. J., 151

Kraut, A. I., 495

Kreitner, R., 250, 383, 393

Kring, W., 204

Kristof, A. L., 5, 64, 173, 208, 209, 210, 459

Kroustalis, C. M., 62, 88

Kuhn, R., 187

Kujacic, M., 411

Kulik, C. T., 237, 247, 395

Kunin, T., 133

L

LaBianca, G., 89, 361, 365

Landau, J., 175, 176

Landis, R. S., 247

Landy, A. L., 225

Landy, F. J., 104

Lapierre, L. M., 224, 225

Lappas, G., 208

Larsen, J. R., Jr., 24

Latack, J. C., 224, 228

Latane, B., 377, 380

Latham, G. P., 246, 265, 247, 248, 250, 265,
    283

Law, K. S., 118, 325

Lawler, E. E., 162, 243, 246, 258, 272, 273,
    274, 276, 278, 280, 393

Lawrence, P. R., 258, 420, 434

Lawson, L., 186

Lazarus, R. S., 205

Leana, C. R., 219

Leary, M. R., 236, 237, 340

Leavitt, H. J., 346

Lebiecki, J. E., 114

Ledford, G. E., 5, 393

Lee, J. Y., 35

Lee, K., 157

Lee, T. W., 72, 76, 182, 183, 184, 467

Lehman, E., 489

Lehman, W. E. K., 192

Leonard, J., 273

LePine, J. A., 103, 104, 390

Levin, I., 141, 142

Levine, J. M., 343, 345, 352, 373, 376

Levy, P. E., 65, 88

Lewin, K., 478, 479, 480

Lewis, A., 342

Lewis, B. P., 200

Lewis, M., 123

Lickel, B., 342

Licuanan, B., 127

Liden, R. C., 322, 427

Liebowitz, S. J., 488

Lievens, F., 64, 65, 88

Likert, J. G., 420

Likert, R., 306, 309, 427

Lim, S., 194

Lin, S., 228

Linville, P. W., 365

Liska, L. Z., 318

Liu, C., 24, 35, 226, 228, 507

Livingstone, L. P., 180

Locke, E. A., 11, 37, 132, 138, 237, 246, 247, 255, 256, 257, 265, 375

Lockhart, D. E., 276

Lofquist, L. H., 135, 136

Lok, P., 155

Long, R. G., 124, 249

Lord, R. G., 24, 25, 243, 249

Lorsch, J. W., 420

Louis, M. R., 67, 442

Lowin, A., 216, 223

Luthans, F., 250, 273, 277, 283, 325, 383, 393

M

Ma, J., 227, 228

Macaulay, J. L., 397

MacFarlane, F., 122

MacKenzie, S. B., 35, 116, 119

Madigan, R., 107

Madison, L. W., 333

Magley, V. J., 194

Maidani, E. A., 257

Majchrzak, A., 177

Malatesta, C., 87

Mann, R. D., 307

Manning, M. R., 203

Maras, P., 363

Margerison, C., 320

Mark, M. M., 506

Marks, M. A., 389, 393 401

Marlowe, D., 35

Marmot, M., 209

Marrow, A. J., 14

Martin, J., 442

Martins, L. L., 225

Martocchio, J. J., 177, 178, 395

Marxer, F., 208

Maslow, A. H., 235, 237, 260

Maslyn, J. M., 322, 427

Mason, H., 467

Mason, L., 467

Mason, R. O., 441, 461

Massar, B., 363

Mathey, J., 468

Mathieu, J. E., 144, 146, 154, 157, 158, 159, 175, 176, 177, 389, 401

Mathieu, J. E., 394

Matteson, M. T., 199

Matthews, A., 367

Mauland, W., 50

Mausner, B., 257

May, D. R., 223, 295, 325

Mayes, B. T., 333

McCann, L. I., 73

McClelland, C. L., 261, 263, 289, 291, 298

McCulloch, J., 127

McDaniel, L. S., 184

McDaniel, M. A., 113, 138

McDonnell, J., 127

McEvoy, G. M., 87, 180

McFadden, S. H., 73

McFarlin, D. B., 243

McGrath, J. E., 38, 378, 379, 380, 381, 382, 398, 407

McGregor, D., 15, 417

McGuire, W., 96

McIntyre, R. M., 396, 397

McKee-Ryan, F., 219

McKenna, D. D., 412, 413, 478

McMahan, G. C., 247, 289, 293

McMahon, J., 315

McMullen, T. J., 191

McNamara, R. S., 124

McNeely, B. L., 117

Meade, A. W., 62, 88

Medsker, G. J., 387, 388, 389, 390, 391, 403

Meglino, B. M., 117, 149, 467

Meichenbaum, D., 222

Meier, K. J., 426

Merritt, D. E., 204, 208, 210, 227

Merton, R. K., 412

Meuter, M. L., 117

Meyer, H. H., 170, 171, 174

Meyer, J. P., 89, 149, 153, 154, 155, 156,
    157, 158, 159, 160, 161, 162, 165, 182,
    281, 359

Michaels, C. E., 149

Miles, R. H., 333

Milgram, S., 37

Milkovich, G. T., 273, 274, 280, 286

Miller, D., 436

Miller, V. D., 78, 79, 81, 82, 84,
    86, 161

Milliken, F. J., 225

Mirvis, P., 477, 479, 486

Mishra, A. K., 443, 447, 465

Mitchell, T. R., 72, 76, 172, 182, 183, 184,
    245, 316, 395, 467

Mitchell, T., 139

Mitra, A., 11, 246, 247, 276

Mitsuhashi, H., 422, 426

Mobley, W. H., 147, 149, 182, 183, 467

Mohamed, M. A. K., 127

Mohrman, S. A., 393, 432, 436

Mone, M. A., 50, 247

Monroy, J., 468

Moore, C., 195

Moore, D. M., 282

Moorhead, G., 4, 288

Moorman, R. H., 118

Moreland, R. L., 343, 345, 352, 373, 376

Moreno, J. L., 347

Morgan, G., 412

Morgan, H., 225

Morgeson, F. P., 186, 295, 296, 297, 298

Morris, C. G., 392, 489

Morrison, E. W., 69, 84, 85, 120, 121, 219,
    270

Moscovici, S., 345

Motowidlo, S. J., 102, 203

Mount, M. K., 114, 115, 116, 141, 174, 225,
    186, 390, 402

Mouton, J. S., 369

Mowday, R. T., 153, 154, 234

Muchinsky, P. M., 150, 152, 245

Mudrack, P. E., 399

Mueller, G. C., 50

Mulaik, S., 52

Mulcahy, C., 199

Mullen, B., 342, 399

Mumford, M. D., 127, 476, 481

Mumford, T. V., 296, 297, 298

Munz, D. C., 503

Murphy, J., 340

Murphy, K. R., 100, 101, 103, 104, 108, 112, 117, 171, 193
Murphy, L. R., 222, 468
Murphy, S. E., 397
Murray, H. A., 235, 238
Murray, M. A., 213
Murtha, T. C., 248

N
Nadler, D. A., 420
Nagel, C. M., 403
Nahrhang, J. D., 296, 297, 298
Naswall, K., 219
Nathan, B. R., 5
National Council on Compensation Insurance, 199
Neal, A., 185
Neale, M. A., 280
Nelson, L., 248
Nelson, T. D., 248
Neubert, M. J., 391, 402
Neuman, G. A., 495, 508
Newman, D. A., 152, 160
Newman, J. E., 16, 201, 206, 207, 209, 211
Newman, J., 280
Newstrom, J. W., 224
Newton, T. J., 213
Ng, E. S. W., 90
Ng, K. Y., 243, 299, 363
Nguyen, N. T., 138
Nicholson, N., 177
Niedhammer, I., 209
Niehoff, B. P., 119
Nielsen, I. K., 213
Northcraft, G. B., 280

Nougaim, K. E., 237
Nunamaker, J. F., Jr., 398
Nunnally, J. C., 43, 133, 507

O
O'Connell, B. J., 188
O'Connor, E. J., 105, 106, 125, 174, 215, 270, 385, 392, 428, 431
O'Donnell, M. P., 226
O'Donnell-Trujillo, N., 355
O'Driscoll, M., 174
O'Leary, E., 355
O'Leary-Kelly, A. M., 68, 69, 85, 161, 213, 395
O'Reilly, C. A., 139, 446, 447, 456, 469
O'Shea, P. G., 391
O'Toole, L. J., 426
och Wilhelmensen, L., 208
Offermann, L. R., 488
Ogilvy, J., 496
Oh, H., 89
Oldham, G. R., 18, 223, 258, 260, 263, 288, 290, 293, 294, 384, 392, 419, 487
Olson, J. M., 189
Olsson, J., 283
Ondrack, D. A., 261
Ones, D. S., 114, 124, 187, 192
O-Reilly, C. A., 127
Organ, D. W., 116, 117, 119, 120, 159
Orlikowski, B., 393
Orvis, K. A., 114
Osburn, H. K., 476, 481
Ostroff, C., 82, 84, 85, 86, 91, 117, 151, 152, 161

Ouchi, W. G., 460, 465

Outerbridge, A. N., 112, 182, 390, 402

Overmeyer-Day, L., 218

Ozeki, C., 6, 225

Ozley, L., 496, 497

P

Pacanowsky, M. E., 452

Packard, J. S., 203

Packer, A. H., 224

Page, R. C., 355

Paladino, M. P., 365

Panzer, F. J., 401

Papper, E. M., 389, 390

Parker, C. P., 321

Parker, S., 86, 108, 487

Parry, M. E., 209

Parsons, C. K., 78

Parsons, T., 412

Patterson, F., 458

Patton, G. K.,

Paul, K. B., 135

Paul, R. J., 320

Pearlman, J., 72

Pearson, C. M., 190, 191, 213

Peeters, M. A. G., 390

Pelletier, K. R., 226

Pemberton, M., 362

Penner, L. A., 118

Perkins, L. A., 90

Perlaki, I., 477

Perlman, B., 73

Perrachio, L., 504, 506

Perrewe, P. L., 208, 210

Peter, R., 209

Peters, L. H., 105, 106, 125, 174, 215, 270, 385, 392, 428

Peters, T. J., 67, 376, 420, 465

Peterson, C., 400

Peterson, M., 467, 468

Peterson, M. F., 227, 228

Peterson, S. J., 277, 283

Petranker, J., 480

Pettigrew, A. M., 441

Petty, M. M., 280, 399

Petty, R. E., 329

Pfeffer, J., 16, 118, 138, 141, 156, 263

Pheysey, D., 429, 431, 436

Phillips, J. L., 390

Piccolo, R. F., 47, 309, 323, 324, 325

Piderit, S. K., 501

Pierce, J. L., 224

Pinder, C. C., 234, 248, 250

Pinneau, S. R., 201, 212

Piotrowski, M., 115

Pittman, T. S., 333

Platten, P. E., 273

Ployhart, R. E., 106, 107, 108, 140

Podsakoff, N. M., 35

Podsakoff, P. M., 35, 47, 116, 119, 142, 150, 152, 172

Poland, T. D., 87

Polos, L., 462

Pond, S., 507

Porras, J. I., 3, 477, 484, 485, 486, 503, 504

Porter, C., 243, 299, 363

Porter, L. W., 153, 154, 333

Potter, P., 223

Powell, C. L., 92

Power, F. R., 219

Powers, W. T., 248

Premack, S. L., 87

Price, R. H., 219

Pritchard, R. D., 170

Prussia, G. E., 149

Puffer, S. M., 16

Pugh, D. S., 429, 431, 436

Pugh, S. D., 118

Pulakos, E. D., 104

Puranam, P., 430

Purser, R. E., 480

Purvanova, R. K., 325

Q

Quam, K., 432, 436

Quick, J. C., 203

Quinn, R. P., 201, 211

Quinones, M. A., 113, 114

R

Raju, N. S., 495, 508

Rao, T. V., 477

Rau, R., 212

Raudenbush, S., 55

Raven, B. H., 327, 329

Ravisi, D., 442

Reed, K., 223

Reed, T. F., 219

Regev, Y., 213

Reid, G. L., 62

Reilly, R. R., 87

Renchin, M. B., 171

Renn, R. W., 261

Rentsch, J. R., 176, 177, 218

Renwick, P. A., 333

Reymen, I. M. M. J., 390

Reynolds, D. H., 193

Rhee, K., 157

Rhodes, S. R., 176, 177

Rhodewalt, F., 315

Richard, P., 209

Riggs, M. L., 386

Riordan, C. M., 3, 213

Rivers, M., 467

Roach, R. M., 399

Robert, G., 122

Roberts, C. K., 40, 41, 204

Robertson, P. J., 3, 477, 484, 485, 486, 503, 504

Robinson, S. L., 187, 219, 270

Roccas, S., 365

Roddenberry, C., 362

Rodgers, R., 487, 508

Rognes, J. K., 358, 368

Rokeach, M., 345

Roman, M. A., 215

Roman, P. M., 191

Ronen, S., 238

Rosen, B., 397, 300

Rosen, C., 278

Rosen, T. H., 192

Rosengren, A., 208

Rosenthal, R. A., 201, 211

Rosenthal, R., 47

Ross, J., 16, 141

Ross, L., 172

Ross, T. L., 280

Ross, W. H., 171

Roth, P. L., 152, 160

Rothstein, M., 149, 186

Rotter, J. B., 188

Rousseau, D., 16

Rousseau, V., 396

Rowland, K. M., 204

Roznowski, M., 182

Rueb, J., 307

Runkel, P. J., 38

Russel, S. S., 30

Russell, M., 192

Russo, M. V., 411, 437

Rutte, C. G., 390

Ryan, K., 119, 159

Ryan, R. M., 254, 255

Rynes, S. L., 64

S

Sablynski, C. J., 72, 76, 184

Sacchi, S., 365

Sackett, P. R., 24

Saks, A. M., 77, 89

Salancik, G. R., 16, 138, 156, 263

Salas, E., 380, 381, 391, 393, 396, 397, 399, 406

Salazar, R. J., 278, 279

Sales, S. M., 204

Salgado, J. F., 112

Salovey, P., 365

Salvaggio, A. N., 152

Salvemini, N. J., 139

Salvendy, G., 295

Sanchez, J. I., 227, 228

Scandura T. A., 25, 37

Scarpello, V., 275

Schacter, S., 340

Schandler, H., 124

Schat, A. C. H., 168

Schaubroeck, J., 23, 65, 204, 208, 210, 223, 227, 406

Scheier, M. F., 248

Schein, E. H., 67, 71, 72, 73, 74, 76, 77, 78, 85, 86, 90, 156, 161, 359, 442, 443, 449, 454, 459, 461, 462, 464, 489, 491, 492, 493, 494, 510

Schillewaert, N., 122

Schleicher, D. J., 151

Schmidt, F. L., 106, 112, 113, 114, 115, 124, 174, 182, 187, 192, 390, 402

Schminke, M., 243, 437

Schmitt, N. S., 174

Schneider, B., 65, 106, 152, 218, 391, 455, 459

Schneider, J., 348

Schneider, R. J., 270, 271, 310

Schopler, J., 362

Schriesheim, C. A., 315

Schuler, R. S., 82, 145, 146, 211, 212

Schultz, M., 442

Schuster, M. H., 279

Schutz, W. C., 340

Schwab, D. P., 71, 180, 181

Schwartz, P., 496

Schwartz, R. D., 23

Schwartz, S. H., 345, 365

Schweiger, D. M., 218, 219

Schwoerer, C. E., 223

Scott, L. R., 186

Scott, W. R.., 436

Scully, J. A., 294

Seabright, M. A., 243

Sears, W., 37

Seashore, S. E., 396, 399

Sechrest, L., 23

Seers, A., 399

Segal, N. L., 141

Selgado, J., 227, 228

Selye, H., 200

Sethna, B. N., 398

Shalley, C. E., 247

Shamir, B., 324

Shapiro, D. L., 234

Shaw, I. F., 506

Shaw, J. D., 11, 246, 247, 276

Shaw, J., 139

Shaw, M. E., 346

Shea, G. P., 5, 304, 376, 385, 387, 390, 394, 432, 504

Sheldon, K. M., 254, 255

Shephard, H. A., 369

Shephard, R. J., 226

Sherif, C. W., 365, 367

Sherif, M., 365, 366, 367

Sherman, S. J., 342

Shim, W., 159

Shirom, A., 202, 212, 217, 504

Shperling, Z., 504

Siebold, G., 365, 397, 399

Siegrist, J., 209, 210

Sifferman, J. J., 211

Silver, W. R., 395

Silvers, R. C., 477

Silvester, J., 458

Sime, W. E., 23, 223, 406

Simpson, D. D., 192

Sims, D. E., 381, 396, 397

Sims, H. P., 315

Simsek, Z., 225

Sin, H-,P., 24

Since, W. D., 422, 426

Sinclair, R. R., 160

Singh, H., 430

Singleton, B., 280

Sinha, J. B., 468

Sitzmann, T. M., 225

Siu, L. O., 227, 228

Skibba, J. S., 135

Skinner, B. F., 254

Skogstad, A., 189, 190

Skov, R. B., 139

Slaughter, J. E., 76

Small, M., 15

Smith, C., 202

Smith, D. B., 152

Smith, E. M., 219

Smith, E. R., 340

Smith, J. C., 222

Smith, K. K., 238, 260

Smith, K., 475

Smith, P. B., 227, 228

Smith, P. C., 30, 134, 135

Snoek, J. D., 201, 211

Snyderman, B., 257

Song, Z., 219

Soose, A., 204

Sorenson, S., 118, 215

Soupata, L., 278

Spangler, W. D., 112

Sparks, K., 202, 212, 217

Spector, P. E., 3, 21, 23, 24, 34, 35, 36, 61, 71, 102, 132, 137, 139, 141, 145, 149, 168, 174, 187, 188, 189, 203, 206, 208,

213, 214, 215, 216, 226, 227, 228, 243,263, 284, 317, 467, 507

Spielberger, C. D., 214

Spiros, R. K., 488

Spitzmuller, C., 30

Staber, U., 126

Stacy, B. A., 213

Stajkovic, A. D., 250, 273

Stalker, G. M., 426, 429, 436

Stamm, C. L., 177

Stanton, J. M., 30

Starke, D., 209

Staw, B. M., 16, 119, 141, 247

Steel, R. P., 176, 177, 181

Steers, R. M., 153, 154, 159, 234

Steil, G., 477, 496

Steiner, D. D., 221

Steiner, I. D., 377

Stetzer, A., 445

Stevens, M. J., 289, 403, 404, 406, 434

Stewart, S. L., 115, 391, 402

Stilwell, D., 321

Stogdill, R. M., 307

Stokes, J. P., 141, 142

Stone, D. L., 193

Stone, V. A., 90

Stone-Romero, E. F., 51

Storms, P. L., 188, 317

Straus, S. G., 398

Strauss, J. P., 115

Stroh, L. K., 16

Sturman, M. C., 109

Styhre, A., 487, 508

Sullivan, S. E., 201

Sulsky, L., 202

Sundstrom, E., 394

Sutton, R. I., 392

Sverke, M., 219

Svyantek, D. J., 508

Swanberg, J., 217

Sweeney, P. D., 243

T

Tabachnick, B. G., 47

Taggar, S., 395

Tajfel, H., 368

Tan, J. A., 135

Taylor, F. W., 10, 414

Taylor, G. A., 90

Taylor, S. E., 200, 362

Teachout, M. S., 113, 114

Teerlink, R., 496, 497

Tepper, B. J., 315

Terpstra, D. E., 508

Tesluk, P. E., 394, 397, 400, 466

Tetrault, L. A., 315

Tetrick, L. E., 199, 203, 261

Tett, R. P., 186

Thayer, P. W., 138, 173, 261, 294

Theodory, G. C., 315

Theorell, T., 208

Thibaut, J. W., 240

Thierry, H., 245

Thomas, J. L., 212, 282

Thomas, K., 355, 358

Thomas, K. M., 90

Thomas, L. T., 225

Thomas, P., 127

Thoreson, C. J., 114, 151

Thoreson, J. D., 114

Thornton, G. C., III., 193
Tiegs, R. B., 261
Tierney, P., 322
Ting-Toomey, S., 228
Tolson, J., 453
Tombaugh, J. R., 219
Toquam, J. L., 397
Torsheim, T., 189, 190
Tosi, H. L., 487
Tracey, J. B., 330, 331, 332
Trevino, L. K., 299
Trevor, C. O., 181
Trice, H. M., 449, 450, 451, 452
Trip, T. M., 243
Trist, E. L., 463, 476
Trubisky, P., 228
Tubre, T. C., 211
Tucker, J. S., 160
Tucker, L. A., 226
Tuckman, B. W., 343, 350, 351, 352, 373
Turban, D. B., 254, 255
Turban, D., 65
Turner, A. N., 258
Turnley, W. H., 333
Tushman, M. L., 420
Tziner, A., 279, 390

U
U.S. Bureau of Labor Statistics, 184, 188
U.S. Department of Health and Human Services, 184
Uhles, A. N., 342
Updegraff, J. A., 200

Ury, W., 368

V
Valacich, J. S., 398
Van de Vliert, E., 145, 261
Van De Vliert, E., 228
Van Dyne, L., 103, 104
Van Eerde, W., 245
Van Fleet, D. D., 213, 303, 304, 306, 307, 309
Van Maanen, J., 23, 67, 71, 72, 73, 74, 76, 77, 78, 86, 90, 161, 453, 457
Van Rooy, D. L., 112
van Ryn, M., 219
Van Scotter, J. R., 102
Van Tuijl, H. F. J. M., 390
Van Vianen, A. E. M., 116, 390
Van Yperen, N. W., 228
Vancouver, J. B., 237, 246
Vandenberg, R. J., 261
VandenHeuvel, A., 177
Vardi, Y., 467
Vecchio, R. P., 315
Veiga, J. F., 225
Venneman, S., 278, 279
Veres, J. G., 87, 88
Vigoda, E., 335
Vijayalakshmi, M., 477
Villanova, P., 215
Vinokur, A. D., 219
Viswesvaran, C., 103, 112, 114, 124, 141, 158, 159, 187, 192
Viteles, M. S., 15
Vivian, J., 363
Vizquel, O. (with Bob Dyer), 91

Vos, M. C., 226

Vroom, V. H., 150, 243, 244, 245, 304, 315, 316, 319, 320

W

Wade, G., 367

Wageman, R., 393, 404, 405, 489

Wagner, J. A., 216

Wagner, J. A., III., 35

Wailes, N., 474

Waldman, D. A., 112

Wall, T., 86, 108, 487

Walumbwa, F. O., 325

Wanberg, C. R., 149, 159, 219

Wanberg, C. R., 219

Wang, D., 118, 325

Wang, H., 118, 325

Wanous, J. P., 70, 87, 160, 238

Waterman, R. H., 67, 376, 420, 465

Watson, D., 16, 141

Watt, J. D., 151

Wayne, S. J., 321, 508

Wayne-Andy, S. J., 322

Webb, E. J., 23

Weber, M., 414

Webster, J., 62, 63, 171

Weekly, J. A., 106, 107, 108, 140

Weiner, Y., 467

Weisberg, J., 279

Weise, D. S., 87, 88

Weiss, D. J., 135, 136

Weiss, H. M., 139, 253, 283

Weiss, J. A., 392

Weitz, J., 141

Welbourne, T. M., 286

Wesson, M. J., 243, 299, 363

Westra, C. D., 397

While, A., 127

Whipple, T., 171

White, B. J., 365, 367

White, L. P., 219

White, M. C., 124

White, S., 139

Whitehead, T. N., 12

Whitney, K., 395, 396

Whyte, G., 391

Wickens, C. D., 184, 295

Wieczorkowska, G., 342

Wieselquist, J., 362

Wildschut, T., 362

Wilkins, A. L., 460, 465

Willander, M., 487, 508

Williams, C. R., 180

Williams, E. A., 25, 37

Williams, J. A., 367

Williams, K., 377, 380

Williams, L. J., 35, 47, 118, 142, 150, 152

Williams, M. L., 138

Wills, T. A., 237, 340

Wilson, J., 467, 468

Wilson, M., 280

Wilson, T. B., 274

Wise, L., 184

Witcher, B., 362

Wofford, J. C., 318

Wolf, G., 16, 55

Wolf, S. ., 68, 69, 85, 161

Wolfe, D. M., 201, 211

Wolfson, A., 495

Wood, R. E., 112

Wooden, M., 177

Woodman, R. W., 508

Woodward, J., 431, 436

Worchel, S., 189

Wright, C., 160

Wright, P. M., 247, 412, 413, 478

Wysocki, J., 315

X

Xie, J. L., 178, 226, 261

Y

Yammarino, F. J., 16

Yeager, S., 506, 507

Yen, H. R., 119

Yetton, P. W., 319, 320

Yi, Y., 35

Yoffie, D., 333

Yost, P. R., 386

Young, J., 456

Young, K. M., 278

Young, T. F., 243

Yu, K. Y. T., 63, 65

Yukl, G., 303, 304, 306, 307, 309, 330, 331, 332, 364

Yun, S., 315

Yzerbyt, V., 365

Z

Zaccaro, S. J., 307, 389, 400

Zajac, D. M., 144, 146, 154, 157, 158, 159, 176, 177

Zammuto, R. F., 431

Zapf, D., 96, 156

Zazanis, M., 400

Zedeck, S., 46

Zempel, J., 204

Zickar, M. J., 12, 13, 76

Zmud, R. W., 507

Zohar, D., 185, 186

Zollo, M., 430

Zuckerman, M., 283

Zwany, A., 238

Zweig, D. I., 77, 89, 171

Subject Index

3M Company, 428

A

Absenteeism. *See* Counterproductive
behavior in organizations; Job
satisfaction; Organizational
commitment
Achievement-oriented leadership,
316
Action research, 14
Action Research Model of organizational
development, 480–482
Administrative management, and
organizational theory, 416–417
Affective-cognitive consistency (ACC) of job
satisfaction, 151. *See also* Job
satisfaction
Affective organizational commitment, 153,
155–156

Agency theory of executive compensation,
286. *See also* Organizational
applications of motivation theory
Agreeableness, and job performance, 115
Alpha level, 49
Altruism, and OCB, 117
Analysis of variance, 45–46
Anticipatory socialization, 70. *See also*
Organizational socialization

B

Bandura, Albert, 249–250
Beehr, Terry, 201
Behaviorally anchored rating scales,
104–105
Bliese, Paul D., 56
Bobko, Philip, 43
Boggs, Wade, 451
Brainstorming, 398

C

Campbell, John, 129
    model of job performance, 98–100,
        109–111. *See also* Productive
        behavior
Cannon, Walter, 200
Center for the Study of Group Dynamics,
    475
Central tendency, 42
Chapman, Derek, 93–94
Charismatic leadership theory, 323
Chatman, Jennifer, 470
Chrysler Corporation, 474
Civic virtue, and OCB, 117
Cluster sampling, 28
Coercive power, 328
Cognitive appraisal, 202
Cognitive Resource Theory of leadership,
    315
Collective vs. individual socialization,
    73–74. *See also* Organizational
    socialization, organizational
    perspective process
Comcon model of decentralized
    communication, 347–348
Common method variance, 35
Comparator, as part of control system, 248
Compliance, and influence, 327. *See also*
    Power in organizations
Conscientiousness, 65, 114–116, 117
Constant (systematic error), 44
Construct validity, 132–133, 155
Continuance organizational commitment,
    153, 156. *See also* Organizational
    commitment

Cooperation (backup-behavior), and team
    effectiveness, 398–399, 402
Coordination, and team effectiveness,
    398–399, 402
Core self-evaluation, and job performance,
    115
Counterproductive behavior in
    organizations:
    absenteeism
        cross-cultural differences in,
            178–179
        defining, 175
        measuring, 175–176
        predictors of, 176–178
    accidents, 184–186
    defined, 167–168
    generalized mistreatment, 188–190
    ineffective job performance
        causes of, 171–174
        detection of, 169–171
        management of, 174–175
        performance reviews, 170
    overview, 195–197
    sexual harassment, 194–195
    substance use, 190–193
    theft, 186–188
    turnover
        impact of, 179–180
        Mobley's vs. Unfolding model of,
            182–184
        predictors of, 180–182
    workplace violence, 188–190
Courtesy, and OCB, 117
Creativity-relevant skills, 124. *See also*
    Innovations in organizations

Cross-level analysis, 54

Cross-product regression, 50–51

D

Declarative knowledge, 107, 109–111

Dejobbing, 16–17

Dell Computer Company, 122

Denison Organizational Culture Survey, 456, 466

Dependent variable, 30

Dictionary of Occupational Titles (DOT), 23, 24, 25

Directive leadership, 316. *See also* Leadership

Discriminator, as part of control system, 248

Diseases of adaptation, 200

Distributive justice, and OCB, 118

E

Eduardo, Salas, 408–409

Effect size, 48

Effectiveness, and job performance, 97–98

Effector, as part of control system, 248

Efficiency, and job performance, 97–98

Effort-to-performance (E → P), 244

Embeddedness, and employee turnover, 184

Employee accidents, 184–186

Employee assistance programs (EAPs), 174, 193. *See also* Counterproductive behavior in organizations

Employee theft, 186–188

Employee turnover. *See* Counterproductive behavior in organizations; Job

satisfaction; Organizational commitment

Equity theory, 118

ERG Theory of motivation, 238

Exemplification, and power, 334

Expectancy. *See* Effort-to-performance (E → P)

Expectancy Theory of job satisfaction and performance, 150

Expectation lowering procedure (ELP), study of, 87–88

Expert power, 328

Extra-role (contextual) job performance, 98, 99–100, 103–104, 117

F

Faces scale, 133–134

Failures in Organization Development and Change (Murvis), 512

Feedback, and motivation, 253–254

Fixed vs. variable socialization, 73, 75–76. *See also* Organizational socialization, organizational perspective process

Formal organizations, 2–3

Formal vs. informal socialization, 73, 74–75. *See also* Organizational socialization, organizational perspective process

Formalization, and team effectiveness, 402

Forsyth, Donelson, 372

F-test, 45

Fundamental attribution error of behavior, 172. *See also* Counterproductive behavior in organizations

G

General adaptation syndrome, and
    occupational stress, 200
General mental ability and, 111–113, 123
General Systems Theory of organizational
    development, 482
Generalized self-efficacy, and job
    performance, 115
Generalizing from Laboratory to Field
    Settings (Locke), 38
Goal priority, and team effectiveness, 402
Goal-Setting Theory of motivation, 246–248
Golden parachutes as executive
    compensation, 287. *See also*
    Organizational applications of
    motivation theory
Groups in organizations:
    characteristics of, 341–343
    communication patterns of, 346–348
    and conflict, 362–366
    improving quality of
        member exchanges, 368–369
        negotiation, 368
        reducing need for interaction, 370–371
        resource-allocation process, 371
        superordinate goals, 366–368
        team development, 369–370
    interactions of, 335
        competition, 357
        interdependence as predictor of, 358
        past history with, 360–361
        types of, 355–357
    membership, 340–341
    Moreland and Levine's model of
        socialization, 352–353

organizational culture of, 359–360
overview, 371, 373
Punctuated Equilibrium Model of
    development, 353–355
social isolation, 341
social networks in, 361–362
Stage model of development, 350–352
status differentials, 348–349
structure of
    role differentiation, 343–344
    normative standards, 344–345
    values, 345–346
    See also Forsyth, Donelson

H

Hackman, Richard, 301
Handbook of Industrial and Organizational
    Psychology (Locke), 131–132
Harley-Davidson, 497
Hawthorne effect, 13
Hawthorne studies, 12–13
Homeostasis, 200
Hub and spokes model of centralized
    communication, 346–347
The Human Side of Enterprise (McGregor),
    418
Human organization, and organizational
    theory, 419–420
Hypothetical construct, motivation as a, 234

I

Ideal bureaucracy, and organizational
    theory, 415–416
Identification, and influence, 327. *See also*
    Power in organizations

Impression management, and OCB, 120

Impression management, and power, 333–334

Independent variable, 30

Industrial/organizational (I/O) psychology, defined, 3
    scientist-practitioner model and, 6 (see also Scientist-practitioner approach to organizational psychology)
    beginning of, 9–12, 15–16
    industrial vs. organizational, 3–5
    See also Organizational psychology; Zickar, Mike J.

Industrial Psychology (Viteles), 15

Informal organizations, 2–3

Information management, and power, 334

Informational power, 328

Innovations in organizations:
    employee attributes to, 122–125
    organizational determinants, 125–128
    overview, 122
    technical vs. administrative, 126

In-role (task) job performance, 98–99, 103–104

Institute for Psychological Research and Application (IPRA), 10

Instrumentality. See Performance-to-outcome (P → O)

Interactional justice, and OCB, 118

Interactional psychology, 208

Interdependence, and team effectiveness, 402, 404–405

Interlocking chain of conferences, and organizational development, 476

Internal consistency reliability, 44

Interpersonal-intergroup discontinuity effect, and group conflict, 362

Interrater reliability, 44

Intimidation, and power, 334

Investiture vs. divestiture socialization, 73, 77–78. See also Organizational socialization, process (organizational perspective)

J

Job autonomy, 216

Job Characteristics Theory of motivation, 257–263, 288–289, 290–294, 296

Job Decision Latitude, and occupational stress, 208

Job Descriptive Index (JDI), 134–135

Job Diagnostic Survey, 290

Job in General (JIG) Scale, 135

Job performance. See Job satisfaction; Organizational Commitment; Productive behavior

Job satisfaction:
    and absenteeism, 146–147
    and attitudinal variables, 144–146
    cross-cultural perspective of, 143–144, 145
    defined, 131–132
    dispositional approach to, 140–142
    and employee turnover, 147–150
    job characteristics approach to, 137–138
    and job performance, 150–152 (see also Productive behavior)
    measurement of, 132–137
    overview, 163–165

Job satisfaction (*continued*)
   predictors of, 137–143
   social information processing approach
      to, 138–140
   See also Organizational commitment
Job Satisfaction Survey (JSS), 136–137
Job-centered vs. employee-centered
      leadership behavior, 309. *See also*
      Leadership
JobShift: How to Prosper in a Workplace
      with Jobs (Bridges), 121

K
Karasek, Robert, 208
Kornhauser, Arthur, 12

L
Latent growth curve modeling, 107–108
Leader–Member Exchange model of
      leadership, 321–323
Leadership:
   authentic, 325–326
   behavioral approach to, 308–309
   charismatic theory of, 323
   contingency approach to, 310
   contingency theory of, 311–316
   cultural differences in, 326
   defined, 303–305
   importance of, 305–306
   Leader–Member Exchange model of, 321–
      323
   vs. management, 304, 305
   overview, 335, 337–338
   Path-Goal Theory of, 316–319
   and power (*see* Power in organizations)

trait approach to, 306–308
transactional theory of, 323–325
transformational theory of, 323
Vroom-Yetton-Jago model of, 319–321
See also Zaccaro, Stephen
Least Preferred Coworker (LPC) Scale,
      313–316. *See also* Leadership
Legitimate power, 328
Lewin, Kurt, 13–14, 475, 476, 480
The Life You Imagine: Life Lessons for Achieving
      Your Dreams (Jeter), 452
Locke, Edwin, 266
Locus of control, and job performance, 115
Lombardi, Vince, 378

M
Management by Objectives (MBO), and
      organizational development, 487
Managerial Behavior, Performance, and
      Effectiveness (Campbell), 129
Maximum control, 30–31
Mean, 42
Mean-squares, 45
Measurement error, 49
Median, 42
Minnesota Satisfaction Questionnaire
      (MSQ), 135–136
Mobley's model of the employee turnover
      process, 147–150, 182
Mode, 42
Moderator variables:
   defined, 48
   detection of, 50–52
Moneyball: The Art of Winning and Unfair
      Game (Lewis), 123

Motivation:
  behavioral approach to, 250–254
  Control Theory of, 248–249
  defined, 234–235
  Equity Theory of, 239–243
  ERG Theory of, 238
  Expectancy Theory of, 243–246
  Goal-Setting Theory of, 246–248
  Job Characteristics Theory of, 257–263
  Motivation-Hygiene Theory of, 256–257
  Need for Achievement Theory of, 238–239
  Need Hierarchy of, 235–238
  organizational applications of (*see* Organizational applications of motivation theory)
  in productive behavior, 109–111, 125
  self-determination theory of, 254–256
  Social Cognitive Theory (SCT) of, 249–250
  summary of theories of, 263, 265–267
  value of theories of, 264–265
Motivation and Morale in Industry (Viteles), 15
Motivation-Hygiene Theory of motivation, 256
Multimethod Job Design Questionnaire, 294
Multiple linear regression, 46–47
Murphy's model of job performance, 100–103, 108–109. *See also* Productive behavior
Murvis, Philip, 512

N
Nadler, David, 439

National Training Laboratories (NTL), 475
Need for Achievement Theory of motivation, 238–239
Need Hierarchy of motivation, 235–238
Neuroticism, and job performance, 115
New Patterns of Management (Likert), 419
Newman, John, 201
Normative organizational commitment, 153, 156–157. *See also* Organizational commitment
Null hypothesis, 45

O
OCB. *See* Organizational citizenship behavior
Occupational Health Psychology (OHP), 202, 203
Occupational Information Network (O*NET), 23–24, 25
Occupational stress:
  clinical/counseling approach to, 201–202
  comparison of models of, 209–210
  cross-cultural research on, 226–228
  Demands–Control model of, 208
  Effort-Reward Imbalance model of, 209
  emotional labor, 220–221
  engineering psychology approach to, 202
  Facet model of, 206–207
  history of, 200–201
  impact on children, 220
  Institute for Social Research (ISR) Model of, 205–206
  interpersonal conflict, 213–214
  job insecurity, 219–220

Occupational stress (*continued*)
  management training, 222–223
  mergers and acquisitions, 218–219
  organizational constraints, 214–215
  organizational psychology approach to,
    202
  overview, 199–200, 229
  perceived control, 215–216
  Person–Environment Fit model of,
    208–209
  reduction of, 223–226
  role stressors, 210–212
  terminology of, 202–205
  work–family conflict, 217–218
  workload, 212–213
On-the-job coaching, 174. *See also*
    Counterproductive behavior in
    organizations
Openness to experience, and job
    performance, 115
Organization ideation, 122. *See also*
    Innovations in organizations
Organizational Behavior Modification
    (OBM), 253–254
Organizational applications of motivation
    theory:
  disciplinary procedures, 298–300
  executive compensation, 284–288
  intangible reward systems, 281–284
  and job design
    history of, 288–289
    humanistic, 289–290
    integrating approaches to, 296–298
    interdisciplinary approach to,
      294–296

Job Characteristics Theory approach,
    290–294
  overview, 269–270, 300–302
  tangible reward systems, 273–274
    ESOPs, 278–279
    fringe benefits, 280
    impact of, 277–278
    incentive pay and bonuses, 276–277
    merit pay, 274–276
    pension plans, 281
    perquisites, 281, 282
    profit- and gain-sharing, 279–280
    stock ownership, 278
  and targeted behaviors, 270–272
  See also Groups in organizations; Team
      effectiveness in organizations
Organizational change and development:
  conditions for success
    consultants, 498–500
    ownership of process, 501–502
    resistance to change, 500–501
    top management support, 498
  defined, 473–475
  effectiveness of, 507–508
  evaluation criteria of, 502–504
  evaluation designs of, 504–506
  history of, 475–477
  group-level interventions of, 487–494
  individual-level interventions of, 486–487
  measuring, 506–507
  organization-wide interventions,
      494–496
  overview, 511, 513
  special issues
    confidentiality, 509–510

multiple clients, 508–509
  terminating relationships, 510–511
theories of change, 483–484
  Burke's model, 484
  Porras and Robertson's model,
    484–486
theories of development
  Action Research Model of, 480–482
  General Systems Theory of, 482
  profession of, 478
  Three-Step Model of, 478–480, 481
  See also Murvis, Philip
Organizational citizenship behavior (OCB):
  overview, 116–117
  reasons for, 117–119
  special issues in, 119–122
Organizational commitment:
  defined, 131, 153
  overview, 152–153, 163–165
  measurement of, 153–155
  predictors of, 155–157
  cross-cultural influences on, 157
  and attitudinal variables, 157–158
  and absenteeism, 158
  and employee turnover, 158–159
  and job performance, 159–160
  predicting performance, 160
  applications of research, 160–163
  See also Job satisfaction
Organizational Commitment questionnaire
    (OCQ), 154–155
Organizational culture:
  academic, 445
  changing, 458–465
  defined, 442–446

Denison model of, 446–447, 466
development of, 454–456
and employee satisfaction, 467–468
manifestations of
  artifacts, 449
  communication, 453–454
  language, 453
  rites, 449–451
  rituals, 451–452
  stories/legends/dramas, 452–453
  symbols, 448
measuring, 456–458
Organizational Culture Profile (OCP),
    446, 456
overview, 441, 468–470
and performance, 465–467
and recruitment/retention, 467
  See also Chatman, Jennifer
Organizational Culture Profile (OCP), 446
Organizational Development and Change
    Division of the Academy of
    Management, 478
Organizational Development Network, 478
Organizational politics, 333–335
Organizational psychology:
  and 9/11, 17
  in context, 3–5
  of counterproductive behavior (*see*
    Counterproductive behavior in
    organizations)
  defined, 1, 2–3
  formal vs. informal organizations, 2–3
  of group dynamics and behavior
    (*see* Groups in organizations)
  and Hawthorne studies, 12–13

Organizational psychology (*continued*)
  indirect benefits of, 1–2
  of job satisfaction (*see* Job satisfaction)
  of leadership and influence processes
    (*see* Leadership)
  of motivation (*see* Motivation)
  of occupational stress (*see* Occupational
    stress)
  vs. organizational behavior, 4
  of organizational change and development
    (*see* Organizational change and
    development)
  of organizational commitment
    (*see* Organizational commitment)
  of organizational culture (*see*
    Organizational culture)
  of organizational socialization
    (*see* Organizational socialization)
  overview, 18–20
  in private organizations, 1
  and productive behavior (*see* Productive
    behavior)
  progression of, 12–17 (*see also* Industrial/
    organizational psychology)
  in public organizations, 1
  research methods in (*see* Research
    methods in organizational
    psychology)
  scientist-practitioner approach (*see*
    Scientist-practitioner approach to
    organizational psychology)
  in social organizations (*see* Social
    organizations)
  statistics in (*see* Statistics in organizational
    psychology)

  of team effectiveness (*see* Team
    effectiveness in organizations)
  theory and design (*see* Organizational
    theory and design)
  and unionization, 13
  and the Vietnam War, 15
  and World War II, 14–15
Organizational socialization:
  into academia, 73
  and conformity, 72
  defined, 67–69
  and diversity, 90–92
  overview, 92, 94
  interactionist perspective process,
    89–90
  newcomer perspective process
    tactics, 78–82
    outcomes of, 82–88
    and realistic expectations, 88
  organizational perspective process
    stages of, 69–72
    tactics, 72–78
  See also Social organizations
Organizational theory and design:
  classical organizational theories,
    414–417
  contingency organizational theories,
    420–421
  coordination-autonomy dilemma, 430
  defined, 412–414
  determinants of design
    culture of organization, 428–429
    environmental uncertainty, 426–427
    managers, 427–428
    size of organization, 429

strategy, 421–426
technology, 430–432
future of, 437–438
humanistic organizational theories,
   417–420
innovations in design
   matrix organization, 434–435
   team-based organization, 432–434
   virtual organization, 435–436
overview, 411–412, 438–440
research on, 436–437
See also Nadler, David
Ownership power, 328

P
Participant observation, 23
Participative decision making, 216
Participative leadership, 316
Path analysis (structural equation modeling),
   52–53
Path-Goal Theory of leadership,
   316–319
Pearson product-moment correlation
   coefficient, 46
Performance-to-outcome (P → O), 244
Pooled interdependence, and group
   dynamics, 358
Power in organizations:
   bases of, 327–330
   defined, 327
   influence tactics, 330–333
   organizational politics, 333–335
   overview, 337–338
   See also Leadership
Prestige power, 328

Prevalence studies, 25
Principled negotiation, and group dynamics,
   368
Private acceptance (internalization), and
   influence, 327, 332. See also Power in
   organizations
Probability sampling, 27
Procedural justice, and OCB, 118
Procedural knowledge, 107, 109–111
Productive behavior:
   defined, 96
   overview, 128, 129
   job performance
      defined, 96–98, 111
      models of, 98–103
      measures of, 103–105
      variability of, 105–106
      instability in, 106–109
      determinants of, 109–116
      and general mental ability,
         111–113
      and job experience, 113–114
      and personality, 114–116
      and job satisfaction, 150–152
      and organizational commitment,
         159–160
   organizational citizenship behavior (see
      Organizational citizenship behavior
      [OCB])
   innovations in organizations (see
      Innovations in organizations)
   See also Campbell, John; Campbell's
      model of job performance; Murphy's
      model of job performance
Productivity, and job performance, 97–98

Promotion of the opposition, and power, 334

Psychology, defined, 3. *See also* Organizational psychology

Punctuated Equilibrium Model of group development, 353–355

Punishment, and motivation, 252–253

Pursuing line responsibility, and power, 334

R

Random assignment, 30

Random coefficient modeling, 55

Random error, 44

Range restriction, 47–48

Range, 42

Realistic job previews (RJPs), study of, 87–88

Reciprocal interdependence, and group dynamics, 358–359

Referent power, 328

Reinforcement, and motivation, 250–252

Reliability, 43–44, 47

Research methods in organizational psychology:
  choosing, 32–33
  methodology
    archival data, 23–25, 32
    experimentation, 30–31, 32
    observational methods, 22–23, 32
    qualitative methods, 24
    quasi-experimentation, 31–32
    survey research, 25–30, 32
  overview, 21–22

special issues
  access to organizations, 38–41
  cross-cultural issues, 41
  generalizing lab findings, 36–38
  self-reports, 34–36
  See also Statistics in organizational psychology

Resistance, and influence, 327. *See also* Power in organizations

Reward power, 328

Role ambiguity, and organizational socialization, 82

Role conflict, and organizational socialization, 82

Role stressors, 201

Rowe, Pat, 93

Rynes, Sara, 93

S

Sample size, 48

Saturn (automotive company), 122

Scientific Management, 10–11, 288, 414–415

Scientist-practitioner approach to organizational psychology:
  in academic careers, 6–7
  example of, 6
  in I/O psychology graduate training, 6–7, 10
  in nonacademic careers, 7, 9
  overview, 5–9
  and practical experience, 7, 8, 9

Self-determination theory of motivation, 254–256

Self-esteem, and job performance, 115

Self Perception Theory of job satisfaction, 139

Self-promotion, and power, 333

Selye, Hans, 200

Sensor, as part of control system, 248

Sequential interdependence, and group dynamics, 358

Serial vs. disjunctive socialization, 73, 76–77. *See also* Organizational socialization, organizational perspective process

Shared mental models, and team effectiveness, 400–401

Siegrist, Johannes, 209

Simple observation, 22–23

Simple random sampling, 27

Social Cognitive Theory (SCT) of motivation, 249–250

Social Comparison Theory of job satisfaction, 139

Social inertia, and groups, 339

Social Information Processing Theory (SIP), 16, 138–140

Social organizations:
  overview, 92, 94
  recruitment process of (applicant's perspective), 63–67
  recruitment process of (organizational perspective)
    planning, 60–61
    methods, 61–63
  recruitment research, 64
  See also Chapman, Derek; Organizational socialization

Society for Industrial and Organizational Psychology (SIOP), 61

Spector, Paul, 164

Sportsmanship, and OCB, 117

Stage model of group development, 350–352

Standard deviation, 43

Standard scores, 43

Standard, as part of control system, 248

Statistical artifacts, 47–48

Statistical minimalist, 43

Statistical significance, 45

Statistics in organizational psychology:
  correlation and regression analysis, 46–47
  descriptive statistics, 42–44
  mean differences, 44–46
  meta-analysis, 47–48
  overview, 55–57
  special issues
    aggregation and levels of analysis, 54–55
    causal modeling, 52–54
    moderator variable, 50–52
    statistical power, 48–50
  See also Bliese, Paul D.; Research methods in organizational psychology

Stewardship theory of executive compensation, 286. *See also* Organizational applications of motivation theory

Stratified random sampling, 27

Stress, meaning of, 204. *See also* Occupational stress

Structural equation modeling (path analysis), 52–53
Succession planning, 60–61
Supportive leadership, 316
Survey Research Center (SRC), 476

T
TADMUS program, 408
Task-relevant skills, 123–124. *See also* Innovations in organizations
Tavistock Clinic, 476
Taylor, Frederick Winslow, 10–11
Team (collective) efficacy, 400
Team effectiveness in organizations:
    affective/cognitive processes of, 399–401
    behavioral processes of, 399
    between-team processes, 401–402
    and conflict, 401
    defined, 376–378
    determinants of
        organizational resources, 392–393
        rewards, 393–395
        task design, 392
        team composition, 390–391
        team goals, 395–396
        within-team processes, 396
    enhancing effectiveness of, 402
        reward systems, 403–405
        selection, 402–403
        training/development, 405–406
    future of, 406
    Gladstein's model of, 381–383
    Hackman's normative model of, 383–385
    McGrath's model of, 378–381
    overview, 375–376, 407, 409
    Shea and Guzzo's model of, 385–387
    summary of models of, 389
    Synthesis model of, 387–389
    See also Groups in organizations; Salas, Eduardo
Team empowerment, 400
Test-retest reliability, 44
Theory of Planned Behavior, 146
Theory X/Y managers, and organizational theory, 418–419
Three-Step Model of Change and Action Research, 475, 478–480, 481
Time lapse data, 63
Transactional leadership theory, 323–325
Transformational leadership theory, 323
t-test, 45
Type I error, 49
Type II error, 49

U
Unfolding model of employee turnover process, 183–184. *See also* Mobley's model of employee turnover process
Utility, and job performance, 97–98

V
Value clarification, 66
Variance, 42
Vertical Dyad Linkage Model of leadership, 321

Vroom-Yetton-Jago model of leadership,
        319–321

W
Weber, Max, 11–12
Work Design Questionnaire (WDQ), 296
Workplace incivility, 191

Y
Yield ratios, 63

Z
Zaccaro, Stephen, 336
Zickar, Mike J., 19